Apache HTTP Server Reference Manual

for Apache version 2.2.17

Apache Software Foundation

Published by Network Theory Ltd

A catalogue record for this book is available from the British Library.

December 2010 First printing.

Published by Network Theory Limited.

Email: info@network-theory.co.uk

ISBN 978-1-906966-03-4

Further information about this book is available from
http://www.network-theory.co.uk/apache/manual/

This book has an unconditional guarantee. If you are not fully satisfied with your purchase for any reason, please contact the publisher at the address above.

This version of the Apache HTTP Server Documentation is converted from XML source files to LaTeX using XSLT. While every care has been taken by the publisher, this book is a reformatted work and may contain conversion errors. The reference version of the documentation can be found on the Apache HTTP Server website at http://httpd.apache.org/docs/2.2/.

Contents

Publisher's Preface

This reference manual documents the Apache HTTP server, the most widely used web server on the internet, serving hundreds of millions of sites.

Apache is *free software*. The term "free software" refers to your freedom to run, copy, distribute, study, change and improve the software. With Apache you have all these freedoms.

You can support free software by becoming an associate member of the Free Software Foundation, which promotes the right to use, study, copy, modify, and redistribute computer programs. It also works to raise awareness of the ethical and political issues of freedom in the use of software. For more information, visit the website www.fsf.org.

The development of Apache is guided by the Apache Software Foundation, a not-for-profit organization working in the public interest. Individuals and organizations using Apache can support its continued development through donations and sponsorship. Further information is available at the website www.apache.org.

Brian Gough
Publisher
December 2010

Notes for this printed edition

This book contains a printed version of the Apache documentation from the Apache 2.2.17 distribution.

While every care has been taken by the publisher, this book is a reformatted work and may contain formatting errors for which the Apache Documentation Project is not responsible.

Please report any errors in this printed edition to the publisher by email at info@network-theory.co.uk. Corrections to the original documentation will be passed onto the Apache Documentation Project as appropriate.

Due to the huge size of the Apache documentation, some parts of the secondary chapters later in this book may not be entirely up to date. All the primary documentation, such as the module directives, should be fully current however.

1 Apache HTTP Server and Supporting Programs

1.1 Server and Supporting Programs

This section documents all the executable programs included with the Apache HTTP Server.

1.1.1 Index

httpd Apache hypertext transfer protocol server

apachectl Apache HTTP server control interface

ab Apache HTTP server benchmarking tool

apxs APache eXtenSion tool

configure Configure the source tree

dbmmanage Create and update user authentication files in DBM format for basic authentication

htcacheclean Clean up the disk cache

htdigest Create and update user authentication files for digest authentication

htdbm Manipulate DBM password databases.

htpasswd Create and update user authentication files for basic authentication

httxt2dbm Create dbm files for use with RewriteMap

logresolve Resolve hostnames for IP-addresses in Apache logfiles

rotatelogs Rotate Apache logs without having to kill the server

suexec Switch User For Exec

Other Programs (p. 48) Support tools with no own manual page.

1.2 httpd - Apache Hypertext Transfer Protocol Server

httpd is the Apache HyperText Transfer Protocol (HTTP) server program. It is designed to be run as a standalone daemon process. When used like this it will create a pool of child processes or threads to handle requests.

In general, httpd should not be invoked directly, but rather should be invoked via apachectl on Unix-based systems or as a service on Windows NT, 2000 and XP (p. 745) and as a console application on Windows 9x and ME (p. 745).

See also:

▷ Starting Apache (p. 49)

▷ Stopping Apache (p. 51)

▷ Configuration Files (p. 54)

▷ Platform-specific Documentation (p. 745)

▷ apachectl (p. 11)

1.2.1 Synopsis

httpd [-d *serverroot*] [-f *config*] [-C *directive*] [-c *directive*] [-D *parameter*] [-e *level*] [-E *file*] [-k start|restart|graceful|stop|graceful-stop] [-R *directory*] [-h] [-l] [-L] [-S] [-t] [-v] [-V] [-X] [-M] [-T]

On Windows systems (p. 745), the following additional arguments are available:

httpd [-k install|config|uninstall] [-n *name*] [-w]

1.2.2 Options

-d serverroot Set the initial value for the ServerRoot directive to *serverroot*. This can be overridden by the ServerRoot directive in the configuration file. The default is /usr/local/apache2.

-f config Uses the directives in the file *config* on startup. If *config* does not begin with a /, then it is taken to be a path relative to the ServerRoot. The default is conf/httpd.conf.

-k start|restart|graceful|stop|graceful-stop Signals httpd to start, restart, or stop. See Stopping Apache (p. 51) for more information.

-C directive Process the configuration *directive* before reading config files.

-c directive Process the configuration *directive* after reading config files.

-D parameter Sets a configuration *parameter* which can be used with <IfDefine> sections in the configuration files to conditionally skip or process commands at server startup and restart. Also can be used to set certain less-common startup parameters including -DNO_DETACH (prevent the parent from forking) and -DFOREGROUND (prevent the parent from calling setsid() et al).

-e level Sets the LogLevel to *level* during server startup. This is useful for temporarily increasing the verbosity of the error messages to find problems during startup.

-E file Send error messages during server startup to *file*.

-R directory When the server is compiled using the SHARED_CORE rule, this specifies the *directory* for the shared object files.

-h Output a short summary of available command line options.

-l Output a list of modules compiled into the server. This will **not** list dynamically loaded modules included using the LoadModule directive.

-L Output a list of directives together with expected arguments and places where the directive is valid.

-M Dump a list of loaded Static and Shared Modules.

-S Show the settings as parsed from the config file (currently only shows the virtualhost settings).

-T **(Available in 2.2.17 and later)** Skip   document   root   check   at startup/restart.

-t Run syntax tests for configuration files only. The program immediately exits after these syntax parsing tests with either a return code of 0 (Syntax OK) or return code not equal to 0 (Syntax Error). If -D DUMP_VHOSTS is also set, details of the virtual host configuration will be printed. If -D DUMP_MODULES is set, all loaded modules will be printed.

-v Print the version of httpd, and then exit.

-V Print the version and build parameters of httpd, and then exit.

-X Run httpd in debug mode. Only one worker will be started and the server will not detach from the console.

The following arguments are available only on the Windows platform (p. 745):

-k install|config|uninstall Install Apache as a Windows NT service; change startup options for the Apache service; and uninstall the Apache service.

-n name The *name* of the Apache service to signal.

-w Keep the console window open on error so that the error message can be read.

1.3 ab - Apache HTTP server benchmarking tool

ab is a tool for benchmarking your Apache Hypertext Transfer Protocol (HTTP) server. It is designed to give you an impression of how your current Apache installation performs. This especially shows you how many requests per second your Apache installation is capable of serving.

See also:

    ▷ httpd (p. 6)

1.3.1 Synopsis

ab [-A *auth-username*:*password*] [-b *windowsize*] [-c
concurrency] [-C *cookie-name=value*] [-d] [-e *csv-file*]
[-f *protocol*] [-g *gnuplot-file*] [-h] [-H *custom-header*
] [-i] [-k] [-n *requests*] [-p *POST-file*] [-P
proxy-auth-username:*password*] [-q] [-r] [-s] [-S] [-t
timelimit] [-T *content-type*] [-u *PUT-file*] [-v *verbosity*]
[-V] [-w] [-x *<table>-attributes*] [-X *proxy*[:*port*]] [
-y *<tr>-attributes*] [-z *<td>-attributes*] [-Z *ciphersuite*]
[http[s]://]*hostname*[:*port*]/*path*

1.3.2 Options

-A auth-username:password Supply BASIC Authentication credentials to the
     server. The username and password are separated by a single : and sent
     on the wire base64 encoded. The string is sent regardless of whether the
     server needs it (*i.e.*, has sent an 401 authentication needed).

-b windowsize Size of TCP send/receive buffer, in bytes.

-c concurrency Number of multiple requests to perform at a time. Default is
     one request at a time.

-C cookie-name=value Add a Cookie: line to the request. The argument is
     typically in the form of a *name=value* pair. This field is repeatable.

-d Do not display the "percentage served within XX [ms] table". (legacy sup-
     port).

-e csv-file Write a Comma separated value (CSV) file which contains for
     each percentage (from 1% to 100%) the time (in milliseconds) it took to
     serve that percentage of the requests. This is usually more useful than
     the 'gnuplot' file; as the results are already 'binned'.

-f protocol Specify SSL/TLS protocol (SSL2, SSL3, TLS1, or ALL).

-g gnuplot-file Write all measured values out as a 'gnuplot' or TSV (Tab
     separate values) file. This file can easily be imported into packages like
     Gnuplot, IDL, Mathematica, Igor or even Excel. The labels are on the
     first line of the file.

-h Display usage information.

-H custom-header Append extra headers to the request. The argument is typically in the form of a valid header line, containing a colon-separated field-value pair (*i.e.*, "Accept-Encoding: zip/zop;8bit").

-i Do HEAD requests instead of GET.

-k Enable the HTTP KeepAlive feature, *i.e.*, perform multiple requests within one HTTP session. Default is no KeepAlive.

-n requests Number of requests to perform for the benchmarking session. The default is to just perform a single request which usually leads to non-representative benchmarking results.

-p POST-file File containing data to POST. Remember to also set -T.

-P proxy-auth-username:password Supply BASIC Authentication credentials to a proxy en-route. The username and password are separated by a single : and sent on the wire base64 encoded. The string is sent regardless of whether the proxy needs it (*i.e.*, has sent an 407 proxy authentication needed).

-q When processing more than 150 requests, ab outputs a progress count on stderr every 10% or 100 requests or so. The -q flag will suppress these messages.

-r Don't exit on socket receive errors.

-s When compiled in (ab -h will show you) use the SSL protected https rather than the http protocol. This feature is experimental and *very* rudimentary. You probably do not want to use it.

-S Do not display the median and standard deviation values, nor display the warning/error messages when the average and median are more than one or two times the standard deviation apart. And default to the min/avg/max values. (legacy support).

-t timelimit Maximum number of seconds to spend for benchmarking. This implies a -n 50000 internally. Use this to benchmark the server within a fixed total amount of time. Per default there is no timelimit.

-T content-type Content-type header to use for POST/PUT data, eg. application/x-www-form-urlencoded. Default: text/plain.

-u PUT-file File containing data to PUT. Remember to also set -T.

-v verbosity Set verbosity level - 4 and above prints information on headers, 3 and above prints response codes (404, 200, etc.), 2 and above prints warnings and info.

-V Display version number and exit.

-w Print out results in HTML tables. Default table is two columns wide, with a white background.

-x <table>-attributes String to use as attributes for <table>. Attributes are inserted <table *here* >.

-X proxy[:port] Use a proxy server for the requests.

-y <tr>-attributes String to use as attributes for <tr>.

-z <td>-attributes String to use as attributes for <td>.

-Z ciphersuite Specify SSL/TLS cipher suite (See openssl ciphers).

1.3.3 Bugs

There are various statically declared buffers of fixed length. Combined with the lazy parsing of the command line arguments, the response headers from the server and other external inputs, this might bite you.

It does not implement HTTP/1.x fully; only accepts some 'expected' forms of responses. The rather heavy use of strstr(3) shows up top in profile, which might indicate a performance problem; *i.e.*, you would measure the ab performance rather than the server's.

1.4 apachectl - Apache HTTP Server Control Interface

apachectl is a front end to the Apache HyperText Transfer Protocol (HTTP) server. It is designed to help the administrator control the functioning of the Apache httpd daemon.

The apachectl script can operate in two modes. First, it can act as a simple front-end to the httpd command that simply sets any necessary environment variables and then invokes httpd, passing through any command line arguments. Second, apachectl can act as a SysV init script, taking simple one-word arguments like start, restart, and stop, and translating them into appropriate signals to httpd.

If your Apache installation uses non-standard paths, you will need to edit the apachectl script to set the appropriate paths to the httpd binary. You can also specify any necessary httpd command line arguments. See the comments in the script for details.

The apachectl script returns a 0 exit value on success, and >0 if an error occurs. For more details, view the comments in the script.

See also:

- ▷ Starting Apache (p. 49)
- ▷ Stopping Apache (p. 51)
- ▷ Configuration Files (p. 54)
- ▷ Platform Docs (p. 745)
- ▷ httpd (p. 6)

1.4.1 Synopsis

When acting in pass-through mode, apachectl can take all the arguments available for the httpd binary.

apachectl [*httpd-argument*]

When acting in SysV init mode, apachectl takes simple, one-word commands, defined below.

apachectl *command*

1.4.2 Options

Only the SysV init-style options are defined here. Other arguments are defined on the httpd manual page.

start Start the Apache httpd daemon. Gives an error if it is already running. This is equivalent to apachectl -k start.

stop Stops the Apache httpd daemon. This is equivalent to apachectl -k stop.

restart Restarts the Apache httpd daemon. If the daemon is not running, it is
started. This command automatically checks the configuration files as in
configtest before initiating the restart to make sure the daemon doesn't
die. This is equivalent to apachectl -k restart.

fullstatus Displays a full status report from mod_status. For this to work, you
need to have mod_status enabled on your server and a text-based browser
such as lynx available on your system. The URL used to access the status
report can be set by editing the STATUSURL variable in the script.

status Displays a brief status report. Similar to the fullstatus option, except
that the list of requests currently being served is omitted.

graceful Gracefully restarts the Apache httpd daemon. If the daemon is not
running, it is started. This differs from a normal restart in that currently
open connections are not aborted. A side effect is that old log files will not
be closed immediately. This means that if used in a log rotation script,
a substantial delay may be necessary to ensure that the old log files are
closed before processing them. This command automatically checks the
configuration files as in configtest before initiating the restart to make
sure Apache doesn't die. This is equivalent to apachectl -k graceful.

graceful-stop Gracefully stops the Apache httpd daemon. This differs from
a normal stop in that currently open connections are not aborted. A side
effect is that old log files will not be closed immediately. This is equivalent
to apachectl -k graceful-stop.

configtest Run a configuration file syntax test. It parses the configuration files
and either reports Syntax Ok or detailed information about the particular
syntax error. This is equivalent to apachectl -t.

The following option was available in earlier versions but has been removed.

startssl To start httpd with SSL support, you should edit your configuration
file to include the relevant directives and then use the normal apachectl
start.

1.5 apxs - APache eXtenSion tool

apxs is a tool for building and installing extension modules for the Apache HyperText Transfer Protocol (HTTP) server. This is achieved by building a dynamic shared object (DSO) from one or more source or object *files* which then can be loaded into the Apache server under runtime via the LoadModule directive from mod_so.

So to use this extension mechanism your platform has to support the DSO feature and your Apache httpd binary has to be built with the mod_so module. The apxs tool automatically complains if this is not the case. You can check this yourself by manually running the command

```
$ httpd -l
```

The module mod_so should be part of the displayed list. If these requirements are fulfilled you can easily extend your Apache server's functionality by installing your own modules with the DSO mechanism by the help of this apxs tool:

```
$ apxs -i -a -c mod_foo.c
gcc -fpic -DSHARED_MODULE -I/path/to/apache/include -c mod_foo.c
ld -Bshareable -o mod_foo.so mod_foo.o
cp mod_foo.so /path/to/apache/modules/mod_foo.so
chmod 755 /path/to/apache/modules/mod_foo.so
[activating module 'foo' in /path/to/apache/etc/httpd.conf]
$ apachectl restart
/path/to/apache/sbin/apachectl restart:  httpd not running,
trying to start
[Tue Mar 31 11:27:55 1998] [debug] mod_so.c(303):  loaded module
foo_module
/path/to/apache/sbin/apachectl restart:  httpd started
$ _
```

The arguments *files* can be any C source file (.c), a object file (.o) or even a library archive (.a). The apxs tool automatically recognizes these extensions and automatically used the C source files for compilation while just using the object and archive files for the linking phase. But when using such pre-compiled objects make sure they are compiled for position independent code (PIC) to be able to use them for a dynamically loaded shared object. For instance with GCC you always just have to use -fpic. For other C compilers consult its manual page or watch for the flags apxs uses to compile the object files.

For more details about DSO support in Apache read the documentation of mod_so or perhaps even read the src/modules/standard/mod_so.c source file.

See also:

▷ apachectl (p. 11)

▷ httpd (p. 6)

1.5.1 Synopsis

apxs -g [-S name=value] -n modname

apxs -q [-S name=value] query ...

apxs -c [-S name=value] [-o dsofile] [-I incdir] [-D
name=value] [-L libdir] [-l libname] [-Wc,compiler-flags
] [-Wl,linker-flags] files ...

apxs -i [-S name=value] [-n modname] [-a] [-A] dso-file
...

apxs -e [-S name=value] [-n modname] [-a] [-A] dso-file
...

1.5.2 Options

Common Options

-n modname This explicitly sets the module name for the -i (install) and -g
(template generation) option. Use this to explicitly specify the module
name. For option -g this is required; for option -i the apxs tool tries to
determine the name from the source or (as a fallback) at least by guessing
it from the filename.

Query Options

-q Performs a query for apxs's knowledge about certain settings. The query pa-
rameters can be one or more of the following strings: CC, CFLAGS, CFLAGS_-
SHLIB, INCLUDEDIR, LD_SHLIB, LDFLAGS_SHLIB, LIBEXECDIR, LIBS_SHLIB,
SBINDIR, SYSCONFDIR, TARGET.

Use this for manually determining settings. For instance use

    INC=-I'apxs -q INCLUDEDIR'

inside your own Makefiles if you need manual access to Apache's C header
files.

Configuration Options

-S name=value This option changes the apxs settings described above.

Template Generation Options

-g This generates a subdirectory name (see option -n) and two files: a sample
module source file named mod_name.c which can be used as a template
for creating your own modules or as a quick start for playing with the
apxs mechanism. And a corresponding Makefile for even easier build and
installing of this module.

DSO Compilation Options

-c This indicates the compilation operation. It first compiles the C source
   files (.c) of *files* into corresponding object files (.o) and then builds a
   dynamically shared object in *dsofile* by linking these object files plus the
   remaining object files (.o and .a) of *files*. If no -o option is specified
   the output file is guessed from the first filename in *files* and thus usually
   defaults to mod_name.so.

-o dsofile Explicitly specifies the filename of the created dynamically shared
   object. If not specified and the name cannot be guessed from the *files* list,
   the fallback name mod_unknown.so is used.

-D name=value This option is directly passed through to the compilation com-
   mand(s). Use this to add your own defines to the build process.

-I incdir This option is directly passed through to the compilation com-
   mand(s). Use this to add your own include directories to the build process.

-L libdir This option is directly passed through to the linker command. Use
   this to add your own library directories to the build process.

-l libname This option is directly passed through to the linker command. Use
   this to add your own libraries to the build process.

-Wc,compiler-flags This option passes *compiler-flags* as additional flags to
   the libtool --mode=compile command. Use this to add local compiler-
   specific options.

-Wl,linker-flags This option passes *linker-flags* as additional flags to the
   libtool --mode=link command. Use this to add local linker-specific options.

DSO Installation and Configuration Options

-i This indicates the installation operation and installs one or more dynamically shared objects into the server's *modules* directory.

-a This activates the module by automatically adding a corresponding
   LoadModule line to Apache's httpd.conf configuration file, or by enabling
   it if it already exists.

-A Same as option -a but the created LoadModule directive is prefixed with a
   hash sign (#), *i.e.*, the module is just prepared for later activation but
   initially disabled.

-e This indicates the editing operation, which can be used with the -a and
   -A options similarly to the -i operation to edit Apache's httpd.conf
   configuration file without attempting to install the module.

1.5.3 Examples

Assume you have an Apache module named mod_foo.c available which should
extend Apache's server functionality. To accomplish this you first have to com-

pile the C source into a shared object suitable for loading into the Apache server
under runtime via the following command:

```
$ apxs -c mod_foo.c
/path/to/libtool --mode=compile gcc ...  -c mod_foo.c
/path/to/libtool --mode=link gcc ...  -o mod_foo.la mod_foo.slo
$ _
```

Then you have to update the Apache configuration by making sure a LoadModule
directive is present to load this shared object. To simplify this step apxs provides
an automatic way to install the shared object in its "modules" directory and
updating the httpd.conf file accordingly. This can be achieved by running:

```
$ apxs -i -a mod_foo.la
/path/to/instdso.sh mod_foo.la /path/to/apache/modules
/path/to/libtool --mode=install cp mod_foo.la
/path/to/apache/modules ...  chmod 755
/path/to/apache/modules/mod_foo.so
[activating module 'foo' in /path/to/apache/conf/httpd.conf]
$ _
```

This way a line named

```
LoadModule foo_module modules/mod_foo.so
```

is added to the configuration file if still not present. If you want to have this
disabled by default use the -A option, *i.e.*

```
$ apxs -i -A mod_foo.c
```

For a quick test of the apxs mechanism you can create a sample Apache module
template plus a corresponding Makefile via:

```
$ apxs -g -n foo
Creating [DIR] foo
Creating [FILE] foo/Makefile
Creating [FILE] foo/modules.mk
Creating [FILE] foo/mod_foo.c
Creating [FILE] foo/.deps
$ _
```

Then you can immediately compile this sample module into a shared object and
load it into the Apache server:

```
$ cd foo
$ make all reload
apxs -c mod_foo.c
/path/to/libtool --mode=compile gcc ...  -c mod_foo.c
/path/to/libtool --mode=link gcc ...  -o mod_foo.la mod_foo.slo
apxs -i -a -n "foo" mod_foo.la
/path/to/instdso.sh mod_foo.la /path/to/apache/modules
/path/to/libtool --mode=install cp mod_foo.la
```

```
/path/to/apache/modules ...  chmod 755
/path/to/apache/modules/mod_foo.so
[activating module 'foo' in /path/to/apache/conf/httpd.conf]
apachectl restart
/path/to/apache/sbin/apachectl restart:  httpd not running,
trying to start
[Tue Mar 31 11:27:55 1998] [debug] mod_so.c(303):  loaded module
foo_module
/path/to/apache/sbin/apachectl restart:  httpd started
$ _
```

1.6 configure - Configure the source tree

The configure script configures the source tree for compiling and installing the Apache HTTP Server on your particular platform. Various options allow the compilation of a server corresponding to your personal requirements.

This script, included in the root directory of the source distribution, is for compilation on Unix and Unix-like systems only. For other platforms, see the platform (p. 745) documentation.

See also:

▷ Compiling and Installing (p. 775)

1.6.1 Synopsis

You should call the configure script from within the root directory of the distribution.

./configure [OPTION]... [VAR=VALUE]...

To assign environment variables (e.g. CC, CFLAGS ...), specify them as VAR=VALUE. See below for descriptions of some of the useful variables.

1.6.2 Options

- Configuration options
- Installation directories
- System types
- Optional features
- Options for support programs

Configuration options

The following options influence the behavior of configure itself.

-C
--config-cache
        This is an alias for --cache-file=config.cache

--cache-file=FILE
        The test results will be cached in file *FILE*. This option is disabled by default.

-h
--help [short|recursive]
        Output the help and exit. With the argument short only options specific to this package will displayed. The argument recursive displays the short help of all the included packages.

-n
--no-create
> The configure script is run normally but does not create output files. This is useful to check the test results before generating makefiles for compilation.

-q
--quiet
> Do not print checking ... messages during the configure process.

--srcdir=DIR
> Defines directory *DIR* to be the source file directory. Default is the directory where configure is located, or the parent directory.

--silent
> Same as --quiet

-V
—version
> Display copyright information and exit.

Installation directories

These options define the installation directory. The installation tree depends on the selected layout.

--prefix=PREFIX Install architecture-independent files in *PREFIX*. By default the installation directory is set to /usr/local/apache2.

--exec-prefix=EPREFIX Install architecture-dependent files in *EPREFIX*. By default the installation directory is set to the *PREFIX* directory.

By default, make install will install all the files in /usr/local/apache2/bin, /usr/local/apache2/lib etc. You can specify an installation prefix other than /usr/local/apache2 using --prefix, for instance --prefix=$HOME.

Define a directory layout

--enable-layout=LAYOUT Configure the source code and build scripts to assume an installation tree based on the layout *LAYOUT*. This allows you to separately specify the locations for each type of file within the Apache HTTP Server installation. The config.layout file contains several example configurations, and you can also create your own custom configuration following the examples. The different layouts in this file are grouped into <Layout FOO>...</Layout> sections and referred to by name as in FOO. The default layout is Apache.

Fine tuning of the installation directories

For better control of the installation directories, use the options below. Please note that the directory defaults are set by autoconf and are overwritten by the corresponding layout setting.

--bindir=DIR Install user executables in *DIR*. The user executables are supporting programs like htpasswd, dbmmanage, etc. which are useful for site administrators. By default *DIR* is set to *EPREFIX*/bin.

--datadir=DIR Install read-only architecture-independent data in *DIR*. By default datadir is set to *PREFIX*/share. This option is offered by autoconf and currently unused.

--includedir=DIR Install C header files in *DIR*. By default includedir is set to *EPREFIX*/include.

--infodir=DIR Install info documentation in *DIR*. By default infodir is set to *PREFIX*/info. This option is currently unused.

--libdir=DIR Install object code libraries in *DIR*. By default libdir is set to *EPREFIX*/lib.

--libexecdir=DIR Install the program executables (i.e., shared modules) in *DIR*. By default libexecdir is set to *EPREFIX*/libexec.

--localstatedir=DIR Install modifiable single-machine data in *DIR*. By default localstatedir is set to *PREFIX*/var. This option is offered by autoconf and currently unused.

--mandir=DIR Install the man documentation in *DIR*. By default mandir is set to *EPREFIX*/man.

--oldincludedir=DIR Install C header files for non-gcc in *DIR*. By default oldincludedir is set to /usr/include. This option is offered by autoconf and currently unused.

--sbindir=DIR Install the system administrator executables in *DIR*. Those are server programs like httpd, apachectl, suexec, etc. which are neccessary to run the Apache HTTP Server. By default sbindir is set to *EPREFIX*/sbin.

--sharedstatedir=DIR Install modifiable architecture-independent data in *DIR*. By default sharedstatedir is set to *PREFIX*/com. This option is offered by autoconf and currently unused.

--sysconfdir=DIR Install read-only single-machine data like the server configuration files httpd.conf, mime.types, etc. in *DIR*. By default sysconfdir is set to *PREFIX*/conf.

System types

These options are used to cross-compile the Apache HTTP Server to run on another system. In normal cases, when building and running the server on the same system, these options are not used.

--build=BUILD Defines the system type of the system on which the tools are being built. It defaults to the result of the script config.guess.

--host=HOST Defines the system type of the system on which the server will run. *HOST* defaults to *BUILD*.

--target=TARGET Configure for building compilers for the system type *TAR-GET*. It defaults to *HOST*. This option is offered by autoconf and not necessary for the Apache HTTP Server.

Optional Features

These options are used to fine tune the features your HTTP server will have.

General syntax

Generally you can use the following syntax to enable or disable a feature:

--disable-FEATURE Do not include *FEATURE*. This is the same as --enable-*FEATURE*=no.

--enable-FEATURE[=ARG] Include *FEATURE*. The default value for *ARG* is yes.

--enable-MODULE=shared The corresponding module will be build as DSO module.

--enable-MODULE=static By default enabled modules are linked statically. You can force this explicitly.

NOTE *configure will not complain about* --enable-foo *even if foo doesn't exist, so you need to type carefully.*

Modules enabled by default

Some modules are compiled by default and have to be disabled explicitly. Use the following options to remove discrete modules from the compilation process.

--disable-actions Disable action triggering on requests, which is provided by mod_actions.

--disable-alias Disable the mapping of requests to different parts of the filesystem, which is provided by mod_alias.

--disable-asis Disable support for as-is filetypes, which is provided by mod_-asis.

--disable-auth Disable user-based access control provided by mod_auth. This module provides for HTTP Basic Authentication, where the usernames and passwords are stored in plain text files.

--disable-autoindex Disable the directory listing functionality provided by mod_autoindex.

--disable-access Disable host-based access control provided by mod_access.

--disable-cgi The module mod_cgi, which provides support for CGI scripts, is enabled by default when using a non-threaded MPM. Use this option to disable CGI support.

--disable-cgid When using the threaded MPMs worker support for CGI scripts is provided by mod_cgid by default. To disable CGI support use this option.

--disable-charset-lite Disable character set translation provided by mod_-charset_lite. This module will be installed by default only on EBCDIC systems.

--disable-dir Disable directory request handling provided by mod_dir.

--disable-env Enable setting and clearing of environment variables, which is provided by mod_env.

--disable-http Disable the HTTP protocol handling. The http module is a basic one, enabling the server to function as an HTTP server. It is only useful to disable it if you want to use another protocol module instead. **Don't disable this module unless you are really sure what you are doing.**
Note: This module will always be linked statically.

--disable-imagemap Disable support for server based imagemaps, which provided by mod_imagemap.

--disable-include Disable Server Side Includes provided by mod_include.

--disable-log-config Disable the logging configuration provided by mod_-log_config. You won't be able to log requests to the server without this module.

--disable-mime The module mod_mime associates the requested filename's extensions with the file's behavior and content (mime-type, language, character set and encoding). Disabling this module is normally not recommended.

--disable-negotiation Disable content negotiation provided by mod_-negotiation.

--disable-setenvif Disable support for basing environment variables on headers, which is provided by mod_setenvif.

--disable-status Enable the process/thread monitoring, which is provided by mod_status.

--disable-userdir Disable the mapping of requests to user-specific directories, which is provided by mod_userdir.

Modules, disabled by default

Some modules are compiled by default and have to be enabled explicitly or by using the keywords most or all (see --enable-mods-shared below for further explanation) to be available. Therefore use the options below.

--enable-auth-anon Enable anonymous user access provided by mod_auth_-anon.

--enable-auth-dbm mod_auth_dbm provides for HTTP Basic Authentication, where the usernames and passwords are stored in DBM type database files. Use this option to enable the module.

--enable-auth-digest Enable RFC2617 Digest authentication provided by mod_auth_digest. This module uses plain text files to store the credentials.

--enable-authnz-ldap Enable LDAP based authentication provided by mod_authnz_ldap.

--enable-cache Enable dynamic file caching provided by mod_cache. This experimental module may be interesting for servers with high load or caching proxy servers. At least one storage management module (e.g. mod_disk_cache or mod_mem_cache) is also necessary.

--enable-cern-meta Enable the CERN-type meta files support provided by mod_cern_meta.

--enable-charset-lite Enable character set translation provided by mod_charset_lite. This module will be installed by default only on EBCDIC systems. On other systems, you have to enable it.

--enable-dav Enable the WebDAV protocol handling provided by mod_dav. Support for filesystem resources is provided by the separate module mod_dav_fs. This module is also automatically enabled with --enable-dav. Note: mod_dav can only be used together with the http protocol module.

--enable-dav-fs Enable DAV support for filesystem resources, which is provided by mod_dav_fs. This module is a provider for the mod_dav module, so you should also use --enable-dav.

--enable-dav-lock Enable mod_dav_lock which provides generic DAV locking support for backend modules. This module needs at least mod_dav to function, so you should also use --enable-dav.

--enable-deflate Enable deflate transfer encoding provided by mod_deflate.

--enable-disk-cache Enable disk caching provided by mod_disk_cache.

--enable-expires Enable Expires header control provided by mod_expires.

--enable-ext-filter Enable the external filter support provided by mod_ext_filter.

--enable-file-cache Enable the file cache provided by mod_file_cache.

--enable-headers Enable control of HTTP headers provided by mod_headers.

--enable-info Enable the server information provided by mod_info.

--enable-ldap Enable LDAP caching and connection pooling services provided by mod_ldap.

--enable-logio Enable logging of input and output bytes including headers provided by mod_logio.

--enable-mem-cache Enable memory caching provided by mod_mem_cache.

--enable-mime-magic Enable automatical determining of MIME types, which
is provided by mod_mime_magic.

--enable-isapi Enable the isapi extension support provided by mod_isapi.

--enable-proxy Enable the proxy/gateway functionality provided by mod_-
proxy. The proxying capabilities for AJP13, CONNECT, FTP, HTTP and
the balancer are provided by the separate modules mod_proxy_ajp,
mod_proxy_connect, mod_proxy_ftp, mod_proxy_http and mod_proxy_-
balancer. These five modules are also automatically enabled with
--enable-proxy.

--enable-proxy-ajp Enable   proxy   support   for   AJP13 (Apache JServ
Protocol 1.3) request handling, which is provided by mod_proxy_ajp.
This module is an extension for the mod_proxy module, so you should
also use --enable-proxy.

--enable-proxy-balancer Enable load balancing support for the AJP13, FTP
and HTTP protocols, which is provided by mod_proxy_balancer. This module is an extension for the mod_proxy module, so you should also use
--enable-proxy.

--enable-proxy-connect Enable proxy support for CONNECT request handling,
which is provided by mod_proxy_connect. This module is an extension for
the mod_proxy module, so you should also use --enable-proxy.

--enable-proxy-ftp Enable proxy support for FTP requests, which is provided
by mod_proxy_ftp. This module is an extension for the mod_proxy module,
so you should also use --enable-proxy.

--enable-proxy-http Enable proxy support for HTTP requests, which is provided by mod_proxy_http. This module is an extension for the mod_proxy
module, so you should also use --enable-proxy.

--enable-rewrite Enable rule based URL manipulation provided by mod_-
rewrite.

--enable-so Enable DSO capability provided by mod_so. This module will be
automatically enabled if you use the --enable-mods-shared option.

--enable-speling Enable the functionality to correct common URL mis-
spellings, which is provided by mod_speling.

--enable-ssl Enable support for SSL/TLS provided by mod_ssl.

--enable-unique-id Enable the generation of per-request unique ids, which is
provided by mod_unique_id.

--enable-usertrack Enable user-session tracking provided by mod_usertrack.

--enable-vhost-alias Enable mass virtual hosting provided by mod_vhost_-
alias.

Modules for developers

The following modules are useful only for developers and testing purposes and are disabled by default. Use the following options to enable them. If you are not sure whether you need one of these modules, omit them.

--enable-bucketeer Enable the manipulation filter for buckets, which is provided by mod_bucketeer.

--enable-case-filter Enable the example uppercase conversion output filter support of mod_case_filter.

--enable-case-filter-in Enable the example uppercase conversion input filter support of mod_case_filter_in.

--enable-echo Enable the ECHO server provided by mod_echo.

--enable-example Enable the example and demo module mod_example.

--enable-optional-fn-export Enable the example for an optional function exporter, which is provided by mod_optional_fn_export.

--enable-optional-fn-import Enable the example for an optional function importer, which is provided by mod_optional_fn_import.

--enable-optional-hook-export Enable the example for an optional hook exporter, which is provided by mod_optional_hook_export.

--enable-optional-hook-import Enable the example optional hook importer, which is provided by mod_optional_hook_import.

MPMs and third-party modules

To add the necessary Multi Processing Module and additional third-party modules use the following options:

--with-module=module-type:module-file[,module-type:module-file]
Add one or more third-party modules to the list of statically linked modules. The module source file *module-file* will be searched in the modules/*module-type* subdirectory of your Apache HTTP server source tree. If it is not found there configure is considering *module-file* to be an absolute file path and tries to copy the source file into the *module-type* subdirectory. If the subdirectory doesn't exist it will be created and populated with a standard Makefile.in.

This option is useful to add small external modules consisting of one source file. For more complex modules you should read the vendor's documentation.

> NOTE *If you want to build a DSO module instead of a statically linked use apxs.*

--with-mpm=MPM Choose the process model for your server. You have to select exactly one Multi-Processing Module (p. 703). Otherwise the default MPM (p. 703) for your operating system will be taken. Possible MPMs are beos, mpmt_os2, prefork, and worker.

Cumulative and other options

--enable-maintainer-mode Turn on debugging and compile time warnings.

--enable-mods-shared=MODULE-LIST Defines a list of modules to be enabled
and build as dynamic shared modules. This means that these modules
have to be loaded dynamically by using the LoadModule directive.

MODULE-LIST is a space separated list of modulenames enclosed by
quotation marks. The module names are given without the preceding
mod_. For example:

    --enable-mods-shared='headers rewrite dav'

Additionally you can use the special keywords all and most. For example,

    --enable-mods-shared=most

will compile most modules and build them as DSO modules.

Caveat: --enable-mods-shared=all does not actually build all modules.
To build all modules then, one might use:

    ./configure \
        --with-ldap \
        --enable-mods-shared="all ssl ldap cache proxy
    authn_alias mem_cache file_cache authnz_ldap
    charset_lite dav_lock disk_cache"

--enable-modules=MODULE-LIST This option behaves similar to
--enable-mods-shared, but will link the given modules statically.
This mean, these modules will always be present while running httpd.
They need not be loaded with LoadModule.

--enable-v4-mapped Allow IPv6 sockets to handle IPv4 connections.

--with-port=PORT This defines the port on which httpd will listen. This port
number is used when generating the configuration file httpd.conf. The
default is 80.

--with-program-name Define an alternative executable name. The default is
httpd.

Optional packages

These options are used to define optional packages.

General syntax

Generally you can use the following syntax to define an optional package:

--with-PACKAGE[=ARG] Use the package PACKAGE. The default value for
ARG is yes.

--without-PACKAGE Do not use the package PACKAGE. This is the same as
--with-PACKAGE=no. This option is provided by autoconf but not very
useful for the Apache HTTP Server.

Specific packages

--with-apr=DIR|FILE The Apache Portable Runtime (APR) is part of the httpd source distribution and will automatically be built together with the HTTP server. If you want to use an already installed APR instead you have to tell configure the path to the apr-config script. You may set the absolute path and name or the directory to the installed APR. apr-config must exist within this directory or the subdirectory bin.

--with-apr-util=DIR|FILE The Apache Portable Runtime Utilities (APU) are part of the httpd source distribution and will automatically be built together with the HTTP server. If you want to use an already installed APU instead you have to tell configure the path to the apu-config script. You may set the absolute path and name or the directory to the installed APU. apu-config must exist within this directory or the subdirectory bin.

--with-ssl=DIR If mod_ssl has been enabled configure searches for an installed OpenSSL. You can set the directory path to the SSL/TLS toolkit instead.

--with-z=DIR configure searches automatically for an installed zlib library if your source configuration requires one (e.g., when mod_deflate is enabled). You can set the directory path to the compression library instead.

Several features of the Apache HTTP Server, including mod_authn_dbm and mod_rewrite's DBM RewriteMap use simple key/value databases for quick lookups of information. SDBM is included in the APU, so this database is always available. If you would like to use other database types, use the following options to enable them:

--with-gdbm[=path] If no *path* is specified, configure will search for the include files and libraries of a GNU DBM installation in the usual search paths. An explicit *path* will cause configure to look in *path*/lib and *path*/include for the relevant files. Finally, the *path* may specify specific include and library paths separated by a colon.

--with-ndbm[=path] Like --with-gdbm, but searches for a New DBM installation.

--with-berkeley-db[=path] Like --with-gdbm, but searches for a Berkeley DB installation.

NOTE *The DBM options are provided by the APU and passed through to its configuration script. They are useless when using an already installed APU defined by --with-apr-util.*

You may use more then one DBM implementation together with your HTTP server. The appropriate DBM type will be configured within the runtime configuration at each time.

Options for support programs

--enable-static-support Build a statically linked version of the support binaries. This means, a stand-alone executable will be built with all the
necessary libraries integrated. Otherwise the support binaries are linked
dynamically by default.

--enable-suexec Use this option to enable suexec, which allows you to set
uid and gid for spawned processes. **Do not use this option unless you
understand all the security implications of running a suid binary
on your server.** Further options to configure suexec are described below.

It is possible to create a statically linked binary of a single support program by
using the following options:

--enable-static-ab Build a statically linked version of ab.

--enable-static-checkgid Build a statically linked version of checkgid.

--enable-static-htdbm Build a statically linked version of htdbm.

--enable-static-htdigest Build a statically linked version of htdigest.

--enable-static-htpasswd Build a statically linked version of htpasswd.

--enable-static-logresolve Build a statically linked version of logresolve.

--enable-static-rotatelogs Build a statically linked version of rotatelogs.

suexec configuration options

The following options are used to fine tune the behavior of suexec. See Configuring and installing suEXEC (p. 47) for further information.

--with-suexec-bin This defines the path to suexec binary.   Default is
--sbindir (see Fine tuning of installation directories).

--with-suexec-caller This defines the user allowed to call suexec. It should
be the same as the user under which httpd normally runs.

--with-suexec-docroot This defines the directory tree under which suexec
access is allowed for executables. Default value is --datadir/htdocs.

--with-suexec-gidmin Define this as the lowest GID allowed to be a target
user for suexec. The default value is 100.

--with-suexec-logfile This defines the filename of the suexec logfile. By
default the logfile is named suexec_log and located in --logfiledir.

--with-suexec-safepath Define the value of the environment variable PATH
to be set for processes started by suexec. Default value is /usr/local/
bin:/usr/bin:/bin.

--with-suexec-userdir This defines the subdirectory under the user's directory that contains all executables for which suexec access is allowed. This
setting is necessary when you want to use suexec together with user-
specific directories (as provided by mod_userdir). The default is public_-
html.

--with-suexec-uidmin Define this as the lowest UID allowed to be a target user for suexec. The default value is 100.

--with-suexec-umask Set umask for processes started by suexec. It defaults to your system settings.

1.6.3 Environment variables

There are some useful environment variables to override the choices made by configure or to help it to find libraries and programs with nonstandard names or locations.

CC Define the C compiler command to be used for compilation.

CFLAGS Set C compiler flags you want to use for compilation.

CPP Define the C preprocessor command to be used.

CPPFLAGS Set C/C++ preprocessor flags, e.g. -I*includedir* if you have headers in a nonstandard directory *includedir*.

LDFLAGS Set linker flags, e.g. -L*libdir* if you have libraries in a nonstandard directory *libdir*.

1.7 dbmmanage - Manage user authentication files in DBM format

dbmmanage is used to create and update the DBM format files used to store usernames and passwords for basic authentication of HTTP users via mod_authn_dbm. Resources available from the Apache HTTP server can be restricted to just the users listed in the files created by dbmmanage. This program can only be used when the usernames are stored in a DBM file. To use a flat-file database see htpasswd.

This manual page only lists the command line arguments. For details of the directives necessary to configure user authentication in httpd see the httpd manual (see below).

See also:

▷ httpd (p. 6)

▷ mod_authn_dbm (p. 167)

▷ mod_authz_dbm (p. 187)

1.7.1 Synopsis

dbmmanage [*encoding*] *filename* add|adduser|check|delete|update *username* [*encpasswd* [*group*[,*group*...]] [*comment*]]]

dbmmanage *filename* view [*username*]

dbmmanage *filename* import

1.7.2 Options

filename The filename of the DBM format file. Usually without the extension .db, .pag, or .dir.

username The user for which the operations are performed. The *username* may not contain a colon (:).

encpasswd This is the already encrypted password to use for the update and add commands. You may use a hyphen (-) if you want to get prompted for the password, but fill in the fields afterwards. Additionally when using the update command, a period (.) keeps the original password untouched.

group A group which the user is member of. A groupname may not contain a colon (:). You may use a hyphen (-) if you don't want to assign the user to a group, but fill in the comment field. Additionally when using the update command, a period (.) keeps the original groups untouched.

comment This is the place for your opaque comments about the user, like realname, mailaddress or such things. The server will ignore this field.

Encodings

-d crypt encryption (default, except on Win32, Netware)

-m MD5 encryption (default on Win32, Netware)

-s SHA1 encryption

-p plaintext (*not recommended*)

Commands

add Adds an entry for *username* to *filename* using the encrypted password
   encpasswd.

> dbmmanage passwords.dat add rbowen foKntnEF3KSXA

adduser Asks for a password and then adds an entry for *username* to *filename*.

> dbmmanage passwords.dat adduser krietz

check Asks for a password and then checks if *username* is in *filename* and if its
   password matches the specified one.

> dbmmanage passwords.dat check rbowen

delete Deletes the *username* entry from *filename*.

> dbmmanage passwords.dat delete rbowen

import Reads *username:password* entries (one per line) from STDIN and adds
   them to *filename*. The passwords already have to be crypted.

update Same as the adduser command, except that it makes sure *username*
   already exists in *filename*.

> dbmmanage passwords.dat update rbowen

view Just displays the contents of the DBM file. If you specify a *username*, it
   displays the particular record only.

> dbmmanage passwords.dat view

1.7.3 Bugs

One should be aware that there are a number of different DBM file formats in
existence, and in all likelihood, libraries for more than one format may exist
on your system. The three primary examples are SDBM, NDBM, the GNU
project's GDBM, and Berkeley DB 2. Unfortunately, all these libraries use
different file formats, and you must make sure that the file format used by
filename is the same format that dbmmanage expects to see. dbmmanage currently
has no way of determining what type of DBM file it is looking at. If used against
the wrong format, will simply return nothing, or may create a different DBM
file with a different name, or at worst, it may corrupt the DBM file if you were
attempting to write to it.

dbmmanage has a list of DBM format preferences, defined by the @AnyDBM::ISA
array near the beginning of the program. Since we prefer the Berkeley DB 2 file

format, the order in which dbmmanage will look for system libraries is Berkeley
DB 2, then NDBM, then GDBM and then SDBM. The first library found will
be the library dbmmanage will attempt to use for all DBM file transactions.
This ordering is slightly different than the standard @AnyDBM::ISA ordering in
Perl, as well as the ordering used by the simple dbmopen() call in Perl, so if
you use any other utilities to manage your DBM files, they must also follow
this preference ordering. Similar care must be taken if using programs in other
languages, like C, to access these files.

One can usually use the file program supplied with most Unix systems to see
what format a DBM file is in.

1.8 htcacheclean - Clean up the disk cache

htcacheclean is used to keep the size of mod_disk_cache's storage within a certain limit. This tool can run either manually or in daemon mode. When running in daemon mode, it sleeps in the background and checks the cache directories at regular intervals for cached content to be removed. You can stop the daemon cleanly by sending it a TERM or INT signal.

See also:

▷ mod_disk_cache (p. 260)

1.8.1 Synopsis

htcacheclean [-D] [-v] [-t] [-r] [-n] -ppath -llimit

htcacheclean [-n] [-t] [-i] -dinterval -ppath -llimit

1.8.2 Options

-dinterval Daemonize and repeat cache cleaning every *interval* minutes. This option is mutually exclusive with the -D, -v and -r options. To shutdown the daemon cleanly, just send it a SIGTERM or SIGINT.

-D Do a dry run and don't delete anything. This option is mutually exclusive with the -d option.

-v Be verbose and print statistics. This option is mutually exclusive with the -d option.

-r Clean thoroughly. This assumes that the Apache web server is not running (otherwise you may get garbage in the cache). This option is mutually exclusive with the -d option and implies the -t option.

-n Be nice. This causes slower processing in favour of other processes. htcacheclean will sleep from time to time so that (a) the disk IO will be delayed and (b) the kernel can schedule other processes in the meantime.

-t Delete all empty directories. By default only cache files are removed; however with some configurations the large number of directories created may require attention. If your configuration requires a very large number of directories, to the point that inode or file allocation table exhaustion may become an issue, use of this option is advised.

-ppath Specify *path* as the root directory of the disk cache. This should be the same value as specified with the CacheRoot directive.

-llimit Specify *limit* as the total disk cache size limit. The value is expressed in bytes by default (or attaching B to the number). Attach K for Kbytes or M for MBytes.

-i Be intelligent and run only when there was a modification of the disk cache. This option is only possible together with the -d option.

1.8.3 Exit Status

htcacheclean returns a zero status ("true") if all operations were successful, 1 otherwise.

1.9 htdbm - Manipulate DBM password databases

htdbm is used to manipulate the DBM format files used to store usernames and passwords for basic authentication of HTTP users via mod_authn_dbm. See the dbmmanage documentation for more information about these DBM files.

See also:

▷ httpd (p. 6)

▷ dbmmanage (p. 30)

▷ mod_authn_dbm (p. 167)

1.9.1 Synopsis

htdbm [-TDBTYPE] [-c] [-m | -d | -p | -s] [-t] [-v] [-x] *filename username*

htdbm -b [-TDBTYPE] [-c] [-m | -d | -p | -s] [-t] [-v] *filename username password*

htdbm -n [-c] [-m | -d | -p | -s] [-t] [-v] *username*

htdbm -nb [-c] [-m | -d | -p | -s] [-t] [-v] *username password*

htdbm -v [-TDBTYPE] [-c] [-m | -d | -p | -s] [-t] [-v] *filename username*

htdbm -vb [-TDBTYPE] [-c] [-m | -d | -p | -s] [-t] [-v] *filename username password*

htdbm -x [-TDBTYPE] [-m | -d | -p | -s] *filename username*

htdbm -l [-TDBTYPE]

1.9.2 Options

-b Use batch mode; *i.e.*, get the password from the command line rather than prompting for it. This option should be used with extreme care, since **the password is clearly visible** on the command line.

-c Create the *passwdfile*. If *passwdfile* already exists, it is rewritten and truncated. This option cannot be combined with the -n option.

-n Display the results on standard output rather than updating a database. This option changes the syntax of the command line, since the *passwdfile* argument (usually the first one) is omitted. It cannot be combined with the -c option.

-m Use MD5 encryption for passwords. On Windows, Netware and TPF, this is the default.

-d Use crypt() encryption for passwords. The default on all platforms but Windows, Netware and TPF. Though possibly supported by htdbm on all platforms, it is not supported by the httpd server on Windows, Netware and TPF.

-s Use SHA encryption for passwords. Facilitates migration from/to Netscape servers using the LDAP Directory Interchange Format (ldif).

-p Use plaintext passwords. Though htdbm will support creation on all platforms, the httpd daemon will only accept plain text passwords on Windows, Netware and TPF.

-l Print each of the usernames and comments from the database on stdout.

-t Interpret the final parameter as a comment. When this option is specified, an additional string can be appended to the command line; this string will be stored in the "Comment" field of the database, associated with the specified username.

-v Verify the username and password. The program will print a message indicating whether the supplied password is valid. If the password is invalid, the program exits with error code 3.

-x Delete user. If the username exists in the specified DBM file, it will be deleted.

filename The filename of the DBM format file. Usually without the extension .db, .pag, or .dir. If -c is given, the DBM file is created if it does not already exist, or updated if it does exist.

username The username to create or update in *passwdfile*. If *username* does not exist in this file, an entry is added. If it does exist, the password is changed.

password The plaintext password to be encrypted and stored in the DBM file. Used only with the -b flag.

-TDBTYPE Type of DBM file (SDBM, GDBM, DB, or "default").

1.9.3 Bugs

One should be aware that there are a number of different DBM file formats in existence, and in all likelihood, libraries for more than one format may exist on your system. The three primary examples are SDBM, NDBM, GNU GDBM, and Berkeley/Sleepycat DB 2/3/4. Unfortunately, all these libraries use different file formats, and you must make sure that the file format used by *filename* is the same format that htdbm expects to see. htdbm currently has no way of determining what type of DBM file it is looking at. If used against the wrong format, will simply return nothing, or may create a different DBM file with a different name, or at worst, it may corrupt the DBM file if you were attempting to write to it.

One can usually use the file program supplied with most Unix systems to see what format a DBM file is in.

1.9.4 Exit Status

htdbm returns a zero status ("true") if the username and password have been successfully added or updated in the DBM File. htdbm returns 1 if it encounters some problem accessing files, 2 if there was a syntax problem with the command line, 3 if the password was entered interactively and the verification entry didn't match, 4 if its operation was interrupted, 5 if a value is too long (username, filename, password, or final computed record), 6 if the username contains illegal characters (see the Restrictions section), and 7 if the file is not a valid DBM password file.

1.9.5 Examples

htdbm /usr/local/etc/apache/.htdbm-users jsmith

Adds or modifies the password for user jsmith. The user is prompted for the password. If executed on a Windows system, the password will be encrypted using the modified Apache MD5 algorithm; otherwise, the system's crypt() routine will be used. If the file does not exist, htdbm will do nothing except return an error.

htdbm -c /home/doe/public_html/.htdbm jane

Creates a new file and stores a record in it for user jane. The user is prompted for the password. If the file exists and cannot be read, or cannot be written, it is not altered and htdbm will display a message and return an error status.

htdbm -mb /usr/web/.htdbm-all jones Pwd4Steve

Encrypts the password from the command line (Pwd4Steve) using the MD5 algorithm, and stores it in the specified file.

1.9.6 Security Considerations

Web password files such as those managed by htdbm should *not* be within the Web server's URI space – that is, they should not be fetchable with a browser.

The use of the -b option is discouraged, since when it is used the unencrypted password appears on the command line.

1.9.7 Restrictions

On the Windows and MPE platforms, passwords encrypted with htdbm are limited to no more than 255 characters in length. Longer passwords will be truncated to 255 characters.

The MD5 algorithm used by htdbm is specific to the Apache software; passwords encrypted using it will not be usable with other Web servers.

Usernames are limited to 255 bytes and may not include the character :.

1.10 htdigest - manage user files for digest authentication

htdigest is used to create and update the flat-files used to store usernames, realm and password for digest authentication of HTTP users. Resources available from the Apache HTTP server can be restricted to just the users listed in the files created by htdigest.

See also:

▷ httpd (p. 6)

▷ mod_auth_digest (p. 152)

1.10.1 Synopsis

htdigest [-c] *passwdfile realm username*

1.10.2 Options

-c Create the *passwdfile*. If *passwdfile* already exists, it is deleted first.

passwdfile Name of the file to contain the username, realm and password. If -c is given, this file is created if it does not already exist, or deleted and recreated if it does exist.

realm The realm name to which the user name belongs.

username The user name to create or update in *passwdfile*. If *username* does not exist is this file, an entry is added. If it does exist, the password is changed.

1.10.3 Security Considerations

This program is not safe as a setuid executable. Do *not* make it setuid.

1.11 htpasswd - Manage user files for basic authentication

htpasswd is used to create and update the flat-files used to store usernames and passwords for basic authentication of HTTP users. If htpasswd cannot access a file, such as not being able to write to the output file or not being able to read the file in order to update it, it returns an error status and makes no changes.

Resources available from the Apache HTTP server can be restricted to just the users listed in the files created by htpasswd. This program can only manage usernames and passwords stored in a flat-file. It can encrypt and display password information for use in other types of data stores, though. To use a DBM database see dbmmanage.

htpasswd encrypts passwords using either a version of MD5 modified for Apache, or the system's crypt() routine. Files managed by htpasswd may contain both types of passwords; some user records may have MD5-encrypted passwords while others in the same file may have passwords encrypted with crypt().

See also:

▷ httpd (p. 6)

▷ The scripts in support/SHA1 which come with the distribution.

1.11.1 Synopsis

htpasswd [-c] [-m] [-D] *passwdfile username*

htpasswd -b [-c] [-m | -d | -p | -s] [-D] *passwdfile username password*

htpasswd -n [-m | -d | -s | -p] *username*

htpasswd -nb [-m | -d | -s | -p] *username password*

1.11.2 Options

-b Use batch mode; *i.e.*, get the password from the command line rather than prompting for it. This option should be used with extreme care, since **the password is clearly visible** on the command line.

-c Create the *passwdfile*. If *passwdfile* already exists, it is rewritten and truncated. This option cannot be combined with the -n option.

-n Display the results on standard output rather than updating a file. This is useful for generating password records acceptable to Apache for inclusion in non-text data stores. This option changes the syntax of the command line, since the *passwdfile* argument (usually the first one) is omitted. It cannot be combined with the -c option.

-m Use MD5 encryption for passwords. On Windows, Netware and TPF, this is the default.

-d Use crypt() encryption for passwords. The default on all platforms but Windows, Netware and TPF. Though possibly supported by htpasswd on all platforms, it is not supported by the httpd server on Windows, Netware and TPF.

-s Use SHA encryption for passwords. Facilitates migration from/to Netscape servers using the LDAP Directory Interchange Format (ldif).

-p Use plaintext passwords. Though htpasswd will support creation on all platforms, the httpd daemon will only accept plain text passwords on Windows, Netware and TPF.

-D Delete user. If the username exists in the specified htpasswd file, it will be deleted.

passwdfile Name of the file to contain the user name and password. If -c is given, this file is created if it does not already exist, or rewritten and truncated if it does exist.

username The username to create or update in *passwdfile*. If *username* does not exist in this file, an entry is added. If it does exist, the password is changed.

password The plaintext password to be encrypted and stored in the file. Only used with the -b flag.

1.11.3 Exit Status

htpasswd returns a zero status ("true") if the username and password have been successfully added or updated in the *passwdfile*. htpasswd returns 1 if it encounters some problem accessing files, 2 if there was a syntax problem with the command line, 3 if the password was entered interactively and the verification entry didn't match, 4 if its operation was interrupted, 5 if a value is too long (username, filename, password, or final computed record), 6 if the username contains illegal characters (see the Restrictions section), and 7 if the file is not a valid password file.

1.11.4 Examples

    htpasswd /usr/local/etc/apache/.htpasswd-users jsmith

Adds or modifies the password for user jsmith. The user is prompted for the password. If executed on a Windows system, the password will be encrypted using the modified Apache MD5 algorithm; otherwise, the system's crypt() routine will be used. If the file does not exist, htpasswd will do nothing except return an error.

    htpasswd -c /home/doe/public_html/.htpasswd jane

Creates a new file and stores a record in it for user jane. The user is prompted for the password. If the file exists and cannot be read, or cannot be written, it is not altered and htpasswd will display a message and return an error status.

    htpasswd -mb /usr/web/.htpasswd-all jones Pwd4Steve

Encrypts the password from the command line (Pwd4Steve) using the MD5
algorithm, and stores it in the specified file.

1.11.5 Security Considerations

Web password files such as those managed by htpasswd should *not* be within the
Web server's URI space – that is, they should not be fetchable with a browser.

This program is not safe as a setuid executable. Do *not* make it setuid.

The use of the -b option is discouraged, since when it is used the unencrypted
password appears on the command line.

When using the crypt() algorithm, note that only the first 8 characters of the
password are used to form the password. If the supplied password is longer, the
extra characters will be silently discarded.

The SHA encryption format does not use salting: for a given password, there is
only one encrypted representation. The crypt() and MD5 formats permute the
representation by prepending a random salt string, to make dictionary attacks
against the passwords more difficult.

1.11.6 Restrictions

On the Windows and MPE platforms, passwords encrypted with htpasswd are
limited to no more than 255 characters in length. Longer passwords will be
truncated to 255 characters.

The MD5 algorithm used by htpasswd is specific to the Apache software; passwords encrypted using it will not be usable with other Web servers.

Usernames are limited to 255 bytes and may not include the character :.

1.12 httxt2dbm - Generate dbm files for use with RewriteMap

httxt2dbm is used to generate dbm files from text input, for use in RewriteMapRewriteMap with the dbm map type.

See also:

> ▷ httpd (p. 6)

> ▷ mod_rewrite (p. 426)

1.12.1 Synopsis

httxt2dbm [-v] [-f *DBM_TYPE*] -i *SOURCE_TXT* -o *OUTPUT_DBM*

1.12.2 Options

-v More verbose output

-f DBM_TYPE Specify the DBM type to be used for the output. If not specified, will use the APR Default. Available types are:
GDBM for GDBM files
SDBM for SDBM files
DB for berkeley DB files
NDBM for NDBM files
default for the default DBM type

-i SOURCE_TXT Input file from which the dbm is to be created. The file should be formated with one record per line, of the form:
key value
See the documentation for RewriteMap for further details of this file's format and meaning.

-o OUTPUT_DBM Name of the output dbm files.

1.12.3 Examples

```
httxt2dbm -i rewritemap.txt -o rewritemap.dbm
httxt2dbm -f SDBM -i rewritemap.txt -o rewritemap.dbm
```

1.13 logresolve - Resolve IP-addresses to hostnames in Apache log files

`logresolve` is a post-processing program to resolve IP-addresses in Apache's access logfiles. To minimize impact on your nameserver, logresolve has its very own internal hash-table cache. This means that each IP number will only be looked up the first time it is found in the log file.

Takes an Apache log file on standard input. The IP addresses must be the first thing on each line and must be separated from the remainder of the line by a space.

1.13.1 Synopsis

`logresolve` [-s *filename*] [-c] < *access_log* > *access_log.new*

1.13.2 Options

-s filename Specifies a filename to record statistics.

-c This causes `logresolve` to apply some DNS checks: after finding the hostname from the IP address, it looks up the IP addresses for the hostname and checks that one of these matches the original address.

1.14 rotatelogs - Piped logging program to rotate Apache logs

rotatelogs is a simple program for use in conjunction with Apache's piped logfile feature. It supports rotation based on a time interval or maximum size of the log.

1.14.1 Synopsis

rotatelogs [-l] [-f] *logfile rotationtime|filesizeM* [*offset*]

1.14.2 Options

-l Causes the use of local time rather than GMT as the base for the interval or for strftime(3) formatting with size-based rotation. Note that using -l in an environment which changes the GMT offset (such as for BST or DST) can lead to unpredictable results!

-f Causes the logfile to be opened immediately, as soon as rotatelogs starts, instead of waiting for the first logfile entry to be read (for non-busy sites, there may be a substantial delay between when the server is started and when the first request is handled, meaning that the associated logfile does not "exist" until then, which causes problems from some automated logging tools). *Available in version 2.2.9 and later.*

logfile The path plus basename of the logfile. If *logfile* includes any '%' characters, it is treated as a format string for strftime(3). Otherwise, the suffix .*nnnnnnnnnn* is automatically added and is the time in seconds. Both formats compute the start time from the beginning of the current period. For example, if a rotation time of 86400 is specified, the hour, minute, and second fields created from the strftime(3) format will all be zero, referring to the beginning of the current 24-hour period (midnight).

rotationtime The time between log file rotations in seconds. The rotation occurs at the beginning of this interval. For example, if the rotation time is 3600, the log file will be rotated at the beginning of every hour; if the rotation time is 86400, the log file will be rotated every night at midnight. (If no data is logged during an interval, no file will be created.)

filesizeM The maximum file size in megabytes followed by the letter M to specify size rather than time.

offset The number of minutes offset from UTC. If omitted, zero is assumed and UTC is used. For example, to use local time in the zone UTC -5 hours, specify a value of -300 for this argument. In most cases, -l should be used instead of specifying an offset.

1.14.3 Examples

CustomLog "|bin/rotatelogs /var/logs/logfile 86400" common

This creates the files /var/logs/logfile.nnnn where nnnn is the system time at which the log nominally starts (this time will always be a multiple of the rotation time, so you can synchronize cron scripts with it). At the end of each rotation time (here after 24 hours) a new log is started.

```
CustomLog "|bin/rotatelogs -l /var/logs/logfile.%Y.%m.%d 86400"
common
```

This creates the files /var/logs/logfile.yyyy.mm.dd where yyyy is the year, mm is the month, and dd is the day of the month. Logging will switch to a new file every day at midnight, local time.

```
CustomLog "|bin/rotatelogs /var/logs/logfile 5M" common
```

This configuration will rotate the logfile whenever it reaches a size of 5 megabytes.

```
ErrorLog "|bin/rotatelogs /var/logs/errorlog.%Y-%m-%d-%H_%M_%S
5M"
```

This configuration will rotate the error logfile whenever it reaches a size of 5 megabytes, and the suffix to the logfile name will be created of the form errorlog.YYYY-mm-dd-HH_MM_SS.

1.14.4 Portability

The following logfile format string substitutions should be supported by all strftime(3) implementations, see the strftime(3) man page for library-specific extensions.

%A	full weekday name (localized)
%a	3-character weekday name (localized)
%B	full month name (localized)
%b	3-character month name (localized)
%c	date and time (localized)
%d	2-digit day of month
%H	2-digit hour (24 hour clock)
%I	2-digit hour (12 hour clock)
%j	3-digit day of year
%M	2-digit minute
%m	2-digit month
%p	am/pm of 12 hour clock (localized)
%S	2-digit second
%U	2-digit week of year (Sunday first day of week)
%W	2-digit week of year (Monday first day of week)
%w	1-digit weekday (Sunday first day of week)
%X	time (localized)
%x	date (localized)
%Y	4-digit year
%y	2-digit year
%Z	time zone name
%%	literal '%'

1.15 suexec - Switch user before executing external programs

suexec is used by the Apache HTTP Server to switch to another user before executing CGI programs. In order to achieve this, it must run as root. Since the HTTP daemon normally doesn't run as root, the suexec executable needs the setuid bit set and must be owned by root. It should never be writable for any other person than root.

For further information about the concepts and and the security model of suexec please refer to the suexec documentation (http://httpd.apache.org/docs/2.2/suexec.html).

1.15.1 Synopsis

suexec -V

1.15.2 Options

-V If you are root, this option displays the compile options of suexec. For security reasons all configuration options are changeable only at compile time.

1.16 Other Programs

The following programs are simple support programs included with the Apache HTTP Server which do not have their own manual pages. They are not installed automatically. You can find them after the configuration process in the support/ directory.

1.16.1 log_server_status

This perl script is designed to be run at a frequent interval by something like cron. It connects to the server and downloads the status information. It reformats the information to a single line and logs it to a file. Adjust the variables at the top of the script to specify the location of the resulting logfile.

1.16.2 split-logfile

This perl script will take a combined Web server access log file and break its contents into separate files. It assumes that the first field of each line is the virtual host identity (put there by "%v"), and that the logfiles should be named that + ".log" in the current directory.

The combined log file is read from stdin. Records read will be appended to any existing log files.

```
split-logfile < access_log
```

2 Using the Apache HTTP Server

2.1 Starting Apache

On Windows, Apache is normally run as a service on Windows NT, 2000 and XP, or as a console application on Windows 9x and ME. For details, see Running Apache as a Service (p. 745) and Running Apache as a Console Application (p. 745).

On Unix, the httpd program is run as a daemon that executes continuously in the background to handle requests. This section describes how to invoke httpd.

See also:

▷ Stopping and Restarting (p. 51)

▷ httpd (p. 6)

▷ apachectl (p. 11)

2.1.1 How Apache Starts

If the Listen specified in the configuration file is default of 80 (or any other port below 1024), then it is necessary to have root privileges in order to start apache, so that it can bind to this privileged port. Once the server has started and performed a few preliminary activities such as opening its log files, it will launch several *child* processes which do the work of listening for and answering requests from clients. The main httpd process continues to run as the root user, but the child processes run as a less privileged user. This is controlled by the selected Multi-Processing Module (p. 703).

The recommended method of invoking the httpd executable is to use the apachectl control script. This script sets certain environment variables that are necessary for httpd to function correctly under some operating systems, and then invokes the httpd binary. apachectl will pass through any command line arguments, so any httpd options may also be used with apachectl. You may also directly edit the apachectl script by changing the HTTPD variable near the top to specify the correct location of the httpd binary and any command-line arguments that you wish to be *always* present.

The first thing that httpd does when it is invoked is to locate and read the configuration file (p. 54) httpd.conf. The location of this file is set at compile-time, but it is possible to specify its location at run time using the -f command-line option as in

```
/usr/local/apache2/bin/apachectl -f /etc/httpd/conf/httpd.conf
```

If all goes well during startup, the server will detach from the terminal and the command prompt will return almost immediately. This indicates that the server is up and running. You can then use your browser to connect to the server and view the test page in the DocumentRoot directory.

2.1.2 Errors During Start-up

If Apache suffers a fatal problem during startup, it will write a message describing the problem either to the console or to the ErrorLog before exiting. One of the most common error messages is "Unable to bind to Port ...". This message is usually caused by either:

- Trying to start the server on a privileged port when not logged in as the root user; or
- Trying to start the server when there is another instance of Apache or some other web server already bound to the same Port.

For further trouble-shooting instructions, consult the Apache FAQ (p. 743).

2.1.3 Starting at Boot-Time

If you want your server to continue running after a system reboot, you should add a call to apachectl to your system startup files (typically rc.local or a file in an rc.N directory). This will start Apache as root. Before doing this ensure that your server is properly configured for security and access restrictions.

The apachectl script is designed to act like a standard SysV init script; it can take the arguments start, restart, and stop and translate them into the appropriate signals to httpd. So you can often simply link apachectl into the appropriate init directory. But be sure to check the exact requirements of your system.

2.1.4 Additional Information

Additional information about the command-line options of httpd and apachectl as well as other support programs included with the server is available on the Server and Supporting Programs (p. 5) page. There is also documentation on all the modules (p. 801) included with the Apache distribution and the directives (p. 805) that they provide.

2.2 Stopping and Restarting

This section covers stopping and restarting Apache on Unix-like systems. Windows NT, 2000 and XP users should see Running Apache as a Service (p. 745) and Windows 9x and ME users should see Running Apache as a Console Application (p. 745) for information on how to control Apache on those platforms.

See also:

▷ httpd (p. 6)

▷ apachectl (p. 11)

▷ Starting (p. 49)

2.2.1 Introduction

In order to stop or restart Apache, you must send a signal to the running httpd processes. There are two ways to send the signals. First, you can use the unix kill command to directly send signals to the processes. You will notice many httpd executables running on your system, but you should not send signals to any of them except the parent, whose pid is in the PidFile. That is to say you shouldn't ever need to send signals to any process except the parent. There are four signals that you can send the parent: TERM, USR1, HUP, and WINCH, which will be described in a moment.

To send a signal to the parent you should issue a command such as:

```
kill -TERM `cat /usr/local/apache2/logs/httpd.pid`
```

The second method of signaling the httpd processes is to use the -k command line options: stop, restart, graceful and graceful-stop, as described below. These are arguments to the httpd binary, but we recommend that you send them using the apachectl control script, which will pass them through to httpd.

After you have signaled httpd, you can read about its progress by issuing:

```
tail -f /usr/local/apache2/logs/error_log
```

Modify those examples to match your ServerRoot and PidFile settings.

2.2.2 Stop Now

Signal: TERM apachectl -k stop

Sending the TERM or stop signal to the parent causes it to immediately attempt to kill off all of its children. It may take it several seconds to complete killing off its children. Then the parent itself exits. Any requests in progress are terminated, and no further requests are served.

2.2.3 Graceful Restart

Signal: USR1 apachectl -k graceful

The USR1 or graceful signal causes the parent process to *advise* the children to exit after their current request (or to exit immediately if they're not serving anything). The parent re-reads its configuration files and re-opens its log files. As each child dies off the parent replaces it with a child from the new *generation* of the configuration, which begins serving new requests immediately.

This code is designed to always respect the process control directive of the MPMs, so the number of processes and threads available to serve clients will be maintained at the appropriate values throughout the restart process. Furthermore, it respects StartServers in the following manner: if after one second at least StartServers new children have not been created, then create enough to pick up the slack. Hence the code tries to maintain both the number of children appropriate for the current load on the server, and respect your wishes with the StartServers parameter.

Users of mod_status will notice that the server statistics are **not** set to zero when a USR1 is sent. The code was written to both minimize the time in which the server is unable to serve new requests (they will be queued up by the operating system, so they're not lost in any event) and to respect your tuning parameters. In order to do this it has to keep the *scoreboard* used to keep track of all children across generations.

The status module will also use a G to indicate those children which are still serving requests started before the graceful restart was given.

At present there is no way for a log rotation script using USR1 to know for certain that all children writing the pre-restart log have finished. We suggest that you use a suitable delay after sending the USR1 signal before you do anything with the old log. For example if most of your hits take less than 10 minutes to complete for users on low bandwidth links then you could wait 15 minutes before doing anything with the old log.

If your configuration file has errors in it when you issue a restart then your parent will not restart; it will exit with an error. In the case of graceful restarts it will also leave children running when it exits. (These are the children which are "gracefully exiting" by handling their last request.) This will cause problems if you attempt to restart the server – it will not be able to bind to its listening ports. Before doing a restart, you can check the syntax of the configuration files with the -t command line argument (see httpd). This still will not guarantee that the server will restart correctly. To check the semantics of the configuration files as well as the syntax, you can try starting httpd as a non-root user. If there are no errors it will attempt to open its sockets and logs and fail because it's not root (or because the currently running httpd already has those ports bound). If it fails for any other reason then it's probably a config file error and the error should be fixed before issuing the graceful restart.

2.2.4 Restart Now

Signal: HUP `apachectl -k restart`

Sending the HUP or `restart` signal to the parent causes it to kill off its children like in TERM, but the parent doesn't exit. It re-reads its configuration files, and re-opens any log files. Then it spawns a new set of children and continues serving hits.

Users of mod_status will notice that the server statistics are set to zero when a HUP is sent.

> *If your configuration file has errors in it when you issue a restart then your parent will not restart; it will exit with an error. See above for a method of avoiding this.*

2.2.5 Graceful Stop

Signal: WINCH `apachectl -k graceful-stop`

The WINCH or `graceful-stop` signal causes the parent process to *advise* the children to exit after their current request (or to exit immediately if they're not serving anything). The parent will then remove its PidFile and cease listening on all ports. The parent will continue to run, and monitor children which are handling requests. Once all children have finalised and exited or the timeout specified by the GracefulShutdownTimeout has been reached, the parent will also exit. If the timeout is reached, any remaining children will be sent the TERM signal to force them to exit.

A TERM signal will immediately terminate the parent process and all children when in the "graceful" state. However as the PidFile will have been removed, you will not be able to use apachectl or httpd to send this signal.

> *The* graceful-stop *signal allows you to run multiple identically configured instances of* httpd *at the same time. This is a powerful feature when performing graceful upgrades of Apache; however it can also cause deadlocks and race conditions with some configurations.*
>
> *Care has been taken to ensure that on-disk files such as the* Lockfile *and* ScriptSock *files contain the server PID, and should coexist without problem. However, if a configuration directive, third-party module or persistent CGI utilises any other on-disk lock or state files, care should be taken to ensure that multiple running instances of* httpd *do not clobber each others files.*
>
> *You should also be wary of other potential race conditions, such as using* rotatelogs *style piped logging. Multiple running instances of* rotatelogs *attempting to rotate the same logfiles at the same time may destroy each other's logfiles.*

2.3 Configuration Files

This section describes the files used to configure the Apache HTTP server.

2.3.1 Main Configuration Files

Related Modules	Related Directives
mod_mime	\<IfDefine\>
	Include
	TypesConfig

Apache is configured by placing directives (p. 805) in plain text configuration files. The main configuration file is usually called httpd.conf. The location of this file is set at compile-time, but may be overridden with the -f command line flag. In addition, other configuration files may be added using the Include directive, and wildcards can be used to include many configuration files. Any directive may be placed in any of these configuration files. Changes to the main configuration files are only recognized by Apache when it is started or restarted.

The server also reads a file containing mime document types; the filename is set by the TypesConfig directive, and is mime.types by default.

2.3.2 Syntax of the Configuration Files

Apache configuration files contain one directive per line. The backslash "\" may be used as the last character on a line to indicate that the directive continues onto the next line. There must be no other characters or white space between the backslash and the end of the line.

Directives in the configuration files are case-insensitive, but arguments to directives are often case sensitive. Lines that begin with the hash character "#" are considered comments, and are ignored. Comments may **not** be included on a line after a configuration directive. Blank lines and white space occurring before a directive are ignored, so you may indent directives for clarity.

The values of shell environment variables can be used in configuration file lines using the syntax ${ENVVAR}. If "ENVVAR" is the name of a valid environment variable, the value of that variable is substituted into that spot in the configuration file line, and processing continues as if that text were found directly in the configuration file. (If the ENVVAR variable is not found, the characters "${ENVVAR}" are left unchanged for use by later stages in the config file processing.)

The maximum length of a line in the configuration file, after environment-variable substitution, joining any continued lines and removing leading and trailing white space, is 8192 characters.

You can check your configuration files for syntax errors without starting the server by using apachectl configtest or the -t command line option.

2.3.3 Modules

Related Modules	Related Directives
mod_so	<IfModule>
	LoadModule

Apache is a modular server. This implies that only the most basic functionality is included in the core server. Extended features are available through modules (p. 801) which can be loaded into Apache. By default, a base (p. 81) set of modules is included in the server at compile-time. If the server is compiled to use dynamically loaded (p. 683) modules, then modules can be compiled separately and added at any time using the LoadModule directive. Otherwise, Apache must be recompiled to add or remove modules. Configuration directives may be included conditional on a presence of a particular module by enclosing them in an <IfModule> block.

To see which modules are currently compiled into the server, you can use the -l command line option.

2.3.4 Scope of Directives

Related Modules	Related Directives
	<Directory>
	<DirectoryMatch>
	<Files>
	<FilesMatch>
	<Location>
	<LocationMatch>
	<VirtualHost>

Directives placed in the main configuration files apply to the entire server. If you wish to change the configuration for only a part of the server, you can scope your directives by placing them in <Directory>, <DirectoryMatch>, <Files>, <FilesMatch>, <Location>, and <LocationMatch> sections. These sections limit the application of the directives which they enclose to particular filesystem locations or URLs. They can also be nested, allowing for very fine grained configuration.

Apache has the capability to serve many different websites simultaneously. This is called Virtual Hosting (p. 541). Directives can also be scoped by placing them inside <VirtualHost> sections, so that they will only apply to requests for a particular website.

Although most directives can be placed in any of these sections, some directives do not make sense in some contexts. For example, directives controlling process creation can only be placed in the main server context. To find which directives can be placed in which sections, check the Context (p. 83) of the directive. For

further information, we provide details on How Directory, Location and Files
sections work (p. 57).

2.3.5 .htaccess Files

Related Modules	Related Directives
	AccessFileName
	AllowOverride

Apache allows for decentralized management of configuration via special files
placed inside the web tree. The special files are usually called .htaccess, but
any name can be specified in the AccessFileName directive. Directives placed
in .htaccess files apply to the directory where you place the file, and all subdirectories. The .htaccess files follow the same syntax as the main configuration files. Since .htaccess files are read on every request, changes made in
these files take immediate effect.

To find which directives can be placed in .htaccess files, check the Context (p.
83) of the directive. The server administrator further controls what directives
may be placed in .htaccess files by configuring the AllowOverride directive in
the main configuration files.

For more information on .htaccess files, see the .htaccess tutorial (p. 667).

2.4 Configuration Sections

Directives in the configuration files (p. 54) may apply to the entire server, or they may be restricted to apply only to particular directories, files, hosts, or URLs. This section describes how to use configuration section containers or .htaccess files to change the scope of other configuration directives.

2.4.1 Types of Configuration Section Containers

Related Modules	Related Directives
core	<Directory>
mod_version	<DirectoryMatch>
mod_proxy	<Files>
	<FilesMatch>
	<IfDefine>
	<IfModule>
	<IfVersion>
	<Location>
	<LocationMatch>
	<Proxy>
	<ProxyMatch>
	<VirtualHost>

There are two basic types of containers. Most containers are evaluated for each request. The enclosed directives are applied only for those requests that match the containers. The <IfDefine>, <IfModule>, and <IfVersion> containers, on the other hand, are evaluated only at server startup and restart. If their conditions are true at startup, then the enclosed directives will apply to all requests. If the conditions are not true, the enclosed directives will be ignored.

The <IfDefine> directive encloses directives that will only be applied if an appropriate parameter is defined on the httpd command line. For example, with the following configuration, all requests will be redirected to another site only if the server is started using httpd -DClosedForNow:

```
<IfDefine ClosedForNow>
Redirect / http://otherserver.example.com/
</IfDefine>
```

The <IfModule> directive is very similar, except it encloses directives that will only be applied if a particular module is available in the server. The module must either be statically compiled in the server, or it must be dynamically compiled and its LoadModule line must be earlier in the configuration file. This directive should only be used if you need your configuration file to work whether or not certain modules are installed. It should not be used to enclose directives that you want to work all the time, because it can suppress useful error messages about missing modules.

In the following example, the MimeMagicFiles directive will be applied only if
mod_mime_magic is available.

```
<IfModule mod_mime_magic.c>
MimeMagicFile conf/magic
</IfModule>
```

The <IfVersion> directive is very similar to <IfDefine> and <IfModule>, except it encloses directives that will only be applied if a particular version of
the server is executing. This module is designed for the use in test suites and
large networks which have to deal with different httpd versions and different
configurations.

```
<IfVersion >= 2.1>
    # this happens only in versions greater or
    # equal 2.1.0.
</IfVersion>
```

<IfDefine>, <IfModule>, and the <IfVersion> can apply negative conditions
by preceding their test with "!". Also, these sections can be nested to achieve
more complex restrictions.

2.4.2 Filesystem and Webspace

The most commonly used configuration section containers are the ones that
change the configuration of particular places in the filesystem or webspace.
First, it is important to understand the difference between the two. The filesystem is the view of your disks as seen by your operating system. For example,
in a default install, Apache resides at /usr/local/apache2 in the Unix filesystem or "c:/Program Files/Apache Group/Apache2" in the Windows filesystem. (Note that forward slashes should always be used as the path separator
in Apache, even for Windows.) In contrast, the webspace is the view of your
site as delivered by the web server and seen by the client. So the path /dir/
in the webspace corresponds to the path /usr/local/apache2/htdocs/dir/ in
the filesystem of a default Apache install on Unix. The webspace need not map
directly to the filesystem, since webpages may be generated dynamically from
databases or other locations.

Filesystem Containers

The <Directory> and <Files> directives, along with their regex counterparts,
apply directives to parts of the filesystem. Directives enclosed in a <Directory>
section apply to the named filesystem directory and all subdirectories of that
directory. The same effect can be obtained using .htaccess files (p. 667). For
example, in the following configuration, directory indexes will be enabled for
the /var/web/dir1 directory and all subdirectories.

```
<Directory /var/web/dir1>
Options +Indexes
</Directory>
```

Directives enclosed in a `<Files>` section apply to any file with the specified name, regardless of what directory it lies in. So for example, the following configuration directives will, when placed in the main section of the configuration file, deny access to any file named `private.html` regardless of where it is found.

```
<Files private.html>
Order allow,deny
Deny from all
</Files>
```

To address files found in a particular part of the filesystem, the `<Files>` and `<Directory>` sections can be combined. For example, the following configuration will deny access to `/var/web/dir1/private.html`, `/var/web/dir1/subdir2/private.html`, `/var/web/dir1/subdir3/private.html`, and any other instance of `private.html` found under the `/var/web/dir1/` directory.

```
<Directory /var/web/dir1>
<Files private.html>
Order allow,deny
Deny from all
</Files>
</Directory>
```

Webspace Containers

The `<Location>` directive and its regex counterpart, on the other hand, change the configuration for content in the webspace. For example, the following configuration prevents access to any URL-path that begins in `/private`. In particular, it will apply to requests for `http://yoursite.example.com/private`, `http://yoursite.example.com/private123`, and `http://yoursite.example.com/private/dir/file.html` as well as any other requests starting with the `/private` string.

```
<Location /private>
Order Allow,Deny
Deny from all
</Location>
```

The `<Location>` directive need not have anything to do with the filesystem. For example, the following example shows how to map a particular URL to an internal Apache handler provided by `mod_status`. No file called `server-status` needs to exist in the filesystem.

```
<Location /server-status>
SetHandler server-status
</Location>
```

Wildcards and Regular Expressions

The <Directory>, <Files>, and <Location> directives can each use shell-style wildcard characters as in fnmatch from the C standard library. The character "*" matches any sequence of characters, "?" matches any single character, and "[*seq*]" matches any character in *seq*. The "/" character will not be matched by any wildcard; it must be specified explicitly.

If even more flexible matching is required, each container has a regu-lar expression (regex) counterpart <DirectoryMatch>, <FilesMatch>, and <LocationMatch> that allow perl-compatible regular expressions to be used in choosing the matches. But see the section below on configuration merging to find out how using regex sections will change how directives are applied.

A non-regex wildcard section that changes the configuration of all user directo-ries could look as follows:

```
<Directory /home/*/public_html>
Options Indexes
</Directory>
```

Using regex sections, we can deny access to many types of image files at once:

```
<FilesMatch \.(?i:gif|jpe?g|png)$>
Order allow,deny
Deny from all
</FilesMatch>
```

What to use When

Choosing between filesystem containers and webspace containers is actually quite easy. When applying directives to objects that reside in the filesystem always use <Directory> or <Files>. When applying directives to objects that do not reside in the filesystem (such as a webpage generated from a database), use <Location>.

It is important to never use <Location> when trying to restrict access to objects in the filesystem. This is because many different webspace locations (URLs) could map to the same filesystem location, allowing your restrictions to be circumvented. For example, consider the following configuration:

```
<Location /dir/>
Order allow,deny
Deny from all
</Location>
```

This works fine if the request is for http://yoursite.example.com/dir/. But what if you are on a case-insensitive filesystem? Then your restriction could be easily circumvented by requesting http://yoursite.example.com/DIR/. The <Directory> directive, in contrast, will apply to any content served from that location, regardless of how it is called. (An exception is filesystem links. The same directory can be placed in more than one part of the filesystem using symbolic links. The `<Directory>` directive will follow the symbolic link without resetting the pathname. Therefore, for the highest level of security, symbolic links should be disabled with the appropriate `Options` directive.)

If you are, perhaps, thinking that none of this applies to you because you use a case-sensitive filesystem, remember that there are many other ways to map multiple webspace locations to the same filesystem location. Therefore you should always use the filesystem containers when you can. There is, however, one exception to this rule. Putting configuration restrictions in a `<Location />` section is perfectly safe because this section will apply to all requests regardless of the specific URL.

2.4.3 Virtual Hosts

The `<VirtualHost>` container encloses directives that apply to specific hosts. This is useful when serving multiple hosts from the same machine with a different configuration for each. For more information, see the Virtual Host Documentation (p. 541).

2.4.4 Proxy

The `<Proxy>` and `<ProxyMatch>` containers apply enclosed configuration directives only to sites accessed through mod_proxy's proxy server that match the specified URL. For example, the following configuration will prevent the proxy server from being used to access the cnn.com website.

```
<Proxy http://cnn.com/*>
Order allow,deny
Deny from all
</Proxy>
```

2.4.5 What Directives are Allowed?

To find out what directives are allowed in what types of configuration sections, check the Context (p. 83) of the directive. Everything that is allowed in `<Directory>` sections is also syntactically allowed in `<DirectoryMatch>`, `<Files>`, `<FilesMatch>`, `<Location>`, `<LocationMatch>`, `<Proxy>`, and `<ProxyMatch>` sections. There are some exceptions, however:

- The `AllowOverride` directive works only in `<Directory>` sections.
- The `FollowSymLinks` and `SymLinksIfOwnerMatch` Options work only in `<Directory>` sections or .htaccess files.
- The `Options` directive cannot be used in `<Files>` and `<FilesMatch>` sections.

2.4.6 How the sections are merged

The configuration sections are applied in a very particular order. Since this can have important effects on how configuration directives are interpreted, it is important to understand how this works.

The order of merging is:

1. `<Directory>` (except regular expressions) and .htaccess done simultaneously (with .htaccess, if allowed, overriding `<Directory>`)

2. `<DirectoryMatch>` (and `<Directory ~>`)

3. `<Files>` and `<FilesMatch>` done simultaneously

4. `<Location>` and `<LocationMatch>` done simultaneously

Apart from `<Directory>`, each group is processed in the order that they appear in the configuration files. `<Directory>` (group 1 above) is processed in the order shortest directory component to longest. So for example, `<Directory /var/web/dir>` will be processed before `<Directory /var/web/dir/subdir>`. If multiple `<Directory>` sections apply to the same directory they are processed in the configuration file order. Configurations included via the Include directive will be treated as if they were inside the including file at the location of the Include directive.

Sections inside `<VirtualHost>` sections are applied *after* the corresponding sections outside the virtual host definition. This allows virtual hosts to override the main server configuration.

When the request is served by mod_proxy, the `<Proxy>` container takes the place of the `<Directory>` container in the processing order.

Later sections override earlier ones.

> TECHNICAL NOTE *There is actually a `<Location>`/`<LocationMatch>` sequence performed just before the name translation phase (where Aliases and DocumentRoots are used to map URLs to filenames). The results of this sequence are completely thrown away after the translation has completed.*

Some Examples

Below is an artificial example to show the order of merging. Assuming they all apply to the request, the directives in this example will be applied in the order A > B > C > D > E.

```
<Location />
E
</Location>
<Files f.html>
D
</Files>
```

```
<VirtualHost *>
<Directory /a/b>
B
</Directory>
</VirtualHost>
<DirectoryMatch "^.*b/">
C
</DirectoryMatch>
<Directory /a/b>
A
</Directory>
```

For a more concrete example, consider the following. Regardless of any access restrictions placed in <Directory> sections, the <Location> section will be evaluated last and will allow unrestricted access to the server. In other words, order of merging is important, so be careful!

```
<Location />
Order deny,allow
Allow from all
</Location>
# Woops!  This <Directory> section will have no effect
<Directory />
Order allow,deny
Allow from all
Deny from badguy.example.com
</Directory>
```

2.5 Server-Wide Configuration

This section explains some of the directives provided by the core server which are used to configure the basic operations of the server.

2.5.1 Server Identification

Related Modules	Related Directives
	ServerName
	ServerAdmin
	ServerSignature
	ServerTokens
	UseCanonicalName
	UseCanonicalPhysicalPort

The ServerAdmin and ServerTokens directives control what information about the server will be presented in server-generated documents such as error messages. The ServerTokens directive sets the value of the Server HTTP response header field.

The ServerName, UseCanonicalName and UseCanonicalPhysicalPort directives are used by the server to determine how to construct self-referential URLs. For example, when a client requests a directory, but does not include the trailing slash in the directory name, Apache must redirect the client to the full name including the trailing slash so that the client will correctly resolve relative references in the document.

2.5.2 File Locations

Related Modules	Related Directives
	CoreDumpDirectory
	DocumentRoot
	ErrorLog
	LockFile
	PidFile
	ScoreBoardFile
	ServerRoot

These directives control the locations of the various files that Apache needs for proper operation. When the pathname used does not begin with a slash (/), the files are located relative to the ServerRoot. Be careful about locating files in paths which are writable by non-root users. See the security tips (p. 677) documentation for more details.

2.5.3 Limiting Resource Usage

Related Modules	Related Directives
	LimitRequestBody
	LimitRequestFields
	LimitRequestFieldsize
	LimitRequestLine
	RLimitCPU
	RLimitMEM
	RLimitNPROC
	ThreadStackSize

The LimitRequest* directives are used to place limits on the amount of resources Apache will use in reading requests from clients. By limiting these values, some kinds of denial of service attacks can be mitigated.

The RLimit* directives are used to limit the amount of resources which can be used by processes forked off from the Apache children. In particular, this will control resources used by CGI scripts and SSI exec commands.

The ThreadStackSize directive is used with some platforms to control the stack size.

2.6 Log Files

In order to effectively manage a web server, it is necessary to get feedback about the activity and performance of the server as well as any problems that may be occurring. The Apache HTTP Server provides very comprehensive and flexible logging capabilities. This section describes how to configure its logging capabilities, and how to understand what the logs contain.

2.6.1 Security Warning

Anyone who can write to the directory where Apache is writing a log file can almost certainly gain access to the uid that the server is started as, which is normally root. Do *NOT* give people write access to the directory the logs are stored in without being aware of the consequences; see the security tips (p. 677) document for details.

In addition, log files may contain information supplied directly by the client, without escaping. Therefore, it is possible for malicious clients to insert control-characters in the log files, so care must be taken in dealing with raw logs.

2.6.2 Error Log

Related Modules	Related Directives
	ErrorLog
	LogLevel

The server error log, whose name and location is set by the ErrorLog directive, is the most important log file. This is the place where Apache httpd will send diagnostic information and record any errors that it encounters in processing requests. It is the first place to look when a problem occurs with starting the server or with the operation of the server, since it will often contain details of what went wrong and how to fix it.

The error log is usually written to a file (typically error_log on Unix systems and error.log on Windows and OS/2). On Unix systems it is also possible to have the server send errors to syslog or pipe them to a program.

The format of the error log is relatively free-form and descriptive. But there is certain information that is contained in most error log entries. For example, here is a typical message.

```
[Wed Oct 11 14:32:52 2000] [error] [client 127.0.0.1] client
denied by server configuration:
/export/home/live/ap/htdocs/test
```

The first item in the log entry is the date and time of the message. The second item lists the severity of the error being reported. The LogLevel directive is used to control the types of errors that are sent to the error log by restricting the severity level. The third item gives the IP address of the client that generated the error. Beyond that is the message itself, which in this case indicates that the server has been configured to deny the client access. The server reports the file-system path (as opposed to the web path) of the requested document.

A very wide variety of different messages can appear in the error log. Most look similar to the example above. The error log will also contain debugging output from CGI scripts. Any information written to stderr by a CGI script will be copied directly to the error log.

It is not possible to customize the error log by adding or removing information. However, error log entries dealing with particular requests have corresponding entries in the access log. For example, the above example entry corresponds to an access log entry with status code 403. Since it is possible to customize the access log, you can obtain more information about error conditions using that log file.

During testing, it is often useful to continuously monitor the error log for any problems. On Unix systems, you can accomplish this using:

```
tail -f error_log
```

2.6.3 Access Log

Related Modules	Related Directives
mod_log_config	CustomLog
mod_setenvif	LogFormat
	SetEnvIf

The server access log records all requests processed by the server. The location and content of the access log are controlled by the CustomLog directive. The LogFormat directive can be used to simplify the selection of the contents of the logs. This section describes how to configure the server to record information in the access log.

Of course, storing the information in the access log is only the start of log management. The next step is to analyze this information to produce useful statistics. Log analysis in general is beyond the scope of this section, and not really part of the job of the web server itself. For more information about this topic, and for applications which perform log analysis, see the "Web Analytics" entry in Wikipedia.[1]

Various versions of Apache httpd have used other modules and directives to control access logging, including mod_log_referer, mod_log_agent, and the TransferLog directive. The CustomLog directive now subsumes the functionality of all the older directives.

The format of the access log is highly configurable. The format is specified using a format string that looks much like a C-style printf(1) format string.

---

[1] http://en.wikipedia.org/wiki/Web_analytics

Some examples are presented in the next sections. For a complete list of the possible contents of the format string, see the mod_log_config format strings (p. 334).

Common Log Format

A typical configuration for the access log might look as follows.

```
LogFormat "%h %l %u %t \"%r\" %>s %b" common
CustomLog logs/access_log common
```

This defines the *nickname* common and associates it with a particular log format string. The format string consists of percent directives, each of which tell the server to log a particular piece of information. Literal characters may also be placed in the format string and will be copied directly into the log output. The quote character (") must be escaped by placing a backslash before it to prevent it from being interpreted as the end of the format string. The format string may also contain the special control characters "\n" for new-line and "\t" for tab.

The CustomLog directive sets up a new log file using the defined *nickname*. The filename for the access log is relative to the ServerRoot unless it begins with a slash.

The above configuration will write log entries in a format known as the Common Log Format (CLF). This standard format can be produced by many different web servers and read by many log analysis programs. The log file entries produced in CLF will look something like this:

```
127.0.0.1 - frank [10/Oct/2000:13:55:36 -0700] "GET
/apache_pb.gif HTTP/1.0" 200 2326
```

Each part of this log entry is described below.

127.0.0.1 (%h) This is the IP address of the client (remote host) which made the request to the server. If HostnameLookups is set to On, then the server will try to determine the hostname and log it in place of the IP address. However, this configuration is not recommended since it can significantly slow the server. Instead, it is best to use a log post-processor such as logresolve to determine the hostnames. The IP address reported here is not necessarily the address of the machine at which the user is sitting. If a proxy server exists between the user and the server, this address will be the address of the proxy, rather than the originating machine.

- (%l) The "hyphen" in the output indicates that the requested piece of information is not available. In this case, the information that is not available is the RFC 1413 identity of the client determined by identd on the clients machine. This information is highly unreliable and should almost never be used except on tightly controlled internal networks. Apache httpd will not even attempt to determine this information unless IdentityCheck is set to On.

frank (%u) This is the userid of the person requesting the document as determined by HTTP authentication. The same value is typically provided to CGI scripts in the REMOTE_USER environment variable. If the status code for the request (see below) is 401, then this value should not be trusted because the user is not yet authenticated. If the document is not password protected, this part will be "-" just like the previous one.

[10/Oct/2000:13:55:36 -0700] (%t) The time that the request was received. The format is:

```
[day/month/year:hour:minute:second zone]
day = 2*digit
month = 3*letter
year = 4*digit
hour = 2*digit
minute = 2*digit
second = 2*digit
zone = ('+' | '-') 4*digit
```

It is possible to have the time displayed in another format by specifying %{format}t in the log format string, where format is as in strftime(3) from the C standard library.

"GET /apache_pb.gif HTTP/1.0" (\"%r\") The request line from the client is given in double quotes. The request line contains a great deal of useful information. First, the method used by the client is GET. Second, the client requested the resource /apache_pb.gif, and third, the client used the protocol HTTP/1.0. It is also possible to log one or more parts of the request line independently. For example, the format string "%m %U%q %H" will log the method, path, query-string, and protocol, resulting in exactly the same output as "%r".

200 (%>s) This is the status code that the server sends back to the client. This information is very valuable, because it reveals whether the request resulted in a successful response (codes beginning in 2), a redirection (codes beginning in 3), an error caused by the client (codes beginning in 4), or an error in the server (codes beginning in 5). The full list of possible status codes can be found in the HTTP specification[2] (RFC2616 section 10).

2326 (%b) The last part indicates the size of the object returned to the client, not including the response headers. If no content was returned to the client, this value will be "-". To log "0" for no content, use %B instead.

Combined Log Format

Another commonly used format string is called the Combined Log Format. It can be used as follows.

```
LogFormat "%h %l %u %t \"%r\" %>s %b \"%{Referer}i\"
\"%{User-agent}i\"" combined
```

---

[2]http://www.w3.org/Protocols/rfc2616/rfc2616.txt

```
CustomLog log/access_log combined
```

This format is exactly the same as the Common Log Format, with the addition of two more fields. Each of the additional fields uses the percent-directive %{header}i, where *header* can be any HTTP request header. The access log under this format will look like:

```
127.0.0.1 - frank [10/Oct/2000:13:55:36 -0700] "GET
/apache_pb.gif HTTP/1.0" 200 2326
"http://www.example.com/start.html" "Mozilla/4.08 [en] (Win98; I
;Nav)"
```

The additional fields are:

"http://www.example.com/start.html" (\"%{Referer}i\") The   "Referer"
   (sic) HTTP request header. This gives the site that the client reports
   having been referred from. (This should be the page that links to or
   includes /apache_pb.gif).

"Mozilla/4.08 [en] (Win98; I ;Nav)" (\"%{User-agent}i\") The   User-
   Agent HTTP request header. This is the identifying information that the
   client browser reports about itself.

Multiple Access Logs

Multiple access logs can be created simply by specifying multiple CustomLog directives in the configuration file. For example, the following directives will create three access logs. The first contains the basic CLF information, while the second and third contain referer and browser information. The last two CustomLog lines show how to mimic the effects of the ReferLog and AgentLog directives.

```
LogFormat "%h %l %u %t \"%r\" %>s %b" common
CustomLog logs/access_log common
CustomLog logs/referer_log "%{Referer}i -> %U"
CustomLog logs/agent_log "%{User-agent}i"
```

This example also shows that it is not necessary to define a nickname with the LogFormat directive. Instead, the log format can be specified directly in the CustomLog directive.

Conditional Logs

There are times when it is convenient to exclude certain entries from the access logs based on characteristics of the client request. This is easily accomplished with the help of environment variables (p. 705). First, an environment variable must be set to indicate that the request meets certain conditions. This is usually accomplished with SetEnvIf. Then the env= clause of the CustomLog directive is used to include or exclude requests where the environment variable is set. Some examples:

```
# Mark requests from the loop-back interface
```

```
SetEnvIf Remote_Addr "127\.0\.0\.1" dontlog
# Mark requests for the robots.txt file
SetEnvIf Request_URI "^/robots\.txt$" dontlog
# Log what remains
CustomLog logs/access_log common env=!dontlog
```

As another example, consider logging requests from english-speakers to one log file, and non-english speakers to a different log file.

```
SetEnvIf Accept-Language "en" english
CustomLog logs/english_log common env=english
CustomLog logs/non_english_log common env=!english
```

Although we have just shown that conditional logging is very powerful and flexible, it is not the only way to control the contents of the logs. Log files are more useful when they contain a complete record of server activity. It is often easier to simply post-process the log files to remove requests that you do not want to consider.

2.6.4 Log Rotation

On even a moderately busy server, the quantity of information stored in the log files is very large. The access log file typically grows 1 MB or more per 10,000 requests. It will consequently be necessary to periodically rotate the log files by moving or deleting the existing logs. This cannot be done while the server is running, because Apache will continue writing to the old log file as long as it holds the file open. Instead, the server must be restarted (p. 51) after the log files are moved or deleted so that it will open new log files.

By using a *graceful* restart, the server can be instructed to open new log files without losing any existing or pending connections from clients. However, in order to accomplish this, the server must continue to write to the old log files while it finishes serving old requests. It is therefore necessary to wait for some time after the restart before doing any processing on the log files. A typical scenario that simply rotates the logs and compresses the old logs to save space is:

```
mv access_log access_log.old
mv error_log error_log.old
apachectl graceful
sleep 600
gzip access_log.old error_log.old
```

Another way to perform log rotation is using piped logs as discussed in the next section.

2.6.5 Piped Logs

Apache httpd is capable of writing error and access log files through a pipe to another process, rather than directly to a file. This capability dramatically increases the flexibility of logging, without adding code to the main server. In order to write logs to a pipe, simply replace the filename with the pipe character "|", followed by the name of the executable which should accept log entries on its standard input. Apache will start the piped-log process when the server starts, and will restart it if it crashes while the server is running. (This last feature is why we can refer to this technique as "reliable piped logging".)

Piped log processes are spawned by the parent Apache httpd process, and inherit the userid of that process. This means that piped log programs usually run as root. It is therefore very important to keep the programs simple and secure.

One important use of piped logs is to allow log rotation without having to restart the server. The Apache HTTP Server includes a simple program called rotatelogs for this purpose. For example, to rotate the logs every 24 hours, you can use:

```
CustomLog "|/usr/local/apache/bin/rotatelogs /var/log/access_log
86400" common
```

Notice that quotes are used to enclose the entire command that will be called for the pipe. Although these examples are for the access log, the same technique can be used for the error log.

A similar but much more flexible log rotation program called cronolog[3] is available at an external site.

As with conditional logging, piped logs are a very powerful tool, but they should not be used where a simpler solution like off-line post-processing is available.

By default the piped log process is spawned using a shell. (usually with /bin/sh -c). Depending on the shell specifics invocation via shell might lead to an additional shell process for the lifetime of the logging pipe program and signal handling problems during restart.

Use "||" instead of "|" to spawn without invoking a shell:

```
# Invoke "rotatelogs" without using a shell
CustomLog "||/usr/local/apache/bin/rotatelogs
/var/log/access_log 86400" common
```

2.6.6 Virtual Hosts

When running a server with many virtual hosts (p. 541), there are several options for dealing with log files. First, it is possible to use logs exactly as in a single-host server. Simply by placing the logging directives outside the <VirtualHost> sections in the main server context, it is possible to log all requests in the same access log and error log. This technique does not allow for easy collection of statistics on individual virtual hosts.

If CustomLog or ErrorLog directives are placed inside a <VirtualHost> section, all requests or errors for that virtual host will be logged only to the specified

---

[3]http://www.cronolog.org/

file. Any virtual host which does not have logging directives will still have its requests sent to the main server logs. This technique is very useful for a small number of virtual hosts, but if the number of hosts is very large, it can be complicated to manage. In addition, it can often create problems with insufficient file descriptors (p. 569).

For the access log, there is a very good compromise. By adding information on the virtual host to the log format string, it is possible to log all hosts to the same log, and later split the log into individual files. For example, consider the following directives.

```
LogFormat "%v %l %u %t \"%r\" %>s %b" comonvhost
CustomLog logs/access_log comonvhost
```

The %v is used to log the name of the virtual host that is serving the request. Then a program like split-logfile (p. 48) can be used to post-process the access log in order to split it into one file per virtual host.

2.6.7 Other Log Files

Related Modules	Related Directives
mod_logio	LogFormat
mod_log_forensic	ForensicLog
mod_cgi	PidFile
mod_rewrite	RewriteLog
	RewriteLogLevel
	ScriptLog
	ScriptLogBuffer
	ScriptLogLength

Logging actual bytes sent and received

mod_logio adds in two additional LogFormat fields (%I and %O) that log the actual number of bytes received and sent on the network.

Forensic Logging

mod_log_forensic provides for forensic logging of client requests. Logging is done before and after processing a request, so the forensic log contains two log lines for each request. The forensic logger is very strict with no customizations. It can be an invaluable debugging and security tool.

PID File

On startup, Apache httpd saves the process id of the parent httpd process to the file logs/httpd.pid. This filename can be changed with the PidFile directive. The process-id is for use by the administrator in restarting and terminating the daemon by sending signals to the parent process; on Windows, use the

-k command line option instead. For more information see the Stopping and Restarting (p. 51) page.

Script Log

In order to aid in debugging, the ScriptLog directive allows you to record the input to and output from CGI scripts. This should only be used in testing - not for live servers. More information is available in the mod_cgi (p. 229) documentation.

Rewrite Log

When using the powerful and complex features of mod_rewrite (p. 426), it is almost always necessary to use the RewriteLog to help in debugging. This log file produces a detailed analysis of how the rewriting engine transforms requests. The level of detail is controlled by the RewriteLogLevel directive.

2.7 Mapping URLs to Filesystem Locations

This section explains how Apache uses the URL of a request to determine the filesystem location from which to serve a file.

2.7.1 Related Modules and Directives

Related Modules	Related Directives
mod_alias	Alias
mod_proxy	AliasMatch
mod_rewrite	CheckSpelling
mod_userdir	DocumentRoot
mod_speling	ErrorDocument
mod_vhost_alias	Options
	ProxyPass
	ProxyPassReverse
	ProxyPassReverseCookieDomain
	ProxyPassReverseCookiePath
	Redirect
	RedirectMatch
	RewriteCond
	RewriteRule
	ScriptAlias
	ScriptAliasMatch
	UserDir

2.7.2 DocumentRoot

In deciding what file to serve for a given request, Apache's default behavior is to take the URL-Path for the request (the part of the URL following the hostname and port) and add it to the end of the DocumentRoot specified in your configuration files. Therefore, the files and directories underneath the DocumentRoot make up the basic document tree which will be visible from the web.

For example, if DocumentRoot were set to /var/www/html then a request for http://www.example.com/fish/guppies.html would result in the file /var/www/html/fish/guppies.html being served to the requesting client.

Apache is also capable of Virtual Hosting (p. 541), where the server receives requests for more than one host. In this case, a different DocumentRoot can be specified for each virtual host, or alternatively, the directives provided by the module mod_vhost_alias can be used to dynamically determine the appropriate place from which to serve content based on the requested IP address or hostname.

The DocumentRoot directive is set in your main server configuration file (httpd.conf) and, possibly, once per additional Virtual Host (p. 541) you create.

2.7.3 Files Outside the DocumentRoot

There are frequently circumstances where it is necessary to allow web access to parts of the filesystem that are not strictly underneath the DocumentRoot. Apache offers several different ways to accomplish this. On Unix systems, symbolic links can bring other parts of the filesystem under the DocumentRoot. For security reasons, Apache will follow symbolic links only if the Options setting for the relevant directory includes FollowSymLinks or SymLinksIfOwnerMatch.

Alternatively, the Alias directive will map any part of the filesystem into the web space. For example, with

```
Alias /docs /var/web
```

the URL http://www.example.com/docs/dir/file.html will be served from /var/web/dir/file.html. The ScriptAlias directive works the same way, with the additional effect that all content located at the target path is treated as CGI scripts.

For situations where you require additional flexibility, you can use the AliasMatch and ScriptAliasMatch directives to do powerful regular expression based matching and substitution. For example,

```
ScriptAliasMatch ^/~([a-zA-Z0-9]+)/cgi-bin/(.+)
/home/$1/cgi-bin/$2
```

will map a request to http://example.com/~user/cgi-bin/script.cgi to the path /home/user/cgi-bin/script.cgi and will treat the resulting file as a CGI script.

2.7.4 User Directories

Traditionally on Unix systems, the home directory of a particular *user* can be referred to as ~user/. The module mod_userdir extends this idea to the web by allowing files under each user's home directory to be accessed using URLs such as the following.

```
http://www.example.com/~user/file.html
```

For security reasons, it is inappropriate to give direct access to a user's home directory from the web. Therefore, the UserDir directive specifies a directory underneath the user's home directory where web files are located. Using the default setting of Userdir public_html, the above URL maps to a file at a directory like /home/user/public_html/file.html where /home/user/ is the user's home directory as specified in /etc/passwd.

There are also several other forms of the Userdir directive which you can use on systems where /etc/passwd does not contain the location of the home directory.

Some people find the "˜" symbol (which is often encoded on the web as %7e) to be awkward and prefer to use an alternate string to represent user directories. This functionality is not supported by mod_userdir. However, if users' home directories are structured in a regular way, then it is possible to use the AliasMatch directive to achieve the desired effect. For example, to make http://www.example.com/upages/user/file.html map to /home/user/ public_html/file.html, use the following AliasMatch directive:

```
AliasMatch ^/upages/([a-zA-Z0-9]+)/?(.*)  /home/$1/public_html/$2
```

2.7.5 URL Redirection

The configuration directives discussed in the above sections tell Apache to get content from a specific place in the filesystem and return it to the client. Sometimes, it is desirable instead to inform the client that the requested content is located at a different URL, and instruct the client to make a new request with the new URL. This is called *redirection* and is implemented by the Redirect directive. For example, if the contents of the directory /foo/ under the DocumentRoot are moved to the new directory /bar/, you can instruct clients to request the content at the new location as follows:

```
Redirect permanent /foo/ http://www.example.com/bar/
```

This will redirect any URL-Path starting in /foo/ to the same URL path on the www.example.com server with /bar/ substituted for /foo/. You can redirect clients to any server, not only the origin server.

Apache also provides a RedirectMatch directive for more complicated rewriting problems. For example, to redirect requests for the site home page to a different site, but leave all other requests alone, use the following configuration:

```
RedirectMatch permanent ^/$
http://www.example.com/startpage.html
```

Alternatively, to temporarily redirect all pages on one site to a particular page on another site, use the following:

```
RedirectMatch temp .*
http://othersite.example.com/startpage.html
```

2.7.6 Reverse Proxy

Apache also allows you to bring remote documents into the URL space of the local server. This technique is called *reverse proxying* because the web server acts like a proxy server by fetching the documents from a remote server and returning them to the client. It is different from normal proxying because, to the client, it appears the documents originate at the reverse proxy server.

In the following example, when clients request documents under the /foo/ directory, the server fetches those documents from the /bar/ directory on internal.example.com and returns them to the client as if they were from the local server.

```
ProxyPass /foo/ http://internal.example.com/bar/
ProxyPassReverse /foo/ http://internal.example.com/bar/
ProxyPassReverseCookieDomain internal.example.com
public.example.com
ProxyPassReverseCookiePath /foo/ /bar/
```

The `ProxyPass` configures the server to fetch the appropriate documents, while the `ProxyPassReverse` directive rewrites redirects originating at `internal.example.com` so that they target the appropriate directory on the local server. Similarly, the `ProxyPassReverseCookieDomain` and `ProxyPassReverseCookiePath` rewrite cookies set by the backend server.

It is important to note, however, that links inside the documents will not be rewritten. So any absolute links on `internal.example.com` will result in the client breaking out of the proxy server and requesting directly from `internal.example.com`. A third-party module `mod_proxy_html`[4] is available to rewrite links in HTML and XHTML.

2.7.7 Rewriting Engine

When even more powerful substitution is required, the rewriting engine provided by `mod_rewrite` can be useful. The directives provided by this module use characteristics of the request such as browser type or source IP address in deciding from where to serve content. In addition, `mod_rewrite` can use external database files or programs to determine how to handle a request. The rewriting engine is capable of performing all three types of mappings discussed above: internal redirects (aliases), external redirects, and proxying. Many practical examples employing `mod_rewrite` are discussed in the detailed `mod_rewrite` documentation (p. 575).

2.7.8 File Not Found

Inevitably, URLs will be requested for which no matching file can be found in the filesystem. This can happen for several reasons. In some cases, it can be a result of moving documents from one location to another. In this case, it is best to use URL redirection to inform clients of the new location of the resource. In this way, you can assure that old bookmarks and links will continue to work, even though the resource is at a new location.

Another common cause of "File Not Found" errors is accidental mistyping of URLs, either directly in the browser, or in HTML links. Apache provides the module `mod_speling` (sic) to help with this problem. When this module is activated, it will intercept "File Not Found" errors and look for a resource with a similar filename. If one such file is found, `mod_speling` will send an HTTP redirect to the client informing it of the correct location. If several "close" files are found, a list of available alternatives will be presented to the client.

---

[4]http://apache.webthing.com/mod_proxy_html/

An especially useful feature of mod_speling, is that it will compare filenames without respect to case. This can help systems where users are unaware of the case-sensitive nature of URLs and the unix filesystem. But using mod_speling for anything more than the occasional URL correction can place additional load on the server, since each "incorrect" request is followed by a URL redirection and a new request from the client.

If all attempts to locate the content fail, Apache returns an error page with HTTP status code 404 (file not found). The appearance of this page is controlled with the ErrorDocument directive and can be customized in a flexible manner as discussed in the Custom error responses (p. 697) document.

3 Apache modules

3.1 Terms Used to Describe Modules

This section describes the terms that are used to describe each Apache module (p. 801).

3.1.1 Description

A brief description of the purpose of the module.

3.1.2 Status

This indicates how tightly bound into the Apache Web server the module is; in other words, you may need to recompile the server in order to gain access to the module and its functionality. Possible values for this attribute are:

MPM A module with status "MPM" is a Multi-Processing Module (p. 703). Unlike the other types of modules, Apache must have one and only one MPM in use at any time. This type of module is responsible for basic request handling and dispatching.

Base A module labeled as having "Base" status is compiled and loaded into the server by default, and is therefore normally available unless you have taken steps to remove the module from your configuration.

Extension A module with "Extension" status is not normally compiled and loaded into the server. To enable the module and its functionality, you may need to change the server build configuration files and re-compile Apache.

Experimental "Experimental" status indicates that the module is available as part of the Apache kit, but you are on your own if you try to use it. The module is being documented for completeness, and is not necessarily supported.

External Modules which are not included with the base Apache distribution ("third-party modules") may use the "External" status. We are not responsible for, nor do we support such modules.

3.1.3 Source File

This quite simply lists the name of the source file which contains the code for the module. This is also the name used by the <IfModule> directive.

3.1.4 Module Identifier

This is a string which identifies the module for use in the LoadModule directive when dynamically loading modules. In particular, it is the name of the external variable of type module in the source file.

3.1.5 Compatibility

If the module was not part of the original Apache version 2 distribution, the version in which it was introduced should be listed here. In addition, if the module is limited to particular platforms, the details will be listed here.

3.2 Terms Used to Describe Directives

This section describes the terms that are used to describe each Apache configuration directive (p. 805).

See also:

▷ Configuration files (p. 54)

3.2.1 Description

A brief description of the purpose of the directive.

3.2.2 Syntax

This indicates the format of the directive as it would appear in a configuration
file. This syntax is extremely directive-specific, and is described in detail in the
directive's definition. Generally, the directive name is followed by a series of
one or more space-separated arguments. If an argument contains a space, the
argument must be enclosed in double quotes. Optional arguments are enclosed
in square brackets. Where an argument can take on more than one possible
value, the possible values are separated by vertical bars "—". Literal text
is presented in the default font, while argument-types for which substitution
is necessary are *emphasized*. Directives which can take a variable number of
arguments will end in "..." indicating that the last argument is repeated.

Directives use a great number of different argument types. A few common ones
are defined below.

URL A complete Uniform Resource Locator including a scheme, hostname, and
    optional pathname as in http://www.example.com/path/to/file.html

URL-path The part of a *url* which follows the scheme and hostname as in
    /path/to/file.html. The *url-path* represents a web-view of a resource,
    as opposed to a file-system view.

file-path The path to a file in the local file-system beginning with the root
    directory as in /usr/local/apache/htdocs/path/to/file.html. Unless
    otherwise specified, a *file-path* which does not begin with a slash will be
    treated as relative to the ServerRoot (p. 87).

directory-path The path to a directory in the local file-system beginning with
    the root directory as in /usr/local/apache/htdocs/path/to/.

filename The name of a file with no accompanying path information as in
    file.html.

regex A Perl-compatible regular expression. The directive definition will spec-
    ify what the *regex* is matching against.

extension In general, this is the part of the *filename* which follows the last
    dot. However, Apache recognizes multiple filename extensions, so if a

filename contains more than one dot, each dot-separated part of the filename following the first dot is an *extension*. For example, the *filename*
`file.html.en` contains two extensions: `.html` and `.en`. For Apache directives, you may specify *extension*s with or without the leading dot. In
addition, *extension*s are not case sensitive.

MIME-type A method of describing the format of a file which consists of a
   major format type and a minor format type, separated by a slash as in
   `text/html`.

env-variable The name of an environment variable (p. 705) defined in the
   Apache configuration process. Note this is not necessarily the same as
   an operating system environment variable. See the environment variable
   documentation (p. 705) for more details.

3.2.3 Default

If the directive has a default value (*i.e.*, if you omit it from your configuration
entirely, the Apache Web server will behave as though you set it to a particular
value), it is described here. If there is no default value, this section should say
"*None*". Note that the default listed here is not necessarily the same as the
value the directive takes in the default httpd.conf distributed with the server.

3.2.4 Context

This indicates where in the server's configuration files the directive is legal. It's
a comma-separated list of one or more of the following values:

server config This means that the directive may be used in the server configuration files (*e.g.*, `httpd.conf`), but **not** within any <VirtualHost> or
   <Directory> containers. It is not allowed in .htaccess files at all.

virtual host This context means that the directive may appear inside
   <VirtualHost> containers in the server configuration files.

directory A directive marked as being valid in this context may be used inside
   <Directory>, <Location>, <Files>, and <Proxy> containers in the server
   configuration files, subject to the restrictions outlined in Configuration
   Sections (p. 57).

.htaccess If a directive is valid in this context, it means that it can appear
   inside *per*-directory .htaccess files. It may not be processed, though
   depending upon the overrides currently active.

The directive is *only* allowed within the designated context; if you try to use
it elsewhere, you'll get a configuration error that will either prevent the server
from handling requests in that context correctly, or will keep the server from
operating at all – *i.e.*, the server won't even start.

The valid locations for the directive are actually the result of a Boolean OR of
all of the listed contexts. In other words, a directive that is marked as being

valid in "server config, .htaccess" can be used in the httpd.conf file and in .htaccess files, but not within any <Directory> or <VirtualHost> containers.

3.2.5 Override

This directive attribute indicates which configuration override must be active in order for the directive to be processed when it appears in a .htaccess file. If the directive's context doesn't permit it to appear in .htaccess files, then no context will be listed.

Overrides are activated by the AllowOverride directive, and apply to a particular scope (such as a directory) and all descendants, unless further modified by other AllowOverride directives at lower levels. The documentation for that directive also lists the possible override names available.

3.2.6 Status

This indicates how tightly bound into the Apache Web server the directive is; in other words, you may need to recompile the server with an enhanced set of modules in order to gain access to the directive and its functionality. Possible values for this attribute are:

Core If a directive is listed as having "Core" status, that means it is part of the innermost portions of the Apache Web server, and is always available.

MPM A directive labeled as having "MPM" status is provided by a Multi-Processing Module (p. 703). This type of directive will be available if and only if you are using one of the MPMs listed on the Module line of the directive definition.

Base A directive labeled as having "Base" status is supported by one of the standard Apache modules which is compiled into the server by default, and is therefore normally available unless you've taken steps to remove the module from your configuration.

Extension A directive with "Extension" status is provided by one of the modules included with the Apache server kit, but the module isn't normally compiled into the server. To enable the directive and its functionality, you will need to change the server build configuration files and re-compile Apache.

Experimental "Experimental" status indicates that the directive is available as part of the Apache kit, but you're on your own if you try to use it. The directive is being documented for completeness, and is not necessarily supported. The module which provides the directive may or may not be compiled in by default; check the top of the page which describes the directive and its module to see if it remarks on the availability.

3.2.7 Module

This quite simply lists the name of the source module which defines the directive.

3.2.8 Compatibility

If the directive wasn't part of the original Apache version 2 distribution, the
version in which it was introduced should be listed here. In addition, if the
directive is available only on certain platforms, it will be noted here.

3.3 Apache Module core

Description:	Core Apache HTTP Server features that are always available
Status:	Core

Directives:

AcceptFilter	LimitRequestBody
AcceptPathInfo	LimitRequestFieldSize
AccessFileName	LimitRequestFields
AddDefaultCharset	LimitRequestLine
AddOutputFilterByType	LimitXMLRequestBody
AllowEncodedSlashes	<Location>
AllowOverride	<LocationMatch>
AuthName	LogLevel
AuthType	MaxKeepAliveRequests
CGIMapExtension	NameVirtualHost
ContentDigest	Options
DefaultType	RLimitCPU
<Directory>	RLimitMEM
<DirectoryMatch>	RLimitNPROC
DocumentRoot	Require
EnableMMAP	Satisfy
EnableSendfile	ScriptInterpreterSource
ErrorDocument	ServerAdmin
ErrorLog	ServerAlias
FileETag	ServerName
<Files>	ServerPath
<FilesMatch>	ServerRoot
ForceType	ServerSignature
HostnameLookups	ServerTokens
<IfDefine>	SetHandler
<IfModule>	SetInputFilter
Include	SetOutputFilter
KeepAlive	TimeOut
KeepAliveTimeout	TraceEnable
<Limit>	UseCanonicalName
<LimitExcept>	UseCanonicalPhysicalPort
LimitInternalRecursion	<VirtualHost>

AcceptFilter Directive

Description:	Configures optimizations for a Protocol's Listener Sockets
Syntax:	AcceptFilter *protocol accept_filter*
Context:	server config
Status:	Core
Module:	core
Compatibility:	Available in Apache 2.1.5 and later

This directive enables operating system specific optimizations for a listening socket by the Protocol type. The basic premise is for the kernel to not send a socket to the server process until either data is received or an entire HTTP Request is buffered. Only FreeBSD's Accept Filters[1] and Linux's more primitive TCP_DEFER_ACCEPT are currently supported.

The default values on FreeBSD are:

```
AcceptFilter http httpready
AcceptFilter https dataready
```

The httpready accept filter buffers entire HTTP requests at the kernel level. Once an entire request is received, the kernel then sends it to the server. See the accf_http(9)[2] man page for more details. Since HTTPS requests are encrypted only the accf_data(9)[3] filter is used.

The default values on Linux are:

```
AcceptFilter http data
AcceptFilter https data
```

Linux's TCP_DEFER_ACCEPT does not support buffering http requests. Any value besides none will enable TCP_DEFER_ACCEPT on that listener. For more details see the Linux tcp(7)[4] man page.

Using none for an argument will disable any accept filters for that protocol. This is useful for protocols that require a server send data first, such as nntp:

```
AcceptFilter nntp none
```

---

[1] http://www.freebsd.org/cgi/man.cgi?query=accept_filter&sektion=9
[2] http://www.freebsd.org/cgi/man.cgi?query=accf_http&sektion=9
[3] http://www.freebsd.org/cgi/man.cgi?query=accf_data&sektion=9
[4] http://homepages.cwi.nl/~aeb/linux/man2html/man7/tcp.7.html

AcceptPathInfo Directive

Description:	Resources accept trailing pathname information
Syntax:	`AcceptPathInfo On|Off|Default`
Default:	`AcceptPathInfo Default`
Context:	server config, virtual host, directory, .htaccess
Override:	FileInfo
Status:	Core
Module:	core
Compatibility:	Available in Apache 2.0.30 and later

This directive controls whether requests that contain trailing pathname information that follows an actual filename (or non-existent file in an existing directory)
will be accepted or rejected. The trailing pathname information can be made
available to scripts in the `PATH_INFO` environment variable.

For example, assume the location `/test/` points to a directory that contains
only the single file `here.html`. Then requests for `/test/here.html/more` and
`/test/nothere.html/more` both collect `/more` as `PATH_INFO`.

The three possible arguments for the `AcceptPathInfo` directive are:

Off A request will only be accepted if it maps to a literal path that exists.
Therefore a request with trailing pathname information after the true
filename such as `/test/here.html/more` in the above example will return
a 404 NOT FOUND error.

On A request will be accepted if a leading path component maps to a file that
exists. The above example `/test/here.html/more` will be accepted if
`/test/here.html` maps to a valid file.

Default The treatment of requests with trailing pathname information is determined by the handler (p. 713) responsible for the request. The core
handler for normal files defaults to rejecting `PATH_INFO` requests. Handlers that serve scripts, such as cgi-script (p. 229) and isapi-handler (p.
318), generally accept `PATH_INFO` by default.

The primary purpose of the `AcceptPathInfo` directive is to allow you to override the handler's choice of accepting or rejecting `PATH_INFO`. This override is
required, for example, when you use a filter (p. 715), such as INCLUDES (p.
302), to generate content based on `PATH_INFO`. The core handler would usually
reject the request, so you can use the following configuration to enable such a
script:

```
<Files "mypaths.shtml">
    Options +Includes
    SetOutputFilter INCLUDES
    AcceptPathInfo On
</Files>
```

AccessFileName Directive

Description:	Name of the distributed configuration file
Syntax:	AccessFileName *filename* [*filename*] ...
Default:	AccessFileName .htaccess
Context:	server config, virtual host
Status:	Core
Module:	core

While processing a request the server looks for the first existing configuration file from this list of names in every directory of the path to the document, if distributed configuration files are enabled for that directory. For example:

```
AccessFileName .acl
```

Before returning the document /usr/local/web/index.html, the server will read /.acl, /usr/.acl, /usr/local/.acl and /usr/local/web/.acl for directives, unless they have been disabled with

```
<Directory />
    AllowOverride None
</Directory>
```

See also:

> ▷ AllowOverride (p. 93)

> ▷ Configuration Files (p. 54)

> ▷ .htaccess Files (p. 667)

AddDefaultCharset Directive

Description:	Default charset parameter to be added when a response content-type is text/plain or text/html
Syntax:	AddDefaultCharset On|Off|*charset*
Default:	AddDefaultCharset Off
Context:	server config, virtual host, directory, .htaccess
Override:	FileInfo
Status:	Core
Module:	core

This directive specifies a default value for the media type charset parameter (the name of a character encoding) to be added to a response if and only if the response's content-type is either text/plain or text/html. This should override any charset specified in the body of the response via a META element, though the exact behavior is often dependent on the user's client configuration. A setting of AddDefaultCharset Off disables this functionality. AddDefaultCharset On enables a default charset of iso-8859-1. Any other value is assumed to be the *charset* to be used, which should be one of the IANA registered charset values[5]

---

[5]http://www.iana.org/assignments/character-sets

for use in MIME media types. For example:

    AddDefaultCharset utf-8

AddDefaultCharset should only be used when all of the text resources to which it applies are known to be in that character encoding and it is too inconvenient to label their charset individually. One such example is to add the charset parameter to resources containing generated content, such as legacy CGI scripts, that might be vulnerable to cross-site scripting attacks due to user-provided data being included in the output. Note, however, that a better solution is to just fix (or delete) those scripts, since setting a default charset does not protect users that have enabled the "auto-detect character encoding" feature on their browser.

See also:

▷ AddCharset (p. 351)

AddOutputFilterByType Directive

Description:	Assigns an output filter to a particular MIME-type
Syntax:	AddOutputFilterByType *filter*[;*filter*...] *MIME-type* [*MIME-type*] ...
Context:	server config, virtual host, directory, .htaccess
Override:	FileInfo
Status:	Core
Module:	core
Compatibility:	Available in Apache 2.0.33 and later; deprecated in Apache 2.1 and later

This directive activates a particular output filter (p. 715) for a request depending on the response MIME-type. Because of certain problems discussed below, this directive is deprecated. The same functionality is available using mod_filter.

The following example uses the DEFLATE filter, which is provided by mod_deflate. It will compress all output (either static or dynamic) which is labeled as text/html or text/plain before it is sent to the client.

    AddOutputFilterByType DEFLATE text/html text/plain

If you want the content to be processed by more than one filter, their names have to be separated by semicolons. It's also possible to use one AddOutputFilterByType directive for each of these filters.

The configuration below causes all script output labeled as text/html to be processed at first by the INCLUDES filter and then by the DEFLATE filter.

    <Location /cgi-bin/>
        Options Includes
        AddOutputFilterByType INCLUDES;DEFLATE text/html
    </Location>

NOTE *Enabling filters with* `AddOutputFilterByType` *may fail partially or completely in some cases. For example, no filters are applied if the MIME-type could not be determined and falls back to the* `DefaultType` *setting, even if the* `DefaultType` *is the same.*

However, if you want to make sure, that the filters will be applied, assign the content type to a resource explicitly, for example with `AddType` *or* `ForceType`. *Setting the content type within a (non-nph) CGI script is also safe.*

See also:

▷ AddOutputFilter (p. 355)

▷ SetOutputFilter (p. 132)

▷ filters (p. 715)

AllowEncodedSlashes Directive

Description:	Determines whether encoded path separators in URLs are allowed to be passed through
Syntax:	`AllowEncodedSlashes On|Off`
Default:	`AllowEncodedSlashes Off`
Context:	server config, virtual host
Status:	Core
Module:	core
Compatibility:	Available in Apache 2.0.46 and later

The `AllowEncodedSlashes` directive allows URLs which contain encoded path separators (`%2F` for / and additionally `%5C` for \ on according systems) to be used. Normally such URLs are refused with a 404 (Not found) error.

Turning `AllowEncodedSlashes On` is mostly useful when used in conjunction with `PATH_INFO`.

NOTE *Allowing encoded slashes does not imply decoding. Occurrences of* `%2F` *or* `%5C` *(only on according systems) will be left as such in the otherwise decoded URL string.*

See also:

▷ AcceptPathInfo (p. 89)

AllowOverride Directive

Description:	Types of directives that are allowed in .htaccess files
Syntax:	AllowOverride All|None|*directive-type*
	[*directive-type*] ...
Default:	AllowOverride All
Context:	directory
Status:	Core
Module:	core

When the server finds an .htaccess file (as specified by AccessFileName) it needs to know which directives declared in that file can override earlier configuration directives.

ONLY AVAILABLE IN <DIRECTORY> SECTIONS *AllowOverride is valid only in <Directory> sections specified without regular expressions, not in <Location>, <DirectoryMatch> or <Files> sections.*

When this directive is set to None, then .htaccess files are completely ignored. In this case, the server will not even attempt to read .htaccess files in the filesystem.

When this directive is set to All, then any directive which has the .htaccess Context (p. 83) is allowed in .htaccess files.

The *directive-type* can be one of the following groupings of directives.

AuthConfig Allow use of the authorization directives (AuthDBMGroupFile, AuthDBMUserFile, AuthGroupFile, AuthName, AuthType, AuthUserFile, Require, *etc.*).

FileInfo Allow use of the directives controlling document types (DefaultType, ErrorDocument, ForceType, LanguagePriority, SetHandler, SetInput-Filter, SetOutputFilter, and mod_mime Add* and Remove* directives, *etc.*), document meta data (Header, RequestHeader, SetEnvIf, SetEnv-IfNoCase, BrowserMatch, CookieExpires, CookieDomain, CookieStyle, CookieTracking, CookieName), mod_rewrite directives RewriteEngine, RewriteOptions, RewriteBase, RewriteCond, RewriteRule) and Action from mod_actions.

Indexes Allow use of the directives controlling directory indexing (Add-Description, AddIcon, AddIconByEncoding, AddIconByType, Default-Icon, DirectoryIndex, FancyIndexing, HeaderName, IndexIgnore, IndexOptions, ReadmeName, *etc.*).

Limit Allow use of the directives controlling host access (Allow, Deny and Order).

Options[=*Option*,...] Allow use of the directives controlling specific directory features (Options and XBitHack). An equal sign may be given followed by a comma (but no spaces) separated lists of options that may be set using the Options command.

Example:

```
AllowOverride AuthConfig Indexes
```

In the example above all directives that are neither in the group AuthConfig nor Indexes cause an internal server error.

For security and performance reasons, do not set AllowOverride to anything other than None in your <Directory /> block. Instead, find (or create) the <Directory> block that refers to the directory where you're actually planning to place a .htaccess file.

See also:

▷ AccessFileName (p. 90)

▷ Configuration Files (p. 54)

▷ .htaccess Files (p. 667)

AuthName Directive

Description:	Authorization realm for use in HTTP authentication
Syntax:	AuthName *auth-domain*
Context:	directory, .htaccess
Override:	AuthConfig
Status:	Core
Module:	core

This directive sets the name of the authorization realm for a directory. This realm is given to the client so that the user knows which username and password to send. AuthName takes a single argument; if the realm name contains spaces, it must be enclosed in quotation marks. It must be accompanied by AuthType and Require directives, and directives such as AuthUserFile and AuthGroupFile to work.

For example:

```
AuthName "Top Secret"
```

The string provided for the AuthName is what will appear in the password dialog provided by most browsers.

See also:

▷ Authentication, Authorization, and Access Control (p. 629)

AuthType Directive

Description:	Type of user authentication
Syntax:	AuthType Basic|Digest
Context:	directory, .htaccess
Override:	AuthConfig
Status:	Core
Module:	core

This directive selects the type of user authentication for a directory. The authentication types available are Basic (implemented by mod_auth_basic) and Digest (implemented by mod_auth_digest).

To implement authentication, you must also use the AuthName and Require directives. In addition, the server must have an authentication-provider module such as mod_authn_file and an authorization module such as mod_authz_user.

See also:

▷ Authentication, Authorization, and Access Control (p. 629)

CGIMapExtension Directive

Description:	Technique for locating the interpreter for CGI scripts
Syntax:	CGIMapExtension *cgi-path* .*extension*
Context:	directory, .htaccess
Override:	FileInfo
Status:	Core
Module:	core
Compatibility:	NetWare only

This directive is used to control how Apache finds the interpreter used to run CGI scripts. For example, setting CGIMapExtension sys:\foo.nlm .foo will cause all CGI script files with a .foo extension to be passed to the FOO interpreter.

ContentDigest Directive

Description:	Enables the generation of Content-MD5 HTTP Response headers
Syntax:	ContentDigest On|Off
Default:	ContentDigest Off
Context:	server config, virtual host, directory, .htaccess
Override:	Options
Status:	Core
Module:	core

This directive enables the generation of Content-MD5 headers as defined in RFC1864 respectively RFC2616.

MD5 is an algorithm for computing a "message digest" (sometimes called "fingerprint") of arbitrary-length data, with a high degree of confidence that any alterations in the data will be reflected in alterations in the message digest.

The Content-MD5 header provides an end-to-end message integrity check (MIC) of the entity-body. A proxy or client may check this header for detecting accidental modification of the entity-body in transit. Example header:

    Content-MD5: AuLb7Dp1rqtRtxz2m9kRpA==

Note that this can cause performance problems on your server since the message digest is computed on every request (the values are not cached).

Content-MD5 is only sent for documents served by the core, and not by any module. For example, SSI documents, output from CGI scripts, and byte range responses do not have this header.

DefaultType Directive

Description:	MIME content-type that will be sent if the server cannot determine a type in any other way
Syntax:	DefaultType *MIME-type|none*
Default:	DefaultType text/plain
Context:	server config, virtual host, directory, .htaccess
Override:	FileInfo
Status:	Core
Module:	core
Compatibility:	The argument none is available in Apache 2.2.7 and later

There will be times when the server is asked to provide a document whose type cannot be determined by its MIME types mappings.

The server SHOULD inform the client of the content-type of the document. If the server is unable to determine this by normal means, it will set it to the configured DefaultType. For example:

    DefaultType image/gif

would be appropriate for a directory which contained many GIF images with filenames missing the .gif extension.

In cases where it can neither be determined by the server nor the administrator (e.g. a proxy), it is preferable to omit the MIME type altogether rather than provide information that may be false. This can be accomplished using

    DefaultType None

DefaultType None is only available in httpd-2.2.7 and later.

Note that unlike ForceType, this directive only provides the default mime-type. All other mime-type definitions, including filename extensions, that might identify the media type will override this default.

Directory Directive

Description:	Enclose a group of directives that apply only to the named file-system directory and sub-directories
Syntax:	`<Directory directory-path> ... </Directory>`
Context:	server config, virtual host
Status:	Core
Module:	core

`<Directory>` and `</Directory>` are used to enclose a group of directives that will apply only to the named directory and sub-directories of that directory. Any directive that is allowed in a directory context may be used. *Directory-path* is either the full path to a directory, or a wild-card string using Unix shell-style matching. In a wild-card string, ? matches any single character, and * matches any sequences of characters. You may also use [] character ranges. None of the wildcards match a '/' character, so `<Directory /*/public_html>` will not match /home/user/public_html, but `<Directory /home/*/public_html>` will match. Example:

```
<Directory /usr/local/httpd/htdocs>
    Options Indexes FollowSymLinks
</Directory>
```

Be careful with the directory-path arguments: They have to literally match the filesystem path which Apache uses to access the files. Directives applied to a particular `<Directory>` will not apply to files accessed from that same directory via a different path, such as via different symbolic links.

Regular expressions can also be used, with the addition of the ~ character. For example:

```
<Directory ~ "^/www/.*/[0-9]{3}">
```

would match directories in /www/ that consisted of three numbers.

If multiple (non-regular expression) `<Directory>` sections match the directory (or one of its parents) containing a document, then the directives are applied in the order of shortest match first, interspersed with the directives from the .htaccess files. For example, with

```
<Directory />
    AllowOverride None
</Directory>
<Directory /home/>
    AllowOverride FileInfo
</Directory>
```

for access to the document /home/web/dir/doc.html the steps are:

- Apply directive `AllowOverride None` (disabling .htaccess files).

- Apply directive `AllowOverride FileInfo` (for directory /home).
- Apply any `FileInfo` directives in `/home/.htaccess`, `/home/web/`
  `.htaccess` and `/home/web/dir/.htaccess` in that order.

Regular expressions are not considered until after all of the normal sections have been applied. Then all of the regular expressions are tested in the order they appeared in the configuration file. For example, with

```
<Directory ~ abc$>
    # ... directives here ...
</Directory>
```

the regular expression section won't be considered until after all normal `<Directory>`s and .htaccess files have been applied. Then the regular expression will match on /home/abc/public_html/abc and the corresponding `<Directory>` will be applied.

Note that the default Apache access for `<Directory />` is Allow from All. This means that Apache will serve any file mapped from an URL. It is recommended that you change this with a block such as

```
<Directory />
    Order Deny,Allow
    Deny from All
</Directory>
```

and then override this for directories you *want* accessible. See the Security Tips (p. 677) page for more details.

The directory sections occur in the `httpd.conf` file. `<Directory>` directives cannot nest, and cannot appear in a `<Limit>` or `<LimitExcept>` section.

See also:

▷ How `<Directory>`, `<Location>` and `<Files>` sections work (p. 57) for an explanation of how these different sections are combined when a request is received

DirectoryMatch Directive

Description:	Enclose directives that apply to file-system directories matching a regular expression and their subdirectories
Syntax:	`<DirectoryMatch regex> ... </DirectoryMatch>`
Context:	server config, virtual host
Status:	Core
Module:	core

`<DirectoryMatch>` and `</DirectoryMatch>` are used to enclose a group of directives which will apply only to the named directory and *sub-directories of that directory*, the same as `<Directory>`. However, it takes as an argument a regular expression. For example:

```
<DirectoryMatch "^/www/(.+/)?[0-9]{3}">
```

would match directories in **/www/** that consisted of three numbers.

END-OF-LINE CHARACTER *The end-of-line character ($) cannot be matched with this directive.*

See also:

▷ Directory (p. 97) for a description of how regular expressions are mixed in with normal Directorys

▷ How <Directory>, <Location> and <Files> sections work (p. 57) for an explanation of how these different sections are combined when a request is received

DocumentRoot Directive

Description:	Directory that forms the main document tree visible from the web
Syntax:	DocumentRoot *directory-path*
Default:	DocumentRoot /usr/local/apache/htdocs
Context:	server config, virtual host
Status:	Core
Module:	core

This directive sets the directory from which **httpd** will serve files. Unless matched by a directive like **Alias**, the server appends the path from the requested URL to the document root to make the path to the document. Example:

```
DocumentRoot /usr/web
```

then an access to http://www.my.host.com/index.html refers to /usr/web/ index.html. If the *directory-path* is not absolute then it is assumed to be relative to the **ServerRoot**.

The **DocumentRoot** should be specified without a trailing slash.

See also:

▷ Mapping URLs to Filesystem Locations (p. 75)

EnableMMAP Directive

Description:	Use memory-mapping to read files during delivery
Syntax:	EnableMMAP On|Off
Default:	EnableMMAP On
Context:	server config, virtual host, directory, .htaccess
Override:	FileInfo
Status:	Core
Module:	core

This directive controls whether the httpd may use memory-mapping if it needs to read the contents of a file during delivery. By default, when the handling of a request requires access to the data within a file – for example, when delivering a server-parsed file using mod_include – Apache memory-maps the file if the OS supports it.

This memory-mapping sometimes yields a performance improvement. But in some environments, it is better to disable the memory-mapping to prevent operational problems:

- On some multiprocessor systems, memory-mapping can reduce the performance of the httpd.

- Deleting or truncating a file while httpd has it memory-mapped can cause httpd to crash with a segmentation fault.

For server configurations that are vulnerable to these problems, you should disable memory-mapping of delivered files by specifying:

```
EnableMMAP Off
```

For NFS mounted files, this feature may be disabled explicitly for the offending files by specifying:

```
<Directory "/path-to-nfs-files">
    EnableMMAP Off
</Directory>
```

Please note that the per-directory and .htaccess configuration of EnableSendfile is not supported by mod_disk_cache. Only global definition of EnableSendfile is taken into account by the module.

EnableSendfile Directive

Description:	Use the kernel sendfile support to deliver files to the client
Syntax:	EnableSendfile On|Off
Default:	EnableSendfile On
Context:	server config, virtual host, directory, .htaccess
Override:	FileInfo
Status:	Core
Module:	core
Compatibility:	Available in version 2.0.44 and later

This directive controls whether httpd may use the sendfile support from the kernel to transmit file contents to the client. By default, when the handling of a request requires no access to the data within a file – for example, when delivering a static file – Apache uses sendfile to deliver the file contents without ever reading the file if the OS supports it.

This sendfile mechanism avoids separate read and send operations, and buffer allocations. But on some platforms or within some filesystems, it is better to disable this feature to avoid operational problems:

- Some platforms may have broken sendfile support that the build system did not detect, especially if the binaries were built on another box and moved to such a machine with broken sendfile support.

- On Linux the use of sendfile triggers TCP-checksum offloading bugs on certain networking cards when using IPv6.

- On Linux on Itanium, sendfile may be unable to handle files over 2GB in size.

- With a network-mounted DocumentRoot (e.g., NFS or SMB), the kernel may be unable to serve the network file through its own cache.

For server configurations that are vulnerable to these problems, you should disable this feature by specifying:

```
EnableSendfile Off
```

For NFS or SMB mounted files, this feature may be disabled explicitly for the offending files by specifying:

```
<Directory "/path-to-nfs-files">
    EnableSendfile Off
</Directory>
```

ErrorDocument Directive

Description:	What the server will return to the client in case of an error
Syntax:	ErrorDocument *error-code* *document*
Context:	server config, virtual host, directory, .htaccess
Override:	FileInfo
Status:	Core
Module:	core
Compatibility:	Quoting syntax for text messages is different in Apache 2.0

In the event of a problem or error, Apache can be configured to do one of four things,

1. output a simple hardcoded error message

2. output a customized message

3. redirect to a local *URL-path* to handle the problem/error

4. redirect to an external *URL* to handle the problem/error

The first option is the default, while options 2-4 are configured using the ErrorDocument directive, which is followed by the HTTP response code and a URL or a message. Apache will sometimes offer additional information regarding the problem/error.

URLs can begin with a slash (/) for local web-paths (relative to the DocumentRoot), or be a full URL which the client can resolve. Alternatively, a message can be provided to be displayed by the browser. Examples:

```
ErrorDocument 500 http://foo.example.com/cgi-bin/tester
ErrorDocument 404 /cgi-bin/bad_urls.pl
ErrorDocument 401 /subscription_info.html
ErrorDocument 403 "Sorry can't allow you access today"
```

Additionally, the special value default can be used to specify Apache's simple hardcoded message. While not required under normal circumstances, default will restore Apache's simple hardcoded message for configurations that would otherwise inherit an existing ErrorDocument.

```
ErrorDocument 404 /cgi-bin/bad_urls.pl

<Directory /web/docs>
     ErrorDocument 404 default
</Directory>
```

Note that when you specify an ErrorDocument that points to a remote URL (ie. anything with a method such as http in front of it), Apache will send a redirect to the client to tell it where to find the document, even if the document ends up being on the same server. This has several implications, the most important being that the client will not receive the original error status code, but instead will receive a redirect status code. This in turn can confuse web robots and other clients which try to determine if a URL is valid using the status code. In addition, if you use a remote URL in an ErrorDocument 401, the client will not know to prompt the user for a password since it will not receive the 401 status code. Therefore, **if you use an ErrorDocument 401 directive then it must refer to a local document.**

Microsoft Internet Explorer (MSIE) will by default ignore server-generated error messages when they are "too small" and substitute its own "friendly" error messages. The size threshold varies depending on the type of error, but in general, if you make your error document greater than 512 bytes, then MSIE will show the server-generated error rather than masking it. More information is available in Microsoft Knowledge Base article Q294807[6].

Although most error messages can be overriden, there are certain circumstances where the internal messages are used regardless of the setting of ErrorDocument. In particular, if a malformed request is detected, normal request processing will be immediately halted and the internal error message returned. This is necessary to guard against security problems caused by bad requests.

If you are using mod_proxy, you may wish to enable ProxyErrorOverride so that you can provide custom error messages on behalf of your Origin servers. If you don't enable ProxyErrorOverride, Apache will not generate custom error documents for proxied content.

Prior to version 2.0, messages were indicated by prefixing them with a single unmatched double quote character.

---

[6]http://support.microsoft.com/default.aspx?scid=kb;en-us;Q294807

See also:

▷ documentation of customizable responses (p. 697)

ErrorLog Directive

Description:	Location where the server will log errors
Syntax:	ErrorLog *file-path* │ syslog[:*facility*]
Default:	ErrorLog logs/error_log (Unix) ErrorLog logs/error.log (Windows and OS/2)
Context:	server config, virtual host
Status:	Core
Module:	core

The ErrorLog directive sets the name of the file to which the server will log any errors it encounters. If the *file-path* is not absolute then it is assumed to be relative to the ServerRoot.

Example
```
ErrorLog /var/log/httpd/error_log
```

If the *file-path* begins with a pipe character "|" then it is assumed to be a command to spawn to handle the error log.

Example
```
ErrorLog "|/usr/local/bin/httpd_errors"
```

See the notes on piped logs (p. 66) for more information.

Using syslog instead of a filename enables logging via syslogd(8) if the system supports it. The default is to use syslog facility local7, but you can override this by using the syslog:*facility* syntax where *facility* can be one of the names usually documented in syslog(1).

Example
```
ErrorLog syslog:user
```

SECURITY: See the security tips (p. 677) document for details on why your security could be compromised if the directory where log files are stored is writable by anyone other than the user that starts the server.

NOTE   *When entering a file path on non-Unix platforms, care should be taken to make sure that only forward slashes are used even though the platform may allow the use of backslashes. In general it is a good idea to always use forward slashes throughout the configuration files.*

See also:

▷ LogLevel (p. 118)

▷ Apache Log Files (p. 66)

FileETag Directive

Description:	File attributes used to create the ETag HTTP response header for static files
Syntax:	FileETag component ...
Default:	FileETag INode MTime Size
Context:	server config, virtual host, directory, .htaccess
Override:	FileInfo
Status:	Core
Module:	core

The FileETag directive configures the file attributes that are used to create the ETag (entity tag) response header field when the document is based on a static file. (The ETag value is used in cache management to save network bandwidth.) In Apache 1.3.22 and earlier, the ETag value was *always* formed from the file's inode, size, and last-modified time (mtime). The FileETag directive allows you to choose which of these – if any – should be used. The recognized keywords are:

INode The file's i-node number will be included in the calculation

MTime The date and time the file was last modified will be included

Size The number of bytes in the file will be included

All All available fields will be used. This is equivalent to:

>   FileETag INode MTime Size

None If a document is file-based, no ETag field will be included in the response

The INode, MTime, and Size keywords may be prefixed with either + or -, which allow changes to be made to the default setting inherited from a broader scope. Any keyword appearing without such a prefix immediately and completely cancels the inherited setting.

If a directory's configuration includes FileETag INode MTime Size, and a subdirectory's includes FileETag -INode, the setting for that subdirectory (which will be inherited by any sub-subdirectories that don't override it) will be equivalent to FileETag MTime Size.

> WARNING *Do not change the default for directories or locations that have WebDAV enabled and use mod_dav_fs as a storage provider. mod_dav_fs uses INode MTime Size as a fixed format for ETag comparisons on conditional requests. These conditional requests will break if the ETag format is changed via FileETag.*

> SERVER SIDE INCLUDES *An ETag is not generated for responses parsed by mod_include, since the response entity can change without a change of the INode, MTime, or Size of the static file with embedded SSI directives.*

Files Directive

Description:	Contains directives that apply to matched filenames
Syntax:	`<Files filename> ... </Files>`
Context:	server config, virtual host, directory, .htaccess
Override:	All
Status:	Core
Module:	core

The `<Files>` directive limits the scope of the enclosed directives by filename. It is comparable to the `<Directory>` and `<Location>` directives. It should be matched with a `</Files>` directive. The directives given within this section will be applied to any object with a basename (last component of filename) matching the specified filename. `<Files>` sections are processed in the order they appear in the configuration file, after the `<Directory>` sections and .htaccess files are read, but before `<Location>` sections. Note that `<Files>` can be nested inside `<Directory>` sections to restrict the portion of the filesystem they apply to.

The *filename* argument should include a filename, or a wild-card string, where ? matches any single character, and * matches any sequences of characters. Regular expressions can also be used, with the addition of the ~ character. For example:

    <Files ~ "\.(gif|jpe?g|png)$">

would match most common Internet graphics formats. `<FilesMatch>` is preferred, however.

Note that unlike `<Directory>` and `<Location>` sections, `<Files>` sections can be used inside .htaccess files. This allows users to control access to their own files, at a file-by-file level.

See also:

> ▷ How `<Directory>`, `<Location>` and `<Files>` sections work (p. 57) for an explanation of how these different sections are combined when a request is received

FilesMatch Directive

Description:	Contains directives that apply to regular-expression matched filenames
Syntax:	`<FilesMatch regex> ... </FilesMatch>`
Context:	server config, virtual host, directory, .htaccess
Override:	All
Status:	Core
Module:	core

The `<FilesMatch>` directive limits the scope of the enclosed directives by filename, just as the `<Files>` directive does. However, it accepts a regular expression. For example:

```
<FilesMatch "\.(gif|jpe?g|png)$">
```

would match most common Internet graphics formats.

See also:

&rhd; How <Directory>, <Location> and <Files> sections work (p. 57) for an
explanation of how these different sections are combined when a request
is received

ForceType Directive

Description:	Forces all matching files to be served with the specified MIME content-type
Syntax:	ForceType *MIME-type*|None
Context:	directory, .htaccess
Override:	FileInfo
Status:	Core
Module:	core
Compatibility:	Moved to the core in Apache 2.0

When placed into an .htaccess file or a <Directory>, or <Location> or <Files>
section, this directive forces all matching files to be served with the content type
identification given by *MIME-type*. For example, if you had a directory full of
GIF files, but did not want to label them all with .gif, you might want to use:

```
ForceType image/gif
```

Note that unlike DefaultType, this directive overrides all mime-type associations, including filename extensions, that might identify the media type.

You can override any ForceType setting by using the value of None:

```
# force all files to be image/gif:
<Location /images>
    ForceType image/gif
</Location>
# but normal mime-type associations here:
<Location /images/mixed>
    ForceType None
</Location>
```

HostnameLookups Directive

Description:	Enables DNS lookups on client IP addresses
Syntax:	HostnameLookups On|Off|Double
Default:	HostnameLookups Off
Context:	server config, virtual host, directory
Status:	Core
Module:	core

This directive enables DNS lookups so that host names can be logged (and passed to CGIs/SSIs in REMOTE_HOST). The value Double refers to doing double-reverse DNS lookup. That is, after a reverse lookup is performed, a forward lookup is then performed on that result. At least one of the IP addresses in the forward lookup must match the original address. (In "tcpwrappers" terminology this is called PARANOID.)

Regardless of the setting, when mod_authz_host is used for controlling access by hostname, a double reverse lookup will be performed. This is necessary for security. Note that the result of this double-reverse isn't generally available unless you set HostnameLookups Double. For example, if only HostnameLookups On and a request is made to an object that is protected by hostname restrictions, regardless of whether the double-reverse fails or not, CGIs will still be passed the single-reverse result in REMOTE_HOST.

The default is Off in order to save the network traffic for those sites that don't truly need the reverse lookups done. It is also better for the end users because they don't have to suffer the extra latency that a lookup entails. Heavily loaded sites should leave this directive Off, since DNS lookups can take considerable amounts of time. The utility logresolve, compiled by default to the bin sub-directory of your installation directory, can be used to look up host names from logged IP addresses offline.

IfDefine Directive

Description:	Encloses directives that will be processed only if a test is true at startup
Syntax:	<IfDefine [!]parameter-name> ... </IfDefine>
Context:	server config, virtual host, directory, .htaccess
Override:	All
Status:	Core
Module:	core

The <IfDefine test>...</IfDefine> section is used to mark directives that are conditional. The directives within an <IfDefine> section are only processed if the test is true. If test is false, everything between the start and end markers is ignored.

The test in the <IfDefine> section directive can be one of two forms:

- parameter-name

- ! *parameter-name*

In the former case, the directives between the start and end markers are only processed if the parameter named *parameter-name* is defined. The second format reverses the test, and only processes the directives if *parameter-name* is not defined.

The *parameter-name* argument is a define as given on the httpd command line via -D*parameter-name*, at the time the server was started.

<IfDefine> sections are nestable, which can be used to implement simple multiple-parameter tests. Example:

```
httpd -DReverseProxy -DUseCache -DMemCache ...
# httpd.conf
<IfDefine ReverseProxy>
    LoadModule proxy_module modules/mod_proxy.so
    LoadModule proxy_http_module modules/mod_proxy_http.so
    <IfDefine UseCache>
        LoadModule cache_module modules/mod_cache.so
        <IfDefine MemCache>
            LoadModule mem_cache_module modules/mod_mem_cache.so
        </IfDefine>
        <IfDefine !MemCache>
            LoadModule disk_cache_module
            modules/mod_disk_cache.so
        </IfDefine>
    </IfDefine>
</IfDefine>
```

IfModule Directive

Description:	Encloses directives that are processed conditional on the presence or absence of a specific module
Syntax:	<IfModule [!]*module-file*|*module-identifier*> ... </IfModule>
Context:	server config, virtual host, directory, .htaccess
Override:	All
Status:	Core
Module:	core
Compatibility:	Module identifiers are available in version 2.1 and later.

The <IfModule *test*>...</IfModule> section is used to mark directives that are conditional on the presence of a specific module. The directives within an <IfModule> section are only processed if the *test* is true. If *test* is false, everything between the start and end markers is ignored.

The *test* in the <IfModule> section directive can be one of two forms:

- *module*

- !*module*

In the former case, the directives between the start and end markers are only processed if the module named *module* is included in Apache – either compiled in or dynamically loaded using LoadModule. The second format reverses the test, and only processes the directives if *module* is **not** included.

The *module* argument can be either the module identifier or the file name of the module, at the time it was compiled. For example, rewrite_module is the identifier and mod_rewrite.c is the file name. If a module consists of several source files, use the name of the file containing the string STANDARD20_MODULE_-STUFF.

<IfModule> sections are nestable, which can be used to implement simple multiple-module tests.

> *This section should only be used if you need to have one configuration file that works whether or not a specific module is available. In normal operation, directives need not be placed in <IfModule> sections.*

Include Directive

Description:	Includes other configuration files from within the server configuration files
Syntax:	Include *file-path*|*directory-path*
Context:	server config, virtual host, directory
Status:	Core
Module:	core
Compatibility:	Wildcard matching available in 2.0.41 and later

This directive allows inclusion of other configuration files from within the server configuration files.

Shell-style (fnmatch()) wildcard characters can be used to include several files at once, in alphabetical order. In addition, if Include points to a directory, rather than a file, Apache will read all files in that directory and any subdirectory. But including entire directories is not recommended, because it is easy to accidentally leave temporary files in a directory that can cause httpd to fail.

The file path specified may be an absolute path, or may be relative to the ServerRoot directory.

Examples:

```
Include /usr/local/apache2/conf/ssl.conf
Include /usr/local/apache2/conf/vhosts/*.conf
```

Or, providing paths relative to your ServerRoot directory:

```
Include conf/ssl.conf
Include conf/vhosts/*.conf
```

See also:

▷ apachectl (p. 11)

KeepAlive Directive

Description:	Enables HTTP persistent connections
Syntax:	KeepAlive On|Off
Default:	KeepAlive On
Context:	server config, virtual host
Status:	Core
Module:	core

The Keep-Alive extension to HTTP/1.0 and the persistent connection feature of HTTP/1.1 provide long-lived HTTP sessions which allow multiple requests to be sent over the same TCP connection. In some cases this has been shown to result in an almost 50% speedup in latency times for HTML documents with many images. To enable Keep-Alive connections, set KeepAlive On.

For HTTP/1.0 clients, Keep-Alive connections will only be used if they are specifically requested by a client. In addition, a Keep-Alive connection with an HTTP/1.0 client can only be used when the length of the content is known in advance. This implies that dynamic content such as CGI output, SSI pages, and server-generated directory listings will generally not use Keep-Alive connections to HTTP/1.0 clients. For HTTP/1.1 clients, persistent connections are the default unless otherwise specified. If the client requests it, chunked encoding will be used in order to send content of unknown length over persistent connections.

When a client uses a Keep-Alive connection it will be counted as a single "request" for the MaxRequestsPerChild directive, regardless of how many requests are sent using the connection.

See also:

▷ MaxKeepAliveRequests (p. 119)

KeepAliveTimeout Directive

Description:	Amount of time the server will wait for subsequent requests on a persistent connection
Syntax:	KeepAliveTimeout *seconds*
Default:	KeepAliveTimeout 5
Context:	server config, virtual host
Status:	Core
Module:	core

The number of seconds Apache will wait for a subsequent request before closing the connection. Once a request has been received, the timeout value specified by the Timeout directive applies.

Setting KeepAliveTimeout to a high value may cause performance problems in heavily loaded servers. The higher the timeout, the more server processes will be kept occupied waiting on connections with idle clients.

In a name-based virtual host context, the value of the first defined virtual host (the default host) in a set of NameVirtualHost will be used. The other values will be ignored.

Limit Directive

Description:	Restrict enclosed access controls to only certain HTTP methods
Syntax:	<Limit method [method] ... > ... </Limit>
Context:	server config, virtual host, directory, .htaccess
Override:	All
Status:	Core
Module:	core

Access controls are normally effective for **all** access methods, and this is the usual desired behavior. **In the general case, access control directives should not be placed within a <Limit> section.**

The purpose of the <Limit> directive is to restrict the effect of the access controls to the nominated HTTP methods. For all other methods, the access restrictions that are enclosed in the <Limit> bracket **will have no effect.** The following example applies the access control only to the methods POST, PUT, and DELETE, leaving all other methods unprotected:

```
<Limit POST PUT DELETE>
    Require valid-user
</Limit>
```

The method names listed can be one or more of: GET, POST, PUT, DELETE, CONNECT, OPTIONS, PATCH, PROPFIND, PROPPATCH, MKCOL, COPY, MOVE, LOCK, and UNLOCK. **The method name is case-sensitive.** If GET is used it will also restrict HEAD requests. The TRACE method cannot be limited.

A <LimitExcept> section should always be used in preference to a <Limit> section when restricting access, since a <LimitExcept> section provides protection against arbitrary methods.

LimitExcept Directive

Description:	Restrict access controls to all HTTP methods except the named ones
Syntax:	`<LimitExcept method [method] ... > ...` `</LimitExcept>`
Context:	server config, virtual host, directory, .htaccess
Override:	All
Status:	Core
Module:	core

`<LimitExcept>` and `</LimitExcept>` are used to enclose a group of access control directives which will then apply to any HTTP access method **not** listed in the arguments; i.e., it is the opposite of a `<Limit>` section and can be used to control both standard and nonstandard/unrecognized methods. See the documentation for `<Limit>` for more details.

For example:

```
<LimitExcept POST GET>
    Require valid-user
</LimitExcept>
```

LimitInternalRecursion Directive

Description:	Determine maximum number of internal redirects and nested subrequests
Syntax:	`LimitInternalRecursion number [number]`
Default:	`LimitInternalRecursion 10`
Context:	server config, virtual host
Status:	Core
Module:	core
Compatibility:	Available in Apache 2.0.47 and later

An internal redirect happens, for example, when using the `Action` directive, which internally redirects the original request to a CGI script. A subrequest is Apache's mechanism to find out what would happen for some URI if it were requested. For example, mod_dir uses subrequests to look for the files listed in the `DirectoryIndex` directive.

`LimitInternalRecursion` prevents the server from crashing when entering an infinite loop of internal redirects or subrequests. Such loops are usually caused by misconfigurations.

The directive stores two different limits, which are evaluated on per-request basis. The first *number* is the maximum number of internal redirects, that may follow each other. The second *number* determines, how deep subrequests may be nested. If you specify only one *number*, it will be assigned to both limits.

Example

LimitInternalRecursion 5

LimitRequestBody Directive

Description:	Restricts the total size of the HTTP request body sent from the client
Syntax:	LimitRequestBody *bytes*
Default:	LimitRequestBody 0
Context:	server config, virtual host, directory, .htaccess
Override:	All
Status:	Core
Module:	core

This directive specifies the number of *bytes* from 0 (meaning unlimited) to 2147483647 (2GB) that are allowed in a request body.

The LimitRequestBody directive allows the user to set a limit on the allowed size of an HTTP request message body within the context in which the directive is given (server, per-directory, per-file or per-location). If the client request exceeds that limit, the server will return an error response instead of servicing the request. The size of a normal request message body will vary greatly depending on the nature of the resource and the methods allowed on that resource. CGI scripts typically use the message body for retrieving form information. Implementations of the PUT method will require a value at least as large as any representation that the server wishes to accept for that resource.

This directive gives the server administrator greater control over abnormal client request behavior, which may be useful for avoiding some forms of denial-of-service attacks.

If, for example, you are permitting file upload to a particular location, and wish to limit the size of the uploaded file to 100K, you might use the following directive:

LimitRequestBody 102400

LimitRequestFieldSize Directive

Description:	Limits the size of the HTTP request header allowed from the client
Syntax:	LimitRequestFieldSize *bytes*
Default:	LimitRequestFieldSize 8190
Context:	server config
Status:	Core
Module:	core

This directive specifies the number of *bytes* that will be allowed in an HTTP request header.

The LimitRequestFieldSize directive allows the server administrator to reduce or increase the limit on the allowed size of an HTTP request header field. A server needs this value to be large enough to hold any one header field from a normal client request. The size of a normal request header field will vary greatly among different client implementations, often depending upon the extent to which a user has configured their browser to support detailed content negotiation. SPNEGO authentication headers can be up to 12392 bytes.

This directive gives the server administrator greater control over abnormal client request behavior, which may be useful for avoiding some forms of denial-of-service attacks.

For example:

    LimitRequestFieldSize 4094

Under normal conditions, the value should not be changed from the default.

LimitRequestFields Directive

Description:	Limits the number of HTTP request header fields that will be accepted from the client
Syntax:	LimitRequestFields *number*
Default:	LimitRequestFields 100
Context:	server config
Status:	Core
Module:	core

Number is an integer from 0 (meaning unlimited) to 32767. The default value is defined by the compile-time constant DEFAULT_LIMIT_REQUEST_FIELDS (100 as distributed).

The LimitRequestFields directive allows the server administrator to modify the limit on the number of request header fields allowed in an HTTP request. A server needs this value to be larger than the number of fields that a normal client request might include. The number of request header fields used by a client rarely exceeds 20, but this may vary among different client implementations, often depending upon the extent to which a user has configured their browser to support detailed content negotiation. Optional HTTP extensions are often expressed using request header fields.

This directive gives the server administrator greater control over abnormal client request behavior, which may be useful for avoiding some forms of denial-of-service attacks. The value should be increased if normal clients see an error response from the server that indicates too many fields were sent in the request.

For example:

    LimitRequestFields 50

LimitRequestLine Directive

Description:	Limit the size of the HTTP request line that will be accepted from the client
Syntax:	LimitRequestLine *bytes*
Default:	LimitRequestLine 8190
Context:	server config
Status:	Core
Module:	core

This directive sets the number of *bytes* that will be allowed on the HTTP request-line.

The LimitRequestLine directive allows the server administrator to reduce or increase the limit on the allowed size of a client's HTTP request-line. Since the request-line consists of the HTTP method, URI, and protocol version, the LimitRequestLine directive places a restriction on the length of a request-URI allowed for a request on the server. A server needs this value to be large enough to hold any of its resource names, including any information that might be passed in the query part of a GET request.

This directive gives the server administrator greater control over abnormal client request behavior, which may be useful for avoiding some forms of denial-of-service attacks.

For example:

    LimitRequestLine 4094

Under normal conditions, the value should not be changed from the default.

LimitXMLRequestBody Directive

Description:	Limits the size of an XML-based request body
Syntax:	LimitXMLRequestBody *bytes*
Default:	LimitXMLRequestBody 1000000
Context:	server config, virtual host, directory, .htaccess
Override:	All
Status:	Core
Module:	core

Limit (in bytes) on maximum size of an XML-based request body. A value of 0 will disable any checking.

Example:

    LimitXMLRequestBody 0

Location Directive

Description:	Applies the enclosed directives only to matching URLs
Syntax:	`<Location URL-path|URL>` ... `</Location>`
Context:	server config, virtual host
Status:	Core
Module:	core

The `<Location>` directive limits the scope of the enclosed directives by URL. It is similar to the `<Directory>` directive, and starts a subsection which is terminated with a `</Location>` directive. `<Location>` sections are processed in the order they appear in the configuration file, after the `<Directory>` sections and `.htaccess` files are read, and after the `<Files>` sections.

`<Location>` sections operate completely outside the filesystem. This has several consequences. Most importantly, `<Location>` directives should not be used to control access to filesystem locations. Since several different URLs may map to the same filesystem location, such access controls may by circumvented.

WHEN TO USE `<LOCATION>`

Use `<Location>` to apply directives to content that lives outside the filesystem. For content that lives in the filesystem, use `<Directory>` and `<Files>`. An exception is `<Location />`, which is an easy way to apply a configuration to the entire server.

For all origin (non-proxy) requests, the URL to be matched is a URL-path of the form `/path/`. *No scheme, hostname, port, or query string may be included.* For proxy requests, the URL to be matched is of the form `scheme://servername/path`, and you must include the prefix.

The URL may use wildcards. In a wild-card string, `?` matches any single character, and `*` matches any sequences of characters. Neither wildcard character matches a `/` in the URL-path.

Regular expressions can also be used, with the addition of the `~` character. For example:

```
<Location ~ "/(extra|special)/data">
```

would match URLs that contained the substring `/extra/data` or `/special/data`. The directive `<LocationMatch>` behaves identical to the regex version of `<Location>`.

The `<Location>` functionality is especially useful when combined with the `SetHandler` directive. For example, to enable status requests, but allow them only from browsers at `example.com`, you might use:

```
<Location /status>
    SetHandler server-status
    Order Deny,Allow
    Deny from all
```

```
      Allow from .example.com
</Location>
```

NOTE ABOUT / (SLASH) *The slash character has special meaning depending on where in a URL it appears. People may be used to its behavior in the filesystem where multiple adjacent slashes are frequently collapsed to a single slash (i.e., /home///foo is the same as /home/foo). In URL-space this is not necessarily true. The <LocationMatch> directive and the regex version of <Location> require you to explicitly specify multiple slashes if that is your intention.*

For example, <LocationMatch ^/abc> would match the request URL /abc but not the request URL //abc. The (non-regex) <Location> directive behaves similarly when used for proxy requests. But when (non-regex) <Location> is used for non-proxy requests it will implicitly match multiple slashes with a single slash. For example, if you specify <Location /abc/def> and the request is to /abc//def then it will match.

See also:

▷ How <Directory>, <Location> and <Files> sections work (p. 57) for an explanation of how these different sections are combined when a request is received

LocationMatch Directive

Description:	Applies the enclosed directives only to regular-expression matching URLs
Syntax:	<LocationMatch regex> ... </LocationMatch>
Context:	server config, virtual host
Status:	Core
Module:	core

The <LocationMatch> directive limits the scope of the enclosed directives by URL, in an identical manner to <Location>. However, it takes a regular expression as an argument instead of a simple string. For example:

```
<LocationMatch "/(extra|special)/data">
```

would match URLs that contained the substring /extra/data or /special/data.

See also:

▷ How <Directory>, <Location> and <Files> sections work (p. 57) for an explanation of how these different sections are combined when a request is received

LogLevel Directive

Description:	Controls the verbosity of the ErrorLog
Syntax:	LogLevel *level*
Default:	LogLevel warn
Context:	server config, virtual host
Status:	Core
Module:	core

LogLevel adjusts the verbosity of the messages recorded in the error logs (see ErrorLog directive). The following *levels* are available, in order of decreasing significance:

Level	Description
emerg	Emergencies - system is unusable.
	e.g. "Child cannot open lock file. Exiting"
alert	Action must be taken immediately.
	e.g. "getpwuid: couldn't determine user name from uid"
crit	Critical Conditions.
	e.g. "socket: Failed to get a socket, exiting child"
error	Error conditions.
	e.g. "Premature end of script headers"
warn	Warning conditions.
	e.g. "child process 1234 did not exit, sending another SIGHUP"
notice	Normal but significant condition.
	e.g. "httpd: caught SIGBUS, attempting to dump core in ... "
info	Informational.
	e.g. "Server seems busy, (you may need to increase StartServers, or Min/MaxSpareServers)... "
debug	Debug-level messages
	e.g. "Opening config file ... "

When a particular level is specified, messages from all other levels of higher significance will be reported as well. *E.g.*, when LogLevel info is specified, then messages with log levels of notice and warn will also be posted.

Using a level of at least crit is recommended.

For example:

```
LogLevel notice
```

NOTE *When logging to a regular file messages of the level notice cannot be suppressed and thus are always logged. However, this doesn't apply when logging is done using syslog.*

MaxKeepAliveRequests Directive

Description:	Number of requests allowed on a persistent connection
Syntax:	MaxKeepAliveRequests *number*
Default:	MaxKeepAliveRequests 100
Context:	server config, virtual host
Status:	Core
Module:	core

The MaxKeepAliveRequests directive limits the number of requests allowed per connection when KeepAlive is on. If it is set to 0, unlimited requests will be allowed. We recommend that this setting be kept to a high value for maximum server performance.

For example:

    MaxKeepAliveRequests 500

NameVirtualHost Directive

Description:	Designates an IP address for name-virtual hosting
Syntax:	NameVirtualHost *addr* [:*port*]
Context:	server config
Status:	Core
Module:	core

The NameVirtualHost directive is a required directive if you want to configure name-based virtual hosts (p. 541).

Although *addr* can be hostname it is recommended that you always use an IP address, e.g.

    NameVirtualHost 111.22.33.44

With the NameVirtualHost directive you specify the IP address on which the server will receive requests for the name-based virtual hosts. This will usually be the address to which your name-based virtual host names resolve. In cases where a firewall or other proxy receives the requests and forwards them on a different IP address to the server, you must specify the IP address of the physical interface on the machine which will be servicing the requests. If you have multiple name-based hosts on multiple addresses, repeat the directive for each address.

NOTE *Note, that the "main server" and any _default_ servers will never be served for a request to a NameVirtualHost IP address (unless for some reason you specify NameVirtualHost but then don't define any VirtualHosts for that address).*

Optionally you can specify a port number on which the name-based virtual hosts should be used, e.g.

```
NameVirtualHost 111.22.33.44:8080
```

IPv6 addresses must be enclosed in square brackets, as shown in the following example:

```
NameVirtualHost [2001:db8::a00:20ff:fea7:ccea]:8080
```

To receive requests on all interfaces, you can use an argument of *:80, or, if you are listening on multiple ports and really want the server to respond on all of them with a particular set of virtual hosts, *

```
NameVirtualHost *:80
```

ARGUMENT TO <VIRTUALHOST> DIRECTIVE *Note that the argument to the <VirtualHost> directive must exactly match the argument to the NameVirtualHost directive.*

```
NameVirtualHost 1.2.3.4
<VirtualHost 1.2.3.4>
# ...
</VirtualHost>
```

See also:

▷ Virtual Hosts documentation (p. 541)

Options Directive

Description:	Configures what features are available in a particular directory
Syntax:	Options [+|-]option [[+|-]option] ...
Default:	Options All
Context:	server config, virtual host, directory, .htaccess
Override:	Options
Status:	Core
Module:	core

The Options directive controls which server features are available in a particular directory.

option can be set to None, in which case none of the extra features are enabled, or one or more of the following:

All All options except for MultiViews. This is the default setting.

ExecCGI Execution of CGI scripts using mod_cgi is permitted.

FollowSymLinks The server will follow symbolic links in this directory.

Even though the server follows the symlink it does not change the pathname used to match against <Directory> sections.

Note also, that this option gets ignored if set inside a <Location> section.

> *Omitting this option should not be considered a security restriction, since symlink testing is subject to race conditions that make it circumventable.*

Includes Server-side includes provided by mod_include are permitted.

IncludesNOEXEC Server-side includes are permitted, but the #exec cmd and #exec cgi are disabled. It is still possible to #include virtual CGI scripts from ScriptAliased directories.

Indexes If a URL which maps to a directory is requested, and there is no DirectoryIndex (*e.g.*, index.html) in that directory, then mod_autoindex will return a formatted listing of the directory.

MultiViews Content negotiated (p. 687) "MultiViews" are allowed using mod_negotiation.

SymLinksIfOwnerMatch The server will only follow symbolic links for which the target file or directory is owned by the same user id as the link.

> NOTE *This option gets ignored if set inside a <Location> section.*
>
> *This option should not be considered a security restriction, since symlink testing is subject to race conditions that make it circumventable.*

Normally, if multiple Options could apply to a directory, then the most specific one is used and others are ignored; the options are not merged. (See how sections are merged (p. 57).) However if *all* the options on the Options directive are preceded by a + or - symbol, the options are merged. Any options preceded by a + are added to the options currently in force, and any options preceded by a - are removed from the options currently in force.

> WARNING *Mixing Options with a + or - with those without is not valid syntax, and is likely to cause unexpected results.*

For example, without any + and - symbols:

```
<Directory /web/docs>
    Options Indexes FollowSymLinks
</Directory>
<Directory /web/docs/spec>
    Options Includes
</Directory>
```

then only Includes will be set for the /web/docs/spec directory. However if the second Options directive uses the + and - symbols:

```
<Directory /web/docs>
    Options Indexes FollowSymLinks
</Directory>
<Directory /web/docs/spec>
    Options +Includes -Indexes
```

```
</Directory>
```

then the options `FollowSymLinks` and `Includes` are set for the `/web/docs/spec` directory.

NOTE *Using -IncludesNOEXEC or -Includes disables server-side includes completely regardless of the previous setting.*

The default in the absence of any other settings is `All`.

RLimitCPU Directive

Description:	Limits the CPU consumption of processes launched by Apache children
Syntax:	`RLimitCPU seconds|max [seconds |max]`
Default:	`Unset; uses operating system defaults`
Context:	server config, virtual host, directory, .htaccess
Override:	All
Status:	Core
Module:	core

Takes 1 or 2 parameters. The first parameter sets the soft resource limit for all processes and the second parameter sets the maximum resource limit. Either parameter can be a number, or `max` to indicate to the server that the limit should be set to the maximum allowed by the operating system configuration. Raising the maximum resource limit requires that the server is running as root, or in the initial startup phase.

This applies to processes forked off from Apache children servicing requests, not the Apache children themselves. This includes CGI scripts and SSI exec commands, but not any processes forked off from the Apache parent such as piped logs.

CPU resource limits are expressed in seconds per process.

See also:

▷ RLimitMEM (p. 122)

▷ RLimitNPROC (p. 123)

RLimitMEM Directive

Description:	Limits the memory consumption of processes launched by Apache children
Syntax:	`RLimitMEM bytes|max [bytes |max]`
Default:	`Unset; uses operating system defaults`
Context:	server config, virtual host, directory, .htaccess
Override:	All
Status:	Core
Module:	core

Takes 1 or 2 parameters. The first parameter sets the soft resource limit for all processes and the second parameter sets the maximum resource limit. Either parameter can be a number, or max to indicate to the server that the limit should be set to the maximum allowed by the operating system configuration. Raising the maximum resource limit requires that the server is running as root, or in the initial startup phase.

This applies to processes forked off from Apache children servicing requests, not the Apache children themselves. This includes CGI scripts and SSI exec commands, but not any processes forked off from the Apache parent such as piped logs.

Memory resource limits are expressed in bytes per process.

See also:

▷ RLimitCPU (p. 122)

▷ RLimitNPROC (p. 123)

RLimitNPROC Directive

Description:	Limits the number of processes that can be launched by processes launched by Apache children
Syntax:	RLimitNPROC number|max [number|max]
Default:	Unset; uses operating system defaults
Context:	server config, virtual host, directory, .htaccess
Override:	All
Status:	Core
Module:	core

Takes 1 or 2 parameters. The first parameter sets the soft resource limit for all processes and the second parameter sets the maximum resource limit. Either parameter can be a number, or max to indicate to the server that the limit should be set to the maximum allowed by the operating system configuration. Raising the maximum resource limit requires that the server is running as root, or in the initial startup phase.

This applies to processes forked off from Apache children servicing requests, not the Apache children themselves. This includes CGI scripts and SSI exec commands, but not any processes forked off from the Apache parent such as piped logs.

Process limits control the number of processes per user.

> NOTE *If CGI processes are not running under user ids other than the web server user id, this directive will limit the number of processes that the server itself can create. Evidence of this situation will be indicated by cannot fork messages in the error_log.*

See also:

▷ RLimitMEM (p. 122)

▷ RLimitCPU (p. 122)

Require Directive

Description:	Selects which authenticated users can access a resource
Syntax:	Require *entity-name* [*entity-name*] ...
Context:	directory, .htaccess
Override:	AuthConfig
Status:	Core
Module:	core

This directive selects which authenticated users can access a resource. The restrictions are processed by authorization modules. Some of the allowed syntaxes provided by `mod_authz_user` and `mod_authz_groupfile` are:

`Require user userid [userid]` ... Only the named users can access the resource.

`Require group group-name [group-name]` ... Only users in the named groups can access the resource.

`Require valid-user` All valid users can access the resource.

Other authorization modules that implement require options include `mod_authnz_ldap`, `mod_authz_dbm`, and `mod_authz_owner`.

`Require` must be accompanied by `AuthName` and `AuthType` directives, and directives such as `AuthUserFile` and `AuthGroupFile` (to define users and groups) in order to work correctly. Example:

```
AuthType Basic
AuthName "Restricted Resource"
AuthUserFile /web/users
AuthGroupFile /web/groups
Require group admin
```

Access controls which are applied in this way are effective for **all** methods. **This is what is normally desired.** If you wish to apply access controls only to specific methods, while leaving other methods unprotected, then place the Require statement into a `<Limit>` section.

If Require is used together with the `Allow` or `Deny` directives, then the interaction of these restrictions is controlled by the `Satisfy` directive.

> REMOVING CONTROLS IN SUBDIRECTORIES *The following example shows how to use the* `Satisfy` *directive to disable access controls in a subdirectory of a protected directory. This technique should be used with caution, because it will also disable any access controls imposed by* `mod_authz_host`.
>
> `<Directory /path/to/protected/>`

```
        Require user david
    </Directory>
    <Directory /path/to/protected/unprotected>
        # All access controls and authentication are disabled
        # in this directory
        Satisfy Any
        Allow from all
    </Directory>
```

See also:

▷ Authentication, Authorization, and Access Control (p. 629)

▷ Satisfy (p. 125)

▷ mod_authz_host (p. 193)

Satisfy Directive

Description:	Interaction between host-level access control and user authentication
Syntax:	`Satisfy Any|All`
Default:	`Satisfy All`
Context:	directory, .htaccess
Override:	AuthConfig
Status:	Core
Module:	core
Compatibility:	Influenced by `<Limit>` and `<LimitExcept>` in version 2.0.51 and later

Access policy if both `Allow` and `Require` used. The parameter can be either `All` or `Any`. This directive is only useful if access to a particular area is being restricted by both username/password *and* client host address. In this case the default behavior (`All`) is to require that the client passes the address access restriction *and* enters a valid username and password. With the `Any` option the client will be granted access if they either pass the host restriction or enter a valid username and password. This can be used to password restrict an area, but to let clients from particular addresses in without prompting for a password.

For example, if you wanted to let people on your network have unrestricted access to a portion of your website, but require that people outside of your network provide a password, you could use a configuration similar to the following:

```
Require valid-user
Order allow,deny
Allow from 192.168.1
Satisfy Any
```

Since version 2.0.51 Satisfy directives can be restricted to particular methods by `<Limit>` and `<LimitExcept>` sections.

See also:

▷ Allow (p. 193)

▷ Require (p. 124)

ScriptInterpreterSource Directive

Description:	Technique for locating the interpreter for CGI scripts
Syntax:	ScriptInterpreterSource
	Registry|Registry-Strict|Script
Default:	ScriptInterpreterSource Script
Context:	server config, virtual host, directory, .htaccess
Override:	FileInfo
Status:	Core
Module:	core
Compatibility:	Win32 only; option Registry-Strict is available in Apache 2.0 and later

This directive is used to control how Apache finds the interpreter used to run CGI scripts. The default setting is Script. This causes Apache to use the interpreter pointed to by the shebang line (first line, starting with #!) in the script. On Win32 systems this line usually looks like:

```
#!C:/Perl/bin/perl.exe
```

or, if perl is in the PATH, simply:

```
#!perl
```

Setting ScriptInterpreterSource Registry will cause the Windows Registry tree HKEY_CLASSES_ROOT to be searched using the script file extension (e.g., .pl) as a search key. The command defined by the registry subkey Shell\ExecCGI\Command or, if it does not exist, by the subkey Shell\Open\Command is used to open the script file. If the registry keys cannot be found, Apache falls back to the behavior of the Script option.

For example, the registry setting to have a script with the .pl extension processed via perl would be:

```
HKEY_CLASSES_ROOT\.pl\Shell\ExecCGI\Command\(Default) =>
C:\Perl\bin\perl.exe -wT
```

SECURITY *Be careful when using ScriptInterpreterSource Registry with ScriptAlias'ed directories, because Apache will try to execute every file within this directory. The Registry setting may cause undesired program calls on files which are typically not executed. For example, the default open command on .htm files on most Windows systems will execute Microsoft Internet Explorer, so any HTTP request for an .htm file existing within the script directory would start the browser in the background on the server. This is a good way to crash your system within a minute or so.*

The option `Registry-Strict` which is new in Apache 2.0 does the same thing as `Registry` but uses only the subkey `Shell\ExecCGI\Command`. The `ExecCGI` key is not a common one. It must be configured manually in the windows registry and hence prevents accidental program calls on your system.

ServerAdmin Directive

Description:	Email address that the server includes in error messages sent to the client
Syntax:	ServerAdmin *email-address* | *URL*
Context:	server config, virtual host
Status:	Core
Module:	core

The `ServerAdmin` sets the contact address that the server includes in any error messages it returns to the client. If the `httpd` doesn't recognize the supplied argument as an URL, it assumes, that it's an *email-address* and prepends it with `mailto:` in hyperlink targets. However, it's recommended to actually use an email address, since there are a lot of CGI scripts that make that assumption. If you want to use an URL, it should point to another server under your control. Otherwise users may not be able to contact you in case of errors.

It may be worth setting up a dedicated address for this, e.g.

    ServerAdmin www-admin@foo.example.com

as users do not always mention that they are talking about the server!

ServerAlias Directive

Description:	Alternate names for a host used when matching requests to name-virtual hosts
Syntax:	ServerAlias *hostname* [*hostname*] ...
Context:	virtual host
Status:	Core
Module:	core

The `ServerAlias` directive sets the alternate names for a host, for use with name-based virtual hosts (p. 543). The `ServerAlias` may include wildcards, if appropriate.

```
<VirtualHost *:80>
ServerName server.domain.com
ServerAlias server server2.domain.com server2
ServerAlias *.example.com
UseCanonicalName Off
# ...
</VirtualHost>
```

See also:

▷ UseCanonicalName (p. 134)

▷ Apache Virtual Host documentation (p. 541)

ServerName Directive

Description:	Hostname and port that the server uses to identify itself
Syntax:	ServerName
	[*scheme*://]*fully-qualified-domain-name*[:*port*]
Context:	server config, virtual host
Status:	Core
Module:	core
Compatibility:	In version 2.0, this directive supersedes the functionality of the Port directive from version 1.3.

The ServerName directive sets the request scheme, hostname and port that the server uses to identify itself. This is used when creating redirection URLs. For example, if the name of the machine hosting the web server is simple.example.com, but the machine also has the DNS alias www.example.com and you wish the web server to be so identified, the following directive should be used:

ServerName www.example.com:80

If no ServerName is specified, then the server attempts to deduce the hostname by performing a reverse lookup on the IP address. If no port is specified in the ServerName, then the server will use the port from the incoming request. For optimal reliability and predictability, you should specify an explicit hostname and port using the ServerName directive.

If you are using name-based virtual hosts (p. 543), the ServerName inside a <VirtualHost> section specifies what hostname must appear in the request's Host: header to match this virtual host.

Sometimes, the server runs behind a device that processes SSL, such as a reverse proxy, load balancer or SSL offload appliance. When this is the case, specify the https:// scheme and the port number to which the clients connect in the ServerName directive to make sure that the server generates the correct self-referential URLs.

See the description of the UseCanonicalName and UseCanonicalPhysicalPort directives for settings which determine whether self-referential URLs (e.g., by the mod_dir module) will refer to the specified port, or to the port number given in the client's request.

See also:

▷ Issues Regarding DNS and Apache (p. 571)

▷ Apache virtual host documentation (p. 541)

▷ UseCanonicalName (p. 134)

    ▷ UseCanonicalPhysicalPort (p. 135)

    ▷ NameVirtualHost (p. 119)

    ▷ ServerAlias (p. 127)

ServerPath Directive

Description:	Legacy URL pathname for a name-based virtual host that is accessed by an incompatible browser
Syntax:	ServerPath *URL-path*
Context:	virtual host
Status:	Core
Module:	core

The `ServerPath` directive sets the legacy URL pathname for a host, for use with name-based virtual hosts (p. 541).

See also:

    ▷ Apache Virtual Host documentation (p. 541)

ServerRoot Directive

Description:	Base directory for the server installation
Syntax:	ServerRoot *directory-path*
Default:	ServerRoot /usr/local/apache
Context:	server config
Status:	Core
Module:	core

The `ServerRoot` directive sets the directory in which the server lives. Typically it will contain the subdirectories `conf/` and `logs/`. Relative paths in other configuration directives (such as `Include` or `LoadModule`, for example) are taken as relative to this directory.

Example
```
ServerRoot /home/httpd
```

See also:

    ▷ the -d option to httpd (p. 49)

    ▷ the security tips (p. 677) for information on how to properly set permissions on the ServerRoot

ServerSignature Directive

Description:	Configures the footer on server-generated documents
Syntax:	ServerSignature On|Off|EMail
Default:	ServerSignature Off
Context:	server config, virtual host, directory, .htaccess
Override:	All
Status:	Core
Module:	core

The ServerSignature directive allows the configuration of a trailing footer line under server-generated documents (error messages, mod_proxy ftp directory listings, mod_info output, ...). The reason why you would want to enable such a footer line is that in a chain of proxies, the user often has no possibility to tell which of the chained servers actually produced a returned error message.

The Off setting, which is the default, suppresses the footer line (and is therefore compatible with the behavior of Apache-1.2 and below). The On setting simply adds a line with the server version number and ServerName of the serving virtual host, and the EMail setting additionally creates a "mailto:" reference to the ServerAdmin of the referenced document.

After version 2.0.44, the details of the server version number presented are controlled by the ServerTokens directive.

See also:

▷ ServerTokens (p. 130)

ServerTokens Directive

Description:	Configures the Server HTTP response header
Syntax:	ServerTokens
	Major|Minor|Min[imal]|Prod[uctOnly]|OS|Full
Default:	ServerTokens Full
Context:	server config
Status:	Core
Module:	core

This directive controls whether Server response header field which is sent back to clients includes a description of the generic OS-type of the server as well as information about compiled-in modules.

ServerTokens Prod[uctOnly] Server sends (*e.g.*):
      Server: Apache

ServerTokens Major Server sends (*e.g.*):
      Server: Apache/2

ServerTokens Minor Server sends (*e.g.*):
      Server: Apache/2.0

ServerTokens Min[imal] Server sends (*e.g.*):
    Server: Apache/2.0.41

ServerTokens OS Server sends (*e.g.*):
    Server: Apache/2.0.41 (Unix)

ServerTokens Full **(or not specified)** Server sends (*e.g.*):
    Server: Apache/2.0.41 (Unix) PHP/4.2.2 MyMod/1.2

This setting applies to the entire server, and cannot be enabled or disabled on a virtualhost-by-virtualhost basis.

After version 2.0.44, this directive also controls the information presented by the ServerSignature directive.

See also:

  ▷ ServerSignature (p. 130)

SetHandler Directive

Description:	Forces all matching files to be processed by a handler
Syntax:	SetHandler *handler-name* | None
Context:	server config, virtual host, directory, .htaccess
Override:	FileInfo
Status:	Core
Module:	core
Compatibility:	Moved into the core in Apache 2.0

When placed into an .htaccess file or a <Directory> or <Location> section, this directive forces all matching files to be parsed through the handler (p. 713) given by *handler-name*. For example, if you had a directory you wanted to be parsed entirely as imagemap rule files, regardless of extension, you might put the following into an .htaccess file in that directory:

    SetHandler imap-file

Another example: if you wanted to have the server display a status report whenever a URL of http://servername/status was called, you might put the following into httpd.conf:

    <Location /status>
        SetHandler server-status
    </Location>

You can override an earlier defined SetHandler directive by using the value None.

See also:

  ▷ AddHandler (p. 353)

SetInputFilter Directive

Description:	Sets the filters that will process client requests and POST input
Syntax:	SetInputFilter *filter* [;*filter*...]
Context:	server config, virtual host, directory, .htaccess
Override:	FileInfo
Status:	Core
Module:	core

The `SetInputFilter` directive sets the filter or filters which will process client requests and POST input when they are received by the server. This is in addition to any filters defined elsewhere, including the `AddInputFilter` directive.

If more than one filter is specified, they must be separated by semicolons in the order in which they should process the content.

See also:

▷ Filters (p. 715) documentation

SetOutputFilter Directive

Description:	Sets the filters that will process responses from the server
Syntax:	SetOutputFilter *filter* [;*filter*...]
Context:	server config, virtual host, directory, .htaccess
Override:	FileInfo
Status:	Core
Module:	core

The `SetOutputFilter` directive sets the filters which will process responses from the server before they are sent to the client. This is in addition to any filters defined elsewhere, including the `AddOutputFilter` directive.

For example, the following configuration will process all files in the /www/data/ directory for server-side includes.

```
<Directory /www/data/>
    SetOutputFilter INCLUDES
</Directory>
```

If more than one filter is specified, they must be separated by semicolons in the order in which they should process the content.

See also:

▷ Filters (p. 715) documentation

TimeOut Directive

Description:	Amount of time the server will wait for certain events before failing a request
Syntax:	TimeOut *seconds*
Default:	TimeOut 300
Context:	server config, virtual host
Status:	Core
Module:	core

The TimeOut directive defines the length of time Apache will wait for I/O in various circumstances:

1. When reading data from the client, the length of time to wait for a TCP packet to arrive if the read buffer is empty.

2. When writing data to the client, the length of time to wait for an acknowledgement of a packet if the send buffer is full.

3. In mod_cgi, the length of time to wait for output from a CGI script.

4. In mod_ext_filter, the length of time to wait for output from a filtering process.

5. In mod_proxy, the default timeout value if ProxyTimeout is not configured.

TraceEnable Directive

Description:	Determines the behaviour on TRACE requests
Syntax:	TraceEnable *[on|off|extended]*
Default:	TraceEnable on
Context:	server config
Status:	Core
Module:	core
Compatibility:	Available in Apache 1.3.34, 2.0.55 and later

This directive overrides the behavior of TRACE for both the core server and mod_proxy. The default TraceEnable on permits TRACE requests per RFC 2616, which disallows any request body to accompany the request. TraceEnable off causes the core server and mod_proxy to return a 405 (Method not allowed) error to the client.

Finally, for testing and diagnostic purposes only, request bodies may be allowed using the non-compliant TraceEnable extended directive. The core (as an origin server) will restrict the request body to 64k (plus 8k for chunk headers if Transfer-Encoding: chunked is used). The core will reflect the full headers and all chunk headers with the response body. As a proxy server, the request body is not restricted to 64k.

UseCanonicalName Directive

Description:	Configures how the server determines its own name and port
Syntax:	UseCanonicalName On|Off|DNS
Default:	UseCanonicalName Off
Context:	server config, virtual host, directory
Status:	Core
Module:	core

In many situations Apache must construct a *self-referential* URL – that is, a URL that refers back to the same server. With UseCanonicalName On Apache will use the hostname and port specified in the ServerName directive to construct the canonical name for the server. This name is used in all self-referential URLs, and for the values of SERVER_NAME and SERVER_PORT in CGIs.

With UseCanonicalName Off Apache will form self-referential URLs using the hostname and port supplied by the client if any are supplied (otherwise it will use the canonical name, as defined above). These values are the same that are used to implement name based virtual hosts (p. 543), and are available with the same clients. The CGI variables SERVER_NAME and SERVER_PORT will be constructed from the client supplied values as well.

An example where this may be useful is on an intranet server where you have users connecting to the machine using short names such as www. You'll notice that if the users type a shortname, and a URL which is a directory, such as http://www/splat, *without the trailing slash* then Apache will redirect them to http://www.domain.com/splat/. If you have authentication enabled, this will cause the user to have to authenticate twice (once for www and once again for www.domain.com – see the FAQ on this subject for more information[7]). But if UseCanonicalName is set Off, then Apache will redirect to http://www/splat/.

There is a third option, UseCanonicalName DNS, which is intended for use with mass IP-based virtual hosting to support ancient clients that do not provide a Host: header. With this option Apache does a reverse DNS lookup on the server IP address that the client connected to in order to work out self-referential URLs.

> WARNING *If CGIs make assumptions about the values of SERVER_NAME they may be broken by this option. The client is essentially free to give whatever value they want as a hostname. But if the CGI is only using SERVER_NAME to construct self-referential URLs then it should be just fine.*

See also:

▷ UseCanonicalPhysicalPort (p. 135)

▷ ServerName (p. 128)

▷ Listen (p. 519)

---

[7] http://httpd.apache.org/docs/misc/FAQ.html#prompted-twice

UseCanonicalPhysicalPort Directive

Description:	Configures how the server determines its own name and port
Syntax:	UseCanonicalPhysicalPort On|Off
Default:	UseCanonicalPhysicalPort Off
Context:	server config, virtual host, directory
Status:	Core
Module:	core

In many situations Apache must construct a *self-referential* URL – that is, a URL that refers back to the same server. With UseCanonicalPhysicalPort On Apache will, when constructing the canonical port for the server to honor the UseCanonicalName directive, provide the actual physical port number being used by this request as a potential port. With UseCanonicalPhysicalPort Off Apache will not ever use the actual physical port number, instead relying on all configured information to construct a valid port number.

NOTE *The ordering of when the physical port is used is as follows:*
UseCanonicalName On

- *Port provided in* Servername
- *Physical port*
- *Default port*

UseCanonicalName Off | DNS

- *Parsed port from* Host: *header*
- *Physical port*
- *Port provided in* Servername
- *Default port*

With UseCanonicalPhysicalPort Off, *the physical ports are removed from the ordering.*

See also:

▷ UseCanonicalName (p. 134)

▷ ServerName (p. 128)

▷ Listen (p. 519)

VirtualHost Directive

Description:	Contains directives that apply only to a specific hostname or IP address
Syntax:	<VirtualHost addr[:port] [addr[:port]] ...> ... </VirtualHost>
Context:	server config
Status:	Core
Module:	core

`<VirtualHost>` and `</VirtualHost>` are used to enclose a group of directives that will apply only to a particular virtual host. Any directive that is allowed in a virtual host context may be used. When the server receives a request for a document on a particular virtual host, it uses the configuration directives enclosed in the `<VirtualHost>` section. *Addr* can be:

- The IP address of the virtual host;
- A fully qualified domain name for the IP address of the virtual host (not recommended);
- The character *, which is used only in combination with `NameVirtualHost` * to match all IP addresses; or
- The string _default_, which is used only with IP virtual hosting to catch unmatched IP addresses.

Example
```
<VirtualHost 10.1.2.3>
    ServerAdmin webmaster@host.example.com
    DocumentRoot /www/docs/host.example.com
    ServerName host.example.com
    ErrorLog logs/host.example.com-error_log
    TransferLog logs/host.example.com-access_log
</VirtualHost>
```

IPv6 addresses must be specified in square brackets because the optional port number could not be determined otherwise. An IPv6 example is shown below:

```
<VirtualHost [2001:db8::a00:20ff:fea7:ccea]>
    ServerAdmin webmaster@host.example.com
    DocumentRoot /www/docs/host.example.com
    ServerName host.example.com
    ErrorLog logs/host.example.com-error_log
    TransferLog logs/host.example.com-access_log
</VirtualHost>
```

Each Virtual Host must correspond to a different IP address, different port number or a different host name for the server. In the former case the server machine must be configured to accept IP packets for multiple addresses. (If the machine does not have multiple network interfaces, then this can be accomplished with the `ifconfig alias` command – if your OS supports it.)

NOTE *The use of `<VirtualHost>` does **not** affect what addresses Apache listens on. You may need to ensure that Apache is listening on the correct addresses using `Listen`.*

When using IP-based virtual hosting, the special name _default_ can be specified in which case this virtual host will match any IP address that is not explicitly listed in another virtual host. In the absence of any _default_ virtual host the "main" server config, consisting of all those definitions outside any VirtualHost section, is used when no IP-match occurs. (But note that any IP address that matches a NameVirtualHost directive will use neither the "main" server config nor the _default_ virtual host. See the name-based virtual hosting (p. 543) documentation for further details.)

You can specify a :port to change the port that is matched. If unspecified then it defaults to the same port as the most recent Listen statement of the main server. You may also specify :* to match all ports on that address. (This is recommended when used with _default_.)

A ServerName should be specified inside each <VirtualHost> block. If it is absent, the ServerName from the "main" server configuration will be inherited.

> SECURITY *See the security tips (p. 677) document for details on why your security could be compromised if the directory where log files are stored is writable by anyone other than the user that starts the server.*

See also:

- ▷ Apache Virtual Host documentation (p. 541)
- ▷ Issues Regarding DNS and Apache (p. 571)
- ▷ Setting which addresses and ports Apache uses (p. 701)
- ▷ How <Directory>, <Location> and <Files> sections work (p. 57) for an explanation of how these different sections are combined when a request is received

3.4 Apache Module mod_actions

Description:	This module provides for executing CGI scripts based on media type or request method.
Status:	Base
Module Identifier:	actions_module
Source File:	mod_actions.c

Summary

This module has two directives. The Action directive lets you run CGI scripts whenever a file of a certain MIME content type is requested. The Script directive lets you run CGI scripts whenever a particular method is used in a request. This makes it much easier to execute scripts that process files.

Directives:

> Action
> Script

See also:

▷ mod_cgi (p. 229)

▷ Dynamic Content with CGI (p. 651)

▷ Apache's Handler Use (p. 713)

Action Directive

Description:	Activates a CGI script for a particular handler or content-type
Syntax:	Action *action-type* *cgi-script* [virtual]
Context:	server config, virtual host, directory, .htaccess
Override:	FileInfo
Status:	Base
Module:	mod_actions
Compatibility:	The virtual modifier and handler passing were introduced in Apache 2.1

This directive adds an action, which will activate *cgi-script* when *action-type* is triggered by the request. The *cgi-script* is the URL-path to a resource that has been designated as a CGI script using ScriptAlias or AddHandler. The *action-type* can be either a handler (p. 713) or a MIME content type. It sends the URL and file path of the requested document using the standard CGI PATH_INFO and PATH_TRANSLATED environment variables. The handler used for the particular request is passed using the REDIRECT_HANDLER variable.

Examples
```
# Requests for files of a particular MIME content type:
Action image/gif /cgi-bin/images.cgi
```

```
# Files of a particular file extension
AddHandler my-file-type .xyz
Action my-file-type /cgi-bin/program.cgi
```

In the first example, requests for files with a MIME content type of image/gif will be handled by the specified cgi script /cgi-bin/images.cgi.

In the second example, requests for files with a file extension of .xyz are handled by the specified cgi script /cgi-bin/program.cgi.

The optional virtual modifier turns off the check whether the requested file really exists. This is useful, for example, if you want to use the Action directive in virtual locations.

Example
```
<Location /news>
    SetHandler news-handler
    Action news-handler /cgi-bin/news.cgi virtual
</Location>
```

See also:

▷ AddHandler (p. 353)

Script Directive

Description:	Activates a CGI script for a particular request method.
Syntax:	Script *method cgi-script*
Context:	server config, virtual host, directory
Status:	Base
Module:	mod_actions

This directive adds an action, which will activate *cgi-script* when a file is requested using the method of *method*. The *cgi-script* is the URL-path to a resource that has been designated as a CGI script using ScriptAlias or AddHandler. The URL and file path of the requested document is sent using the standard CGI PATH_INFO and PATH_TRANSLATED environment variables.

*Any arbitrary method name may be used. **Method names are case-sensitive,** so Script PUT and Script put have two entirely different effects.*

Note that the Script command defines default actions only. If a CGI script is called, or some other resource that is capable of handling the requested method internally, it will do so. Also note that Script with a method of GET will only be called if there are query arguments present (*e.g.*, foo.html?hi). Otherwise, the request will proceed normally.

Examples
```
# For <ISINDEX>-style searching
Script GET /cgi-bin/search
```

```
# A CGI PUT handler
Script PUT /~bob/put.cgi
```

3.5 Apache Module mod_alias

Description:	Provides for mapping different parts of the host filesystem in the document tree and for URL redirection
Status:	Base
Module Identifier:	alias_module
Source File:	mod_alias.c

Summary

The directives contained in this module allow for manipulation and control of URLs as requests arrive at the server. The Alias and ScriptAlias directives are used to map between URLs and filesystem paths. This allows for content which is not directly under the DocumentRoot served as part of the web document tree. The ScriptAlias directive has the additional effect of marking the target directory as containing only CGI scripts.

The Redirect directives are used to instruct clients to make a new request with a different URL. They are often used when a resource has moved to a new location.

mod_alias is designed to handle simple URL manipulation tasks. For more complicated tasks such as manipulating the query string, use the tools provided by mod_rewrite.

Directives:

> Alias
> AliasMatch
> Redirect
> RedirectMatch
> RedirectPermanent
> RedirectTemp
> ScriptAlias
> ScriptAliasMatch

See also:

> ▷ mod_rewrite (p. 426)
> ▷ Mapping URLs to the filesystem (p. 75)

3.5.1 Order of Processing

Aliases and Redirects occuring in different contexts are processed like other directives according to standard merging rules (p. 57). But when multiple Aliases or Redirects occur in the same context (for example, in the same <VirtualHost> section) they are processed in a particular order.

First, all Redirects are processed before Aliases are processed, and therefore a request that matches a Redirect or RedirectMatch will never have Aliases applied. Second, the Aliases and Redirects are processed in the order they appear in the configuration files, with the first match taking precedence.

For this reason, when two or more of these directives apply to the same subpath, you must list the most specific path first in order for all the directives to have an effect. For example, the following configuration will work as expected:

```
Alias /foo/bar /baz
Alias /foo /gaq
```

But if the above two directives were reversed in order, the /foo Alias would always match before the /foo/bar Alias, so the latter directive would be ignored.

Alias Directive

Description:	Maps URLs to filesystem locations
Syntax:	Alias *URL-path* *file-path|directory-path*
Context:	server config, virtual host
Status:	Base
Module:	mod_alias

The Alias directive allows documents to be stored in the local filesystem other than under the DocumentRoot. URLs with a (%-decoded) path beginning with *url-path* will be mapped to local files beginning with *directory-path*. The *url-path* is case-sensitive, even on case-insensitive file systems.

Example:
```
Alias /image /ftp/pub/image
```

A request for http://myserver/image/foo.gif would cause the server to return the file /ftp/pub/image/foo.gif. Only complete path segments are matched, so the above alias would not match a request for http://myserver/imagefoo.gif. For more complex matching using regular expressions, see the AliasMatch directive.

Note that if you include a trailing / on the *url-path* then the server will require a trailing / in order to expand the alias. That is, if you use

```
Alias /icons/ /usr/local/apache/icons/
```

then the url /icons will not be aliased.

Note that you may need to specify additional <Directory> sections which cover the *destination* of aliases. Aliasing occurs before <Directory> sections are checked, so only the destination of aliases are affected. (Note however <Location> sections are run through once before aliases are performed, so they will apply.)

In particular, if you are creating an Alias to a directory outside of your DocumentRoot, you may need to explicitly permit access to the target directory.

Example:
```
Alias /image /ftp/pub/image
<Directory /ftp/pub/image>
    Order allow,deny
    Allow from all
</Directory>
```

AliasMatch Directive

Description:	Maps URLs to filesystem locations using regular expressions
Syntax:	AliasMatch *regex file-path|directory-path*
Context:	server config, virtual host
Status:	Base
Module:	mod_alias

This directive is equivalent to `Alias`, but makes use of regular expressions, instead of simple prefix matching. The supplied regular expression is matched against the URL-path, and if it matches, the server will substitute any parenthesized matches into the given string and use it as a filename. For example, to activate the /icons directory, one might use:

```
AliasMatch ^/icons(.*) /usr/local/apache/icons$1
```

The full range of regular expression power is available. For example, it is possible to construct an alias with case-insensitive matching of the url-path:

```
AliasMatch (?i)^/image(.*) /ftp/pub/image$1
```

One subtle difference between `Alias` and `AliasMatch` is that `Alias` will automatically copy any additional part of the URI, past the part that matched, onto the end of the file path on the right side, while `AliasMatch` will not. This means that in almost all cases, you will want the regular expression to match the entire request URI from beginning to end, and to use substitution on the right side.

In other words, just changing `Alias` to `AliasMatch` will not have the same effect. At a minimum, you need to add ^ to the beginning of the regular expression and add (.*)$ to the end, and add $1 to the end of the replacement.

For example, suppose you want to replace this with AliasMatch:

```
Alias /image/ /ftp/pub/image/
```

This is NOT equivalent - don't do this! This will send all requests that have /image/ anywhere in them to /ftp/pub/image/:

```
AliasMatch /image/ /ftp/pub/image/
```

This is what you need to get the same effect:

```
AliasMatch ^/image/(.*)$ /ftp/pub/image/$1
```

Of course, there's no point in using `AliasMatch` where `Alias` would work. `AliasMatch` lets you do more complicated things. For example, you could serve different kinds of files from different directories:

```
AliasMatch ^/image/(.*)\.jpg$ /files/jpg.images/$1.jpg
AliasMatch ^/image/(.*)\.gif$ /files/gif.images/$1.gif
```

Redirect Directive

Description:	Sends an external redirect asking the client to fetch a different URL
Syntax:	Redirect [*status*] *URL–path URL*
Context:	server config, virtual host, directory, .htaccess
Override:	FileInfo
Status:	Base
Module:	mod_alias

The Redirect directive maps an old URL into a new one by asking the client to refetch the resource at the new location.

The old *URL-path* is a case-sensitive (%-decoded) path beginning with a slash. A relative path is not allowed. The new *URL* should be an absolute URL beginning with a scheme and hostname, but a URL-path beginning with a slash may also be used, in which case the scheme and hostname of the current server will be added.

Then any request beginning with *URL-Path* will return a redirect request to the client at the location of the target *URL*. Additional path information beyond the matched *URL-Path* will be appended to the target URL.

Example:
```
Redirect /service http://foo2.example.com/service
```

If the client requests http://example.com/service/foo.txt, it will be told to access http://foo2.example.com/service/foo.txt instead. Only complete path segments are matched, so the above example would not match a request for http://example.com/servicefoo.txt. For more complex matching using regular expressions, see the RedirectMatch directive.

NOTE *Redirect directives take precedence over Alias and ScriptAlias directives, irrespective of their ordering in the configuration file.*

If no *status* argument is given, the redirect will be "temporary" (HTTP status 302). This indicates to the client that the resource has moved temporarily. The *status* argument can be used to return other HTTP status codes:

permanent Returns a permanent redirect status (301) indicating that the resource has moved permanently.

temp Returns a temporary redirect status (302). This is the default.

seeother Returns a "See Other" status (303) indicating that the resource has been replaced.

gone Returns a "Gone" status (410) indicating that the resource has been permanently removed. When this status is used the *URL* argument should be omitted.

Other status codes can be returned by giving the numeric status code as the value of *status*. If the status is between 300 and 399, the *URL* argument must be present, otherwise it must be omitted. Note that the status must be known to the Apache code (see the function send_error_response in http_protocol.c).

Example:
```
Redirect permanent /one http://example.com/two
Redirect 303 /three http://example.com/other
```

RedirectMatch Directive

Description:	Sends an external redirect based on a regular expression match of the current URL
Syntax:	RedirectMatch [*status*] *regex URL*
Context:	server config, virtual host, directory, .htaccess
Override:	FileInfo
Status:	Base
Module:	mod_alias

This directive is equivalent to Redirect, but makes use of regular expressions, instead of simple prefix matching. The supplied regular expression is matched against the URL-path, and if it matches, the server will substitute any parenthesized matches into the given string and use it as a filename. For example, to redirect all GIF files to like-named JPEG files on another server, one might use:

```
RedirectMatch (.*)\.gif$ http://www.anotherserver.com$1.jpg
```

RedirectPermanent Directive

Description:	Sends an external permanent redirect asking the client to fetch a different URL
Syntax:	RedirectPermanent *URL-path URL*
Context:	server config, virtual host, directory, .htaccess
Override:	FileInfo
Status:	Base
Module:	mod_alias

This directive makes the client know that the Redirect is permanent (status 301). Exactly equivalent to Redirect permanent.

RedirectTemp Directive

Description:	Sends an external temporary redirect asking the client to fetch a different URL
Syntax:	RedirectTemp URL-path URL
Context:	server config, virtual host, directory, .htaccess
Override:	FileInfo
Status:	Base
Module:	mod_alias

This directive makes the client know that the Redirect is only temporary (status 302). Exactly equivalent to Redirect temp.

ScriptAlias Directive

Description:	Maps a URL to a filesystem location and designates the target as a CGI script
Syntax:	ScriptAlias URL-path file-path|directory-path
Context:	server config, virtual host
Status:	Base
Module:	mod_alias

The ScriptAlias directive has the same behavior as the Alias directive, except that in addition it marks the target directory as containing CGI scripts that will be processed by mod_cgi's cgi-script handler. URLs with a case-sensitive (%-decoded) path beginning with URL-path will be mapped to scripts beginning with the second argument, which is a full pathname in the local filesystem.

Example:
```
ScriptAlias /cgi-bin/ /web/cgi-bin/
```

A request for http://myserver/cgi-bin/foo would cause the server to run the script /web/cgi-bin/foo. This configuration is essentially equivalent to:

```
Alias /cgi-bin/ /web/cgi-bin/
<Location /cgi-bin >
    SetHandler cgi-script
    Options +ExecCGI
</Location>
```

It is safer to avoid placing CGI scripts under the DocumentRoot in order to avoid accidentally revealing their source code if the configuration is ever changed. The ScriptAlias makes this easy by mapping a URL and designating CGI scripts at the same time. If you do choose to place your CGI scripts in a directory already accessible from the web, do not use ScriptAlias. Instead, use <Directory>, SetHandler, and Options as in:

```
<Directory /usr/local/apache2/htdocs/cgi-bin >
    SetHandler cgi-script
```

```
Options ExecCGI
</Directory>
```

This is necessary since multiple URL-paths can map to the same filesystem location, potentially bypassing the ScriptAlias and revealing the source code of the CGI scripts if they are not restricted by a Directory section.

See also:

▷ CGI Tutorial (p. 651)

ScriptAliasMatch Directive

Description:	Maps a URL to a filesystem location using a regular expression and designates the target as a CGI script
Syntax:	ScriptAliasMatch *regex file-path|directory-path*
Context:	server config, virtual host
Status:	Base
Module:	mod_alias

This directive is equivalent to ScriptAlias, but makes use of regular expressions, instead of simple prefix matching. The supplied regular expression is matched against the URL-path, and if it matches, the server will substitute any parenthesized matches into the given string and use it as a filename. For example, to activate the standard /cgi-bin, one might use:

```
ScriptAliasMatch ^/cgi-bin(.*) /usr/local/apache/cgi-bin$1
```

As for AliasMatch, the full range of regular expression power is available. For example, it is possible to construct an alias with case-insensitive matching of the url-path:

```
ScriptAliasMatch (?i)^/cgi-bin(.*) /usr/local/apache/cgi-bin$1
```

The considerations related to the difference between Alias and AliasMatch also apply to the difference between ScriptAlias and ScriptAliasMatch. See AliasMatch for details.

3.6 Apache Module mod_asis

Description:	Sends files that contain their own HTTP headers
Status:	Base
Module Identifier:	asis_module
Source File:	mod_asis.c

Summary

This module provides the handler send-as-is which causes Apache to send the document without adding most of the usual HTTP headers.

This can be used to send any kind of data from the server, including redirects and other special HTTP responses, without requiring a CGI script or an NPH script.

For historical reasons, this module will also process any file with the mime type httpd/send-as-is.

This module provides no directives.

See also:

▷ mod_headers (p. 289)

▷ mod_cern_meta (p. 227)

▷ Apache's Handler Use (p. 713)

3.6.1 Usage

In the server configuration file, associate files with the send-as-is handler *e.g.*

```
AddHandler send-as-is asis
```

The contents of any file with a .asis extension will then be sent by Apache to the client with almost no changes. In particular, HTTP headers are derived from the file itself according to mod_cgi rules, so an asis file must include valid headers, and may also use the CGI Status: header to determine the HTTP response code.

Here's an example of a file whose contents are sent *as is* so as to tell the client that a file has redirected.

```
Status:  301 Now where did I leave that URL
Location:  http://xyz.abc.com/foo/bar.html
Content-type:  text/html

<html>
<head>
<title>Lame excuses'R'us</title>
</head>
<body>
<h1>Fred's exceptionally wonderful page has moved to
```

```
<a href="http://xyz.abc.com/foo/bar.html">Joe's</a> site.
</h1>
</body>
</html>
```

NOTES: *The server always adds a* Date: *and* Server: *header to the data returned to the client, so these should not be included in the file. The server does not add a* Last-Modified *header; it probably should.*

3.7 Apache Module mod_auth_basic

Description:	Basic authentication
Status:	Base
Module Identifier:	auth_basic_module
Source File:	mod_auth_basic.c
Compatibility:	Available in Apache 2.1 and later

Summary

This module allows the use of HTTP Basic Authentication to restrict access by looking up users in the given providers. HTTP Digest Authentication is provided by mod_auth_digest. This module should usually be combined with at least one authentication module such as mod_authn_file and one authorization module such as mod_authz_user.

Directives:

    AuthBasicAuthoritative
    AuthBasicProvider

See also:

▷ AuthName (p. 94)

▷ AuthType (p. 95)

▷ Require (p. 124)

▷ Satisfy (p. 125)

▷ Authentication howto (p. 629)

AuthBasicAuthoritative Directive

Description:	Sets whether authorization and authentication are passed to lower level modules
Syntax:	AuthBasicAuthoritative On|Off
Default:	AuthBasicAuthoritative On
Context:	directory, .htaccess
Override:	AuthConfig
Status:	Base
Module:	mod_auth_basic

Normally, each authorization module listed in AuthBasicProvider will attempt to verify the user, and if the user is not found in any provider, access will be denied. Setting the AuthBasicAuthoritative directive explicitly to Off allows for both authentication and authorization to be passed on to other non-provider-based modules if there is no userID or rule matching the supplied userID. This should only be necessary when combining mod_auth_basic with third-party modules that are not configured with the AuthBasicProvider directive. When using such modules, the order of processing is determined in the modules' source code and is not configurable.

AuthBasicProvider Directive

Description:	Sets the authentication provider(s) for this location
Syntax:	AuthBasicProvider *provider-name* [*provider-name*] ...
Default:	AuthBasicProvider file
Context:	directory, .htaccess
Override:	AuthConfig
Status:	Base
Module:	mod_auth_basic

The AuthBasicProvider directive sets which provider is used to authenticate the users for this location. The default file provider is implemented by the mod_authn_file module. Make sure that the chosen provider module is present in the server.

Example
```
<Location /secure>
    AuthType basic
    AuthName "private area"
    AuthBasicProvider dbm
    AuthDBMType SDBM
    AuthDBMUserFile /www/etc/dbmpasswd
    Require valid-user
</Location>
```

Providers are implemented by mod_authn_dbm, mod_authn_file, mod_authn_dbd, and mod_authnz_ldap.

3.8 Apache Module mod_auth_digest

Description:	User authentication using MD5 Digest Authentication.
Status:	Extension
Module Identifier:	auth_digest_module
Source File:	mod_auth_digest.c

Summary

This module implements HTTP Digest Authentication (RFC2617[8]), and provides a more secure alternative to mod_auth_basic.

Directives:

> AuthDigestAlgorithm
> AuthDigestDomain
> AuthDigestNcCheck
> AuthDigestNonceFormat
> AuthDigestNonceLifetime
> AuthDigestProvider
> AuthDigestQop
> AuthDigestShmemSize

See also:

- ▷ AuthName (p. 94)
- ▷ AuthType (p. 95)
- ▷ Require (p. 124)
- ▷ Satisfy (p. 125)
- ▷ Authentication howto (p. 629)

3.8.1 Using Digest Authentication

Using MD5 Digest authentication is very simple. Simply set up authentication normally, using AuthType Digest and AuthDigestProvider instead of the normal AuthType Basic and AuthBasicProvider. Then add a AuthDigestDomain directive containing at least the root URI(s) for this protection space.

Appropriate user (text) files can be created using the htdigest tool.

Example:
```
<Location /private/>
    AuthType Digest
    AuthName "private area"
    AuthDigestDomain /private/ http://mirror.my.dom/private2/

    AuthDigestProvider file
    AuthUserFile /web/auth/.digest_pw
```

---

[8]http://www.faqs.org/rfcs/rfc2617.html

```
    Require valid-user
</Location>
```

NOTE *Digest authentication is more secure than Basic authentication, but only works with supporting browsers. As of September 2004, major browsers that support digest authentication include Amaya[9], Konqueror[10], MS Internet Explorer[11] for Mac OS X and Windows (although the Windows version fails when used with a query string – see "Working with MS Internet Explorer" below for a workaround), Mozilla[12], Netscape[13] 7, Opera[14], and Safari[15]. lynx[16] does not support digest authentication. Since digest authentication is not as widely implemented as basic authentication, you should use it only in environments where all users will have supporting browsers.*

3.8.2 Working with MS Internet Explorer

The Digest authentication implementation in previous Internet Explorer for Windows versions (5 and 6) had issues, namely that GET requests with a query string were not RFC compliant. There are a few ways to work around this issue.

The first way is to use POST requests instead of GET requests to pass data to your program. This method is the simplest approach if your application can work with this limitation.

Since version 2.0.51 Apache also provides a workaround in the AuthDigest-EnableQueryStringHack environment variable. If AuthDigestEnableQuery-StringHack is set for the request, Apache will take steps to work around the MSIE bug and remove the query string from the digest comparison. Using this method would look similar to the following.

Using Digest Authentication with MSIE:
```
BrowserMatch "MSIE" AuthDigestEnableQueryStringHack=On
```

This workaround is not necessary for MSIE 7, though enabling it does not cause any compatibility issues or significant overhead.

See the BrowserMatch directive for more details on conditionally setting environment variables.

---

[9] http://www.w3.org/Amaya/
[10] http://konqueror.kde.org/
[11] http://www.microsoft.com/windows/ie/
[12] http://www.mozilla.org
[13] http://channels.netscape.com/ns/browsers/download.jsp
[14] http://www.opera.com/
[15] http://www.apple.com/safari/
[16] http://lynx.isc.org/

AuthDigestAlgorithm Directive

Description:	Selects the algorithm used to calculate the challenge and response hashes in digest authentication
Syntax:	AuthDigestAlgorithm MD5|MD5-sess
Default:	AuthDigestAlgorithm MD5
Context:	directory, .htaccess
Override:	AuthConfig
Status:	Extension
Module:	mod_auth_digest

The `AuthDigestAlgorithm` directive selects the algorithm used to calculate the challenge and response hashes.

MD5-sess is not correctly implemented yet.

AuthDigestDomain Directive

Description:	URIs that are in the same protection space for digest authentication
Syntax:	AuthDigestDomain URI [URI] ...
Context:	directory, .htaccess
Override:	AuthConfig
Status:	Extension
Module:	mod_auth_digest

The `AuthDigestDomain` directive allows you to specify one or more URIs which are in the same protection space (*i.e.* use the same realm and username/password info). The specified URIs are prefixes; the client will assume that all URIs "below" these are also protected by the same username/password. The URIs may be either absolute URIs (*i.e.* including a scheme, host, port, etc.) or relative URIs.

This directive *should* always be specified and contain at least the (set of) root URI(s) for this space. Omitting to do so will cause the client to send the Authorization header for *every request* sent to this server. Apart from increasing the size of the request, it may also have a detrimental effect on performance if `AuthDigestNcCheck` is on.

The URIs specified can also point to different servers, in which case clients (which understand this) will then share username/password info across multiple servers without prompting the user each time.

AuthDigestNcCheck Directive

Description:	Enables or disables checking of the nonce-count sent by the server
Syntax:	AuthDigestNcCheck On|Off
Default:	AuthDigestNcCheck Off
Context:	server config
Status:	Extension
Module:	mod_auth_digest

Not implemented yet.

AuthDigestNonceFormat Directive

Description:	Determines how the nonce is generated
Syntax:	AuthDigestNonceFormat *format*
Context:	directory, .htaccess
Override:	AuthConfig
Status:	Extension
Module:	mod_auth_digest

Not implemented yet.

AuthDigestNonceLifetime Directive

Description:	How long the server nonce is valid
Syntax:	AuthDigestNonceLifetime *seconds*
Default:	AuthDigestNonceLifetime 300
Context:	directory, .htaccess
Override:	AuthConfig
Status:	Extension
Module:	mod_auth_digest

The `AuthDigestNonceLifetime` directive controls how long the server nonce is valid. When the client contacts the server using an expired nonce the server will send back a 401 with `stale=true`. If *seconds* is greater than 0 then it specifies the amount of time for which the nonce is valid; this should probably never be set to less than 10 seconds. If *seconds* is less than 0 then the nonce never expires.

AuthDigestProvider Directive

Description:	Sets the authentication provider(s) for this location
Syntax:	AuthDigestProvider *provider-name* [*provider-name*] ...
Default:	AuthDigestProvider file
Context:	directory, .htaccess
Override:	AuthConfig
Status:	Extension
Module:	mod_auth_digest

The AuthDigestProvider directive sets which provider is used to authenticate the users for this location. The default file provider is implemented by the mod_authn_file module. Make sure that the chosen provider module is present in the server.

See mod_authn_dbm, mod_authn_file, and mod_authn_dbd for providers.

AuthDigestQop Directive

Description:	Determines the quality-of-protection to use in digest authentication
Syntax:	AuthDigestQop none|auth|auth-int [auth|auth-int]
Default:	AuthDigestQop auth
Context:	directory, .htaccess
Override:	AuthConfig
Status:	Extension
Module:	mod_auth_digest

The AuthDigestQop directive determines the **quality-of-protection** to use. auth will only do authentication (username/password); auth-int is authentication plus integrity checking (an MD5 hash of the entity is also computed and checked); none will cause the module to use the old RFC-2069 digest algorithm (which does not include integrity checking). Both auth and auth-int may be specified, in which the case the browser will choose which of these to use. none should only be used if the browser for some reason does not like the challenge it receives otherwise.

auth-int is not implemented yet.

AuthDigestShmemSize Directive

Description:	The amount of shared memory to allocate for keeping track of clients
Syntax:	AuthDigestShmemSize *size*
Default:	AuthDigestShmemSize 1000
Context:	server config
Status:	Extension
Module:	mod_auth_digest

The AuthDigestShmemSize directive defines the amount of shared memory, that will be allocated at the server startup for keeping track of clients. Note that the shared memory segment cannot be set less than the space that is necessary for tracking at least *one* client. This value is dependant on your system. If you want to find out the exact value, you may simply set AuthDigestShmemSize to the value of 0 and read the error message after trying to start the server.

The *size* is normally expressed in Bytes, but you may let the number follow a K or an M to express your value as KBytes or MBytes. For example, the following directives are all equivalent:

```
AuthDigestShmemSize 1048576
AuthDigestShmemSize 1024K
AuthDigestShmemSize 1M
```

3.9 Apache Module mod_authn_alias

Description:	Provides the ability to create extended authentication providers based on actual providers
Status:	Extension
Module Identifier:	authn_alias_module
Source File:	mod_authn_alias.c
Compatibility:	Available in Apache 2.1 and later

Summary

This module allows extended authentication providers to be created within the configuration file and assigned an alias name. The alias providers can then be referenced through the directives AuthBasicProvider or AuthDigestProvider in the same way as a base authentication provider. Besides the ability to create and alias an extended provider, it also allows the same extended authentication provider to be reference by multiple locations.

Directives:

<AuthnProviderAlias>

3.9.1 Examples

This example checks for passwords in two different text files.

Checking multiple text password files
```
# Check here first
<AuthnProviderAlias file file1>
    AuthUserFile /www/conf/passwords1
</AuthnProviderAlias>
# Then check here
<AuthnProviderAlias file file2>
    AuthUserFile /www/conf/passwords2
</AuthnProviderAlias>
<Directory /var/web/pages/secure>
    AuthBasicProvider file1 file2

    AuthType Basic
    AuthName "Protected Area"
    Require valid-user
</Directory>
```

The example below creates two different LDAP authentication provider aliases based on the LDAP provider. This allows a single authenticated location to be serviced by multiple ldap hosts:

Checking multiple LDAP servers
```
LoadModule authn_alias_module modules/mod_authn_alias.so

<AuthnProviderAlias ldap ldap-alias1>
```

```
        AuthLDAPBindDN cn=youruser,o=ctx
        AuthLDAPBindPassword yourpassword
        AuthLDAPURL ldap://ldap.host/o=ctx
</AuthnProviderAlias>

<AuthnProviderAlias ldap ldap-other-alias>
        AuthLDAPBindDN cn=yourotheruser,o=dev
        AuthLDAPBindPassword yourotherpassword
        AuthLDAPURL ldap://other.ldap.host/o=dev?cn
</AuthnProviderAlias>

Alias /secure /webpages/secure
<Directory /webpages/secure>
        Order deny,allow
        Allow from all

        AuthBasicProvider ldap-other-alias ldap-alias1

        AuthType Basic
        AuthName LDAP_Protected_Place
        AuthzLDAPAuthoritative off
        Require valid-user
</Directory>
```

AuthnProviderAlias Directive

Description:	Enclose a group of directives that represent an extension of a base authentication provider and referenced by the specified alias
Syntax:	`<AuthnProviderAlias baseProvider Alias>` ... `</AuthnProviderAlias>`
Context:	server config
Status:	Extension
Module:	mod_authn_alias

`<AuthnProviderAlias>` and `</AuthnProviderAlias>` are used to enclose a group of authentication directives that can be referenced by the alias name using one of the directives `AuthBasicProvider` or `AuthDigestProvider`.

3.10 Apache Module mod_authn_anon

Description:	Allows "anonymous" user access to authenticated areas
Status:	Extension
Module Identifier:	authn_anon_module
Source File:	mod_authn_anon.c
Compatibility:	Available in Apache 2.1 and later

Summary

This module provides authentication front-ends such as mod_auth_basic to authenticate users similar to anonymous-ftp sites, *i.e.* have a 'magic' user id 'anonymous' and the email address as a password. These email addresses can be logged.

Combined with other (database) access control methods, this allows for effective user tracking and customization according to a user profile while still keeping the site open for 'unregistered' users. One advantage of using Auth-based user tracking is that, unlike magic-cookies and funny URL pre/postfixes, it is completely browser independent and it allows users to share URLs.

When using mod_auth_basic, this module is invoked via the AuthBasicProvider directive with the anon value.

Directives:

> Anonymous
> Anonymous_LogEmail
> Anonymous_MustGiveEmail
> Anonymous_NoUserID
> Anonymous_VerifyEmail

3.10.1 Example

The example below is combined with "normal" htpasswd-file based authentication and allows users in additionally as 'guests' with the following properties:

- It insists that the user enters a userID. (Anonymous_NoUserID)
- It insists that the user enters a password. (Anonymous_MustGiveEmail)
- The password entered must be a valid email address, *i.e.* contain at least one '@' and a '.'. (Anonymous_VerifyEmail)
- The userID must be one of anonymous guest www test welcome and comparison is **not** case sensitive. (Anonymous)
- And the Email addresses entered in the passwd field are logged to the error log file. (Anonymous_LogEmail)

Example
```
<Directory /foo>
```

```
              AuthName "Use 'anonymous' & Email address for guest entry"
              AuthType Basic
              AuthBasicProvider file anon
              AuthUserFile /path/to/your/.htpasswd

              Anonymous_NoUserID off
              Anonymous_MustGiveEmail on
              Anonymous_VerifyEmail on
              Anonymous_LogEmail on
              Anonymous anonymous guest www test welcome

              Order Deny,Allow
              Allow from all

              Require valid-user
          </Directory>
```

Anonymous Directive

Description:	Specifies userIDs that are allowed access without password verification
Syntax:	Anonymous *user* [*user*] ...
Context:	directory, .htaccess
Override:	AuthConfig
Status:	Extension
Module:	mod_authn_anon

A list of one or more 'magic' userIDs which are allowed access without password verification. The userIDs are space separated. It is possible to use the ' and " quotes to allow a space in a userID as well as the \ escape character.

Please note that the comparison is **case-IN-sensitive**.

It's strongly recommended that the magic username 'anonymous' is always one of the allowed userIDs.

Example:

```
Anonymous anonymous "Not Registered" "I don't know"
```

This would allow the user to enter without password verification by using the userIDs "anonymous", "AnonyMous", "Not Registered" and "I Don't Know".

As of Apache 2.1 it is possible to specify the userID as "*". That allows *any* supplied userID to be accepted.

Anonymous_LogEmail Directive

Description:	Sets whether the password entered will be logged in the error log
Syntax:	Anonymous_LogEmail On|Off
Default:	Anonymous_LogEmail On
Context:	directory, .htaccess
Override:	AuthConfig
Status:	Extension
Module:	mod_authn_anon

When set On, the default, the 'password' entered (which hopefully contains a sensible email address) is logged in the error log.

Anonymous_MustGiveEmail Directive

Description:	Specifies whether blank passwords are allowed
Syntax:	Anonymous_MustGiveEmail On|Off
Default:	Anonymous_MustGiveEmail On
Context:	directory, .htaccess
Override:	AuthConfig
Status:	Extension
Module:	mod_authn_anon

Specifies whether the user must specify an email address as the password. This prohibits blank passwords.

Anonymous_NoUserID Directive

Description:	Sets whether the userID field may be empty
Syntax:	Anonymous_NoUserID On|Off
Default:	Anonymous_NoUserID Off
Context:	directory, .htaccess
Override:	AuthConfig
Status:	Extension
Module:	mod_authn_anon

When set On, users can leave the userID (and perhaps the password field) empty. This can be very convenient for MS-Explorer users who can just hit return or click directly on the OK button; which seems a natural reaction.

Anonymous_VerifyEmail Directive

Description:	Sets whether to check the password field for a correctly formatted email address
Syntax:	`Anonymous_VerifyEmail On|Off`
Default:	`Anonymous_VerifyEmail Off`
Context:	directory, .htaccess
Override:	AuthConfig
Status:	Extension
Module:	mod_authn_anon

When set `On` the 'password' entered is checked for at least one '@' and a '.' to encourage users to enter valid email addresses (see the above `Anonymous_-LogEmail`).

3.11 Apache Module mod_authn_dbd

Description:	User authentication using an SQL database
Status:	Extension
Module Identifier:	authn_dbd_module
Source File:	mod_authn_dbd.c
Compatibility:	Available in Apache 2.1 and later

Summary

This module provides authentication front-ends such as mod_auth_digest and mod_auth_basic to authenticate users by looking up users in SQL tables. Similar functionality is provided by, for example, mod_authn_file.

This module relies on mod_dbd to specify the backend database driver and connection parameters, and manage the database connections.

When using mod_auth_basic or mod_auth_digest, this module is invoked via the AuthBasicProvider or AuthDigestProvider with the dbd value.

Directives:

>   AuthDBDUserPWQuery
>   AuthDBDUserRealmQuery

See also:

> ▷ AuthName (p. 94)
>
> ▷ AuthType (p. 95)
>
> ▷ AuthBasicProvider (p. 151)
>
> ▷ AuthDigestProvider (p. 155)
>
> ▷ DBDriver (p. 250)
>
> ▷ DBDParams (p. 249)

3.11.1 Configuration Example

This simple example shows use of this module in the context of the Authentication and DBD frameworks. Please note that you need to load an authorization module, such as mod_authz_user, to get it working.

```
# mod_dbd configuration
DBDriver pgsql
DBDParams "dbname=apacheauth user=apache password=xxxxxx"

DBDMin   4
DBDKeep  8
DBDMax   20
DBDExptime 300
```

```
<Directory /usr/www/myhost/private>
    # core authentication and mod_auth_basic configuration
    # for mod_authn_dbd
    AuthType Basic
    AuthName "My Server"
    AuthBasicProvider dbd

    # core authorization configuration
    Require valid-user

    # mod_authn_dbd SQL query to authenticate a user
    AuthDBDUserPWQuery \
        "SELECT password FROM authn WHERE user = %s"
</Directory>
```

3.11.2 Exposing Login Information

If httpd was built against APR version 1.3.0 or higher, then whenever a query is made to the database server, all column values in the first row returned by the query are placed in the environment, using environment variables with the prefix "AUTHENTICATE_".

If a database query for example returned the username, full name and telephone number of a user, a CGI program will have access to this information without the need to make a second independent database query to gather this additional information.

This has the potential to dramatically simplify the coding and configuration required in some web applications.

AuthDBDUserPWQuery Directive

Description:	SQL query to look up a password for a user
Syntax:	AuthDBDUserPWQuery query
Context:	directory
Status:	Extension
Module:	mod_authn_dbd

The AuthDBDUserPWQuery specifies an SQL query to look up a password for a specified user. The user's ID will be passed as a single string parameter when the SQL query is executed. It may be referenced within the query statement using a %s format specifier.

```
AuthDBDUserPWQuery \
    "SELECT password FROM authn WHERE user = %s"
```

The first column value of the first row returned by the query statement should be a string containing the encrypted password. Subsequent rows will be ignored. If no rows are returned, the user will not be authenticated through mod_authn_dbd.

If httpd was built against APR version 1.3.0 or higher, any additional column values in the first row returned by the query statement will be stored as environment variables with names of the form AUTHENTICATE_COLUMN.

AuthDBDUserRealmQuery Directive

Description:	SQL query to look up a password hash for a user and realm.
Syntax:	AuthDBDUserRealmQuery query
Context:	directory
Status:	Extension
Module:	mod_authn_dbd

The AuthDBDUserRealmQuery specifies an SQL query to look up a password for a specified user and realm. The user's ID and the realm, in that order, will be passed as string parameters when the SQL query is executed. They may be referenced within the query statement using %s format specifiers.

```
AuthDBDUserRealmQuery \
    "SELECT password FROM authn WHERE user = %s AND realm = %s"
```

The first column value of the first row returned by the query statement should be a string containing the encrypted password. Subsequent rows will be ignored. If no rows are returned, the user will not be authenticated through mod_authn_dbd.

If httpd was built against APR version 1.3.0 or higher, any additional column values in the first row returned by the query statement will be stored as environment variables with names of the form AUTHENTICATE_COLUMN.

3.12 Apache Module mod_authn_dbm

Description:	User authentication using DBM files
Status:	Extension
Module Identifier:	authn_dbm_module
Source File:	mod_authn_dbm.c
Compatibility:	Available in Apache 2.1 and later

Summary

This module provides authentication front-ends such as mod_auth_digest and mod_auth_basic to authenticate users by looking up users in **dbm** password files. Similar functionality is provided by mod_authn_file.

When using mod_auth_basic or mod_auth_digest, this module is invoked via the AuthBasicProvider or AuthDigestProvider with the dbm value.

Directives:

> AuthDBMType
> AuthDBMUserFile

See also:

> ▷ AuthName (p. 94)
>
> ▷ AuthType (p. 95)
>
> ▷ AuthBasicProvider (p. 151)
>
> ▷ AuthDigestProvider (p. 155)

AuthDBMType Directive

Description:	Sets the type of database file that is used to store passwords
Syntax:	AuthDBMType default|SDBM|GDBM|NDBM|DB
Default:	AuthDBMType default
Context:	directory, .htaccess
Override:	AuthConfig
Status:	Extension
Module:	mod_authn_dbm

Sets the type of database file that is used to store the passwords. The default database type is determined at compile time. The availability of other types of database files also depends on compile-time settings (p. 775).

It is crucial that whatever program you use to create your password files is configured to use the same type of database.

AuthDBMUserFile Directive

Description:	Sets the name of a database file containing the list of users and passwords for authentication
Syntax:	AuthDBMUserFile *file-path*
Context:	directory, .htaccess
Override:	AuthConfig
Status:	Extension
Module:	mod_authn_dbm

The `AuthDBMUserFile` directive sets the name of a DBM file containing the list of users and passwords for user authentication. *File-path* is the absolute path to the user file.

The user file is keyed on the username. The value for a user is the encrypted password, optionally followed by a colon and arbitrary data. The colon and the data following it will be ignored by the server.

> SECURITY: *Make sure that the `AuthDBMUserFile` is stored outside the document tree of the web-server; do not put it in the directory that it protects. Otherwise, clients will be able to download the `AuthDBMUserFile`.*

Important compatibility note: The implementation of dbmopen in the apache modules reads the string length of the hashed values from the DBM data structures, rather than relying upon the string being NULL-appended. Some applications, such as the Netscape web server, rely upon the string being NULL-appended, so if you are having trouble using DBM files interchangeably between applications this may be a part of the problem.

A perl script called dbmmanage is included with Apache. This program can be used to create and update DBM format password files for use with this module.

3.13 Apache Module mod_authn_default

Description:	Authentication fallback module
Status:	Base
Module Identifier:	authn_default_module
Source File:	mod_authn_default.c
Compatibility:	Available in Apache 2.1 and later

Summary

This module is designed to be the fallback module, if you don't have configured an authentication module like mod_auth_basic. It simply rejects any credentials supplied by the user.

Directives:

> AuthDefaultAuthoritative

AuthDefaultAuthoritative Directive

Description:	Sets whether authentication is passed to lower level modules
Syntax:	AuthDefaultAuthoritative On|Off
Default:	AuthDefaultAuthoritative On
Context:	directory, .htaccess
Override:	AuthConfig
Status:	Base
Module:	mod_authn_default

Setting the AuthDefaultAuthoritative directive explicitly to Off allows for authentication to be passed on to lower level modules (as defined in the modules.c files).

NOTE *Normally there are no lower level modules, since* mod_authn_-default *is defined to be already on a very low level. Therefore you should leave the value of* AuthDefaultAuthoritative *as default (*On*).*

3.14 Apache Module mod_authn_file

Description:	User authentication using text files
Status:	Base
Module Identifier:	authn_file_module
Source File:	mod_authn_file.c
Compatibility:	Available in Apache 2.1 and later

Summary

This module provides authentication front-ends such as mod_auth_digest and mod_auth_basic to authenticate users by looking up users in plain text password files. Similar functionality is provided by mod_authn_dbm.

When using mod_auth_basic or mod_auth_digest, this module is invoked via the AuthBasicProvider or AuthDigestProvider with the file value.

Directives:

> AuthUserFile

See also:

> ▷ AuthBasicProvider (p. 151)
> ▷ AuthDigestProvider (p. 155)
> ▷ htpasswd (p. 39)
> ▷ htdigest (p. 38)

AuthUserFile Directive

Description:	Sets the name of a text file containing the list of users and passwords for authentication
Syntax:	AuthUserFile *file-path*
Context:	directory, .htaccess
Override:	AuthConfig
Status:	Base
Module:	mod_authn_file

The AuthUserFile directive sets the name of a textual file containing the list of users and passwords for user authentication. *File-path* is the path to the user file. If it is not absolute, it is treated as relative to the ServerRoot.

Each line of the user file contains a username followed by a colon, followed by the encrypted password. If the same user ID is defined multiple times, mod_authn_file will use the first occurrence to verify the password.

The utility htpasswd which is installed as part of the binary distribution, or which can be found in src/support, is used to maintain the password file for *HTTP Basic Authentication*. See the man page (p. 39) for more details. In short:

Create a password file Filename with username as the initial ID. It will prompt for the password:

htpasswd -c Filename username

Add or modify username2 in the password file Filename:

htpasswd Filename username2

Note that searching large text files is *very* inefficient; AuthDBMUserFile should be used instead.

If you are using *HTTP Digest Authentication*, the htpasswd tool is not sufficient. You have to use htdigest instead. Note that you cannot mix user data for Digest Authentication and Basic Authentication within the same file.

SECURITY *Make sure that the AuthUserFile is stored outside the document tree of the web-server. Do not put it in the directory that it protects. Otherwise, clients may be able to download the AuthUserFile.*

3.15 Apache Module mod_authnz_ldap

Description:	Allows an LDAP directory to be used to store the database for HTTP Basic authentication.
Status:	Extension
Module Identifier:	authnz_ldap_module
Source File:	mod_authnz_ldap.c
Compatibility:	Available in version 2.1 and later

Summary

This module provides authentication front-ends such as mod_auth_basic to authenticate users through an LDAP directory.

mod_authnz_ldap supports the following features:

- Known to support the OpenLDAP SDK[17] (both 1.x and 2.x), Novell LDAP SDK[18] and the iPlanet (Netscape)[19] SDK.
- Complex authorization policies can be implemented by representing the policy with LDAP filters.
- Uses extensive caching of LDAP operations via mod_ldap (p. 323).
- Support for LDAP over SSL (requires the Netscape SDK) or TLS (requires the OpenLDAP 2.x SDK or Novell LDAP SDK).

When using mod_auth_basic, this module is invoked via the AuthBasicProvider directive with the ldap value.

Directives:

AuthLDAPBindAuthoritative	AuthLDAPGroupAttribute
AuthLDAPBindDN	AuthLDAPGroupAttributeIsDN
AuthLDAPBindPassword	AuthLDAPRemoteUserAttribute
AuthLDAPCharsetConfig	AuthLDAPRemoteUserIsDN
AuthLDAPCompareDNOnServer	AuthLDAPUrl
AuthLDAPDereferenceAliases	AuthzLDAPAuthoritative

See also:

▷ mod_ldap (p. 323)

▷ mod_auth_basic (p. 150)

▷ mod_authz_user (p. 201)

▷ mod_authz_groupfile (p. 191)

[17]http://www.openldap.org/
[18]http://developer.novell.com/ndk/cldap.htm
[19]http://www.iplanet.com/downloads/developer/

3.15.1 Contents

- Operation

    - The Authentication Phase
    - The Authorization Phase

- The Require Directives

    - Require ldap-user
    - Require ldap-group
    - Require ldap-dn
    - Require ldap-attribute
    - Require ldap-filter

- Examples
- Using TLS
- Using SSL
- Exposing Login Information
- Using Microsoft FrontPage with mod_authnz_ldap

    - How It Works
    - Caveats

3.15.2 Operation

There are two phases in granting access to a user. The first phase is authentication, in which the mod_authnz_ldap authentication provider verifies that the user's credentials are valid. This is also called the *search/bind* phase. The second phase is authorization, in which mod_authnz_ldap determines if the authenticated user is allowed access to the resource in question. This is also known as the *compare* phase.

mod_authnz_ldap registers both an authn_ldap authentication provider and an authz_ldap authorization handler. The authn_ldap authentication provider can be enabled through the AuthBasicProvider directive using the ldap value. The authz_ldap handler extends the Require directive's authorization types by adding ldap-user, ldap-dn and ldap-group values.

The Authentication Phase

During the authentication phase, mod_authnz_ldap searches for an entry in the directory that matches the username that the HTTP client passes. If a single unique match is found, then mod_authnz_ldap attempts to bind to the directory server using the DN of the entry plus the password provided by the HTTP client. Because it does a search, then a bind, it is often referred to as the search/bind phase. Here are the steps taken during the search/bind phase.

1. Generate a search filter by combining the attribute and filter provided in the `AuthLDAPURL` directive with the username passed by the HTTP client.

2. Search the directory using the generated filter. If the search does not return exactly one entry, deny or decline access.

3. Fetch the distinguished name of the entry retrieved from the search and attempt to bind to the LDAP server using the DN and the password passed by the HTTP client. If the bind is unsuccessful, deny or decline access.

The following directives are used during the search/bind phase

`AuthLDAPURL`	Specifies the LDAP server, the base DN, the attribute to use in the search, as well as the extra search filter to use.
`AuthLDAPBindDN`	An optional DN to bind with during the search phase.
`AuthLDAPBindPassword`	An optional password to bind with during the search phase.

The Authorization Phase

During the authorization phase, mod_authnz_ldap attempts to determine if the user is authorized to access the resource. Many of these checks require mod_-authnz_ldap to do a compare operation on the LDAP server. This is why this phase is often referred to as the compare phase. mod_authnz_ldap accepts the following `Require` directives to determine if the credentials are acceptable:

- Grant access if there is a `Require ldap-user` directive, and the username in the directive matches the username passed by the client.

- Grant access if there is a `Require ldap-dn` directive, and the DN in the directive matches the DN fetched from the LDAP directory.

- Grant access if there is a `Require ldap-group` directive, and the DN fetched from the LDAP directory (or the username passed by the client) occurs in the LDAP group.

- Grant access if there is a `Require ldap-attribute` directive, and the attribute fetched from the LDAP directory matches the given value.

- Grant access if there is a `Require ldap-filter` directive, and the search filter successfully finds a single user object that matches the dn of the authenticated user.

- otherwise, deny or decline access

Other `Require` values may also be used which may require loading additional authorization modules. Note that if you use a `Require` value from another authorization module, you will need to ensure that `AuthzLDAPAuthoritative` is set to off to allow the authorization phase to fall back to the module providing the alternate `Require` value. When no LDAP-specific `Require` direc-

tives are used, authorization is allowed to fall back to other modules as if
AuthzLDAPAuthoritative was set to off.

- Grant access to all successfully authenticated users if there is a Require
  valid-user directive. (requires mod_authz_user)
- Grant access if there is a Require group directive, and mod_authz_-
  groupfile has been loaded with the AuthGroupFile directive set.
- others...

mod_authnz_ldap uses the following directives during the compare phase:

AuthLDAPURL	The attribute specified in the URL is used in compare operations for the Require ldap-user operation.
AuthLDAPCompareDNOnServer	Determines the behavior of the Require ldap-dn directive.
AuthLDAPGroupAttribute	Determines the attribute to use for comparisons in the Require ldap-group directive.
AuthLDAPGroupAttributeIsDN	Specifies whether to use the user DN or the username when doing comparisons for the Require ldap-group directive.

3.15.3 The Require Directives

Apache's Require directives are used during the authorization phase to ensure
that a user is allowed to access a resource. mod_authnz_ldap extends the authorization types with ldap-user, ldap-dn, ldap-group, ldap-attribute and
ldap-filter. Other authorization types may also be used but may require that
additional authorization modules be loaded.

Require ldap-user

The Require ldap-user directive specifies what usernames can access the resource. Once mod_authnz_ldap has retrieved a unique DN from the directory, it
does an LDAP compare operation using the username specified in the Require
ldap-user to see if that username is part of the just-fetched LDAP entry. Multiple users can be granted access by putting multiple usernames on the line,
separated with spaces. If a username has a space in it, then it must be surrounded with double quotes. Multiple users can also be granted access by using
multiple Require ldap-user directives, with one user per line. For example,
with a AuthLDAPURL of ldap://ldap/o=Airius?cn (i.e., cn is used for searches),
the following Require directives could be used to restrict access:

```
Require ldap-user "Barbara Jenson"
Require ldap-user "Fred User"
Require ldap-user "Joe Manager"
```

Because of the way that mod_authnz_ldap handles this directive, Barbara Jenson could sign on as *Barbara Jenson, Babs Jenson* or any other cn that she has in her LDAP entry. Only the single Require ldap-user line is needed to support all values of the attribute in the user's entry.

If the uid attribute was used instead of the cn attribute in the URL above, the above three lines could be condensed to

```
Require ldap-user bjenson fuser jmanager
```

Require ldap-group

This directive specifies an LDAP group whose members are allowed access. It takes the distinguished name of the LDAP group. Note: Do not surround the group name with quotes. For example, assume that the following entry existed in the LDAP directory:

```
dn:   cn=Administrators, o=Airius
objectClass:   groupOfUniqueNames
uniqueMember:   cn=Barbara Jenson, o=Airius
uniqueMember:   cn=Fred User, o=Airius
```

The following directive would grant access to both Fred and Barbara:

```
Require ldap-group cn=Administrators, o=Airius
```

Behavior of this directive is modified by the AuthLDAPGroupAttribute and AuthLDAPGroupAttributeIsDN directives.

Require ldap-dn

The Require ldap-dn directive allows the administrator to grant access based on distinguished names. It specifies a DN that must match for access to be granted. If the distinguished name that was retrieved from the directory server matches the distinguished name in the Require ldap-dn, then authorization is granted. Note: do not surround the distinguished name with quotes.

The following directive would grant access to a specific DN:

```
Require ldap-dn cn=Barbara Jenson, o=Airius
```

Behavior of this directive is modified by the AuthLDAPCompareDNOnServer directive.

Require ldap-attribute

The Require ldap-attribute directive allows the administrator to grant access based on attributes of the authenticated user in the LDAP directory. If the attribute in the directory matches the value given in the configuration, access is granted.

The following directive would grant access to anyone with the attribute employeeType = active

```
Require ldap-attribute employeeType=active
```

Multiple attribute/value pairs can be specified on the same line separated by spaces or they can be specified in multiple `Require ldap-attribute` directives. The effect of listing multiple attribute/values pairs is an OR operation. Access will be granted if any of the listed attribute values match the value of the corresponding attribute in the user object. If the value of the attribute contains a space, only the value must be within double quotes.

The following directive would grant access to anyone with the city attribute equal to "San Jose" or status equal to "Active"

```
Require ldap-attribute city="San Jose" status=active
```

Require ldap-filter

The `Require ldap-filter` directive allows the administrator to grant access based on a complex LDAP search filter. If the dn returned by the filter search matches the authenticated user dn, access is granted.

The following directive would grant access to anyone having a cell phone and is in the marketing department

```
Require ldap-filter &(cell=*)(department=marketing)
```

The difference between the `Require ldap-filter` directive and the `Require ldap-attribute` directive is that `ldap-filter` performs a search operation on the LDAP directory using the specified search filter rather than a simple attribute comparison. If a simple attribute comparison is all that is required, the comparison operation performed by `ldap-attribute` will be faster than the search operation used by `ldap-filter` especially within a large directory.

3.15.4 Examples

- Grant access to anyone who exists in the LDAP directory, using their UID for searches.

  ```
  AuthLDAPURL "ldap://ldap1.airius.com:389/ou=People,
  o=Airius?uid?sub?(objectClass=*)"
  Require valid-user
  ```

- The next example is the same as above but with the fields that have useful defaults omitted. Also, note the use of a redundant LDAP server.

  ```
  AuthLDAPURL "ldap://ldap1.airius.com
  ldap2.airius.com/ou=People, o=Airius"
  Require valid-user
  ```

- The next example is similar to the previous one, but it uses the common name instead of the UID. Note that this could be problematical if multiple people in the directory share the same cn, because a search on cn **must** return exactly one entry. That's why this approach is not recommended:

it's a better idea to choose an attribute that is guaranteed unique in your directory, such as uid.

```
AuthLDAPURL "ldap://ldap.airius.com/ou=People, o=Airius?cn"
Require valid-user
```

- Grant access to anybody in the Administrators group. The users must authenticate using their UID.

```
AuthLDAPURL ldap://ldap.airius.com/o=Airius?uid
Require ldap-group cn=Administrators, o=Airius
```

- The next example assumes that everyone at Airius who carries an alphanumeric pager will have an LDAP attribute of qpagePagerID. The example will grant access only to people (authenticated via their UID) who have alphanumeric pagers:

```
AuthLDAPURL
ldap://ldap.airius.com/o=Airius?uid??(qpagePagerID=*)
Require valid-user
```

- The next example demonstrates the power of using filters to accomplish complicated administrative requirements. Without filters, it would have been necessary to create a new LDAP group and ensure that the group's members remain synchronized with the pager users. This becomes trivial with filters. The goal is to grant access to anyone who has a pager, plus grant access to Joe Manager, who doesn't have a pager, but does need to access the same resource:

```
AuthLDAPURL ldap://ldap.airius.com/o=Airius?uid??
(|(qpagePagerID=*)(uid=jmanager))
Require valid-user
```

This last may look confusing at first, so it helps to evaluate what the search filter will look like based on who connects, as shown below. If Fred User connects as fuser, the filter would look like

```
(&(|(qpagePagerID=*)(uid=jmanager))(uid=fuser))
```

The above search will only succeed if *fuser* has a pager. When Joe Manager connects as *jmanager*, the filter looks like

```
(&(|(qpagePagerID=*)(uid=jmanager))(uid=jmanager))
```

The above search will succeed whether *jmanager* has a pager or not.

3.15.5 Using TLS

To use TLS, see the mod_ldap directives LDAPTrustedClientCert, LDAPTrusted-GlobalCert and LDAPTrustedMode.

An optional second parameter can be added to the AuthLDAPURL to override the default connection type set by LDAPTrustedMode. This will allow the connection established by an *ldap://* Url to be upgraded to a secure connection on the same port.

3.15.6 Using SSL

To use SSL, see the mod_ldap directives LDAPTrustedClientCert, LDAPTrusted-GlobalCert and LDAPTrustedMode.

To specify a secure LDAP server, use *ldaps://* in the AuthLDAPURL directive, instead of *ldap://*.

3.15.7 Exposing Login Information

When this module performs authentication, LDAP attributes specified in the AuthLDAPUrl directive are placed in environment variables with the prefix "AUTHENTICATE_".

If the attribute field contains the username, common name and telephone number of a user, a CGI program will have access to this information without the need to make a second independent LDAP query to gather this additional information.

This has the potential to dramatically simplify the coding and configuration required in some web applications.

3.15.8 Using Microsoft FrontPage with mod_authnz_ldap

Normally, FrontPage uses FrontPage-web-specific user/group files (i.e., the mod_authn_file and mod_authz_groupfile modules) to handle all authentication. Unfortunately, it is not possible to just change to LDAP authentication by adding the proper directives, because it will break the *Permissions* forms in the FrontPage client, which attempt to modify the standard text-based authorization files.

Once a FrontPage web has been created, adding LDAP authentication to it is a matter of adding the following directives to *every* .htaccess file that gets created in the web

```
AuthLDAPURL             "the url"
AuthGroupFile mygroupfile
Require group mygroupfile
```

How It Works

FrontPage restricts access to a web by adding the Require valid-user directive to the .htaccess files. The Require valid-user directive will succeed for any user who is valid *as far as LDAP is concerned*. This means that anybody who has an entry in the LDAP directory is considered a valid user, whereas FrontPage considers only those people in the local user file to be valid. By substituting the ldap-group with group file authorization, Apache is allowed to consult the local user file (which is managed by FrontPage) - instead of LDAP - when handling authorizing the user.

Once directives have been added as specified above, FrontPage users will be able to perform all management operations from the FrontPage client.

Caveats

- When choosing the LDAP URL, the attribute to use for authentication should be something that will also be valid for putting into a mod_authn_-file user file. The user ID is ideal for this.

- When adding users via FrontPage, FrontPage administrators should choose usernames that already exist in the LDAP directory (for obvious reasons). Also, the password that the administrator enters into the form is ignored, since Apache will actually be authenticating against the password in the LDAP database, and not against the password in the local user file. This could cause confusion for web administrators.

- Apache must be compiled with mod_auth_basic, mod_authn_file and mod_authz_groupfile in order to use FrontPage support. This is because Apache will still use the mod_authz_groupfile group file for determine the extent of a user's access to the FrontPage web.

- The directives must be put in the .htaccess files. Attempting to put them inside <Location> or <Directory> directives won't work. This is because mod_authnz_ldap has to be able to grab the AuthGroupFile directive that is found in FrontPage .htaccess files so that it knows where to look for the valid user list. If the mod_authnz_ldap directives aren't in the same .htaccess file as the FrontPage directives, then the hack won't work, because mod_authnz_ldap will never get a chance to process the .htaccess file, and won't be able to find the FrontPage-managed user file.

AuthLDAPBindAuthoritative Directive

Description:	Determines if other authentication providers are used when a user can be mapped to a DN but the server cannot successfully bind with the user's credentials.
Syntax:	AuthLDAPBindAuthoritative *off*|*on*
Default:	AuthLDAPBindAuthoritative on
Context:	directory, .htaccess
Override:	AuthConfig
Status:	Extension
Module:	mod_authnz_ldap
Compatibility:	Available in versions later than 2.2.14

By default, subsequent authentication providers are only queried if a user cannot be mapped to a DN, but not if the user can be mapped to a DN and their password cannot be verified with an LDAP bind. If AuthLDAPBindAuthoritative is set to *off*, other configured authentication modules will have a chance to validate the user if the LDAP bind (with the current user's credentials) fails for any reason.

This allows users present in both LDAP and AuthUserFile to authenticate when the LDAP server is available but the user's account is locked or password is otherwise unusable.

See also:

▷ AuthUserFile (p. 170)

▷ AuthBasicProvider (p. 151)

AuthLDAPBindDN Directive

Description:	Optional DN to use in binding to the LDAP server
Syntax:	AuthLDAPBindDN *distinguished-name*
Context:	directory, .htaccess
Override:	AuthConfig
Status:	Extension
Module:	mod_authnz_ldap

An optional DN used to bind to the server when searching for entries. If not provided, mod_authnz_ldap will use an anonymous bind.

AuthLDAPBindPassword Directive

Description:	Password used in conjuction with the bind DN
Syntax:	AuthLDAPBindPassword *password*
Context:	directory, .htaccess
Override:	AuthConfig
Status:	Extension
Module:	mod_authnz_ldap

A bind password to use in conjunction with the bind DN. Note that the bind password is probably sensitive data, and should be properly protected. You should only use the AuthLDAPBindDN and AuthLDAPBindPassword if you absolutely need them to search the directory.

AuthLDAPCharsetConfig Directive

Description:	Language to charset conversion configuration file
Syntax:	AuthLDAPCharsetConfig *file-path*
Context:	server config
Status:	Extension
Module:	mod_authnz_ldap

The AuthLDAPCharsetConfig directive sets the location of the language to charset conversion configuration file. *File-path* is relative to the ServerRoot. This file specifies the list of language extensions to character sets. Most administrators use the provided charset.conv file, which associates common language extensions to character sets.

The file contains lines in the following format:

Language-Extension charset [Language-String] ...

The case of the extension does not matter. Blank lines, and lines beginning with a hash character (#) are ignored.

AuthLDAPCompareDNOnServer Directive

Description:	Use the LDAP server to compare the DNs
Syntax:	AuthLDAPCompareDNOnServer on|off
Default:	AuthLDAPCompareDNOnServer on
Context:	directory, .htaccess
Override:	AuthConfig
Status:	Extension
Module:	mod_authnz_ldap

When set, mod_authnz_ldap will use the LDAP server to compare the DNs. This is the only foolproof way to compare DNs. mod_authnz_ldap will search the directory for the DN specified with the Require dn directive, then, retrieve the DN and compare it with the DN retrieved from the user entry. If this directive is not set, mod_authnz_ldap simply does a string comparison. It is possible to get false negatives with this approach, but it is much faster. Note the mod_ldap cache can speed up DN comparison in most situations.

AuthLDAPDereferenceAliases Directive

Description:	When will the module de-reference aliases
Syntax:	AuthLDAPDereferenceAliases never|searching|finding|always
Default:	AuthLDAPDereferenceAliases Always
Context:	directory, .htaccess
Override:	AuthConfig
Status:	Extension
Module:	mod_authnz_ldap

This directive specifies when mod_authnz_ldap will de-reference aliases during LDAP operations. The default is always.

AuthLDAPGroupAttribute Directive

Description:	LDAP attributes used to check for group membership
Syntax:	AuthLDAPGroupAttribute *attribute*
Default:	AuthLDAPGroupAttribute member uniquemember
Context:	directory, .htaccess
Override:	AuthConfig
Status:	Extension
Module:	mod_authnz_ldap

This directive specifies which LDAP attributes are used to check for group membership. Multiple attributes can be used by specifying this directive multiple times. If not specified, then mod_authnz_ldap uses the member and uniquemember attributes.

AuthLDAPGroupAttributeIsDN Directive

Description:	Use the DN of the client username when checking for group membership
Syntax:	AuthLDAPGroupAttributeIsDN on|off
Default:	AuthLDAPGroupAttributeIsDN on
Context:	directory, .htaccess
Override:	AuthConfig
Status:	Extension
Module:	mod_authnz_ldap

When set on, this directive says to use the distinguished name of the client username when checking for group membership. Otherwise, the username will be used. For example, assume that the client sent the username bjenson, which corresponds to the LDAP DN cn=Babs Jenson, o=Airius. If this directive is set, mod_authnz_ldap will check if the group has cn=Babs Jenson, o=Airius as a member. If this directive is not set, then mod_authnz_ldap will check if the group has bjenson as a member.

AuthLDAPRemoteUserAttribute Directive

Description:	Use the value of the attribute returned during the user query to set the REMOTE_USER environment variable
Syntax:	AuthLDAPRemoteUserAttribute uid
Default:	none
Context:	directory, .htaccess
Override:	AuthConfig
Status:	Extension
Module:	mod_authnz_ldap

If this directive is set, the value of the REMOTE_USER environment variable will be set to the value of the attribute specified. Make sure that this attribute is included in the list of attributes in the AuthLDAPUrl definition, otherwise this directive will have no effect. This directive, if present, takes precedence over AuthLDAPRemoteUserIsDN. This directive is useful should you want people to log into a website using an email address, but a backend application expects the username as a userid.

AuthLDAPRemoteUserIsDN Directive

Description:	Use the DN of the client username to set the REMOTE-USER environment variable
Syntax:	AuthLDAPRemoteUserIsDN on|off
Default:	AuthLDAPRemoteUserIsDN off
Context:	directory, .htaccess
Override:	AuthConfig
Status:	Extension
Module:	mod_authnz_ldap

If this directive is set to on, the value of the REMOTE_USER environment variable will be set to the full distinguished name of the authenticated user, rather than just the username that was passed by the client. It is turned off by default.

AuthLDAPUrl Directive

Description:	URL specifying the LDAP search parameters
Syntax:	AuthLDAPUrl *url* *[NONE|SSL|TLS|STARTTLS]*
Context:	directory, .htaccess
Override:	AuthConfig
Status:	Extension
Module:	mod_authnz_ldap

An RFC 2255 URL which specifies the LDAP search parameters to use. The syntax of the URL is

```
ldap://host:port/basedn?attribute?scope?filter
```

ldap For regular ldap, use the string ldap. For secure LDAP, use ldaps instead. Secure LDAP is only available if Apache was linked to an LDAP library with SSL support.

host:port The name/port of the ldap server (defaults to localhost:389 for ldap, and localhost:636 for ldaps). To specify multiple, redundant LDAP servers, just list all servers, separated by spaces. mod_authnz_ldap will try connecting to each server in turn, until it makes a successful connection.

Once a connection has been made to a server, that connection remains active for the life of the httpd process, or until the LDAP server goes down.

If the LDAP server goes down and breaks an existing connection, mod_authnz_ldap will attempt to re-connect, starting with the primary server, and trying each redundant server in turn. Note that this is different than a true round-robin search.

basedn The DN of the branch of the directory where all searches should start from. At the very least, this must be the top of your directory tree, but could also specify a subtree in the directory.

attribute The attribute to search for. Although RFC 2255 allows a comma-separated list of attributes, only the first attribute will be used, no matter how many are provided. If no attributes are provided, the default is to use uid. It's a good idea to choose an attribute that will be unique across all entries in the subtree you will be using.

scope The scope of the search. Can be either one or sub. Note that a scope of base is also supported by RFC 2255, but is not supported by this module. If the scope is not provided, or if base scope is specified, the default is to use a scope of sub.

filter A valid LDAP search filter. If not provided, defaults to (objectClass=*), which will search for all objects in the tree. Filters are limited to approximately 8000 characters (the definition of MAX_STRING_LEN in the Apache source code). This should be more than sufficient for any application.

When doing searches, the attribute, filter and username passed by the HTTP client are combined to create a search filter that looks like (&(*filter*)(*attribute*=*username*)).

For example, consider an URL of ldap://ldap.airius.com/o=Airius?cn?sub?(posixid=*). When a client attempts to connect using a username of Babs Jenson, the resulting search filter will be (&(posixid=*)(cn=Babs Jenson)).

An optional parameter can be added to allow the LDAP Url to override the connection type. This parameter can be one of the following:

NONE Establish an unsecure connection on the default LDAP port. This is the same as ldap:// on port 389.

SSL Establish a secure connection on the default secure LDAP port. This is the same as ldaps://

TLS — STARTTLS Establish an upgraded secure connection on the default LDAP port. This connection will be initiated on port 389 by default and then upgraded to a secure connection on the same port.

See above for examples of AuthLDAPURL URLs.

When AuthLDAPURL is enabled in a particular context, but some other module has performed authentication for the request, the server will try to map the username to a DN during authorization regardless of whether or not LDAP-specific requirements are present. To ignore the failures to map a username to a DN during authorization, set AuthzLDAPAutoritative to "off".

AuthzLDAPAuthoritative Directive

Description:	Prevent other authentication modules from authenticating the user if this one fails
Syntax:	AuthzLDAPAuthoritative on|off
Default:	AuthzLDAPAuthoritative on
Context:	directory, .htaccess
Override:	AuthConfig
Status:	Extension
Module:	mod_authnz_ldap

Set to off if this module should let other authorization modules attempt to authorize the user, should authorization with this module fail. Control is only passed on to lower modules if there is no DN or rule that matches the supplied user name (as passed by the client).

When no LDAP-specific Require directives are used, authorization is allowed to fall back to other modules as if AuthzLDAPAuthoritative was set to off.

3.16 Apache Module mod_authz_dbm

Description:	Group authorization using DBM files
Status:	Extension
Module Identifier:	authz_dbm_module
Source File:	mod_authz_dbm.c
Compatibility:	Available in Apache 2.1 and later

Summary

This module provides authorization capabilities so that authenticated users can be allowed or denied access to portions of the web site by group membership. Similar functionality is provided by mod_authz_groupfile.

Directives:

    AuthDBMGroupFile
    AuthzDBMAuthoritative
    AuthzDBMType

See also:

▷ Require (p. 124)

▷ Satisfy (p. 125)

AuthDBMGroupFile Directive

Description:	Sets the name of the database file containing the list of user groups for authorization
Syntax:	AuthDBMGroupFile *file-path*
Context:	directory, .htaccess
Override:	AuthConfig
Status:	Extension
Module:	mod_authz_dbm

The AuthDBMGroupFile directive sets the name of a DBM file containing the list of user groups for user authorization. *File-path* is the absolute path to the group file.

The group file is keyed on the username. The value for a user is a comma-separated list of the groups to which the users belongs. There must be no whitespace within the value, and it must never contain any colons.

SECURITY *Make sure that the AuthDBMGroupFile is stored outside the document tree of the web-server. Do not put it in the directory that it protects. Otherwise, clients will be able to download the AuthDBMGroupFile unless otherwise protected.*

Combining Group and Password DBM files: In some cases it is easier to manage a single database which contains both the password and group details for each user. This simplifies any support programs that need to be written: they now only have to deal with writing to and locking a single DBM file. This can be accomplished by first setting the group and password files to point to the same DBM:

```
AuthDBMGroupFile /www/userbase
AuthDBMUserFile /www/userbase
```

The key for the single DBM is the username. The value consists of

```
Encrypted Password :  List of Groups [ :  (ignored) ]
```

The password section contains the encrypted password as before. This is followed by a colon and the comma separated list of groups. Other data may optionally be left in the DBM file after another colon; it is ignored by the authorization module. This is what www.telescope.org uses for its combined password and group database.

AuthzDBMAuthoritative Directive

Description:	Sets whether authorization will be passed on to lower level modules
Syntax:	AuthzDBMAuthoritative On|Off
Default:	AuthzDBMAuthoritative On
Context:	directory, .htaccess
Override:	AuthConfig
Status:	Extension
Module:	mod_authz_dbm

Setting the AuthzDBMAuthoritative directive explicitly to Off allows group authorization to be passed on to lower level modules (as defined in the modules.c file) if there is no group found for the supplied userID. If there are any groups specified, the usual checks will be applied and a failure will give an Authentication Required reply.

So if a userID appears in the database of more than one module, or if a valid Require directive applies to more than one module, then the first module will verify the credentials and no access is passed on, regardless of the AuthAuthoritative setting.

A common use for this is in conjunction with one of the auth providers; such as mod_authn_dbm or mod_authn_file. Whereas this DBM module supplies the bulk of the user credential checking; a few (administrator) related accesses fall through to a lower level with a well protected .htpasswd file.

By default, control is not passed on and an unknown group will result in an Authentication Required reply. Not setting it thus keeps the system secure and forces an NCSA compliant behaviour.

SECURITY *Do consider the implications of allowing a user to allow fall-through in his .htaccess file and verify that this is really what you want.*

Generally it is easier to just secure a single .htpasswd *file than it is to secure a database which might have more access interfaces.*

AuthzDBMType Directive

Description:	Sets the type of database file that is used to store list of user groups
Syntax:	AuthzDBMType default|SDBM|GDBM|NDBM|DB
Default:	AuthzDBMType default
Context:	directory, .htaccess
Override:	AuthConfig
Status:	Extension
Module:	mod_authz_dbm

Sets the type of database file that is used to store the list of user groups. The default database type is determined at compile time. The availability of other types of database files also depends on compile-time settings (p. 775).

It is crucial that whatever program you use to create your group files is configured to use the same type of database.

3.17 Apache Module mod_authz_default

Description:	Authorization fallback module
Status:	Base
Module Identifier:	authz_default_module
Source File:	mod_authz_default.c
Compatibility:	Available in Apache 2.1 and later

Summary

This module is designed to be the fallback module, if you don't have configured an authorization module like mod_authz_user or mod_authz_groupfile. It simply rejects any authorization request.

Directives:

AuthzDefaultAuthoritative

AuthzDefaultAuthoritative Directive

Description:	Sets whether authorization is passed to lower level modules
Syntax:	AuthzDefaultAuthoritative On|Off
Default:	AuthzDefaultAuthoritative On
Context:	directory, .htaccess
Override:	AuthConfig
Status:	Base
Module:	mod_authz_default

Setting the AuthzDefaultAuthoritative directive explicitly to Off allows for authorization to be passed on to lower level modules (as defined in the modules.c files).

NOTE *Normally there are no lower level modules, since mod_authz_-*
default is defined to be already on a very low level. Therefore you
should leave the value of AuthzDefaultAuthoritative as default (On).

3.18 Apache Module mod_authz_groupfile

Description:	Group authorization using plaintext files
Status:	Base
Module Identifier:	authz_groupfile_module
Source File:	mod_authz_groupfile.c
Compatibility:	Available in Apache 2.1 and later

Summary

This module provides authorization capabilities so that authenticated users can be allowed or denied access to portions of the web site by group membership. Similar functionality is provided by mod_authz_dbm.

Directives:

    AuthGroupFile
    AuthzGroupFileAuthoritative

See also:

 ▷ Require (p. 124)

 ▷ Satisfy (p. 125)

AuthGroupFile Directive

Description:	Sets the name of a text file containing the list of user groups for authorization
Syntax:	AuthGroupFile *file-path*
Context:	directory, .htaccess
Override:	AuthConfig
Status:	Base
Module:	mod_authz_groupfile

The AuthGroupFile directive sets the name of a textual file containing the list of user groups for user authorization. *File-path* is the path to the group file. If it is not absolute, it is treated as relative to the ServerRoot.

Each line of the group file contains a groupname followed by a colon, followed by the member usernames separated by spaces.

Example:
    mygroup: bob joe anne

Note that searching large text files is *very* inefficient; AuthDBMGroupFile provides a much better performance.

> SECURITY *Make sure that the AuthGroupFile is stored outside the document tree of the web-server; do not put it in the directory that it protects. Otherwise, clients may be able to download the AuthGroupFile.*

AuthzGroupFileAuthoritative Directive

Description:	Sets whether authorization will be passed on to lower level modules
Syntax:	AuthzGroupFileAuthoritative On|Off
Default:	AuthzGroupFileAuthoritative On
Context:	directory, .htaccess
Override:	AuthConfig
Status:	Base
Module:	mod_authz_groupfile

Setting the AuthzGroupFileAuthoritative directive explicitly to Off allows for group authorization to be passed on to lower level modules (as defined in the modules.c files) if there is **no group** matching the supplied userID.

By default, control is not passed on and an unknown group will result in an Authentication Required reply. Not setting it thus keeps the system secure and forces an NCSA compliant behaviour.

SECURITY *Do consider the implications of allowing a user to allow fall-through in his .htaccess file and verify that this is really what you want. Generally it is easier to just secure a single .htpasswd file than it is to secure a database which might have more access interfaces.*

3.19 Apache Module mod_authz_host

Description:	Group authorizations based on host (name or IP address)
Status:	Base
Module Identifier:	authz_host_module
Source File:	mod_authz_host.c
Compatibility:	Available in Apache 2.1 and later

Summary

The directives provided by mod_authz_host are used in <Directory>, <Files>, and <Location> sections as well as .htaccess (p. 87) files to control access to particular parts of the server. Access can be controlled based on the client hostname, IP address, or other characteristics of the client request, as captured in environment variables (p. 705). The Allow and Deny directives are used to specify which clients are or are not allowed access to the server, while the Order directive sets the default access state, and configures how the Allow and Deny directives interact with each other.

Both host-based access restrictions and password-based authentication may be implemented simultaneously. In that case, the Satisfy directive is used to determine how the two sets of restrictions interact.

In general, access restriction directives apply to all access methods (GET, PUT, POST, etc). This is the desired behavior in most cases. However, it is possible to restrict some methods, while leaving other methods unrestricted, by enclosing the directives in a <Limit> section.

Directives:

> Allow
> Deny
> Order

See also:

> ▷ Satisfy (p. 125)

> ▷ Require (p. 124)

Allow Directive

Description:	Controls which hosts can access an area of the server
Syntax:	Allow from all|*host*|env=[!]*env-variable* [*host*|env=[!]*env-variable*] ...
Context:	directory, .htaccess
Override:	Limit
Status:	Base
Module:	mod_authz_host

The `Allow` directive affects which hosts can access an area of the server. Access can be controlled by hostname, IP address, IP address range, or by other characteristics of the client request captured in environment variables.

The first argument to this directive is always `from`. The subsequent arguments can take three different forms. If `Allow from all` is specified, then all hosts are allowed access, subject to the configuration of the Deny and Order directives as discussed below. To allow only particular hosts or groups of hosts to access the server, the *host* can be specified in any of the following formats:

A (partial) domain-name   *Example:*
```
Allow from apache.org
Allow from .net example.edu
```

Hosts whose names match, or end in, this string are allowed access. Only complete components are matched, so the above example will match `foo.apache.org` but it will not match `fooapache.org`. This configuration will cause Apache to perform a double reverse DNS lookup on the client IP address, regardless of the setting of the `HostnameLookups` directive. It will do a reverse DNS lookup on the IP address to find the associated hostname, and then do a forward lookup on the hostname to assure that it matches the original IP address. Only if the forward and reverse DNS are consistent and the hostname matches will access be allowed.

A full IP address   *Example:*
```
Allow from 10.1.2.3
Allow from 192.168.1.104 192.168.1.205
```

An IP address of a host allowed access

A partial IP address   *Example:*
```
Allow from 10.1
Allow from 10 172.20 192.168.2
```

The first 1 to 3 bytes of an IP address, for subnet restriction.

A network/netmask pair   *Example:*
```
Allow from 10.1.0.0/255.255.0.0
```

A network a.b.c.d, and a netmask w.x.y.z. For more fine-grained subnet restriction.

A network/nnn CIDR specification   *Example:*
```
Allow from 10.1.0.0/16
```

Similar to the previous case, except the netmask consists of nnn high-order 1 bits.

Note that the last three examples above match exactly the same set of hosts.

IPv6 addresses and IPv6 subnets can be specified as shown below:
```
Allow from 2001:db8::a00:20ff:fea7:ccea
Allow from 2001:db8::a00:20ff:fea7:ccea/10
```

The third format of the arguments to the `Allow` directive allows access to the server to be controlled based on the existence of an environment variable (p. 705). When `Allow from env=env-variable` is specified, then the request is allowed access if the environment variable *env-variable* exists. When `Allow from env=!env-variable` is specified, then the request is allowed access if the environment variable *env-variable* doesn't exist. The server provides the ability to set environment variables in a flexible way based on characteristics of the client request using the directives provided by `mod_setenvif`. Therefore, this directive can be used to allow access based on such factors as the clients `User-Agent` (browser type), `Referer`, or other HTTP request header fields.

Example:
```
SetEnvIf User-Agent ^KnockKnock/2\.0 let_me_in
<Directory /docroot>
    Order Deny,Allow
    Deny from all
    Allow from env=let_me_in
</Directory>
```

In this case, browsers with a user-agent string beginning with `KnockKnock/2.0` will be allowed access, and all others will be denied.

Deny Directive

Description:	Controls which hosts are denied access to the server
Syntax:	`Deny from all`|*host*|`env=[!]`*env-variable* [*host*|`env=[!]`*env-variable*] ...
Context:	directory, .htaccess
Override:	Limit
Status:	Base
Module:	mod_authz_host

This directive allows access to the server to be restricted based on hostname, IP address, or environment variables. The arguments for the `Deny` directive are identical to the arguments for the `Allow` directive.

Order Directive

Description:	Controls the default access state and the order in which `Allow` and `Deny` are evaluated.
Syntax:	`Order` *ordering*
Default:	`Order Deny,Allow`
Context:	directory, .htaccess
Override:	Limit
Status:	Base
Module:	mod_authz_host

The `Order` directive, along with the `Allow` and `Deny` directives, controls a three-pass access control system. The first pass processes either all `Allow` or all `Deny`

directives, as specified by the Order directive. The second pass parses the rest
of the directives (Deny or Allow). The third pass applies to all requests which
do not match either of the first two.

Note that all Allow and Deny directives are processed, unlike a typical firewall,
where only the first match is used. The last match is effective (also unlike a
typical firewall). Additionally, the order in which lines appear in the configuration files is not significant – all Allow lines are processed as one group, all Deny
lines are considered as another, and the default state is considered by itself.

Ordering is one of:

Allow,Deny First, all Allow directives are evaluated; at least one must match,
   or the request is rejected. Next, all Deny directives are evaluated. If any
   matches, the request is rejected. Last, any requests which do not match
   an Allow or a Deny directive are denied by default.

Deny,Allow First, all Deny directives are evaluated; if any match, the request
   is denied **unless** it also matches an Allow directive. Any requests which
   do not match any Allow or Deny directives are permitted.

Mutual-failure This order has the same effect as Order Allow,Deny and is
   deprecated in its favor.

Keywords may only be separated by a comma; *no whitespace* is allowed between
them.

Match	Allow,Deny result	Deny,Allow result
Match Allow only	Request allowed	Request allowed
Match Deny only	Request denied	Request denied
No match	Default to second direc-tive: Denied	Default to second direc-tive: Allowed
Match both Allow & Deny	Final match controls: Denied	Final match controls: Allowed

In the following example, all hosts in the apache.org domain are allowed access;
all other hosts are denied access.

```
Order Deny,Allow
Deny from all
Allow from apache.org
```

In the next example, all hosts in the apache.org domain are allowed access,
except for the hosts which are in the foo.apache.org subdomain, who are denied
access. All hosts not in the apache.org domain are denied access because the
default state is to Deny access to the server.

```
Order Allow,Deny
Allow from apache.org
Deny from foo.apache.org
```

On the other hand, if the Order in the last example is changed to Deny,Allow,
all hosts will be allowed access. This happens because, regardless of the actual

ordering of the directives in the configuration file, the `Allow from apache.org` will be evaluated last and will override the `Deny from foo.apache.org`. All hosts not in the `apache.org` domain will also be allowed access because the default state is `Allow`.

The presence of an `Order` directive can affect access to a part of the server even in the absence of accompanying `Allow` and `Deny` directives because of its effect on the default access state. For example,

```
<Directory /www>
    Order Allow,Deny
</Directory>
```

will `Deny` all access to the `/www` directory because the default access state is set to `Deny`.

The `Order` directive controls the order of access directive processing only within each phase of the server's configuration processing. This implies, for example, that an `Allow` or `Deny` directive occurring in a `<Location>` section will always be evaluated after an `Allow` or `Deny` directive occurring in a `<Directory>` section or `.htaccess` file, regardless of the setting of the `Order` directive. For details on the merging of configuration sections, see the documentation on How Directory, Location and Files sections work (p. 57).

3.20 Apache Module mod_authz_owner

Description:	Authorization based on file ownership
Status:	Extension
Module Identifier:	authz_owner_module
Source File:	mod_authz_owner.c
Compatibility:	Available in Apache 2.1 and later

Summary

This module authorizes access to files by comparing the userid used for HTTP authentication (the web userid) with the file-system owner or group of the requested file. The supplied username and password must be already properly verified by an authentication module, such as mod_auth_basic or mod_auth_-digest. mod_authz_owner recognizes two arguments for the Require directive, file-owner and file-group, as follows:

file-owner The supplied web-username must match the system's name for the owner of the file being requested. That is, if the operating system says the requested file is owned by jones, then the username used to access it through the web must be jones as well.

file-group The name of the system group that owns the file must be present in a group database, which is provided, for example, by mod_authz_-groupfile or mod_authz_dbm, and the web-username must be a member of that group. For example, if the operating system says the requested file is owned by (system) group accounts, the group accounts must appear in the group database and the web-username used in the request must be a member of that group.

> NOTE   *If mod_authz_owner is used in order to authorize a resource that is not actually present in the filesystem (i.e. a virtual resource), it will deny the access.*
>
> *Particularly it will never authorize content negotiated "MultiViews" (p. 687) resources.*

Directives:

AuthzOwnerAuthoritative

See also:

▷ Require (p. 124)

▷ Satisfy (p. 125)

3.20.1 Configuration Examples

Require file-owner

Consider a multi-user system running the Apache Web server, with each user having his or her own files in ~/public_html/private. Assuming that there is a single AuthDBMUserFile database that lists all of their web-usernames, and that these usernames match the system's usernames that actually own the files on the server, then the following stanza would allow only the user himself access to his own files. User jones would not be allowed to access files in /home/smith/public_html/private unless they were owned by jones instead of smith.

```
<Directory /home/*/public_html/private>
    AuthType Basic
    AuthName MyPrivateFiles
    AuthBasicProvider dbm
    AuthDBMUserFile /usr/local/apache2/etc/.htdbm-all
    Satisfy All
    Require file-owner
</Directory>
```

Require file-group

Consider a system similar to the one described above, but with some users that share their project files in ~/public_html/project-foo. The files are owned by the system group foo and there is a single AuthDBMGroupFile database that contains all of the web-usernames and their group membership, *i.e.* they must be at least member of a group named foo. So if jones and smith are both member of the group foo, then both will be authorized to access the project-foo directories of each other.

```
<Directory /home/*/public_html/project-foo>
    AuthType Basic
    AuthName "Project Foo Files"
    AuthBasicProvider dbm

    # combined user/group database
    AuthDBMUserFile /usr/local/apache2/etc/.htdbm-all
    AuthDBMGroupFile /usr/local/apache2/etc/.htdbm-all

    Satisfy All
    Require file-group
</Directory>
```

AuthzOwnerAuthoritative Directive

Description:	Sets whether authorization will be passed on to lower level modules
Syntax:	AuthzOwnerAuthoritative On|Off
Default:	AuthzOwnerAuthoritative On
Context:	directory, .htaccess
Override:	AuthConfig
Status:	Extension
Module:	mod_authz_owner

Setting the AuthzOwnerAuthoritative directive explicitly to Off allows for user authorization to be passed on to lower level modules (as defined in the modules.c files) if:

- in the case of file-owner the file-system owner does not match the supplied web-username or could not be determined, or

- in the case of file-group the file-system group does not contain the supplied web-username or could not be determined.

Note that setting the value to Off also allows the combination of file-owner and file-group, so access will be allowed if either one or the other (or both) match.

By default, control is not passed on and an authorization failure will result in an "Authentication Required" reply. Not setting it to Off thus keeps the system secure and forces an NCSA compliant behaviour.

3.21 Apache Module mod_authz_user

Description:	User Authorization
Status:	Base
Module Identifier:	authz_user_module
Source File:	mod_authz_user.c
Compatibility:	Available in Apache 2.1 and later

Summary

This module provides authorization capabilities so that authenticated users can be allowed or denied access to portions of the web site. mod_authz_user grants access if the authenticated user is listed in a Require user directive. Alternatively Require valid-user can be used to grant access to all successfully authenticated users.

Directives:

AuthzUserAuthoritative

See also:

▷ Require (p. 124)

▷ Satisfy (p. 125)

AuthzUserAuthoritative Directive

Description:	Sets whether authorization will be passed on to lower level modules
Syntax:	AuthzUserAuthoritative On|Off
Default:	AuthzUserAuthoritative On
Context:	directory, .htaccess
Override:	AuthConfig
Status:	Base
Module:	mod_authz_user

Setting the AuthzUserAuthoritative directive explicitly to Off allows for user authorization to be passed on to lower level modules (as defined in the modules.c files) if there is **no user** matching the supplied userID.

By default, control is not passed on and an unknown user will result in an Authentication Required reply. Not setting it to Off thus keeps the system secure and forces an NCSA compliant behaviour.

3.22 Apache Module mod_autoindex

Description:	Generates directory indexes, automatically, similar to the Unix ls command or the Win32 dir shell command
Status:	Base
Module Identifier:	autoindex_module
Source File:	mod_autoindex.c

Summary

The index of a directory can come from one of two sources:

- A file written by the user, typically called index.html. The DirectoryIndex directive sets the name of this file. This is controlled by mod_dir.

- Otherwise, a listing generated by the server. The other directives control the format of this listing. The AddIcon, AddIconByEncoding and AddIconByType are used to set a list of icons to display for various file types; for each file listed, the first icon listed that matches the file is displayed. These are controlled by mod_autoindex.

The two functions are separated so that you can completely remove (or replace) automatic index generation should you want to.

Automatic index generation is enabled with using Options +Indexes. See the Options directive for more details.

If the FancyIndexing option is given with the IndexOptions directive, the column headers are links that control the order of the display. If you select a header link, the listing will be regenerated, sorted by the values in that column. Selecting the same header repeatedly toggles between ascending and descending order. These column header links are suppressed with IndexOptions directive's SuppressColumnSorting option.

Note that when the display is sorted by "Size", it's the *actual* size of the files that's used, not the displayed value - so a 1010-byte file will always be displayed before a 1011-byte file (if in ascending order) even though they both are shown as "1K".

Directives:

AddAlt	HeaderName
AddAltByEncoding	IndexHeadInsert
AddAltByType	IndexIgnore
AddDescription	IndexOptions
AddIcon	IndexOrderDefault
AddIconByEncoding	IndexStyleSheet
AddIconByType	ReadmeName
DefaultIcon	

3.22.1 Autoindex Request Query Arguments

Apache 2.0.23 reorganized the Query Arguments for Column Sorting, and introduced an entire group of new query options. To effectively eliminate all client control over the output, the `IndexOptions IgnoreClient` option was introduced.

The column sorting headers themselves are self-referencing hyperlinks that add the sort query options shown below. Any option below may be added to any request for the directory resource.

- `C=N` sorts the directory by file name
- `C=M` sorts the directory by last-modified date, then file name
- `C=S` sorts the directory by size, then file name
- `C=D` sorts the directory by description, then file name
- `O=A` sorts the listing in Ascending Order
- `O=D` sorts the listing in Descending Order
- `F=0` formats the listing as a simple list (not FancyIndexed)
- `F=1` formats the listing as a FancyIndexed list
- `F=2` formats the listing as an HTMLTable FancyIndexed list
- `V=0` disables version sorting
- `V=1` enables version sorting
- `P=pattern` lists only files matching the given *pattern*

Note that the 'P'attern query argument is tested *after* the usual `IndexIgnore` directives are processed, and all file names are still subjected to the same criteria as any other autoindex listing. The Query Arguments parser in `mod_autoindex` will stop abruptly when an unrecognized option is encountered. The Query Arguments must be well formed, according to the table above.

The simple example below, which can be clipped and saved in a header.html file, illustrates these query options. Note that the unknown "X" argument, for the submit button, is listed last to assure the arguments are all parsed before `mod_autoindex` encounters the X=Go input.

```
<form action="" method="get">
    Show me a <select name="F">
        <option value="0"> Plain list</option>
        <option value="1" selected="selected"> Fancy
        list</option>
        <option value="2"> Table list</option>
    </select>
    Sorted by <select name="C">
```

```
        <option value="N" selected="selected"> Name</option>
        <option value="M"> Date Modified</option>
        <option value="S"> Size</option>
        <option value="D"> Description</option>
    </select>
    <select name="O">
        <option value="A" selected="selected">
        Ascending</option>
        <option value="D"> Descending</option>
    </select>
    <select name="V">
        <option value="0" selected="selected"> in Normal
        order</option>
        <option value="1"> in Version order</option>
    </select>
    Matching <input type="text" name="P" value="*" />
    <input type="submit" name="X" value="Go" />
</form>
```

AddAlt Directive

Description:	Alternate text to display for a file, instead of an icon selected by filename
Syntax:	AddAlt *string file* [*file*] ...
Context:	server config, virtual host, directory, .htaccess
Override:	Indexes
Status:	Base
Module:	mod_autoindex

AddAlt provides the alternate text to display for a file, instead of an icon, for FancyIndexing. *File* is a file extension, partial filename, wild-card expression or full filename for files to describe. If *String* contains any whitespace, you have to enclose it in quotes (" or '). This alternate text is displayed if the client is image-incapable, has image loading disabled, or fails to retrieve the icon.

Examples
```
AddAlt "PDF file" *.pdf
AddAlt Compressed *.gz *.zip *.Z
```

AddAltByEncoding Directive

Description:	Alternate text to display for a file instead of an icon selected by MIME-encoding
Syntax:	AddAltByEncoding *string MIME-encoding [MIME-encoding]* ...
Context:	server config, virtual host, directory, .htaccess
Override:	Indexes
Status:	Base
Module:	mod_autoindex

AddAltByEncoding provides the alternate text to display for a file, instead of an icon, for FancyIndexing. *MIME-encoding* is a valid content-encoding, such as x-compress. If *String* contains any whitespace, you have to enclose it in quotes (" or '). This alternate text is displayed if the client is image-incapable, has image loading disabled, or fails to retrieve the icon.

Example
    AddAltByEncoding gzip x-gzip

AddAltByType Directive

Description:	Alternate text to display for a file, instead of an icon selected by MIME content-type
Syntax:	AddAltByType *string MIME-type [MIME-type]* ...
Context:	server config, virtual host, directory, .htaccess
Override:	Indexes
Status:	Base
Module:	mod_autoindex

AddAltByType sets the alternate text to display for a file, instead of an icon, for FancyIndexing. *MIME-type* is a valid content-type, such as text/html. If *String* contains any whitespace, you have to enclose it in quotes (" or '). This alternate text is displayed if the client is image-incapable, has image loading disabled, or fails to retrieve the icon.

Example
    AddAltByType 'plain text' text/plain

AddDescription Directive

Description:	Description to display for a file
Syntax:	AddDescription *string file [file]* ...
Context:	server config, virtual host, directory, .htaccess
Override:	Indexes
Status:	Base
Module:	mod_autoindex

This sets the description to display for a file, for FancyIndexing. *File* is a file extension, partial filename, wild-card expression or full filename for files to describe. *String* is enclosed in double quotes (").

Example
```
AddDescription "The planet Mars" /web/pics/mars.gif
```

The typical, default description field is 23 bytes wide. 6 more bytes are added by the IndexOptions SuppressIcon option, 7 bytes are added by the IndexOptions SuppressSize option, and 19 bytes are added by the IndexOptions SuppressLastModified option. Therefore, the widest default the description column is ever assigned is 55 bytes.

See the DescriptionWidth IndexOptions keyword for details on overriding the size of this column, or allowing descriptions of unlimited length.

> CAUTION *Descriptive text defined with AddDescription may contain HTML markup, such as tags and character entities. If the width of the description column should happen to truncate a tagged element (such as cutting off the end of a bolded phrase), the results may affect the rest of the directory listing.*

AddIcon Directive

Description:	Icon to display for a file selected by name
Syntax:	AddIcon *icon name* [*name*] ...
Context:	server config, virtual host, directory, .htaccess
Override:	Indexes
Status:	Base
Module:	mod_autoindex

This sets the icon to display next to a file ending in *name* for FancyIndexing. *Icon* is either a (%-escaped) relative URL to the icon, or of the format (*alttext*,*url*) where *alttext* is the text tag given for an icon for non-graphical browsers.

Name is either ^^DIRECTORY^^ for directories, ^^BLANKICON^^ for blank lines (to format the list correctly), a file extension, a wildcard expression, a partial filename or a complete filename.

Examples
```
AddIcon (IMG,/icons/image.xbm) .gif .jpg .xbm
AddIcon /icons/dir.xbm ^^DIRECTORY^^
AddIcon /icons/backup.xbm *~
```

AddIconByType should be used in preference to AddIcon, when possible.

AddIconByEncoding Directive

Description:	Icon to display next to files selected by MIME content-encoding
Syntax:	AddIconByEncoding *icon MIME-encoding* [*MIME-encoding*] ...
Context:	server config, virtual host, directory, .htaccess
Override:	Indexes
Status:	Base
Module:	mod_autoindex

This sets the icon to display next to files with FancyIndexing. *Icon* is either a (%-escaped) relative URL to the icon, or of the format (alttext,url) where *alttext* is the text tag given for an icon for non-graphical browsers.

MIME-encoding is a valid content-encoding, such as x-compress.

Example
    AddIconByEncoding /icons/compress.xbm x-compress

AddIconByType Directive

Description:	Icon to display next to files selected by MIME content-type
Syntax:	AddIconByType *icon MIME-type* [*MIME-type*] ...
Context:	server config, virtual host, directory, .htaccess
Override:	Indexes
Status:	Base
Module:	mod_autoindex

This sets the icon to display next to files of type *MIME-type* for FancyIndexing. *Icon* is either a (%-escaped) relative URL to the icon, or of the format (alttext,url) where *alttext* is the text tag given for an icon for non-graphical browsers.

MIME-type is a wildcard expression matching required the mime types.

Example
    AddIconByType (IMG,/icons/image.xbm) image/*

DefaultIcon Directive

Description:	Icon to display for files when no specific icon is configured
Syntax:	DefaultIcon *url-path*
Context:	server config, virtual host, directory, .htaccess
Override:	Indexes
Status:	Base
Module:	mod_autoindex

The DefaultIcon directive sets the icon to display for files when no specific icon is known, for FancyIndexing. *Url-path* is a (%-escaped) relative URL to the icon.

> *Example*
> DefaultIcon /icon/unknown.xbm

HeaderName Directive

Description:	Name of the file that will be inserted at the top of the index listing
Syntax:	HeaderName *filename*
Context:	server config, virtual host, directory, .htaccess
Override:	Indexes
Status:	Base
Module:	mod_autoindex

The HeaderName directive sets the name of the file that will be inserted at the top of the index listing. *Filename* is the name of the file to include.

> *Example*
> HeaderName HEADER.html

> *Both HeaderName and ReadmeName now treat Filename as a URI path relative to the one used to access the directory being indexed. If Filename begins with a slash, it will be taken to be relative to the DocumentRoot.*

> > *Example*
> > HeaderName /include/HEADER.html

> *Filename must resolve to a document with a major content type of text/* (e.g., text/html, text/plain, etc.). This means that filename may refer to a CGI script if the script's actual file type (as opposed to its output) is marked as text/html such as with a directive like:*

> > AddType text/html .cgi

> *Content negotiation (p. 687) will be performed if Options MultiViews is in effect. If filename resolves to a static text/html document (not a CGI script) and either one of the options Includes or IncludesNOEXEC is enabled, the file will be processed for server-side includes (see the mod_include documentation).*

If the file specified by HeaderName contains the beginnings of an HTML document (<html>, <head>, etc.) then you will probably want to set IndexOptions +SuppressHTMLPreamble, so that these tags are not repeated.

IndexHeadInsert Directive

Description:	Inserts text in the HEAD section of an index page.
Syntax:	IndexHeadInsert *"markup ..."*
Context:	server config, virtual host, directory, .htaccess
Override:	Indexes
Status:	Base
Module:	mod_autoindex
Compatibility:	Available in Apache 2.2.11 and later

The IndexHeadInsert directive specifies a string to insert in the *<head>* section of the HTML generated for the index page.

Example
```
IndexHeadInsert "<link rel=\"sitemap\" href=\"/sitemap.html\">"
```

IndexIgnore Directive

Description:	Adds to the list of files to hide when listing a directory
Syntax:	IndexIgnore *file* [*file*] ...
Context:	server config, virtual host, directory, .htaccess
Override:	Indexes
Status:	Base
Module:	mod_autoindex

The IndexIgnore directive adds to the list of files to hide when listing a directory. *File* is a shell-style wildcard expression or full filename. Multiple IndexIgnore directives add to the list, rather than the replacing the list of ignored files. By default, the list contains . (the current directory).

```
IndexIgnore README .htaccess *.bak *~
```

IndexOptions Directive

Description:	Various configuration settings for directory indexing
Syntax:	IndexOptions [+|-]*option* [[+|-]*option*] ...
Context:	server config, virtual host, directory, .htaccess
Override:	Indexes
Status:	Base
Module:	mod_autoindex

The IndexOptions directive specifies the behavior of the directory indexing. *Option* can be one of

Charset=*character-set* (*Apache 2.0.61 and later*) The Charset keyword allows you to specify the character set of the generated page. The default is either *ISO-8859-1* or *UTF-8*, depending on whether the underlying file system is unicode or not.

Example:

```
IndexOptions Charset=UTF-8
```

Type=*MIME content-type* (*Apache 2.0.61 and later*) The Type keyword allows you to specify the MIME content-type of the generated page. The default is *text/html*.

Example:
```
IndexOptions Type=text/plain
```

DescriptionWidth=[*n* — *] (*Apache 2.0.23 and later*) The DescriptionWidth keyword allows you to specify the width of the description column in characters.

-DescriptionWidth (or unset) allows mod_autoindex to calculate the best width.

DescriptionWidth=n fixes the column width to *n* bytes wide.

DescriptionWidth=* grows the column to the width necessary to accommodate the longest description string.

See the section on AddDescription for dangers inherent in truncating descriptions.

FancyIndexing This turns on fancy indexing of directories.

FoldersFirst (*Apache 2.0.23 and later*) If this option is enabled, subdirectory listings will *always* appear first, followed by normal files in the directory. The listing is basically broken into two components, the files and the subdirectories, and each is sorted separately and then displayed subdirectories-first. For instance, if the sort order is descending by name, and FoldersFirst is enabled, subdirectory Zed will be listed before subdirectory Beta, which will be listed before normal files Gamma and Alpha. **This option only has an effect if FancyIndexing is also enabled.**

HTMLTable (*Apache HTTP Server 2.0.23 and later*) This option with FancyIndexing constructs a simple table for the fancy directory listing. It is necessary for utf-8 enabled platforms or if file names or description text will alternate between left-to-right and right-to-left reading order.

IconsAreLinks This makes the icons part of the anchor for the filename, for fancy indexing.

IconHeight[=*pixels*] Presence of this option, when used with IconWidth, will cause the server to include height and width attributes in the img tag for the file icon. This allows browser to precalculate the page layout without having to wait until all the images have been loaded. If no value is given for the option, it defaults to the standard height of the icons supplied with the Apache software.

IconWidth[=*pixels*] Presence of this option, when used with IconHeight, will cause the server to include height and width attributes in the img tag for the file icon. This allows browser to precalculate the page layout without having to wait until all the images have been loaded. If no value is given for the option, it defaults to the standard width of the icons supplied with the Apache software.

IgnoreCase If this option is enabled, names are sorted in a case-insensitive manner. For instance, if the sort order is ascending by name, and IgnoreCase is enabled, file Zeta will be listed after file alfa (Note: file GAMMA will always be listed before file gamma).

IgnoreClient This option causes mod-autoindex to ignore all query variables from the client, including sort order (implies SuppressColumnSorting.)

NameWidth=[*n* — *] The NameWidth keyword allows you to specify the width of the filename column in bytes.

-NameWidth (or unset) allows mod-autoindex to calculate the best width.

NameWidth=*n* fixes the column width to *n* bytes wide.

NameWidth=* grows the column to the necessary width.

ScanHTMLTitles This enables the extraction of the title from HTML documents for fancy indexing. If the file does not have a description given by AddDescription then httpd will read the document for the value of the title element. This is CPU and disk intensive.

ShowForbidden If specified, Apache will show files normally hidden because the subrequest returned HTTP_UNAUTHORIZED or HTTP_FORBIDDEN

SuppressColumnSorting If specified, Apache will not make the column headings in a FancyIndexed directory listing into links for sorting. The default behavior is for them to be links; selecting the column heading will sort the directory listing by the values in that column. **Prior to Apache 2.0.23, this also disabled parsing the Query Arguments for the sort string.** That behavior is now controlled by IndexOptions IgnoreClient in Apache 2.0.23.

SuppressDescription This will suppress the file description in fancy indexing listings. By default, no file descriptions are defined, and so the use of this option will regain 23 characters of screen space to use for something else. See AddDescription for information about setting the file description. See also the DescriptionWidth index option to limit the size of the description column.

SuppressHTMLPreamble If the directory actually contains a file specified by the HeaderName directive, the module usually includes the contents of the file after a standard HTML preamble (<html>, <head>, *et cetera*). The SuppressHTMLPreamble option disables this behaviour, causing the module to start the display with the header file contents. The header file must contain appropriate HTML instructions in this case. If there is no header file, the preamble is generated as usual.

SuppressIcon (*Apache 2.0.23 and later*) This will suppress the icon in fancy indexing listings. Combining both SuppressIcon and SuppressRules yields proper HTML 3.2 output, which by the final specification prohibits img and hr elements from the pre block (used to format FancyIndexed listings.)

SuppressLastModified This will suppress the display of the last modification date, in fancy indexing listings.

SuppressRules (*Apache 2.0.23 and later*) This will suppress the horizontal rule lines (hr elements) in directory listings. Combining both SuppressIcon and SuppressRules yields proper HTML 3.2 output, which by the final specification prohibits img and hr elements from the pre block (used to format FancyIndexed listings.)

SuppressSize This will suppress the file size in fancy indexing listings.

TrackModified (*Apache 2.0.23 and later*) This returns the Last-Modified and ETag values for the listed directory in the HTTP header. It is only valid if the operating system and file system return appropriate stat() results. Some Unix systems do so, as do OS2's JFS and Win32's NTFS volumes. OS2 and Win32 FAT volumes, for example, do not. Once this feature is enabled, the client or proxy can track changes to the list of files when they perform a HEAD request. Note some operating systems correctly track new and removed files, but do not track changes for sizes or dates of the files within the directory. **Changes to the size or date stamp of an existing file will not update the** Last-Modified **header on all Unix platforms.** If this is a concern, leave this option disabled.

VersionSort (*Apache 2.0a3 and later*) The VersionSort keyword causes files containing version numbers to sort in a natural way. Strings are sorted as usual, except that substrings of digits in the name and description are compared according to their numeric value.

> *Example:*
> foo-1.7
> foo-1.7.2
> foo-1.7.12
> foo-1.8.2
> foo-1.8.2a
> foo-1.12

If the number starts with a zero, then it is considered to be a fraction:

> foo-1.001
> foo-1.002
> foo-1.030
> foo-1.04

XHTML (*Apache 2.0.49 and later*) The XHTML keyword forces mod_-autoindex to emit XHTML 1.0 code instead of HTML 3.2.

Incremental IndexOptions Apache 1.3.3 introduced some significant changes in the handling of IndexOptions directives. In particular:

- Multiple IndexOptions directives for a single directory are now merged together. The result of:
  <Directory /foo>

```
                    IndexOptions HTMLTable
                    IndexOptions SuppressColumnsorting
                </Directory>
```
will be the equivalent of
```
    IndexOptions HTMLTable SuppressColumnsorting
```
- The addition of the incremental syntax (*i.e.*, prefixing keywords with + or -).

Whenever a '+' or '-' prefixed keyword is encountered, it is applied to the current IndexOptions settings (which may have been inherited from an upper-level directory). However, whenever an unprefixed keyword is processed, it clears all inherited options and any incremental settings encountered so far. Consider the following example:

```
    IndexOptions +ScanHTMLTitles -IconsAreLinks FancyIndexing
    IndexOptions +SuppressSize
```

The net effect is equivalent to IndexOptions FancyIndexing +SuppressSize, because the unprefixed FancyIndexing discarded the incremental keywords before it, but allowed them to start accumulating again afterward.

To unconditionally set the IndexOptions for a particular directory, clearing the inherited settings, specify keywords without any + or - prefixes.

IndexOrderDefault Directive

Description:	Sets the default ordering of the directory index
Syntax:	IndexOrderDefault Ascending|Descending Name|Date|Size|Description
Default:	IndexOrderDefault Ascending Name
Context:	server config, virtual host, directory, .htaccess
Override:	Indexes
Status:	Base
Module:	mod_autoindex

The IndexOrderDefault directive is used in combination with the FancyIndexing index option. By default, fancyindexed directory listings are displayed in ascending order by filename; the IndexOrderDefault allows you to change this initial display order.

IndexOrderDefault takes two arguments. The first must be either Ascending or Descending, indicating the direction of the sort. The second argument must be one of the keywords Name, Date, Size, or Description, and identifies the primary key. The secondary key is *always* the ascending filename.

You can force a directory listing to only be displayed in a particular order by combining this directive with the SuppressColumnSorting index option; this will prevent the client from requesting the directory listing in a different order.

IndexStyleSheet Directive

Description:	Adds a CSS stylesheet to the directory index
Syntax:	IndexStyleSheet *url-path*
Context:	server config, virtual host, directory, .htaccess
Override:	Indexes
Status:	Base
Module:	mod_autoindex

The `IndexStyleSheet` directive sets the name of the file that will be used as the CSS for the index listing.

Example
```
IndexStyleSheet "/css/style.css"
```

ReadmeName Directive

Description:	Name of the file that will be inserted at the end of the index listing
Syntax:	ReadmeName *filename*
Context:	server config, virtual host, directory, .htaccess
Override:	Indexes
Status:	Base
Module:	mod_autoindex

The `ReadmeName` directive sets the name of the file that will be appended to the end of the index listing. *Filename* is the name of the file to include, and is taken to be relative to the location being indexed. If *Filename* begins with a slash, it will be taken to be relative to the `DocumentRoot`.

Example
```
ReadmeName FOOTER.html
```

Example 2
```
ReadmeName /include/FOOTER.html
```

See also `HeaderName`, where this behavior is described in greater detail.

3.23 Apache Module mod-cache

Description:	Content cache keyed to URIs.
Status:	Extension
Module Identifier:	cache_module
Source File:	mod_cache.c

Summary

This module should be used with care and can be used to circumvent Allow and Deny directives. You should not enable caching for any content to which you wish to limit access by client host name, address or environment variable.

mod-cache implements an RFC 2616[20] compliant HTTP content cache that can be used to cache either local or proxied content. mod-cache requires the services of one or more storage management modules. Two storage management modules are included in the base Apache distribution:

mod-disk-cache implements a disk based storage manager.

mod-mem-cache implements a memory based storage manager. mod-mem-cache can be configured to operate in two modes: caching open file descriptors or caching objects in heap storage. mod-mem-cache can be used to cache locally generated content or to cache backend server content for mod_proxy when configured using ProxyPass (aka **reverse proxy**)

Content is stored in and retrieved from the cache using URI based keys. Content with access protection is not cached.

Further details, discussion, and examples, are provided in the Caching Guide (p. 639).

Directives:

CacheDefaultExpire	CacheLastModifiedFactor
CacheDisable	CacheLock
CacheEnable	CacheLockMaxAge
CacheIgnoreCacheControl	CacheLockPath
CacheIgnoreHeaders	CacheMaxExpire
CacheIgnoreNoLastMod	CacheStoreNoStore
CacheIgnoreQueryString	CacheStorePrivate
CacheIgnoreURLSessionIdentifiers	

See also:

▷ Caching Guide (p. 639)

---

[20]http://www.ietf.org/rfc/rfc2616.txt

3.23.1 Related Modules and Directives

Related Modules	Related Directives
mod_disk_cache	CacheRoot
mod_mem_cache	CacheDirLevels
	CacheDirLength
	CacheMinFileSize
	CacheMaxFileSize
	MCacheSize
	MCacheMaxObjectCount
	MCacheMinObjectSize
	MCacheMaxObjectSize
	MCacheRemovalAlgorithm
	MCacheMaxStreamingBuffer

3.23.2 Sample Configuration

Sample httpd.conf

```
#
# Sample Cache Configuration
#
LoadModule cache_module modules/mod_cache.so

<IfModule mod_cache.c>
    #LoadModule disk_cache_module modules/mod_disk_cache.so
    # If you want to use mod_disk_cache instead of mod_mem_cache,
    # uncomment the line above and comment out the LoadModule
    line below.
    <IfModule mod_disk_cache.c>

        CacheRoot c:/cacheroot
        CacheEnable disk /
        CacheDirLevels 5
        CacheDirLength 3

    </IfModule>

    LoadModule mem_cache_module modules/mod_mem_cache.so
    <IfModule mod_mem_cache.c>

        CacheEnable mem /
        MCacheSize 4096
        MCacheMaxObjectCount 100
        MCacheMinObjectSize 1
        MCacheMaxObjectSize 2048

    </IfModule>

    # When acting as a proxy, don't cache the list of security
    updates
    CacheDisable http://security.update.server/update-list/
</IfModule>
```

3.23.3 Avoiding the Thundering Herd

When a cached entry becomes stale, mod_cache will submit a conditional request to the backend, which is expected to confirm whether the cached entry is still fresh, and send an updated entity if not.

A small but finite amount of time exists between the time the cached entity becomes stale, and the time the stale entity is fully refreshed. On a busy server, a significant number of requests might arrive during this time, and cause a **thundering herd** of requests to strike the backend suddenly and unpredictably.

To keep the thundering herd at bay, the CacheLock directive can be used to define a directory in which locks are created for URLs **in flight**. The lock is used as a **hint** by other requests to either suppress an attempt to cache (someone else has gone to fetch the entity), or to indicate that a stale entry is being refreshed (stale content will be returned in the mean time).

Initial caching of an entry

When an entity is cached for the first time, a lock will be created for the entity until the response has been fully cached. During the lifetime of the lock, the cache will suppress the second and subsequent attempt to cache the same entity. While this doesn't hold back the thundering herd, it does stop the cache attempting to cache the same entity multiple times simultaneously.

Refreshment of a stale entry

When an entity reaches its freshness lifetime and becomes stale, a lock will be created for the entity until the response has either been confirmed as still fresh, or replaced by the backend. During the lifetime of the lock, the second and subsequent incoming request will cause stale data to be returned, and the thundering herd is kept at bay.

Locks and Cache-Control: no-cache

Locks are used as a **hint only** to enable the cache to be more gentle on backend servers, however the lock can be overridden if necessary. If the client sends a request with a Cache-Control header forcing a reload, any lock that may be present will be ignored, and the client's request will be honoured immediately and the cached entry refreshed.

As a further safety mechanism, locks have a configurable maximum age. Once this age has been reached, the lock is removed, and a new request is given the opportunity to create a new lock. This maximum age can be set using the CacheLockMaxAge directive, and defaults to 5 seconds.

Example configuration

Enabling the cache lock
```
#
# Enable the cache lock
```

```
#
<IfModule mod_cache.c>
    CacheLock on
    CacheLockPath /tmp/mod_cache-lock
    CacheLockMaxAge 5
</IfModule>
```

CacheDefaultExpire Directive

Description:	The default duration to cache a document when no expiry date is specified.
Syntax:	CacheDefaultExpire *seconds*
Default:	CacheDefaultExpire 3600 (one hour)
Context:	server config, virtual host
Status:	Extension
Module:	mod_cache

The CacheDefaultExpire directive specifies a default time, in seconds, to cache a document if neither an expiry date nor last-modified date are provided with the document. The value specified with the CacheMaxExpire directive does *not* override this setting.

```
CacheDefaultExpire 86400
```

CacheDisable Directive

Description:	Disable caching of specified URLs
Syntax:	CacheDisable *url-string*
Context:	server config, virtual host
Status:	Extension
Module:	mod_cache

The CacheDisable directive instructs mod_cache to *not* cache urls at or below *url-string*.

Example
```
CacheDisable /local_files
```

The no-cache environment variable can be set to disable caching on a finer grained set of resources in versions 2.2.12 and later.

See also:

▷ Environment Variables in Apache (p. 705)

CacheEnable Directive

Description:	Enable caching of specified URLs using a specified storage manager
Syntax:	CacheEnable *cache_type url-string*
Context:	server config, virtual host
Status:	Extension
Module:	mod_cache

The CacheEnable directive instructs mod_cache to cache urls at or below *url-string*. The cache storage manager is specified with the *cache_type* argument. *cache_type* mem instructs mod_cache to use the memory based storage manager implemented by mod_mem_cache. *cache_type* disk instructs mod_cache to use the disk based storage manager implemented by mod_disk_cache. *cache_type* fd instructs mod_cache to use the file descriptor cache implemented by mod_-mem_cache.

In the event that the URL space overlaps between different CacheEnable directives (as in the example below), each possible storage manager will be run until the first one that actually processes the request. The order in which the storage managers are run is determined by the order of the CacheEnable directives in the configuration file.

```
CacheEnable mem /manual
CacheEnable fd /images
CacheEnable disk /
```

When acting as a forward proxy server, *url-string* can also be used to specify remote sites and proxy protocols which caching should be enabled for.

```
# Cache proxied url's
CacheEnable disk /

# Cache FTP-proxied url's
CacheEnable disk ftp://

# Cache content from www.apache.org
CacheEnable disk http://www.apache.org/
```

The no-cache environment variable can be set to disable caching on a finer grained set of resources in versions 2.2.12 and later.

See also:

▷ Environment Variables in Apache (p. 705)

CacheIgnoreCacheControl Directive

Description:	Ignore request to not serve cached content to client
Syntax:	CacheIgnoreCacheControl On|Off
Default:	CacheIgnoreCacheControl Off
Context:	server config, virtual host
Status:	Extension
Module:	mod_cache

Ordinarily, requests containing a Cache-Control: no-cache or Pragma: no-cache header value will not be served from the cache. The CacheIgnoreCacheControl directive allows this behavior to be overridden. CacheIgnoreCacheControl On tells the server to attempt to serve the resource from the cache even if the request contains no-cache header values. Resources requiring authorization will *never* be cached.

```
CacheIgnoreCacheControl On
```

> WARNING: *This directive will allow serving from the cache even if the client has requested that the document not be served from the cache. This might result in stale content being served.*

See also:

- ▷ CacheStorePrivate (p. 225)
- ▷ CacheStoreNoStore (p. 225)

CacheIgnoreHeaders Directive

Description:	Do not store the given HTTP header(s) in the cache.
Syntax:	CacheIgnoreHeaders header-string [header-string] ...
Default:	CacheIgnoreHeaders None
Context:	server config, virtual host
Status:	Extension
Module:	mod_cache

According to RFC 2616, hop-by-hop HTTP headers are not stored in the cache. The following HTTP headers are hop-by-hop headers and thus do not get stored in the cache in *any* case regardless of the setting of CacheIgnoreHeaders:

- Connection
- Keep-Alive
- Proxy-Authenticate
- Proxy-Authorization
- TE
- Trailers

- Transfer-Encoding

- Upgrade

CacheIgnoreHeaders specifies additional HTTP headers that should not to be stored in the cache. For example, it makes sense in some cases to prevent cookies from being stored in the cache.

CacheIgnoreHeaders takes a space separated list of HTTP headers that should not be stored in the cache. If only hop-by-hop headers not should be stored in the cache (the RFC 2616 compliant behaviour), CacheIgnoreHeaders can be set to None.

Example 1
    CacheIgnoreHeaders Set-Cookie

Example 2
    CacheIgnoreHeaders None

WARNING: *If headers like Expires which are needed for proper cache management are not stored due to a CacheIgnoreHeaders setting, the behaviour of mod_cache is undefined.*

CacheIgnoreNoLastMod Directive

Description:	Ignore the fact that a response has no Last Modified header.
Syntax:	CacheIgnoreNoLastMod On|Off
Default:	CacheIgnoreNoLastMod Off
Context:	server config, virtual host
Status:	Extension
Module:	mod_cache

Ordinarily, documents without a last-modified date are not cached. Under some circumstances the last-modified date is removed (during mod_include process-ing for example) or not provided at all. The CacheIgnoreNoLastMod directive provides a way to specify that documents without last-modified dates should be considered for caching, even without a last-modified date. If neither a last-modified date nor an expiry date are provided with the document then the value specified by the CacheDefaultExpire directive will be used to generate an expiration date.

    CacheIgnoreNoLastMod On

CacheIgnoreQueryString Directive

Description:	Ignore query string when caching
Syntax:	`CacheIgnoreQueryString On|Off`
Default:	`CacheIgnoreQueryString Off`
Context:	server config, virtual host
Status:	Extension
Module:	mod_cache
Compatibility:	Available in Apache 2.2.6 and later

Ordinarily, requests with query string parameters are cached separately for each unique query string. This is according to RFC 2616/13.9 done only if an expiration time is specified. The `CacheIgnoreQueryString` directive tells the cache to cache requests even if no expiration time is specified, and to reply with a cached reply even if the query string differs. From a caching point of view the request is treated as if having no query string when this directive is enabled.

```
CacheIgnoreQueryString On
```

CacheIgnoreURLSessionIdentifiers Directive

Description:	Ignore defined session identifiers encoded in the URL when caching
Syntax:	`CacheIgnoreURLSessionIdentifiers identifier [identifier] ...`
Default:	`CacheIgnoreURLSessionIdentifiers None`
Context:	server config, virtual host
Status:	Extension
Module:	mod_cache

Sometimes applications encode the session identifier into the URL as in the following examples:

- `/someapplication/image.gif;jsessionid=123456789`
- `/someapplication/image.gif?PHPSESSIONID=12345678`

This causes cacheable resources to be stored separately for each session, which is often not desired. `CacheIgnoreURLSessionIdentifiers` lets define a list of identifiers that are removed from the key that is used to identify an entity in the cache, such that cacheable resources are not stored separately for each session.

`CacheIgnoreURLSessionIdentifiers None` clears the list of ignored identifiers. Otherwise, each identifier is added to the list.

Example 1
```
CacheIgnoreURLSessionIdentifiers jsessionid
```

Example 2
```
CacheIgnoreURLSessionIdentifiers None
```

CacheLastModifiedFactor Directive

Description:	The factor used to compute an expiry date based on the LastModified date.
Syntax:	CacheLastModifiedFactor *float*
Default:	CacheLastModifiedFactor 0.1
Context:	server config, virtual host
Status:	Extension
Module:	mod_cache

In the event that a document does not provide an expiry date but does provide a last-modified date, an expiry date can be calculated based on the time since the document was last modified. The CacheLastModifiedFactor directive specifies a *factor* to be used in the generation of this expiry date according to the following formula:

```
expiry-period = time-since-last-modified-date * factor expiry-date
= current-date + expiry-period
```

For example, if the document was last modified 10 hours ago, and *factor* is 0.1 then the expiry-period will be set to 10*0.1 = 1 hour. If the current time was 3:00pm then the computed expiry-date would be 3:00pm + 1hour = 4:00pm.

If the expiry-period would be longer than that set by CacheMaxExpire, then the latter takes precedence.

```
CacheLastModifiedFactor 0.5
```

CacheLock Directive

Description:	Enable the thundering herd lock.
Syntax:	CacheLock *on/off*
Default:	CacheLock off
Context:	server config, virtual host
Status:	Extension
Module:	mod_cache
Compatibility:	Available in Apache 2.2.15 and later

The CacheLock directive enables the thundering herd lock for the given URL space.

In a minimal configuration the following directive is all that is needed to enable the thundering herd lock in the default system temp directory.

```
# Enable chache lock
CacheLock on
```

CacheLockMaxAge Directive

Description:	Set the maximum possible age of a cache lock.
Syntax:	CacheLockMaxAge *integer*
Default:	CacheLockMaxAge 5
Context:	server config, virtual host
Status:	Extension
Module:	mod_cache

The CacheLockMaxAge directive specifies the maximum age of any cache lock.

A lock older than this value in seconds will be ignored, and the next incoming request will be given the opportunity to re-establish the lock. This mechanism prevents a slow client taking an excessively long time to refresh an entity.

CacheLockPath Directive

Description:	Set the lock path directory.
Syntax:	CacheLockPath *directory*
Default:	CacheLockPath /tmp/mod_cache-lock
Context:	server config, virtual host
Status:	Extension
Module:	mod_cache

The CacheLockPath directive allows you to specify the directory in which the locks are created. By default, the system's temporary folder is used. Locks consist of empty files that only exist for stale URLs in flight, so is significantly less resource intensive than the traditional disk cache.

CacheMaxExpire Directive

Description:	The maximum time in seconds to cache a document
Syntax:	CacheMaxExpire *seconds*
Default:	CacheMaxExpire 86400 (one day)
Context:	server config, virtual host
Status:	Extension
Module:	mod_cache

The CacheMaxExpire directive specifies the maximum number of seconds for which cacheable HTTP documents will be retained without checking the origin server. Thus, documents will be out of date at most this number of seconds. This maximum value is enforced even if an expiry date was supplied with the document.

    CacheMaxExpire 604800

CacheStoreNoStore Directive

Description:	Attempt to cache requests or responses that have been marked as no-store.
Syntax:	CacheStoreNoStore On|Off
Default:	CacheStoreNoStore Off
Context:	server config, virtual host
Status:	Extension
Module:	mod_cache

Ordinarily, requests or responses with Cache-Control: no-store header values will not be stored in the cache. The CacheStoreNoCache directive allows this behavior to be overridden. CacheStoreNoCache On tells the server to attempt to cache the resource even if it contains no-store header values. Resources requiring authorization will *never* be cached.

```
CacheStoreNoStore On
```

WARNING: *As described in RFC 2616, the no-store directive is intended to "prevent the inadvertent release or retention of sensitive information (for example, on backup tapes)." Enabling this option could store sensitive information in the cache. You are hereby warned.*

See also:

▷ CacheIgnoreCacheControl (p. 220)

▷ CacheStorePrivate (p. 225)

CacheStorePrivate Directive

Description:	Attempt to cache responses that the server has marked as private
Syntax:	CacheStorePrivate On|Off
Default:	CacheStorePrivate Off
Context:	server config, virtual host
Status:	Extension
Module:	mod_cache

Ordinarily, responses with Cache-Control: private header values will not be stored in the cache. The CacheStorePrivate directive allows this behavior to be overridden. CacheStorePrivate On tells the server to attempt to cache the resource even if it contains private header values. Resources requiring authorization will *never* be cached.

```
CacheStorePrivate On
```

WARNING: *This directive will allow caching even if the upstream server has requested that the resource not be cached. This directive is only ideal for a 'private' cache.*

See also:

▷ CacheIgnoreCacheControl (p. 220)

▷ CacheStoreNoStore (p. 225)

3.24 Apache Module mod_cern_meta

Description:	CERN httpd metafile semantics
Status:	Extension
Module Identifier:	cern_meta_module
Source File:	mod_cern_meta.c

Summary

Emulate the CERN HTTPD Meta file semantics. Meta files are HTTP headers that can be output in addition to the normal range of headers for each file accessed. They appear rather like the Apache .asis files, and are able to provide a crude way of influencing the Expires: header, as well as providing other curiosities. There are many ways to manage meta information, this one was chosen because there is already a large number of CERN users who can exploit this module.

More information on the CERN metafile semantics[21] is available.

Directives:

    MetaDir
    MetaFiles
    MetaSuffix

See also:

   ▷ mod_headers (p. 289)

   ▷ mod_asis (p. 148)

MetaDir Directive

Description:	Name of the directory to find CERN-style meta information files
Syntax:	MetaDir *directory*
Default:	MetaDir .web
Context:	server config, virtual host, directory, .htaccess
Override:	Indexes
Status:	Extension
Module:	mod_cern_meta

Specifies the name of the directory in which Apache can find meta information files. The directory is usually a 'hidden' subdirectory of the directory that contains the file being accessed. Set to "." to look in the same directory as the file:

    MetaDir .

Or, to set it to a subdirectory of the directory containing the files:

---

[21]http://www.w3.org/pub/WWW/Daemon/User/Config/General.html#MetaDir

```
MetaDir .meta
```

MetaFiles Directive

Description:	Activates CERN meta-file processing
Syntax:	`MetaFiles on|off`
Default:	`MetaFiles off`
Context:	server config, virtual host, directory, .htaccess
Override:	Indexes
Status:	Extension
Module:	mod_cern_meta

Turns on/off Meta file processing on a per-directory basis.

MetaSuffix Directive

Description:	File name suffix for the file containing CERN-style meta information
Syntax:	`MetaSuffix suffix`
Default:	`MetaSuffix .meta`
Context:	server config, virtual host, directory, .htaccess
Override:	Indexes
Status:	Extension
Module:	mod_cern_meta

Specifies the file name suffix for the file containing the meta information. For example, the default values for the two directives will cause a request to DOCUMENT_ROOT/somedir/index.html to look in DOCUMENT_-ROOT/somedir/.web/index.html.meta and will use its contents to generate additional MIME header information.

Example:
```
MetaSuffix .meta
```

3.25 Apache Module mod_cgi

Description:	Execution of CGI scripts
Status:	Base
Module Identifier:	cgi_module
Source File:	mod_cgi.c

Summary

Any file that has the handler cgi-script will be treated as a CGI script, and run by the server, with its output being returned to the client. Files acquire this handler either by having a name containing an extension defined by the AddHandler directive, or by being in a ScriptAlias directory.

For an introduction to using CGI scripts with Apache, see our tutorial on Dynamic Content With CGI (p. 651).

When using a multi-threaded MPM under Unix, the module mod_cgid should be used in place of this module. At the user level, the two modules are essentially identical.

For backward-compatibility, the CGI script handler will also be activated for any file with the mime-type application/x-httpd-cgi. The use of the magic mime-type is deprecated.

Directives:

> ScriptLog
> ScriptLogBuffer
> ScriptLogLength

See also:

▷ AcceptPathInfo (p. 89)

▷ Options (p. 120)

▷ ScriptAlias (p. 146)

▷ AddHandler (p. 353)

▷ Running CGI programs under different user IDs (p. 719)

▷ CGI Specification[22]

3.25.1 CGI Environment variables

The server will set the CGI environment variables as described in the CGI specification[23], with the following provisions:

PATH_INFO This will not be available if the AcceptPathInfo directive is explicitly set to off. The default behavior, if AcceptPathInfo is not

---

[22]http://hoohoo.ncsa.uiuc.edu/cgi/
[23]http://hoohoo.ncsa.uiuc.edu/cgi/

given, is that `mod_cgi` will accept path info (trailing `/more/path/info` following the script filename in the URI), while the core server will return a 404 NOT FOUND error for requests with additional path info. Omitting the `AcceptPathInfo` directive has the same effect as setting it `On` for `mod_cgi` requests.

REMOTE_HOST This will only be set if `HostnameLookups` is set to on (it is off by default), and if a reverse DNS lookup of the accessing host's address indeed finds a host name.

REMOTE_IDENT This will only be set if `IdentityCheck` is set to on and the accessing host supports the ident protocol. Note that the contents of this variable cannot be relied upon because it can easily be faked, and if there is a proxy between the client and the server, it is usually totally useless.

REMOTE_USER This will only be set if the CGI script is subject to authentication.

3.25.2 CGI Debugging

Debugging CGI scripts has traditionally been difficult, mainly because it has not been possible to study the output (standard output and error) for scripts which are failing to run properly. These directives, included in Apache 1.2 and later, provide more detailed logging of errors when they occur.

CGI Logfile Format

When configured, the CGI error log logs any CGI which does not execute properly. Each CGI script which fails to operate causes several lines of information to be logged. The first two lines are always of the format:

```
%% [time] request-line
%% HTTP-status CGI-script-filename
```

If the error is that the CGI script cannot be run, the log file will contain an extra two lines:

```
%%error
error-message
```

Alternatively, if the error is the result of the script returning incorrect header information (often due to a bug in the script), the following information is logged:

```
%request
All HTTP request headers received
POST or PUT entity (if any)
%response
All headers output by the CGI script
%stdout
CGI standard output
```

%stderr
CGI standard error

(The %stdout and %stderr parts may be missing if the script did not output anything on standard output or standard error).

ScriptLog Directive

Description:	Location of the CGI script error logfile
Syntax:	ScriptLog *file-path*
Context:	server config, virtual host
Status:	Base
Module:	mod_cgi, mod_cgid

The ScriptLog directive sets the CGI script error logfile. If no ScriptLog is given, no error log is created. If given, any CGI errors are logged into the filename given as argument. If this is a relative file or path it is taken relative to the ServerRoot.

Example
ScriptLog logs/cgi_log

This log will be opened as the user the child processes run as, *i.e.* the user specified in the main User directive. This means that either the directory the script log is in needs to be writable by that user or the file needs to be manually created and set to be writable by that user. If you place the script log in your main logs directory, do **NOT** change the directory permissions to make it writable by the user the child processes run as.

Note that script logging is meant to be a debugging feature when writing CGI scripts, and is not meant to be activated continuously on running servers. It is not optimized for speed or efficiency, and may have security problems if used in a manner other than that for which it was designed.

ScriptLogBuffer Directive

Description:	Maximum amount of PUT or POST requests that will be recorded in the scriptlog
Syntax:	ScriptLogBuffer *bytes*
Default:	ScriptLogBuffer 1024
Context:	server config, virtual host
Status:	Base
Module:	mod_cgi, mod_cgid

The size of any PUT or POST entity body that is logged to the file is limited, to prevent the log file growing too big too quickly if large bodies are being received. By default, up to 1024 bytes are logged, but this can be changed with this directive.

ScriptLogLength Directive

Description:	Size limit of the CGI script logfile
Syntax:	ScriptLogLength *bytes*
Default:	ScriptLogLength 10385760
Context:	server config, virtual host
Status:	Base
Module:	mod_cgi, mod_cgid

ScriptLogLength can be used to limit the size of the CGI script logfile. Since the logfile logs a lot of information per CGI error (all request headers, all script output) it can grow to be a big file. To prevent problems due to unbounded growth, this directive can be used to set an maximum file-size for the CGI logfile. If the file exceeds this size, no more information will be written to it.

3.26 Apache Module mod_cgid

Description:	Execution of CGI scripts using an external CGI daemon
Status:	Base
Module Identifier:	cgid_module
Source File:	mod_cgid.c
Compatibility:	Unix threaded MPMs only

Summary

Except for the optimizations and the additional ScriptSock directive noted below, mod_cgid behaves similarly to mod_cgi. **See the mod_cgi summary for additional details about Apache and CGI.**

On certain Unix operating systems, forking a process from a multi-threaded server is a very expensive operation because the new process will replicate all the threads of the parent process. In order to avoid incurring this expense on each CGI invocation, mod_cgid creates an external daemon that is responsible for forking child processes to run CGI scripts. The main server communicates with this daemon using a unix domain socket.

This module is used by default instead of mod_cgi whenever a multi-threaded MPM is selected during the compilation process. At the user level, this module is identical in configuration and operation to mod_cgi. The only exception is the additional directive ScriptSock which gives the name of the socket to use for communication with the cgi daemon.

Directives:

> ScriptLog (p. 231)
> ScriptLogBuffer (p. 231)
> ScriptLogLength (p. 232)
> ScriptSock

See also:

> ▷ mod_cgi (p. 229)

> ▷ Running CGI programs under different user IDs (p. 719)

ScriptSock Directive

Description:	The filename prefix of the socket to use for communication with the CGI daemon
Syntax:	ScriptSock *file-path*
Default:	ScriptSock logs/cgisock
Context:	server config
Status:	Base
Module:	mod_cgid

This directive sets the filename prefix of the socket to use for communication with the CGI daemon, an extension corresponding to the process ID of the server will be appended. The socket will be opened using the permissions of the user who starts Apache (usually root). To maintain the security of communications with CGI scripts, it is important that no other user has permission to write in the directory where the socket is located.

Example
```
ScriptSock /var/run/cgid.sock
```

3.27 Apache Module mod_charset_lite

Description:	Specify character set translation or recoding
Status:	Extension
Module Identifier:	charset_lite_module
Source File:	mod_charset_lite.c

Summary

mod_charset_lite allows the server to change the character set of responses before sending them to the client. In an EBCDIC environment, Apache always translates HTTP protocol content (e.g. response headers) from the code page of the Apache process locale to ISO-8859-1, but not the body of responses. In any environment, mod_charset_lite can be used to specify that response bodies should be translated. For example, if files are stored in EBCDIC, then mod_charset_lite can translate them to ISO-8859-1 before sending them to the client.

This module provides a small subset of configuration mechanisms implemented by Russian Apache and its associated mod_charset.

Directives:

> CharsetDefault
> CharsetOptions
> CharsetSourceEnc

3.27.1 Common Problems

Invalid character set names

The character set name parameters of CharsetSourceEnc and CharsetDefault must be acceptable to the translation mechanism used by APR on the system where mod_charset_lite is deployed. These character set names are not standardized and are usually not the same as the corresponding values used in http headers. Currently, APR can only use iconv(3), so you can easily test your character set names using the iconv(1) program, as follows:

```
iconv -f charsetsourceenc-value -t charsetdefault-value
```

Mismatch between character set of content and translation rules

If the translation rules don't make sense for the content, translation can fail in various ways, including:

- The translation mechanism may return a bad return code, and the connection will be aborted.

- The translation mechanism may silently place special characters (e.g., question marks) in the output buffer when it cannot translate the input buffer.

CharsetDefault Directive

Description:	Charset to translate into
Syntax:	CharsetDefault charset
Context:	server config, virtual host, directory, .htaccess
Override:	FileInfo
Status:	Extension
Module:	mod_charset_lite

The CharsetDefault directive specifies the charset that content in the associated container should be translated to.

The value of the *charset* argument must be accepted as a valid character set name by the character set support in APR. Generally, this means that it must be supported by iconv.

Example
```
<Directory /export/home/trawick/apacheinst/htdocs/convert>
    CharsetSourceEnc UTF-16BE
    CharsetDefault ISO-8859-1
</Directory>
```

CharsetOptions Directive

Description:	Configures charset translation behavior
Syntax:	CharsetOptions option [option] ...
Default:	CharsetOptions DebugLevel=0 NoImplicitAdd
Context:	server config, virtual host, directory, .htaccess
Override:	FileInfo
Status:	Extension
Module:	mod_charset_lite

The CharsetOptions directive configures certain behaviors of mod_charset_-lite. *Option* can be one of

DebugLevel=n The DebugLevel keyword allows you to specify the level of debug messages generated by mod_charset_lite. By default, no messages are generated. This is equivalent to DebugLevel=0. With higher numbers, more debug messages are generated, and server performance will be degraded. The actual meanings of the numeric values are described with the definitions of the DBGLVL_ constants near the beginning of mod_-charset_lite.c.

ImplicitAdd | NoImplicitAdd The ImplicitAdd keyword specifies that mod_-charset_lite should implicitly insert its filter when the configuration specifies that the character set of content should be translated. If the filter chain is explicitly configured using the AddOutputFilter directive, NoImplicitAdd should be specified so that mod_charset_lite doesn't add its filter.

TranslateAllMimeTypes | NoTranslateAllMimeTypes Normally,   mod_-
charset_lite will only perform translation on a small subset of possible
mimetypes. When the **TranslateAllMimeTypes** keyword is specified for
a given configuration section, translation is performed without regard for
mimetype.

CharsetSourceEnc Directive

Description:	Source charset of files
Syntax:	CharsetSourceEnc *charset*
Context:	server config, virtual host, directory, .htaccess
Override:	FileInfo
Status:	Extension
Module:	mod_charset_lite

The CharsetSourceEnc directive specifies the source charset of files in the associated container.

The value of the *charset* argument must be accepted as a valid character set
name by the character set support in APR. Generally, this means that it must
be supported by iconv.

Example
```
<Directory /export/home/trawick/apacheinst/htdocs/convert>
    CharsetSourceEnc UTF-16BE
    CharsetDefault ISO-8859-1
</Directory>
```

The character set names in this example work with the iconv translation support
in Solaris 8.

3.28 Apache Module mod_dav

Description:	Distributed Authoring and Versioning (WebDAV[24]) functionality
Status:	Extension
Module Identifier:	dav_module
Source File:	mod_dav.c

Summary

This module provides class 1 and class 2 WebDAV[25] ('Web-based Distributed Authoring and Versioning') functionality for Apache. This extension to the HTTP protocol allows creating, moving, copying, and deleting resources and collections on a remote web server.

Directives:

> Dav
> DavDepthInfinity
> DavMinTimeout

See also:

 ▷ DavLockDB (p. 242)

 ▷ LimitXMLRequestBody (p. 115)

 ▷ WebDAV Resources[26]

3.28.1 Enabling WebDAV

To enable mod_dav, add the following to a container in your httpd.conf file:

> Dav On

This enables the DAV file system provider, which is implemented by the mod_dav_fs module. Therefore, that module must be compiled into the server or loaded at runtime using the LoadModule directive.

In addition, a location for the DAV lock database must be specified in the global section of your httpd.conf file using the DavLockDB directive:

> DavLockDB /usr/local/apache2/var/DavLock

The directory containing the lock database file must be writable by the User and Group under which Apache is running.

You may wish to add a <Limit> clause inside the <Location> directive to limit access to DAV-enabled locations. If you want to set the maximum amount of bytes that a DAV client can send at one request, you have to use the

---

[24]http://www.webdav.org/
[25]http://www.webdav.org
[26]http://www.webdav.org

LimitXMLRequestBody directive. The "normal" LimitRequestBody directive has no effect on DAV requests.

Full Example

```
DavLockDB /usr/local/apache2/var/DavLock

<Location /foo>
    Order Allow,Deny
    Allow from all
    Dav On

    AuthType Basic
    AuthName DAV
    AuthUserFile user.passwd

    <LimitExcept GET OPTIONS>
        Require user admin
    </LimitExcept>
</Location>
```

mod_dav is a descendant of Greg Stein's mod_dav for Apache 1.3[27]. More information about the module is available from that site.

3.28.2 Security Issues

Since DAV access methods allow remote clients to manipulate files on the server, you must take particular care to assure that your server is secure before enabling mod_dav.

Any location on the server where DAV is enabled should be protected by authentication. The use of HTTP Basic Authentication is not recommended. You should use at least HTTP Digest Authentication, which is provided by the mod_auth_digest module. Nearly all WebDAV clients support this authentication method. An alternative is Basic Authentication over an SSL (p. 616) enabled connection.

In order for mod_dav to manage files, it must be able to write to the directories and files under its control using the User and Group under which Apache is running. New files created will also be owned by this User and Group. For this reason, it is important to control access to this account. The DAV repository is considered private to Apache; modifying files outside of Apache (for example using FTP or filesystem-level tools) should not be allowed.

mod_dav may be subject to various kinds of denial-of-service attacks. The LimitXMLRequestBody directive can be used to limit the amount of memory consumed in parsing large DAV requests. The DavDepthInfinity directive can be used to prevent PROPFIND requests on a very large repository from consuming large amounts of memory. Another possible denial-of-service attack involves a client simply filling up all available disk space with many large files. There is

---

[27]http://www.webdav.org/mod_dav/

no direct way to prevent this in Apache, so you should avoid giving DAV access
to untrusted users.

3.28.3 Complex Configurations

One common request is to use mod_dav to manipulate dynamic files (PHP scripts,
CGI scripts, etc). This is difficult because a GET request will always run the
script, rather than downloading its contents. One way to avoid this is to map
two different URLs to the content, one of which will run the script, and one of
which will allow it to be downloaded and manipulated with DAV.

```
Alias /phparea /home/gstein/php_files
Alias /php-source /home/gstein/php_files
<Location /php-source>
    DAV On
    ForceType text/plain
</Location>
```

With this setup, http://example.com/phparea can be used to access the output
of the PHP scripts, and http://example.com/php-source can be used with a
DAV client to manipulate them.

Dav Directive

Description:	Enable WebDAV HTTP methods
Syntax:	Dav On|Off|*provider-name*
Default:	Dav Off
Context:	directory
Status:	Extension
Module:	mod_dav

Use the Dav directive to enable the WebDAV HTTP methods for the given
container:

```
<Location /foo>
    Dav On
</Location>
```

The value On is actually an alias for the default provider filesystem which is
served by the mod_dav_fs module. Note, that once you have DAV enabled for
some location, it *cannot* be disabled for sublocations. For a complete configuration example have a look at the section above.

> *Do not enable WebDAV until you have secured your server. Otherwise
> everyone will be able to distribute files on your system.*

DavDepthInfinity Directive

Description:	Allow PROPFIND, Depth: Infinity requests
Syntax:	DavDepthInfinity on|off
Default:	DavDepthInfinity off
Context:	server config, virtual host, directory
Status:	Extension
Module:	mod_dav

Use the DavDepthInfinity directive to allow the processing of PROPFIND requests containing the header 'Depth: Infinity'. Because this type of request could constitute a denial-of-service attack, by default it is not allowed.

DavMinTimeout Directive

Description:	Minimum amount of time the server holds a lock on a DAV resource
Syntax:	DavMinTimeout seconds
Default:	DavMinTimeout 0
Context:	server config, virtual host, directory
Status:	Extension
Module:	mod_dav

When a client requests a DAV resource lock, it can also specify a time when the lock will be automatically removed by the server. This value is only a request, and the server can ignore it or inform the client of an arbitrary value.

Use the DavMinTimeout directive to specify, in seconds, the minimum lock timeout to return to a client. Microsoft Web Folders defaults to a timeout of 120 seconds; the DavMinTimeout can override this to a higher value (like 600 seconds) to reduce the chance of the client losing the lock due to network latency.

Example
```
<Location /MSWord>
    DavMinTimeout 600
</Location>
```

3.29 Apache Module mod_dav_fs

Description:	filesystem provider for mod_dav
Status:	Extension
Module Identifier:	dav_fs_module
Source File:	mod_dav_fs.c

Summary

This module *requires* the service of mod_dav. It acts as a support module for mod_dav and provides access to resources located in the server's file system. The formal name of this provider is filesystem. mod_dav backend providers will be invoked by using the Dav directive:

Example
```
Dav filesystem
```

Since filesystem is the default provider for mod_dav, you may simply use the value On instead.

Directives:

DavLockDB

See also:

▷ mod_dav (p. 238)

DavLockDB Directive

Description:	Location of the DAV lock database
Syntax:	DavLockDB *file-path*
Context:	server config, virtual host
Status:	Extension
Module:	mod_dav_fs

Use the DavLockDB directive to specify the full path to the lock database, excluding an extension. If the path is not absolute, it will be taken relative to ServerRoot. The implementation of mod_dav_fs uses a SDBM database to track user locks.

Example
```
DavLockDB var/DavLock
```

The directory containing the lock database file must be writable by the User and Group under which Apache is running. For security reasons, you should create a directory for this purpose rather than changing the permissions on an existing directory. In the above example, Apache will create files in the var/ directory under the ServerRoot with the base filename DavLock and extension name chosen by the server.

3.30 Apache Module mod_dav_lock

Description:	generic locking module for mod_dav
Status:	Extension
Module Identifier:	dav_lock_module
Source File:	mod_dav_lock.c
Compatibility:	Available in version 2.1 and later

Summary

This module implements a generic locking API which can be used by any backend provider of mod_dav. It *requires* at least the service of mod_dav. But without a backend provider which makes use of it, it's useless and should not be loaded into the server. A sample backend module which actually utilizes mod_dav_lock is mod_dav_svn[28], the subversion provider module.

Note that mod_dav_fs does *not* need this generic locking module, because it uses its own more specialized version.

In order to make mod_dav_lock functional, you just have to specify the location of the lock database using the DavGenericLockDB directive described below.

> DEVELOPER'S NOTE *In order to retrieve the pointer to the locking provider function, you have to use the ap_lookup_provider API with the arguments dav-lock, generic, and 0.*

Directives:

DavGenericLockDB

See also:

▷ mod_dav (p. 238)

DavGenericLockDB Directive

Description:	Location of the DAV lock database
Syntax:	DavGenericLockDB *file-path*
Context:	server config, virtual host, directory
Status:	Extension
Module:	mod_dav_lock

Use the DavGenericLockDB directive to specify the full path to the lock database, excluding an extension. If the path is not absolute, it will be interpreted relative to ServerRoot. The implementation of mod_dav_lock uses a SDBM database to track user locks.

Example
DavGenericLockDB var/DavLock

---

[28]http://subversion.tigris.org/

The directory containing the lock database file must be writable by the User and Group under which Apache is running. For security reasons, you should create a directory for this purpose rather than changing the permissions on an existing directory. In the above example, Apache will create files in the var/ directory under the ServerRoot with the base filename DavLock and an extension added by the server.

3.31 Apache Module mod_dbd

Description:	Manages SQL database connections
Status:	Extension
Module Identifier:	dbd_module
Source File:	mod_dbd.c
Compatibility:	Version 2.1 and later

Summary

mod_dbd manages SQL database connections using APR. It provides database connections on request to modules requiring SQL database functions, and takes care of managing databases with optimal efficiency and scalability for both threaded and non-threaded MPMs. For details, see the APR[29] website and this overview of the Apache DBD Framework[30] by its original developer.

Directives:

> DBDExptime
> DBDKeep
> DBDMax
> DBDMin
> DBDParams
> DBDPersist
> DBDPrepareSQL
> DBDriver

See also:

> ▷ Password Formats (p. 771)

3.31.1 Connection Pooling

This module manages database connections, in a manner optimised for the platform. On non-threaded platforms, it provides a persistent connection in the manner of classic LAMP (Linux, Apache, Mysql, Perl/PHP/Python). On threaded platforms, it provides an altogether more scalable and efficient *connection pool*, as described in this article at ApacheTutor[31]. Note that mod_dbd supersedes the modules presented in that article.

3.31.2 Apache DBD API

mod_dbd exports five functions for other modules to use. The API is as follows:

```
typedef struct {
    apr_dbd_t *handle;
```

---

[29]http://apr.apache.org/
[30]http://people.apache.org/~niq/dbd.html
[31]http://www.apachetutor.org/dev/reslist

```
      apr_dbd_driver_t *driver;
      apr_hash_t *prepared;
} ap_dbd_t;

/* Export functions to access the database */

/* acquire a connection that MUST be explicitly closed.
 * Returns NULL on error
 */
AP_DECLARE(ap_dbd_t*) ap_dbd_open(apr_pool_t*, server_rec*);

/* release a connection acquired with ap_dbd_open */
AP_DECLARE(void) ap_dbd_close(server_rec*, ap_dbd_t*);

/* acquire a connection that will have the lifetime of
 * a request and MUST NOT be explicitly closed. Return
 * NULL on error. This is the preferred function for
 * most applications.
 */
AP_DECLARE(ap_dbd_t*) ap_dbd_acquire(request_rec*);

/* acquire a connection that will have the lifetime of
 * a connection and MUST NOT be explicitly closed.
 * Return NULL on error.
 */
AP_DECLARE(ap_dbd_t*) ap_dbd_cacquire(request_rec*);

/* Prepare a statement for use by a client module */
AP_DECLARE(void) ap_dbd_prepare(server_rec*, const char*,
                                const char*);

/* Also export them as optional functions for modules
   that prefer it */
APR_DECLARE_OPTIONAL_FN(ap_dbd_t*, ap_dbd_open,
                        (apr_pool_t*, server_rec*));
APR_DECLARE_OPTIONAL_FN(void, ap_dbd_close,
                        (server_rec*, ap_dbd_t*));
APR_DECLARE_OPTIONAL_FN(ap_dbd_t*, ap_dbd_acquire,
                        (request_rec*));
APR_DECLARE_OPTIONAL_FN(ap_dbd_t*, ap_dbd_cacquire,
                        (conn_rec*));
APR_DECLARE_OPTIONAL_FN(void, ap_dbd_prepare,
                        (server_rec*, const char*, const char*));
```

3.31.3 SQL Prepared Statements

mod_dbd supports SQL prepared statements on behalf of modules that may wish
to use them. Each prepared statement must be assigned a name (label), and
they are stored in a hash: the prepared field of an ap_dbd_t. Hash entries are
of type apr_dbd_prepared_t and can be used in any of the apr_dbd prepared
statement SQL query or select commands.

It is up to DBD user modules to use the prepared statements and document
what statements can be specified in httpd.conf, or to provide their own directives
and use ap_dbd_prepare.

3.31.4 SECURITY WARNING

Any web/database application needs to secure itself against SQL injection attacks. In most cases, Apache DBD is safe, because applications use prepared
statements, and untrusted inputs are only ever used as data. Of course, if you
use it via third-party modules, you should ascertain what precautions they may
require.

However, the *FreeTDS* driver is inherently **unsafe**. The underlying library
doesn't support prepared statements, so the driver emulates them, and the
untrusted input is merged into the SQL statement.

It can be made safe by *untainting* all inputs: a process inspired by Perl's taint
checking. Each input is matched against a regexp, and only the match is used,
according to the Perl idiom:

```
$untrusted =~ /([a-z]+)/;
  $trusted = $1;
```

To use this, the untainting regexps must be included in the prepared statements
configured. The regexp follows immediately after the % in the prepared statement, and is enclosed in curly brackets {}. For example, if your application
expects alphanumeric input, you can use:

```
"SELECT foo FROM bar WHERE input = %s"
```

with other drivers, and suffer nothing worse than a failed query. But with
FreeTDS you'd need:

```
"SELECT foo FROM bar WHERE input = %{([A-Za-z0-9]+)}s"
```

Now anything that doesn't match the regexp's $1 match is discarded, so the
statement is safe.

An alternative to this may be the third-party ODBC driver, which offers the
security of genuine prepared statements.

DBDExptime Directive

Description:	Keepalive time for idle connections
Syntax:	DBDExptime *time-in-seconds*
Default:	DBDExptime 300
Context:	server config, virtual host
Status:	Extension
Module:	mod_dbd

Set the time to keep idle connections alive when the number of connections specified in DBDKeep has been exceeded (threaded platforms only).

DBDKeep Directive

Description:	Maximum sustained number of connections
Syntax:	DBDKeep *number*
Default:	DBDKeep 2
Context:	server config, virtual host
Status:	Extension
Module:	mod_dbd

Set the maximum number of connections per process to be sustained, other than for handling peak demand (threaded platforms only).

DBDMax Directive

Description:	Maximum number of connections
Syntax:	DBDMax *number*
Default:	DBDMax 10
Context:	server config, virtual host
Status:	Extension
Module:	mod_dbd

Set the hard maximum number of connections per process (threaded platforms only).

DBDMin Directive

Description:	Minimum number of connections
Syntax:	DBDMin *number*
Default:	DBDMin 1
Context:	server config, virtual host
Status:	Extension
Module:	mod_dbd

Set the minimum number of connections per process (threaded platforms only).

DBDParams Directive

Description:	Parameters for database connection
Syntax:	DBDParams *param1=value1*[,*param2=value2*]
Context:	server config, virtual host
Status:	Extension
Module:	mod_dbd

As required by the underlying driver. Typically this will be used to pass whatever cannot be defaulted amongst username, password, database name, hostname and port number for connection.

Connection string parameters for current drivers include:

FreeTDS (for MSSQL and SyBase - see SECURITY note) username, password, appname, dbname, host, charset, lang, server

MySQL host, port, user, pass, dbname, sock, flags, fldsz, group, reconnect

ODBC datasource, user, password, connect, ctimeout, stimeout, access, tx-mode, bufsize

Oracle user, pass, dbname, server

PostgreSQL The connection string is passed straight through to PQconnectdb

SQLite2 The connection string is split on a colon, and part1:part2 is used as sqlite_open(part1, atoi(part2), NULL)

SQLite3 The connection string is passed straight through to sqlite3_open

DBDPersist Directive

Description:	Whether to use persistent connections
Syntax:	DBDPersist On|Off
Context:	server config, virtual host
Status:	Extension
Module:	mod_dbd

If set to Off, persistent and pooled connections are disabled. A new database connection is opened when requested by a client, and closed immediately on release. This option is for debugging and low-usage servers.

The default is to enable a pool of persistent connections (or a single LAMP-style persistent connection in the case of a non-threaded server), and should almost always be used in operation.

Prior to version 2.2.2, this directive accepted only the values 0 and 1 instead of Off and On, respectively.

DBDPrepareSQL Directive

Description:	Define an SQL prepared statement
Syntax:	DBDPrepareSQL *"SQL statement" label*
Context:	server config, virtual host
Status:	Extension
Module:	mod_dbd

For modules such as authentication that repeatedly use a single SQL statement, optimum performance is achieved by preparing the statement at startup rather than every time it is used. This directive prepares an SQL statement and assigns it a label.

DBDriver Directive

Description:	Specify an SQL driver
Syntax:	DBDriver *name*
Context:	server config, virtual host
Status:	Extension
Module:	mod_dbd

Selects an apr_dbd driver by name. The driver must be installed on your system (on most systems, it will be a shared object or DLL). For example, DBDriver mysql will select the MySQL driver in apr_dbd_mysql.so.

3.32 Apache Module mod_deflate

Description:	Compress content before it is delivered to the client
Status:	Extension
Module Identifier:	deflate_module
Source File:	mod_deflate.c

Summary

The mod_deflate module provides the DEFLATE output filter that allows output from your server to be compressed before being sent to the client over the network.

Directives:

    DeflateBufferSize
    DeflateCompressionLevel
    DeflateFilterNote
    DeflateMemLevel
    DeflateWindowSize

See also:

▷ Filters (p. 715)

3.32.1 Sample Configurations

This is a simple sample configuration for the impatient.

Compress only a few types
    AddOutputFilterByType DEFLATE text/html text/plain text/xml

The following configuration, while resulting in more compressed content, is also much more complicated. Do not use this unless you fully understand all the configuration details.

Compress everything except images
    <Location />
        # Insert filter
        SetOutputFilter DEFLATE

        # Netscape 4.x has some problems...
        BrowserMatch ^Mozilla/4 gzip-only-text/html

        # Netscape 4.06-4.08 have some more problems
        BrowserMatch ^Mozilla/4\.0[678] no-gzip

        # MSIE masquerades as Netscape, but it is fine
        BrowserMatch \bMSIE !no-gzip !gzip-only-text/html
        # Don't compress images
        SetEnvIfNoCase Request_URI \
            \.(?:gif|jpe?g|png)$ no-gzip dont-vary

```
    # Make sure proxies don't deliver the wrong content
    Header append Vary User-Agent env=!dont-vary
</Location>
```

3.32.2 Enabling Compression

Output Compression

Compression is implemented by the DEFLATE filter (p. 715). The following directive will enable compression for documents in the container where it is placed:

```
    SetOutputFilter DEFLATE
```

Some popular browsers cannot handle compression of all content so you may
want to set the gzip-only-text/html note to 1 to only allow HTML files to be
compressed (see below). If you set this to *anything but 1* it will be ignored.

If you want to restrict the compression to particular MIME types in general, you
may use the AddOutputFilterByType directive. Here is an example of enabling
compression only for the HTML files of the Apache documentation:

```
    <Directory "/your-server-root/manual">
        AddOutputFilterByType DEFLATE text/html
    </Directory>
```

For browsers that have problems even with compression of all file types, use
the BrowserMatch directive to set the no-gzip note for that particular browser
so that no compression will be performed. You may combine no-gzip with
gzip-only-text/html to get the best results. In that case the former overrides
the latter. Take a look at the following excerpt from the configuration example
defined in the section above:

```
    BrowserMatch ^Mozilla/4 gzip-only-text/html
    BrowserMatch ^Mozilla/4\.0[678] no-gzip
    BrowserMatch \bMSIE !no-gzip !gzip-only-text/html
```

At first we probe for a User-Agent string that indicates a Netscape Navigator
version of 4.x. These versions cannot handle compression of types other than
text/html. The versions 4.06, 4.07 and 4.08 also have problems with decompressing HTML files. Thus, we completely turn off the deflate filter for them.

The third BrowserMatch directive fixes the guessed identity of the user agent,
because the Microsoft Internet Explorer identifies itself also as "Mozilla/4" but
is actually able to handle requested compression. Therefore we match against
the additional string "MSIE" (\b means "word boundary") in the User-Agent
Header and turn off the restrictions defined before.

NOTE   *The DEFLATE filter is always inserted after RESOURCE filters like
         PHP or SSI. It never touches internal subrequests.*

NOTE   *There is a environment variable force-gzip, set via SetEnv, which
         will ignore the accept-encoding setting of your browser and will send*

compressed output.

Output Decompression

The mod_deflate module also provides a filter for inflating/uncompressing a gzip compressed response body. In order to activate this feature you have to insert the INFLATE filter into the outputfilter chain using SetOutputFilter or AddOutputFilter, for example:

```
<Location /dav-area>
    ProxyPass http://example.com/
    SetOutputFilter INFLATE
</Location>
```

This Example will uncompress gzip'ed output from example.com, so other filters can do further processing with it.

Input Decompression

The mod_deflate module also provides a filter for decompressing a gzip compressed request body. In order to activate this feature you have to insert the DEFLATE filter into the input filter chain using SetInputFilter or AddInputFilter, for example:

```
<Location /dav-area>
    SetInputFilter DEFLATE
</Location>
```

Now if a request contains a Content-Encoding: gzip header, the body will be automatically decompressed. Few browsers have the ability to gzip request bodies. However, some special applications actually do support request compression, for instance some WebDAV[32] clients.

> NOTE ON CONTENT-LENGTH *If you evaluate the request body yourself, don't trust the Content-Length header! The Content-Length header reflects the length of the incoming data from the client and not the byte count of the decompressed data stream.*

3.32.3 Dealing with proxy servers

The mod_deflate module sends a Vary: Accept-Encoding HTTP response header to alert proxies that a cached response should be sent only to clients that send the appropriate Accept-Encoding request header. This prevents compressed content from being sent to a client that will not understand it.

If you use some special exclusions dependent on, for example, the User-Agent header, you must manually configure an addition to the Vary header to alert proxies of the additional restrictions. For example, in a typical configuration where the addition of the DEFLATE filter depends on the User-Agent, you should add:

---

[32]http://www.webdav.org

```
Header append Vary User-Agent
```

If your decision about compression depends on other information than request
headers (e.g. HTTP version), you have to set the Vary header to the value *.
This prevents compliant proxies from caching entirely.

Example
```
Header set Vary *
```

DeflateBufferSize Directive

Description:	Fragment size to be compressed at one time by zlib
Syntax:	DeflateBufferSize value
Default:	DeflateBufferSize 8096
Context:	server config, virtual host
Status:	Extension
Module:	mod_deflate

The DeflateBufferSize directive specifies the size in bytes of the fragments
that zlib should compress at one time.

DeflateCompressionLevel Directive

Description:	How much compression do we apply to the output
Syntax:	DeflateCompressionLevel value
Default:	Zlib's default
Context:	server config, virtual host
Status:	Extension
Module:	mod_deflate
Compatibility:	This directive is available since Apache 2.0.45

The DeflateCompressionLevel directive specifies what level of compression
should be used, the higher the value, the better the compression, but the more
CPU time is required to achieve this.

The value must be between 1 (less compression) and 9 (more compression).

DeflateFilterNote Directive

Description:	Places the compression ratio in a note for logging
Syntax:	DeflateFilterNote [type] notename
Context:	server config, virtual host
Status:	Extension
Module:	mod_deflate
Compatibility:	type is available since Apache 2.0.45

The DeflateFilterNote directive specifies that a note about compression ratios
should be attached to the request. The name of the note is the value specified
for the directive. You can use that note for statistical purposes by adding the
value to your access log (p. 66).

Example
```
DeflateFilterNote ratio

LogFormat '"%r" %b (%{ratio}n) "%{User-agent}i"' deflate
CustomLog logs/deflate_log deflate
```

If you want to extract more accurate values from your logs, you can use the *type* argument to specify the type of data left as a note for logging. *type* can be one of:

Input Store the byte count of the filter's input stream in the note.

Output Store the byte count of the filter's output stream in the note.

Ratio Store the compression ratio (output/input * 100) in the note. This is the default, if the *type* argument is omitted.

Thus you may log it this way:

Accurate Logging
```
DeflateFilterNote Input instream
DeflateFilterNote Output outstream
DeflateFilterNote Ratio ratio

LogFormat '"%r" %{outstream}n/%{instream}n (%{ratio}n%%)'
deflate
CustomLog logs/deflate_log deflate
```

See also:

   ▷ mod_log_config (p. 334)

DeflateMemLevel Directive

Description:	How much memory should be used by zlib for compression
Syntax:	DeflateMemLevel value
Default:	DeflateMemLevel 9
Context:	server config, virtual host
Status:	Extension
Module:	mod_deflate

The DeflateMemLevel directive specifies how much memory should be used by zlib for compression (a value between 1 and 9).

DeflateWindowSize Directive

Description:	Zlib compression window size
Syntax:	DeflateWindowSize value
Default:	DeflateWindowSize 15
Context:	server config, virtual host
Status:	Extension
Module:	mod_deflate

The `DeflateWindowSize` directive specifies the zlib compression window size (a value between 1 and 15). Generally, the higher the window size, the higher the compression ratio that can be expected.

3.33 Apache Module mod_dir

Description:	Provides for "trailing slash" redirects and serving directory index files
Status:	Base
Module Identifier:	dir_module
Source File:	mod_dir.c

Summary

The index of a directory can come from one of two sources:

- A file written by the user, typically called index.html. The DirectoryIndex directive sets the name of this file. This is controlled by mod_dir.

- Otherwise, a listing generated by the server. This is provided by mod_autoindex.

The two functions are separated so that you can completely remove (or replace) automatic index generation should you want to.

A "trailing slash" redirect is issued when the server receives a request for a URL http://servername/foo/dirname where dirname is a directory. Directories require a trailing slash, so mod_dir issues a redirect to http://servername/foo/dirname/.

Directives:

> DirectoryIndex
> DirectorySlash
> FallbackResource

DirectoryIndex Directive

Description:	List of resources to look for when the client requests a directory
Syntax:	DirectoryIndex local-url [local-url] ...
Default:	DirectoryIndex index.html
Context:	server config, virtual host, directory, .htaccess
Override:	Indexes
Status:	Base
Module:	mod_dir

The DirectoryIndex directive sets the list of resources to look for, when the client requests an index of the directory by specifying a / at the end of the directory name. *Local-url* is the (%-encoded) URL of a document on the server relative to the requested directory; it is usually the name of a file in the directory. Several URLs may be given, in which case the server will return the first one that it finds. If none of the resources exist and the Indexes option is set, the server will generate its own listing of the directory.

Example
DirectoryIndex index.html

then a request for http://myserver/docs/ would return http://myserver/docs/index.html if it exists, or would list the directory if it did not.

Note that the documents do not need to be relative to the directory;

DirectoryIndex index.html index.txt /cgi-bin/index.pl

would cause the CGI script /cgi-bin/index.pl to be executed if neither index.html or index.txt existed in a directory.

DirectorySlash Directive

Description:	Toggle trailing slash redirects on or off
Syntax:	DirectorySlash On|Off
Default:	DirectorySlash On
Context:	server config, virtual host, directory, .htaccess
Override:	Indexes
Status:	Base
Module:	mod_dir
Compatibility:	Available in version 2.0.51 and later

The DirectorySlash directive determines, whether mod_dir should fixup URLs pointing to a directory or not.

Typically if a user requests a resource without a trailing slash, which points to a directory, mod_dir redirects him to the same resource, but *with* trailing slash for some good reasons:

- The user is finally requesting the canonical URL of the resource.
- mod_autoindex works correctly. Since it doesn't emit the path in the link, it would point to the wrong path.
- DirectoryIndex will be evaluated *only* for directories requested with trailing slash.
- Relative URL references inside html pages will work correctly.

Well, if you don't want this effect *and* the reasons above don't apply to you, you can turn off the redirect with:

```
# see security warning below!
<Location /some/path>
    DirectorySlash Off
    SetHandler some-handler
</Location>
```

SECURITY WARNING *Turning off the trailing slash redirect may result in an information disclosure. Consider a situation where mod_autoindex* *is active (Options +Indexes) and DirectoryIndex is set to a valid resource (say, index.html) and there's no other special handler defined for that URL. In this case a request with a trailing slash would show the index.html file. **But a request without trailing slash would list the directory contents.***

FallbackResource Directive

Description:	Define a default URL for requests that don't map to a file
Syntax:	FallbackResource *local-url*
Default:	None - httpd will return 404 (Not Found)
Context:	server config, virtual host, directory, .htaccess
Override:	Indexes
Status:	Base
Module:	mod_dir

Use this to set a handler for any URL that doesn't map to anything in your filesystem, and would otherwise return HTTP 404 (Not Found). For example

```
FallbackResource default.php
```

will cause requests for non-existent files to be handled by default.php, while requests for files that exist are unaffected.

3.34 Apache Module mod_disk_cache

Description:	Content cache storage manager keyed to URIs
Status:	Extension
Module Identifier:	disk_cache_module
Source File:	mod_disk_cache.c

Summary

mod_disk_cache implements a disk based storage manager. It is primarily of use in conjunction with mod_cache.

Content is stored in and retrieved from the cache using URI based keys. Content with access protection is not cached.

htcacheclean can be used to maintain the cache size at a maximum level.

NOTE: *mod_disk_cache requires the services of mod_cache.*

NOTE: *mod_disk_cache uses the sendfile feature to serve files from the cache when supported by the platform, and when enabled with EnableSendfile. However, per-directory and .htaccess configuration of EnableSendfile are ignored by mod_disk_cache as the corresponding settings are not available to the module when a request is being served from the cache.*

Directives:

    CacheDirLength
    CacheDirLevels
    CacheMaxFileSize
    CacheMinFileSize
    CacheRoot

CacheDirLength Directive

Description:	The number of characters in subdirectory names
Syntax:	CacheDirLength *length*
Default:	CacheDirLength 2
Context:	server config, virtual host
Status:	Extension
Module:	mod_disk_cache

The CacheDirLength directive sets the number of characters for each subdirectory name in the cache hierarchy.

The result of CacheDirLevels CacheDirLength must not be higher than 20.*

CacheDirLength 4

CacheDirLevels Directive

Description:	The number of levels of subdirectories in the cache.
Syntax:	CacheDirLevels *levels*
Default:	CacheDirLevels 3
Context:	server config, virtual host
Status:	Extension
Module:	mod_disk_cache

The `CacheDirLevels` directive sets the number of subdirectory levels in the cache. Cached data will be saved this many directory levels below the `CacheRoot` directory.

> *The result of CacheDirLevels* CacheDirLength must not be higher than 20.*

    CacheDirLevels 5

CacheMaxFileSize Directive

Description:	The maximum size (in bytes) of a document to be placed in the cache
Syntax:	CacheMaxFileSize *bytes*
Default:	CacheMaxFileSize 1000000
Context:	server config, virtual host
Status:	Extension
Module:	mod_disk_cache

The `CacheMaxFileSize` directive sets the maximum size, in bytes, for a document to be considered for storage in the cache.

    CacheMaxFileSize 64000

CacheMinFileSize Directive

Description:	The minimum size (in bytes) of a document to be placed in the cache
Syntax:	CacheMinFileSize *bytes*
Default:	CacheMinFileSize 1
Context:	server config, virtual host
Status:	Extension
Module:	mod_disk_cache

The `CacheMinFileSize` directive sets the minimum size, in bytes, for a document to be considered for storage in the cache.

    CacheMinFileSize 64

CacheRoot Directive

Description:	The directory root under which cache files are stored
Syntax:	CacheRoot *directory*
Context:	server config, virtual host
Status:	Extension
Module:	mod_disk_cache

The CacheRoot directive defines the name of the directory on the disk to contain cache files. If the mod_disk_cache module has been loaded or compiled into the Apache server, this directive *must* be defined. Failing to provide a value for CacheRoot will result in a configuration file processing error. The CacheDirLevels and CacheDirLength directives define the structure of the directories under the specified root directory.

    CacheRoot c:/cacheroot

3.35 Apache Module mod_dumpio

Description:	Dumps all I/O to error log as desired.
Status:	Extension
Module Identifier:	dumpio_module
Source File:	mod_dumpio.c

Summary

mod_dumpio allows for the logging of all input received by Apache and/or all output sent by Apache to be logged (dumped) to the error.log file.

The data logging is done right after SSL decoding (for input) and right before SSL encoding (for output). As can be expected, this can produce extreme volumes of data, and should only be used when debugging problems.

Directives:

> DumpIOInput
> DumpIOLogLevel
> DumpIOOutput

3.35.1 Enabling dumpio Support

To enable the module, it should be compiled and loaded in to your running Apache configuration. Logging can then be enabled or disabled via the below directives.

DumpIOInput Directive

Description:	Dump all input data to the error log
Syntax:	DumpIOInput On|Off
Default:	DumpIOInput Off
Context:	server config
Status:	Extension
Module:	mod_dumpio
Compatibility:	DumpIOInput is only available in Apache 2.1.3 and later.

Enable dumping of all input.

Example
> DumpIOInput On

DumpIOLogLevel Directive

Description:	Controls the logging level of the DumpIO output
Syntax:	DumpIOLogLevel *level*
Default:	DumpIOLogLevel debug
Context:	server config
Status:	Extension
Module:	mod_dumpio
Compatibility:	DumpIOLogLevel is only available in Apache 2.2.4 and later.

Enable dumping of all output at a specific LogLevel level.

Example
```
DumpIOLogLevel notice
```

COMPATIBILITY *Prior to 2.2.4 mod_dumpio would only dump to the log when LogLevel was set to debug*

DumpIOOutput Directive

Description:	Dump all output data to the error log
Syntax:	DumpIOOutput On|Off
Default:	DumpIOOutput Off
Context:	server config
Status:	Extension
Module:	mod_dumpio
Compatibility:	DumpIOOutput is only available in Apache 2.1.3 and later.

Enable dumping of all output.

Example
```
DumpIOOutput On
```

3.36 Apache Module mod_echo

Description:	A simple echo server to illustrate protocol modules
Status:	Experimental
Module Identifier:	echo_module
Source File:	mod_echo.c
Compatibility:	Available in Apache 2.0 and later

Summary

This module provides an example protocol module to illustrate the concept. It provides a simple echo server. Telnet to it and type stuff, and it will echo it.

Directives:

> ProtocolEcho

ProtocolEcho Directive

Description:	Turn the echo server on or off
Syntax:	ProtocolEcho On|Off
Default:	ProtocolEcho Off
Context:	server config, virtual host
Status:	Experimental
Module:	mod_echo
Compatibility:	ProtocolEcho is only available in 2.0 and later.

The ProtocolEcho directive enables or disables the echo server.

Example
> ProtocolEcho On

3.37 Apache Module mod_env

Description:	Modifies the environment which is passed to CGI scripts and SSI pages
Status:	Base
Module Identifier:	env_module
Source File:	mod_env.c

Summary

This module allows for control of the environment that will be provided to CGI scripts and SSI pages. Environment variables may be passed from the shell which invoked the httpd process. Alternatively, environment variables may be set or unset within the configuration process.

Directives:

> PassEnv
> SetEnv
> UnsetEnv

See also:

> ▷ Environment Variables (p. 705)

PassEnv Directive

Description:	Passes environment variables from the shell
Syntax:	PassEnv *env-variable* [*env-variable*] ...
Context:	server config, virtual host, directory, .htaccess
Override:	FileInfo
Status:	Base
Module:	mod_env

Specifies one or more environment variables to pass to CGI scripts and SSI pages from the environment of the shell which invoked the httpd process.

Example
    PassEnv LD_LIBRARY_PATH

SetEnv Directive

Description:	Sets environment variables
Syntax:	SetEnv *env-variable value*
Context:	server config, virtual host, directory, .htaccess
Override:	FileInfo
Status:	Base
Module:	mod_env

Sets an environment variable, which is then passed on to CGI scripts and SSI pages.

Example
```
SetEnv SPECIAL_PATH /foo/bin
```

The internal environment variables set by this directive are set after most early request processing directives are run, such as access control and URI-to-filename mapping. If the environment variable you're setting is meant as input into this early phase of processing such as the RewriteRule directive, you should instead set the environment variable with SetEnvIf.

UnsetEnv Directive

Description:	Removes variables from the environment
Syntax:	UnsetEnv *env-variable* [*env-variable*] ...
Context:	server config, virtual host, directory, .htaccess
Override:	FileInfo
Status:	Base
Module:	mod_env

Removes one or more environment variables from those passed on to CGI scripts and SSI pages.

Example
```
UnsetEnv LD_LIBRARY_PATH
```

3.38 Apache Module mod_example

Description:	Illustrates the Apache module API
Status:	Experimental
Module Identifier:	example_module
Source File:	mod_example.c

Summary

Some files in the modules/experimental directory under the Apache distribution directory tree are provided as an example to those that wish to write modules that use the Apache API.

The main file is mod_example.c, which illustrates all the different callback mechanisms and call syntaxes. By no means does an add-on module need to include routines for all of the callbacks - quite the contrary!

The example module is an actual working module. If you link it into your server, enable the "example-handler" handler for a location, and then browse to that location, you will see a display of some of the tracing the example module did as the various callbacks were made.

Directives:

Example

3.38.1 Compiling the example module

To include the example module in your server, follow the steps below:

1. Run configure with --enable-example option.
2. Make the server (run "make").

To add another module of your own:

1. cp modules/experimental/mod_example.c modules/new_module/*mod_-myexample.c*
2. Modify the file.
3. Create modules/new_module/config.m4.

   a) Add APACHE_MODPATH_INIT(new_module).
   b) Copy APACHE_MODULE line with "example" from modules/experimental/config.m4.
   c) Replace the first argument "example" with *myexample*.
   d) Replace the second argument with brief description of your module. It will be used in configure --help.
   e) If your module needs additional C compiler flags, linker flags or libraries, add them to CFLAGS, LDFLAGS and LIBS accordingly. See other config.m4 files in modules directory for examples.

     f) Add `APACHE_MODPATH_FINISH`.

4. Create `module/new_module/Makefile.in`. If your module doesn't need special build instructions, all you need to have in that file is include `$(top_srcdir)/build/special.mk`.

5. Run `./buildconf` from the top-level directory.

6. Build the server with `--enable-myexample`

3.38.2 Using the mod_example Module

To activate the example module, include a block similar to the following in your `httpd.conf` file:

```
<Location /example-info>
SetHandler example-handler
</Location>
```

As an alternative, you can put the following into a `.htaccess` (p. 87) file and then request the file "test.example" from that location:

```
AddHandler example-handler .example
```

After reloading/restarting your server, you should be able to browse to this location and see the brief display mentioned earlier.

Example Directive

Description:	Demonstration directive to illustrate the Apache module API
Syntax:	Example
Context:	server config, virtual host, directory, .htaccess
Status:	Experimental
Module:	mod_example

The `Example` directive just sets a demonstration flag which the example module's content handler displays. It takes no arguments. If you browse to an URL to which the example content-handler applies, you will get a display of the routines within the module and how and in what order they were called to service the document request. The effect of this directive one can observe under the point "Example directive declared here: YES/NO".

3.39 Apache Module mod_expires

Description:	Generation of Expires and Cache-Control HTTP headers according to user-specified criteria
Status:	Extension
Module Identifier:	expires_module
Source File:	mod_expires.c

Summary

This module controls the setting of the Expires HTTP header and the max-age directive of the Cache-Control HTTP header in server responses. The expiration date can set to be relative to either the time the source file was last modified, or to the time of the client access.

These HTTP headers are an instruction to the client about the document's validity and persistence. If cached, the document may be fetched from the cache rather than from the source until this time has passed. After that, the cache copy is considered "expired" and invalid, and a new copy must be obtained from the source.

To modify Cache-Control directives other than max-age (see RFC 2616 section 14.9[33]), you can use the Header directive.

Directives:

    ExpiresActive
    ExpiresByType
    ExpiresDefault

3.39.1 Alternate Interval Syntax

The ExpiresDefault and ExpiresByType directives can also be defined in a more readable syntax of the form:

    ExpiresDefault "<base> [plus] {<num> <type>}*"
    ExpiresByType type/encoding "<base> [plus] {<num> <type>}*"

where <base> is one of:

- access
- now (equivalent to 'access')
- modification

The plus keyword is optional. <num> should be an integer value [acceptable to atoi()], and <type> is one of:

- years
- months

---

[33]http://www.w3.org/Protocols/rfc2616/rfc2616-sec14.html#sec14.9

- weeks
- days
- hours
- minutes
- seconds

For example, any of the following directives can be used to make documents expire 1 month after being accessed, by default:

```
ExpiresDefault "access plus 1 month"
ExpiresDefault "access plus 4 weeks"
ExpiresDefault "access plus 30 days"
```

The expiry time can be fine-tuned by adding several '<num> <type>' clauses:

```
ExpiresByType text/html "access plus 1 month 15 days 2 hours"
ExpiresByType image/gif "modification plus 5 hours 3 minutes"
```

Note that if you use a modification date based setting, the Expires header will **not** be added to content that does not come from a file on disk. This is due to the fact that there is no modification time for such content.

ExpiresActive Directive

Description:	Enables generation of Expires headers
Syntax:	ExpiresActive On|Off
Context:	server config, virtual host, directory, .htaccess
Override:	Indexes
Status:	Extension
Module:	mod_expires

This directive enables or disables the generation of the Expires and Cache-Control headers for the document realm in question. (That is, if found in an .htaccess file, for instance, it applies only to documents generated from that directory.) If set to Off, the headers will not be generated for any document in the realm (unless overridden at a lower level, such as an .htaccess file overriding a server config file). If set to On, the headers will be added to served documents according to the criteria defined by the ExpiresByType and ExpiresDefault directives (*q.v.*).

Note that this directive does not guarantee that an Expires or Cache-Control header will be generated. If the criteria aren't met, no header will be sent, and the effect will be as though this directive wasn't even specified.

ExpiresByType Directive

Description:	Value of the Expires header configured by MIME type
Syntax:	ExpiresByType *MIME-type* *<code>seconds*
Context:	server config, virtual host, directory, .htaccess
Override:	Indexes
Status:	Extension
Module:	mod_expires

This directive defines the value of the Expires header and the max-age directive of the Cache-Control header generated for documents of the specified type (*e.g.*, text/html). The second argument sets the number of seconds that will be added to a base time to construct the expiration date. The Cache-Control: max-age is calculated by subtracting the request time from the expiration date and expressing the result in seconds.

The base time is either the last modification time of the file, or the time of the client's access to the document. Which should be used is specified by the <code> field; M means that the file's last modification time should be used as the base time, and A means the client's access time should be used.

The difference in effect is subtle. If M is used, all current copies of the document in all caches will expire at the same time, which can be good for something like a weekly notice that's always found at the same URL. If A is used, the date of expiration is different for each client; this can be good for image files that don't change very often, particularly for a set of related documents that all refer to the same images (*i.e.*, the images will be accessed repeatedly within a relatively short timespan).

Example:
```
# enable expirations
ExpiresActive On
# expire GIF images after a month in the client's cache
ExpiresByType image/gif A2592000
# HTML documents are good for a week from the
# time they were changed
ExpiresByType text/html M604800
```

Note that this directive only has effect if ExpiresActive On has been specified. It overrides, for the specified MIME type *only*, any expiration date set by the ExpiresDefault directive.

You can also specify the expiration time calculation using an alternate syntax, described earlier in this section.

ExpiresDefault Directive

Description:	Default algorithm for calculating expiration time
Syntax:	ExpiresDefault *<code>seconds*
Context:	server config, virtual host, directory, .htaccess
Override:	Indexes
Status:	Extension
Module:	mod_expires

This directive sets the default algorithm for calculating the expiration time for all documents in the affected realm. It can be overridden on a type-by-type basis by the ExpiresByType directive. See the description of that directive for details about the syntax of the argument, and the alternate syntax description as well.

3.40 Apache Module mod_ext_filter

Description:	Pass the response body through an external program before delivery to the client
Status:	Extension
Module Identifier:	ext_filter_module
Source File:	mod_ext_filter.c

Summary

mod_ext_filter presents a simple and familiar programming model for filters (p. 715). With this module, a program which reads from stdin and writes to stdout (i.e., a Unix-style filter command) can be a filter for Apache. This filtering mechanism is much slower than using a filter which is specially written for the Apache API and runs inside of the Apache server process, but it does have the following benefits:

- the programming model is much simpler

- any programming/scripting language can be used, provided that it allows the program to read from standard input and write to standard output

- existing programs can be used unmodified as Apache filters

Even when the performance characteristics are not suitable for production use, mod_ext_filter can be used as a prototype environment for filters.

Directives:

> ExtFilterDefine
> ExtFilterOptions

See also:

> ▷ Filters (p. 715)

3.40.1 Examples

Generating HTML from some other type of response

```
# mod_ext_filter directive to define a filter
# to HTML-ize text/c files using the external
# program /usr/bin/enscript, with the type of
# the result set to text/html
ExtFilterDefine c-to-html mode=output \
    intype=text/c outtype=text/html \
    cmd="/usr/bin/enscript --color -W html -Ec -o - -"

<Directory "/export/home/trawick/apacheinst/htdocs/c">
    # core directive to cause the new filter to
    # be run on output
    SetOutputFilter c-to-html
```

```
            # mod_mime directive to set the type of .c
            # files to text/c
            AddType text/c .c

            # mod_ext_filter directive to set the debug
            # level just high enough to see a log message
            # per request showing the configuration in force
            ExtFilterOptions DebugLevel=1
        </Directory>
```

Implementing a content encoding filter

Note: this gzip example is just for the purposes of illustration. Please refer to mod_deflate for a practical implementation.

```
    # mod_ext_filter directive to define the external filter
    ExtFilterDefine gzip mode=output cmd=/bin/gzip

    <Location /gzipped>
        # core directive to cause the gzip filter to be
        # run on output
        SetOutputFilter gzip

        # mod_header directive to add
        # "Content-Encoding:  gzip" header field
        Header set Content-Encoding gzip
    </Location>
```

Slowing down the server

```
    # mod_ext_filter directive to define a filter
    # which runs everything through cat; cat doesn't
    # modify anything; it just introduces extra pathlength
    # and consumes more resources
    ExtFilterDefine slowdown mode=output cmd=/bin/cat \
        preservescontentlength

    <Location />
        # core directive to cause the slowdown filter to
        # be run several times on output
        #
        SetOutputFilter slowdown;slowdown;slowdown
    </Location>
```

Using sed to replace text in the response

```
    # mod_ext_filter directive to define a filter which
    # replaces text in the response
    #
    ExtFilterDefine fixtext mode=output intype=text/html \
        cmd="/bin/sed s/verdana/arial/g"

    <Location />
```

```
            # core directive to cause the fixtext filter to
            # be run on output
            SetOutputFilter fixtext
        </Location>
```

Tracing another filter

```
    # Trace the data read and written by mod_deflate
    # for a particular client (IP 192.168.1.31)
    # experiencing compression problems.
    # This filter will trace what goes into mod_deflate.
    ExtFilterDefine tracebefore \
        cmd="/bin/tracefilter.pl /tmp/tracebefore" \
        EnableEnv=trace_this_client

    # This filter will trace what goes after mod_deflate.
    # Note that without the ftype parameter, the default
    # filter type of AP_FTYPE_RESOURCE would cause the
    # filter to be placed *before* mod_deflate in the filter
    # chain.  Giving it a numeric value slightly higher than
    # AP_FTYPE_CONTENT_SET will ensure that it is placed
    # after mod_deflate.
    ExtFilterDefine traceafter \
        cmd="/bin/tracefilter.pl /tmp/traceafter" \
        EnableEnv=trace_this_client ftype=21

    <Directory /usr/local/docs>
        SetEnvIf Remote_Addr 192.168.1.31 trace_this_client
        SetOutputFilter tracebefore;deflate;traceafter
    </Directory>
```

Here is the filter which traces the data:
```
    #!/usr/local/bin/perl -w
    use strict;
    open(SAVE, ">$ARGV[0]")
        or die "can't open $ARGV[0]:  $?";
    while (<STDIN>) {
        print SAVE $_;
        print $_;
    }
    close(SAVE);
```

ExtFilterDefine Directive

Description:	Define an external filter
Syntax:	ExtFilterDefine *filtername parameters*
Context:	server config
Status:	Extension
Module:	mod_ext_filter

The ExtFilterDefine directive defines the characteristics of an external filter, including the program to run and its arguments.

filtername specifies the name of the filter being defined. This name can then be used in SetOutputFilter directives. It must be unique among all registered filters. *At the present time, no error is reported by the register-filter API, so a problem with duplicate names isn't reported to the user.*

Subsequent parameters can appear in any order and define the external command to run and certain other characteristics. The only required parameter is cmd=. These parameters are:

cmd=cmdline The cmd= keyword allows you to specify the external command to
run. If there are arguments after the program name, the command line
should be surrounded in quotation marks (*e.g.*, cmd="/bin/mypgm arg1
arg2".) Normal shell quoting is not necessary since the program is run
directly, bypassing the shell. Program arguments are blank-delimited. A
backslash can be used to escape blanks which should be part of a program argument. Any backslashes which are part of the argument must be
escaped with backslash themselves. In addition to the standard CGI environment variables, DOCUMENT_URI, DOCUMENT_PATH_INFO, and
QUERY_STRING_UNESCAPED will also be set for the program.

mode=mode Use mode=output (the default) for filters which process the response.
Use mode=input for filters which process the request. mode=input is available in Apache 2.1 and later.

intype=imt This parameter specifies the internet media type (*i.e.*, MIME type)
of documents which should be filtered. By default, all documents are
filtered. If intype= is specified, the filter will be disabled for documents
of other types.

outtype=imt This parameter specifies the internet media type (*i.e.*, MIME
type) of filtered documents. It is useful when the filter changes the internet media type as part of the filtering operation. By default, the internet
media type is unchanged.

PreservesContentLength The PreservesContentLength keyword specifies
that the filter preserves the content length. This is not the default, as
most filters change the content length. In the event that the filter doesn't
modify the length, this keyword should be specified.

ftype=filtertype This parameter specifies the numeric value for filter type
that the filter should be registered as. The default value, AP_FTYPE_-
RESOURCE, is sufficient in most cases. If the filter needs to operate at a
different point in the filter chain than resource filters, then this parameter
will be necessary. See the AP_FTYPE_foo definitions in util_filter.h for
appropriate values.

disableenv=env This parameter specifies the name of an environment variable
which, if set, will disable the filter.

enableenv=env This parameter specifies the name of an environment variable
which must be set, or the filter will be disabled.

ExtFilterOptions Directive

Description:	Configure mod_ext_filter options
Syntax:	ExtFilterOptions *option* [*option*] ...
Default:	ExtFilterOptions DebugLevel=0 NoLogStderr
Context:	directory
Status:	Extension
Module:	mod_ext_filter

The ExtFilterOptions directive specifies special processing options for mod_-
ext_filter. *Option* can be one of

DebugLevel=n The DebugLevel keyword allows you to specify the level of debug
messages generated by mod_ext_filter. By default, no debug messages
are generated. This is equivalent to DebugLevel=0. With higher numbers, more debug messages are generated, and server performance will be
degraded. The actual meanings of the numeric values are described with
the definitions of the DBGLVL_ constants near the beginning of mod_-
ext_filter.c.

Note: The core directive LogLevel should be used to cause debug messages
to be stored in the Apache error log.

LogStderr | NoLogStderr The LogStderr keyword specifies that messages
written to standard error by the external filter program will be saved
in the Apache error log. NoLogStderr disables this feature.

Onfail=[abort|remove] (new in httpd version 2.2.12). Determines how
to proceed if the external filter program cannot be started. With abort
(the default value) the request will be aborted. With remove, the filter is
removed and the request continues without it.

Example
ExtFilterOptions LogStderr DebugLevel=0

Messages written to the filter's standard error will be stored in the Apache error
log. No debug messages will be generated by mod_ext_filter.

3.41 Apache Module mod_file_cache

Description:	Caches a static list of files in memory
Status:	Experimental
Module Identifier:	file_cache_module
Source File:	mod_file_cache.c

Summary

This module should be used with care. You can easily create a broken site using mod_file_cache, so read this section carefully.

Caching frequently requested files that change very infrequently is a technique for reducing server load. mod_file_cache provides two techniques for caching frequently requested *static* files. Through configuration directives, you can direct mod_file_cache to either open then mmap() a file, or to pre-open a file and save the file's open *file handle*. Both techniques reduce server load when processing requests for these files by doing part of the work (specifically, the file I/O) for serving the file when the server is started rather than during each request.

Notice: You cannot use this for speeding up CGI programs or other files which are served by special content handlers. It can only be used for regular files which are usually served by the Apache core content handler.

This module is an extension of and borrows heavily from the mod_mmap_static module in Apache 1.3.

Directives:

> CacheFile
> MMapFile

3.41.1 Using mod_file_cache

mod_file_cache caches a list of statically configured files via MMapFile or CacheFile directives in the main server configuration.

Not all platforms support both directives. You will receive an error message in the server error log if you attempt to use an unsupported directive. If given an unsupported directive, the server will start but the file will not be cached. On platforms that support both directives, you should experiment with both to see which works best for you.

MMapFile Directive

The MMapFile directive of mod_file_cache maps a list of statically configured files into memory through the system call mmap(). This system call is available on most modern Unix derivates, but not on all. There are sometimes system-specific limits on the size and number of files that can be mmap()ed; experimentation is probably the easiest way to find out.

This mmap()ing is done once at server start or restart, only. So whenever one of the mapped files changes on the filesystem you *have* to restart the server (see the Stopping and Restarting (p. 51) documentation). To reiterate that point: if the files are modified *in place* without restarting the server you may end up serving requests that are completely bogus. You should update files by unlinking the old copy and putting a new copy in place. Most tools such as rdist and mv do this. The reason why this modules doesn't take care of changes to the files is that this check would need an extra stat() every time which is a waste and against the intent of I/O reduction.

CacheFile Directive

The CacheFile directive of mod_file_cache opens an active *handle* or *file descriptor* to the file (or files) listed in the configuration directive and places these open file handles in the cache. When the file is requested, the server retrieves the handle from the cache and passes it to the sendfile() (or TransmitFile() on Windows), socket API.

This file handle caching is done once at server start or restart, only. So whenever one of the cached files changes on the filesystem you *have* to restart the server (see the Stopping and Restarting (p. 51) documentation). To reiterate that point: if the files are modified *in place* without restarting the server you may end up serving requests that are completely bogus. You should update files by unlinking the old copy and putting a new copy in place. Most tools such as rdist and mv do this.

> NOTE *Don't bother asking for a directive which recursively caches all the files in a directory. Try this instead... See the* Include *directive, and consider this command:*
>
> ```
> find /www/htdocs -type f -print \
> | sed -e 's/.*/mmapfile &/' > /www/conf/mmap.conf
> ```

CacheFile Directive

Description:	Cache a list of file handles at startup time
Syntax:	CacheFile file-path [file-path] ...
Context:	server config
Status:	Experimental
Module:	mod_file_cache

The CacheFile directive opens handles to one or more files (given as whitespace separated arguments) and places these handles into the cache at server startup time. Handles to cached files are automatically closed on a server shutdown. When the files have changed on the filesystem, the server should be restarted to re-cache them.

Be careful with the *file-path* arguments: They have to literally match the filesystem path Apache's URL-to-filename translation handlers create. We cannot compare inodes or other stuff to match paths through symbolic links *etc.* because that again would cost extra stat() system calls which is not acceptable. This module may or may not work with filenames rewritten by mod_alias or mod_rewrite.

Example
CacheFile /usr/local/apache/htdocs/index.html

MMapFile Directive

Description:	Map a list of files into memory at startup time
Syntax:	MMapFile *file-path* [*file-path*] ...
Context:	server config
Status:	Experimental
Module:	mod_file_cache

The MMapFile directive maps one or more files (given as whitespace separated arguments) into memory at server startup time. They are automatically unmapped on a server shutdown. When the files have changed on the filesystem at least a HUP or USR1 signal should be send to the server to re-mmap() them.

Be careful with the *file-path* arguments: They have to literally match the filesystem path Apache's URL-to-filename translation handlers create. We cannot compare inodes or other stuff to match paths through symbolic links *etc.* because that again would cost extra stat() system calls which is not acceptable. This module may or may not work with filenames rewritten by mod_alias or mod_rewrite.

Example
MMapFile /usr/local/apache/htdocs/index.html

3.42 Apache Module mod_filter

Description:	Context-sensitive smart filter configuration module
Status:	Base
Module Identifier:	filter_module
Source File:	mod_filter.c
Compatibility:	Version 2.1 and later

Summary

This module enables smart, context-sensitive configuration of output content filters. For example, apache can be configured to process different content-types through different filters, even when the content-type is not known in advance (e.g. in a proxy).

mod_filter works by introducing indirection into the filter chain. Instead of inserting filters in the chain, we insert a filter harness which in turn dispatches conditionally to a filter provider. Any content filter may be used as a provider to mod_filter; no change to existing filter modules is required (although it may be possible to simplify them).

Directives:

> FilterChain
> FilterDeclare
> FilterProtocol
> FilterProvider
> FilterTrace

3.42.1 Smart Filtering

In the traditional filtering model, filters are inserted unconditionally using AddOutputFilter and family. Each filter then needs to determine whether to run, and there is little flexibility available for server admins to allow the chain to be configured dynamically.

mod_filter by contrast gives server administrators a great deal of flexibility in configuring the filter chain. In fact, filters can be inserted based on any Request Header, Response Header or Environment Variable. This generalises the limited flexibility offered by AddOutputFilterByType, and fixes it to work correctly with dynamic content, regardless of the content generator. The ability to dispatch based on Environment Variables offers the full flexibility of configuration with mod_rewrite to anyone who needs it.

3.42.2 Filter Declarations, Providers and Chains

In the traditional model, output filters are a simple chain from the content generator (handler) to the client. This works well provided the filter chain can be correctly configured, but presents problems when the filters need to be configured dynamically based on the outcome of the handler.

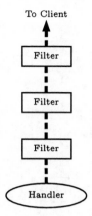

Figure 3.1: The traditional filter model

mod_filter works by introducing indirection into the filter chain. Instead of inserting filters in the chain, we insert a filter harness which in turn dispatches conditionally to a filter provider. Any content filter may be used as a provider to mod_filter; no change to existing filter modules is required (although it may be possible to simplify them). There can be multiple providers for one filter, but no more than one provider will run for any single request.

A filter chain comprises any number of instances of the filter harness, each of which may have any number of providers. A special case is that of a single provider with unconditional dispatch: this is equivalent to inserting the provider filter directly into the chain.

3.42.3 Configuring the Chain

There are three stages to configuring a filter chain with mod_filter. For details of the directives, see below.

Declare Filters The FilterDeclare directive declares a filter, assigning it a name and filter type. Required only if the filter is not the default type AP_FTYPE_RESOURCE.

Register Providers The FilterProvider directive registers a provider with a filter. The filter may have been declared with FilterDeclare; if not, FilterProvider will implicitly declare it with the default type AP_-FTYPE_RESOURCE. The provider must have been registered with ap_-register_output_filter by some module. The remaining arguments to FilterProvider are a dispatch criterion and a match string. The former may be an HTTP request or response header, an environment variable,

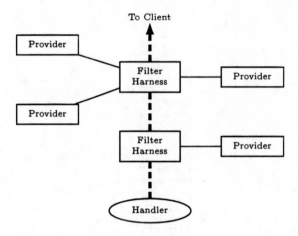

Figure 3.2: The mod_filter model

or the Handler used by this request. The latter is matched to it for each request, to determine whether this provider will be used to implement the filter for this request.

Configure the Chain The above directives build components of a smart filter chain, but do not configure it to run. The FilterChain directive builds a filter chain from smart filters declared, offering the flexibility to insert filters at the beginning or end of the chain, remove a filter, or clear the chain.

3.42.4 Filtering and Response Status

mod_filter normally only runs filters on responses with HTTP status 200 (OK). If you want to filter documents with other response statuses, you can set the *filter-errordocs* environment variable, and it will work on all responses regardless of status. To refine this further, you can use expression conditions with FilterProvider.

3.42.5 Examples

Server side Includes (SSI) A simple case of using mod_filter in place of AddOutputFilterByType

```
FilterDeclare SSI
FilterProvider SSI INCLUDES resp=Content-Type $text/html
FilterChain SSI
```

Server side Includes (SSI) The same as the above but dispatching on handler (classic SSI behaviour; .shtml files get processed).

```
FilterProvider SSI INCLUDES Handler server-parsed
FilterChain SSI
```

Emulating mod_gzip with mod_deflate Insert INFLATE filter only if "gzip" is NOT in the Accept-Encoding header. This filter runs with ftype CONTENT_SET.

```
FilterDeclare gzip CONTENT_SET
FilterProvider gzip inflate req=Accept-Encoding !$gzip
FilterChain gzip
```

Image Downsampling Suppose we want to downsample all web images, and have filters for GIF, JPEG and PNG.

```
FilterProvider unpack jpeg_unpack Content-Type $image/jpeg
FilterProvider unpack gif_unpack Content-Type $image/gif
FilterProvider unpack png_unpack Content-Type $image/png

FilterProvider downsample downsample_filter Content-Type
$image
FilterProtocol downsample "change=yes"

FilterProvider repack jpeg_pack Content-Type $image/jpeg
FilterProvider repack gif_pack Content-Type $image/gif
FilterProvider repack png_pack Content-Type $image/png
<Location /image-filter>
    FilterChain unpack downsample repack
</Location>
```

3.42.6 Protocol Handling

Historically, each filter is responsible for ensuring that whatever changes it makes are correctly represented in the HTTP response headers, and that it does not run when it would make an illegal change. This imposes a burden on filter authors to re-implement some common functionality in every filter:

- Many filters will change the content, invalidating existing content tags, checksums, hashes, and lengths.

- Filters that require an entire, unbroken response in input need to ensure they don't get byteranges from a backend.

- Filters that transform output in a filter need to ensure they don't violate a Cache-Control: no-transform header from the backend.

- Filters may make responses uncacheable.

mod_filter aims to offer generic handling of these details of filter implementation, reducing the complexity required of content filter modules. This is work-in-progress; the FilterProtocol implements some of this functionality for back-compatibility with Apache 2.0 modules. For httpd 2.1 and later, the ap_register_output_filter_protocol and ap_filter_protocol API enables filter modules to declare their own behaviour.

At the same time, mod_filter should not interfere with a filter that wants to handle all aspects of the protocol. By default (i.e. in the absence of any FilterProtocol directives), mod_filter will leave the headers untouched.

At the time of writing, this feature is largely untested, as modules in common use are designed to work with 2.0. Modules using it should test it carefully.

FilterChain Directive

Description:	Configure the filter chain
Syntax:	FilterChain [+=-@!] *filter-name* ...
Context:	server config, virtual host, directory, .htaccess
Override:	Options
Status:	Base
Module:	mod_filter

This configures an actual filter chain, from declared filters. FilterChain takes any number of arguments, each optionally preceded with a single-character control that determines what to do:

+filter-name Add *filter-name* to the end of the filter chain

@filter-name Insert *filter-name* at the start of the filter chain

-filter-name Remove *filter-name* from the filter chain

=filter-name Empty the filter chain and insert *filter-name*

! Empty the filter chain

filter-name Equivalent to +*filter-name*

FilterDeclare Directive

Description:	Declare a smart filter
Syntax:	FilterDeclare *filter-name [type]*
Context:	server config, virtual host, directory, .htaccess
Override:	Options
Status:	Base
Module:	mod_filter

This directive declares an output filter together with a header or environment variable that will determine runtime configuration. The first argument is a *filter-name* for use in FilterProvider, FilterChain and FilterProtocol directives.

The final (optional) argument is the type of filter, and takes values of ap_filter_type - namely RESOURCE (the default), CONTENT_SET, PROTOCOL, TRANSCODE, CONNECTION or NETWORK.

FilterProtocol Directive

Description:	Deal with correct HTTP protocol handling
Syntax:	FilterProtocol *filter-name* [*provider-name*] *proto-flags*
Context:	server config, virtual host, directory, .htaccess
Override:	Options
Status:	Base
Module:	mod_filter

This directs mod_filter to deal with ensuring the filter doesn't run when it shouldn't, and that the HTTP response headers are correctly set taking into account the effects of the filter.

There are two forms of this directive. With three arguments, it applies specifically to a *filter-name* and a *provider-name* for that filter. With two arguments it applies to a *filter-name* whenever the filter runs *any* provider.

proto-flags is one or more of

change=yes The filter changes the content, including possibly the content length

change=1:1 The filter changes the content, but will not change the content length

byteranges=no The filter cannot work on byteranges and requires complete input

proxy=no The filter should not run in a proxy context

proxy=transform The filter transforms the response in a manner incompatible with the HTTP Cache-Control: no-transform header.

cache=no The filter renders the output uncacheable (eg by introducing randomised content changes)

FilterProvider Directive

Description:	Register a content filter
Syntax:	FilterProvider *filter-name* *provider-name* [req|resp|env]=*dispatch match*
Context:	server config, virtual host, directory, .htaccess
Override:	Options
Status:	Base
Module:	mod_filter

This directive registers a *provider* for the smart filter. The provider will be called if and only if the *match* declared here matches the value of the header or environment variable declared as *dispatch*.

provider-name must have been registered by loading a module that registers the name with ap_register_output_filter.

The *dispatch* argument is a string with optional req=, resp= or env= prefix causing it to dispatch on (respectively) the request header, response header, or environment variable named. In the absence of a prefix, it defaults to a response header. A special case is the word handler, which causes mod_filter to dispatch on the content handler.

The *match* argument specifies a match that will be applied to the filter's *dispatch* criterion. The *match* may be a string match (exact match or substring), a regex, an integer (greater, lessthan or equals), or unconditional. The first characters of the *match* argument determines this:

First, if the first character is an exclamation mark (!), this reverses the rule, so the provider will be used if and only if the match *fails*.

Second, it interprets the first character excluding any leading ! as follows:

Character	Description
(none)	exact match
$	substring match
/	regex match (delimited by a second /)
=	integer equality
<	integer less-than
<=	integer less-than or equal
>	integer greater-than
>=	integer greater-than or equal
*	Unconditional match

FilterTrace Directive

Description:	Get debug/diagnostic information from mod_filter
Syntax:	FilterTrace *filter-name* *level*
Context:	server config, virtual host, directory
Status:	Base
Module:	mod_filter

This directive generates debug information from mod_filter. It is designed to help test and debug providers (filter modules), although it may also help with mod_filter itself.

The debug output depends on the *level* set:

0 (**default**) No debug information is generated.

1 mod_filter will record buckets and brigades passing through the filter to the error log, before the provider has processed them. This is similar to the information generated by mod_diagnostics[34].

2 (**not yet implemented**) Will dump the full data passing through to a temp-file before the provider. **For single-user debug only**; this will not support concurrent hits.

---

[34]http://apache.webthing.com/mod_diagnostics/

3.43 Apache Module mod_headers

Description:	Customization of HTTP request and response headers
Status:	Extension
Module Identifier:	headers_module
Source File:	mod_headers.c

Summary

This module provides directives to control and modify HTTP request and response headers. Headers can be merged, replaced or removed.

Directives:

> Header
> RequestHeader

3.43.1 Order of Processing

The directives provided by mod_headers can occur almost anywhere within the server configuration, and can be limited in scope by enclosing them in configuration sections (p. 57).

Order of processing is important and is affected both by the order in the configuration file and by placement in configuration sections (p. 57). These two directives have a different effect if reversed:

> RequestHeader append MirrorID "mirror 12"
> RequestHeader unset MirrorID

This way round, the MirrorID header is not set. If reversed, the MirrorID header is set to "mirror 12".

3.43.2 Early and Late Processing

mod_headers can be applied either early or late in the request. The normal mode is late, when *Request* Headers are set immediately before running the content generator and *Response* Headers just as the response is sent down the wire. Always use Late mode in an operational server.

Early mode is designed as a test/debugging aid for developers. Directives defined using the early keyword are set right at the beginning of processing the request. This means they can be used to simulate different requests and set up test cases, but it also means that headers may be changed at any time by other modules before generating a Response.

Because early directives are processed before the request path's configuration is traversed, early headers can only be set in a main server or virtual host context. Early directives cannot depend on a request path, so they will fail in contexts such as <Directory> or <Location>.

3.43.3 Examples

1. Copy all request headers that begin with "TS" to the response headers:

   ```
   Header echo ^TS
   ```

2. Add a header, MyHeader, to the response including a timestamp for when the request was received and how long it took to begin serving the request. This header can be used by the client to intuit load on the server or in isolating bottlenecks between the client and the server.

   ```
   Header set MyHeader "%D %t"
   ```

   results in this header being added to the response:

   ```
   MyHeader:  D=3775428 t=991424704447256
   ```

3. Say hello to Joe

   ```
   Header set MyHeader "Hello Joe.  It took %D microseconds \
   for Apache to serve this request."
   ```

   results in this header being added to the response:

   ```
   MyHeader:  Hello Joe.  It took D=3775428 microseconds for
   Apache to serve this request.
   ```

4. Conditionally send MyHeader on the response if and only if header MyRequestHeader is present on the request. This is useful for constructing headers in response to some client stimulus. Note that this example requires the services of the mod_setenvif module.

   ```
   SetEnvIf MyRequestHeader myvalue HAVE_MyRequestHeader
   Header set MyHeader "%D %t mytext" env=HAVE_MyRequestHeader
   ```

   If the header MyRequestHeader: myvalue is present on the HTTP request, the response will contain the following header:

   ```
   MyHeader:  D=3775428 t=991424704447256 mytext
   ```

5. Enable DAV to work with Apache running HTTP through SSL hardware (problem description[35]) by replacing *https:* with *http:* in the *Destination* header:

   ```
   RequestHeader edit Destination ^https: http:  early
   ```

6. Set the same header value under multiple non-exclusive conditions, but do not duplicate the value in the final header. If all of the following conditions applied to a request (i.e., if the CGI, NO_CACHE and NO_STORE environment variables all existed for the request):

   ```
   Header merge Cache-Control no-cache env=CGI
   Header merge Cache-Control no-cache env=NO_CACHE
   Header merge Cache-Control no-store env=NO_STORE
   ```

   then the response would contain the following header:

   ```
   Cache-Control:  no-cache, no-store
   ```

---

[35]http://svn.haxx.se/users/archive-2006-03/0549.shtml

If append was used instead of merge, then the response would contain the following header:

```
Cache-Control:  no-cache, no-cache, no-store
```

Header Directive

Description:	Configure HTTP response headers
Syntax:	Header [condition]
	set|append|merge|add|unset|echo|edit header
	[value] [early|env=[!]variable]
Context:	server config, virtual host, directory, .htaccess
Override:	FileInfo
Status:	Extension
Module:	mod_headers
Compatibility:	The merge argument is available in version 2.2.9 and later.
	The edit argument is available in version 2.2.4 and later.

This directive can replace, merge or remove HTTP response headers. The header is modified just after the content handler and output filters are run, allowing outgoing headers to be modified.

By default, this directive only affects successful responses (responses in the 2xx range). The optional *condition* can be either onsuccess (default) or always (all status codes, including successful responses). A value of always may be needed to influence headers set by some internal modules even for successful responses, and is always needed to affect non-2xx responses such as redirects or client errors.

CGI *To manipulate headers set by CGI scripts, it is necessary to specify always for the first parameter.*

The action it performs is determined by the first argument (second argument if a *condition* is specified). This can be one of the following values:

set The response header is set, replacing any previous header with this name. The *value* may be a format string.

append The response header is appended to any existing header of the same name. When a new value is merged onto an existing header it is separated from the existing header with a comma. This is the HTTP standard way of giving a header multiple values.

merge The response header is appended to any existing header of the same name, unless the value to be appended already appears in the header's comma-delimited list of values. When a new value is merged onto an existing header it is separated from the existing header with a comma. This is the HTTP standard way of giving a header multiple values. Values are compared in a case sensitive manner, and after all format specifiers have been processed. Values in double quotes are considered different from otherwise identical unquoted values. *Available in version 2.2.9 and later.*

add The response header is added to the existing set of headers, even if this header already exists. This can result in two (or more) headers having the same name. This can lead to unforeseen consequences, and in general set, append or merge should be used instead.

unset The response header of this name is removed, if it exists. If there are multiple headers of the same name, all will be removed. *value* must be omitted.

echo Request headers with this name are echoed back in the response headers. *header* may be a regular expression. *value* must be omitted.

edit If this request header exists, its value is transformed according to a regular expression search-and-replace. The *value* argument is a regular expression, and the *replacement* is a replacement string, which may contain backreferences. *Available in version 2.2.4 and later.*

This argument is followed by a *header* name, which can include the final colon, but it is not required. Case is ignored for set, append, merge, add, unset and edit. The *header* name for echo is case sensitive and may be a regular expression.

For set, append, merge and add a *value* is specified as the next argument. If *value* contains spaces, it should be surrounded by double quotes. *value* may be a character string, a string containing format specifiers or a combination of both. The following format specifiers are supported in *value*:

Format	Description
%%	The percent sign
%t	The time the request was received in Universal Coordinated Time since the epoch (Jan. 1, 1970) measured in microseconds. The value is preceded by t=.
%D	The time from when the request was received to the time the headers are sent on the wire. This is a measure of the duration of the request. The value is preceded by D=. The value is measured in microseconds.
%{FOOBAR}e	The contents of the environment variable (p. 705) FOOBAR.
%{FOOBAR}s	The contents of the SSL environment variable (p. 458) FOOBAR, if mod_ssl is enabled.

NOTE *The %s format specifier is only available in Apache 2.1 and later; it can be used instead of %e to avoid the overhead of enabling SSLOptions +StdEnvVars. If SSLOptions +StdEnvVars must be enabled anyway for some other reason, %e will be more efficient than %s.*

For edit there is both a *value* argument which is a regular expression, and an additional *replacement* string.

The Header directive may be followed by an an additional argument, which may be used to specify conditions under which the action will be taken, or may be the keyword early to specify early processing. If the environment variable (p. 705) specified in the env=... argument exists (or if the environment variable does not exist and env=!... is specified) then the action specified by the Header directive will take effect. Otherwise, the directive will have no effect on the request.

Except in early mode, the Header directives are processed just before the response is sent to the network. These means that it is possible to set and/or override most headers, except for those headers added by the header filter.

RequestHeader Directive

Description:	Configure HTTP request headers
Syntax:	RequestHeader set|append|merge|add|unset|edit header [value] [replacement] [early|env=[!]variable]
Context:	server config, virtual host, directory, .htaccess
Override:	FileInfo
Status:	Extension
Module:	mod_headers
Compatibility:	The merge argument is available in version 2.2.9 and later. The edit argument is available in version 2.2.4 and later.

This directive can replace, merge, change or remove HTTP request headers. The header is modified just before the content handler is run, allowing incoming headers to be modified. The action it performs is determined by the first argument. This can be one of the following values:

set The request header is set, replacing any previous header with this name.

append The request header is appended to any existing header of the same name. When a new value is merged onto an existing header it is separated from the existing header with a comma. This is the HTTP standard way of giving a header multiple values.

merge The response header is appended to any existing header of the same name, unless the value to be appended already appears in the existing header's comma-delimited list of values. When a new value is merged onto an existing header it is separated from the existing header with a comma. This is the HTTP standard way of giving a header multiple values. Values are compared in a case sensitive manner, and after all format specifiers have been processed. Values in double quotes are considered different from otherwise identical unquoted values. *Available in version 2.2.9 and later.*

add The request header is added to the existing set of headers, even if this header already exists. This can result in two (or more) headers having the same name. This can lead to unforeseen consequences, and in general set, append or merge should be used instead.

unset The request header of this name is removed, if it exists. If there are multiple headers of the same name, all will be removed. *value* must be omitted.

edit If this request header exists, its value is transformed according to a regular expression search-and-replace. The *value* argument is a regular expression, and the *replacement* is a replacement string, which may contain
backreferences. *Available in version 2.2.4 and later.*

This argument is followed by a header name, which can include the final colon,
but it is not required. Case is ignored. For set, append, merge and add a
value is given as the third argument. If a *value* contains spaces, it should be
surrounded by double quotes. For unset, no *value* should be given. *value* may
be a character string, a string containing format specifiers or a combination of
both. The supported format specifiers are the same as for the Header; please
have a look there for details. For edit both a *value* and a *replacement* are
required, and are a regular expression and a replacement string respectively.

The RequestHeader directive may be followed by an additional argument, which
may be used to specify conditions under which the action will be taken, or may
be the keyword early to specify early processing. If the environment variable
(p. 705) specified in the env=... argument exists (or if the environment variable
does not exist and env=!... is specified) then the action specified by the
RequestHeader directive will take effect. Otherwise, the directive will have
no effect on the request.

Except in early mode, the RequestHeader directive is processed just before the
request is run by its handler in the fixup phase. This should allow headers generated by the browser, or by Apache input filters to be overridden or modified.

3.44 Apache Module mod_ident

Description:	RFC 1413 ident lookups
Status:	Extension
Module Identifier:	ident_module
Source File:	mod_ident.c
Compatibility:	Available in Apache 2.1 and later

Summary

This module queries an RFC 1413[36] compatible daemon on a remote host to look up the owner of a connection.

Directives:

> IdentityCheck
> IdentityCheckTimeout

See also:

> ▷ mod_log_config (p. 334)

IdentityCheck Directive

Description:	Enables logging of the RFC 1413 identity of the remote user
Syntax:	IdentityCheck On|Off
Default:	IdentityCheck Off
Context:	server config, virtual host, directory
Status:	Extension
Module:	mod_ident
Compatibility:	Moved out of core in Apache 2.1

This directive enables RFC 1413[37]-compliant logging of the remote user name for each connection, where the client machine runs identd or something similar. This information is logged in the access log using the %...l format string (p. 334).

> *The information should not be trusted in any way except for rudimentary usage tracking.*

Note that this can cause serious latency problems accessing your server since every request requires one of these lookups to be performed. When firewalls or proxy servers are involved, each lookup might possibly fail and add a latency duration as defined by the IdentityCheckTimeout directive to each hit. So in general this is not very useful on public servers accessible from the Internet.

---

[36]http://www.ietf.org/rfc/rfc1413.txt
[37]http://www.ietf.org/rfc/rfc1413.txt

IdentityCheckTimeout Directive

Description:	Determines the timeout duration for ident requests
Syntax:	IdentityCheckTimeout *seconds*
Default:	IdentityCheckTimeout 30
Context:	server config, virtual host, directory
Status:	Extension
Module:	mod_ident

This directive specifies the timeout duration of an ident request. The default value of 30 seconds is recommended by RFC 1413[38], mainly because of possible network latency. However, you may want to adjust the timeout value according to your local network speed.

---

[38]http://www.ietf.org/rfc/rfc1413.txt

3.45 Apache Module mod_imagemap

Description:	Server-side imagemap processing
Status:	Base
Module Identifier:	imagemap_module
Source File:	mod_imagemap.c

Summary

This module processes .map files, thereby replacing the functionality of the imagemap CGI program. Any directory or document type configured to use the handler imap-file (using either AddHandler or SetHandler) will be processed by this module.

The following directive will activate files ending with .map as imagemap files:

```
AddHandler imap-file map
```

Note that the following is still supported:

```
AddType application/x-httpd-imap map
```

However, we are trying to phase out "magic MIME types" so we are deprecating this method.

Directives:

```
ImapBase
ImapDefault
ImapMenu
```

3.45.1 New Features

The imagemap module adds some new features that were not possible with previously distributed imagemap programs.

- URL references relative to the Referer: information.
- Default <base> assignment through a new map directive base.
- No need for imagemap.conf file.
- Point references.
- Configurable generation of imagemap menus.

3.45.2 Imagemap File

The lines in the imagemap files can have one of several formats:

```
directive value [x,y ...]
directive value "Menu text" [x,y ...]
directive value x,y ...  "Menu text"
```

The directive is one of base, default, poly, circle, rect, or point. The value is an absolute or relative URL, or one of the special values listed below. The coordinates are x, y pairs separated by whitespace. The quoted text is used as the text of the link if a imagemap menu is generated. Lines beginning with '#' are comments.

Imagemap File Directives

There are six directives allowed in the imagemap file. The directives can come in any order, but are processed in the order they are found in the imagemap file.

base **Directive** Has the effect of <base href="*value*">. The non-absolute URLs of the map-file are taken relative to this value. The base directive overrides ImapBase as set in a .htaccess file or in the server configuration files. In the absence of an ImapBase configuration directive, base defaults to http://server_name/.

base_uri is synonymous with base. Note that a trailing slash on the URL is significant.

default **Directive** The action taken if the coordinates given do not fit any of the poly, circle or rect directives, and there are no point directives. Defaults to nocontent in the absence of an ImapDefault configuration setting, causing a status code of 204 No Content to be returned. The client should keep the same page displayed.

poly **Directive** Takes three to one-hundred points, and is obeyed if the user selected coordinates fall within the polygon defined by these points.

circle Takes the center coordinates of a circle and a point on the circle. Is obeyed if the user selected point is with the circle.

rect **Directive** Takes the coordinates of two opposing corners of a rectangle. Obeyed if the point selected is within this rectangle.

point **Directive** Takes a single point. The point directive closest to the user selected point is obeyed if no other directives are satisfied. Note that default will not be followed if a point directive is present and valid coordinates are given.

Values

The values for each of the directives can be any of the following:

a **URL** The URL can be relative or absolute URL. Relative URLs can contain '..' syntax and will be resolved relative to the base value.

base itself will not be resolved according to the current value. A statement base mailto: will work properly, though.

map Equivalent to the URL of the imagemap file itself. No coordinates are sent with this, so a menu will be generated unless ImapMenu is set to none.

menu Synonymous with map.

referer Equivalent to the URL of the referring document. Defaults to
http://servername/ if no Referer: header was present.

nocontent Sends a status code of 204 No Content, telling the client to keep
the same page displayed. Valid for all but base.

error Fails with a 500 Server Error. Valid for all but base, but sort of silly
for anything but default.

Coordinates

0,0 200,200 A coordinate consists of an *x* and a *y* value separated by a comma.
The coordinates are separated from each other by whitespace. To accommodate the way Lynx handles imagemaps, should a user select the
coordinate 0,0, it is as if no coordinate had been selected.

Quoted Text

"Menu Text" After the value or after the coordinates, the line optionally may
contain text within double quotes. This string is used as the text for the
link if a menu is generated:

```
<a href="http://example.com/">Menu text</a>
```

If no quoted text is present, the name of the link will be used as the text:

```
<a href="http://example.com/">http://example.com</a>
```

If you want to use double quotes within this text, you have to write them
as ".

3.45.3 Example Mapfile

```
#Comments are printed in a 'formatted' or 'semiformatted' menu.
#And can contain html tags.  <hr>
base referer
poly map "Could I have a menu, please?" 0,0 0,10 10,10 10,0
rect ..  0,0 77,27 "the directory of the referer"
circle http://www.inetnebr.example.com/lincoln/feedback/ 195,0
305,27
rect another_file "in same directory as referer" 306,0 419,27
point http://www.zyzzyva.example.com/ 100,100
point http://www.tripod.example.com/ 200,200
rect mailto:nate@tripod.example.com 100,150 200,0 "Bugs?"
```

3.45.4 Referencing your mapfile

HTML example
```
<a href="/maps/imagemap1.map">
    <img ismap src="/images/imagemap1.gif">
</a>
```

XHTML example
```
<a href="/maps/imagemap1.map">
    <img ismap="ismap" src="/images/imagemap1.gif" />
</a>
```

ImapBase Directive

Description:	Default base for imagemap files
Syntax:	ImapBase map|referer|*URL*
Default:	ImapBase http://servername/
Context:	server config, virtual host, directory, .htaccess
Override:	Indexes
Status:	Base
Module:	mod_imagemap

The ImapBase directive sets the default base used in the imagemap files. Its value is overridden by a base directive within the imagemap file. If not present, the base defaults to http://*servername*/.

See also:

▷ UseCanonicalName (p. 134)

ImapDefault Directive

Description:	Default action when an imagemap is called with coordinates that are not explicitly mapped
Syntax:	ImapDefault error|nocontent|map|referer|*URL*
Default:	ImapDefault nocontent
Context:	server config, virtual host, directory, .htaccess
Override:	Indexes
Status:	Base
Module:	mod_imagemap

The ImapDefault directive sets the default default used in the imagemap files. Its value is overridden by a default directive within the imagemap file. If not present, the default action is nocontent, which means that a 204 No Content is sent to the client. In this case, the client should continue to display the original page.

ImapMenu Directive

Description:	Action if no coordinates are given when calling an imagemap
Syntax:	ImapMenu none|formatted|semiformatted|unformatted
Context:	server config, virtual host, directory, .htaccess
Override:	Indexes
Status:	Base
Module:	mod_imagemap

The ImapMenu directive determines the action taken if an imagemap file is called without valid coordinates.

none If ImapMenu is none, no menu is generated, and the default action is performed.

formatted A formatted menu is the simplest menu. Comments in the imagemap file are ignored. A level one header is printed, then an hrule, then the links each on a separate line. The menu has a consistent, plain look close to that of a directory listing.

semiformatted In the semiformatted menu, comments are printed where they occur in the imagemap file. Blank lines are turned into HTML breaks. No header or hrule is printed, but otherwise the menu is the same as a formatted menu.

unformatted Comments are printed, blank lines are ignored. Nothing is printed that does not appear in the imagemap file. All breaks and headers must be included as comments in the imagemap file. This gives you the most flexibility over the appearance of your menus, but requires you to treat your map files as HTML instead of plaintext.

3.46 Apache Module mod_include

Description:	Server-parsed HTML documents (Server Side Includes)
Status:	Base
Module Identifier:	include_module
Source File:	mod_include.c
Compatibility:	Implemented as an output filter since Apache 2.0

Summary

This module provides a filter which will process files before they are sent to the client. The processing is controlled by specially formatted SGML comments, referred to as **elements**. These elements allow conditional text, the inclusion of other files or programs, as well as the setting and printing of environment variables.

Directives:

SSIETag
SSIEnableAccess
SSIEndTag
SSIErrorMsg
SSILastModified
SSIStartTag
SSITimeFormat
SSIUndefinedEcho
XBitHack

See also:

▷ Options (p. 120)

▷ AcceptPathInfo (p. 89)

▷ Filters (p. 715)

▷ SSI Tutorial (p. 659)

3.46.1 Enabling Server-Side Includes

Server Side Includes are implemented by the INCLUDES filter (p. 715). If documents containing server-side include directives are given the extension .shtml, the following directives will make Apache parse them and assign the resulting document the mime type of text/html:

```
AddType text/html .shtml
AddOutputFilter INCLUDES .shtml
```

The following directive must be given for the directories containing the shtml files (typically in a <Directory> section, but this directive is also valid in .htaccess files if AllowOverride Options is set):

```
Options +Includes
```

For backwards compatibility, the `server-parsed` handler (p. 713) also activates the INCLUDES filter. As well, Apache will activate the INCLUDES filter for any document with mime type `text/x-server-parsed-html` or `text/x-server-parsed-html3` (and the resulting output will have the mime type `text/html`).

For more information, see our Tutorial on Server Side Includes (p. 659).

3.46.2 PATH_INFO with Server Side Includes

Files processed for server-side includes no longer accept requests with `PATH_INFO` (trailing pathname information) by default. You can use the `AcceptPathInfo` directive to configure the server to accept requests with `PATH_INFO`.

3.46.3 Basic Elements

The document is parsed as an HTML document, with special commands embedded as SGML comments. A command has the syntax:

```
<!--#element attribute=value attribute=value ...  -->
```

The value will often be enclosed in double quotes, but single quotes (') and backticks (`) are also possible. Many commands only allow a single attribute-value pair. Note that the comment terminator (`-->`) should be preceded by whitespace to ensure that it isn't considered part of an SSI token. Note that the leading `<!--#` is *one* token and may not contain any whitespaces.

The allowed elements are listed in the following table:

Element	Description
config	configure output formats
echo	print variables
exec	execute external programs
fsize	print size of a file
flastmod	print last modification time of a file
include	include a file
printenv	print all available variables
set	set a value of a variable

SSI elements may be defined by modules other than `mod_include`. In fact, the `exec` element is provided by `mod_cgi`, and will only be available if this module is loaded.

The config Element

This command controls various aspects of the parsing. The valid attributes are:

echomsg (*Apache 2.1 and later*) The value is a message that is sent back to the client if the echo element attempts to echo an undefined variable. This overrides any SSIUndefinedEcho directives.

errmsg The value is a message that is sent back to the client if an error occurs while parsing the document. This overrides any SSIErrorMsg directives.

sizefmt The value sets the format to be used when displaying the size of a file. Valid values are bytes for a count in bytes, or abbrev for a count in Kb or Mb as appropriate, for example a size of 1024 bytes will be printed as "1K".

timefmt The value is a string to be used by the strftime(3) library routine when printing dates.

The echo Element

This command prints one of the include variables defined below. If the variable is unset, the result is determined by the SSIUndefinedEcho directive. Any dates printed are subject to the currently configured timefmt.

Attributes:

var The value is the name of the variable to print.

encoding Specifies how Apache should encode special characters contained in the variable before outputting them. If set to none, no encoding will be done. If set to url, then URL encoding (also known as %-encoding; this is appropriate for use within URLs in links, etc.) will be performed. At the start of an echo element, the default is set to entity, resulting in entity encoding (which is appropriate in the context of a block-level HTML element, e.g. a paragraph of text). This can be changed by adding an encoding attribute, which will remain in effect until the next encoding attribute is encountered or the element ends, whichever comes first.

The encoding attribute must *precede* the corresponding var attribute to be effective, and only special characters as defined in the ISO-8859-1 character encoding will be encoded. This encoding process may not have the desired result if a different character encoding is in use.

> *In order to avoid cross-site scripting issues, you should always encode user supplied data.*

The exec Element

The exec command executes a given shell command or CGI script. It requires mod_cgi to be present in the server. If Options IncludesNOEXEC is set, this command is completely disabled. The valid attributes are:

cgi The value specifies a (%-encoded) URL-path to the CGI script. If the path does not begin with a slash (/), then it is taken to be relative to the current document. The document referenced by this path is invoked as a CGI script, even if the server would not normally recognize it as such.

However, the directory containing the script must be enabled for CGI scripts (with `ScriptAlias` or `Options ExecCGI`).

The CGI script is given the `PATH_INFO` and query string (`QUERY_STRING`) of the original request from the client; these *cannot* be specified in the URL path. The include variables will be available to the script in addition to the standard CGI (p. 229) environment.

Example
```
<!--#exec cgi="/cgi-bin/example.cgi" -->
```

If the script returns a `Location:` header instead of output, then this will be translated into an HTML anchor.

The `include virtual` element should be used in preference to `exec cgi`. In particular, if you need to pass additional arguments to a CGI program, using the query string, this cannot be done with `exec cgi`, but can be done with `include virtual`, as shown here:

```
<!--#include virtual="/cgi-bin/example.cgi?argument=value"
-->
```

cmd The server will execute the given string using /bin/sh. The include variables are available to the command, in addition to the usual set of CGI variables.

The use of `#include virtual` is almost always prefered to using either `#exec cgi` or `#exec cmd`. The former (`#include virtual`) uses the standard Apache sub-request mechanism to include files or scripts. It is much better tested and maintained.

In addition, on some platforms, like Win32, and on Unix when using suexec (p. 719), you cannot pass arguments to a command in an exec directive, or otherwise include spaces in the command. Thus, while the following will work under a non-suexec configuration on unix, it will not produce the desired result under Win32, or when running suexec:

```
<!--#exec cmd="perl /path/to/perlscript arg1 arg2" -->
```

The fsize Element

This command prints the size of the specified file, subject to the sizefmt format specification. Attributes:

file The value is a path relative to the directory containing the current document being parsed.

virtual The value is a (%-encoded) URL-path. If it does not begin with a slash (/) then it is taken to be relative to the current document. Note, that this does *not* print the size of any CGI output, but the size of the CGI script itself.

The flastmod Element

This command prints the last modification date of the specified file, subject to the timefmt format specification. The attributes are the same as for the fsize command.

The include Element

This command inserts the text of another document or file into the parsed file. Any included file is subject to the usual access control. If the directory containing the parsed file has Options (p. 87) IncludesNOEXEC set, then only documents with a text MIME-type (text/plain, text/html etc.) will be included. Otherwise CGI scripts are invoked as normal using the complete URL given in the command, including any query string.

An attribute defines the location of the document; the inclusion is done for each attribute given to the include command. The valid attributes are:

file The value is a path relative to the directory containing the current document being parsed. It cannot contain ../, nor can it be an absolute path. Therefore, you cannot include files that are outside of the document root, or above the current document in the directory structure. The virtual attribute should always be used in preference to this one.

virtual The value is a (%-encoded) URL-path. The URL cannot contain a scheme or hostname, only a path and an optional query string. If it does not begin with a slash (/) then it is taken to be relative to the current document.

A URL is constructed from the attribute, and the output the server would return if the URL were accessed by the client is included in the parsed output. Thus included files can be nested.

If the specified URL is a CGI program, the program will be executed and its output inserted in place of the directive in the parsed file. You may include a query string in a CGI url:

```
<!--#include virtual="/cgi-bin/example.cgi?argument=value"
-->
```

include virtual should be used in preference to exec cgi to include the output of CGI programs into an HTML document.

The printenv Element

This prints out a listing of all existing variables and their values. Special characters are entity encoded (see the echo element for details) before being output. There are no attributes.

Example
```
<!--#printenv -->
```

The set Element

This sets the value of a variable. Attributes:

var The name of the variable to set.

value The value to give a variable.

Example
```
<!--#set var="category" value="help" -->
```

3.46.4 Include Variables

In addition to the variables in the standard CGI environment, these are available for the echo command, for if and elif, and to any program invoked by the document.

DATE_GMT The current date in Greenwich Mean Time.

DATE_LOCAL The current date in the local time zone.

DOCUMENT_NAME The filename (excluding directories) of the document requested by the user.

DOCUMENT_URI The (%-decoded) URL path of the document requested by the user. Note that in the case of nested include files, this is *not* the URL for the current document. Note also that if the URL is modified internally (e.g. by an alias or directoryindex), the modified URL is shown.

LAST_MODIFIED The last modification date of the document requested by the user.

QUERY_STRING_UNESCAPED If a query string is present, this variable contains the (%-decoded) query string, which is *escaped* for shell usage (special characters like & etc. are preceded by backslashes).

3.46.5 Variable Substitution

Variable substitution is done within quoted strings in most cases where they may reasonably occur as an argument to an SSI directive. This includes the config, exec, flastmod, fsize, include, echo, and set directives, as well as the arguments to conditional operators. You can insert a literal dollar sign into the string using backslash quoting:

```
<!--#if expr="$a = \$test" -->
```

If a variable reference needs to be substituted in the middle of a character sequence that might otherwise be considered a valid identifier in its own right, it can be disambiguated by enclosing the reference in braces, *à la* shell substitution:

```
<!--#set var="Zed" value="${REMOTE_HOST}_${REQUEST_METHOD}" -->
```

This will result in the Zed variable being set to "X_Y" if REMOTE_HOST is "X" and REQUEST_METHOD is "Y".

The below example will print "in foo" if the DOCUMENT_URI is /foo/file.html, "in bar" if it is /bar/file.html and "in neither" otherwise:

```
<!--#if expr='"$DOCUMENT_URI" = "/foo/file.html"' -->
    in foo
<!--#elif expr='"$DOCUMENT_URI" = "/bar/file.html"' -->
    in bar
<!--#else -->
    in neither
<!--#endif -->
```

3.46.6 Flow Control Elements

The basic flow control elements are:

```
<!--#if expr="test_condition" -->
<!--#elif expr="test_condition" -->
<!--#else -->
<!--#endif -->
```

The if element works like an if statement in a programming language. The test condition is evaluated and if the result is true, then the text until the next elif, else or endif element is included in the output stream.

The elif or else statements are used to put text into the output stream if the original *test_condition* was false. These elements are optional.

The endif element ends the if element and is required.

test_condition is one of the following:

string
:   true if *string* is not empty

-A string
:   true if the URL represented by the string is accessible by configuration, false otherwise. This test only has an effect if SSIEnableAccess is on. This is useful where content on a page is to be hidden from users who are not authorized to view the URL, such as a link to that URL. Note that the URL is only tested for whether access would be granted, not whether the URL exists.

    Example
    ```
    <!--#if expr="-A /private" -->
        Click <a href="/private">here</a> to access private
        information.
    <!--#endif -->
    ```

string1 = string2
string1 == string2
string1 != string2
:   Compare *string1* with *string2*. If *string2* has the form */string2/* then it

is treated as a regular expression. Regular expressions are implemented by the PCRE[39] engine and have the same syntax as those in perl 5[40]. Note that == is just an alias for = and behaves exactly the same way.

If you are matching positive (= or ==), you can capture grouped parts of the regular expression. The captured parts are stored in the special variables $1 .. $9.

Example
```
<!--#if expr="$QUERY_STRING = /^sid=([a-zA-Z0-9]+)/" -->
    <!--#set var="session" value="$1" -->
<!--#endif -->
```

string1 < string2
string1 <= string2
string1 > string2
string1 >= string2

Compare *string1* with *string2*. Note, that strings are compared *literally* (using strcmp(3)). Therefore the string "100" is less than "20".

(test_condition)
true if *test_condition* is true

! test_condition
true if *test_condition* is false

test_condition1 && test_condition2
true if both *test_condition1* and *test_condition2* are true

test_condition1 || test_condition2
true if either *test_condition1* or *test_condition2* is true

"=" and "!=" bind more tightly than "&&" and "||". "!" binds most tightly. Thus, the following are equivalent:

```
<!--#if expr="$a = test1 && $b = test2" -->
<!--#if expr="($a = test1) && ($b = test2)" -->
```

The boolean operators && and || share the same priority. So if you want to bind such an operator more tightly, you should use parentheses.

Anything that's not recognized as a variable or an operator is treated as a string. Strings can also be quoted: 'string'. Unquoted strings can't contain whitespace (blanks and tabs) because it is used to separate tokens such as variables. If multiple strings are found in a row, they are concatenated using blanks. So,

string1   string2 results in *string1 string2*
and
'string1   string2' results in *string1   string2*.

---

[39]http://www.pcre.org
[40]http://www.perl.com

OPTIMIZATION OF BOOLEAN EXPRESSIONS *If the expressions become more complex and slow down processing significantly, you can try to optimize them according to the evaluation rules:*

- *Expressions are evaluated from left to right*
- *Binary boolean operators (&& and ||) are short circuited wherever possible. In conclusion with the rule above that means, mod_include evaluates at first the left expression. If the left result is sufficient to determine the end result, processing stops here. Otherwise it evaluates the right side and computes the end result from both left and right results.*
- *Short circuit evaluation is turned off as long as there are regular expressions to deal with. These must be evaluated to fill in the backreference variables ($1 .. $9).*

If you want to look how a particular expression is handled, you can recompile mod_include using the -DDEBUG_INCLUDE compiler option. This inserts for every parsed expression tokenizer information, the parse tree and how it is evaluated into the output sent to the client.

ESCAPING SLASHES IN REGEX STRINGS *All slashes which are not intended to act as delimiters in your regex must be escaped. This is regardless of their meaning to the regex engine.*

SSIETag Directive

Description:	Controls whether ETags are generated by the server.
Syntax:	SSIETag on|off
Default:	SSIETag off
Context:	directory, .htaccess
Status:	Base
Module:	mod_include
Compatibility:	Available in version 2.2.15 and later.

Under normal circumstances, a file filtered by mod_include may contain elements that are either dynamically generated, or that may have changed independently of the original file. As a result, by default the server is asked not to generate an ETag header for the response by adding no-etag to the request notes.

The SSIETag directive suppresses this behaviour, and allows the server to generate an ETag header. This can be used to enable caching of the output. Note that a backend server or dynamic content generator may generate an ETag of its own, ignoring no-etag, and this ETag will be passed by mod_include regardless of the value of this setting. SSIETag can take on the following values:

off no-etag will be added to the request notes, and the server is asked not to generate an ETag. Where a server ignores the value of no-etag and generates an ETag anyway, the ETag will be respected.

on Existing ETags will be respected, and ETags generated by the server will be
passed on in the response.

SSIEnableAccess Directive

Description:	Enable the -A flag during conditional flow control processing.
Syntax:	SSIEnableAccess on|off
Default:	SSIEnableAccess off
Context:	directory, .htaccess
Status:	Base
Module:	mod_include

The SSIEnableAccess directive controls whether the -A test is enabled during
conditional flow control processing. SSIEnableAccess can take on the following
values:

off <!--#if expr="-A /foo"--> will be interpreted as a series of string and regular
   expression tokens, the -A has no special meaning.

on <!--#if expr="-A /foo"--> will evaluate to false if the URL /foo is inaccessible
   by configuration, or true otherwise.

SSIEndTag Directive

Description:	String that ends an include element
Syntax:	SSIEndTag tag
Default:	SSIEndTag "-->"
Context:	server config, virtual host
Status:	Base
Module:	mod_include
Compatibility:	Available in version 2.0.30 and later.

This directive changes the string that mod_include looks for to mark the end of
an include element.

Example
   SSIEndTag "%>"

See also:

▷ SSIStartTag (p. 313)

SSIErrorMsg Directive

Description:	Error message displayed when there is an SSI error
Syntax:	SSIErrorMsg *message*
Default:	SSIErrorMsg "[an error occurred while processing this directive]"
Context:	server config, virtual host, directory, .htaccess
Override:	All
Status:	Base
Module:	mod_include
Compatibility:	Available in version 2.0.30 and later.

The SSIErrorMsg directive changes the error message displayed when mod_-include encounters an error. For production servers you may consider changing the default error message to "<!-- Error -->" so that the message is not presented to the user.

This directive has the same effect as the <!--#config errmsg=*message* --> element.

Example
  SSIErrorMsg "<!-- Error -->"

SSILastModified Directive

Description:	Controls whether Last-Modified headers are generated by the server.
Syntax:	SSILastModified on|off
Default:	SSILastModified off
Context:	directory, .htaccess
Status:	Base
Module:	mod_include
Compatibility:	Available in version 2.2.15 and later.

Under normal circumstances, a file filtered by mod_include may contain elements that are either dynamically generated, or that may have changed independently of the original file. As a result, by default the Last-Modified header is stripped from the response.

The SSILastModified directive overrides this behaviour, and allows the Last-Modified header to be respected if already present, or set if the header is not already present. This can be used to enable caching of the output. SSILastModified can take on the following values:

off The Last-Modified header will be stripped from responses, unless the XBitHack directive is set to full as described below.

on The Last-Modified header will be respected if already present in a response, and added to the response if the response is a file and the header is missing. The SSILastModified directive takes precedence over XBitHack.

SSIStartTag Directive

Description:	String that starts an include element
Syntax:	SSIStartTag *tag*
Default:	SSIStartTag "<!--#"
Context:	server config, virtual host
Status:	Base
Module:	mod_include
Compatibility:	Available in version 2.0.30 and later.

This directive changes the string that mod_include looks for to mark an include element to process.

You may want to use this option if you have 2 servers parsing the output of a file each processing different commands (possibly at different times).

Example
```
SSIStartTag "<%"
SSIEndTag "%>"
```

The example given above, which also specifies a matching SSIEndTag, will allow you to use SSI directives as shown in the example below:

SSI directives with alternate start and end tags
```
<%printenv %>
```

See also:

▷ SSIEndTag (p. 311)

SSITimeFormat Directive

Description:	Configures the format in which date strings are displayed
Syntax:	SSITimeFormat *formatstring*
Default:	SSITimeFormat "%A, %d-%b-%Y %H:%M:%S %Z"
Context:	server config, virtual host, directory, .htaccess
Override:	All
Status:	Base
Module:	mod_include
Compatibility:	Available in version 2.0.30 and later.

This directive changes the format in which date strings are displayed when echoing DATE environment variables. The *formatstring* is as in strftime(3) from the C standard library.

This directive has the same effect as the <!--#config timefmt=*formatstring* --> element.

Example
```
SSITimeFormat "%R, %B %d, %Y"
```

The above directive would cause times to be displayed in the format "22:26,

June 14, 2002".

SSIUndefinedEcho Directive

Description:	String displayed when an unset variable is echoed
Syntax:	SSIUndefinedEcho *string*
Default:	SSIUndefinedEcho "(none)"
Context:	server config, virtual host, directory, .htaccess
Override:	All
Status:	Base
Module:	mod_include
Compatibility:	Available in version 2.0.34 and later.

This directive changes the string that mod_include displays when a variable is not set and "echoed".

Example
    SSIUndefinedEcho "<!-- undef -->"

XBitHack Directive

Description:	Parse SSI directives in files with the execute bit set
Syntax:	XBitHack on|off|full
Default:	XBitHack off
Context:	server config, virtual host, directory, .htaccess
Override:	Options
Status:	Base
Module:	mod_include

The XBitHack directive controls the parsing of ordinary html documents. This directive only affects files associated with the MIME-type text/html. XBitHack can take on the following values:

off No special treatment of executable files.

on Any text/html file that has the user-execute bit set will be treated as a server-parsed HTML document.

full As for on but also test the group-execute bit. If it is set, then set the Last-modified date of the returned file to be the last modified time of the file. If it is not set, then no last-modified date is sent. Setting this bit allows clients and proxies to cache the result of the request.

> NOTE *You would not want to use the full option, unless you assure the group-execute bit is unset for every SSI script which might #include a CGI or otherwise produces different output on each hit (or could potentially change on subsequent requests).*
>
> *The SSILastModified directive takes precedence over the XBitHack directive when SSILastModified is set to on.*

3.47 Apache Module mod_info

Description:	Provides a comprehensive overview of the server config-uration
Status:	Extension
Module Identifier:	info_module
Source File:	mod_info.c

Summary

To configure mod_info, add the following to your httpd.conf file.

```
<Location /server-info>
    SetHandler server-info
</Location>
```

You may wish to use mod_authz_host inside the <Location> directive to limit access to your server configuration information:

```
<Location /server-info>
    SetHandler server-info
    Order deny,allow
    Deny from all
    Allow from yourcompany.com
</Location>
```

Once configured, the server information is obtained by accessing http://your.host.example.com/server-info

Directives:

```
AddModuleInfo
```

3.47.1 Security Issues

Once mod_info is loaded into the server, its handler capability is available in *all* configuration files, including per-directory files (*e.g.*, .htaccess). This may have security-related ramifications for your site.

In particular, this module can leak sensitive information from the configuration directives of other Apache modules such as system paths, usernames/passwords, database names, etc. Therefore, this module should **only** be used in a controlled environment and always with caution.

You will probably want to use mod_authz_host to limit access to your server configuration information.

Access control
```
<Location /server-info>
    SetHandler server-info
    Order allow,deny
    # Allow access from server itself
```

```
      Allow from 127.0.0.1
      # Additionally, allow access from local workstation
      Allow from 192.168.1.17
</Location>
```

3.47.2 Selecting the information shown

By default, the server information includes a list of all enabled modules, and
for each module, a description of the directives understood by that module, the
hooks implemented by that module, and the relevant directives from the current
configuration.

Other views of the configuration information are available by appending a query
to the server-info request. For example, http://your.host.example.com/
server-info?config will show all configuration directives.

?<module-name> Only information relevant to the named module

?config Just the configuration directives, not sorted by module

?hooks Only the list of Hooks each module is attached to

?list Only a simple list of enabled modules

?server Only the basic server information

3.47.3 Known Limitations

mod_info provides its information by reading the parsed configuration, rather
than reading the original configuration file. There are a few limitations as a
result of the way the parsed configuration tree is created:

- Directives which are executed immediately rather than being stored in
  the parsed configuration are not listed. These include ServerRoot,
  LoadModule, and LoadFile.

- Directives which control the configuration file itself, such as Include,
  <IfModule> and <IfDefine> are not listed, but the included configuration directives are.

- Comments are not listed. (This may be considered a feature.)

- Configuration directives from .htaccess files are not listed (since they do
  not form part of the permanent server configuration).

- Container directives such as <Directory> are listed normally, but mod_-
  info cannot figure out the line number for the closing </Directory>.

- Directives generated by third party modules such as mod_perl[41] might not
  be listed.

---

[41]http://perl.apache.org

AddModuleInfo Directive

Description:	Adds additional information to the module information displayed by the server-info handler
Syntax:	AddModuleInfo *module-name string*
Context:	server config, virtual host
Status:	Extension
Module:	mod_info
Compatibility:	Apache 1.3 and above

This allows the content of *string* to be shown as HTML interpreted, **Additional Information** for the module *module-name*. Example:

```
AddModuleInfo mod_deflate.c 'See <a \
    href="http://www.apache.org/docs/2.2/mod/mod_deflate.html">\
    http://www.apache.org/docs/2.2/mod/mod_deflate.html</a>'
```

3.48 Apache Module mod_isapi

Description:	ISAPI Extensions within Apache for Windows
Status:	Base
Module Identifier:	isapi_module
Source File:	mod_isapi.c
Compatibility:	Win32 only

Summary

This module implements the Internet Server extension API. It allows Internet Server extensions (*e.g.* ISAPI .dll modules) to be served by Apache for Windows, subject to the noted restrictions.

ISAPI extension modules (.dll files) are written by third parties. The Apache Group does not author these modules, so we provide no support for them. Please contact the ISAPI's author directly if you are experiencing problems running their ISAPI extension. **Please *do not* post such problems to Apache's lists or bug reporting pages.**

Directives:

> ISAPIAppendLogToErrors
> ISAPIAppendLogToQuery
> ISAPICacheFile
> ISAPIFakeAsync
> ISAPILogNotSupported
> ISAPIReadAheadBuffer

3.48.1 Usage

In the server configuration file, use the AddHandler directive to associate ISAPI files with the isapi-handler handler, and map it to them with their file extensions. To enable any .dll file to be processed as an ISAPI extension, edit the httpd.conf file and add the following line:

> AddHandler isapi-handler .dll

> *In older versions of the Apache server,* isapi-isa *was the proper handler name, rather than* isapi-handler. *For compatibility, configurations may continue using* isapi-isa *through all versions of Apache prior to 2.3.0.*

There is no capability within the Apache server to leave a requested module loaded. However, you may preload and keep a specific module loaded by using the following syntax in your httpd.conf:

> ISAPICacheFile c:/WebWork/Scripts/ISAPI/mytest.dll

Whether or not you have preloaded an ISAPI extension, all ISAPI extensions are governed by the same permissions and restrictions as CGI scripts. That is,

Options ExecCGI must be set for the directory that contains the ISAPI .dll file.

Review the Additional Notes and the Programmer's Journal for additional details and clarification of the specific ISAPI support offered by mod_isapi.

3.48.2 Additional Notes

Apache's ISAPI implementation conforms to all of the ISAPI 2.0 specification, except for some "Microsoft-specific" extensions dealing with asynchronous I/O. Apache's I/O model does not allow asynchronous reading and writing in a manner that the ISAPI could access. If an ISA tries to access unsupported features, including async I/O, a message is placed in the error log to help with debugging. Since these messages can become a flood, the directive ISAPILogNotSupported Off exists to quiet this noise.

Some servers, like Microsoft IIS, load the ISAPI extension into the server and keep it loaded until memory usage is too high, or unless configuration options are specified. Apache currently loads and unloads the ISAPI extension each time it is requested, unless the ISAPICacheFile directive is specified. This is inefficient, but Apache's memory model makes this the most effective method. Many ISAPI modules are subtly incompatible with the Apache server, and unloading these modules helps to ensure the stability of the server.

Also, remember that while Apache supports ISAPI Extensions, it **does not support ISAPI Filters**. Support for filters may be added at a later date, but no support is planned at this time.

3.48.3 Programmer's Journal

If you are programming Apache 2.0 mod_isapi modules, you must limit your calls to ServerSupportFunction to the following directives:

HSE_REQ_SEND_URL_REDIRECT_RESP Redirect the user to another location.
> This must be a fully qualified URL (*e.g.* http://server/location).

HSE_REQ_SEND_URL Redirect the user to another location.
> This cannot be a fully qualified URL, you are not allowed to pass the protocol or a server name (*e.g.* simply /location).
> This redirection is handled by the server, not the browser.

> WARNING   *In their recent documentation, Microsoft appears to have abandoned the distinction between the two HSE_REQ_SEND_- URL functions. Apache continues to treat them as two distinct functions with different requirements and behaviors.*

HSE_REQ_SEND_RESPONSE_HEADER Apache accepts a response body following the header if it follows the blank line (two consecutive newlines) in the headers string argument. This body cannot contain NULLs, since the headers argument is NULL terminated.

HSE_REQ_DONE_WITH_SESSION Apache considers this a no-op, since the session will be finished when the ISAPI returns from processing.

HSE_REQ_MAP_URL_TO_PATH Apache will translate a virtual name to a physical name.

HSE_APPEND_LOG_PARAMETER This logged message may be captured in any of the following logs:

- in the \"%{isapi-parameter}n\" component in a CustomLog directive
- in the %q log component with the ISAPIAppendLogToQuery On directive
- in the error log with the ISAPIAppendLogToErrors On directive

The first option, the %{isapi-parameter}n component, is always available and preferred.

HSE_REQ_IS_KEEP_CONN Will return the negotiated Keep-Alive status.

HSE_REQ_SEND_RESPONSE_HEADER_EX Will behave as documented, although the fKeepConn flag is ignored.

HSE_REQ_IS_CONNECTED Will report false if the request has been aborted.

Apache returns FALSE to any unsupported call to ServerSupportFunction, and sets the GetLastError value to ERROR_INVALID_PARAMETER.

ReadClient retrieves the request body exceeding the initial buffer (defined by ISAPIReadAheadBuffer). Based on the ISAPIReadAheadBuffer setting (number of bytes to buffer prior to calling the ISAPI handler) shorter requests are sent complete to the extension when it is invoked. If the request is longer, the ISAPI extension must use ReadClient to retrieve the remaining request body.

WriteClient is supported, but only with the HSE_IO_SYNC flag or no option flag (value of 0). Any other WriteClient request will be rejected with a return value of FALSE, and a GetLastError value of ERROR_INVALID_PARAMETER.

GetServerVariable is supported, although extended server variables do not exist (as defined by other servers.) All the usual Apache CGI environment variables are available from GetServerVariable, as well as the ALL_HTTP and ALL_RAW values.

Apache 2.0 mod_isapi supports additional features introduced in later versions of the ISAPI specification, as well as limited emulation of async I/O and the TransmitFile semantics. Apache also supports preloading ISAPI .dlls for performance, neither of which were not available under Apache 1.3 mod_isapi.

ISAPIAppendLogToErrors Directive

Description:	Record HSE_APPEND_LOG_PARAMETER requests from ISAPI extensions to the error log
Syntax:	ISAPIAppendLogToErrors on|off
Default:	ISAPIAppendLogToErrors off
Context:	server config, virtual host, directory, .htaccess
Override:	FileInfo
Status:	Base
Module:	mod_isapi

Record HSE_APPEND_LOG_PARAMETER requests from ISAPI extensions to the server error log.

ISAPIAppendLogToQuery Directive

Description:	Record HSE_APPEND_LOG_PARAMETER requests from ISAPI extensions to the query field
Syntax:	ISAPIAppendLogToQuery on|off
Default:	ISAPIAppendLogToQuery on
Context:	server config, virtual host, directory, .htaccess
Override:	FileInfo
Status:	Base
Module:	mod_isapi

Record HSE_APPEND_LOG_PARAMETER requests from ISAPI extensions to the query field (appended to the CustomLog %q component).

ISAPICacheFile Directive

Description:	ISAPI .dll files to be loaded at startup
Syntax:	ISAPICacheFile file-path [file-path] ...
Context:	server config, virtual host
Status:	Base
Module:	mod_isapi

Specifies a space-separated list of file names to be loaded when the Apache server is launched, and remain loaded until the server is shut down. This directive may be repeated for every ISAPI .dll file desired. The full path name of each file should be specified. If the path name is not absolute, it will be treated relative to ServerRoot.

ISAPIFakeAsync Directive

Description:	Fake asynchronous support for ISAPI callbacks
Syntax:	ISAPIFakeAsync on|off
Default:	ISAPIFakeAsync off
Context:	server config, virtual host, directory, .htaccess
Override:	FileInfo
Status:	Base
Module:	mod_isapi

While set to on, asynchronous support for ISAPI callbacks is simulated.

ISAPILogNotSupported Directive

Description:	Log unsupported feature requests from ISAPI extensions
Syntax:	ISAPILogNotSupported on|off
Default:	ISAPILogNotSupported off
Context:	server config, virtual host, directory, .htaccess
Override:	FileInfo
Status:	Base
Module:	mod_isapi

Logs all requests for unsupported features from ISAPI extensions in the server error log. This may help administrators to track down problems. Once set to on and all desired ISAPI modules are functioning, it should be set back to off.

ISAPIReadAheadBuffer Directive

Description:	Size of the Read Ahead Buffer sent to ISAPI extensions
Syntax:	ISAPIReadAheadBuffer size
Default:	ISAPIReadAheadBuffer 49152
Context:	server config, virtual host, directory, .htaccess
Override:	FileInfo
Status:	Base
Module:	mod_isapi

Defines the maximum size of the Read Ahead Buffer sent to ISAPI extensions when they are initially invoked. All remaining data must be retrieved using the ReadClient callback; some ISAPI extensions may not support the ReadClient function. Refer questions to the ISAPI extension's author.

3.49 Apache Module mod_ldap

Description:	LDAP connection pooling and result caching services for use by other LDAP modules
Status:	Extension
Module Identifier:	ldap_module
Source File:	util_ldap.c
Compatibility:	Available in version 2.0.41 and later

Summary

This module was created to improve the performance of websites relying on backend connections to LDAP servers. In addition to the functions provided by the standard LDAP libraries, this module adds an LDAP connection pool and an LDAP shared memory cache.

To enable this module, LDAP support must be compiled into apr-util. This is achieved by adding the --with-ldap flag to the configure script when building Apache.

SSL/TLS support is dependant on which LDAP toolkit has been linked to APR. As of this writing, APR-util supports: OpenLDAP SDK[42] (2.x or later), Novell LDAP SDK[43], Mozilla LDAP SDK[44], native Solaris LDAP SDK (Mozilla based), native Microsoft LDAP SDK, or the iPlanet (Netscape)[45] SDK. See the APR[46] website for details.

Directives:

LDAPCacheEntries
LDAPCacheTTL
LDAPConnectionTimeout
LDAPOpCacheEntries
LDAPOpCacheTTL
LDAPSharedCacheFile

LDAPSharedCacheSize
LDAPTrustedClientCert
LDAPTrustedGlobalCert
LDAPTrustedMode
LDAPVerifyServerCert

3.49.1 Example Configuration

The following is an example configuration that uses mod_ldap to increase the performance of HTTP Basic authentication provided by mod_authnz_ldap.

```
# Enable the LDAP connection pool and shared
# memory cache.  Enable the LDAP cache status
# handler.  Requires that mod_ldap and mod_authnz_ldap
# be loaded.  Change the "yourdomain.example.com" to
```

---

[42]http://www.openldap.org/
[43]http://developer.novell.com/ndk/cldap.htm
[44]http://www.mozilla.org/directory/csdk.html
[45]http://www.iplanet.com/downloads/developer/
[46]http://apr.apache.org

```
# match your domain.
LDAPSharedCacheSize 500000
LDAPCacheEntries 1024
LDAPCacheTTL 600
LDAPOpCacheEntries 1024
LDAPOpCacheTTL 600

<Location /ldap-status>
    SetHandler ldap-status
    Order deny,allow
    Deny from all
    Allow from yourdomain.example.com
    AuthLDAPURL ldap://127.0.0.1/dc=example,dc=com?uid?one
    AuthzLDAPAuthoritative off
    Require valid-user
</Location>
```

3.49.2 LDAP Connection Pool

LDAP connections are pooled from request to request. This allows the LDAP server to remain connected and bound ready for the next request, without the need to unbind/connect/rebind. The performance advantages are similar to the effect of HTTP keepalives.

On a busy server it is possible that many requests will try and access the same LDAP server connection simultaneously. Where an LDAP connection is in use, Apache will create a new connection alongside the original one. This ensures that the connection pool does not become a bottleneck.

There is no need to manually enable connection pooling in the Apache configuration. Any module using this module for access to LDAP services will share the connection pool.

3.49.3 LDAP Cache

For improved performance, mod_ldap uses an aggressive caching strategy to minimize the number of times that the LDAP server must be contacted. Caching can easily double or triple the throughput of Apache when it is serving pages protected with mod_authnz_ldap. In addition, the load on the LDAP server will be significantly decreased.

mod_ldap supports two types of LDAP caching during the search/bind phase with a *search/bind cache* and during the compare phase with two *operation caches*. Each LDAP URL that is used by the server has its own set of these three caches.

The Search/Bind Cache

The process of doing a search and then a bind is the most time-consuming aspect of LDAP operation, especially if the directory is large. The search/bind cache is used to cache all searches that resulted in successful binds. Negative results (*i.e.*, unsuccessful searches, or searches that did not result in a successful bind) are not cached. The rationale behind this decision is that connections with invalid credentials are only a tiny percentage of the total number of connections, so by not caching invalid credentials, the size of the cache is reduced.

mod_ldap stores the username, the DN retrieved, the password used to bind, and the time of the bind in the cache. Whenever a new connection is initiated with the same username, mod_ldap compares the password of the new connection with the password in the cache. If the passwords match, and if the cached entry is not too old, mod_ldap bypasses the search/bind phase.

The search and bind cache is controlled with the LDAPCacheEntries and LDAPCacheTTL directives.

Operation Caches

During attribute and distinguished name comparison functions, mod_ldap uses two operation caches to cache the compare operations. The first compare cache is used to cache the results of compares done to test for LDAP group membership. The second compare cache is used to cache the results of comparisons done between distinguished names.

The behavior of both of these caches is controlled with the LDAPOpCacheEntries and LDAPOpCacheTTL directives.

Monitoring the Cache

mod_ldap has a content handler that allows administrators to monitor the cache performance. The name of the content handler is ldap-status, so the following directives could be used to access the mod_ldap cache information:

```
<Location /server/cache-info>
    SetHandler ldap-status
</Location>
```

By fetching the URL http://servername/cache-info, the administrator can get a status report of every cache that is used by mod_ldap cache. Note that if Apache does not support shared memory, then each httpd instance has its own cache, so reloading the URL will result in different information each time, depending on which httpd instance processes the request.

3.49.4 Using SSL/TLS

The ability to create SSL and TLS connections to an LDAP server is defined by the directives LDAPTrustedGlobalCert, LDAPTrustedClientCert and LDAPTrustedMode. These directives specify the CA and optional client certificates to be used, as well as the type of encryption to be used on the connection (none, SSL or TLS/STARTTLS).

```
# Establish an SSL LDAP connection on port 636.  Requires that
```

```
# mod_ldap and mod_authnz_ldap be loaded.  Change the
# "yourdomain.example.com" to match your domain.
LDAPTrustedGlobalCert CA_DER /certs/certfile.der
<Location /ldap-status>
    SetHandler ldap-status
    Order deny,allow
    Deny from all
    Allow from yourdomain.example.com
    AuthLDAPURL ldaps://127.0.0.1/dc=example,dc=com?uid?one
    AuthzLDAPAuthoritative off
    Require valid-user
</Location>

# Establish a TLS LDAP connection on port 389.  Requires that
# mod_ldap and mod_authnz_ldap be loaded.  Change the
# "yourdomain.example.com" to match your domain.
LDAPTrustedGlobalCert CA_DER /certs/certfile.der
<Location /ldap-status>
    SetHandler ldap-status
    Order deny,allow
    Deny from all
    Allow from yourdomain.example.com
    AuthLDAPURL ldap://127.0.0.1/dc=example,dc=com?uid?one TLS
    AuthzLDAPAuthoritative off
    Require valid-user
</Location>
```

3.49.5 SSL/TLS Certificates

The different LDAP SDKs have widely different methods of setting and handling both CA and client side certificates.

If you intend to use SSL or TLS, read this section CAREFULLY so as to understand the differences between configurations on the different LDAP toolkits supported.

Netscape/Mozilla/iPlanet SDK

CA certificates are specified within a file called cert7.db. The SDK will not talk to any LDAP server whose certificate was not signed by a CA specified in this file. If client certificates are required, an optional key3.db file may be specified with an optional password. The secmod file can be specified if required. These files are in the same format as used by the Netscape Communicator or Mozilla web browsers. The easiest way to obtain these files is to grab them from your browser installation.

Client certificates are specified per connection using the LDAPTrusted-ClientCert directive by referring to the certificate "nickname". An optional password may be specified to unlock the certificate's private key.

The SDK supports SSL only. An attempt to use STARTTLS will cause an error when an attempt is made to contact the LDAP server at runtime.

```
# Specify a Netscape CA certificate file
LDAPTrustedGlobalCert CA_CERT7_DB /certs/cert7.db
# Specify an optional key3.db file for client certificate
support
LDAPTrustedGlobalCert CERT_KEY3_DB /certs/key3.db
# Specify the secmod file if required
LDAPTrustedGlobalCert CA_SECMOD /certs/secmod
<Location /ldap-status>
    SetHandler ldap-status
    Order deny,allow
    Deny from all
    Allow from yourdomain.example.com
    LDAPTrustedClientCert CERT_NICKNAME <nickname> [password]
    AuthLDAPURL ldaps://127.0.0.1/dc=example,dc=com?uid?one
    AuthzLDAPAuthoritative off
    Require valid-user
</Location>
```

Novell SDK

One or more CA certificates must be specified for the Novell SDK to work correctly. These certificates can be specified as binary DER or Base64 (PEM) encoded files.

Note: Client certificates are specified globally rather than per connection, and so must be specified with the LDAPTrustedGlobalCert directive as below. Trying to set client certificates via the LDAPTrustedClientCert directive will cause an error to be logged when an attempt is made to connect to the LDAP server..

The SDK supports both SSL and STARTTLS, set using the LDAPTrustedMode parameter. If an ldaps:// URL is specified, SSL mode is forced, override this directive.

```
# Specify two CA certificate files
LDAPTrustedGlobalCert CA_DER /certs/cacert1.der
LDAPTrustedGlobalCert CA_BASE64 /certs/cacert2.pem
# Specify a client certificate file and key
LDAPTrustedGlobalCert CERT_BASE64 /certs/cert1.pem
LDAPTrustedGlobalCert KEY_BASE64 /certs/key1.pem [password]
# Do not use this directive, as it will throw an error
#LDAPTrustedClientCert CERT_BASE64 /certs/cert1.pem
```

OpenLDAP SDK

One or more CA certificates must be specified for the OpenLDAP SDK to work correctly. These certificates can be specified as binary DER or Base64 (PEM) encoded files.

Client certificates are specified per connection using the LDAPTrustedClientCert directive.

The documentation for the SDK claims to support both SSL and START-TLS, however STARTTLS does not seem to work on all versions of the SDK. The SSL/TLS mode can be set using the LDAPTrustedMode parameter. If an ldaps:// URL is specified, SSL mode is forced. The OpenLDAP documentation notes that SSL (ldaps://) support has been deprecated to be replaced with TLS, although the SSL functionality still works.

```
# Specify two CA certificate files
LDAPTrustedGlobalCert CA_DER /certs/cacert1.der
LDAPTrustedGlobalCert CA_BASE64 /certs/cacert2.pem
<Location /ldap-status>
    SetHandler ldap-status
    Order deny,allow
    Deny from all
    Allow from yourdomain.example.com
    LDAPTrustedClientCert CERT_BASE64 /certs/cert1.pem
    LDAPTrustedClientCert KEY_BASE64 /certs/key1.pem
    AuthLDAPURL ldaps://127.0.0.1/dc=example,dc=com?uid?one
    AuthzLDAPAuthoritative off
    Require valid-user
</Location>
```

Solaris SDK

SSL/TLS for the native Solaris LDAP libraries is not yet supported. If required, install and use the OpenLDAP libraries instead.

Microsoft SDK

SSL/TLS certificate configuration for the native Microsoft LDAP libraries is done inside the system registry, and no configuration directives are required.

Both SSL and TLS are supported by using the ldaps:// URL format, or by using the LDAPTrustedMode directive accordingly.

Note: The status of support for client certificates is not yet known for this toolkit.

LDAPCacheEntries Directive

Description:	Maximum number of entries in the primary LDAP cache
Syntax:	LDAPCacheEntries *number*
Default:	LDAPCacheEntries 1024
Context:	server config
Status:	Extension
Module:	mod_ldap

Specifies the maximum size of the primary LDAP cache. This cache contains successful search/binds. Set it to 0 to turn off search/bind caching. The default size is 1024 cached searches.

LDAPCacheTTL Directive

Description:	Time that cached items remain valid
Syntax:	LDAPCacheTTL *seconds*
Default:	LDAPCacheTTL 600
Context:	server config
Status:	Extension
Module:	mod_ldap

Specifies the time (in seconds) that an item in the search/bind cache remains valid. The default is 600 seconds (10 minutes).

LDAPConnectionTimeout Directive

Description:	Specifies the socket connection timeout in seconds
Syntax:	LDAPConnectionTimeout *seconds*
Context:	server config
Status:	Extension
Module:	mod_ldap

This directive configures the LDAP_OPT_NETWORK_TIMEOUT option in the underlying LDAP client library, when available. This value typically controls how long the LDAP client library will wait for the TCP connection to the LDAP server to complete.

If a connection is not successful with the timeout period, either an error will be returned or the LDAP client library will attempt to connect to a secondary LDAP server if one is specified (via a space-separated list of hostnames in the AuthLDAPURL).

The default is 10 seconds, if the LDAP client library linked with the server supports the LDAP_OPT_NETWORK_TIMEOUT option.

LDAPConnectionTimeout is only available when the LDAP client library linked with the server supports the LDAP_OPT_NETWORK_TIME-OUT option, and the ultimate behavior is dictated entirely by the LDAP client library.

LDAPOpCacheEntries Directive

Description:	Number of entries used to cache LDAP compare operations
Syntax:	LDAPOpCacheEntries *number*
Default:	LDAPOpCacheEntries 1024
Context:	server config
Status:	Extension
Module:	mod_ldap

This specifies the number of entries mod_ldap will use to cache LDAP compare operations. The default is 1024 entries. Setting it to 0 disables operation caching.

LDAPOpCacheTTL Directive

Description:	Time that entries in the operation cache remain valid
Syntax:	LDAPOpCacheTTL *seconds*
Default:	LDAPOpCacheTTL 600
Context:	server config
Status:	Extension
Module:	mod_ldap

Specifies the time (in seconds) that entries in the operation cache remain valid. The default is 600 seconds.

LDAPSharedCacheFile Directive

Description:	Sets the shared memory cache file
Syntax:	LDAPSharedCacheFile *directory-path/filename*
Context:	server config
Status:	Extension
Module:	mod_ldap

Specifies the directory path and file name of the shared memory cache file. If not set, anonymous shared memory will be used if the platform supports it.

LDAPSharedCacheSize Directive

Description:	Size in bytes of the shared-memory cache
Syntax:	LDAPSharedCacheSize *bytes*
Default:	LDAPSharedCacheSize 500000
Context:	server config
Status:	Extension
Module:	mod_ldap

Specifies the number of bytes to allocate for the shared memory cache. The default is 500kb. If set to 0, shared memory caching will not be used.

LDAPTrustedClientCert Directive

Description:	Sets the file containing or nickname referring to a per connection client certificate. Not all LDAP toolkits support per connection client certificates.
Syntax:	LDAPTrustedClientCert type directory-path/filename/nickname [password]
Context:	server config, virtual host, directory, .htaccess
Status:	Extension
Module:	mod_ldap

It specifies the directory path, file name or nickname of a per connection client certificate used when establishing an SSL or TLS connection to an LDAP server. Different locations or directories may have their own independent client certificate settings. Some LDAP toolkits (notably Novell) do not support per connection client certificates, and will throw an error on LDAP server connection if you try to use this directive (Use the LDAPTrustedGlobalCert directive instead for Novell client certificates - See the SSL/TLS certificate guide above for details). The type specifies the kind of certificate parameter being set, depending on the LDAP toolkit being used. Supported types are:

- CERT_DER - binary DER encoded client certificate
- CERT_BASE64 - PEM encoded client certificate
- CERT_NICKNAME - Client certificate "nickname" (Netscape SDK)
- KEY_DER - binary DER encoded private key
- KEY_BASE64 - PEM encoded private key

LDAPTrustedGlobalCert Directive

Description:	Sets the file or database containing global trusted Certificate Authority or global client certificates
Syntax:	LDAPTrustedGlobalCert type directory-path/filename [password]
Context:	server config
Status:	Extension
Module:	mod_ldap

It specifies the directory path and file name of the trusted CA certificates and/or system wide client certificates mod_ldap should use when establishing an SSL or TLS connection to an LDAP server. Note that all certificate information specified using this directive is applied globally to the entire server installation. Some LDAP toolkits (notably Novell) require all client certificates to be set globally using this directive. Most other toolkits require clients certificates to be set per Directory or per Location using LDAPTrustedClientCert. If you get this wrong, an error may be logged when an attempt is made to contact the LDAP server, or the connection may silently fail (See the SSL/TLS certificate

guide above for details). The type specifies the kind of certificate parameter
being set, depending on the LDAP toolkit being used. Supported types are:

- CA_DER - binary DER encoded CA certificate
- CA_BASE64 - PEM encoded CA certificate
- CA_CERT7_DB - Netscape cert7.db CA certificate database file
- CA_SECMOD - Netscape secmod database file
- CERT_DER - binary DER encoded client certificate
- CERT_BASE64 - PEM encoded client certificate
- CERT_KEY3_DB - Netscape key3.db client certificate database file
- CERT_NICKNAME - Client certificate "nickname" (Netscape SDK)
- CERT_PFX - PKCS#12 encoded client certificate (Novell SDK)
- KEY_DER - binary DER encoded private key
- KEY_BASE64 - PEM encoded private key
- KEY_PFX - PKCS#12 encoded private key (Novell SDK)

LDAPTrustedMode Directive

Description:	Specifies the SSL/TLS mode to be used when connecting to an LDAP server.
Syntax:	LDAPTrustedMode type
Context:	server config, virtual host
Status:	Extension
Module:	mod_ldap

The following modes are supported:

- NONE - no encryption
- SSL - ldaps:// encryption on default port 636
- TLS - STARTTLS encryption on default port 389

Not all LDAP toolkits support all the above modes. An error message will be
logged at runtime if a mode is not supported, and the connection to the LDAP
server will fail.

If an ldaps:// URL is specified, the mode becomes SSL and the setting of
LDAPTrustedMode is ignored.

LDAPVerifyServerCert Directive

Description:	Force server certificate verification
Syntax:	LDAPVerifyServerCert On|Off
Default:	LDAPVerifyServerCert On
Context:	server config
Status:	Extension
Module:	mod_ldap

Specifies whether to force the verification of a server certificate when establishing an SSL connection to the LDAP server.

3.50 Apache Module mod_log_config

Description:	Logging of the requests made to the server
Status:	Base
Module Identifier:	log_config_module
Source File:	mod_log_config.c

Summary

This module provides for flexible logging of client requests. Logs are written in a customizable format, and may be written directly to a file, or to an external program. Conditional logging is provided so that individual requests may be included or excluded from the logs based on characteristics of the request.

Three directives are provided by this module: TransferLog to create a log file, LogFormat to set a custom format, and CustomLog to define a log file and format in one step. The TransferLog and CustomLog directives can be used multiple times in each server to cause each request to be logged to multiple files.

Directives:

> BufferedLogs
> CookieLog
> CustomLog
> LogFormat
> TransferLog

See also:

▷ Apache Log Files (p. 66)

3.50.1 Custom Log Formats

The format argument to the LogFormat and CustomLog directives is a string. This string is used to log each request to the log file. It can contain literal characters copied into the log files and the C-style control characters "\n" and "\t" to represent new-lines and tabs. Literal quotes and backslashes should be escaped with backslashes.

The characteristics of the request itself are logged by placing "%" directives in the format string, which are replaced in the log file by the values as follows:

Format String	Description
%%	The percent sign
%a	Remote IP-address
%A	Local IP-address
%B	Size of response in bytes, excluding HTTP headers.
%b	Size of response in bytes, excluding HTTP headers. In CLF format, *i.e.* a '-' rather than a 0 when no bytes are sent.

%{Foobar}C	The contents of cookie *Foobar* in the request sent to the server. Only version 0 cookies are fully supported.
%D	The time taken to serve the request, in microseconds.
%{FOOBAR}e	The contents of the environment variable *FOOBAR*
%f	Filename
%h	Remote host
%H	The request protocol
%{Foobar}i	The contents of *Foobar*: header line(s) in the request sent to the server. Changes made by other modules (e.g. mod_headers) affect this.
%k	Number of keepalive requests handled on this connection. Interesting if KeepAlive is being used, so that, for example, a '1' means the first keepalive request after the initial one, '2' the second, etc...; otherwise this is always 0 (indicating the initial request). Available in versions 2.2.11 and later.
%l	Remote logname (from identd, if supplied). This will return a dash unless mod_ident is present and IdentityCheck is set On.
%m	The request method
%{Foobar}n	The contents of note *Foobar* from another module.
%{Foobar}o	The contents of *Foobar*: header line(s) in the reply.
%p	The canonical port of the server serving the request
%{format}p	The canonical port of the server serving the request or the server's actual port or the client's actual port. Valid formats are canonical, local, or remote.
%P	The process ID of the child that serviced the request.
%{format}P	The process ID or thread id of the child that serviced the request. Valid formats are pid, tid, and hextid. hextid requires APR 1.2.0 or higher.
%q	The query string (prepended with a ? if a query string exists, otherwise an empty string)
%r	First line of request
%R	The handler generating the response (if any).
%s	Status. For requests that got internally redirected, this is the status of the *original* request — %>s for the last.
%t	Time the request was received (standard English format)
%{format}t	The time, in the form given by format, which should be in strftime(3) format. (potentially localized)
%T	The time taken to serve the request, in seconds.
%u	Remote user (from auth; may be bogus if return status (%s) is 401)
%U	The URL path requested, not including any query string.
%v	The canonical ServerName of the server serving the request.
%V	The server name according to the UseCanonicalName setting.

%X	Connection status when response is completed:

      X =   connection aborted before the response completed.

      + =   connection may be kept alive after the response is sent.

      - =   connection will be closed after the response is sent.

(This directive was %c in late versions of Apache 1.3, but this conflicted with the historical ssl %{var}c syntax.)

%I	Bytes received, including request and headers, cannot be zero. You need to enable mod_logio to use this.
%O	Bytes sent, including headers, cannot be zero. You need to enable mod_logio to use this.

Modifiers

Particular items can be restricted to print only for responses with specific HTTP status codes by placing a comma-separated list of status codes immediately following the "%". For example, "%400,501{User-agent}i" logs User-agent on 400 errors and 501 errors only. For other status codes, the literal string "-" will be logged. The status code list may be preceded by a "!" to indicate negation: "%!200,304,302{Referer}i" logs Referer on all requests that do *not* return one of the three specified codes.

The modifiers "<" and ">" can be used for requests that have been internally redirected to choose whether the original or final (respectively) request should be consulted. By default, the % directives %s, %U, %T, %D, and %r look at the original request while all others look at the final request. So for example, %>s can be used to record the final status of the request and %<u can be used to record the original authenticated user on a request that is internally redirected to an unauthenticated resource.

Some Notes

For security reasons, starting with version 2.0.46, non-printable and other special characters in %r, %i and %o are escaped using \xhh sequences, where hh stands for the hexadecimal representation of the raw byte. Exceptions from this rule are " and \, which are escaped by prepending a backslash, and all whitespace characters, which are written in their C-style notation (\n, \t, etc). In versions prior to 2.0.46, no escaping was performed on these strings so you had to be quite careful when dealing with raw log files.

In httpd 2.0, unlike 1.3, the %b and %B format strings do not represent the number of bytes sent to the client, but simply the size in bytes of the HTTP response (which will differ, for instance, if the connection is aborted, or if SSL is used). The %O format provided by mod_logio will log the actual number of bytes sent over the network.

Note: mod_cache is implemented as a quick-handler and not as a standard handler. Therefore, the %R format string will not return any handler information when content caching is involved.

Examples

Some commonly used log format strings are:

Common Log Format (CLF) "%h %l %u %t \"%r\" %>s %b"

Common Log Format with Virtual Host "%v %h %l %u %t \"%r\" %>s %b"

NCSA extended/combined log format "%h %l %u %t \"%r\" %>s %b \"%{Referer}i\" \"%{User-agent}i\""

Referer log format "%{Referer}i -> %U"

Agent (Browser) log format "%{User-agent}i"

3.50.2 Security Considerations

See the security tips (p. 677) document for details on why your security could be compromised if the directory where logfiles are stored is writable by anyone other than the user that starts the server.

BufferedLogs Directive

Description:	Buffer log entries in memory before writing to disk
Syntax:	BufferedLogs On|Off
Default:	BufferedLogs Off
Context:	server config
Status:	Base
Module:	mod_log_config
Compatibility:	Available in versions 2.0.41 and later.

The BufferedLogs directive causes mod_log_config to store several log entries in memory and write them together to disk, rather than writing them after each request. On some systems, this may result in more efficient disk access and hence higher performance. It may be set only once for the entire server; it cannot be configured per virtual-host.

This directive is experimental and should be used with caution.

CookieLog Directive

Description:	Sets filename for the logging of cookies
Syntax:	CookieLog *filename*
Context:	server config, virtual host
Status:	Base
Module:	mod_log_config
Compatibility:	This directive is deprecated.

The CookieLog directive sets the filename for logging of cookies. The filename is relative to the ServerRoot. This directive is included only for compatibility with mod_cookies, and is deprecated.

CustomLog Directive

Description:	Sets filename and format of log file
Syntax:	CustomLog *file*|*pipe format*|*nickname* [env=[!]*environment-variable*]
Context:	server config, virtual host
Status:	Base
Module:	mod_log_config

The CustomLog directive is used to log requests to the server. A log format is specified, and the logging can optionally be made conditional on request characteristics using environment variables.

The first argument, which specifies the location to which the logs will be written, can take one of the following two types of values:

file A filename, relative to the ServerRoot.

pipe The pipe character "|", followed by the path to a program to receive the log information on its standard input. See the notes on piped logs (p. 66) for more information.

> SECURITY: *If a program is used, then it will be run as the user who started httpd. This will be root if the server was started by root; be sure that the program is secure.*

> NOTE *When entering a file path on non-Unix platforms, care should be taken to make sure that only forward slashes are used even though the platform may allow the use of backslashes. In general it is a good idea to always use forward slashes throughout the configuration files.*

The second argument specifies what will be written to the log file. It can specify either a *nickname* defined by a previous LogFormat directive, or it can be an explicit *format* string as described in the log formats section.

For example, the following two sets of directives have exactly the same effect:

```
# CustomLog with format nickname
LogFormat "%h %l %u %t \"%r\" %>s %b" common
CustomLog logs/access_log common
# CustomLog with explicit format string
CustomLog logs/access_log "%h %l %u %t \"%r\" %>s %b"
```

The third argument is optional and controls whether or not to log a particular request based on the presence or absence of a particular variable in the server environment. If the specified environment variable (p. 705) is set for the request (or is not set, in the case of a 'env=!name' clause), then the request will be logged.

Environment variables can be set on a per-request basis using the mod_setenvif and/or mod_rewrite modules. For example, if you want to record requests for all GIF images on your server in a separate logfile but not in your main log, you can use:

```
SetEnvIf Request_URI \.gif$ gif-image
CustomLog gif-requests.log common env=gif-image
CustomLog nongif-requests.log common env=!gif-image
```

Or, to reproduce the behavior of the old RefererIgnore directive, you might use the following:

```
SetEnvIf Referer example\.com localreferer
CustomLog referer.log referer env=!localreferer
```

LogFormat Directive

Description:	Describes a format for use in a log file
Syntax:	LogFormat format|nickname [nickname]
Default:	LogFormat "%h %l %u %t \"%r\" %>s %b"
Context:	server config, virtual host
Status:	Base
Module:	mod_log_config

This directive specifies the format of the access log file.

The LogFormat directive can take one of two forms. In the first form, where only one argument is specified, this directive sets the log format which will be used by logs specified in subsequent TransferLog directives. The single argument can specify an explicit format as discussed in the custom log formats section above. Alternatively, it can use a nickname to refer to a log format defined in a previous LogFormat directive as described below.

The second form of the LogFormat directive associates an explicit format with a nickname. This nickname can then be used in subsequent LogFormat or CustomLog directives rather than repeating the entire format string. A LogFormat directive that defines a nickname **does nothing else** – that is, it *only* defines the nickname, it doesn't actually apply the format and make it the default. Therefore, it will not affect subsequent `TransferLog` directives. In addition, `LogFormat` cannot use one nickname to define another nickname. Note that the nickname should not contain percent signs (%).

Example
```
LogFormat "%v %h %l %u %t \"%r\" %>s %b" vhost_common
```

TransferLog Directive

Description:	Specify location of a log file
Syntax:	TransferLog file|pipe
Context:	server config, virtual host
Status:	Base
Module:	mod_log_config

This directive has exactly the same arguments and effect as the `CustomLog` directive, with the exception that it does not allow the log format to be specified explicitly or for conditional logging of requests. Instead, the log format is determined by the most recently specified `LogFormat` directive which does not define a nickname. Common Log Format is used if no other format has been specified.

Example
```
LogFormat "%h %l %u %t \"%r\" %>s %b \"%{Referer}i\"
\"%{User-agent}i\""
TransferLog logs/access_log
```

3.51 Apache Module mod_log_forensic

Description:	Forensic Logging of the requests made to the server
Status:	Extension
Module Identifier:	log_forensic_module
Source File:	mod_log_forensic.c
Compatibility:	mod_unique_id is no longer required since version 2.1

Summary

This module provides for forensic logging of client requests. Logging is done before and after processing a request, so the forensic log contains two log lines for each request. The forensic logger is very strict, which means:

- The format is fixed. You cannot modify the logging format at runtime.
- If it cannot write its data, the child process exits immediately and may dump core (depending on your CoreDumpDirectory configuration).

The check_forensic script, which can be found in the distribution's support directory, may be helpful in evaluating the forensic log output.

Directives:

    ForensicLog

See also:

  ▷ Apache Log Files (p. 66)

  ▷ mod_log_config (p. 334)

3.51.1 Forensic Log Format

Each request is logged two times. The first time is *before* it's processed further (that is, after receiving the headers). The second log entry is written *after* the request processing at the same time where normal logging occurs.

In order to identify each request, a unique request ID is assigned. This forensic ID can be cross logged in the normal transfer log using the %{forensic-id}n format string. If you're using mod_unique_id, its generated ID will be used.

The first line logs the forensic ID, the request line and all received headers, separated by pipe characters (|). A sample line looks like the following (all on one line):

```
+yQtJf8CoAB4AAFNXBIEAAAAA|GET /manual/de/images/down.gif
HTTP/1.1|Host:localhost%3a8080|User-Agent:Mozilla/5.0 (X11; U;
Linux i686; en-US; rv%3a1.6) Gecko/20040216
Firefox/0.8|Accept:image/png, etc...
```

The plus character at the beginning indicates that this is the first log line of this request. The second line just contains a minus character and the ID again:

`-yQtJf8CoAB4AAFNXBIEAAAAA`

The check_forensic script takes as its argument the name of the logfile. It looks for those +/- ID pairs and complains if a request was not completed.

3.51.2 Security Considerations

See the security tips (p. 677) document for details on why your security could be compromised if the directory where logfiles are stored is writable by anyone other than the user that starts the server.

ForensicLog Directive

Description:	Sets filename of the forensic log
Syntax:	ForensicLog *filename*|*pipe*
Context:	server config, virtual host
Status:	Extension
Module:	mod_log_forensic

The ForensicLog directive is used to log requests to the server for forensic analysis. Each log entry is assigned a unique ID which can be associated with the request using the normal CustomLog directive. mod_log_forensic creates a token called forensic-id, which can be added to the transfer log using the %{forensic-id}n format string.

The argument, which specifies the location to which the logs will be written, can take one of the following two types of values:

filename A filename, relative to the ServerRoot.

pipe The pipe character "|", followed by the path to a program to receive the log information on its standard input. The program name can be specified relative to the ServerRoot directive.

> SECURITY: *If a program is used, then it will be run as the user who started httpd. This will be root if the server was started by root; be sure that the program is secure or switches to a less privileged user.*

> NOTE *When entering a file path on non-Unix platforms, care should be taken to make sure that only forward slashes are used even though the platform may allow the use of backslashes. In general it is a good idea to always use forward slashes throughout the configuration files.*

3.52 Apache Module mod_logio

Description:	Logging of input and output bytes per request
Status:	Extension
Module Identifier:	logio_module
Source File:	mod_logio.c

Summary

This module provides the logging of input and output number of bytes received/sent per request. The numbers reflect the actual bytes as received on the network, which then takes into account the headers and bodies of requests and responses. The counting is done before SSL/TLS on input and after SSL/TLS on output, so the numbers will correctly reflect any changes made by encryption.

This module requires mod_log_config.

> *When KeepAlive connections are used with SSL, the overhead of the SSL handshake is reflected in the byte count of the first request on the connection. When per-directory SSL renegotiation occurs, the bytes are associated with the request that triggered the renegotiation.*

This module provides no directives.

See also:

▷ mod_log_config (p. 334)

▷ Apache Log Files (p. 66)

3.52.1 Custom Log Formats

This modules adds two new logging directives. The characteristics of the request itself are logged by placing "%" directives in the format string, which are replaced in the log file by the values as follows:

Format String	Description
%...I	Bytes received, including request and headers, cannot be zero.
%...O	Bytes sent, including headers, cannot be zero.

Usually, the functionality is used like this:

Combined I/O log format: "%h %l %u %t \"%r\" %>s %b
\"%{Referer}i\" \"%{User-agent}i\" %I %O"

3.53 Apache Module mod_mem_cache

Description:	Content cache keyed to URIs
Status:	Extension
Module Identifier:	mem_cache_module
Source File:	mod_mem_cache.c

Summary

This module *requires* the service of mod_cache. It acts as a support module for mod_cache and provides a memory based storage manager. mod_mem_cache can be configured to operate in two modes: caching open file descriptors or caching objects in heap storage. mod_mem_cache is most useful when used to cache locally generated content or to cache backend server content for mod_proxy configured for ProxyPass (aka **reverse proxy**).

Content is stored in and retrieved from the cache using URI based keys. Content with access protection is not cached.

> NOTE *In most cases mod_disk_cache should be the preferred choice. This is explained further in the Caching Guide (p. 639). In particular, this module's cache is per-process, which can be partially mitigated by configuring threaded MPMS to use fewer child processes via configuration of larger values for ThreadsPerChild. This module's cache is also limited to storing a single variant (see HTTP Vary: header) of each resource in the cache.*

Directives:

> MCacheMaxObjectCount
> MCacheMaxObjectSize
> MCacheMaxStreamingBuffer
> MCacheMinObjectSize
> MCacheRemovalAlgorithm
> MCacheSize

See also:

> ▷ mod_cache (p. 215)

> ▷ mod_disk_cache (p. 260)

MCacheMaxObjectCount Directive

Description:	The maximum number of objects allowed to be placed in the cache
Syntax:	MCacheMaxObjectCount *value*
Default:	MCacheMaxObjectCount 1009
Context:	server config
Status:	Extension
Module:	mod_mem_cache

The MCacheMaxObjectCount directive sets the maximum number of objects to be cached. The value is used to create the open hash table. If a new object needs to be inserted in the cache and the maximum number of objects has been reached, an object will be removed to allow the new object to be cached. The object to be removed is selected using the algorithm specified by MCacheRemovalAlgorithm.

Example
    MCacheMaxObjectCount 13001

MCacheMaxObjectSize Directive

Description:	The maximum size (in bytes) of a document allowed in the cache
Syntax:	MCacheMaxObjectSize *bytes*
Default:	MCacheMaxObjectSize 10000
Context:	server config
Status:	Extension
Module:	mod_mem_cache

The MCacheMaxObjectSize directive sets the maximum allowable size, in bytes, of a document for it to be considered cacheable.

Example
    MCacheMaxObjectSize 6400000

NOTE *The value of MCacheMaxObjectSize must be greater than the value specified by the MCacheMinObjectSize directive.*

MCacheMaxStreamingBuffer Directive

Description:	Maximum amount of a streamed response to buffer in memory before declaring the response uncacheable
Syntax:	MCacheMaxStreamingBuffer *size_in_bytes*
Default:	MCacheMaxStreamingBuffer the smaller of 100000 or MCacheMaxObjectSize
Context:	server config
Status:	Extension
Module:	mod_mem_cache

The `MCacheMaxStreamingBuffer` directive specifies the maximum number of bytes of a streamed response to buffer before deciding that the response is too big to cache. A streamed response is one in which the entire content is not immediately available and in which the `Content-Length` may not be known. Sources of streaming responses include proxied responses and the output of CGI scripts. By default, a streamed response will *not* be cached unless it has a `Content-Length` header. The reason for this is to avoid using a large amount of memory to buffer a partial response that might end up being too large to fit in the cache. The `MCacheMaxStreamingBuffer` directive allows buffering of streamed responses that don't contain a `Content-Length` up to the specified maximum amount of space. If the maximum buffer space is reached, the buffered content is discarded and the attempt to cache is abandoned.

NOTE: *Using a nonzero value for MCacheMaxStreamingBuffer will not delay the transmission of the response to the client. As soon as mod-mem_cache copies a block of streamed content into a buffer, it sends the block on to the next output filter for delivery to the client.*

```
# Enable caching of streamed responses up to 64KB:
MCacheMaxStreamingBuffer 65536
```

MCacheMinObjectSize Directive

Description:	The minimum size (in bytes) of a document to be allowed in the cache
Syntax:	MCacheMinObjectSize *bytes*
Default:	MCacheMinObjectSize 1
Context:	server config
Status:	Extension
Module:	mod_mem_cache

The `MCacheMinObjectSize` directive sets the minimum size in bytes of a document for it to be considered cacheable.

Example
```
MCacheMinObjectSize 10000
```

MCacheRemovalAlgorithm Directive

Description:	The algorithm used to select documents for removal from the cache
Syntax:	MCacheRemovalAlgorithm LRU|GDSF
Default:	MCacheRemovalAlgorithm GDSF
Context:	server config
Status:	Extension
Module:	mod_mem_cache

The `MCacheRemovalAlgorithm` directive specifies the algorithm used to select documents for removal from the cache. Two choices are available:

LRU **(Least Recently Used)** LRU removes the documents that have not been accessed for the longest time.

GDSF **(GreadyDual-Size)** GDSF assigns a priority to cached documents based on the cost of a cache miss and the size of the document. Documents with the lowest priority are removed first.

Example
```
MCacheRemovalAlgorithm GDSF
MCacheRemovalAlgorithm LRU
```

MCacheSize Directive

Description:	The maximum amount of memory used by the cache in KBytes
Syntax:	MCacheSize *KBytes*
Default:	MCacheSize 100
Context:	server config
Status:	Extension
Module:	mod_mem_cache

The MCacheSize directive sets the maximum amount of memory to be used by the cache, in KBytes (1024-byte units). If a new object needs to be inserted in the cache and the size of the object is greater than the remaining memory, objects will be removed until the new object can be cached. The object to be removed is selected using the algorithm specified by MCacheRemovalAlgorithm.

Example
```
MCacheSize 700000
```

NOTE *The MCacheSize value must be greater than the value specified by the MCacheMaxObjectSize directive.*

3.54 Apache Module mod_mime

Description:	Associates the requested filename's extensions with the file's behavior (handlers and filters) and content (mime-type, language, character set and encoding)
Status:	Base
Module Identifier:	mime_module
Source File:	mod_mime.c

Summary

This module is used to associate various bits of "meta information" with files by their filename extensions. This information relates the filename of the document to its mime-type, language, character set and encoding. This information is sent to the browser, and participates in content negotiation, so the user's preferences are respected when choosing one of several possible files to serve. See mod_-negotiation for more information about content negotiation (p. 687).

The directives AddCharset, AddEncoding, AddLanguage and AddType are all used to map file extensions onto the meta-information for that file. Respectively they set the character set, content-encoding, content-language, and MIME-type (content-type) of documents. The directive TypesConfig is used to specify a file which also maps extensions onto MIME types.

In addition, mod_mime may define the handler (p. 713) and filters (p. 715) that originate and process content. The directives AddHandler, AddOutputFilter, and AddInputFilter control the modules or scripts that serve the document. The MultiviewsMatch directive allows mod_negotiation to consider these file extensions to be included when testing Multiviews matches.

While mod_mime associates meta-information with filename extensions, the core server provides directives that are used to associate all the files in a given container (e.g., <Location>, <Directory>, or <Files>) with particular meta-information. These directives include ForceType, SetHandler, SetInputFilter, and SetOutputFilter. The core directives override any filename extension mappings defined in mod_mime.

Note that changing the meta-information for a file does not change the value of the Last-Modified header. Thus, previously cached copies may still be used by a client or proxy, with the previous headers. If you change the meta-information (language, content type, character set or encoding) you may need to 'touch' affected files (updating their last modified date) to ensure that all visitors are receive the corrected content headers.

Directives:

AddCharset	AddInputFilter
AddEncoding	AddLanguage
AddHandler	AddOutputFilter

AddType	RemoveHandler
DefaultLanguage	RemoveInputFilter
ModMimeUsePathInfo	RemoveLanguage
MultiviewsMatch	RemoveOutputFilter
RemoveCharset	RemoveType
RemoveEncoding	TypesConfig

See also:

▷ MimeMagicFile (p. 366)

▷ AddDefaultCharset (p. 90)

▷ ForceType (p. 106)

▷ DefaultType (p. 96)

▷ SetHandler (p. 131)

▷ SetInputFilter (p. 132)

▷ SetOutputFilter (p. 132)

3.54.1 Files with Multiple Extensions

Files can have more than one extension, and the order of the extensions is *normally* irrelevant. For example, if the file welcome.html.fr maps onto content type text/html and language French then the file welcome.fr.html will map onto exactly the same information. If more than one extension is given that maps onto the same type of meta-information, then the one to the right will be used, except for languages and content encodings. For example, if .gif maps to the MIME-type image/gif and .html maps to the MIME-type text/html, then the file welcome.gif.html will be associated with the MIME-type text/html.

Languages and content encodings are treated accumulative, because one can assign more than one language or encoding to a particular resource. For example, the file welcome.html.en.de will be delivered with Content-Language: en, de and Content-Type: text/html.

Care should be taken when a file with multiple extensions gets associated with both a MIME-type and a handler. This will usually result in the request being handled by the module associated with the handler. For example, if the .imap extension is mapped to the handler imap-file (from mod_imagemap) and the .html extension is mapped to the MIME-type text/html, then the file world.imap.html will be associated with both the imap-file handler and text/html MIME-type. When it is processed, the imap-file handler will be used, and so it will be treated as a mod_imagemap imagemap file.

If you would prefer only the last dot-separated part of the filename to be mapped to a particular piece of meta-data, then do not use the Add* directives. For example, if you wish to have the file foo.html.cgi processed as a CGI script, but not the file bar.cgi.html, then instead of using AddHandler cgi-script .cgi, use

Configure handler based on final extension only
```
<FilesMatch \.cgi$>
    SetHandler cgi-script
</FilesMatch>
```

3.54.2 Content encoding

A file of a particular MIME-type can additionally be encoded a particular way to simplify transmission over the Internet. While this usually will refer to compression, such as gzip, it can also refer to encryption, such a pgp or to an encoding such as UUencoding, which is designed for transmitting a binary file in an ASCII (text) format.

The HTTP/1.1 RFC[47], section 14.11 puts it this way:

> The Content-Encoding entity-header field is used as a modifier to the media-type. When present, its value indicates what additional content codings have been applied to the entity-body, and thus what decoding mechanisms must be applied in order to obtain the media-type referenced by the Content-Type header field. Content-Encoding is primarily used to allow a document to be compressed without losing the identity of its underlying media type.

By using more than one file extension (see section above about multiple file extensions), you can indicate that a file is of a particular *type*, and also has a particular *encoding*.

For example, you may have a file which is a Microsoft Word document, which is pkzipped to reduce its size. If the .doc extension is associated with the Microsoft Word file type, and the .zip extension is associated with the pkzip file encoding, then the file Resume.doc.zip would be known to be a pkzip'ed Word document.

Apache sends a Content-encoding header with the resource, in order to tell the client browser about the encoding method.

```
Content-encoding:  pkzip
```

3.54.3 Character sets and languages

In addition to file type and the file encoding, another important piece of information is what language a particular document is in, and in what character set the file should be displayed. For example, the document might be written in the Vietnamese alphabet, or in Cyrillic, and should be displayed as such. This information, also, is transmitted in HTTP headers.

The character set, language, encoding and mime type are all used in the process of content negotiation (See mod_negotiation) to determine which document to give to the client, when there are alternative documents in more than one

---

[47]http://www.ietf.org/rfc/rfc2616.txt

character set, language, encoding or MIME type. All filename extensions associations created with AddCharset, AddEncoding, AddLanguage and AddType directives (and extensions listed in the MimeMagicFile) participate in this select
process. Filename extensions that are only associated using the AddHandler,
AddInputFilter or AddOutputFilter directives may be included or excluded
from matching by using the MultiviewsMatch directive.

Charset

To convey this further information, Apache optionally sends a
Content-Language header, to specify the language that the document is
in, and can append additional information onto the Content-Type header to
indicate the particular character set that should be used to correctly render
the information.

```
Content-Language:  en, fr
Content-Type:  text/plain; charset=ISO-8859-1
```

The language specification is the two-letter abbreviation for the language. The
charset is the name of the particular character set which should be used.

AddCharset Directive

Description:	Maps the given filename extensions to the specified content charset
Syntax:	AddCharset *charset extension* [*extension*] ...
Context:	server config, virtual host, directory, .htaccess
Override:	FileInfo
Status:	Base
Module:	mod_mime

The AddCharset directive maps the given filename extensions to the specified
content charset. *charset* is the MIME charset parameter[48] of filenames containing *extension*. This mapping is added to any already in force, overriding any
mappings that already exist for the same *extension*.

Example
```
AddLanguage ja .ja
AddCharset EUC-JP .euc
AddCharset ISO-2022-JP .jis
AddCharset SHIFT_JIS .sjis
```

Then the document xxxx.ja.jis will be treated as being a Japanese document whose charset is ISO-2022-JP (as will the document xxxx.jis.ja). The
AddCharset directive is useful for both to inform the client about the character encoding of the document so that the document can be interpreted and
displayed appropriately, and for content negotiation (p. 687), where the server
returns one from several documents based on the client's charset preference.

---

[48]http://www.iana.org/assignments/character-sets

The *extension* argument is case-insensitive and can be specified with or without a leading dot. Filenames may have multiple extensions and the *extension* argument will be compared against each of them.

See also:

▷ mod_negotiation (p. 367)

▷ AddDefaultCharset (p. 90)

AddEncoding Directive

Description:	Maps the given filename extensions to the specified encoding type
Syntax:	AddEncoding *MIME-enc extension* [*extension*] ...
Context:	server config, virtual host, directory, .htaccess
Override:	FileInfo
Status:	Base
Module:	mod_mime

The AddEncoding directive maps the given filename extensions to the specified encoding type. *MIME-enc* is the MIME encoding to use for documents containing the *extension*. This mapping is added to any already in force, overriding any mappings that already exist for the same *extension*.

Example
```
AddEncoding x-gzip .gz
AddEncoding x-compress .Z
```

This will cause filenames containing the .gz extension to be marked as encoded using the x-gzip encoding, and filenames containing the .Z extension to be marked as encoded with x-compress.

Old clients expect x-gzip and x-compress, however the standard dictates that they're equivalent to gzip and compress respectively. Apache does content encoding comparisons by ignoring any leading x-. When responding with an encoding Apache will use whatever form (*i.e.*, x-foo or foo) the client requested. If the client didn't specifically request a particular form Apache will use the form given by the AddEncoding directive. To make this long story short, you should always use x-gzip and x-compress for these two specific encodings. More recent encodings, such as deflate should be specified without the x-.

The *extension* argument is case-insensitive and can be specified with or without a leading dot. Filenames may have multiple extensions and the *extension* argument will be compared against each of them.

AddHandler Directive

Description:	Maps the filename extensions to the specified handler
Syntax:	AddHandler *handler-name extension* [*extension*] ...
Context:	server config, virtual host, directory, .htaccess
Override:	FileInfo
Status:	Base
Module:	mod_mime

Files having the name *extension* will be served by the specified *handler-name (p. 713)*. This mapping is added to any already in force, overriding any mappings that already exist for the same *extension*. For example, to activate CGI scripts with the file extension .cgi, you might use:

```
AddHandler cgi-script .cgi
```

Once that has been put into your httpd.conf file, any file containing the .cgi extension will be treated as a CGI program.

The *extension* argument is case-insensitive and can be specified with or without a leading dot. Filenames may have multiple extensions and the *extension* argument will be compared against each of them.

See also:

  ▷ SetHandler (p. 131)

AddInputFilter Directive

Description:	Maps filename extensions to the filters that will process client requests
Syntax:	AddInputFilter *filter*[;*filter*...] *extension* [*extension*] ...
Context:	server config, virtual host, directory, .htaccess
Override:	FileInfo
Status:	Base
Module:	mod_mime
Compatibility:	AddInputFilter is only available in Apache 2.0.26 and later.

AddInputFilter maps the filename extension *extension* to the filters (p. 715) which will process client requests and POST input when they are received by the server. This is in addition to any filters defined elsewhere, including the SetInputFilter directive. This mapping is merged over any already in force, overriding any mappings that already exist for the same *extension*.

If more than one *filter* is specified, they must be separated by semicolons in the order in which they should process the content. The *filter* is case-insensitive.

The *extension* argument is case-insensitive and can be specified with or without a leading dot. Filenames may have multiple extensions and the *extension* argument will be compared against each of them.

See also:

   ▷ RemoveInputFilter (p. 360)

   ▷ SetInputFilter (p. 132)

AddLanguage Directive

Description:	Maps the given filename extension to the specified content language
Syntax:	AddLanguage *MIME-lang extension* [*extension*] ...
Context:	server config, virtual host, directory, .htaccess
Override:	FileInfo
Status:	Base
Module:	mod_mime

The AddLanguage directive maps the given filename extension to the specified content language. *MIME-lang* is the MIME language of filenames containing *extension*. This mapping is added to any already in force, overriding any mappings that already exist for the same *extension*.

Example
```
AddEncoding x-compress .Z
AddLanguage en .en
AddLanguage fr .fr
```

Then the document xxxx.en.Z will be treated as being a compressed English document (as will the document xxxx.Z.en). Although the content language is reported to the client, the browser is unlikely to use this information. The AddLanguage directive is more useful for content negotiation (p. 687), where the server returns one from several documents based on the client's language preference.

If multiple language assignments are made for the same extension, the last one encountered is the one that is used. That is, for the case of:

```
AddLanguage en .en
AddLanguage en-gb .en
AddLanguage en-us .en
```

documents with the extension .en would be treated as being en-us.

The *extension* argument is case-insensitive and can be specified with or without a leading dot. Filenames may have multiple extensions and the *extension* argument will be compared against each of them.

See also:

   ▷ mod_negotiation (p. 367)

AddOutputFilter Directive

Description:	Maps filename extensions to the filters that will process responses from the server
Syntax:	AddOutputFilter *filter*[;*filter*...] *extension* [*extension*] ...
Context:	server config, virtual host, directory, .htaccess
Override:	FileInfo
Status:	Base
Module:	mod_mime
Compatibility:	AddOutputFilter is only available in Apache 2.0.26 and later.

The AddOutputFilter directive maps the filename extension *extension* to the filters (p. 715) which will process responses from the server before they are sent to the client. This is in addition to any filters defined elsewhere, including SetOutputFilter and AddOutputFilterByType directive. This mapping is merged over any already in force, overriding any mappings that already exist for the same *extension*.

For example, the following configuration will process all .shtml files for server-side includes and will then compress the output using mod_deflate.

```
AddOutputFilter INCLUDES;DEFLATE shtml
```

If more than one filter is specified, they must be separated by semicolons in the order in which they should process the content. The *filter* argument is case-insensitive.

The *extension* argument is case-insensitive and can be specified with or without a leading dot. Filenames may have multiple extensions and the *extension* argument will be compared against each of them.

See also:

   ▷ RemoveOutputFilter (p. 361)

   ▷ SetOutputFilter (p. 132)

AddType Directive

Description:	Maps the given filename extensions onto the specified content type
Syntax:	AddType *MIME-type extension* [*extension*] ...
Context:	server config, virtual host, directory, .htaccess
Override:	FileInfo
Status:	Base
Module:	mod_mime

The AddType directive maps the given filename extensions onto the specified content type. *MIME-type* is the MIME type to use for filenames containing *extension.* This mapping is added to any already in force, overriding any mappings that already exist for the same *extension.* This directive can be used to add mappings not listed in the MIME types file (see the `TypesConfig` directive).

Example
```
AddType image/gif .gif
```

It is recommended that new MIME types be added using the `AddType` directive rather than changing the `TypesConfig` file.

The *extension* argument is case-insensitive and can be specified with or without a leading dot. Filenames may have multiple extensions and the *extension* argument will be compared against each of them.

See also:

▷ DefaultType (p. 96)

▷ ForceType (p. 106)

DefaultLanguage Directive

Description:	Sets all files in the given scope to the specified language
Syntax:	DefaultLanguage *MIME-lang*
Context:	server config, virtual host, directory, .htaccess
Override:	FileInfo
Status:	Base
Module:	mod_mime

The `DefaultLanguage` directive tells Apache that all files in the directive's scope (*e.g.*, all files covered by the current `<Directory>` container) that don't have an explicit language extension (such as `.fr` or `.de` as configured by `AddLanguage`) should be considered to be in the specified *MIME-lang* language. This allows entire directories to be marked as containing Dutch content, for instance, without having to rename each file. Note that unlike using extensions to specify languages, `DefaultLanguage` can only specify a single language.

If no `DefaultLanguage` directive is in force, and a file does not have any language extensions as configured by `AddLanguage`, then that file will be considered to have no language attribute.

Example
```
DefaultLanguage en
```

See also:

▷ mod_negotiation (p. 367)

ModMimeUsePathInfo Directive

Description:	Tells mod_mime to treat path_info components as part of the filename
Syntax:	ModMimeUsePathInfo On|Off
Default:	ModMimeUsePathInfo Off
Context:	directory
Status:	Base
Module:	mod_mime
Compatibility:	Available in Apache 2.0.41 and later

The ModMimeUsePathInfo directive is used to combine the filename with the path_info URL component to apply mod_mime's directives to the request. The default value is Off - therefore, the path_info component is ignored.

This directive is recommended when you have a virtual filesystem.

Example
```
ModMimeUsePathInfo On
```

If you have a request for /bar/foo.shtml where /bar is a Location and ModMimeUsePathInfo is On, mod_mime will treat the incoming request as /bar/foo.shtml and directives like AddOutputFilter INCLUDES .shtml will add the INCLUDES filter to the request. If ModMimeUsePathInfo is not set, the INCLUDES filter will not be added.

See also:

▷ AcceptPathInfo (p. 89)

MultiviewsMatch Directive

Description:	The types of files that will be included when searching for a matching file with MultiViews
Syntax:	MultiviewsMatch Any|NegotiatedOnly|Filters|Handlers [Handlers|Filters]
Default:	MultiviewsMatch NegotiatedOnly
Context:	server config, virtual host, directory, .htaccess
Override:	FileInfo
Status:	Base
Module:	mod_mime
Compatibility:	Available in Apache 2.0.26 and later.

MultiviewsMatch permits three different behaviors for mod_negotiation (p. 367)'s Multiviews feature. Multiviews allows a request for a file, *e.g.* index.html, to match any negotiated extensions following the base request, *e.g.* index.html.en, index.html.fr, or index.html.gz.

The NegotiatedOnly option provides that every extension following the base name must correlate to a recognized mod_mime extension for content negotiation, *e.g.* Charset, Content-Type, Language, or Encoding. This is the strictest implementation with the fewest unexpected side effects, and is the default behavior.

To include extensions associated with Handlers and/or Filters, set the MultiviewsMatch directive to either Handlers, Filters, or both option keywords. If all other factors are equal, the smallest file will be served, *e.g.* in deciding between index.html.cgi of 500 bytes and index.html.pl of 1000 bytes, the .cgi file would win in this example. Users of .asis files might prefer to use the Handler option, if .asis files are associated with the asis-handler.

You may finally allow Any extensions to match, even if mod_mime doesn't recognize the extension. This was the behavior in Apache 1.3, and can cause unpredicatable results, such as serving .old or .bak files the webmaster never expected to be served.

For example, the following configuration will allow handlers and filters to participate in Multviews, but will exclude unknown files:

    MultiviewsMatch Handlers Filters

MultiviewsMatch is not allowed in a <Location> or <LocationMatch> section.

See also:

▷ Options (p. 120)

▷ mod_negotiation (p. 367)

RemoveCharset Directive

Description:	Removes any character set associations for a set of file extensions
Syntax:	RemoveCharset *extension* [*extension*] ...
Context:	virtual host, directory, .htaccess
Override:	FileInfo
Status:	Base
Module:	mod_mime
Compatibility:	RemoveCharset is only available in Apache 2.0.24 and later.

The RemoveCharset directive removes any character set associations for files with the given extensions. This allows .htaccess files in subdirectories to undo any associations inherited from parent directories or the server config files.

The *extension* argument is case-insensitive and can be specified with or without a leading dot.

Example
RemoveCharset .html .shtml

RemoveEncoding Directive

Description:	Removes any content encoding associations for a set of file extensions
Syntax:	RemoveEncoding extension [extension] ...
Context:	virtual host, directory, .htaccess
Override:	FileInfo
Status:	Base
Module:	mod_mime

The RemoveEncoding directive removes any encoding associations for files with the given extensions. This allows .htaccess files in subdirectories to undo any associations inherited from parent directories or the server config files. An example of its use might be:

```
/foo/.htaccess:
  AddEncoding x-gzip .gz
  AddType text/plain .asc
  <Files *.gz.asc>
      RemoveEncoding .gz
  </Files>
```

This will cause foo.gz to be marked as being encoded with the gzip method, but foo.gz.asc as an unencoded plaintext file.

> NOTE *RemoveEncoding directives are processed after any AddEncoding directives, so it is possible they may undo the effects of the latter if both occur within the same directory configuration.*

The *extension* argument is case-insensitive and can be specified with or without a leading dot.

RemoveHandler Directive

Description:	Removes any handler associations for a set of file extensions
Syntax:	RemoveHandler extension [extension] ...
Context:	virtual host, directory, .htaccess
Override:	FileInfo
Status:	Base
Module:	mod_mime

The RemoveHandler directive removes any handler associations for files with the given extensions. This allows .htaccess files in subdirectories to undo any associations inherited from parent directories or the server config files. An example of its use might be:

```
/foo/.htaccess:
  AddHandler server-parsed .html
```

```
/foo/bar/.htaccess:
```

```
RemoveHandler .html
```

This has the effect of returning .html files in the /foo/bar directory to being treated as normal files, rather than as candidates for parsing (see the mod_-include module).

The *extension* argument is case-insensitive and can be specified with or without a leading dot.

RemoveInputFilter Directive

Description:	Removes any input filter associations for a set of file extensions
Syntax:	RemoveInputFilter *extension* [*extension*] ...
Context:	virtual host, directory, .htaccess
Override:	FileInfo
Status:	Base
Module:	mod_mime
Compatibility:	RemoveInputFilter is only available in Apache 2.0.26 and later.

The RemoveInputFilter directive removes any input filter (p. 715) associations for files with the given extensions. This allows .htaccess files in subdirectories to undo any associations inherited from parent directories or the server config files.

The *extension* argument is case-insensitive and can be specified with or without a leading dot.

See also:

▷ AddInputFilter (p. 353)

▷ SetInputFilter (p. 132)

RemoveLanguage Directive

Description:	Removes any language associations for a set of file extensions
Syntax:	RemoveLanguage *extension* [*extension*] ...
Context:	virtual host, directory, .htaccess
Override:	FileInfo
Status:	Base
Module:	mod_mime
Compatibility:	RemoveLanguage is only available in Apache 2.0.24 and later.

The RemoveLanguage directive removes any language associations for files with the given extensions. This allows .htaccess files in subdirectories to undo any associations inherited from parent directories or the server config files.

The *extension* argument is case-insensitive and can be specified with or without a leading dot.

RemoveOutputFilter Directive

Description:	Removes any output filter associations for a set of file extensions
Syntax:	RemoveOutputFilter *extension* [*extension*] ...
Context:	virtual host, directory, .htaccess
Override:	FileInfo
Status:	Base
Module:	mod_mime
Compatibility:	RemoveOutputFilter is only available in Apache 2.0.26 and later.

The RemoveOutputFilter directive removes any output filter (p. 715) associations for files with the given extensions. This allows .htaccess files in subdirectories to undo any associations inherited from parent directories or the server config files.

The *extension* argument is case-insensitive and can be specified with or without a leading dot.

Example
```
RemoveOutputFilter shtml
```

See also:

▷ AddOutputFilter (p. 355)

RemoveType Directive

Description:	Removes any content type associations for a set of file extensions
Syntax:	RemoveType *extension* [*extension*] ...
Context:	virtual host, directory, .htaccess
Override:	FileInfo
Status:	Base
Module:	mod_mime

The RemoveType directive removes any MIME type associations for files with the given extensions. This allows .htaccess files in subdirectories to undo any associations inherited from parent directories or the server config files. An example of its use might be:

/foo/.htaccess:
```
RemoveType .cgi
```

This will remove any special handling of .cgi files in the /foo/ directory and any beneath it, causing the files to be treated as being of the DefaultType.

NOTE *RemoveType directives are processed after any AddType directives, so it is possible they may undo the effects of the latter if both occur within the same directory configuration.*

The *extension* argument is case-insensitive and can be specified with or without a leading dot.

TypesConfig Directive

Description:	The location of the mime.types file
Syntax:	TypesConfig *file-path*
Default:	TypesConfig conf/mime.types
Context:	server config
Status:	Base
Module:	mod_mime

The TypesConfig directive sets the location of the MIME types configuration file. *File-path* is relative to the ServerRoot. This file sets the default list of mappings from filename extensions to content types. Most administrators use the provided mime.types file, which associates common filename extensions with IANA registered content types. The current list is maintained at http://www.iana.org/assignments/media-types/index.html. This simplifies the httpd.conf file by providing the majority of media-type definitions, and may be overridden by AddType directives as needed. You should not edit the mime.types file, because it may be replaced when you upgrade your server.

The file contains lines in the format of the arguments to an AddType directive:

MIME-type [*extension*] ...

The case of the extension does not matter. Blank lines, and lines beginning with a hash character (#) are ignored.

*Please do **not** send requests to the Apache HTTP Server Project to add any new entries in the distributed mime.types file unless (1) they are already registered with IANA, and (2) they use widely accepted, non-conflicting filename extensions across platforms. category/x-subtype requests will be automatically rejected, as will any new two-letter extensions as they will likely conflict later with the already crowded language and character set namespace.*

See also:

▷ mod_mime_magic (p. 363)

3.55 Apache Module mod_mime_magic

Description:	Determines the MIME type of a file by looking at a few bytes of its contents
Status:	Extension
Module Identifier:	mime_magic_module
Source File:	mod_mime_magic.c

Summary

This module determines the MIME type of files in the same way the Unix file(1) command works: it looks at the first few bytes of the file. It is intended as a "second line of defense" for cases that mod_mime can't resolve.

This module is derived from a free version of the file(1) command for Unix, which uses "magic numbers" and other hints from a file's contents to figure out what the contents are. This module is active only if the magic file is specified by the MimeMagicFile directive.

Directives:

MimeMagicFile

3.55.1 Format of the Magic File

The contents of the file are plain ASCII text in 4-5 columns. Blank lines are allowed but ignored. Commented lines use a hash mark (#). The remaining lines are parsed for the following columns:

Column	Description
1	byte number to begin checking from
	">" indicates a dependency upon the previous non-">" line
2	type of data to match
	byte single character
	short machine-order 16-bit integer
	long machine-order 32-bit integer
	string arbitrary-length string
	date long integer date (seconds since Unix epoch/1970)
	beshort big-endian 16-bit integer
	belong big-endian 32-bit integer
	bedate big-endian 32-bit integer date
	leshort little-endian 16-bit integer
	lelong little-endian 32-bit integer
	ledate little-endian 32-bit integer date
3	contents of data to match
4	MIME type if matched
5	MIME encoding if matched (optional)

For example, the following magic file lines would recognize some audio formats:

```
# Sun/NeXT audio data
0        string    .snd
>12      belong    1        audio/basic
>12      belong    2        audio/basic
>12      belong    3        audio/basic
>12      belong    4        audio/basic
>12      belong    5        audio/basic
>12      belong    6        audio/basic
>12      belong    7        audio/basic
>12      belong    23       audio/x-adpcm
```

Or these would recognize the difference between *.doc files containing Microsoft Word or FrameMaker documents. (These are incompatible file formats which use the same file suffix.)

```
# Frame
0   string   \<MakerFile        application/x-frame
0   string   \<MIFFile          application/x-frame
0   string   \<MakerDictionary  application/x-frame
0   string   \<MakerScreenFon   application/x-frame
0   string   \<MML              application/x-frame
0   string   \<Book             application/x-frame
0   string   \<Maker            application/x-frame

# MS-Word
0   string   \376\067\0\043          application/msword
0   string   \320\317\021\340\241\261  application/msword
0   string   \333\245-\0\0\0         application/msword
```

An optional MIME encoding can be included as a fifth column. For example, this can recognize gzipped files and set the encoding for them.

```
# gzip (GNU zip, not to be confused with
#       [Info-ZIP/PKWARE] zip archiver)

0   string   \037\213 application/octet-stream  x-gzip
```

3.55.2 Performance Issues

This module is not for every system. If your system is barely keeping up with its load or if you're performing a web server benchmark, you may not want to enable this because the processing is not free.

However, an effort was made to improve the performance of the original file(1) code to make it fit in a busy web server. It was designed for a server where there are thousands of users who publish their own documents. This is probably very common on intranets. Many times, it's helpful if the server can make more intelligent decisions about a file's contents than the file name allows ... even if just to reduce the "why doesn't my page work" calls when users improperly name their own files. You have to decide if the extra work suits your environment.

3.55.3 Notes

The following notes apply to the mod_mime_magic module and are included here
for compliance with contributors' copyright restrictions that require their ac-
knowledgment.

> mod_mime_magic: MIME type lookup via file magic numbers
> Copyright (c) 1996-1997 Cisco Systems, Inc.

> This software was submitted by Cisco Systems to the Apache Group
> in July 1997. Future revisions and derivatives of this source code must
> acknowledge Cisco Systems as the original contributor of this module.
> All other licensing and usage conditions are those of the Apache Group.

> Some of this code is derived from the free version of the file command
> originally posted to comp.sources.unix. Copyright info for that program
> is included below as required.

> - Copyright (c) Ian F. Darwin, 1987. Written by Ian F. Darwin.

> This software is not subject to any license of the American Telephone
> and Telegraph Company or of the Regents of the University of Califor-
> nia.

> Permission is granted to anyone to use this software for any purpose on
> any computer system, and to alter it and redistribute it freely, subject
> to the following restrictions:

> 1. The author is not responsible for the consequences of use of this
>   software, no matter how awful, even if they arise from flaws in it.
> 2. The origin of this software must not be misrepresented, either by
>   explicit claim or by omission. Since few users ever read sources,
>   credits must appear in the documentation.
> 3. Altered versions must be plainly marked as such, and must not be
>   misrepresented as being the original software. Since few users ever
>   read sources, credits must appear in the documentation.
> 4. This notice may not be removed or altered.

> For compliance with Mr Darwin's terms: this has been very significantly
> modified from the free "file" command.

> - all-in-one file for compilation convenience when moving from one
>   version of Apache to the next.
> - Memory allocation is done through the Apache API's pool struc-
>   ture.
> - All functions have had necessary Apache API request or server
>   structures passed to them where necessary to call other Apache
>   API routines. (i.e., usually for logging, files, or memory allocation
>   in itself or a called function.)

- *struct magic has been converted from an array to a single-ended linked list because it only grows one record at a time, it's only accessed sequentially, and the Apache API has no equivalent of* realloc()*.*
- *Functions have been changed to get their parameters from the server configuration instead of globals. (It should be reentrant now but has not been tested in a threaded environment.)*
- *Places where it used to print results to stdout now saves them in a list where they're used to set the MIME type in the Apache request record.*
- *Command-line flags have been removed since they will never be used here.*

MimeMagicFile Directive

Description:	Enable MIME-type determination based on file contents using the specified magic file
Syntax:	MimeMagicFile *file-path*
Context:	server config, virtual host
Status:	Extension
Module:	mod_mime_magic

The MimeMagicFile directive can be used to enable this module. The default file is distributed at conf/magic. Non-rooted paths are relative to the ServerRoot. Virtual hosts will use the same file as the main server unless a more specific setting is used, in which case the more specific setting overrides the main server's file.

Example
MimeMagicFile conf/magic

3.56 Apache Module mod_negotiation

Description:	Provides for content negotiation (p. 687)
Status:	Base
Module Identifier:	negotiation_module
Source File:	mod_negotiation.c

Summary

Content negotiation, or more accurately content selection, is the selection of the document that best matches the clients capabilities, from one of several available documents. There are two implementations of this.

- A type map (a file with the handler type-map) which explicitly lists the files containing the variants.

- A MultiViews search (enabled by the MultiViews Options), where the server does an implicit filename pattern match, and choose from amongst the results.

Directives:

    CacheNegotiatedDocs
    ForceLanguagePriority
    LanguagePriority

See also:

- ▷ Options (p. 120)
- ▷ mod_mime (p. 348)
- ▷ Content Negotiation (p. 687)
- ▷ Environment Variables (p. 705)

3.56.1 Type maps

A type map has a format similar to RFC822 mail headers. It contains document descriptions separated by blank lines, with lines beginning with a hash character ('#') treated as comments. A document description consists of several header records; records may be continued on multiple lines if the continuation lines start with spaces. The leading space will be deleted and the lines concatenated. A header record consists of a keyword name, which always ends in a colon, followed by a value. Whitespace is allowed between the header name and value, and between the tokens of value. The headers allowed are:

Content-Encoding: The encoding of the file. Apache only recognizes encodings that are defined by an AddEncoding directive. This normally includes the encodings x-compress for compress'd files, and x-gzip for gzip'd files. The x- prefix is ignored for encoding comparisons.

Content-Language: The language(s) of the variant, as an Internet standard language tag (RFC 1766[49]). An example is en, meaning English. If the variant contains more than one language, they are separated by a comma.

Content-Length: The length of the file, in bytes. If this header is not present, then the actual length of the file is used.

Content-Type: The MIME media type of the document, with optional parameters. Parameters are separated from the media type and from one another by a semi-colon, with a syntax of name=value. Common parameters include:

> level an integer specifying the version of the media type. For text/html this defaults to 2, otherwise 0.
>
> qs a floating-point number with a value in the range 0.0 to 1.0, indicating the relative 'quality' of this variant compared to the other available variants, independent of the client's capabilities. For example, a JPEG file is usually of higher source quality than an ASCII file if it is attempting to represent a photograph. However, if the resource being represented is ASCII art, then an ASCII file would have a higher source quality than a JPEG file. All qs values are therefore specific to a given resource.

> *Example*
> Content-Type: image/jpeg; qs=0.8

URI: URI of the file containing the variant (of the given media type, encoded with the given content encoding). These are interpreted as URLs relative to the map file; they must be on the same server (!), and they must refer to files to which the client would be granted access if they were to be requested directly.

Body: New in Apache 2.0, the actual content of the resource may be included in the type-map file using the Body header. This header must contain a string that designates a delimiter for the body content. Then all following lines in the type map file will be considered part of the resource body until the delimiter string is found.

> *Example:*
> ```
> Body:----xyz----
> <html>
> <body>
> <p>Content of the page.</p>
> </body>
> </html>
> ----xyz----
> ```

---

[49]http://www.ietf.org/rfc/rfc1766.txt

3.56.2 MultiViews

A MultiViews search is enabled by the MultiViews Options. If the server receives a request for /some/dir/foo and /some/dir/foo does *not* exist, then the server reads the directory looking for all files named foo.*, and effectively fakes up a type map which names all those files, assigning them the same media types and content-encodings it would have if the client had asked for one of them by name. It then chooses the best match to the client's requirements, and returns that document.

The MultiViewsMatch directive configures whether Apache will consider files that do not have content negotiation meta-information assigned to them when choosing files.

CacheNegotiatedDocs Directive

Description:	Allows content-negotiated documents to be cached by proxy servers
Syntax:	CacheNegotiatedDocs On|Off
Default:	CacheNegotiatedDocs Off
Context:	server config, virtual host
Status:	Base
Module:	mod_negotiation
Compatibility:	The syntax changed in version 2.0.

If set, this directive allows content-negotiated documents to be cached by proxy servers. This could mean that clients behind those proxies could retrieve versions of the documents that are not the best match for their abilities, but it will make caching more efficient.

This directive only applies to requests which come from HTTP/1.0 browsers. HTTP/1.1 provides much better control over the caching of negotiated documents, and this directive has no effect in responses to HTTP/1.1 requests.

Prior to version 2.0, CacheNegotiatedDocs did not take an argument; it was turned on by the presence of the directive by itself.

ForceLanguagePriority Directive

Description:	Action to take if a single acceptable document is not found
Syntax:	ForceLanguagePriority None|Prefer|Fallback [Prefer|Fallback]
Default:	ForceLanguagePriority Prefer
Context:	server config, virtual host, directory, .htaccess
Override:	FileInfo
Status:	Base
Module:	mod_negotiation
Compatibility:	Available in version 2.0.30 and later

The ForceLanguagePriority directive uses the given LanguagePriority to satisfy negotiation where the server could otherwise not return a single matching document.

ForceLanguagePriority Prefer uses LanguagePriority to serve a one valid result, rather than returning an HTTP result 300 (MULTIPLE CHOICES) when there are several equally valid choices. If the directives below were given, and the user's Accept-Language header assigned en and de each as quality .500 (equally acceptable) then the first matching variant, en, will be served.

```
LanguagePriority en fr de
ForceLanguagePriority Prefer
```

ForceLanguagePriority Fallback uses LanguagePriority to serve a valid result, rather than returning an HTTP result 406 (NOT ACCEPTABLE). If the directives below were given, and the user's Accept-Language only permitted an es language response, but such a variant isn't found, then the first variant from the LanguagePriority list below will be served.

```
LanguagePriority en fr de
ForceLanguagePriority Fallback
```

Both options, Prefer and Fallback, may be specified, so either the first matching variant from LanguagePriority will be served if more than one variant is acceptable, or first available document will be served if none of the variants matched the client's acceptable list of languages.

See also:

▷ AddLanguage (p. 354)

LanguagePriority Directive

Description:	The precedence of language variants for cases where the client does not express a preference
Syntax:	LanguagePriority *MIME-lang* [*MIME-lang*] ...
Context:	server config, virtual host, directory, .htaccess
Override:	FileInfo
Status:	Base
Module:	mod_negotiation

The LanguagePriority sets the precedence of language variants for the case where the client does not express a preference, when handling a MultiViews request. The list of *MIME-lang* are in order of decreasing preference.

Example:
```
LanguagePriority en fr de
```

For a request for foo.html, where foo.html.fr and foo.html.de both existed, but the browser did not express a language preference, then foo.html.fr would be returned.

Note that this directive only has an effect if a 'best' language cannot be determined by any other means or the ForceLanguagePriority directive is not None. In general, the client determines the language preference, not the server.

See also:

▷ AddLanguage (p. 354)

3.57 Apache Module mod_nw_ssl

Description:	Enable SSL encryption for NetWare
Status:	Base
Module Identifier:	nwssl_module
Source File:	mod_nw_ssl.c
Compatibility:	NetWare only

Summary

This module enables SSL encryption for a specified port. It takes advantage of the SSL encryption functionality that is built into the NetWare operating system.

Directives:

    NWSSLTrustedCerts
    NWSSLUpgradeable
    SecureListen

NWSSLTrustedCerts Directive

Description:	List of additional client certificates
Syntax:	NWSSLTrustedCerts *filename* [*filename*] ...
Context:	server config
Status:	Base
Module:	mod_nw_ssl

Specifies a list of client certificate files (DER format) that are used when creating a proxied SSL connection. Each client certificate used by a server must be listed separately in its own .der file.

NWSSLUpgradeable Directive

Description:	Allows a connection to be upgraded to an SSL connection upon request
Syntax:	NWSSLUpgradeable [*IP-address*:]*portnumber*
Context:	server config
Status:	Base
Module:	mod_nw_ssl

Allow a connection that was created on the specified address and/or port to be upgraded to an SSL connection upon request from the client. The address and/or port must have already be defined previously with a Listen directive.

SecureListen Directive

Description:	Enables SSL encryption for the specified port
Syntax:	SecureListen [*IP-address*:]*portnumber*
	Certificate-Name [MUTUAL]
Context:	server config
Status:	Base
Module:	mod_nw_ssl

Specifies the port and the eDirectory based certificate name that will be used to enable SSL encryption. An optional third parameter also enables mutual authentication.

3.58 Apache Module mod_proxy

Description:	HTTP/1.1 proxy/gateway server
Status:	Extension
Module Identifier:	proxy_module
Source File:	mod_proxy.c

Summary

WARNING *Do not enable proxying with ProxyRequests until you have*
secured your server. Open proxy servers are dangerous both to your
network and to the Internet at large.

This module implements a proxy/gateway for Apache. It implements proxying
capability for AJP13 (Apache JServe Protocol version 1.3), FTP, CONNECT (for
SSL), HTTP/0.9, HTTP/1.0, and HTTP/1.1. The module can be configured to
connect to other proxy modules for these and other protocols.

Apache's proxy features are divided into several modules in addition to mod_-
proxy: mod_proxy_http, mod_proxy_ftp, mod_proxy_ajp, mod_proxy_balancer,
and mod_proxy_connect. Thus, if you want to use one or more of the particular
proxy functions, load mod_proxy *and* the appropriate module(s) into the server
(either statically at compile-time or dynamically via the LoadModule directive).

In addition, extended features are provided by other modules. Caching is provided by mod_cache and related modules. The ability to contact remote servers
using the SSL/TLS protocol is provided by the SSLProxy* directives of mod_-
ssl. These additional modules will need to be loaded and configured to take
advantage of these features.

Directives:

AllowCONNECT
BalancerMember
NoProxy
<Proxy>
ProxyBadHeader
ProxyBlock
ProxyDomain
ProxyErrorOverride
ProxyFtpDirCharset
ProxyIOBufferSize
<ProxyMatch>
ProxyMaxForwards
ProxyPass
ProxyPassInterpolateEnv

ProxyPassMatch
ProxyPassReverse
ProxyPassReverseCookieDomain
ProxyPassReverseCookiePath
ProxyPreserveHost
ProxyReceiveBufferSize
ProxyRemote
ProxyRemoteMatch
ProxyRequests
ProxySet
ProxyStatus
ProxyTimeout
ProxyVia

See also:

▷ mod_cache (p. 215)

▷ mod_proxy_http (p. 419)

▷ mod_proxy_ftp (p. 416)

▷ mod_proxy_connect (p. 415)

▷ mod_proxy_balancer (p. 408)

▷ mod_ssl (p. 458)

3.58.1 Forward Proxies and Reverse Proxies/Gateways

Apache can be configured in both a **forward** and **reverse** proxy (also known as **gateway**) mode.

An ordinary **forward proxy** is an intermediate server that sits between the client and the *origin server*. In order to get content from the origin server, the client sends a request to the proxy naming the origin server as the target and the proxy then requests the content from the origin server and returns it to the client. The client must be specially configured to use the forward proxy to access other sites.

A typical usage of a forward proxy is to provide Internet access to internal clients that are otherwise restricted by a firewall. The forward proxy can also use caching (as provided by mod_cache) to reduce network usage.

The forward proxy is activated using the ProxyRequests directive. Because forward proxies allow clients to access arbitrary sites through your server and to hide their true origin, it is essential that you secure your server so that only authorized clients can access the proxy before activating a forward proxy.

A **reverse proxy** (or **gateway**), by contrast, appears to the client just like an ordinary web server. No special configuration on the client is necessary. The client makes ordinary requests for content in the name-space of the reverse proxy. The reverse proxy then decides where to send those requests, and returns the content as if it was itself the origin.

A typical usage of a reverse proxy is to provide Internet users access to a server that is behind a firewall. Reverse proxies can also be used to balance load among several back-end servers, or to provide caching for a slower back-end server. In addition, reverse proxies can be used simply to bring several servers into the same URL space.

A reverse proxy is activated using the ProxyPass directive or the [P] flag to the RewriteRule directive. It is **not** necessary to turn ProxyRequests on in order to configure a reverse proxy.

3.58.2 Basic Examples

The examples below are only a very basic idea to help you get started. Please read the documentation on the individual directives.

In addition, if you wish to have caching enabled, consult the documentation
from mod_cache.

Reverse Proxy
```
ProxyPass /foo http://foo.example.com/bar
ProxyPassReverse /foo http://foo.example.com/bar
```

Forward Proxy
```
ProxyRequests On
ProxyVia On

<Proxy *>
    Order deny,allow
    Deny from all
    Allow from internal.example.com
</Proxy>
```

3.58.3 Workers

The proxy manages the configuration of origin servers and their communication
parameters in objects called **workers**. There are two built-in workers, the
default forward proxy worker and the default reverse proxy worker. Additional
workers can be configured explicitly.

The two default workers have a fixed configuration and will be used if no other
worker matches the request. They do not use HTTP Keep-Alive or connection
pooling. The TCP connections to the origin server will instead be opened and
closed for each request.

Explicitly configured workers are identified by their URL. They are usually
created and configured using ProxyPass or ProxyPassMatch when used for a
reverse proxy:

```
ProxyPass /example http://backend.example.com
connectiontimeout=5 timeout=30
```

This will create a worker associated with the origin server URL
http://backend.example.com and using the given timeout values. When used
in a forward proxy, workers are usually defined via the ProxySet directive:

```
ProxySet http://backend.example.com connectiontimeout=5
timeout=30
```

or alternatively using Proxy and ProxySet:

```
<Proxy http://backend.example.com>
    ProxySet connectiontimeout=5 timeout=30
</Proxy>
```

Using explicitly configured workers in the forward mode is not very common,
because forward proxies usually communicate with many different origin servers.
Creating explicit workers for some of the origin servers can still be useful, if they
are used very often. Explicitly configured workers have no concept of forward

or reverse proxying by themselves. They encapsulate a common concept of communication with origin servers. A worker created by `ProxyPass` for use in a reverse proxy will be also used for forward proxy requests whenever the URL to the origin server matches the worker URL and vice versa.

The URL identifying a direct worker is the URL of its origin server including any path components given:

```
ProxyPass /examples http://backend.example.com/examples
ProxyPass /docs http://backend.example.com/docs
```

This example defines two different workers, each using a separate connection pool and configuration.

WORKER SHARING *Worker sharing happens if the worker URLs overlap, which occurs when the URL of some worker is a leading substring of the URL of another worker defined later in the configuration file. In the following example*

```
ProxyPass /apps http://backend.example.com/ timeout=60
ProxyPass /examples http://backend.example.com/examples
timeout=10
```

the second worker isn't actually created. Instead the first worker is used. The benefit is, that there is only one connection pool, so connections are more often reused. Note that all configuration attributes given explicitly for the later worker and some configuration defaults will overwrite the configuration given for the first worker. This will be logged as a warning. In the above example the resulting timeout value for the URL /apps will be 10 instead of 60!

If you want to avoid worker sharing, sort your worker definitions by URL length, starting with the longest worker URLs. If you want to maximize worker sharing use the reverse sort order. See also the related warning about ordering ProxyPass directives.

Explicitly configured workers come in two flavors: **direct workers** and (load) **balancer workers**. They support many important configuration attributes which are described below in the `ProxyPass` directive. The same attributes can also be set using `ProxySet`.

The set of options available for a direct worker depends on the protocol, which is specified in the origin server URL. Available protocols include `ajp`, `ftp`, `http` and `scgi`.

Balancer workers are virtual workers that use direct workers known as their members to actually handle the requests. Each balancer can have multiple members. When it handles a request, it chooses a member based on the configured load balancing algorithm.

A balancer worker is created if its worker URL uses `balancer` as the protocol scheme. The balancer URL uniquely identifies the balancer worker. Members are added to a balancer using `BalancerMember`.

3.58.4 Controlling access to your proxy

You can control who can access your proxy via the `<Proxy>` control block as in
the following example:

```
<Proxy *>
    Order Deny,Allow
    Deny from all
    Allow from 192.168.0
</Proxy>
```

For more information on access control directives, see `mod_authz_host`.

Strictly limiting access is essential if you are using a forward proxy (using the
`ProxyRequests` directive). Otherwise, your server can be used by any client to
access arbitrary hosts while hiding his or her true identity. This is dangerous
both for your network and for the Internet at large. When using a reverse proxy
(using the `ProxyPass` directive with `ProxyRequests Off`), access control is less
critical because clients can only contact the hosts that you have specifically
configured.

3.58.5 Slow Startup

If you're using the `ProxyBlock` directive, hostnames' IP addresses are looked up
and cached during startup for later match test. This may take a few seconds
(or more) depending on the speed with which the hostname lookups occur.

3.58.6 Intranet Proxy

An Apache proxy server situated in an intranet needs to forward external requests through the company's firewall (for this, configure the `ProxyRemote` directive to forward the respective *scheme* to the firewall proxy). However, when
it has to access resources within the intranet, it can bypass the firewall when accessing hosts. The `NoProxy` directive is useful for specifying which hosts belong
to the intranet and should be accessed directly.

Users within an intranet tend to omit the local domain name from
their WWW requests, thus requesting "http://somehost/" instead of
`http://somehost.example.com/`. Some commercial proxy servers let them get
away with this and simply serve the request, implying a configured local domain. When the `ProxyDomain` directive is used and the server is configured for
proxy service, Apache can return a redirect response and send the client to the
correct, fully qualified, server address. This is the preferred method since the
user's bookmark files will then contain fully qualified hosts.

3.58.7 Protocol Adjustments

For circumstances where mod_proxy is sending requests to an origin server that doesn't properly implement keepalives or HTTP/1.1, there are two environment variables (p. 705) that can force the request to use HTTP/1.0 with no keepalive. These are set via the SetEnv directive.

These are the force-proxy-request-1.0 and proxy-nokeepalive notes.

```
<Location /buggyappserver/>
    ProxyPass http://buggyappserver:7001/foo/
    SetEnv force-proxy-request-1.0 1
    SetEnv proxy-nokeepalive 1
</Location>
```

3.58.8 Request Bodies

Some request methods such as POST include a request body. The HTTP protocol requires that requests which include a body either use chunked transfer encoding or send a Content-Length request header. When passing these requests on to the origin server, mod_proxy_http will always attempt to send the Content-Length. But if the body is large and the original request used chunked encoding, then chunked encoding may also be used in the upstream request. You can control this selection using environment variables (p. 705). Setting proxy-sendcl ensures maximum compatibility with upstream servers by always sending the Content-Length, while setting proxy-sendchunked minimizes resource usage by using chunked encoding.

3.58.9 Reverse Proxy Request Headers

When acting in a reverse-proxy mode (using the ProxyPass directive, for example), mod_proxy_http adds several request headers in order to pass information to the origin server. These headers are:

X-Forwarded-For The IP address of the client.

X-Forwarded-Host The original host requested by the client in the Host HTTP request header.

X-Forwarded-Server The hostname of the proxy server.

Be careful when using these headers on the origin server, since they will contain more than one (comma-separated) value if the original request already contained one of these headers. For example, you can use %{X-Forwarded-For}i in the log format string of the origin server to log the original clients IP address, but you may get more than one address if the request passes through several proxies.

See also the ProxyPreserveHost and ProxyVia directives, which control other request headers.

AllowCONNECT Directive

Description:	Ports that are allowed to CONNECT through the proxy
Syntax:	AllowCONNECT port [port] ...
Default:	AllowCONNECT 443 563
Context:	server config, virtual host
Status:	Extension
Module:	mod_proxy

The AllowCONNECT directive specifies a list of port numbers to which the proxy CONNECT method may connect. Today's browsers use this method when a https connection is requested and proxy tunneling over HTTP is in effect.

By default, only the default https port (443) and the default snews port (563) are enabled. Use the AllowCONNECT directive to override this default and allow connections to the listed ports only.

Note that you'll need to have mod_proxy_connect present in the server in order to get the support for the CONNECT at all.

BalancerMember Directive

Description:	Add a member to a load balancing group
Syntax:	BalancerMember [balancerurl] url [key=value [key=value ...]]
Context:	directory
Status:	Extension
Module:	mod_proxy
Compatibility:	BalancerMember is only available in Apache 2.2 and later.

This directive adds a member to a load balancing group. It could be used within a <Proxy balancer://...> container directive, and can take any of the key value pairs available to ProxyPass directives.

The balancerurl is only needed when not in <Proxy balancer://...> container directive. It corresponds to the url of a balancer defined in ProxyPass directive.

NoProxy Directive

Description:	Hosts, domains, or networks that will be connected to directly
Syntax:	NoProxy host [host] ...
Context:	server config, virtual host
Status:	Extension
Module:	mod_proxy

This directive is only useful for Apache proxy servers within intranets. The NoProxy directive specifies a list of subnets, IP addresses, hosts and/or domains, separated by spaces. A request to a host which matches one or more of these is always served directly, without forwarding to the configured ProxyRemote proxy server(s).

Example
```
ProxyRemote * http://firewall.example.com:81
NoProxy .example.com 192.168.112.0/21
```

The *host* arguments to the `NoProxy` directive are one of the following type list:

Domain A **Domain** is a partially qualified DNS domain name, preceded by a period. It represents a list of hosts which logically belong to the same DNS domain or zone (*i.e.*, the suffixes of the hostnames are all ending in *Domain*).

    Examples
```
.com .apache.org.
```

To distinguish *Domains* from *Hostnames* (both syntactically and semantically; a DNS domain can have a DNS A record, too!), *Domains* are always written with a leading period.

> NOTE *Domain name comparisons are done without regard to the case, and Domains are always assumed to be anchored in the root of the DNS tree, therefore two domains* `.ExAmple.com` *and* `.example.com.` *(note the trailing period) are considered equal. Since a domain comparison does not involve a DNS lookup, it is much more efficient than subnet comparison.*

SubNet A **SubNet** is a partially qualified internet address in numeric (dotted quad) form, optionally followed by a slash and the netmask, specified as the number of significant bits in the *SubNet*. It is used to represent a subnet of hosts which can be reached over a common network interface. In the absence of the explicit net mask it is assumed that omitted (or zero valued) trailing digits specify the mask. (In this case, the netmask can only be multiples of 8 bits wide.) Examples:

`192.168` **or** `192.168.0.0` the subnet 192.168.0.0 with an implied netmask of 16 valid bits (sometimes used in the netmask form `255.255.0.0`)

`192.168.112.0/21` the subnet 192.168.112.0/21 with a netmask of 21 valid bits (also used in the form `255.255.248.0`)

As a degenerate case, a *SubNet* with 32 valid bits is the equivalent to an *IPAddr*, while a *SubNet* with zero valid bits (*e.g.*, 0.0.0.0/0) is the same as the constant *_Default_*, matching any IP address.

IPAddr A **IPAddr** represents a fully qualified internet address in numeric (dotted quad) form. Usually, this address represents a host, but there need not necessarily be a DNS domain name connected with the address.

    Example
```
192.168.123.7
```

> NOTE *An IPAddr does not need to be resolved by the DNS system, so it can result in more effective apache performance.*

Hostname A **Hostname** is a fully qualified DNS domain name which can be
resolved to one or more *IPAddrs* via the DNS domain name service. It
represents a logical host (in contrast to *Domains*, see above) and must be
resolvable to at least one *IPAddr* (or often to a list of hosts with different
IPAddrs).

> *Examples*
> prep.ai.example.com
> www.apache.org

> NOTE *In many situations, it is more effective to specify an IPAddr
> in place of a Hostname since a DNS lookup can be avoided. Name
> resolution in Apache can take a remarkable deal of time when the
> connection to the name server uses a slow PPP link.*

> *Hostname comparisons are done without regard to the case,
> and Hostnames are always assumed to be anchored in the root
> of the DNS tree, therefore two hosts WWW.ExAmple.com and
> www.example.com. (note the trailing period) are considered equal.*

See also:

▷ DNS Issues (p. 571)

Proxy Directive

Description:	Container for directives applied to proxied resources
Syntax:	<Proxy *wildcard-url*> ...</Proxy>
Context:	server config, virtual host
Status:	Extension
Module:	mod_proxy

Directives placed in <Proxy> sections apply only to matching proxied content.
Shell-style wildcards are allowed.

For example, the following will allow only hosts in yournetwork.example.com
to access content via your proxy server:

```
<Proxy *>
    Order Deny,Allow
    Deny from all
    Allow from yournetwork.example.com
</Proxy>
```

The following example will process all files in the foo directory of example.com
through the INCLUDES filter when they are sent through the proxy server:

```
<Proxy http://example.com/foo/*>
    SetOutputFilter INCLUDES
</Proxy>
```

See also:

▷ ProxyMatch (p. 385)

ProxyBadHeader Directive

Description:	Determines how to handle bad header lines in a response
Syntax:	ProxyBadHeader IsError|Ignore|StartBody
Default:	ProxyBadHeader IsError
Context:	server config, virtual host
Status:	Extension
Module:	mod_proxy
Compatibility:	Available in Apache 2.0.44 and later

The `ProxyBadHeader` directive determines the behaviour of mod_proxy if it receives syntactically invalid header lines (*i.e.* containing no colon). The following arguments are possible:

`IsError` Abort the request and end up with a 502 (Bad Gateway) response. This is the default behaviour.

`Ignore` Treat bad header lines as if they weren't sent.

`StartBody` When receiving the first bad header line, finish reading the headers and treat the remainder as body. This helps to work around buggy backend servers which forget to insert an empty line between the headers and the body.

ProxyBlock Directive

Description:	Words, hosts, or domains that are banned from being proxied
Syntax:	ProxyBlock *|word|host|domain [word|host|domain] ...
Context:	server config, virtual host
Status:	Extension
Module:	mod_proxy

The `ProxyBlock` directive specifies a list of words, hosts and/or domains, separated by spaces. HTTP, HTTPS, and FTP document requests to sites whose names contain matched words, hosts or domains are *blocked* by the proxy server. The proxy module will also attempt to determine IP addresses of list items which may be hostnames during startup, and cache them for match test as well. That may slow down the startup time of the server.

Example
```
ProxyBlock joes-garage.com some-host.co.uk rocky.wotsamattau.edu
```

rocky.wotsamattau.edu would also be matched if referenced by IP address.

Note that wotsamattau would also be sufficient to match wotsamattau.edu.

Note also that
```
ProxyBlock *
```

blocks connections to all sites.

ProxyDomain Directive

Description:	Default domain name for proxied requests
Syntax:	ProxyDomain *Domain*
Context:	server config, virtual host
Status:	Extension
Module:	mod_proxy

This directive is only useful for Apache proxy servers within intranets. The ProxyDomain directive specifies the default domain which the apache proxy server will belong to. If a request to a host without a domain name is encountered, a redirection response to the same host with the configured *Domain* appended will be generated.

> *Example*
> ProxyRemote * http://firewall.example.com:81
> NoProxy .example.com 192.168.112.0/21
> ProxyDomain .example.com

ProxyErrorOverride Directive

Description:	Override error pages for proxied content
Syntax:	ProxyErrorOverride On|Off
Default:	ProxyErrorOverride Off
Context:	server config, virtual host
Status:	Extension
Module:	mod_proxy
Compatibility:	Available in version 2.0 and later

This directive is useful for reverse-proxy setups, where you want to have a common look and feel on the error pages seen by the end user. This also allows for included files (via mod_include's SSI) to get the error code and act accordingly (default behavior would display the error page of the proxied server, turning this on shows the SSI Error message).

This directive does not affect the processing of informational (1xx), normal success (2xx), or redirect (3xx) responses.

ProxyFtpDirCharset Directive

Description:	Define the character set for proxied FTP listings
Syntax:	ProxyFtpDirCharset *character set*
Default:	ProxyFtpDirCharset ISO-8859-1
Context:	server config, virtual host, directory
Status:	Extension
Module:	mod_proxy
Compatibility:	Available in Apache 2.2.7 and later

The `ProxyFtpDirCharset` directive defines the character set to be set for FTP directory listings in HTML generated by mod_proxy_ftp.

ProxyIOBufferSize Directive

Description:	Determine size of internal data throughput buffer
Syntax:	ProxyIOBufferSize *bytes*
Default:	ProxyIOBufferSize 8192
Context:	server config, virtual host
Status:	Extension
Module:	mod_proxy

The `ProxyIOBufferSize` directive adjusts the size of the internal buffer, which is used as a scratchpad for the data between input and output. The size must be less or equal 8192.

In almost every case there's no reason to change that value.

ProxyMatch Directive

Description:	Container for directives applied to regular-expression-matched proxied resources
Syntax:	<ProxyMatch *regex*> ...</ProxyMatch>
Context:	server config, virtual host
Status:	Extension
Module:	mod_proxy

The `<ProxyMatch>` directive is identical to the `<Proxy>` directive, except it matches URLs using regular expressions.

See also:

▷ Proxy (p. 382)

ProxyMaxForwards Directive

Description:	Maximium number of proxies that a request can be forwarded through
Syntax:	ProxyMaxForwards *number*
Default:	ProxyMaxForwards -1
Context:	server config, virtual host
Status:	Extension
Module:	mod_proxy
Compatibility:	Available in Apache 2.0 and later; default behaviour changed in 2.2.7

The `ProxyMaxForwards` directive specifies the maximum number of proxies through which a request may pass, if there's no Max-Forwards header supplied with the request. This may be set to prevent infinite proxy loops, or a DoS attack.

Example
```
ProxyMaxForwards 15
```

Note that setting `ProxyMaxForwards` is a violation of the HTTP/1.1 protocol (RFC2616), which forbids a `Proxy` setting `Max-Forwards` if the Client didn't set it. Earlier Apache versions would always set it. A negative `ProxyMaxForwards` value, including the default -1, gives you protocol-compliant behaviour, but may leave you open to loops.

ProxyPass Directive

Description:	Maps remote servers into the local server URL-space
Syntax:	ProxyPass [path] !|url [key=value key=value ...]] [nocanon] [interpolate]
Context:	server config, virtual host, directory
Status:	Extension
Module:	mod_proxy

This directive allows remote servers to be mapped into the space of the local server; the local server does not act as a proxy in the conventional sense, but appears to be a mirror of the remote server. The local server is often called a **reverse proxy** or **gateway**. The *path* is the name of a local virtual path; *url* is a partial URL for the remote server and cannot include a query string.

*The ProxyRequests directive should usually be set **off** when using ProxyPass.*

Suppose the local server has address `http://example.com/`; then
```
ProxyPass /mirror/foo/ http://backend.example.com/
```
will cause a local request for `http://example.com/mirror/foo/bar` to be internally converted into a proxy request to `http://backend.example.com/bar`.

If the first argument ends with a trailing /, the second argument should also end with a trailing / and vice versa. Otherwise the resulting requests to the backend may miss some needed slashes and not deliver the expected results.

The ! directive is useful in situations where you don't want to reverse-proxy a subdirectory, *e.g.*
```
ProxyPass /mirror/foo/i !
ProxyPass /mirror/foo http://backend.example.com
```
will proxy all requests to `/mirror/foo` to `backend.example.com` *except* requests made to `/mirror/foo/i`.

ORDERING PROXYPASS DIRECTIVES *The configured ProxyPass and*

*ProxyPassMatch rules are checked in the order of configuration. The
first rule that matches wins. So usually you should sort conflicting
ProxyPass rules starting with the longest URLs first. Otherwise later
rules for longer URLS will be hidden by any earlier rule which uses a
leading substring of the URL. Note that there is some relation with
worker sharing.*

*For the same reasons exclusions must come before the general ProxyPass
directives.*

As of Apache 2.1, the ability to use pooled connections to a backend server is
available. Using the key=value parameters it is possible to tune this connection
pooling. The default for a Hard Maximum for the number of connections is the
number of threads per process in the active MPM. In the Prefork MPM, this is
always 1, while with the Worker MPM it is controlled by the ThreadsPerChild.

Setting min will determine how many connections will always be open to the
backend server. Up to the Soft Maximum or smax number of connections will
be created on demand. Any connections above smax are subject to a time to
live or ttl. Apache will never create more than the Hard Maximum or max
connections to the backend server.

```
ProxyPass /example http://backend.example.com smax=5 max=20
ttl=120 retry=300
```

Parameter	Description
min	(Default: 0) Minimum number of connections that will always be open to the backend server.
max	(Default: 1...n) Hard Maximum number of connections that will be allowed to the backend server. The default for a Hard Maximum for the number of connections is the number of threads per process in the active MPM. In the Prefork MPM, this is always 1, while with the Worker MPM it is controlled by the ThreadsPerChild. Apache will never create more than the Hard Maximum connections to the backend server.
smax	(Default: max) Upto the Soft Maximum number of connections will be created on demand. Any connections above smax are subject to a time to live or ttl.
acquire	(Default: -) If set this will be the maximum time to wait for a free connection in the connection pool, in milliseconds. If there are no free connections in the pool the Apache will return SERVER_BUSY status to the client.
connectiontimeout	(Default: timeout) Connect timeout in seconds. The number of seconds Apache waits for the creation of a connection to the backend to complete. By adding a postfix of ms the timeout can be also set in milliseconds.

disablereuse   (Default: Off) This parameter should be used when
                   you want to force mod_proxy to immediately close a
                   connection to the backend after being used, and thus,
                   disable its persistent connection and pool for that
                   backend. This helps in various situations where a
                   firewall between Apache and the backend server (re-
                   gardless of protocol) tends to silently drop connections
                   or when backends themselves may be under round-
                   robin DNS. To disable connection pooling reuse, set
                   this property value to On.

flushpackets   (Default: off) Determines whether the proxy module
                   will auto-flush the output brigade after each "chunk"
                   of data. 'off' means that it will flush only when needed,
                   'on' means after each chunk is sent and 'auto' means
                   poll/wait for a period of time and flush if no input has
                   been received for 'flushwait' milliseconds. Currently
                   this is in effect only for AJP.

flushwait   (Default: 10) The time to wait for additional input,
                   in milliseconds, before flushing the output brigade if
                   'flushpackets' is 'auto'.

keepalive   (Default: Off) This parameter should be used when
                   you have a firewall between your Apache and the back-
                   end server, who tend to drop inactive connections.
                   This flag will tell the Operating System to send KEEP_-
                   ALIVE messages on inactive connections (interval de-
                   pends on global OS settings, generally 120ms), and
                   thus prevent the firewall to drop the connection. To
                   enable keepalive set this property value to On.

lbset   (Default: 0) Sets the load balancer cluster set that
                   the worker is a member of. The load balancer will try
                   all members of a lower numbered lbset before trying
                   higher numbered ones.

ping   (Default: 0) Ping property tells webserver to send a
                   CPING request on ajp13 connection before forwarding a
                   request. The parameter is the delay in seconds to wait
                   for the CPONG reply. This features has been added to
                   avoid problem with hung and busy Tomcat's and re-
                   quire ajp13 ping/pong support which has been imple-
                   mented on Tomcat 3.3.2+, 4.1.28+ and 5.0.13+. This
                   will increase the network traffic during the normal op-
                   eration which could be an issue, but it will lower the
                   traffic in case some of the cluster nodes are down or
                   busy. Currently this has an effect only for AJP. By
                   adding a postfix of ms the delay can be also set in
                   milliseconds.

loadfactor	(Default: 1) Worker load factor. Used with BalancerMember. It is a number between 1 and 100 and defines the normalized weighted load applied to the worker.
redirect	(Default: -) Redirection Route of the worker. This value is usually set dynamically to enable safe removal of the node from the cluster. If set all requests without session id will be redirected to the BalancerMember that has route parametar equal as this value.
retry	(Default: 60) Connection pool worker retry timeout in seconds. If the connection pool worker to the backend server is in the error state, Apache will not forward any requests to that server until the timeout expires. This enables to shut down the backend server for maintenance, and bring it back online later. A value of 0 means always retry workers in an error state with no timeout.
route	(Default: -) Route of the worker when used inside load balancer. The route is a value appended to session id.
status	(Default: -) Single letter value defining the initial status of this worker: 'D' is disabled, 'S' is stopped, 'I' is ignore-errors, 'H' is hot-standby and 'E' is in an error state. Status can be set (which is the default) by prepending with '+' or cleared by prepending with '-'. Thus, a setting of 'S-E' sets this worker to Stopped and clears the in-error flag.
timeout	(Default: ProxyTimeout) Connection timeout in seconds. The number of seconds Apache waits for data sent by / to the backend.
ttl	(Default: -) Time To Live for the inactive connections above the smax connections in seconds. Apache will close all connections that has not been used inside that time period.

If the Proxy directive scheme starts with the balancer:// (eg: balancer://cluster/, any path information is ignored) then a virtual worker that does not really communicate with the backend server will be created. Instead it is responsible for the management of several "real" workers. In that case the special set of parameters can be add to this virtual worker. See mod_proxy_balancer for more information about how the balancer works.

Parameter	Description
lbmethod	(Default: byrequests) Balancer load-balance method. Select the load-balancing scheduler method to use. Either byrequests, to perform weighted request counting, bytraffic, to perform weighted traffic byte count balancing, or bybusyness, to perform pending request balancing. Default is byrequests.
maxattempts	(Default: 1) Maximum number of failover attempts before giving up.
nofailover	(Default: Off) If set to On the session will break if the worker is in error state or disabled. Set this value to On if backend servers do not support session replication.
stickysession	(Default: -) Balancer sticky session name. The value is usually set to something like JSESSIONID or PHPSESSIONID, and it depends on the backend application server that support sessions. If the backend application server uses different name for cookies and url encoded id (like servlet containers) use — to to separate them. The first part is for the cookie the second for the path.
scolonpathdelim	(Default: Off) If set to On the semi-colon character ';' will be used as an additional sticky session path deliminator/separator. This is mainly used to emulate mod_jk's behavior when dealing with paths such as JSESSIONID=6736bcf34;foo=aabfa
timeout	(Default: 0) Balancer timeout in seconds. If set this will be the maximum time to wait for a free worker. Default is not to wait.
failonstatus	(Default: -) A single or comma-separated list of HTTP status codes. If set this will force the worker into error state when the backend returns any status code in the list. Worker recovery behaves the same as other worker errors.

A sample balancer setup

```
ProxyPass /special-area http://special.example.com smax=5 max=10
ProxyPass / balancer://mycluster/
stickysession=JSESSIONID|jsessionid nofailover=On
<Proxy balancer://mycluster>
    BalancerMember http://1.2.3.4:8009
    BalancerMember http://1.2.3.5:8009 smax=10
    # Less powerful server, don't send as many requests there
    BalancerMember http://1.2.3.6:8009 smax=1 loadfactor=20
</Proxy>
```

Setting up a hot-standby, that will only be used if no other members are available

```
ProxyPass / balancer://hotcluster/
<Proxy balancer://hotcluster>
    BalancerMember http://1.2.3.4:8009 loadfactor=1
    BalancerMember http://1.2.3.5:8009 loadfactor=2
    # The below is the hot standby
    BalancerMember http://1.2.3.6:8009 status=+H
    ProxySet lbmethod=bytraffic
</Proxy>
```

Normally, mod_proxy will canonicalise ProxyPassed URLs. But this may be incompatible with some backends, particularly those that make use of *PATH_INFO*. The optional *nocanon* keyword suppresses this, and passes the URL path "raw" to the backend. Note that may affect the security of your backend, as it removes the normal limited protection against URL-based attacks provided by the proxy.

The optional *interpolate* keyword (available in httpd 2.2.9 and later), in combination with ProxyPassInterpolateEnv causes the ProxyPass to interpolate environment variables, using the syntax *${VARNAME}*. Note that many of the standard CGI-derived environment variables will not exist when this interpolation happens, so you may still have to resort to mod_rewrite for complex rules.

When used inside a <Location> section, the first argument is omitted and the local directory is obtained from the <Location>. The same will occur inside a <LocationMatch> section, however ProxyPass does not interpret the regexp as such, so it is necessary to use ProxyPassMatch in this situation instead.

If you require a more flexible reverse-proxy configuration, see the RewriteRule directive with the [P] flag.

ProxyPassInterpolateEnv Directive

Description:	Enable Environment Variable interpolation in Reverse Proxy configurations
Syntax:	ProxyPassInterpolateEnv On|Off
Default:	ProxyPassInterpolateEnv Off
Context:	server config, virtual host, directory
Status:	Extension
Module:	mod_proxy
Compatibility:	Available in httpd 2.2.9 and later

This directive, together with the *interpolate* argument to ProxyPass, ProxyPassReverse, ProxyPassReverseCookieDomain and ProxyPassReverseCookiePath enables reverse proxies to be dynamically configured using environment variables, which may be set by another module such as mod_rewrite. It affects the ProxyPass, ProxyPassReverse, ProxyPassReverseCookieDomain, and ProxyPassReverseCookiePath directives, and causes them to substitute the value of an environment variable varname for the string ${varname} in configuration directives.

Keep this turned off (for server performance) unless you need it!

ProxyPassMatch Directive

Description:	Maps remote servers into the local server URL-space using regular expressions
Syntax:	ProxyPassMatch [regex] !|url [key=value [key=value ...]]
Context:	server config, virtual host, directory
Status:	Extension
Module:	mod_proxy
Compatibility:	available in Apache 2.2.5 and later

This directive is equivalent to ProxyPass, but makes use of regular expressions, instead of simple prefix matching. The supplied regular expression is matched against the *url*, and if it matches, the server will substitute any parenthesized matches into the given string and use it as a new *url*.

Suppose the local server has address http://example.com/; then

ProxyPassMatch ^(/.*\.gif)$ http://backend.example.com$1

will cause a local request for http://example.com/foo/bar.gif to be internally converted into a proxy request to http://backend.example.com/foo/bar.gif.

NOTE   *The URL argument must be parsable as a URL before regexp substitutions (as well as after). This limits the matches you can use. For instance, if we had used*

ProxyPassMatch ^(/.*\.gif)$
http://backend.example.com:8000$1

in our previous example, it would fail with a syntax error at server startup. This is a bug (PR 46665 in the ASF bugzilla), and the workaround is to reformulate the match:

ProxyPassMatch ^/(.*\.gif)$
http://backend.example.com:8000/$1

The ! directive is useful in situations where you don't want to reverse-proxy a subdirectory.

When used inside a <LocationMatch> section, the first argument is omitted and the regexp is obtained from the <LocationMatch>.

If you require a more flexible reverse-proxy configuration, see the RewriteRule directive with the [P] flag.

ProxyPassReverse Directive

Description:	Adjusts the URL in HTTP response headers sent from a reverse proxied server
Syntax:	ProxyPassReverse [path] url [interpolate]
Context:	server config, virtual host, directory
Status:	Extension
Module:	mod_proxy

This directive lets Apache adjust the URL in the Location, Content-Location and URI headers on HTTP redirect responses. This is essential when Apache is used as a reverse proxy (or gateway) to avoid bypassing the reverse proxy because of HTTP redirects on the backend servers which stay behind the reverse proxy.

Only the HTTP response headers specifically mentioned above will be rewritten. Apache will not rewrite other response headers, nor will it rewrite URL references inside HTML pages. This means that if the proxied content contains absolute URL references, they will bypass the proxy. A third-party module that will look inside the HTML and rewrite URL references is Nick Kew's mod_proxy_html[50].

path is the name of a local virtual path. *url* is a partial URL for the remote server - the same way they are used for the ProxyPass directive.

For example, suppose the local server has address http://example.com/; then

```
ProxyPass /mirror/foo/ http://backend.example.com/
ProxyPassReverse /mirror/foo/ http://backend.example.com/
ProxyPassReverseCookieDomain backend.example.com
public.example.com
ProxyPassReverseCookiePath / /mirror/foo/
```

will not only cause a local request for the http://example.com/ mirror/foo/bar to be internally converted into a proxy request to http://backend.example.com/bar (the functionality ProxyPass provides here). It also takes care of redirects the server backend.example.com sends: when http://backend.example.com/bar is redirected by him to http://backend.example.com/quux Apache adjusts this to http://example.com/mirror/foo/quux before forwarding the HTTP redirect response to the client. Note that the hostname used for constructing the URL is chosen in respect to the setting of the UseCanonicalName directive.

Note that this ProxyPassReverse directive can also be used in conjunction with the proxy pass-through feature (RewriteRule ... [P]) from mod_rewrite because it doesn't depend on a corresponding ProxyPass directive.

The optional *interpolate* keyword (available in httpd 2.2.9 and later), used together with ProxyPassInterpolateEnv, enables interpolation of environment

---

[50]http://apache.webthing.com/mod_proxy_html/

variables specified using the format *${VARNAME}*.

When used inside a <Location> section, the first argument is omitted and the local directory is obtained from the <Location>. The same occurs inside a <LocationMatch> section, but will probably not work as intended, as ProxyPassReverse will interpret the regexp literally as a path; if needed in this situation, specify the ProxyPassReverse outside the section, or in a separate <Location> section.

ProxyPassReverseCookieDomain Directive

Description:	Adjusts the Domain string in Set-Cookie headers from a reverse-proxied server
Syntax:	ProxyPassReverseCookieDomain *internal-domain public-domain* [*interpolate*]
Context:	server config, virtual host, directory
Status:	Extension
Module:	mod_proxy

Usage is basically similar to ProxyPassReverse, but instead of rewriting headers that are a URL, this rewrites the domain string in Set-Cookie headers.

ProxyPassReverseCookiePath Directive

Description:	Adjusts the Path string in Set-Cookie headers from a reverse-proxied server
Syntax:	ProxyPassReverseCookiePath *internal-path public-path* [*interpolate*]
Context:	server config, virtual host, directory
Status:	Extension
Module:	mod_proxy

Usage is basically similar to ProxyPassReverse, but instead of rewriting headers that are a URL, this rewrites the path string in Set-Cookie headers.

ProxyPreserveHost Directive

Description:	Use incoming Host HTTP request header for proxy request
Syntax:	ProxyPreserveHost On|Off
Default:	ProxyPreserveHost Off
Context:	server config, virtual host
Status:	Extension
Module:	mod_proxy
Compatibility:	Available in Apache 2.0.31 and later.

When enabled, this option will pass the Host: line from the incoming request to the proxied host, instead of the hostname specified in the ProxyPass line.

This option should normally be turned Off. It is mostly useful in special configurations like proxied mass name-based virtual hosting, where the original Host header needs to be evaluated by the backend server.

ProxyReceiveBufferSize Directive

Description:	Network buffer size for proxied HTTP and FTP connections
Syntax:	ProxyReceiveBufferSize *bytes*
Default:	ProxyReceiveBufferSize 0
Context:	server config, virtual host
Status:	Extension
Module:	mod_proxy

The `ProxyReceiveBufferSize` directive specifies an explicit (TCP/IP) network buffer size for proxied HTTP and FTP connections, for increased throughput. It has to be greater than 512 or set to 0 to indicate that the system's default buffer size should be used.

Example
```
ProxyReceiveBufferSize 2048
```

ProxyRemote Directive

Description:	Remote proxy used to handle certain requests
Syntax:	ProxyRemote *match remote-server*
Context:	server config, virtual host
Status:	Extension
Module:	mod_proxy

This defines remote proxies to this proxy. *match* is either the name of a URL-scheme that the remote server supports, or a partial URL for which the remote server should be used, or * to indicate the server should be contacted for all requests. *remote-server* is a partial URL for the remote server. Syntax:

```
remote-server = scheme://hostname[:port]
```

scheme is effectively the protocol that should be used to communicate with the remote server; only http and https are supported by this module. When using https, the requests are forwarded through the remote proxy using the HTTP CONNECT method.

Example
```
ProxyRemote
http://goodguys.example.com/ http://mirrorguys.example.com:8000
ProxyRemote * http://cleverproxy.localdomain
ProxyRemote ftp http://ftpproxy.mydomain:8080
```

In the last example, the proxy will forward FTP requests, encapsulated as yet another HTTP proxy request, to another proxy which can handle them.

This option also supports reverse proxy configuration - a backend webserver can be embedded within a virtualhost URL space even if that server is hidden by another forward proxy.

ProxyRemoteMatch Directive

Description:	Remote proxy used to handle requests matched by regular expressions
Syntax:	ProxyRemoteMatch *regex remote-server*
Context:	server config, virtual host
Status:	Extension
Module:	mod_proxy

The ProxyRemoteMatch is identical to the ProxyRemote directive, except the first argument is a regular expression match against the requested URL.

ProxyRequests Directive

Description:	Enables forward (standard) proxy requests
Syntax:	ProxyRequests On|Off
Default:	ProxyRequests Off
Context:	server config, virtual host
Status:	Extension
Module:	mod_proxy

This allows or prevents Apache from functioning as a forward proxy server. (Setting ProxyRequests to Off does not disable use of the ProxyPass directive.)

In a typical reverse proxy or gateway configuration, this option should be set to Off.

In order to get the functionality of proxying HTTP or FTP sites, you need also mod_proxy_http or mod_proxy_ftp (or both) present in the server.

> WARNING *Do not enable proxying with ProxyRequests until you have secured your server. Open proxy servers are dangerous both to your network and to the Internet at large.*

See also:

▷ Forward and Reverse Proxies/Gateways

ProxySet Directive

Description:	Set various Proxy balancer or member parameters
Syntax:	ProxySet *url key=value [key=value ...]*
Context:	directory
Status:	Extension
Module:	mod_proxy
Compatibility:	ProxySet is only available in Apache 2.2 and later.

This directive is used as an alternate method of setting any of the parameters available to Proxy balancers and workers normally done via the ProxyPass directive. If used within a <Proxy *balancer url*|*worker url*> container directive, the *url* argument is not required. As a side effect the respective balancer or worker gets created. This can be useful when doing reverse proxying via a RewriteRule instead of a ProxyPass directive.

```
<Proxy balancer://hotcluster>
    BalancerMember http://www2.example.com:8009 loadfactor=1
    BalancerMember http://www3.example.com:8009 loadfactor=2
    ProxySet lbmethod=bytraffic
</Proxy>

<Proxy http://backend>
    ProxySet keepalive=On
</Proxy>

ProxySet balancer://foo lbmethod=bytraffic timeout=15

ProxySet ajp://backend:7001 timeout=15
```

WARNING *Keep in mind that the same parameter key can have a different meaning depending whether it is applied to a balancer or a worker as shown by the two examples above regarding timeout.*

ProxyStatus Directive

Description:	Show Proxy LoadBalancer status in mod_status
Syntax:	ProxyStatus Off|On|Full
Default:	ProxyStatus Off
Context:	server config, virtual host
Status:	Extension
Module:	mod_proxy
Compatibility:	Available in version 2.2 and later

This directive determines whether or not proxy loadbalancer status data is displayed via the mod_status server-status page.

NOTE *Full is synonymous with On*

ProxyTimeout Directive

Description:	Network timeout for proxied requests
Syntax:	ProxyTimeout *seconds*
Default:	Value of Timeout
Context:	server config, virtual host
Status:	Extension
Module:	mod_proxy
Compatibility:	Available in Apache 2.0.31 and later

This directive allows a user to specify a timeout on proxy requests. This is useful when you have a slow/buggy appserver which hangs, and you would rather just return a timeout and fail gracefully instead of waiting however long it takes the server to return.

ProxyVia Directive

Description:	Information provided in the Via HTTP response header for proxied requests
Syntax:	ProxyVia On|Off|Full|Block
Default:	ProxyVia Off
Context:	server config, virtual host
Status:	Extension
Module:	mod_proxy

This directive controls the use of the Via: HTTP header by the proxy. Its intended use is to control the flow of proxy requests along a chain of proxy servers. See RFC 2616[51] (HTTP/1.1), section 14.45 for an explanation of Via: header lines.

- If set to Off, which is the default, no special processing is performed. If a request or reply contains a Via: header, it is passed through unchanged.

- If set to On, each request and reply will get a Via: header line added for the current host.

- If set to Full, each generated Via: header line will additionally have the Apache server version shown as a Via: comment field.

- If set to Block, every proxy request will have all its Via: header lines removed. No new Via: header will be generated.

---

[51]http://www.ietf.org/rfc/rfc2616.txt

3.59 Apache Module mod_proxy_ajp

Description:	AJP support module for mod_proxy
Status:	Extension
Module Identifier:	proxy_ajp_module
Source File:	mod_proxy_ajp.c
Compatibility:	Available in version 2.1 and later

Summary

This module *requires* the service of mod_proxy. It provides support for the Apache JServ Protocol version 1.3 (hereafter *AJP13*).

Thus, in order to get the ability of handling AJP13 protocol, mod_proxy and mod_proxy_ajp have to be present in the server.

> WARNING *Do not enable proxying until you have secured your server (p. 374). Open proxy servers are dangerous both to your network and to the Internet at large.*

This module provides no directives.

See also:

▷ mod_proxy (p. 374)

3.59.1 Overview of the protocol

The AJP13 protocol is packet-oriented. A binary format was presumably chosen over the more readable plain text for reasons of performance. The web server communicates with the servlet container over TCP connections. To cut down on the expensive process of socket creation, the web server will attempt to maintain persistent TCP connections to the servlet container, and to reuse a connection for multiple request/response cycles.

Once a connection is assigned to a particular request, it will not be used for any others until the request-handling cycle has terminated. In other words, requests are not multiplexed over connections. This makes for much simpler code at either end of the connection, although it does cause more connections to be open at once.

Once the web server has opened a connection to the servlet container, the connection can be in one of the following states:

- Idle
  No request is being handled over this connection.

- Assigned
  The connecton is handling a specific request.

Once a connection is assigned to handle a particular request, the basic request informaton (e.g. HTTP headers, etc) is sent over the connection in a highly condensed form (e.g. common strings are encoded as integers). Details of that format are below in Request Packet Structure. If there is a body to the request (content-length > 0), that is sent in a separate packet immediately after.

At this point, the servlet container is presumably ready to start processing the request. As it does so, it can send the following messages back to the web server:

- SEND_HEADERS
  Send a set of headers back to the browser.

- SEND_BODY_CHUNK
  Send a chunk of body data back to the browser.

- GET_BODY_CHUNK
  Get further data from the request if it hasn't all been transferred yet. This is necessary because the packets have a fixed maximum size and arbitrary amounts of data can be included the body of a request (for uploaded files, for example). (Note: this is unrelated to HTTP chunked tranfer.)

- END_RESPONSE
  Finish the request-handling cycle.

Each message is accompanied by a differently formatted packet of data. See Response Packet Structures below for details.

3.59.2 Basic Packet Structure

There is a bit of an XDR heritage to this protocol, but it differs in lots of ways (no 4 byte alignment, for example).

Byte order: I am not clear about the endian-ness of the individual bytes. I'm guessing the bytes are little-endian, because that's what XDR specifies, and I'm guessing that sys/socket library is magically making that so (on the C side). If anyone with a better knowledge of socket calls can step in, that would be great.

There are four data types in the protocol: bytes, booleans, integers and strings.

Byte A single byte.

Boolean A single byte, 1 = true, 0 = false. Using other non-zero values as true (i.e. C-style) may work in some places, but it won't in others.

Integer A number in the range of 0 to 2^{16} (32768). Stored in 2 bytes with the high-order byte first.

String A variable-sized string (length bounded by 2^{16}). Encoded with the length packed into two bytes first, followed by the string (including the terminating '\0'). Note that the encoded length does **not** include the trailing '\0' – it is like strlen. This is a touch confusing on the Java side, which is littered with odd autoincrement statements to skip over these terminators. I believe the reason this was done was to allow the C code to be extra efficient when reading strings which the servlet container is sending back – with the terminating \0 character, the C code can pass around references into a single buffer, without copying. If the \0 was missing, the C code would have to copy things out in order to get its notion of a string.

Packet Size

According to much of the code, the max packet size is 8 * 1024 bytes (8K). The actual length of the packet is encoded in the header.

Packet Headers

Packets sent from the server to the container begin with 0x1234. Packets sent from the container to the server begin with AB (that's the ASCII code for A followed by the ASCII code for B). After those first two bytes, there is an integer (encoded as above) with the length of the payload. Although this might suggest that the maximum payload could be as large as 2^{16}, in fact, the code sets the maximum to be 8K.

Packet Format (Server->Container)					
Byte	0	1	2	3	4...(n+3)
Contents	0x12	0x34	Data	Length (n)	Data

Packet Format (Container->Server)					
Byte	0	1	2	3	4...(n+3)
Contents	A	B	Data	Length (n)	Data

For most packets, the first byte of the payload encodes the type of message. The exception is for request body packets sent from the server to the container – they are sent with a standard packet header (0x1234 and then length of the packet), but without any prefix code after that.

The web server can send the following messages to the servlet container:

Code	Type of Packet	Meaning
2	Forward Request	Begin the request-processing cycle with the following data.
7	Shutdown	The web server asks the container to shut itself down.
8	Ping	The web server asks the container to take control (secure login phase).
10	CPing	The web server asks the container to respond quickly with a CPong.
none	Data	Size (2 bytes) and corresponding body data.

To ensure some basic security, the container will only actually do the Shutdown if the request comes from the same machine on which it's hosted.

The first Data packet is send immediately after the Forward Request by the web server.

The servlet container can send the following types of messages to the webserver:

Code	Type of Packet	Meaning
3	Send Body Chunk	Send a chunk of the body from the servlet container to the web server (and presumably, onto the browser).
4	Send Headers	Send the response headers from the servlet container to the web server (and presumably, onto the browser).
5	End Response	Marks the end of the response (and thus the request-handling cycle).
6	Get Body Chunk	Get further data from the request if it hasn't all been transferred yet.
9	CPong Reply	The reply to a CPing request

Each of the above messages has a different internal structure, detailed below.

3.59.3 Request Packet Structure

For messages from the server to the container of type *Forward Request*:

```
AJP13_FORWARD_REQUEST :=
      prefix_code       (byte) 0x02 = JK_AJP13_FORWARD_REQUEST
      method            (byte)
      protocol          (string)
      req_uri           (string)
      remote_addr       (string)
      remote_host       (string)
      server_name       (string)
      server_port       (integer)
      is_ssl            (boolean)
      num_headers       (integer)
      request_headers  *(req_header_name req_header_value)
      attributes       *(attribut_name attribute_value)
      request_terminator (byte) 0xFF
```

The request_headers have the following structure:

```
req_header_name :=
      sc_req_header_name | (string)
                       [see below for how this is parsed]

sc_req_header_name := 0xA0xx (integer)

req_header_value := (string)
```

The attributes are optional and have the following structure:

```
attribute_name := sc_a_name | (sc_a_req_attribute string)
```

```
attribute_value := (string)
```

Not that the all-important header is content-length, because it determines whether or not the container looks for another packet immediately.

Detailed description of the elements of Forward Request

Request prefix

For all requests, this will be 2. See above for details on other Prefix codes.

Method

The HTTP method, encoded as a single byte:

Command Name	Code
OPTIONS	1
GET	2
HEAD	3
POST	4
PUT	5
DELETE	6
TRACE	7
PROPFIND	8
PROPPATCH	9
MKCOL	10
COPY	11
MOVE	12
LOCK	13
UNLOCK	14
ACL	15
REPORT	16
VERSION-CONTROL	17
CHECKIN	18
CHECKOUT	19
UNCHECKOUT	20
SEARCH	21
MKWORKSPACE	22
UPDATE	23
LABEL	24
MERGE	25
BASELINE_CONTROL	26
MKACTIVITY	27

Later version of ajp13, will transport additional methods, even if they are not in this list.

protocol, req_uri, remote_addr, remote_host, server_name, server_port, is_ssl

These are all fairly self-explanatory. Each of these is required, and will be sent for every request.

Headers

The structure of request_headers is the following: First, the number of headers num_headers is encoded. Then, a series of header name req_header_name / value req_header_value pairs follows. Common header names are encoded as integers, to save space. If the header name is not in the list of basic headers, it is encoded normally (as a string, with prefixed length). The list of common headers sc_req_header_nameand their codes is as follows (all are case-sensitive):

Name	Code value	Code name
accept	0xA001	SC_REQ_ACCEPT
accept-charset	0xA002	SC_REQ_ACCEPT_CHARSET
accept-encoding	0xA003	SC_REQ_ACCEPT_ENCODING
accept-language	0xA004	SC_REQ_ACCEPT_LANGUAGE
authorization	0xA005	SC_REQ_AUTHORIZATION
connection	0xA006	SC_REQ_CONNECTION
content-type	0xA007	SC_REQ_CONTENT_TYPE
content-length	0xA008	SC_REQ_CONTENT_LENGTH
cookie	0xA009	SC_REQ_COOKIE
cookie2	0xA00A	SC_REQ_COOKIE2
host	0xA00B	SC_REQ_HOST
pragma	0xA00C	SC_REQ_PRAGMA
referer	0xA00D	SC_REQ_REFERER
user-agent	0xA00E	SC_REQ_USER_AGENT

The Java code that reads this grabs the first two-byte integer and if it sees an '0xA0' in the most significant byte, it uses the integer in the second byte as an index into an array of header names. If the first byte is not 0xA0, it assumes that the two-byte integer is the length of a string, which is then read in.

This works on the assumption that no header names will have length greater than 0x9999 (==0xA000 - 1), which is perfectly reasonable, though somewhat arbitrary.

NOTE: *The content-length header is extremely important. If it is present and non-zero, the container assumes that the request has a body (a POST request, for example), and immediately reads a separate packet off the input stream to get that body.*

Attributes

The attributes prefixed with a ? (e.g. ?context) are all optional. For each, there is a single byte code to indicate the type of attribute, and then its value (string or integer). They can be sent in any order (though the C code always sends them in the order listed below). A special terminating code is sent to signal the end of the list of optional attributes. The list of byte codes is:

Information	Code Value	Type Of Value	Note
?context	0x01	-	Not currently implemented
?servlet_path	0x02	-	Not currently implemented
?remote_user	0x03	String	
?auth_type	0x04	String	
?query_string	0x05	String	
?jvm_route	0x06	String	
?ssl_cert	0x07	String	
?ssl_cipher	0x08	String	
?ssl_session	0x09	String	
?req_attribute	0x0A	String	Name (the name of the attribute follows)
?ssl_key_size	0x0B	Integer	
are_done	0xFF	-	request_terminator

The context and servlet_path are not currently set by the C code, and most of the Java code completely ignores whatever is sent over for those fields (and some of it will actually break if a string is sent along after one of those codes). I don't know if this is a bug or an unimplemented feature or just vestigial code, but it's missing from both sides of the connection.

The remote_user and auth_type presumably refer to HTTP-level authentication, and communicate the remote user's username and the type of authentication used to establish their identity (e.g. Basic, Digest).

The query_string, ssl_cert, ssl_cipher, and ssl_session refer to the corresponding pieces of HTTP and HTTPS.

The jvm_route, is used to support sticky sessions – associating a user's sesson with a particular Tomcat instance in the presence of multiple, load-balancing servers.

Beyond this list of basic attributes, any number of other attributes can be sent via the req_attribute code 0x0A. A pair of strings to represent the attribute name and value are sent immediately after each instance of that code. Environment values are passed in via this method.

Finally, after all the attributes have been sent, the attribute terminator, 0xFF, is sent. This signals both the end of the list of attributes and also then end of the Request Packet.

3.59.4 Response Packet Structure

For messages which the container can send back to the server.

```
AJP13_SEND_BODY_CHUNK :=
  prefix_code   3
  chunk_length  (integer)
  chunk        *(byte)
  chunk_terminator (byte) 0x00

AJP13_SEND_HEADERS :=
  prefix_code       4
  http_status_code  (integer)
  http_status_msg   (string)
  num_headers       (integer)
  response_headers *(res_header_name header_value)

res_header_name :=
    sc_res_header_name | (string)
                        [see below for how this is parsed]

sc_res_header_name := 0xA0 (byte)

header_value := (string)

AJP13_END_RESPONSE :=
  prefix_code   5
  reuse         (boolean)


AJP13_GET_BODY_CHUNK :=
  prefix_code      6
  requested_length (integer)
```

Details:

Send Body Chunk

The chunk is basically binary data, and is sent directly back to the browser.

Send Headers

The status code and message are the usual HTTP things (e.g. 200 and OK). The response header names are encoded the same way the request header names are. See header_encoding above for details about how the codes are distinguished from the strings.
The codes for common headers are:

Name	Code value
Content-Type	0xA001
Content-Language	0xA002
Content-Length	0xA003
Date	0xA004
Last-Modified	0xA005
Location	0xA006
Set-Cookie	0xA007
Set-Cookie2	0xA008
Servlet-Engine	0xA009
Status	0xA00A
WWW-Authenticate	0xA00B

After the code or the string header name, the header value is immediately encoded.

End Response

Signals the end of this request-handling cycle. If the reuse flag is true (==1), this TCP connection can now be used to handle new incoming requests. If reuse is false (anything other than 1 in the actual C code), the connection should be closed.

Get Body Chunk

The container asks for more data from the request (if the body was too large to fit in the first packet sent over or when the request is chunked). The server will send a body packet back with an amount of data which is the minimum of the request_length, the maximum send body size (8186 (8 Kbytes - 6)), and the number of bytes actually left to send from the request body.

If there is no more data in the body (i.e. the servlet container is trying to read past the end of the body), the server will send back an *empty* packet, which is a body packet with a payload length of 0. (0x12,0x34,0x00,0x00)

3.60 Apache Module mod_proxy_balancer

Description:	mod_proxy extension for load balancing
Status:	Extension
Module Identifier:	proxy_balancer_module
Source File:	mod_proxy_balancer.c
Compatibility:	Available in version 2.1 and later

Summary

This module *requires* the service of mod_proxy. It provides load balancing support for HTTP, FTP and AJP13 protocols

Thus, in order to get the ability of load balancing, mod_proxy and mod_proxy_balancer have to be present in the server.

> WARNING *Do not enable proxying until you have secured your server (p. 374). Open proxy servers are dangerous both to your network and to the Internet at large.*

This module provides no directives.

See also:

▷ mod_proxy (p. 374)

3.60.1 Load balancer scheduler algorithm

At present, there are 3 load balancer scheduler algorithms available for use: Request Counting, Weighted Traffic Counting and Pending Request Counting. These are controlled via the lbmethod value of the Balancer definition. See the ProxyPass directive for more information.

3.60.2 Load balancer stickyness

The balancer supports stickyness. When a request is proxied to some back-end, then all following requests from the same user should be proxied to the same back-end. Many load balancers implement this feature via a table that maps client IP addresses to back-ends. This approach is transparent to clients and back-ends, but suffers from some problems: unequal load distribution if clients are themselves hidden behind proxies, stickyness errors when a client uses a dynamic IP address that changes during a session and loss of stickyness, if the mapping table overflows.

The module mod_proxy_balancer implements stickyness on top of two alternative means: cookies and URL encoding. Providing the cookie can be either done by the back-end or by the Apache web server itself. The URL encoding is usually done on the back-end.

3.60.3 Examples of a balancer configuration

Before we dive into the technical details, here's an example of how you might use mod_proxy_balancer to provide load balancing between two back-end servers:

```
<Proxy balancer://mycluster>
BalancerMember http://192.168.1.50:80
BalancerMember http://192.168.1.51:80
</Proxy>
ProxyPass /test balancer://mycluster
```

Another example of how to provide load balancing with stickyness using mod_headers, even if the back-end server does not set a suitable session cookie:

```
Header add Set-Cookie "ROUTEID=.%{BALANCER_WORKER_ROUTE}e;
path=/" env=BALANCER_ROUTE_CHANGED
<Proxy balancer://mycluster>
BalancerMember http://192.168.1.50:80 route=1
BalancerMember http://192.168.1.51:80 route=2
ProxySet stickysession=ROUTEID
</Proxy>
ProxyPass /test balancer://mycluster
```

3.60.4 Request Counting Algorithm

Enabled via lbmethod=byrequests, the idea behind this scheduler is that we distribute the requests among the various workers to ensure that each gets their configured share of the number of requests. It works as follows:

lbfactor is *how much we expect this worker to work*, or *the workers's work quota*. This is a normalized value representing their "share" of the amount of work to be done.

lbstatus is *how urgent this worker has to work to fulfill its quota of work*.

The **worker** is a member of the load balancer, usually a remote host serving one of the supported protocols.

We distribute each worker's work quota to the worker, and then see which of them needs to work most urgently (biggest lbstatus). This worker is then selected for work, and its lbstatus reduced by the total work quota we distributed to all workers. Thus the sum of all lbstatus does not change(*) and we distribute the requests as desired.

If some workers are disabled, the others will still be scheduled correctly.

```
for each worker in workers
    worker lbstatus += worker lbfactor
    total factor    += worker lbfactor
    if worker lbstatus > candidate lbstatus
        candidate = worker
```

```
candidate lbstatus -= total factor
```

If a balancer is configured as follows:

worker	a	b	c	d
lbfactor	25	25	25	25
lbstatus	0	0	0	0

And b gets disabled, the following schedule is produced:

worker	a	b	c	d
lbstatus	-50	0	25	25
lbstatus	-25	0	-25	50
lbstatus (repeat)	0	0	0	0

That is it schedules: a c d a c d a c d ... Please note that:

worker	a	b	c	d
lbfactor	25	25	25	25

Has the exact same behavior as:

worker	a	b	c	d
lbfactor	1	1	1	1

This is because all values of **lbfactor** are normalized with respect to the others.
For:

worker	a	b	c
lbfactor	1	4	1

worker b will, on average, get 4 times the requests that a and c will.

The following asymmetric configuration works as one would expect:

worker	a	b
lbfactor	70	30
lbstatus	*-30*	30
lbstatus	40	*-40*
lbstatus	*10*	-10
lbstatus	*-20*	20
lbstatus	*-50*	50
lbstatus	20	*-20*
lbstatus	*-10*	10
lbstatus	*-40*	40
lbstatus	30	*-30*
lbstatus	*0*	0
(repeat)		

That is after 10 schedules, the schedule repeats and 7 a are selected with 3 b interspersed.

3.60.5 Weighted Traffic Counting Algorithm

Enabled via lbmethod=bytraffic, the idea behind this scheduler is very similar to the Request Counting method, with the following changes:

lbfactor is *how much traffic, in bytes, we want this worker to handle.* This is also a normalized value representing their "share" of the amount of work to be done, but instead of simply counting the number of requests, we take into account the amount of traffic this worker has seen.

If a balancer is configured as follows:

worker	a	b	c
lbfactor	1	2	1

Then we mean that we want b to process twice the amount of bytes than a or c should. It does not necessarily mean that b would handle twice as many requests, but it would process twice the I/O. Thus, the size of the request and response are applied to the weighting and selection algorithm.

3.60.6 Pending Request Counting Algorithm

Enabled via lbmethod=bybusyness, this scheduler keeps track of how many requests each worker is assigned at present. A new request is automatically assigned to the worker with the lowest number of active requests. This is useful in the case of workers that queue incoming requests independently of Apache, to ensure that queue length stays even and a request is always given to the worker most likely to service it fastest.

In the case of multiple least-busy workers, the statistics (and weightings) used by the Request Counting method are used to break the tie. Over time, the distribution of work will come to resemble that characteristic of byrequests.

3.60.7 Exported Environment Variables

At present there are 6 environment variables exported:

BALANCER_SESSION_STICKY This is assigned the *stickysession* value
used for the current request. It is the name of the cookie or request
parameter used for sticky sessions

BALANCER_SESSION_ROUTE This is assigned the *route* parsed from the
current request.

BALANCER_NAME This is assigned the name of the balancer used for the
current request. The value is something like balancer://foo.

BALANCER_WORKER_NAME This is assigned the name of the
worker used for the current request. The value is something like
http://hostA:1234.

BALANCER_WORKER_ROUTE This is assigned the *route* of the worker
that will be used for the current request.

BALANCER_ROUTE_CHANGED This is set to 1 if the session route does
not match the worker route (BALANCER_SESSION_ROUTE != BAL-
ANCER_WORKER_ROUTE) or the session does not yet have an established route. This can be used to determine when/if the client needs to
be sent an updated route when sticky sessions are used.

3.60.8 Enabling Balancer Manager Support

This module *requires* the service of mod_status. Balancer manager enables
dynamic update of balancer members. You can use balancer manager to change
the balance factor or a particular member, or put it in the off line mode.

Thus, in order to get the ability of load balancer management, mod_status and
mod_proxy_balancer have to be present in the server.

To enable load balancer management for browsers from the example.com domain
add this code to your httpd.conf configuration file

```
<Location /balancer-manager>
SetHandler balancer-manager

Order Deny,Allow
Deny from all
Allow from .example.com
</Location>
```

You can now access load balancer manager by using a Web browser to access
the page http://your.server.name/balancer-manager

3.60.9 Details on load balancer stickyness

When using cookie based stickyness, you need to configure the name of the cookie that contains the information about which back-end to use. This is done via the *stickysession* attribute added to either ProxyPass or ProxySet. The name of the cookie is case-sensitive. The balancer extracts the value of the cookie and looks for a member worker with *route* equal to that value. The *route* must also be set in either ProxyPass or ProxySet. The cookie can either be set by the back-end, or as shown in the above example by the Apache web server itself.

Some back-ends use a slightly different form of stickyness cookie, for instance Apache Tomcat. Tomcat adds the name of the Tomcat instance to the end of its session id cookie, separated with a dot (.) from the session id. Thus if the Apache web server finds a dot in the value of the stickyness cookie, it only uses the part behind the dot to search for the route. In order to let Tomcat know about its instance name, you need to set the attribute jvmRoute inside the Tomcat configuration file conf/server.xml to the value of the *route* of the worker that connects to the respective Tomcat. The name of the session cookie used by Tomcat (and more generally by Java web applications based on servlets) is JSESSIONID (upper case) but can be configured to something else.

The second way of implementing stickyness is URL encoding. The web server searches for a query parameter in the URL of the request. The name of the parameter is specified again using *stickysession*. The value of the parameter is used to lookup a member worker with *route* equal to that value. Since it is not easy to extract and manipulate all URL links contained in responses, generally the work of adding the parameters to each link is done by the back-end generating the content. In some cases it might be feasible doing this via the web server using mod_substitute. This can have negative impact on performance though.

The Java standards implement URL encoding slightly different. They use a path info appended to the URL using a semicolon (;) as the separator and add the session id behind. As in the cookie case, Apache Tomcat can include the configured jvmRoute in this path info. To let Apache find this sort of path info, you neet to set scolonpathdelim to On in ProxyPass or ProxySet.

Finally you can support cookies and URL encoding at the same time, by configuring the name of the cookie and the name of the URL parameter separated by a vertical bar (|) as in the following example:

```
ProxyPass /test balancer://mycluster
stickysession=JSESSIONID|jsessionid scolonpathdelim=On <Proxy
balancer://mycluster>
BalancerMember http://192.168.1.50:80 route=node1
BalancerMember http://192.168.1.51:80 route=node2
</Proxy>
```

If the cookie and the request parameter both provide routing information for the same request, the information from the request parameter is used.

3.60.10 Troubleshooting load balancer stickyness

If you experience stickyness errors, e.g. users loose their application sessions and need to login again, you first want to check whether this is because the back-ends are sometimes unavailable or whether your configuration is wrong. To find out about possible stability problems with the back-ends, check your Apache error log for proxy error messages.

To verify your configuration, first check, whether the stickyness is based on a cookie or on URL encoding. Next step would be logging the appropriate data in the access log by using an enhanced LogFormat. The following fields are useful:

%{MYCOOKIE}C The value contained in the cookie with name MYCOOKIE. The name should be the same given in the *stickysession* attribute.

%{Set-Cookie}o This logs any cookie set by the back-end. You can track, whether the back-end sets the session cookie you expect, and to which value it is set.

%{BALANCER_SESSION_STICKY}e The name of the cookie or request parameter used to lookup the routing information.

%{BALANCER_SESSION_ROUTE}e The route information found in the request.

%{BALANCER_WORKER_ROUTE}e The route of the worker chosen.

%{BALANCER_ROUTE_CHANGED}e Set to 1 if the route in the request is different from the route of the worker, i.e. the request couldn't be handled sticky.

Common reasons for loss of session are session timeouts, which are usually configurable on the back-end server.

The balancer also logs detailed information about handling stickyness to the error log, if the log level is set to debug or higher. This is an easy way to troubleshoot stickyness problems, but the log volume might be to high for production servers under high load.

3.61 Apache Module mod_proxy_connect

Description:	mod_proxy extension for CONNECT request handling
Status:	Extension
Module Identifier:	proxy_connect_module
Source File:	mod_proxy_connect.c

Summary

This module *requires* the service of mod_proxy. It provides support for the CONNECT HTTP method. This method is mainly used to tunnel SSL requests through proxy servers.

Thus, in order to get the ability of handling CONNECT requests, mod_proxy and mod_proxy_connect have to be present in the server.

CONNECT is also used, when the server needs to send an HTTPS request through a forward proxy. In this case the server acts as a CONNECT client. This functionality is part of mod_proxy and mod_proxy_connect is not needed in this case.

> WARNING *Do not enable proxying until you have secured your server (p. 374). Open proxy servers are dangerous both to your network and to the Internet at large.*

This module provides no directives.

See also:

▷ AllowCONNECT (p. 380)

▷ mod_proxy (p. 374)

3.62 Apache Module mod_proxy_ftp

Description:	FTP support module for mod_proxy
Status:	Extension
Module Identifier:	proxy_ftp_module
Source File:	mod_proxy_ftp.c

Summary

This module *requires* the service of mod_proxy. It provides support for the proxying FTP sites. Note that FTP support is currently limited to the GET method.

Thus, in order to get the ability of handling FTP proxy requests, mod_proxy and mod_proxy_ftp have to be present in the server.

> WARNING *Do not enable proxying until you have secured your server (p. 374). Open proxy servers are dangerous both to your network and to the Internet at large.*

This module provides no directives.

See also:

▷ mod_proxy (p. 374)

3.62.1 Why doesn't file type xxx download via FTP?

You probably don't have that particular file type defined as application/octet-stream in your proxy's mime.types configuration file. A useful line can be

```
application/octet-stream    bin dms lha lzh exe class tgz taz
```

Alternatively you may prefer to default everything to binary:

```
DefaultType application/octet-stream
```

3.62.2 How can I force an FTP ASCII download of File xxx?

In the rare situation where you must download a specific file using the FTP ASCII transfer method (while the default transfer is in binary mode), you can override mod_proxy's default by suffixing the request with ;type=a to force an ASCII transfer. (FTP Directory listings are always executed in ASCII mode, however.)

3.62.3 How can I do FTP upload?

Currently, only GET is supported for FTP in mod_proxy. You can of course use HTTP upload (POST or PUT) through an Apache proxy.

3.62.4 How can I access FTP files outside of my home directory?

An FTP URI is interpreted relative to the home directory of the user who is logging in. Alas, to reach higher directory levels you cannot use /../, as the dots are interpreted by the browser and not actually sent to the FTP server. To address this problem, the so called **Squid %2f hack** was implemented in the Apache FTP proxy; it is a solution which is also used by other popular proxy servers like the Squid Proxy Cache[52]. By prepending /%2f to the path of your request, you can make such a proxy change the FTP starting directory to / (instead of the home directory). For example, to retrieve the file /etc/motd, you would use the URL:

    ftp://user@host/%2f/etc/motd

3.62.5 How can I hide the FTP cleartext password in my browser's URL line?

To log in to an FTP server by username and password, Apache uses different strategies. In the absence of a user name and password in the URL altogether, Apache sends an anonymous login to the FTP server, *i.e.*,

    user: anonymous
    password: apache_proxy@

This works for all popular FTP servers which are configured for anonymous access.

For a personal login with a specific username, you can embed the user name into the URL, like in:

    ftp://username@host/myfile

If the FTP server asks for a password when given this username (which it should), then Apache will reply with a 401 (Authorization required) response, which causes the Browser to pop up the username/password dialog. Upon entering the password, the connection attempt is retried, and if successful, the requested resource is presented. The advantage of this procedure is that your browser does not display the password in cleartext (which it would if you had used

    ftp://username:password@host/myfile

in the first place).

> NOTE *The password which is transmitted in such a way is not encrypted on its way. It travels between your browser and the Apache proxy server in a base64-encoded cleartext string, and between the Apache proxy and the FTP server as plaintext. You should therefore think twice before accessing your FTP server via HTTP (or before accessing your personal files via FTP at all!) When using insecure channels, an eavesdropper*

---

[52]http://www.squid-cache.org/

might intercept your password on its way.

3.63 Apache Module mod_proxy_http

Description:	HTTP support module for mod_proxy
Status:	Extension
Module Identifier:	proxy_http_module
Source File:	mod_proxy_http.c

Summary

This module *requires* the service of mod_proxy. It provides the features used for proxying HTTP and HTTPS requests. mod_proxy_http supports HTTP/0.9, HTTP/1.0 and HTTP/1.1. It does *not* provide any caching abilities. If you want to set up a caching proxy, you might want to use the additional service of the mod_cache module.

Thus, in order to get the ability of handling HTTP proxy requests, mod_proxy and mod_proxy_http have to be present in the server.

> WARNING *Do not enable proxying until you have secured your server (p. 374). Open proxy servers are dangerous both to your network and to the Internet at large.*

This module provides no directives.

See also:

> ▷ mod_proxy (p. 374)

> ▷ mod_proxy_connect (p. 415)

3.63.1 Environment Variables

In addition to the configuration directives that control the behaviour of mod_proxy, there are a number of **environment variables** that control the HTTP protocol provider:

proxy-sendextracrlf Causes proxy to send an extra CR-LF newline on the end of a request. This is a workaround for a bug in some browsers.

force-proxy-request-1.0 Forces the proxy to send requests to the backend as HTTP/1.0 and disables HTTP/1.1 features.

proxy-nokeepalive Forces the proxy to close the backend connection after each request.

proxy-chain-auth If the proxy requires authentication, it will read and consume the proxy authentication credentials sent by the client. With *proxy-chain-auth* it will *also* forward the credentials to the next proxy in the chain. This may be necessary if you have a chain of proxies that share authentication information. **Security Warning:** Do not set this unless you know you need it, as it forwards sensitive information!

proxy-sendcl HTTP/1.0 required all HTTP requests that include a body (e.g. POST requests) to include a *Content-Length* header. This environment variable forces the Apache proxy to send this header to the backend server, regardless of what the Client sent to the proxy. It ensures compatibility when proxying for an HTTP/1.0 or unknown backend. However, it may require the entire request to be buffered by the proxy, so it becomes very inefficient for large requests.

proxy-sendchunks or proxy-sendchunked This is the opposite of *proxy-sendcl*. It allows request bodies to be sent to the backend using chunked transfer encoding. This allows the request to be efficiently streamed, but requires that the backend server supports HTTP/1.1.

proxy-interim-response This variable takes values RFC or Suppress. Earlier httpd versions would suppress HTTP interim (1xx) responses sent from the backend. This is technically a violation of the HTTP protocol. In practice, if a backend sends an interim response, it may itself be extending the protocol in a manner we know nothing about, or just broken. So this is now configurable: set proxy-interim-response RFC to be fully protocol compliant, or proxy-interim-response Suppress to suppress interim responses.

proxy-initial-not-pooled If this variable is set no pooled connection will be reused if the client connection is an initial connection. This avoids the "proxy: error reading status line from remote server" error message caused by the race condition that the backend server closed the pooled connection after the connection check by the proxy and before data sent by the proxy reached the backend. It has to be kept in mind that setting this variable downgrades performance, especially with HTTP/1.0 clients.

3.64 Apache Module mod_proxy_scgi

Description:	SCGI gateway module for mod_proxy
Status:	Extension
Module Identifier:	proxy_scgi_module
Source File:	mod_proxy_scgi.c
Compatibility:	Available in version 2.2.14 and later

Summary

This module *requires* the service of mod_proxy. It provides support for the SCGI protocol, version 1[53].

Thus, in order to get the ability of handling the SCGI protocol, mod_proxy and mod_proxy_scgi have to be present in the server.

> WARNING *Do not enable proxying until you have secured your server (p. 374). Open proxy servers are dangerous both to your network and to the Internet at large.*

Directives:

```
ProxySCGIInternalRedirect
ProxySCGISendfile
```

See also:

▷ mod_proxy (p. 374)

▷ mod_proxy_balancer (p. 408)

3.64.1 Examples

Remember, in order to make the following examples work, you have to enable mod_proxy and mod_proxy_scgi.

Simple gateway
```
ProxyPass /scgi-bin/ scgi://localhost:4000/
```

The balanced gateway needs mod_proxy_balancer in addition to the already mentioned proxy modules.

Balanced gateway
```
ProxyPass /scgi-bin/ balancer://somecluster/
<Proxy balancer://somecluster/>
    BalancerMember scgi://localhost:4000/
    BalancerMember scgi://localhost:4001/
</Proxy>
```

---

[53]http://python.ca/scgi/protocol.txt

ProxySCGIInternalRedirect Directive

Description:	Enable or disable internal redirect responses from the back-end
Syntax:	ProxySCGIInternalRedirect On|Off
Default:	ProxySCGIInternalRedirect On
Context:	server config, virtual host, directory
Status:	Extension
Module:	mod_proxy_scgi

The ProxySCGIInternalRedirect enables the backend to internally redirect the gateway to a different URL. This feature origins in mod_cgi, which internally redirects the response, if the response status is OK (200) and the response contains a Location header and its value starts with a slash (/). This value is interpreted as a new local URL that Apache internally redirects to.

mod_proxy_scgi does the same as mod_cgi in this regard, except that you can turn off the feature.

Example
```
ProxySCGIInternalRedirect Off
```

ProxySCGISendfile Directive

Description:	Enable evaluation of *X-Sendfile* pseudo response header
Syntax:	ProxySCGISendfile On|Off|*Headername*
Default:	ProxySCGISendfile Off
Context:	server config, virtual host, directory
Status:	Extension
Module:	mod_proxy_scgi

The ProxySCGISendfile directive enables the SCGI backend to let files serve directly by the gateway. This is useful performance purposes – the httpd can use sendfile or other optimizations, which are not possible if the file comes over the backend socket.

The ProxySCGISendfile argument determines the gateway behaviour:

Off No special handling takes place.

On The gateway looks for a backend response header called X-Sendfile and interprets the value as filename to serve. The header is removed from the final response headers. This is equivalent to ProxySCGIRequest X-Sendfile.

anything else Similar to On, but instead of the hardcoded header name the argument is applied as header name.

Example
```
# Use the default header (X-Sendfile)
ProxySCGISendfile On
```

```
# Use a different header
ProxySCGISendfile X-Send-Static
```

3.65 Apache Module mod_reqtimeout

Description:	Set timeout and minimum data rate for receiving requests
Status:	Experimental
Module Identifier:	reqtimeout_module
Source File:	mod_reqtimeout.c
Compatibility:	Available in Apache 2.2.15 and later

Directives:

> RequestReadTimeout

3.65.1 Examples

1. Allow 10 seconds to receive the request including the headers and 30 seconds for receiving the request body:

   > RequestReadTimeout header=10 body=30

2. Allow at least 10 seconds to receive the request body. If the client sends data, increase the timeout by 1 second for every 1000 bytes received, with no upper limit for the timeout (exept for the limit given indirectly by LimitRequestBody):

   > RequestReadTimeout body=10,MinRate=1000

3. Allow at least 10 seconds to receive the request including the headers. If the client sends data, increase the timeout by 1 second for every 500 bytes received. But do not allow more than 30 seconds for the request including the headers:

   > RequestReadTimeout header=10-30,MinRate=500

RequestReadTimeout Directive

Description:	Set timeout values for receiving request headers and body from client.
Syntax:	RequestReadTimeout [header=*timeout* [[-*maxtimeout*],MinRate=*rate*] [body=*timeout* [[-*maxtimeout*],MinRate=*rate*]
Default:	Unset; no limit
Context:	server config, virtual host
Status:	Experimental
Module:	mod_reqtimeout

This directive can set various timeouts for receiving the request headers and the request body from the client. If the client fails to send headers or body within the configured time, a 408 REQUEST TIMEOUT error is sent.

For SSL virtual hosts, the header timeout values include the time needed to do the initial SSL handshake. The body timeout values include the time needed for SSL renegotiation (if necessary).

When an `AcceptFilter` is in use (usually the case on Linux and FreeBSD), the socket is not sent to the server process before at least one byte (or the whole request for `httpready`) is received. The header timeout configured with `RequestReadTimeout` is only effective after the server process has received the socket.

For each of the two timeout types (header or body), there are three ways to specify the timeout:

- **Fixed timeout value:**

    type=timeout

    The time in seconds allowed for reading all of the request headers or body, respectively. A value of 0 means no limit.

- **Timeout value that is increased when data is received:**

    type=timeout,MinRate=data_rate

    Same as above, but whenever data is received, the timeout value is increased according to the specified minimum data rate (in bytes per second).

- **Timeout value that is increased when data is received, with an upper bound:**

    type=timeout-maxtimeout,MinRate=data_rate

    Same as above, but the timeout will not be increased above the second value of the specified timeout range.

3.66 Apache Module mod_rewrite

Description:	Provides a rule-based rewriting engine to rewrite requested URLs on the fly
Status:	Extension
Module Identifier:	rewrite_module
Source File:	mod_rewrite.c
Compatibility:	Available in Apache 1.3 and later

Summary

This module uses a rule-based rewriting engine (based on a regular-expression parser) to rewrite requested URLs on the fly. It supports an unlimited number of rules and an unlimited number of attached rule conditions for each rule, to provide a really flexible and powerful URL manipulation mechanism. The URL manipulations can depend on various tests, of server variables, environment variables, HTTP headers, or time stamps. Even external database lookups in various formats can be used to achieve highly granular URL matching.

This module operates on the full URLs (including the path-info part) both in per-server context (httpd.conf) and per-directory context (.htaccess) and can generate query-string parts on result. The rewritten result can lead to internal sub-processing, external request redirection or even to an internal proxy throughput.

Further details, discussion, and examples, are provided in the detailed mod_-rewrite documentation (p. 575).

Directives:

>   RewriteBase
>   RewriteCond
>   RewriteEngine
>   RewriteLock
>   RewriteLog
>   RewriteLogLevel
>   RewriteMap
>   RewriteOptions
>   RewriteRule

See also:

▷ Rewrite Flags

3.66.1 Quoting Special Characters

As of Apache 1.3.20, special characters in *TestString* and *Substitution* strings can be escaped (that is, treated as normal characters without their usual special meaning) by prefixing them with a backslash ('\') character. In other words, you can include an actual dollar-sign character in a *Substitution* string by using

'\$'; this keeps mod_rewrite from trying to treat it as a backreference.

3.66.2 Environment Variables

This module keeps track of two additional (non-standard) CGI/SSI environment variables named SCRIPT_URL and SCRIPT_URI. These contain the *logical* Web-view to the current resource, while the standard CGI/SSI variables SCRIPT_NAME and SCRIPT_FILENAME contain the *physical* System-view.

Notice: These variables hold the URI/URL *as they were initially requested*, that is, *before* any rewriting. This is important to note because the rewriting process is primarily used to rewrite logical URLs to physical pathnames.

```
SCRIPT_NAME=/sw/lib/w3s/tree/global/u/rse/.www/index.html
SCRIPT_FILENAME=/u/rse/.www/index.html
SCRIPT_URL=/u/rse/
SCRIPT_URI=http://en1.engelschall.com/u/rse/
```

3.66.3 Rewriting in Virtual Hosts

By default, mod_rewrite configuration settings from the main server context are not inherited by virtual hosts. To make the main server settings apply to virtual hosts, you must place the following directives in each <VirtualHost> section:

```
RewriteEngine On
RewriteOptions Inherit
```

3.66.4 Practical Solutions

For numerous examples of common, and not-so-common, uses for mod_rewrite, see the Rewrite Guide (p. 591), and the Advanced Rewrite Guide (p. 599) documents.

RewriteBase Directive

Description:	Sets the base URL for per-directory rewrites
Syntax:	RewriteBase *URL-path*
Default:	See usage for information.
Context:	directory, .htaccess
Override:	FileInfo
Status:	Extension
Module:	mod_rewrite

The RewriteBase directive explicitly sets the base URL for per-directory rewrites. As you will see below, RewriteRule can be used in per-directory config files (.htaccess). In such a case, it will act locally, stripping the local directory prefix before processing, and applying rewrite rules only to the remainder. When processing is complete, the prefix is automatically added back to the path. The default setting is; RewriteBase *physical-directory-path*

When a substitution occurs for a new URL, this module has to re-inject the URL into the server processing. To be able to do this it needs to know what the corresponding URL-prefix or URL-base is. By default this prefix is the corresponding filepath itself. **However, for most websites, URLs are NOT directly related to physical filename paths, so this assumption will often be wrong!** Therefore, you can use the RewriteBase directive to specify the correct URL-prefix.

*If your webserver's URLs are **not** directly related to physical file paths, you will need to use RewriteBase in every .htaccess file where you want to use RewriteRule directives.*

For example, assume the following per-directory config file:

```
#
# /abc/def/.htaccess -- per-dir config file for directory
# /abc/def
# Remember: /abc/def is the physical path of /xyz, i.e., the
#           server has a 'Alias /xyz /abc/def' directive e.g.
#

RewriteEngine On

# let the server know that we were reached via /xyz and not
# via the physical path prefix /abc/def
RewriteBase /xyz

# now the rewriting rules
RewriteRule ^oldstuff\.html$ newstuff.html
```

In the above example, a request to /xyz/oldstuff.html gets correctly rewritten to the physical file /abc/def/newstuff.html.

FOR APACHE HACKERS *The following list gives detailed information about the internal processing steps:*

```
Request:
  /xyz/oldstuff.html

Internal Processing:
  /xyz/oldstuff.html      -> /abc/def/oldstuff.html
                               (per-server Alias)
  /abc/def/oldstuff.html -> /abc/def/newstuff.html
                               (per-dir    RewriteRule)
  /abc/def/newstuff.html -> /xyz/newstuff.html
                               (per-dir    RewriteBase)
  /xyz/newstuff.html      -> /abc/def/newstuff.html
                               (per-server Alias)
```

Result:
/abc/def/newstuff.html

This seems very complicated, but is in fact correct Apache internal pro-cessing. Because the per-directory rewriting comes late in the process, the rewritten request has to be re-injected into the Apache kernel, as if it were a new request. (See mod_rewrite technical details (p. 588).) This is not the serious overhead it may seem to be - this re-injection is completely internal to the Apache server (and the same procedure is used by many other operations within Apache).

RewriteCond Directive

Description:	Defines a condition under which rewriting will take place
Syntax:	RewriteCond *TestString CondPattern*
Context:	server config, virtual host, directory, .htaccess
Override:	FileInfo
Status:	Extension
Module:	mod_rewrite

The RewriteCond directive defines a rule condition. One or more RewriteCond can precede a RewriteRule directive. The following rule is then only used if both the current state of the URI matches its pattern, **and** if these conditions are met.

TestString is a string which can contain the following expanded constructs in addition to plain text:

- **RewriteRule backreferences**: These are backreferences of the form $N (0 <= N <= 9), which provide access to the grouped parts (in parentheses) of the pattern, from the RewriteRule which is subject to the current set of RewriteCond conditions..

- **RewriteCond backreferences**: These are backreferences of the form %N (1 <= N <= 9), which provide access to the grouped parts (again, in parentheses) of the pattern, from the last matched RewriteCond in the current set of conditions.

- **RewriteMap expansions**: These are expansions of the form ${mapname:key|default}. See the documentation for RewriteMap for more details.

- **Server-Variables**: These are variables of the form %{ *NAME_OF_-VARIABLE* } where *NAME_OF_VARIABLE* can be a string taken from the following list:

HTTP headers:	connection & request:	
HTTP_USER_AGENT	REMOTE_ADDR	
HTTP_REFERER	REMOTE_HOST	
HTTP_COOKIE	REMOTE_PORT	
HTTP_FORWARDED	REMOTE_USER	
HTTP_HOST	REMOTE_IDENT	
HTTP_PROXY_CON-	REQUEST_METHOD	
NECTION	SCRIPT_FILENAME	
HTTP_ACCEPT	PATH_INFO	
	QUERY_STRING	
	AUTH_TYPE	
server internals:	**date and time:**	**specials:**
DOCUMENT_ROOT	TIME_YEAR	API_VERSION
SERVER_ADMIN	TIME_MON	THE_REQUEST
SERVER_NAME	TIME_DAY	REQUEST_URI
SERVER_ADDR	TIME_HOUR	REQUEST_FILE-
SERVER_PORT	TIME_MIN	NAME
SERVER_PROTOCOL	TIME_SEC	IS_SUBREQ
SERVER_SOFTWARE	TIME_WDAY	HTTPS
	TIME	

These variables all correspond to the similarly named HTTP MIME-headers, C variables of the Apache server or struct tm fields of the Unix system. Most are documented elsewhere in the Manual or in the CGI specification. Those that are special to mod_rewrite include those below.

IS_SUBREQ *Will contain the text "true" if the request currently being processed is a sub-request, "false" otherwise. Sub-requests may be generated by modules that need to resolve additional files or URIs in order to complete their tasks.*

API_VERSION *This is the version of the Apache module API (the internal interface between server and module) in the current httpd build, as defined in* include/ap_mmn.h. *The module API version corresponds to the version of Apache in use (in the release version of Apache 1.3.14, for instance, it is 19990320:10), but is mainly of interest to module authors.*

THE_REQUEST *The full HTTP request line sent by the browser to the server (e.g.,* "GET /index.html HTTP/1.1"). *This does not include any additional headers sent by the browser.*

REQUEST_URI *The resource requested in the HTTP request line. (In the example above, this would be "/index.html".)*

REQUEST_FILENAME *The full local filesystem path to the file or script matching the request, if this has already been determined by the server at the time* REQUEST_FILENAME *is referenced. Otherwise, such as when used in virtual host context, the same value as* REQUEST_URI.

HTTPS *Will contain the text "on" if the connection is using SSL/TLS, or "off" otherwise. (This variable can be safely*

> *used regardless of whether or not mod_ssl is loaded.)*

Other things you should be aware of:

1. The variables SCRIPT_FILENAME and REQUEST_FILENAME contain the same value - the value of the filename field of the internal request_rec structure of the Apache server. The first name is the commonly known CGI variable name while the second is the appropriate counterpart of REQUEST_URI (which contains the value of the uri field of request_-rec).

   If a substitution occurred and the rewriting continues, the value of both variables will be updated accordingly.

   If used in per-server context (*i.e.*, before the request is mapped to the filesystem) SCRIPT_FILENAME and REQUEST_FILENAME cannot contain the full local filesystem path since the path is unknown at this stage of processing. Both variables will initially contain the value of REQUEST_URI in that case. In order to obtain the full local filesystem path of the request in per-server context, use an URL-based look-ahead %{LA-U:REQUEST_FILENAME} to determine the final value of REQUEST_-FILENAME.

2. %{ENV:variable}, where *variable* can be any environment variable, is also available. This is looked-up via internal Apache structures and (if not found there) via getenv() from the Apache server process.

3. %{SSL:variable}, where *variable* is the name of an SSL environment variable (p. 458), can be used whether or not mod_ssl is loaded, but will always expand to the empty string if it is not. Example: %{SSL:SSL_-CIPHER_USEKEYSIZE} may expand to 128.

4. %{HTTP:header}, where *header* can be any HTTP MIME-header name, can always be used to obtain the value of a header sent in the HTTP request. Example: %{HTTP:Proxy-Connection} is the value of the HTTP header "Proxy-Connection:". If an HTTP header is used in a condition, this header is added to the Vary header of the response in case the condition evaluates to true for the request. It is **not** added if the condition evaluates to false for the request. Adding the HTTP header to the Vary header of the response is needed for proper caching.

   It has to be kept in mind that conditions follow a short circuit logic in the case of the 'ornext|OR' flag so that certain conditions might not be evaluated at all.

5. %{LA-U:variable} can be used for look-aheads which perform an internal (URL-based) sub-request to determine the final value of *variable*. This can be used to access a variable for rewriting which is not available at the current stage, but will be set in a later phase. For instance, to rewrite according to the REMOTE_USER variable from within the per-server context (httpd.conf file) you must use %{LA-U:REMOTE_USER} - this variable is set

by the authorization phases, which come *after* the URL translation phase (during which mod_rewrite operates).

On the other hand, because mod_rewrite implements its per-directory context (.htaccess file) via the Fixup phase of the API and because the authorization phases come *before* this phase, you just can use %{REMOTE_-USER} in that context.

6. %{LA-F:variable} can be used to perform an internal (filename-based) sub-request, to determine the final value of *variable*. Most of the time, this is the same as LA-U above.

CondPattern is the condition pattern, a regular expression which is applied to the current instance of the *TestString*. *TestString* is first evaluated, before being matched against *CondPattern*.

Remember: *CondPattern* is a *perl compatible regular expression* with some additions:

1. You can prefix the pattern string with a '!' character (exclamation mark) to specify a **non**-matching pattern.

2. There are some special variants of *CondPatterns*. Instead of real regular expression strings you can also use one of the following:

   - '**<CondPattern**' (lexicographically precedes)
     Treats the *CondPattern* as a plain string and compares it lexicographically to *TestString*. True if *TestString* lexicographically precedes *CondPattern*.
   - '**>CondPattern**' (lexicographically follows)
     Treats the *CondPattern* as a plain string and compares it lexicographically to *TestString*. True if *TestString* lexicographically follows *CondPattern*.
   - '**=CondPattern**' (lexicographically equal)
     Treats the *CondPattern* as a plain string and compares it lexicographically to *TestString*. True if *TestString* is lexicographically equal to *CondPattern* (the two strings are exactly equal, character for character). If *CondPattern* is "" (two quotation marks) this compares *TestString* to the empty string.
   - '**-d**' (is directory)
     Treats the *TestString* as a pathname and tests whether or not it exists, and is a directory.
   - '**-f**' (is regular file)
     Treats the *TestString* as a pathname and tests whether or not it exists, and is a regular file.
   - '**-s**' (is regular file, with size)
     Treats the *TestString* as a pathname and tests whether or not it exists, and is a regular file with size greater than zero.

- '-l' (is symbolic link)
  Treats the *TestString* as a pathname and tests whether or not it exists, and is a symbolic link.
- '-x' (has executable permissions)
  Treats the *TestString* as a pathname and tests whether or not it exists, and has executable permissions. These permissions are determined according to the underlying OS.
- '-F' (is existing file, via subrequest)
  Checks whether or not *TestString* is a valid file, accessible via all the server's currently-configured access controls for that path. This uses an internal subrequest to do the check, so use it with care - it can impact your server's performance!
- '-U' (is existing URL, via subrequest)
  Checks whether or not *TestString* is a valid URL, accessible via all the server's currently-configured access controls for that path. This uses an internal subrequest to do the check, so use it with care - it can impact your server's performance!

NOTE: *All of these tests can also be prefixed by an exclamation mark ('!') to negate their meaning.*

3. You can also set special flags for *CondPattern* by appending [*flags*] as the third argument to the RewriteCond directive, where *flags* is a comma-separated list of any of the following flags:

- 'nocase|NC' (no case)
  This makes the test case-insensitive - differences between 'A-Z' and 'a-z' are ignored, both in the expanded *TestString* and the *CondPattern*. This flag is effective only for comparisons between *TestString* and *CondPattern*. It has no effect on filesystem and subrequest checks.
- 'ornext|OR' (or next condition)
  Use this to combine rule conditions with a local OR instead of the implicit AND. Typical example:
  ```
  RewriteCond %{REMOTE_HOST} ^host1.* [OR]
  RewriteCond %{REMOTE_HOST} ^host2.* [OR]
  RewriteCond %{REMOTE_HOST} ^host3.*
  RewriteRule ...some special stuff for any
                      of these hosts...
  ```
  Without this flag you would have to write the condition/rule pair three times.
- 'novary|NV' (no vary)
  If a HTTP header is used in the condition, this flag prevents this header from being added to the Vary header of the response.
  Using this flag might break proper caching of the response if the representation of this response varies on the value of this header. So this flag should be only used if the meaning of the Vary header is well understood.

Example:

To rewrite the Homepage of a site according to the "User-Agent:" header of the request, you can use the following:

```
RewriteCond %{HTTP_USER_AGENT} ^Mozilla.*
RewriteRule ^/$ /homepage.max.html [L]

RewriteCond %{HTTP_USER_AGENT} ^Lynx.*
RewriteRule ^/$ /homepage.min.html [L]

RewriteRule ^/$ /homepage.std.html [L]
```

Explanation: If you use a browser which identifies itself as 'Mozilla' (including Netscape Navigator, Mozilla etc), then you get the max homepage (which could include frames, or other special features). If you use the Lynx browser (which is terminal-based), then you get the min homepage (which could be a version designed for easy, text-only browsing). If neither of these conditions apply (you use any other browser, or your browser identifies itself as something non-standard), you get the std (standard) homepage.

RewriteEngine Directive

Description:	Enables or disables runtime rewriting engine
Syntax:	RewriteEngine on|off
Default:	RewriteEngine off
Context:	server config, virtual host, directory, .htaccess
Override:	FileInfo
Status:	Extension
Module:	mod_rewrite

The RewriteEngine directive enables or disables the runtime rewriting engine. If it is set to off this module does no runtime processing at all. It does not even update the SCRIPT_URx environment variables.

Use this directive to disable the module instead of commenting out all the RewriteRule directives!

Note that rewrite configurations are not inherited by virtual hosts. This means that you need to have a RewriteEngine on directive for each virtual host in which you wish to use rewrite rules.

RewriteMap directives of the type prg are not started during server initialization if they're defined in a context that does not have RewriteEngine set to on.

RewriteLock Directive

Description:	Sets the name of the lock file used for `RewriteMap` synchronization
Syntax:	RewriteLock *file-path*
Context:	server config
Status:	Extension
Module:	mod_rewrite

This directive sets the filename for a synchronization lockfile which mod_rewrite needs to communicate with `RewriteMap` *programs*. Set this lockfile to a local path (not on a NFS-mounted device) when you want to use a rewriting map-program. It is not required for other types of rewriting maps.

RewriteLog Directive

Description:	Sets the name of the file used for logging rewrite engine processing
Syntax:	RewriteLog *file-path*
Context:	server config, virtual host
Status:	Extension
Module:	mod_rewrite

The `RewriteLog` directive sets the name of the file to which the server logs any rewriting actions it performs. If the name does not begin with a slash ('/') then it is assumed to be relative to the *Server Root*. The directive should occur only once per server config.

> *To disable the logging of rewriting actions it is not recommended to set Filename to /dev/null, because although the rewriting engine does not then output to a logfile it still creates the logfile output internally.* **This will slow down the server with no advantage to the administrator!** *To disable logging either remove or comment out the RewriteLog directive or use RewriteLogLevel 0!*

SECURITY

> *See the Apache Security Tips (p. 677) document for details on how your security could be compromised if the directory where logfiles are stored is writable by anyone other than the user that starts the server.*

Example
```
RewriteLog "/usr/local/var/apache/logs/rewrite.log"
```

RewriteLogLevel Directive

Description:	Sets the verbosity of the log file used by the rewrite engine
Syntax:	RewriteLogLevel *Level*
Default:	RewriteLogLevel 0
Context:	server config, virtual host
Status:	Extension
Module:	mod_rewrite

The `RewriteLogLevel` directive sets the verbosity level of the rewriting logfile. The default level 0 means no logging, while 9 or more means that practically all actions are logged.

To disable the logging of rewriting actions simply set *Level* to 0. This disables all rewrite action logs.

> *Using a high value for Level will slow down your Apache server dramatically! Use the rewriting logfile at a Level greater than 2 only for debugging!*

Example
```
RewriteLogLevel 3
```

RewriteMap Directive

Description:	Defines a mapping function for key-lookup
Syntax:	RewriteMap *MapName MapType:MapSource*
Context:	server config, virtual host
Status:	Extension
Module:	mod_rewrite
Compatibility:	The choice of different dbm types is available in Apache 2.0.41 and later

The `RewriteMap` directive defines a *Rewriting Map* which can be used inside rule substitution strings by the mapping-functions to insert/substitute fields through a key lookup. The source of this lookup can be of various types.

The *MapName* is the name of the map and will be used to specify a mapping-function for the substitution strings of a rewriting rule via one of the following constructs:

${ *MapName* : *LookupKey* }
${ *MapName* : *LookupKey* | *DefaultValue* }

When such a construct occurs, the map *MapName* is consulted and the key *LookupKey* is looked-up. If the key is found, the map-function construct is substituted by *SubstValue*. If the key is not found then it is substituted by *DefaultValue* or by the empty string if no *DefaultValue* was specified.

For example, you might define a `RewriteMap` as:

```
RewriteMap examplemap txt:/path/to/file/map.txt
```

You would then be able to use this map in a `RewriteRule` as follows:

```
RewriteRule ^/ex/(.*) ${examplemap:$1}
```

The following combinations for *MapType* and *MapSource* can be used:

- **Standard Plain Text**
  MapType: txt, MapSource: Unix filesystem path to valid regular file

  This is the standard rewriting map feature where the *MapSource* is a plain ASCII file containing either blank lines, comment lines (starting with a '#' character) or pairs like the following - one per line.

  MatchingKey SubstValue

  ```
  ##
  ##  map.txt -- rewriting map
  ##

  Ralf.S.Engelschall    rse    # Bastard Operator From Hell
  Mr.Joe.Average        joe    # Mr. Average

  RewriteMap real-to-user txt:/path/to/file/map.txt
  ```

- **Randomized Plain Text**
  MapType: rnd, MapSource: Unix filesystem path to valid regular file

  This is identical to the Standard Plain Text variant above but with a special post-processing feature: After looking up a value it is parsed according to contained "|" characters which have the meaning of "or". In other words they indicate a set of alternatives from which the actual returned value is chosen randomly. For example, you might use the following map file and directives to provide a random load balancing between several back-end servers, via a reverse-proxy. Images are sent to one of the servers in the 'static' pool, while everything else is sent to one of the 'dynamic' pool.

  Example:

  ```
  ##
  ##  map.txt -- rewriting map
  ##

  static    www1|www2|www3|www4
  dynamic   www5|www6
  ```

  Configuration directives
  ```
  RewriteMap servers rnd:/path/to/file/map.txt

  RewriteRule ^/(.*\.(png|gif|jpg))
  http://${servers:static}/$1 [NC,P,L]
  RewriteRule ^/(.*) http://${servers:dynamic}/$1 [P,L]
  ```

- **Hash File**

  MapType: dbm[=*type*], MapSource: Unix filesystem path to valid regular file

  Here the source is a binary format DBM file containing the same contents as a *Plain Text* format file, but in a special representation which is optimized for really fast lookups. The *type* can be sdbm, gdbm, ndbm, or db depending on compile-time settings (p. 775). If the *type* is omitted, the compile-time default will be chosen.

  To create a DBM file from a source text file, use the httxt2dbm (p. 42) utility.

  ```
  $ httxt2dbm -i mapfile.txt -o mapfile.map
  ```

- **Internal Function**

  MapType: int, MapSource: Internal Apache function

  Here, the source is an internal Apache function. Currently you cannot create your own, but the following functions already exist:

  - **toupper**:
    Converts the key to all upper case.
  - **tolower**:
    Converts the key to all lower case.
  - **escape**:
    Translates special characters in the key to hex-encodings.
  - **unescape**:
    Translates hex-encodings in the key back to special characters.

- **External Rewriting Program**

  MapType: prg, MapSource: Unix filesystem path to valid regular file

  Here the source is a program, not a map file. To create it you can use a language of your choice, but the result has to be an executable program (either object-code or a script with the magic cookie trick '#!/path/to/interpreter' as the first line).

  This program is started once, when the Apache server is started, and then communicates with the rewriting engine via its stdin and stdout filehandles. For each map-function lookup it will receive the key to lookup as a newline-terminated string on stdin. It then has to give back the looked-up value as a newline-terminated string on stdout or the four-character string "NULL" if it fails (*i.e.*, there is no corresponding value for the given key). A trivial program which will implement a 1:1 map (*i.e.*, key == value) could be:

  External rewriting programs are not started if they're defined in a context that does not have RewriteEngine set to on.

  ```
  #!/usr/bin/perl
  $| = 1;
  while (<STDIN>) {
  ```

```
        # ...put here any transformations or lookups...
        print $_;
}
```

But be very careful:

1. *"Keep it simple, stupid"* (KISS). If this program hangs, it will cause Apache to hang when trying to use the relevant rewrite rule.
2. A common mistake is to use buffered I/O on stdout. Avoid this, as it will cause a deadloop! "$|=1" is used above, to prevent this.
3. The RewriteLock directive can be used to define a lockfile which mod_rewrite can use to synchronize communication with the mapping program. By default no such synchronization takes place.

The RewriteMap directive can occur more than once. For each mapping-function use one RewriteMap directive to declare its rewriting mapfile. While you cannot **declare** a map in per-directory context it is of course possible to **use** this map in per-directory context.

NOTE *For plain text and DBM format files the looked-up keys are cached in-core until the mtime of the mapfile changes or the server does a restart. This way you can have map-functions in rules which are used for every request. This is no problem, because the external lookup only happens once!*

RewriteOptions Directive

Description:	Sets some special options for the rewrite engine
Syntax:	RewriteOptions *Options*
Context:	server config, virtual host, directory, .htaccess
Override:	FileInfo
Status:	Extension
Module:	mod_rewrite
Compatibility:	MaxRedirects is no longer available in version 2.1 and later

The RewriteOptions directive sets some special options for the current per-server or per-directory configuration. The *Option* string can currently only be one of the following:

inherit This forces the current configuration to inherit the configuration of the parent. In per-virtual-server context, this means that the maps, conditions and rules of the main server are inherited. In per-directory context this means that conditions and rules of the parent directory's .htaccess configuration are inherited.

RewriteRule Directive

Description:	Defines rules for the rewriting engine
Syntax:	RewriteRule *Pattern Substitution* [*flags*]
Context:	server config, virtual host, directory, .htaccess
Override:	FileInfo
Status:	Extension
Module:	mod_rewrite

The `RewriteRule` directive is the real rewriting workhorse. The directive can occur more than once, with each instance defining a single rewrite rule. The order in which these rules are defined is important - this is the order in which they will be applied at run-time.

Pattern is a perl compatible regular expression. On the first RewriteRule it is applied to the URL-path (p. 83) of the request; subsequent patterns are applied to the output of the last matched RewriteRule.

> WHAT IS MATCHED? *The Pattern will initially be matched against the part of the URL after the hostname and port, and before the query string. If you wish to match against the hostname, port, or query string, use a RewriteCond with the %{HTTP_HOST}, %{SERVER_PORT}, or %{QUERY_STRING} variables respectively.*

For some hints on regular expressions, see the mod_rewrite Introduction (p. 577).

In mod_rewrite, the NOT character ('!') is also available as a possible pattern prefix. This enables you to negate a pattern; to say, for instance: *"if the current URL does NOT match this pattern"*. This can be used for exceptional cases, where it is easier to match the negative pattern, or as a last default rule.

> NOTE *When using the NOT character to negate a pattern, you cannot include grouped wildcard parts in that pattern. This is because, when the pattern does NOT match (ie, the negation matches), there are no contents for the groups. Thus, if negated patterns are used, you cannot use $N in the substitution string!*

The *Substitution* of a rewrite rule is the string that replaces the original URL-path that was matched by *Pattern*. The *Substitution* may be a:

file-system path Designates the location on the file-system of the resource to be delivered to the client.

URL-path A DocumentRoot-relative path to the resource to be served. Note that mod_rewrite tries to guess whether you have specified a file-system path or a URL-path by checking to see if the first segment of the path exists at the root of the file-system. For example, if you specify a *Substitution* string of /www/file.html, then this will be treated as a URL-path *unless* a directory named www exists at the root or your file-system, in which case it will be treated as a file-system path. If you wish other

URL-mapping directives (such as `Alias`) to be applied to the resulting URL-path, use the [PT] flag as described below.

Absolute URL If an absolute URL is specified, mod_rewrite checks to see whether the hostname matches the current host. If it does, the scheme and hostname are stripped out and the resulting path is treated as a URL-path. Otherwise, an external redirect is performed for the given URL. To force an external redirect back to the current host, see the [R] flag below.

- (dash) A dash indicates that no substitution should be performed (the existing path is passed through untouched). This is used when a flag (see below) needs to be applied without changing the path.

In addition to plain text, the *Substition* string can include

1. back-references (`$N`) to the RewriteRule pattern
2. back-references (`%N`) to the last matched RewriteCond pattern
3. server-variables as in rule condition test-strings (`%{VARNAME}`)
4. mapping-function calls (`${mapname:key|default}`)

Back-references are identifiers of the form $N (N=0..9), which will be replaced by the contents of the Nth group of the matched *Pattern*. The server-variables are the same as for the *TestString* of a RewriteCond directive. The mapping-functions come from the RewriteMap directive and are explained there. These three types of variables are expanded in the order above.

As already mentioned, all rewrite rules are applied to the *Substitution* (in the order in which they are defined in the config file). The URL is **completely replaced** by the *Substitution* and the rewriting process continues until all rules have been applied, or it is explicitly terminated by a L flag.

MODIFYING THE QUERY STRING *By default, the query string is passed through unchanged. You can, however, create URLs in the substitution string containing a query string part. Simply use a question mark inside the substitution string to indicate that the following text should be re-injected into the query string. When you want to erase an existing query string, end the substitution string with just a question mark. To combine new and old query strings, use the [QSA] flag.*

Additionally you can set special actions to be performed by appending [*flags*] as the third argument to the RewriteRule directive. *Flags* is a comma-separated list, surrounded by square brackets, of any of the following flags:

'B' (escape backreferences) Apache has to unescape URLs before mapping them, so backreferences will be unescaped at the time they are applied. Using the B flag, non-alphanumeric characters in backreferences will be escaped. For example, consider the rule:

```
RewriteRule ^(.*)$ index.php?show=$1
```

This will map /C++ to index.php?show=/C++. But it will also map
/C%2b%2b to index.php?show=/C++, because the %2b has been unescaped.
With the B flag, it will instead map to index.php?show=/C%2b%2b.

This escaping is particularly necessary in a proxy situation, when the
backend may break if presented with an unescaped URL.

'chain|C' (**chained with next rule**) This flag chains the current rule with
the next rule (which itself can be chained with the following rule, and
so on). This has the following effect: if a rule matches, then processing
continues as usual - the flag has no effect. If the rule does **not** match,
then all following chained rules are skipped. For instance, it can be used
to remove the ".www" part, inside a per-directory rule set, when you let
an external redirect happen (where the ".www" part should not occur!).

'cookie|CO=*NAME*:*VAL*:*domain*[:*lifetime*[:*path*[:*secure*[:*httponly*]]]]'
(**set cookie**)

This sets a cookie in the client's browser. The cookie's name is specified
by *NAME* and the value is *VAL*. The *domain* field is the domain of the
cookie, such as '.apache.org', the optional *lifetime* is the lifetime of the
cookie in minutes, and the optional *path* is the path of the cookie. If
secure is set to 'secure', 'true' or '1', the cookie is only transmitted via
secured connections. If *httponly* is set to 'HttpOnly', 'true' or '1', the
HttpOnly flag is used, making the cookie not accessible to JavaScript
code on browsers that support this feature.

'discardpathinfo|DPI' (discard PATH_INFO) In per-directory context, the
URI each RewriteRule compares against is the concatenation of the current values of the URI and PATH_INFO.

The current URI can be the initial URI as requested by the client, the
result of a previous round of mod_rewrite processing, or the result of a
prior rule in the current round of mod_rewrite processing.

In contrast, the PATH_INFO that is appended to the URI before each rule
reflects only the value of PATH_INFO before this round of mod_rewrite
processing. As a consequence, if large portions of the URI are matched
and copied into a substitution in multiple RewriteRule directives, without
regard for which parts of the URI came from the current PATH_INFO,
the final URI may have multiple copies of PATH_INFO appended to it.

Use this flag on any substitution where the PATH_INFO that resulted
from the previous mapping of this request to the filesystem is not of interest. This flag permanently forgets the PATH_INFO established before
this round of mod_rewrite processing began. PATH_INFO will not be recalculated until the current round of mod_rewrite processing completes.
Subsequent rules during this round of processing will see only the direct
result of substitutions, without any PATH_INFO appended.

'env|E=*VAR*[:*VAL*]' (**set environment variable**) This forces an environ-
ment variable named *VAR* to be set. The value will be *VAL* if provided,
where *VAL* can contain regexp backreferences ($N and %N) which will

be expanded. You can use this flag more than once, to set more than one variable. The variables can later be dereferenced in many situations, most commonly from within XSSI (via `<!--#echo var="VAR"-->`) or CGI (`$ENV{'VAR'}`). You can also dereference the variable in a later Rewrite-Cond pattern, using `%{ENV:VAR}`. Use this to strip information from URLs, while maintaining a record of that information.

'forbidden|F' (force URL to be forbidden) This forces the current URL to be forbidden - it immediately sends back a HTTP response of 403 (FORBIDDEN). Use this flag in conjunction with appropriate Rewrite-Conds to conditionally block some URLs.

'gone|G' (force URL to be gone) This forces the current URL to be gone - it immediately sends back a HTTP response of 410 (GONE). Use this flag to mark pages which no longer exist as gone.

'handler|H=*Content-handler*' (force Content handler) Force   the Content-handler of the target file to be *Content-handler*. For instance, this can be used to simulate the mod_alias directive ScriptAlias, which internally forces all files inside the mapped directory to have a handler of "cgi-script".

'last|L' (last rule) Stop the rewriting process here and don't apply any more rewrite rules. This corresponds to the Perl last command or the break command in C. Use this flag to prevent the currently rewritten URL from being rewritten further by following rules. Remember, however, that if the RewriteRule generates an internal redirect (which frequently occurs when rewriting in a per-directory context), this will reinject the request and will cause processing to be repeated starting from the first RewriteRule.

'next|N' (next round) Re-run the rewriting process (starting again with the first rewriting rule). This time, the URL to match is no longer the original URL, but rather the URL returned by the last rewriting rule. This corresponds to the Perl next command or the continue command in C. Use this flag to restart the rewriting process - to immediately go to the top of the loop. **Be careful not to create an infinite loop!**

'nocase|NC' (no case) This makes the *Pattern* case-insensitive, ignoring difference between 'A-Z' and 'a-z' when *Pattern* is matched against the current URL.

'noescape|NE' (no URI escaping of output) This flag prevents mod_rewrite from applying the usual URI escaping rules to the result of a rewrite. Ordinarily, special characters (such as '%', '$', ';', and so on) will be escaped into their hexcode equivalents ('%25', '%24', and '%3B', respectively); this flag prevents this from happening. This allows percent symbols to appear in the output, as in

```
RewriteRule /foo/(.*) /bar?arg=P1\%3d$1 [R,NE]
```

which would turn '/foo/zed' into a safe request for '/bar?arg=P1=zed'.

'nosubreq|NS' (not for internal sub-requests) This flag forces the rewriting engine to skip a rewriting rule if the current request is an internal sub-request. For instance, sub-requests occur internally in Apache when mod_include tries to find out information about possible directory default files (index.xxx files). On sub-requests it is not always useful, and can even cause errors, if the complete set of rules are applied. Use this flag to exclude some rules.

To decide whether or not to use this rule: if you prefix URLs with CGI-scripts, to force them to be processed by the CGI-script, it's likely that you will run into problems (or significant overhead) on sub-requests. In these cases, use this flag.

'proxy|P' **(force proxy)** This flag forces the substitution part to be internally sent as a proxy request and immediately (rewrite processing stops here) put through the proxy module (p. 374). You must make sure that the substitution string is a valid URI (typically starting with http://*hostname*) which can be handled by the Apache proxy module. If not, you will get an error from the proxy module. Use this flag to achieve a more powerful implementation of the ProxyPass (p. 374) directive, to map remote content into the namespace of the local server.

Note: mod_proxy must be enabled in order to use this flag.

'passthrough|PT' **(pass through to next handler)** This flag forces the rewrite engine to set the uri field of the internal request_rec structure to the value of the filename field. This flag is just a hack to enable post-processing of the output of RewriteRule directives, using Alias, ScriptAlias, Redirect, and other directives from various URI-to-filename translators. For example, to rewrite /abc to /def using mod_-rewrite, and then /def to /ghi using mod_alias:

```
RewriteRule ^/abc(.*) /def$1 [PT]
Alias /def /ghi
```

If you omit the PT flag, mod_rewrite will rewrite uri=/abc/... to filename=/def/... as a full API-compliant URI-to-filename translator should do. Then mod_alias will try to do a URI-to-filename transition, which will fail.

Note: **You must use this flag if you want to mix directives from different modules which allow URL-to-filename translators**. The typical example is the use of mod_alias and mod_rewrite.

The PT flag implies the L flag: rewriting will be stopped in order to pass the request to the next phase of processing.

'qsappend|QSA' **(query string append)** This flag forces the rewrite engine to append a query string part of the substitution string to the existing string, instead of replacing it. Use this when you want to add more data to the query string via a rewrite rule.

'redirect|R [=*code*]' **(force redirect)** Prefix   *Substitution*   with http://thishost[:thisport]/ (which makes the new URL a URI) to force a external redirection. If no *code* is given, a HTTP response of

302 (MOVED TEMPORARILY) will be returned. If you want to use other response codes, simply specify the appropriate number or use one of the following symbolic names: temp (default), permanent, seeother. Use this for rules to canonicalize the URL and return it to the client - to translate "/~" into "/u/", or to always append a slash to /u/*user*, etc. **Note:** When you use this flag, make sure that the substitution field is a valid URL! Otherwise, you will be redirecting to an invalid location. Remember that this flag on its own will only prepend http://thishost[:thisport]/ to the URL, and rewriting will continue. Usually, you will want to stop rewriting at this point, and redirect immediately. To stop rewriting, you should add the 'L' flag.

While this is typically used for redirects, any valid status code can be given here. If the status code is outside the redirect range (300-399), then the *Substitution* string is dropped and rewriting is stopped as if the L flag was used.

'skip|S=*num*' (**skip next rule(s)**) This flag forces the rewriting engine to skip the next *num* rules in sequence, if the current rule matches. Use this to make pseudo if-then-else constructs: The last rule of the then-clause becomes skip=N, where N is the number of rules in the else-clause. (This is **not** the same as the 'chain—C' flag!)

'type|T=*MIME-type*' (**force MIME type**) Force the MIME-type of the target file to be *MIME-type*. This can be used to set up the content-type based on some conditions. For example, the following snippet allows .php files to be *displayed* by mod_php if they are called with the .phps extension:

```
RewriteRule ^(.+\.php)s$ $1
[T=application/x-httpd-php-source]
```

HOME DIRECTORY EXPANSION *When the substitution string begins with a string resembling "/~user" (via explicit text or backreferences), mod_-rewrite performs home directory expansion independent of the presence or configuration of mod_userdir.*

This expansion does not occur when the PT flag is used on the RewriteRule directive.

PER-DIRECTORY REWRITES

The rewrite engine may be used in .htaccess (p. 667) files. To enable the rewrite engine for these files you need to set "RewriteEngine On" and "Options FollowSymLinks" must be enabled. If your administrator has disabled override of FollowSymLinks for a user's directory, then you cannot use the rewrite engine. This restriction is required for security reasons.

When using the rewrite engine in .htaccess files the per-directory pre-fix (which always is the same for a specific directory) is automatically removed for the pattern matching and automatically added after the

*substitution has been done. This feature is essential for many sorts
of rewriting; without this, you would always have to match the parent
directory, which is not always possible. There is one exception: If a
substitution string starts with* http://, *then the directory prefix will
not be added, and an external redirect (or proxy throughput, if using
flag P) is forced. See the* RewriteBase *directive for more information.*

The rewrite engine may also be used in <Directory> *sections with the
same prefix-matching rules as would be applied to* .htaccess *files. It is
usually simpler, however, to avoid the prefix substitution complication
by putting the rewrite rules in the main server or virtual host context,
rather than in a* <Directory> *section.*

Although rewrite rules are syntactically permitted in <Location> *sections, this should never be necessary and is unsupported.*

Here are all possible substitution combinations and their meanings:

Inside per-server configuration (httpd.conf**) for request "GET
/somepath/pathinfo"**

> *Given Rule:*
> *Resulting Substitution:*

> ^/somepath(.*) otherpath$1
>> invalid, not supported
> ^/somepath(.*) otherpath$1 [R]
>> invalid, not supported
> ^/somepath(.*) otherpath$1 [P]
>> invalid, not supported

> ^/somepath(.*) /otherpath$1
>> /otherpath/pathinfo
> ^/somepath(.*) /otherpath$1 [R]
>> http://thishost/otherpath/pathinfo
>> via external redirection
> ^/somepath(.*) /otherpath$1 [P]
>> doesn't make sense, not supported

> ^/somepath(.*) http://thishost/otherpath$1
>> /otherpath/pathinfo
> ^/somepath(.*) http://thishost/otherpath$1 [R]
>> http://thishost/otherpath/pathinfo
>> via external redirection
> ^/somepath(.*) http://thishost/otherpath$1 [P]
>> doesn't make sense, not supported

```
^/somepath(.*) http://otherhost/otherpath$1
    http://otherhost/otherpath/pathinfo
    via external redirection
^/somepath(.*) http://otherhost/otherpath$1 [R]
    http://otherhost/otherpath/pathinfo
    via external redirection (the [R] flag is redundant)
^/somepath(.*) http://otherhost/otherpath$1 [P]
    http://otherhost/otherpath/pathinfo
    via internal proxy
```

Inside per-directory configuration for /somepath
(/physical/path/to/somepath/.htacccess, **with** RewriteBase /somepath)
for request "GET /somepath/localpath/pathinfo"

Given Rule:
Resulting Substitution:

```
^localpath(.*) otherpath$1
    /somepath/otherpath/pathinfo
^localpath(.*) otherpath$1 [R]
    http://thishost/somepath/otherpath/pathinfo
    via external redirection
^localpath(.*) otherpath$1 [P]
    doesn't make sense, not supported

^localpath(.*) /otherpath$1
    /otherpath/pathinfo
^localpath(.*) /otherpath$1 [R]
    http://thishost/otherpath/pathinfo
    via external redirection
^localpath(.*) /otherpath$1 [P]
    doesn't make sense, not supported

^localpath(.*) http://thishost/otherpath$1
    /otherpath/pathinfo
^localpath(.*) http://thishost/otherpath$1 [R]
    http://thishost/otherpath/pathinfo
    via external redirection
^localpath(.*) http://thishost/otherpath$1 [P]
    doesn't make sense, not supported

^localpath(.*) http://otherhost/otherpath$1
    http://otherhost/otherpath/pathinfo
    via external redirection
```

^localpath(.*) http://otherhost/otherpath$1 [R]
   http://otherhost/otherpath/pathinfo
   via external redirection (the [R] flag is redundant)

^localpath(.*) http://otherhost/otherpath$1 [P]
   http://otherhost/otherpath/pathinfo
   via internal proxy

3.67 Apache Module mod_setenvif

Description:	Allows the setting of environment variables based on characteristics of the request
Status:	Base
Module Identifier:	setenvif_module
Source File:	mod_setenvif.c

Summary

The mod_setenvif module allows you to set environment variables according to whether different aspects of the request match regular expressions you specify. These environment variables can be used by other parts of the server to make decisions about actions to be taken.

The directives are considered in the order they appear in the configuration files. So more complex sequences can be used, such as this example, which sets netscape if the browser is mozilla but not MSIE.

```
BrowserMatch ^Mozilla netscape
BrowserMatch MSIE !netscape
```

Directives:

```
BrowserMatch
BrowserMatchNoCase
SetEnvIf
SetEnvIfNoCase
```

See also:

▷ Environment Variables in Apache (p. 705)

BrowserMatch Directive

Description:	Sets environment variables conditional on HTTP User-Agent
Syntax:	BrowserMatch *regex* *[!]env-variable*[=*value*] [[!]*env-variable*[=*value*]] ...
Context:	server config, virtual host, directory, .htaccess
Override:	FileInfo
Status:	Base
Module:	mod_setenvif

The BrowserMatch is a special case of the SetEnvIf directive that sets environment variables conditional on the User-Agent HTTP request header. The following two lines have the same effect:

```
BrowserMatchNoCase Robot is_a_robot
SetEnvIfNoCase User-Agent Robot is_a_robot
```

Some additional examples:

```
BrowserMatch ^Mozilla forms jpeg=yes browser=netscape
BrowserMatch "^Mozilla/[2-3]" tables agif frames javascript
BrowserMatch MSIE !javascript
```

BrowserMatchNoCase Directive

Description:	Sets environment variables conditional on User-Agent without respect to case
Syntax:	BrowserMatchNoCase *regex* *[!]env-variable* *[=value]* *[[!]env-variable [=value]]* ...
Context:	server config, virtual host, directory, .htaccess
Override:	FileInfo
Status:	Base
Module:	mod_setenvif
Compatibility:	Apache 1.2 and above (in Apache 1.2 this directive was found in the now-obsolete mod_browser module)

The BrowserMatchNoCase directive is semantically identical to the BrowserMatch directive. However, it provides for case-insensitive matching. For example:

```
BrowserMatchNoCase mac platform=macintosh
BrowserMatchNoCase win platform=windows
```

The BrowserMatch and BrowserMatchNoCase directives are special cases of the SetEnvIf and SetEnvIfNoCase directives. The following two lines have the same effect:

```
BrowserMatchNoCase Robot is_a_robot
SetEnvIfNoCase User-Agent Robot is_a_robot
```

SetEnvIf Directive

Description:	Sets environment variables based on attributes of the request
Syntax:	SetEnvIf *attribute* *regex* *[!]env-variable* *[=value]* *[[!]env-variable [=value]]* ...
Context:	server config, virtual host, directory, .htaccess
Override:	FileInfo
Status:	Base
Module:	mod_setenvif

The SetEnvIf directive defines environment variables based on attributes of the request. The *attribute* specified in the first argument can be one of three things:

1. An HTTP request header field (see RFC2616[54] for more information about these); for example: Host, User-Agent, Referer, and Accept-Language. A regular expression may be used to specify a set of request headers.

2. One of the following aspects of the request:

---

[54]http://www.rfc-editor.org/rfc/rfc2616.txt

- Remote_Host - the hostname (if available) of the client making the request
- Remote_Addr - the IP address of the client making the request
- Server_Addr - the IP address of the server on which the request was received (only with versions later than 2.0.43)
- Request_Method - the name of the method being used (GET, POST, *et cetera*)
- Request_Protocol - the name and version of the protocol with which the request was made (*e.g.*, "HTTP/0.9", "HTTP/1.1", *etc.*)
- Request_URI - the resource requested on the HTTP request line – generally the portion of the URL following the scheme and host portion without the query string. See the RewriteCond directive of mod_rewrite for extra information on how to match your query string.

3. The name of an environment variable in the list of those associated with the request. This allows SetEnvIf directives to test against the result of prior matches. Only those environment variables defined by earlier SetEnvIf[NoCase] directives are available for testing in this manner. 'Earlier' means that they were defined at a broader scope (such as server-wide) or previously in the current directive's scope. Environment variables will be considered only if there was no match among request characteristics and a regular expression was not used for the *attribute*.

The second argument (*regex*) is a regular expression. If the *regex* matches against the *attribute*, then the remainder of the arguments are evaluated.

The rest of the arguments give the names of variables to set, and optionally values to which they should be set. These take the form of

1. *varname*, or
2. !*varname*, or
3. *varname=value*

In the first form, the value will be set to "1". The second will remove the given variable if already defined, and the third will set the variable to the literal value given by *value*. Since version 2.0.51 Apache will recognize occurrences of $1..$9 within *value* and replace them by parenthesized subexpressions of *regex*.

Example:
```
SetEnvIf Request_URI "\.gif$" object_is_image=gif
SetEnvIf Request_URI "\.jpg$" object_is_image=jpg
SetEnvIf Request_URI "\.xbm$" object_is_image=xbm
 :
SetEnvIf Referer www\.mydomain\.example\.com intra_site_referral
 :
SetEnvIf object_is_image xbm XBIT_PROCESSING=1
 :
SetEnvIf ^TS* ^[a-z].* HAVE_TS
```

The first three will set the environment variable object_is_image if the request was for an image file, and the fourth sets intra_site_referral if the referring page was somewhere on the www.mydomain.example.com Web site.

The last example will set environment variable HAVE_TS if the request contains any headers that begin with "TS" whose values begins with any character in the set [a-z].

See also:

▷ Environment Variables in Apache (p. 705), for additional examples.

SetEnvIfNoCase Directive

Description:	Sets environment variables based on attributes of the request without respect to case
Syntax:	SetEnvIfNoCase *attribute* *regex* [!]*env-variable* [=*value*] [[!]*env-variable* [=*value*]] ...
Context:	server config, virtual host, directory, .htaccess
Override:	FileInfo
Status:	Base
Module:	mod_setenvif
Compatibility:	Apache 1.3 and above

The SetEnvIfNoCase is semantically identical to the SetEnvIf directive, and differs only in that the regular expression matching is performed in a case-insensitive manner. For example:

```
SetEnvIfNoCase Host Apache\.Org site=apache
```

This will cause the site environment variable to be set to "apache" if the HTTP request header field Host: was included and contained Apache.Org, apache.org, or any other combination.

3.68 Apache Module mod_so

Description:	Loading of executable code and modules into the server at start-up or restart time
Status:	Extension
Module Identifier:	so_module
Source File:	mod_so.c
Compatibility:	This is a Base module (always included) on Windows

Summary

On selected operating systems this module can be used to load modules into Apache at runtime via the Dynamic Shared Object (p. 683) (DSO) mechanism, rather than requiring a recompilation.

On Unix, the loaded code typically comes from shared object files (usually with .so extension); on Windows this may either the .so or .dll extension.

> WARNING *Apache 1.3 modules cannot be directly used with Apache 2.0 - the module must be modified to dynamically load or compile into Apache 2.0.*

Directives:

```
LoadFile
LoadModule
```

3.68.1 Creating Loadable Modules for Windows

> NOTE *The module name format changed for Windows with Apache 1.3.15 and 2.0 - the modules are now named as mod_foo.so*
>
> *While mod_so still loads modules with ApacheModuleFoo.dll names, the new naming convention is preferred; if you are converting your loadable module for 2.0, please fix the name to this 2.0 convention.*

The Apache module API is unchanged between the Unix and Windows versions. Many modules will run on Windows with no or little change from Unix, although others rely on aspects of the Unix architecture which are not present in Windows, and will not work.

When a module does work, it can be added to the server in one of two ways. As with Unix, it can be compiled into the server. Because Apache for Windows does not have the Configure program of Apache for Unix, the module's source file must be added to the ApacheCore project file, and its symbols must be added to the os\win32\modules.c file.

The second way is to compile the module as a DLL, a shared library that can be loaded into the server at runtime, using the LoadModule directive. These module DLLs can be distributed and run on any Apache for Windows installation, without recompilation of the server.

To create a module DLL, a small change is necessary to the module's source
file: The module record must be exported from the DLL (which will be created
later; see below). To do this, add the AP_MODULE_DECLARE_DATA (defined in the
Apache header files) to your module's module record definition. For example,
if your module has:

```
module foo_module;
```

Replace the above with:

```
module AP_MODULE_DECLARE_DATA foo_module;
```

Note that this will only be activated on Windows, so the module can continue
to be used, unchanged, with Unix if needed. Also, if you are familiar with .DEF
files, you can export the module record with that method instead.

Now, create a DLL containing your module. You will need to link this against
the libhttpd.lib export library that is created when the libhttpd.dll shared
library is compiled. You may also have to change the compiler settings to ensure
that the Apache header files are correctly located. You can find this library in
your server root's modules directory. It is best to grab an existing module .dsp
file from the tree to assure the build environment is configured correctly, or
alternately compare the compiler and link options to your .dsp.

This should create a DLL version of your module. Now simply place it in the
modules directory of your server root, and use the LoadModule directive to load
it.

LoadFile Directive

Description:	Link in the named object file or library
Syntax:	LoadFile *filename* [*filename*] ...
Context:	server config
Status:	Extension
Module:	mod_so

The LoadFile directive links in the named object files or libraries when the
server is started or restarted; this is used to load additional code which may
be required for some module to work. *Filename* is either an absolute path or
relative to ServerRoot (p. 87).

For example:

```
LoadFile libexec/libxmlparse.so
```

LoadModule Directive

Description:	Links in the object file or library, and adds to the list of active modules
Syntax:	LoadModule *module filename*
Context:	server config
Status:	Extension
Module:	mod_so

The LoadModule directive links in the object file or library *filename* and adds the module structure named *module* to the list of active modules. *Module* is the name of the external variable of type module in the file, and is listed as the Module Identifier (p. 81) in the module documentation. Example:

    LoadModule status_module modules/mod_status.so

loads the named module from the modules subdirectory of the ServerRoot.

3.69 Apache Module mod_speling

Description:	Attempts to correct mistaken URLs that users might have entered by ignoring capitalization and by allowing up to one misspelling
Status:	Extension
Module Identifier:	speling_module
Source File:	mod_speling.c

Summary

Requests to documents sometimes cannot be served by the core apache server because the request was misspelled or miscapitalized. This module addresses this problem by trying to find a matching document, even after all other modules gave up. It does its work by comparing each document name in the requested directory against the requested document name **without regard to case**, and allowing **up to one misspelling** (character insertion / omission / transposition or wrong character). A list is built with all document names which were matched using this strategy.

If, after scanning the directory,

- no matching document was found, Apache will proceed as usual and return a "document not found" error.

- only one document is found that "almost" matches the request, then it is returned in the form of a redirection response.

- more than one document with a close match was found, then the list of the matches is returned to the client, and the client can select the correct candidate.

Directives:

    CheckCaseOnly
    CheckSpelling

CheckCaseOnly Directive

Description:	Limits the action of the speling module to case corrections
Syntax:	CheckCaseOnly on|off
Default:	CheckCaseOnly Off
Context:	server config, virtual host, directory, .htaccess
Override:	Options
Status:	Extension
Module:	mod_speling

When set, this directive limits the action of the spelling correction to lower/upper case changes. Other potential corrections are not performed.

CheckSpelling Directive

Description:	Enables the spelling module
Syntax:	CheckSpelling on|off
Default:	CheckSpelling Off
Context:	server config, virtual host, directory, .htaccess
Override:	Options
Status:	Extension
Module:	mod_speling
Compatibility:	CheckSpelling was available as a separately available module for Apache 1.1, but was limited to miscapitalizations. As of Apache 1.3, it is part of the Apache distribution. Prior to Apache 1.3.2, the CheckSpelling directive was only available in the "server" and "virtual host" contexts.

This directive enables or disables the spelling module. When enabled, keep in mind that

- the directory scan which is necessary for the spelling correction will have an impact on the server's performance when many spelling corrections have to be performed at the same time.

- the document trees should not contain sensitive files which could be matched inadvertently by a spelling "correction".

- the module is unable to correct misspelled user names (as in http://my.host/~apahce/), just file names or directory names.

- spelling corrections apply strictly to existing files, so a request for the <Location /status> may get incorrectly treated as the negotiated file "/stats.html".

mod_speling should not be enabled in DAV (p. 238) enabled directories, because it will try to "spell fix" newly created resource names against existing filenames, e.g., when trying to upload a new document doc43.html it might redirect to an existing document doc34.html, which is not what was intended.

3.70 Apache Module mod_ssl

Description:	Strong cryptography using the Secure Sockets Layer (SSL) and Transport Layer Security (TLS) protocols
Status:	Extension
Module Identifier:	ssl_module
Source File:	mod_ssl.c

Summary

This module provides SSL v2/v3 and TLS v1 support for the Apache HTTP Server. It was contributed by Ralf S. Engeschall based on his mod_ssl project and originally derived from work by Ben Laurie.

This module relies on OpenSSL[55] to provide the cryptography engine.

Further details, discussion, and examples are provided in the SSL documentation (p. 616).

Directives:

SSLCACertificateFile	SSLProxyCARevocationFile
SSLCACertificatePath	SSLProxyCARevocationPath
SSLCADNRequestFile	SSLProxyCheckPeerCN
SSLCADNRequestPath	SSLProxyCheckPeerExpire
SSLCARevocationFile	SSLProxyCipherSuite
SSLCARevocationPath	SSLProxyEngine
SSLCertificateChainFile	SSLProxyMachineCertificateFile
SSLCertificateFile	SSLProxyMachineCertificatePath
SSLCertificateKeyFile	SSLProxyProtocol
SSLCipherSuite	SSLProxyVerify
SSLCryptoDevice	SSLProxyVerifyDepth
SSLEngine	SSLRandomSeed
SSLFIPS	SSLRenegBufferSize
SSLHonorCipherOrder	SSLRequire
SSLInsecureRenegotiation	SSLRequireSSL
SSLMutex	SSLSessionCache
SSLOptions	SSLSessionCacheTimeout
SSLPassPhraseDialog	SSLStrictSNIVHostCheck
SSLProtocol	SSLUserName
SSLProxyCACertificateFile	SSLVerifyClient
SSLProxyCACertificatePath	SSLVerifyDepth

3.70.1 Environment Variables

This module provides a lot of SSL information as additional environment variables to the SSI and CGI namespace. The generated variables are listed in the

---

[55]http://www.openssl.org/

table below.

Variable Name:	Value Type:	Description:
HTTPS	flag	HTTPS is being used.
SSL_PROTOCOL	string	The SSL protocol version (SSLv2, SSLv3, TLSv1)
SSL_SESSION_ID	string	The hex-encoded SSL session id
SSL_CIPHER	string	The cipher specification name
SSL_CIPHER_EXPORT	string	true if cipher is an export cipher
SSL_CIPHER_USEKEYSIZE	number	Number of cipher bits (actually used)
SSL_CIPHER_ALGKEYSIZE	number	Number of cipher bits (possible)
SSL_COMPRESS_METHOD	string	SSL compression method negotiated
SSL_VERSION_INTERFACE	string	The mod_ssl program version
SSL_VERSION_LIBRARY	string	The OpenSSL program version
SSL_CLIENT_M_VERSION	string	The version of the client certificate
SSL_CLIENT_M_SERIAL	string	The serial of the client certificate
SSL_CLIENT_S_DN	string	Subject DN in client's certificate
SSL_CLIENT_S_DN_$x509$	string	Component of client's Subject DN
SSL_CLIENT_I_DN	string	Issuer DN of client's certificate
SSL_CLIENT_I_DN_$x509$	string	Component of client's Issuer DN
SSL_CLIENT_V_START	string	Validity of client's certificate (start time)
SSL_CLIENT_V_END	string	Validity of client's certificate (end time)
SSL_CLIENT_V_REMAIN	string	Number of days until client's certificate expires
SSL_CLIENT_A_SIG	string	Algorithm used for the signature of client's certificate
SSL_CLIENT_A_KEY	string	Algorithm used for the public key of client's certificate
SSL_CLIENT_CERT	string	PEM-encoded client certificate
SSL_CLIENT_CERT_CHAIN_n	string	PEM-encoded certificates in client certificate chain

SSL_CLIENT_VERIFY	string	NONE, SUCCESS, GENEROUS or FAILED: *reason*
SSL_SERVER_M_VERSION	string	The version of the server certificate
SSL_SERVER_M_SERIAL	string	The serial of the server certificate
SSL_SERVER_S_DN	string	Subject DN in server's certificate
SSL_SERVER_S_DN_*x509*	string	Component of server's Subject DN
SSL_SERVER_I_DN	string	Issuer DN of server's certificate
SSL_SERVER_I_DN_*x509*	string	Component of server's Issuer DN
SSL_SERVER_V_START	string	Validity of server's certificate (start time)
SSL_SERVER_V_END	string	Validity of server's certificate (end time)
SSL_SERVER_A_SIG	string	Algorithm used for the signature of server's certificate
SSL_SERVER_A_KEY	string	Algorithm used for the public key of server's certificate
SSL_SERVER_CERT	string	PEM-encoded server certificate

x509 specifies a component of an X.509 DN; one of C,ST,L,O,OU,CN,T,I,G, S,D,UID,Email. In Apache 2.1 and later, *x509* may also include a numeric _n suffix. If the DN in question contains multiple attributes of the same name, this suffix is used as an index to select a particular attribute. For example, where the server certificate subject DN included two OU fields, SSL_SERVER_S_DN_OU_0 and SSL_SERVER_S_DN_OU_1 could be used to reference each.

SSL_CLIENT_V_REMAIN is only available in version 2.1 and later.

3.70.2 Custom Log Formats

When mod_ssl is built into Apache or at least loaded (under DSO situation) additional functions exist for the Custom Log Format (p. 334) of mod_log_-config. First there is an additional "%{*varname*}x" eXtension format function which can be used to expand any variables provided by any module, especially those provided by mod_ssl which can you find in the above table.

Example
```
CustomLog logs/ssl_request_log \"%t %h %{SSL_PROTOCOL}x
%{SSL_CIPHER}x \"%r\" %b"
```

SSLCACertificateFile Directive

Description:	File of concatenated PEM-encoded CA Certificates for Client Auth
Syntax:	SSLCACertificateFile *file-path*
Context:	server config, virtual host
Status:	Extension
Module:	mod_ssl

This directive sets the *all-in-one* file where you can assemble the Certificates of Certification Authorities (CAs) whose *clients* you deal with. These are used for Client Authentication. Such a file is simply the concatenation of the various PEM-encoded Certificate files, in order of preference. This can be used alternatively and/or additionally to SSLCACertificatePath.

Example
```
SSLCACertificateFile
/usr/local/apache2/conf/ssl.crt/ca-bundle-client.crt
```

SSLCACertificatePath Directive

Description:	Directory of PEM-encoded CA Certificates for Client Auth
Syntax:	SSLCACertificatePath *directory-path*
Context:	server config, virtual host
Status:	Extension
Module:	mod_ssl

This directive sets the directory where you keep the Certificates of Certification Authorities (CAs) whose clients you deal with. These are used to verify the client certificate on Client Authentication.

The files in this directory have to be PEM-encoded and are accessed through hash filenames. So usually you can't just place the Certificate files there: you also have to create symbolic links named *hash-value*.N. And you should always make sure this directory contains the appropriate symbolic links. Use the Makefile which comes with mod_ssl to accomplish this task.

Example
```
SSLCACertificatePath /usr/local/apache2/conf/ssl.crt/
```

SSLCADNRequestFile Directive

Description:	File of concatenated PEM-encoded CA Certificates for defining acceptable CA names
Syntax:	SSLCADNRequestFile *file-path*
Context:	server config, virtual host
Status:	Extension
Module:	mod_ssl

When a client certificate is requested by mod_ssl, a list of *acceptable Certificate*

Authority names is sent to the client in the SSL handshake. These CA names can be used by the client to select an appropriate client certificate out of those it has available.

If neither of the directives SSLCADNRequestPath or SSLCADNRequestFile are given, then the set of acceptable CA names sent to the client is the names of all the CA certificates given by the SSLCACertificateFile and SSLCACertificatePath directives; in other words, the names of the CAs which will actually be used to verify the client certificate.

In some circumstances, it is useful to be able to send a set of acceptable CA names which differs from the actual CAs used to verify the client certificate - for example, if the client certificates are signed by intermediate CAs. In such cases, SSLCADNRequestPath and/or SSLCADNRequestFile can be used; the acceptable CA names are then taken from the complete set of certificates in the directory and/or file specified by this pair of directives.

SSLCADNRequestFile must specify an *all-in-one* file containing a concatenation of PEM-encoded CA certificates.

Example
SSLCADNRequestFile /usr/local/apache2/conf/ca-names.crt

SSLCADNRequestPath Directive

Description:	Directory of PEM-encoded CA Certificates for defining acceptable CA names
Syntax:	SSLCADNRequestPath *directory-path*
Context:	server config, virtual host
Status:	Extension
Module:	mod_ssl

This optional directive can be used to specify the set of *acceptable CA names* which will be sent to the client when a client certificate is requested. See the SSLCADNRequestFile directive for more details.

The files in this directory have to be PEM-encoded and are accessed through hash filenames. So usually you can't just place the Certificate files there: you also have to create symbolic links named *hash-value*.N. And you should always make sure this directory contains the appropriate symbolic links. Use the Makefile which comes with mod_ssl to accomplish this task.

Example
SSLCADNRequestPath /usr/local/apache2/conf/ca-names.crt/

SSLCARevocationFile Directive

Description:	File of concatenated PEM-encoded CA CRLs for Client Auth
Syntax:	SSLCARevocationFile *file-path*
Context:	server config, virtual host
Status:	Extension
Module:	mod_ssl

This directive sets the *all-in-one* file where you can assemble the Certificate Revocation Lists (CRLs) of Certification Authorities (CAs) whose *clients* you deal with. These are used for Client Authentication. Such a file is simply the concatenation of the various PEM-encoded CRL files, in order of preference. This can be used alternatively and/or additionally to SSLCARevocationPath.

Example
```
SSLCARevocationFile
/usr/local/apache2/conf/ssl.crl/ca-bundle-client.crl
```

SSLCARevocationPath Directive

Description:	Directory of PEM-encoded CA CRLs for Client Auth
Syntax:	SSLCARevocationPath *directory-path*
Context:	server config, virtual host
Status:	Extension
Module:	mod_ssl

This directive sets the directory where you keep the Certificate Revocation Lists (CRLs) of Certification Authorities (CAs) whose clients you deal with. These are used to revoke the client certificate on Client Authentication.

The files in this directory have to be PEM-encoded and are accessed through hash filenames. So usually you have not only to place the CRL files there. Additionally you have to create symbolic links named *hash-value*.rN. And you should always make sure this directory contains the appropriate symbolic links. Use the Makefile which comes with mod_ssl to accomplish this task.

Example
```
SSLCARevocationPath /usr/local/apache2/conf/ssl.crl/
```

SSLCertificateChainFile Directive

Description:	File of PEM-encoded Server CA Certificates
Syntax:	SSLCertificateChainFile *file-path*
Context:	server config, virtual host
Status:	Extension
Module:	mod_ssl

This directive sets the optional *all-in-one* file where you can assemble the certificates of Certification Authorities (CAs) which form the certificate chain of the server certificate. This starts with the issuing CA certificate of the server certificate and can range up to the root CA certificate. Such a file is simply the concatenation of the various PEM-encoded CA Certificate files, usually in certificate chain order.

This should be used alternatively and/or additionally to SSLCACertificatePath for explicitly constructing the server certificate chain which is sent to the browser in addition to the server certificate. It is especially useful to avoid conflicts with CA certificates when using client authentication. Because although placing a CA certificate of the server certificate chain into SSLCACertificatePath has the same effect for the certificate chain construction, it has the side-effect that client certificates issued by this same CA certificate are also accepted on client authentication.

But be careful: Providing the certificate chain works only if you are using a *single* RSA *or* DSA based server certificate. If you are using a coupled RSA+DSA certificate pair, this will work only if actually both certificates use the *same* certificate chain. Else the browsers will be confused in this situation.

Example
```
SSLCertificateChainFile /usr/local/apache2/conf/ssl.crt/ca.crt
```

SSLCertificateFile Directive

Description:	Server PEM-encoded X.509 Certificate file
Syntax:	SSLCertificateFile *file-path*
Context:	server config, virtual host
Status:	Extension
Module:	mod_ssl

This directive points to the PEM-encoded Certificate file for the server and optionally also to the corresponding RSA or DSA Private Key file for it (contained in the same file). If the contained Private Key is encrypted the Pass Phrase dialog is forced at startup time. This directive can be used up to two times (referencing different filenames) when both a RSA and a DSA based server certificate is used in parallel.

Example
```
SSLCertificateFile /usr/local/apache2/conf/ssl.crt/server.crt
```

SSLCertificateKeyFile Directive

Description:	Server PEM-encoded Private Key file
Syntax:	SSLCertificateKeyFile *file-path*
Context:	server config, virtual host
Status:	Extension
Module:	mod_ssl

This directive points to the PEM-encoded Private Key file for the server. If the Private Key is not combined with the Certificate in the SSLCertificateFile, use this additional directive to point to the file with the stand-alone Private Key.

When SSLCertificateFile is used and the file contains both the Certificate and the Private Key this directive need not be used. But we strongly discourage this practice. Instead we recommend you to separate the Certificate and the Private Key. If the contained Private Key is encrypted, the Pass Phrase dialog is forced at startup time. This directive can be used up to two times (referencing different filenames) when both a RSA and a DSA based private key is used in parallel.

Example
```
SSLCertificateKeyFile /usr/local/apache2/conf/ssl.key/server.key
```

SSLCipherSuite Directive

Description:	Cipher Suite available for negotiation in SSL handshake
Syntax:	SSLCipherSuite *cipher-spec*
Default:	SSLCipherSuite ALL:!ADH:RC4+RSA:+HIGH: +MEDIUM:+LOW:+SSLv2:+EXP
Context:	server config, virtual host, directory, .htaccess
Override:	AuthConfig
Status:	Extension
Module:	mod_ssl

This complex directive uses a colon-separated *cipher-spec* string consisting of OpenSSL cipher specifications to configure the Cipher Suite the client is permitted to negotiate in the SSL handshake phase. Notice that this directive can be used both in per-server and per-directory context. In per-server context it applies to the standard SSL handshake when a connection is established. In per-directory context it forces an SSL renegotiation with the reconfigured Cipher Suite after the HTTP request was read but before the HTTP response is sent.

An SSL cipher specification in *cipher-spec* is composed of 4 major attributes plus a few extra minor ones:

- *Key Exchange Algorithm*:
  RSA or Diffie-Hellman variants.

- *Authentication Algorithm*:
  RSA, Diffie-Hellman, DSS or none.

- *Cipher/Encryption Algorithm*:
  DES, Triple-DES, RC4, RC2, IDEA or none.

- *MAC Digest Algorithm*:
  MD5, SHA or SHA1.

An SSL cipher can also be an export cipher and is either a SSLv2 or SSLv3/TLSv1 cipher (here TLSv1 is equivalent to SSLv3). To specify which ciphers to use, one can either specify all the Ciphers, one at a time, or use aliases to specify the preference and order for the ciphers (see Table 3.5).

Table 3.5:

Tag	Description
	Key Exchange Algorithm:
kRSA	RSA key exchange
kDHr	Diffie-Hellman key exchange with RSA key
kDHd	Diffie-Hellman key exchange with DSA key
kEDH	Ephemeral (temp.key) Diffie-Hellman key exchange (no cert)
	Authentication Algorithm:
aNULL	No authentication
aRSA	RSA authentication
aDSS	DSS authentication
aDH	Diffie-Hellman authentication
	Cipher Encoding Algorithm:
eNULL	No encoding
DES	DES encoding
3DES	Triple-DES encoding
RC4	RC4 encoding
RC2	RC2 encoding
IDEA	IDEA encoding
	MAC Digest Algorithm:
MD5	MD5 hash function
SHA1	SHA1 hash function
SHA	SHA hash function
	Aliases:
SSLv2	all SSL version 2.0 ciphers
SSLv3	all SSL version 3.0 ciphers
TLSv1	all TLS version 1.0 ciphers
EXP	all export ciphers
EXPORT40	all 40-bit export ciphers only
EXPORT56	all 56-bit export ciphers only
LOW	all low strength ciphers (no export, single DES)
MEDIUM	all ciphers with 128 bit encryption
HIGH	all ciphers using Triple-DES
RSA	all ciphers using RSA key exchange
DH	all ciphers using Diffie-Hellman key exchange
EDH	all ciphers using Ephemeral Diffie-Hellman key exchange
ADH	all ciphers using Anonymous Diffie-Hellman key exchange
DSS	all ciphers using DSS authentication
NULL	all ciphers using no encryption

Now where this becomes interesting is that these can be put together to specify the order and ciphers you wish to use. To speed this up there are also aliases (SSLv2, SSLv3, TLSv1, EXP, LOW, MEDIUM, HIGH) for certain groups of ciphers. These tags can be joined together with prefixes to form the *cipher-spec*. Available prefixes are:

- none: add cipher to list
- +: add ciphers to list and pull them to current location in list
- -: remove cipher from list (can be added later again)
- !: kill cipher from list completely (can **not** be added later again)

A simpler way to look at all of this is to use the "openssl ciphers -v" command which provides a nice way to successively create the correct *cipher-spec* string. The default *cipher-spec* string is "ALL:!ADH:RC4+RSA:+HIGH:+MEDIUM:+LOW:+SSLv2:+EXP" which means the following: first, remove from consideration any ciphers that do not authenticate, i.e. for SSL only the Anonymous Diffie-Hellman ciphers. Next, use ciphers using RC4 and RSA. Next include the high, medium and then the low security ciphers. Finally *pull* all SSLv2 and export ciphers to the end of the list.

```
$ openssl ciphers -v 'ALL:!ADH:RC4+RSA:+HIGH:+MEDIUM:+LOW:+SSLv2
:+EXP'
NULL-SHA    SSLv3 Kx=RSA      Au=RSA Enc=None    Mac=SHA1
NULL-MD5    SSLv3 Kx=RSA      Au=RSA Enc=None    Mac=MD5
...
EXP-RC4-MD5 SSLv3 Kx=RSA(512) Au=RSA Enc=RC4(40) Mac=MD5 export
EXP-RC4-MD5 SSLv2 Kx=RSA(512) Au=RSA Enc=RC4(40) Mac=MD5 export
```

The complete list of particular RSA & DH ciphers for SSL is given in Table 3.7.

Example
```
SSLCipherSuite RSA:!EXP:!NULL:+HIGH:+MEDIUM:-LOW
```

SSLCryptoDevice Directive

Description:	Enable use of a cryptographic hardware accelerator
Syntax:	SSLCryptoDevice *engine*
Default:	SSLCryptoDevice builtin
Context:	server config
Status:	Extension
Module:	mod_ssl
Compatibility:	Available in Apache 2.1 and later, if using -engine flavor of OpenSSL 0.9.6, or OpenSSL 0.9.7 or later

This directive enables use of a cryptographic hardware accelerator board to offload some of the SSL processing overhead. This directive can only be used if the SSL toolkit is built with "engine" support; OpenSSL 0.9.7 and later releases have "engine" support by default, the separate "-engine" releases of OpenSSL 0.9.6 must be used.

Table 3.7:

Cipher-Tag	Protocol	Key Ex.	Auth.	Enc.	MAC	Type
RSA Ciphers:						
DES-CBC3-SHA	SSLv3	RSA	RSA	3DES(168)	SHA1	
DES-CBC3-MD5	SSLv2	RSA	RSA	3DES(168)	MD5	
IDEA-CBC-SHA	SSLv3	RSA	RSA	IDEA(128)	SHA1	
RC4-SHA	SSLv3	RSA	RSA	RC4(128)	SHA1	
RC4-MD5	SSLv3	RSA	RSA	RC4(128)	MD5	
IDEA-CBC-MD5	SSLv2	RSA	RSA	IDEA(128)	MD5	
RC2-CBC-MD5	SSLv2	RSA	RSA	RC2(128)	MD5	
RC4-MD5	SSLv2	RSA	RSA	RC4(128)	MD5	
DES-CBC-SHA	SSLv3	RSA	RSA	DES(56)	SHA1	
RC4-64-MD5	SSLv2	RSA	RSA	RC4(64)	MD5	
DES-CBC-MD5	SSLv2	RSA	RSA	DES(56)	MD5	
EXP-DES-CBC -SHA	SSLv3	RSA(512)	RSA	DES(40)	SHA1	export
EXP-RC2-CBC -MD5	SSLv3	RSA(512)	RSA	RC2(40)	MD5	export
EXP-RC4-MD5	SSLv3	RSA(512)	RSA	RC4(40)	MD5	export
EXP-RC2-CBC -MD5	SSLv2	RSA(512)	RSA	RC2(40)	MD5	export
EXP-RC4-MD5	SSLv2	RSA(512)	RSA	RC4(40)	MD5	export
NULL-SHA	SSLv3	RSA	RSA	None	SHA1	
NULL-MD5	SSLv3	RSA	RSA	None	MD5	
Diffie-Hellman Ciphers:						
ADH-DES-CBC3 -SHA	SSLv3	DH	None	3DES(168)	SHA1	
ADH-DES-CBC -SHA	SSLv3	DH	None	DES(56)	SHA1	
ADH-RC4-MD5	SSLv3	DH	None	RC4(128)	MD5	
EDH-RSA-DES -CBC3-SHA	SSLv3	DH	RSA	3DES(168)	SHA1	
EDH-DSS-DES -CBC3-SHA	SSLv3	DH	DSS	3DES(168)	SHA1	
EDH-RSA-DES -CBC-SHA	SSLv3	DH	RSA	DES(56)	SHA1	
EDH-DSS-DES -CBC-SHA	SSLv3	DH	DSS	DES(56)	SHA1	
EXP-EDH-RSA -DES-CBC-SHA	SSLv3	DH(512)	RSA	DES(40)	SHA1	export
EXP-EDH-DSS -DES-CBC-SHA	SSLv3	DH(512)	DSS	DES(40)	SHA1	export
EXP-ADH-DES -CBC-SHA	SSLv3	DH(512)	None	DES(40)	SHA1	export
EXP-ADH-RC4 -MD5	SSLv3	DH(512)	None	RC4(40)	MD5	export

To discover which engine names are supported, run the command "openssl engine".

Example
```
# For a Broadcom accelerator:
SSLCryptoDevice ubsec
```

SSLEngine Directive

Description:	SSL Engine Operation Switch
Syntax:	SSLEngine on|off|optional
Default:	SSLEngine off
Context:	server config, virtual host
Status:	Extension
Module:	mod_ssl

This directive toggles the usage of the SSL/TLS Protocol Engine. This is usually used inside a <VirtualHost> section to enable SSL/TLS for a particular virtual host. By default the SSL/TLS Protocol Engine is disabled for both the main server and all configured virtual hosts.

Example
```
<VirtualHost _default_:443>
SSLEngine on
...
</VirtualHost>
```

In Apache 2.1 and later, SSLEngine can be set to optional. This enables support for RFC 2817[56], Upgrading to TLS Within HTTP/1.1. At this time no web browsers support RFC 2817.

SSLFIPS Directive

Description:	SSL FIPS mode Switch
Syntax:	SSLFIPS on|off
Default:	SSLFIPS off
Context:	server config
Status:	Extension
Module:	mod_ssl

This directive toggles the usage of the SSL library FIPS_mode flag. It must be set in the global server context and cannot be configured with conflicting settings (SSLFIPS on followed by SSLFIPS off or similar). The mode applies to all SSL library operations.

If httpd was compiled against an SSL library which did not support the FIPS_mode flag, SSLFIPS on will fail. Refer to the FIPS 140-2 Security Policy document of the SSL provider library for specific requirements to use mod_ssl

---

[56]http://www.ietf.org/rfc/rfc2817.txt

in a FIPS 140-2 approved mode of operation; note that mod_ssl itself is not validated, but may be described as using FIPS 140-2 validated cryptographic module, when all components are assembled and operated under the guidelines imposed by the applicable Security Policy.

SSLHonorCipherOrder Directive

Description:	Option to prefer the server's cipher preference order
Syntax:	SSLHonorCipherOrder *flag*
Context:	server config, virtual host
Status:	Extension
Module:	mod_ssl
Compatibility:	Available in Apache 2.1 and later, if using OpenSSL 0.9.7 or later

When choosing a cipher during an SSLv3 or TLSv1 handshake, normally the client's preference is used. If this directive is enabled, the server's preference will be used instead.

Example
SSLHonorCipherOrder on

SSLInsecureRenegotiation Directive

Description:	Option to enable support for insecure renegotiation
Syntax:	SSLInsecureRenegotiation *flag*
Default:	SSLInsecureRenegotiation off
Context:	server config, virtual host
Status:	Extension
Module:	mod_ssl
Compatibility:	Available in httpd 2.2.15 and later, if using OpenSSL 0.9.8m or later

As originally specified, all versions of the SSL and TLS protocols (up to and including TLS/1.2) were vulnerable to a Man-in-the-Middle attack (CVE-2009-3555[57]) during a renegotiation. This vulnerability allowed an attacker to "prefix" a chosen plaintext to the HTTP request as seen by the web server. A protocol extension was developed which fixed this vulnerability if supported by both client and server.

If mod_ssl is linked against OpenSSL version 0.9.8m or later, by default renegotiation is only supported with clients supporting the new protocol extension. If this directive is enabled, renegotiation will be allowed with old (unpatched) clients, albeit insecurely.

SECURITY WARNING *If this directive is enabled, SSL connections will be vulnerable to the Man-in-the-Middle prefix attack as described in CVE-*

---

[57]http://cve.mitre.org/cgi-bin/cvename.cgi?name=CAN-2009-3555

2009-3555[58].

Example
```
SSLInsecureRenegotiation on
```

The SSL_SECURE_RENEG environment variable can be used from an SSI or CGI
script to determine whether secure renegotiation is supported for a given SSL
connection.

SSLMutex Directive

Description:	Semaphore for internal mutual exclusion of operations
Syntax:	SSLMutex *type*
Default:	SSLMutex none
Context:	server config
Status:	Extension
Module:	mod_ssl

This configures the SSL engine's semaphore (aka. lock) which is used for mutual
exclusion of operations which have to be done in a synchronized way between
the pre-forked Apache server processes. This directive can only be used in the
global server context because it's only useful to have one global mutex. This
directive is designed to closely match the AcceptMutex directive.

The following Mutex *types* are available:

- none | no

  This is the default where no Mutex is used at all. Use it at your own risk.
  But because currently the Mutex is mainly used for synchronizing write
  access to the SSL Session Cache you can live without it as long as you
  accept a sometimes garbled Session Cache. So it's not recommended to
  leave this the default. Instead configure a real Mutex.

- posixsem

  This is an elegant Mutex variant where a Posix Semaphore is used when
  possible. It is only available when the underlying platform and APR
  supports it.

- sysvsem

  This is a somewhat elegant Mutex variant where a SystemV IPC
  Semaphore is used when possible. It is possible to "leak" SysV semaphores
  if processes crash before the semaphore is removed. It is only available
  when the underlying platform and APR supports it.

- sem

  This directive tells the SSL Module to pick the "best" semaphore implementation available to it, choosing between Posix and SystemV IPC, in
  that order. It is only available when the underlying platform and APR
  supports at least one of the 2.

---

[58]http://cve.mitre.org/cgi-bin/cvename.cgi?name=CAN-2009-3555

- `pthread`

  This directive tells the SSL Module to use Posix thread mutexes. It is only available if the underlying platform and APR supports it.

- `fcntl:/path/to/mutex`

  This is a portable Mutex variant where a physical (lock-)file and the `fcntl()` function are used as the Mutex. Always use a local disk filesystem for `/path/to/mutex` and never a file residing on a NFS- or AFS-filesystem. It is only available when the underlying platform and APR supports it. Note: Internally, the Process ID (PID) of the Apache parent process is automatically appended to `/path/to/mutex` to make it unique, so you don't have to worry about conflicts yourself. Notice that this type of mutex is not available under the Win32 environment. There you *have* to use the semaphore mutex.

- `flock:/path/to/mutex`

  This is similar to the `fcntl:/path/to/mutex` method with the exception that the `flock()` function is used to provide file locking. It is only available when the underlying platform and APR supports it.

- `file:/path/to/mutex`

  This directive tells the SSL Module to pick the "best" file locking implementation available to it, choosing between `fcntl` and `flock`, in that order. It is only available when the underlying platform and APR supports at least one of the 2.

- `default | yes`

  This directive tells the SSL Module to pick the default locking implementation as determined by the platform and APR.

Example
SSLMutex file:/usr/local/apache/logs/ssl_mutex

SSLOptions Directive

Description:	Configure various SSL engine run-time options
Syntax:	SSLOptions [+|-]*option* ...
Context:	server config, virtual host, directory, .htaccess
Override:	Options
Status:	Extension
Module:	mod_ssl

This directive can be used to control various run-time options on a per-directory basis. Normally, if multiple SSLOptions could apply to a directory, then the most specific one is taken completely; the options are not merged. However if *all* the options on the SSLOptions directive are preceded by a plus (+) or minus (-) symbol, the options are merged. Any options preceded by a + are added to the options currently in force, and any options preceded by a - are removed from the options currently in force.

The available *options* are:

- StdEnvVars

  When this option is enabled, the standard set of SSL related CGI/SSI
  environment variables are created. This per default is disabled for performance reasons, because the information extraction step is a rather expensive operation. So one usually enables this option for CGI and SSI
  requests only.

- ExportCertData

  When this option is enabled, additional CGI/SSI environment variables
  are created: SSL_SERVER_CERT, SSL_CLIENT_CERT and SSL_CLIENT_CERT_-
  CHAIN_n (with n = 0,1,2,..). These contain the PEM-encoded X.509 Certificates of server and client for the current HTTPS connection and can be
  used by CGI scripts for deeper Certificate checking. Additionally all other
  certificates of the client certificate chain are provided, too. This bloats up
  the environment a little bit which is why you have to use this option to
  enable it on demand.

- FakeBasicAuth

  When this option is enabled, the Subject Distinguished Name (DN)
  of the Client X509 Certificate is translated into a HTTP Basic Authorization username. This means that the standard Apache authentication methods can be used for access control. The user name is
  just the Subject of the Client's X509 Certificate (which can be determined by running OpenSSL's openssl x509 command: openssl x509
  -noout -subject -in *certificate*.crt). Note that no password is obtained from the user. Every entry in the user file needs this password: "xxj31ZMTZzkVA", which is the DES-encrypted version of the word
  'password'. Those who live under MD5-based encryption (for instance
  under FreeBSD or BSD/OS, etc.) should use the following MD5 hash of
  the same word: "$1$0XLyS...$0wx8s2/m9/gfkcRVXzgoE/".

- StrictRequire

  This *forces* forbidden access when SSLRequireSSL or SSLRequire successfully decided that access should be forbidden. Usually the default
  is that in the case where a "Satisfy any" directive is used, and other
  access restrictions are passed, denial of access due to SSLRequireSSL
  or SSLRequire is overridden (because that's how the Apache Satisfy
  mechanism should work.) But for strict access restriction you can use
  SSLRequireSSL and/or SSLRequire in combination with an "SSLOptions
  +StrictRequire". Then an additional "Satisfy Any" has no chance once
  mod_ssl has decided to deny access.

- OptRenegotiate

  This enables optimized SSL connection renegotiation handling when SSL
  directives are used in per-directory context. By default a strict scheme
  is enabled where *every* per-directory reconfiguration of SSL parameters

causes a *full* SSL renegotiation handshake. When this option is used mod_-
ssl tries to avoid unnecessary handshakes by doing more granular (but
still safe) parameter checks. Nevertheless these granular checks sometimes
maybe not what the user expects, so enable this on a per-directory basis
only, please.

Example
```
SSLOptions +FakeBasicAuth -StrictRequire
<Files ~ "\.(cgi|shtml)$">
SSLOptions +StdEnvVars -ExportCertData
<Files>
```

SSLPassPhraseDialog Directive

Description:	Type of pass phrase dialog for encrypted private keys
Syntax:	SSLPassPhraseDialog *type*
Default:	SSLPassPhraseDialog builtin
Context:	server config
Status:	Extension
Module:	mod_ssl

When Apache starts up it has to read the various Certificate (see
SSLCertificateFile) and Private Key (see SSLCertificateKeyFile) files of
the SSL-enabled virtual servers. Because for security reasons the Private Key
files are usually encrypted, mod_ssl needs to query the administrator for a Pass
Phrase in order to decrypt those files. This query can be done in two ways
which can be configured by *type*:

- builtin

  This is the default where an interactive terminal dialog occurs at startup
  time just before Apache detaches from the terminal. Here the administrator has to manually enter the Pass Phrase for each encrypted Private
  Key file. Because a lot of SSL-enabled virtual hosts can be configured,
  the following reuse-scheme is used to minimize the dialog: When a Private
  Key file is encrypted, all known Pass Phrases (at the beginning there are
  none, of course) are tried. If one of those known Pass Phrases succeeds
  no dialog pops up for this particular Private Key file. If none succeeded,
  another Pass Phrase is queried on the terminal and remembered for the
  next round (where it perhaps can be reused).

  This scheme allows mod_ssl to be maximally flexible (because for N encrypted Private Key files you *can* use N different Pass Phrases - but then
  you have to enter all of them, of course) while minimizing the terminal
  dialog (i.e. when you use a single Pass Phrase for all N Private Key files
  this Pass Phrase is queried only once).

- |/path/to/program [args...]

  This mode allows an external program to be used which acts as a pipe to a
  particular input device; the program is sent the standard prompt text used

for the builtin mode on stdin, and is expected to write password strings on stdout. If several passwords are needed (or an incorrect password is entered), additional prompt text will be written subsequent to the first password being returned, and more passwords must then be written back.

- exec:/path/to/program

Here an external program is configured which is called at startup for each encrypted Private Key file. It is called with two arguments (the first is of the form "servername:portnumber", the second is either "RSA" or "DSA"), which indicate for which server and algorithm it has to print the corresponding Pass Phrase to stdout. The intent is that this external program first runs security checks to make sure that the system is not compromised by an attacker, and only when these checks are passed successfully it provides the Pass Phrase.

Both these security checks, and the way the Pass Phrase is determined, can be as complex as you like. mod_ssl just defines the interface: an executable program which provides the Pass Phrase on stdout. Nothing more or less! So, if you're really paranoid about security, here is your interface. Anything else has to be left as an exercise to the administrator, because local security requirements are so different.

The reuse-algorithm above is used here, too. In other words: the external program is called only once per unique Pass Phrase.

Example
SSLPassPhraseDialog exec:/usr/local/apache/sbin/pp-filter

SSLProtocol Directive

Description:	Configure usable SSL protocol flavors
Syntax:	SSLProtocol [+|-]*protocol* ...
Default:	SSLProtocol all
Context:	server config, virtual host
Override:	Options
Status:	Extension
Module:	mod_ssl

This directive can be used to control the SSL protocol flavors mod_ssl should use when establishing its server environment. Clients then can only connect with one of the provided protocols.

The available (case-insensitive) *protocol*s are:

- SSLv2

This is the Secure Sockets Layer (SSL) protocol, version 2.0. It is the original SSL protocol as designed by Netscape Corporation. Though its use has been deprecated, because of weaknesses in the security of the protocol.

- SSLv3

  This is the Secure Sockets Layer (SSL) protocol, version 3.0, from the
  Netscape Corporation. It is the successor to SSLv2 and the predecessor
  to TLSv1. It's supported by almost all popular browsers.

- TLSv1

  This is the Transport Layer Security (TLS) protocol, version 1.0. It is
  the successor to SSLv3 and is defined in RFC2246[59]. Which has been
  obsoleted by RFC4346[60].

- All

  This is a shortcut for "+SSLv2 +SSLv3 +TLSv1" and a convenient way for
  enabling all protocols except one when used in combination with the minus
  sign on a protocol as the example above shows.

Example
```
# enable SSLv3 and TLSv1, but not SSLv2
SSLProtocol all -SSLv2
```

SSLProxyCACertificateFile Directive

Description:	File of concatenated PEM-encoded CA Certificates for Remote Server Auth
Syntax:	SSLProxyCACertificateFile *file-path*
Context:	server config, virtual host
Status:	Extension
Module:	mod_ssl

This directive sets the *all-in-one* file where you can assemble the Certificates of
Certification Authorities (CAs) whose *remote servers* you deal with. These are
used for Remote Server Authentication. Such a file is simply the concatenation
of the various PEM-encoded Certificate files, in order of preference. This can
be used alternatively and/or additionally to SSLProxyCACertificatePath.

Example
```
SSLProxyCACertificateFile
/usr/local/apache2/conf/ssl.crt/ca-bundle-remote-server.crt
```

SSLProxyCACertificatePath Directive

Description:	Directory of PEM-encoded CA Certificates for Remote Server Auth
Syntax:	SSLProxyCACertificatePath *directory-path*
Context:	server config, virtual host
Status:	Extension
Module:	mod_ssl

---

[59]http://www.ietf.org/rfc/rfc2246.txt
[60]http://www.ietf.org/rfc/rfc4346.txt

This directive sets the directory where you keep the Certificates of Certification Authorities (CAs) whose remote servers you deal with. These are used to verify the remote server certificate on Remote Server Authentication.

The files in this directory have to be PEM-encoded and are accessed through hash filenames. So usually you can't just place the Certificate files there: you also have to create symbolic links named *hash-value*.N. And you should always make sure this directory contains the appropriate symbolic links. Use the Makefile which comes with mod_ssl to accomplish this task.

Example
```
SSLProxyCACertificatePath /usr/local/apache2/conf/ssl.crt/
```

SSLProxyCARevocationFile Directive

Description:	File of concatenated PEM-encoded CA CRLs for Remote Server Auth
Syntax:	SSLProxyCARevocationFile *file-path*
Context:	server config, virtual host
Status:	Extension
Module:	mod_ssl

This directive sets the *all-in-one* file where you can assemble the Certificate Revocation Lists (CRLs) of Certification Authorities (CAs) whose *remote servers* you deal with. These are used for Remote Server Authentication. Such a file is simply the concatenation of the various PEM-encoded CRL files, in order of preference. This can be used alternatively and/or additionally to SSLProxyCARevocationPath.

Example
```
SSLProxyCARevocationFile
/usr/local/apache2/conf/ssl.crl/ca-bundle-remote-server.crl
```

SSLProxyCARevocationPath Directive

Description:	Directory of PEM-encoded CA CRLs for Remote Server Auth
Syntax:	SSLProxyCARevocationPath *directory-path*
Context:	server config, virtual host
Status:	Extension
Module:	mod_ssl

This directive sets the directory where you keep the Certificate Revocation Lists (CRLs) of Certification Authorities (CAs) whose remote servers you deal with. These are used to revoke the remote server certificate on Remote Server Authentication.

The files in this directory have to be PEM-encoded and are accessed through hash filenames. So usually you have not only to place the CRL files there. Additionally you have to create symbolic links named *hash-value*.rN. And you should always make sure this directory contains the appropriate symbolic links. Use the Makefile which comes with mod_ssl to accomplish this task.

Example
SSLProxyCARevocationPath /usr/local/apache2/conf/ssl.crl/

SSLProxyCheckPeerCN Directive

Description:	Whether to check the remote server certificates CN field
Syntax:	SSLProxyCheckPeerCN on|off
Default:	SSLProxyCheckPeerCN off
Context:	server config, virtual host
Status:	Extension
Module:	mod_ssl

This directive sets whether the remote server certificates CN field is compared against the hostname of the request URL. If both are not equal a 502 status code (Bad Gateway) is sent.

Example
SSLProxyCheckPeerCN on

SSLProxyCheckPeerExpire Directive

Description:	Whether to check if remote server certificate is expired
Syntax:	SSLProxyCheckPeerExpire on|off
Default:	SSLProxyCheckPeerExpire off
Context:	server config, virtual host
Status:	Extension
Module:	mod_ssl

This directive sets whether it is checked if the remote server certificate is expired or not. If the check fails a 502 status code (Bad Gateway) is sent.

Example
SSLProxyCheckPeerExpire on

SSLProxyCipherSuite Directive

Description:	Cipher Suite available for negotiation in SSL proxy handshake
Syntax:	SSLProxyCipherSuite cipher-spec
Default:	SSLProxyCipherSuite ALL:!ADH:RC4+RSA:+HIGH:+MEDIUM:+LOW:+SSLv2:+EXP
Context:	server config, virtual host, directory, .htaccess
Override:	AuthConfig
Status:	Extension
Module:	mod_ssl

Equivalent to SSLCipherSuite, but for the proxy connection. Please refer to

SSLCipherSuite for additional information.

SSLProxyEngine Directive

Description:	SSL Proxy Engine Operation Switch
Syntax:	SSLProxyEngine on|off
Default:	SSLProxyEngine off
Context:	server config, virtual host
Status:	Extension
Module:	mod_ssl

This directive toggles the usage of the SSL/TLS Protocol Engine for proxy. This is usually used inside a <VirtualHost> section to enable SSL/TLS for proxy usage in a particular virtual host. By default the SSL/TLS Protocol Engine is disabled for proxy image both for the main server and all configured virtual hosts.

Example
```
<VirtualHost _default_:443>
SSLProxyEngine on
...
</VirtualHost>
```

SSLProxyMachineCertificateFile Directive

Description:	File of concatenated PEM-encoded client certificates and keys to be used by the proxy
Syntax:	SSLProxyMachineCertificateFile *filename*
Context:	server config
Override:	Not applicable
Status:	Extension
Module:	mod_ssl

This directive sets the all-in-one file where you keep the certificates and keys used for authentication of the proxy server to remote servers.

This referenced file is simply the concatenation of the various PEM-encoded certificate files, in order of preference. Use this directive alternatively or additionally to SSLProxyMachineCertificatePath.

Currently there is no support for encrypted private keys

Example
```
SSLProxyMachineCertificateFile
/usr/local/apache2/conf/ssl.crt/proxy.pem
```

SSLProxyMachineCertificatePath Directive

Description:	Directory of PEM-encoded client certificates and keys to be used by the proxy
Syntax:	SSLProxyMachineCertificatePath *directory*
Context:	server config
Override:	Not applicable
Status:	Extension
Module:	mod_ssl

This directive sets the directory where you keep the certificates and keys used for authentication of the proxy server to remote servers.

The files in this directory must be PEM-encoded and are accessed through hash filenames. Additionally, you must create symbolic links named *hash-value*.N. And you should always make sure this directory contains the appropriate symbolic links. Use the Makefile which comes with mod_ssl to accomplish this task.

Currently there is no support for encrypted private keys

Example
SSLProxyMachineCertificatePath
/usr/local/apache2/conf/proxy.crt/

SSLProxyProtocol Directive

Description:	Configure usable SSL protocol flavors for proxy usage
Syntax:	SSLProxyProtocol [+|-]*protocol* ...
Default:	SSLProxyProtocol all
Context:	server config, virtual host
Override:	Options
Status:	Extension
Module:	mod_ssl

This directive can be used to control the SSL protocol flavors mod_ssl should use when establishing its server environment for proxy . It will only connect to servers using one of the provided protocols.

Please refer to SSLProtocol for additional information.

SSLProxyVerify Directive

Description:	Type of remote server Certificate verification
Syntax:	SSLProxyVerify *level*
Default:	SSLProxyVerify none
Context:	server config, virtual host, directory, .htaccess
Override:	AuthConfig
Status:	Extension
Module:	mod_ssl

When a proxy is configured to forward requests to a remote SSL server, this directive can be used to configure certificate verification of the remote server. Notice that this directive can be used both in per-server and per-directory context. In per-server context it applies to the remote server authentication process used in the standard SSL handshake when a connection is established by the proxy. In per-directory context it forces an SSL renegotiation with the reconfigured remote server verification level after the HTTP request was read but before the HTTP response is sent.

> Note that even when certificate verification is enabled, mod_ssl does not check whether the commonName (hostname) attribute of the server certificate matches the hostname used to connect to the server. In other words, the proxy does not guarantee that the SSL connection to the backend server is "secure" beyond the fact that the certificate is signed by one of the CAs configured using the SSLProxyCACertificatePath and/or SSLProxyCACertificateFile directives. In order to get this check done please have a look at SSLProxyCheckPeerCN and SSLProxyCheckPeerExpire directives which are off by default.

The following levels are available for *level*:

- **none**: no remote server Certificate is required at all
- **optional**: the remote server *may* present a valid Certificate
- **require**: the remote server *has to* present a valid Certificate
- **optional_no_ca**: the remote server may present a valid Certificate but it need not to be (successfully) verifiable.

In practice only levels **none** and **require** are really interesting, because level **optional** doesn't work with all servers and level **optional_no_ca** is actually against the idea of authentication (but can be used to establish SSL test pages, etc.)

Example
SSLProxyVerify require

SSLProxyVerifyDepth Directive

Description:	Maximum depth of CA Certificates in Remote Server Certificate verification
Syntax:	SSLProxyVerifyDepth *number*
Default:	SSLProxyVerifyDepth 1
Context:	server config, virtual host, directory, .htaccess
Override:	AuthConfig
Status:	Extension
Module:	mod_ssl

This directive sets how deeply mod_ssl should verify before deciding that the remote server does not have a valid certificate. Notice that this directive can be used both in per-server and per-directory context. In per-server context it applies to the client authentication process used in the standard SSL handshake when a connection is established. In per-directory context it forces an SSL renegotiation with the reconfigured remote server verification depth after the HTTP request was read but before the HTTP response is sent.

The depth actually is the maximum number of intermediate certificate issuers, i.e. the number of CA certificates which are max allowed to be followed while verifying the remote server certificate. A depth of 0 means that self-signed remote server certificates are accepted only; the default depth of 1 means the remote server certificate can be self-signed or has to be signed by a CA which is directly known to the server (i.e. the CA's certificate is under SSLProxyCACertificatePath), etc.

Example
SSLProxyVerifyDepth 10

SSLRandomSeed Directive

Description:	Pseudo Random Number Generator (PRNG) seeding source
Syntax:	SSLRandomSeed *context source* [*bytes*]
Context:	server config
Status:	Extension
Module:	mod_ssl

This configures one or more sources for seeding the Pseudo Random Number Generator (PRNG) in OpenSSL at startup time (*context* is startup) and/or just before a new SSL connection is established (*context* is connect). This directive can only be used in the global server context because the PRNG is a global facility.

The following *source* variants are available:

- builtin This is the always available builtin seeding source. Its usage consumes minimum CPU cycles under runtime and hence can be always used without drawbacks. The source used for seeding the PRNG contains of the current time, the current process id and (when applicable) a randomly choosen 1KB extract of the inter-process scoreboard structure of Apache. The drawback is that this is not really a strong source and at startup time (where the scoreboard is still not available) this source just produces a few bytes of entropy. So you should always, at least for the startup, use an additional seeding source.

- file:/path/to/source

  This variant uses an external file /path/to/source as the source for seeding the PRNG. When *bytes* is specified, only the first *bytes* number of bytes of the file form the entropy (and *bytes* is given to /path/to/source as the first argument). When *bytes* is not specified the whole file forms the entropy (and 0 is given to /path/to/source as the first argument). Use this especially at startup time, for instance with an available

/dev/random and/or /dev/urandom device (which usually exist on modern
Unix derivates like FreeBSD and Linux).

But be careful: Usually /dev/random provides only as much entropy data
as it actually has, i.e. when you request 512 bytes of entropy, but the
device currently has only 100 bytes available two things can happen: On
some platforms you receive only the 100 bytes while on other platforms
the read blocks until enough bytes are available (which can take a long
time). Here using an existing /dev/urandom is better, because it never
blocks and actually gives the amount of requested data. The drawback is
just that the quality of the received data may not be the best.

On some platforms like FreeBSD one can even control how the entropy is actually generated, i.e. by which system interrupts. More details one can find under *rndcontrol(8)* on those platforms. Alternatively, when your system lacks such a random device, you can use
tool like EGD[61] (Entropy Gathering Daemon) and run its client program with the exec:/path/to/program/ variant (see below) or use
egd:/path/to/egd-socket (see below).

- exec:/path/to/program

This variant uses an external executable /path/to/program as the source
for seeding the PRNG. When *bytes* is specified, only the first *bytes* number of bytes of its stdout contents form the entropy. When *bytes* is not
specified, the entirety of the data produced on stdout form the entropy.
Use this only at startup time when you need a very strong seeding with
the help of an external program (for instance as in the example above
with the truerand utility you can find in the mod_ssl distribution which
is based on the AT&T *truerand* library). Using this in the connection
context slows down the server too dramatically, of course. So usually you
should avoid using external programs in that context.

- egd:/path/to/egd-socket (Unix only)

This variant uses the Unix domain socket of the external Entropy Gathering Daemon (EGD) (see http://www.lothar.com/tech /crypto/[62]) to seed
the PRNG. Use this if no random device exists on your platform.

Example
```
SSLRandomSeed startup builtin
SSLRandomSeed startup file:/dev/random
SSLRandomSeed startup file:/dev/urandom 1024
SSLRandomSeed startup exec:/usr/local/bin/truerand 16
SSLRandomSeed connect builtin
SSLRandomSeed connect file:/dev/random
SSLRandomSeed connect file:/dev/urandom 1024
```

---

[61]http://www.lothar.com/tech/crypto/
[62]http://www.lothar.com/tech/crypto/

SSLRenegBufferSize Directive

Description:	Set the size for the SSL renegotiation buffer
Syntax:	SSLRenegBufferSize *bytes*
Default:	SSLRenegBufferSize 131072
Context:	directory, .htaccess
Override:	AuthConfig
Status:	Extension
Module:	mod_ssl

If an SSL renegotiation is required in per-location context, for example, any use of SSLVerifyClient in a Directory or Location block, then mod_ssl must buffer any HTTP request body into memory until the new SSL handshake can be performed. This directive can be used to set the amount of memory that will be used for this buffer.

Note that in many configurations, the client sending the request body will be untrusted so a denial of service attack by consumption of memory must be considered when changing this configuration setting.

Example
SSLRenegBufferSize 262144

SSLRequire Directive

Description:	Allow access only when an arbitrarily complex boolean expression is true
Syntax:	SSLRequire *expression*
Context:	directory, .htaccess
Override:	AuthConfig
Status:	Extension
Module:	mod_ssl

This directive specifies a general access requirement which has to be fulfilled in order to allow access. It is a very powerful directive because the requirement specification is an arbitrarily complex boolean expression containing any number of access checks.

The implementation of SSLRequire is not thread safe. Using SSLRequire inside .htaccess files on a threaded MPM (p. 703) may cause random crashes.

The *expression* must match the following syntax (given as a BNF grammar notation):

```
    expr      ::= "true" | "false"
              | "!" expr
              | expr "&&" expr
```

```
                    | expr "||" expr
                    | "(" expr ")"
                    | comp

   comp      ::= word "==" word | word "eq" word
                 | word "!=" word | word "ne" word
                 | word "<"  word | word "lt" word
                 | word "<=" word | word "le" word
                 | word ">"  word | word "gt" word
                 | word ">=" word | word "ge" word
                 | word "in" "{" wordlist "}"
                 | word "in" "OID(" word ")"
                 | word "=~" regex
                 | word "!~" regex

   wordlist ::= word
               | wordlist "," word

   word      ::= digit
               | cstring
               | variable
               | function

   digit    ::= [0-9]+
   cstring  ::= "..."
   variable ::= "%{" varname "}"
   function ::= funcname "(" funcargs ")"
```

while for varname any variable from Tables 3.9 and 3.10 can be used. Finally for funcname the following functions are available:

- file(*filename*)

  This function takes one string argument and expands to the contents of the file. This is especially useful for matching this contents against a regular expression, etc.

Notice that *expression* is first parsed into an internal machine representation and then evaluated in a second step. Actually, in Global and Per-Server Class context *expression* is parsed at startup time and at runtime only the machine representation is executed. For Per-Directory context this is different: here *expression* has to be parsed and immediately executed for every request.

   Example
```
   SSLRequire ( %{SSL_CIPHER} !~ m/^(EXP|NULL)-/ \
   and %{SSL_CLIENT_S_DN_O} eq "Snake Oil, Ltd." \
   and %{SSL_CLIENT_S_DN_OU} in {"Staff", "CA", "Dev"} \
   and %{TIME_WDAY} >= 1 and %{TIME_WDAY} <= 5 \
   and %{TIME_HOUR} >= 8 and %{TIME_HOUR} <= 20 ) \
```

      or %{REMOTE_ADDR} =~ m/^192\.76\.162\.[0-9]+$/

The OID() function expects to find zero or more instances of the given OID in
the client certificate, and compares the left-hand side string against the value
of matching OID attributes. Every matching OID is checked, until a match is
found.

Table 3.9: Standard CGI/1.0 and Apache variables:

HTTP_USER_AGENT	PATH_INFO	AUTH_TYPE
HTTP_REFERER	QUERY_STRING	SERVER_SOFTWARE
HTTP_COOKIE	REMOTE_HOST	API_VERSION
HTTP_FORWARDED	REMOTE_IDENT	TIME_YEAR
HTTP_HOST	IS_SUBREQ	TIME_MON
HTTP_PROXY_CONNECTION	DOCUMENT_ROOT	TIME_DAY
HTTP_ACCEPT	SERVER_ADMIN	TIME_HOUR
HTTP:headername	SERVER_NAME	TIME_MIN
THE_REQUEST	SERVER_PORT	TIME_SEC
REQUEST_METHOD	SERVER_PROTOCOL	TIME_WDAY
REQUEST_SCHEME	REMOTE_ADDR	TIME
REQUEST_URI	REMOTE_USER	ENV:variablename
REQUEST_FILENAME		

SSLRequireSSL Directive

Description:	Deny access when SSL is not used for the HTTP request
Syntax:	SSLRequireSSL
Context:	directory, .htaccess
Override:	AuthConfig
Status:	Extension
Module:	mod_ssl

This directive forbids access unless HTTP over SSL (i.e. HTTPS) is enabled
for the current connection. This is very handy inside the SSL-enabled virtual
host or directories for defending against configuration errors that expose stuff
that should be protected. When this directive is present all requests are denied
which are not using SSL.

   Example
   SSLRequireSSL

Table 3.10: SSL-related variables:

HTTPS	SSL_CLIENT_M_VERSION	SSL_SERVER_M_VERSION
	SSL_CLIENT_M_SERIAL	SSL_SERVER_M_SERIAL
SSL_PROTOCOL	SSL_CLIENT_V_START	SSL_SERVER_V_START
SSL_SESSION_ID	SSL_CLIENT_V_END	SSL_SERVER_V_END
SSL_CIPHER	SSL_CLIENT_S_DN	SSL_SERVER_S_DN
SSL_CIPHER_EXPORT	SSL_CLIENT_S_DN_C	SSL_SERVER_S_DN_C
SSL_CIPHER_ALGKEYSIZE	SSL_CLIENT_S_DN_ST	SSL_SERVER_S_DN_ST
SSL_CIPHER_USEKEYSIZE	SSL_CLIENT_S_DN_L	SSL_SERVER_S_DN_L
SSL_VERSION_LIBRARY	SSL_CLIENT_S_DN_O	SSL_SERVER_S_DN_O
SSL_VERSION_INTERFACE	SSL_CLIENT_S_DN_OU	SSL_SERVER_S_DN_OU
	SSL_CLIENT_S_DN_CN	SSL_SERVER_S_DN_CN
	SSL_CLIENT_S_DN_T	SSL_SERVER_S_DN_T
	SSL_CLIENT_S_DN_I	SSL_SERVER_S_DN_I
	SSL_CLIENT_S_DN_G	SSL_SERVER_S_DN_G
	SSL_CLIENT_S_DN_S	SSL_SERVER_S_DN_S
	SSL_CLIENT_S_DN_D	SSL_SERVER_S_DN_D
	SSL_CLIENT_S_DN_UID	SSL_SERVER_S_DN_UID
	SSL_CLIENT_S_DN_Email	SSL_SERVER_S_DN_Email
	SSL_CLIENT_I_DN	SSL_SERVER_I_DN
	SSL_CLIENT_I_DN_C	SSL_SERVER_I_DN_C
	SSL_CLIENT_I_DN_ST	SSL_SERVER_I_DN_ST
	SSL_CLIENT_I_DN_L	SSL_SERVER_I_DN_L
	SSL_CLIENT_I_DN_O	SSL_SERVER_I_DN_O
	SSL_CLIENT_I_DN_OU	SSL_SERVER_I_DN_OU
	SSL_CLIENT_I_DN_CN	SSL_SERVER_I_DN_CN
	SSL_CLIENT_I_DN_T	SSL_SERVER_I_DN_T
	SSL_CLIENT_I_DN_I	SSL_SERVER_I_DN_I
	SSL_CLIENT_I_DN_G	SSL_SERVER_I_DN_G
	SSL_CLIENT_I_DN_S	SSL_SERVER_I_DN_S
	SSL_CLIENT_I_DN_D	SSL_SERVER_I_DN_D
	SSL_CLIENT_I_DN_UID	SSL_SERVER_I_DN_UID
	SSL_CLIENT_I_DN_Email	SSL_SERVER_I_DN_Email
	SSL_CLIENT_A_SIG	SSL_SERVER_A_SIG
	SSL_CLIENT_A_KEY	SSL_SERVER_A_KEY
	SSL_CLIENT_CERT	SSL_SERVER_CERT
	SSL_CLIENT_CERT_CHAIN_n	
	SSL_CLIENT_VERIFY	

SSLSessionCache Directive

Description:	Type of the global/inter-process SSL Session Cache
Syntax:	SSLSessionCache *type*
Default:	SSLSessionCache none
Context:	server config
Status:	Extension
Module:	mod_ssl

This configures the storage type of the global/inter-process SSL Session Cache. This cache is an optional facility which speeds up parallel request processing. For requests to the same server process (via HTTP keep-alive), OpenSSL already caches the SSL session information locally. But because modern clients request inlined images and other data via parallel requests (usually up to four parallel requests are common) those requests are served by *different* pre-forked server processes. Here an inter-process cache helps to avoid unneccessary session handshakes.

The following four storage *types* are currently supported:

- none

  This disables the global/inter-process Session Cache. This will incur a noticeable speed penalty and may cause problems if using certain browsers, particularly if client certificates are enabled. This setting is not recommended.

- nonenotnull

  This disables any global/inter-process Session Cache. However it does force OpenSSL to send a non-null session ID to accommodate buggy clients that require one.

- dbm:/path/to/datafile

  This makes use of a DBM hashfile on the local disk to synchronize the local OpenSSL memory caches of the server processes. This session cache may suffer reliability issues under high load.

- shm:/path/to/datafile[(*size*)]

  This makes use of a high-performance cyclic buffer (approx. *size* bytes in size) inside a shared memory segment in RAM (established via /path/to/datafile) to synchronize the local OpenSSL memory caches of the server processes. This is the recommended session cache.

- dc:UNIX:/path/to/socket

  This makes use of the distcache[63] distributed session caching libraries. The argument should specify the location of the server or proxy to be used using the distcache address syntax; for example, UNIX:/path/to/socket specifies a UNIX domain socket (typically a local dc_client proxy); IP:server.example.com:9001 specifies an IP address.

---

[63]http://www.distcache.org/

Examples
```
SSLSessionCache dbm:/usr/local/apache/logs/ssl_gcache_data
SSLSessionCache
shm:/usr/local/apache/logs/ssl_gcache_data(512000)
```

SSLSessionCacheTimeout Directive

Description:	Number of seconds before an SSL session expires in the Session Cache
Syntax:	SSLSessionCacheTimeout *seconds*
Default:	SSLSessionCacheTimeout 300
Context:	server config, virtual host
Status:	Extension
Module:	mod_ssl

This directive sets the timeout in seconds for the information stored in the global/inter-process SSL Session Cache and the OpenSSL internal memory cache. It can be set as low as 15 for testing, but should be set to higher values like 300 in real life.

Example
```
SSLSessionCacheTimeout 600
```

SSLStrictSNIVHostCheck Directive

Description:	Whether to allow non SNI clients to access a name based virtual host.
Syntax:	SSLStrictSNIVHostCheck on|off
Default:	SSLStrictSNIVHostCheck off
Context:	server config, virtual host
Status:	Extension
Module:	mod_ssl
Compatibility:	Available in Apache 2.2.12 and later

This directive sets whether a non SNI client is allowed to access a name based virtual host. If set to on in the non default name based virtual host, non SNI clients are not allowed to access this particular virtual host. If set to on in the default name based virtual host, non SNI clients are not allowed to access any name based virtual host belonging to this IP / port combination.

This option is only available if httpd was compiled against an SNI capable version of OpenSSL.

Example
```
SSLStrictSNIVHostCheck on
```

SSLUserName Directive

Description:	Variable name to determine user name
Syntax:	SSLUserName *varname*
Context:	server config, directory, .htaccess
Override:	AuthConfig
Status:	Extension
Module:	mod_ssl
Compatibility:	Available in Apache 2.0.51 and later

This directive sets the "user" field in the Apache request object. This is used by lower modules to identify the user with a character string. In particular, this may cause the environment variable REMOTE_USER to be set. The *varname* can be any of the SSL environment variables.

Note that this directive has no effect if the FakeBasicAuth option is used (see SSLOptions).

Example
SSLUserName SSL_CLIENT_S_DN_CN

SSLVerifyClient Directive

Description:	Type of Client Certificate verification
Syntax:	SSLVerifyClient *level*
Default:	SSLVerifyClient none
Context:	server config, virtual host, directory, .htaccess
Override:	AuthConfig
Status:	Extension
Module:	mod_ssl

This directive sets the Certificate verification level for the Client Authentication. Notice that this directive can be used both in per-server and per-directory context. In per-server context it applies to the client authentication process used in the standard SSL handshake when a connection is established. In per-directory context it forces an SSL renegotiation with the reconfigured client verification level after the HTTP request was read but before the HTTP response is sent.

The following levels are available for *level*:

- **none**: no client Certificate is required at all
- **optional**: the client *may* present a valid Certificate
- **require**: the client *has to* present a valid Certificate
- **optional_no_ca**: the client may present a valid Certificate but it need not to be (successfully) verifiable.

In practice only levels **none** and **require** are really interesting, because level **optional** doesn't work with all browsers and level **optional_no_ca** is actually against the idea of authentication (but can be used to establish SSL test pages, etc.)

Example
```
SSLVerifyClient require
```

SSLVerifyDepth Directive

Description:	Maximum depth of CA Certificates in Client Certificate verification
Syntax:	SSLVerifyDepth *number*
Default:	SSLVerifyDepth 1
Context:	server config, virtual host, directory, .htaccess
Override:	AuthConfig
Status:	Extension
Module:	mod_ssl

This directive sets how deeply mod_ssl should verify before deciding that the clients don't have a valid certificate. Notice that this directive can be used both in per-server and per-directory context. In per-server context it applies to the client authentication process used in the standard SSL handshake when a connection is established. In per-directory context it forces an SSL renegotiation with the reconfigured client verification depth after the HTTP request was read but before the HTTP response is sent.

The depth actually is the maximum number of intermediate certificate issuers, i.e. the number of CA certificates which are max allowed to be followed while verifying the client certificate. A depth of 0 means that self-signed client certificates are accepted only; the default depth of 1 means the client certificate can be self-signed or has to be signed by a CA which is directly known to the server (i.e. the CA's certificate is under SSLCACertificatePath), etc.

Example
```
SSLVerifyDepth 10
```

3.71 Apache Module mod_status

Description:	Provides information on server activity and performance
Status:	Base
Module Identifier:	status_module
Source File:	mod_status.c

Summary

The Status module allows a server administrator to find out how well their server is performing. A HTML page is presented that gives the current server statistics in an easily readable form. If required this page can be made to automatically refresh (given a compatible browser). Another page gives a simple machine-readable list of the current server state.

The details given are:

- The number of worker serving requests
- The number of idle workers
- The status of each worker, the number of requests that worker has performed and the total number of bytes served by the worker (*)
- A total number of accesses and byte count served (*)
- The time the server was started/restarted and the time it has been running for
- Averages giving the number of requests per second, the number of bytes served per second and the average number of bytes per request (*)
- The current percentage CPU used by each worker and in total by Apache (*)
- The current hosts and requests being processed (*)

The lines marked "(*)" are only available if ExtendedStatus is On.

Directives:

    ExtendedStatus
    SeeRequestTail

3.71.1 Enabling Status Support

To enable status reports only for browsers from the example.com domain add this code to your httpd.conf configuration file

    <Location /server-status>
    SetHandler server-status

    Order Deny,Allow
    Deny from all

```
Allow from .example.com
</Location>
```

You can now access server statistics by using a Web browser to access the page
http://your.server.name/server-status

3.71.2 Automatic Updates

You can get the status page to update itself automatically if you have a
browser that supports "refresh". Access the page http://your.server.name/
server-status?refresh=N to refresh the page every N seconds.

3.71.3 Machine Readable Status File

A machine-readable version of the status file is available by accessing the page
http://your.server.name/server-status?auto. This is useful when automatically run; see the Perl program in the /support directory of Apache, log_-
server_status.

> *It should be noted that if* mod_status *is compiled into the server,
> its handler capability is available in all configuration files, includ-
> ing per-directory files (e.g.,* .htaccess*). This may have security-
> related ramifications for your site.*

ExtendedStatus Directive

Description:	Keep track of extended status information for each request
Syntax:	ExtendedStatus On|Off
Default:	ExtendedStatus Off
Context:	server config
Status:	Base
Module:	mod_status
Compatibility:	ExtendedStatus is only available in Apache 1.3.2 and later.

This setting applies to the entire server, and cannot be enabled or disabled on a
virtualhost-by-virtualhost basis. The collection of extended status information
can slow down the server.

SeeRequestTail Directive

Description:	Determine if mod_status displays the first 63 characters of a request or the last 63, assuming the request itself is greater than 63 chars.
Syntax:	SeeRequestTail On|Off
Default:	SeeRequestTail Off
Context:	server config
Status:	Base
Module:	mod_status
Compatibility:	Available in Apache 2.2.7 and later.

mod_status with ExtendedStatus On displays the actual request being handled. For historical purposes, only 63 characters of the request are actually stored for display purposes. This directive controls whether the 1st 63 characters are stored (the previous behavior and the default) or if the last 63 characters are. This is only applicable, of course, if the length of the request is 64 characters or greater.

If Apache is handling a request like GET /disk1/storage/apache/htdocs/ images/imagestore1/food/apples.jpg HTTP/1.1 mod_status displays as follows:

Off	GET /disk1/storage/apache/htdocs/images/imagestore1/food/apples
On	orage/apache/htdocs/images/imagestore1/food/apples.jpg HTTP/1.1

3.72 Apache Module mod_substitute

Description:	Perform search and replace operations on response bodies
Status:	Extension
Module Identifier:	substitute_module
Source File:	mod_substitute.c
Compatibility:	Available in Apache 2.2.7 and later

Summary

mod_substitute provides a mechanism to perform both regular expression and fixed string substitutions on response bodies.

Directives:

> Substitute

Substitute Directive

Description:	Pattern to filter the response content
Syntax:	Substitute s/pattern/substitution/[infq]
Context:	directory, .htaccess
Override:	FileInfo
Status:	Extension
Module:	mod_substitute

The Substitute directive specifies a search and replace pattern to apply to the response body.

The meaning of the pattern can be modified by using any combination of these flags:

i Perform a case-insensitive match.

n By default the pattern is treated as a regular expression. Using the n flag forces the pattern to be treated as a fixed string.

f The f flag causes mod_substitute to flatten the result of a substitution allowing for later substitutions to take place on the boundary of this one. This is the default.

q The q flag causes mod_substitute to not flatten the buckets after each substitution. This can result in a much faster response and a decrease in memory utilization, but should only be used if there is no possibility that the result of one substitution will ever match a pattern or regex of a subsequent one.

Example
```
<Location />
    AddOutputFilterByType SUBSTITUTE text/html
    Substitute s/foo/bar/ni
```

```
</Location>
```

If either the pattern or the substitution contains a slash character then an
alternative delimiter should be used:

Example of using an alternate delimiter
```
<Location />
     AddOutputFilterByType SUBSTITUTE text/html
     Substitute "s|<BR */?>|<br />|i"
</Location>
```

3.73 Apache Module mod_suexec

Description:	Allows CGI scripts to run as a specified user and Group
Status:	Extension
Module Identifier:	suexec_module
Source File:	mod_suexec.c
Compatibility:	Available in Apache 2.0 and later

Summary

This module, in combination with the suexec support program allows CGI scripts to run as a specified user and Group.

Directives:

SuexecUserGroup

See also:

▷ SuEXEC support (p. 719)

SuexecUserGroup Directive

Description:	User and group for CGI programs to run as
Syntax:	SuexecUserGroup *User Group*
Context:	server config, virtual host
Status:	Extension
Module:	mod_suexec
Compatibility:	SuexecUserGroup is only available in 2.0 and later.

The SuexecUserGroup directive allows you to specify a user and group for CGI programs to run as. Non-CGI requests are still processed with the user specified in the User directive. This directive replaces the Apache 1.3 configuration of using the User and Group directives inside VirtualHosts.

Example
SuexecUserGroup nobody nogroup

3.74 Apache Module mod_unique_id

Description:	Provides an environment variable with a unique identifier for each request
Status:	Extension
Module Identifier:	unique_id_module
Source File:	mod_unique_id.c

Summary

This module provides a magic token for each request which is guaranteed to be unique across "all" requests under very specific conditions. The unique identifier is even unique across multiple machines in a properly configured cluster of machines. The environment variable UNIQUE_ID is set to the identifier for each request. Unique identifiers are useful for various reasons which are beyond the scope of this section.

This module provides no directives.

3.74.1 Theory

First a brief recap of how the Apache server works on Unix machines. This feature currently isn't supported on Windows NT. On Unix machines, Apache creates several children; the children process requests one at a time. Each child can serve multiple requests in its lifetime. For the purpose of this discussion, the children don't share any data with each other. We'll refer to the children as **httpd processes**.

Your website has one or more machines under your administrative control. Together we'll call them a cluster of machines. Each machine can possibly run multiple instances of Apache. All of these collectively are considered "the universe", and with certain assumptions we'll show that in this universe we can generate unique identifiers for each request, without extensive communication between machines in the cluster.

The machines in your cluster should satisfy these requirements. (Even if you have only one machine you should synchronize its clock with NTP.)

- The machines' times are synchronized via NTP or other network time protocol.
- The machines' hostnames all differ, such that the module can do a hostname lookup on the hostname and receive a different IP address for each machine in the cluster.

As far as operating system assumptions go, we assume that pids (process ids) fit in 32-bits. If the operating system uses more than 32-bits for a pid, the fix is trivial but must be performed in the code.

Given those assumptions, at a single point in time we can identify any httpd process on any machine in the cluster from all other httpd processes. The machine's IP address and the pid of the httpd process are sufficient to do this. So in order to generate unique identifiers for requests we need only distinguish between different points in time.

To distinguish time we will use a Unix timestamp (seconds since January 1, 1970 UTC), and a 16-bit counter. The timestamp has only one second granularity, so the counter is used to represent up to 65536 values during a single second. The quadruple *(ip_addr, pid, time_stamp, counter)* is sufficient to enumerate 65536 requests per second per httpd process. There are issues however with pid reuse over time, and the counter is used to alleviate this issue.

When an httpd child is created, the counter is initialized with (current microseconds divided by 10) modulo 65536 (this formula was chosen to eliminate some variance problems with the low order bits of the microsecond timers on some systems). When a unique identifier is generated, the time stamp used is the time the request arrived at the web server. The counter is incremented every time an identifier is generated (and allowed to roll over).

The kernel generates a pid for each process as it forks the process, and pids are allowed to roll over (they're 16-bits on many Unixes, but newer systems have expanded to 32-bits). So over time the same pid will be reused. However unless it is reused within the same second, it does not destroy the uniqueness of our quadruple. That is, we assume the system does not spawn 65536 processes in a one second interval (it may even be 32768 processes on some Unixes, but even this isn't likely to happen).

Suppose that time repeats itself for some reason. That is, suppose that the system's clock is screwed up and it revisits a past time (or it is too far forward, is reset correctly, and then revisits the future time). In this case we can easily show that we can get pid and time stamp reuse. The choice of initializer for the counter is intended to help defeat this. Note that we really want a random number to initialize the counter, but there aren't any readily available numbers on most systems (*i.e.*, you can't use rand() because you need to seed the generator, and can't seed it with the time because time, at least at one second resolution, has repeated itself). This is not a perfect defense.

How good a defense is it? Suppose that one of your machines serves at most 500 requests per second (which is a very reasonable upper bound at this writing, because systems generally do more than just shovel out static files). To do that it will require a number of children which depends on how many concurrent clients you have. But we'll be pessimistic and suppose that a single child is able to serve 500 requests per second. There are 1000 possible starting counter values such that two sequences of 500 requests overlap. So there is a 1.5% chance that if time (at one second resolution) repeats itself this child will repeat a counter value, and uniqueness will be broken. This was a very pessimistic example, and with real world values it's even less likely to occur. If your system is such that it's still likely to occur, then perhaps you should make the counter 32 bits (by editing the code).

You may be concerned about the clock being "set back" during summer daylight savings. However this isn't an issue because the times used here are UTC, which "always" go forward. Note that x86 based Unixes may need proper configuration for this to be true – they should be configured to assume that the motherboard clock is on UTC and compensate appropriately. But even still, if you're running NTP then your UTC time will be correct very shortly after reboot.

The UNIQUE_ID environment variable is constructed by encoding the 112-bit (32-bit IP address, 32 bit pid, 32 bit time stamp, 16 bit counter) quadruple using the alphabet [A-Za-z0-9@-] in a manner similar to MIME base64 encoding, producing 19 characters. The MIME base64 alphabet is actually [A-Za-z0-9+/] however + and / need to be specially encoded in URLs, which makes them less desirable. All values are encoded in network byte ordering so that the encoding is comparable across architectures of different byte ordering. The actual ordering of the encoding is: time stamp, IP address, pid, counter. This ordering has a purpose, but it should be emphasized that applications should not dissect the encoding. Applications should treat the entire encoded UNIQUE_-ID as an opaque token, which can be compared against other UNIQUE_IDs for equality only.

The ordering was chosen such that it's possible to change the encoding in the future without worrying about collision with an existing database of UNIQUE_-IDs. The new encodings should also keep the time stamp as the first element, and can otherwise use the same alphabet and bit length. Since the time stamps are essentially an increasing sequence, it's sufficient to have a *flag second* in which all machines in the cluster stop serving and request, and stop using the old encoding format. Afterwards they can resume requests and begin issuing the new encodings.

This we believe is a relatively portable solution to this problem. It can be extended to multithreaded systems like Windows NT, and can grow with future needs. The identifiers generated have essentially an infinite life-time because future identifiers can be made longer as required. Essentially no communication is required between machines in the cluster (only NTP synchronization is required, which is low overhead), and no communication between httpd processes is required (the communication is implicit in the pid value assigned by the kernel). In very specific situations the identifier can be shortened, but more information needs to be assumed (for example the 32-bit IP address is overkill for any site, but there is no portable shorter replacement for it).

3.75 Apache Module mod_userdir

Description:	User-specific directories
Status:	Base
Module Identifier:	userdir_module
Source File:	mod_userdir.c

Summary

This module allows user-specific directories to be accessed using the
http://example.com/~user/ syntax.

Directives:

> UserDir

See also:

 ▷ Mapping URLs to the Filesystem (p. 75)

 ▷ public_html tutorial (p. 673)

UserDir Directive

Description:	Location of the user-specific directories
Syntax:	UserDir *directory-filename* [*directory-filename*] . . .
Context:	server config, virtual host
Status:	Base
Module:	mod_userdir

The UserDir directive sets the real directory in a user's home directory to use
when a request for a document for a user is received. *Directory-filename* is one
of the following:

- The name of a directory or a pattern such as those shown below.

- The keyword disabled. This turns off *all* username-to-directory translations except those explicitly named with the enabled keyword (see below).

- The keyword disabled followed by a space-delimited list of usernames.
  Usernames that appear in such a list will *never* have directory translation
  performed, even if they appear in an enabled clause.

- The keyword enabled followed by a space-delimited list of usernames.
  These usernames will have directory translation performed even if a global
  disable is in effect, but not if they also appear in a disabled clause.

If neither the enabled nor the disabled keywords appear in the Userdir directive, the argument is treated as a filename pattern, and is used to turn the
name into a directory specification. A request for http://www.example.com/
~bob/one/two.html will be translated to:

UserDir directive used
  ⇒ *Translated path*
UserDir public_html
  ⇒ ~bob/public_html/one/two.html
UserDir /usr/web
  ⇒ /usr/web/bob/one/two.html
UserDir /home/*/www
  ⇒ /home/bob/www/one/two.html

The following directives will send redirects to the client:

UserDir directive used
  ⇒ *Translated path*
UserDir http://www.example.com/users
  ⇒ http://www.example.com/users/bob/one/two.html
UserDir http://www.example.com/*/usr
  ⇒ http://www.example.com/bob/usr/one/two.html
UserDir http://www.example.com/~*/
  ⇒ http://www.example.com/~bob/one/two.html

Be careful when using this directive; for instance, "UserDir ./"
would map "/~root" *to* "/" - *which is probably undesirable.*
It is strongly recommended that your configuration include a
"UserDir disabled root" *declaration. See also the* Directory *di-*
rective and the Security Tips (p. 677) page for more information.

Additional examples:

To allow a few users to have UserDir directories, but not anyone else, use the
following:

```
UserDir disabled
UserDir enabled user1 user2 user3
```

To allow most users to have UserDir directories, but deny this to a few, use the
following:

```
UserDir disabled user4 user5 user6
```

It is also possible to specify alternative user directories. If you use a command
like:

```
Userdir public_html /usr/web http://www.example.com/
```

with a request for http://www.example.com/~bob/one/two.html, it will try to
find the page at ~bob/public_html/one/two.html first, then /usr/web/bob/
one/two.html, and finally it will send a redirect to http://www.example.com/
bob/one/two.html.

If you add a redirect, it must be the last alternative in the list. Apache cannot
determine if the redirect succeeded or not, so if you have the redirect earlier in
the list, that will always be the alternative that is used.

User directory substitution is not active by default in versions 2.1.4 and later. In earlier versions, UserDir public_html was assumed if no UserDir directive was present.

See also:

> ▷ public_html tutorial (p. 673)

3.76 Apache Module mod_usertrack

Description:	*Clickstream* logging of user activity on a site
Status:	Extension
Module Identifier:	usertrack_module
Source File:	mod_usertrack.c

Summary

Previous releases of Apache have included a module which generates a 'click-stream' log of user activity on a site using cookies. This was called the "cookies" module, mod_cookies. In Apache 1.2 and later this module has been renamed the "user tracking" module, mod_usertrack. This module has been simplified and new directives added.

Directives:

> CookieDomain
> CookieExpires
> CookieName
> CookieStyle
> CookieTracking

3.76.1 Logging

Previously, the cookies module (now the user tracking module) did its own logging, using the CookieLog directive. In this release, this module does no logging at all. Instead, a configurable log format file should be used to log user click-streams. This is possible because the logging module now allows multiple log files. The cookie itself is logged by using the text %{cookie}n in the log file format. For example:

> CustomLog logs/clickstream "%{cookie}n %r %t"

For backward compatibility the configurable log module implements the old CookieLog directive, but this should be upgraded to the above CustomLog directive.

3.76.2 2-digit or 4-digit dates for cookies?

(the following is from message <022701bda43d$9d32bbb0$1201a8c0@christian.office.sane.com> in the new-httpd archives)

From: "Christian Allen" <christian@sane.com>
Subject: Re: Apache Y2K bug in mod_usertrack.c
Date: Tue, 30 Jun 1998 11:41:56 -0400

Did some work with cookies and dug up some info that might be useful.

True, Netscape claims that the correct format NOW is four digit
dates, and four digit dates do in fact work... for Netscape 4.x
(Communicator), that is. However, 3.x and below do NOT accept them.
It seems that Netscape originally had a 2-digit standard, and then
with all of the Y2K hype and probably a few complaints, changed to
a four digit date for Communicator. Fortunately, 4.x also
understands the 2-digit format, and so the best way to ensure that
your expiration date is legible to the client's browser is to use
2-digit dates.

However, this does not limit expiration dates to the year 2000; if
you use an expiration year of "13", for example, it is interpreted
as 2013, NOT 1913! In fact, you can use an expiration year of up to
"37", and it will be understood as "2037" by both MSIE and Netscape
versions 3.x and up (not sure about versions previous to those).
Not sure why Netscape used that particular year as its cut-off
point, but my guess is that it was in respect to UNIX's 2038
problem. Netscape/MSIE 4.x seem to be able to understand 2-digit
years beyond that, at least until "50" for sure (I think they
understand up until about "70", but not for sure).

Summary: Mozilla 3.x and up understands two digit dates up until
"37" (2037). Mozilla 4.x understands up until at least "50" (2050)
in 2-digit form, but also understands 4-digit years, which can
probably reach up until 9999. Your best bet for sending a long-life
cookie is to send it for some time late in the year "37".

CookieDomain Directive

Description:	The domain to which the tracking cookie applies
Syntax:	CookieDomain *domain*
Context:	server config, virtual host, directory, .htaccess
Override:	FileInfo
Status:	Extension
Module:	mod_usertrack

This directive controls the setting of the domain to which the tracking cookie
applies. If not present, no domain is included in the cookie header field.

The domain string **must** begin with a dot, and **must** include at least one
embedded dot. That is, .example.com is legal, but foo.example.com and .com
are not.

*Most browsers in use today will not allow cookies to be set for a
two-part top level domain, such as .co.uk, although such a domain
ostensibly fulfills the requirements above.*

These domains are equivalent to top level domains such as .com, *and allowing such cookies may be a security risk. Thus, if you are under a two-part top level domain, you should still use your actual domain, as you would with any other top level domain (for example, use* .foo.co.uk).

CookieExpires Directive

Description:	Expiry time for the tracking cookie
Syntax:	CookieExpires *expiry-period*
Context:	server config, virtual host, directory, .htaccess
Override:	FileInfo
Status:	Extension
Module:	mod_usertrack

When used, this directive sets an expiry time on the cookie generated by the usertrack module. The *expiry-period* can be given either as a number of seconds, or in the format such as "2 weeks 3 days 7 hours". Valid denominations are: years, months, weeks, days, hours, minutes and seconds. If the expiry time is in any format other than one number indicating the number of seconds, it must be enclosed by double quotes.

If this directive is not used, cookies last only for the current browser session.

CookieName Directive

Description:	Name of the tracking cookie
Syntax:	CookieName *token*
Default:	CookieName Apache
Context:	server config, virtual host, directory, .htaccess
Override:	FileInfo
Status:	Extension
Module:	mod_usertrack

This directive allows you to change the name of the cookie this module uses for its tracking purposes. By default the cookie is named "Apache".

You must specify a valid cookie name; results are unpredictable if you use a name containing unusual characters. Valid characters include A-Z, a-z, 0-9, "_", and "-".

CookieStyle Directive

Description:	Format of the cookie header field
Syntax:	CookieStyle *Netscape|Cookie|Cookie2|RFC2109|RFC2965*
Default:	CookieStyle Netscape
Context:	server config, virtual host, directory, .htaccess
Override:	FileInfo
Status:	Extension
Module:	mod_usertrack

This directive controls the format of the cookie header field. The three formats allowed are:

- **Netscape**, which is the original but now deprecated syntax. This is the default, and the syntax Apache has historically used.

- **Cookie** or **RFC2109**, which is the syntax that superseded the Netscape syntax.

- **Cookie2** or **RFC2965**, which is the most current cookie syntax.

Not all clients can understand all of these formats, but you should use the newest one that is generally acceptable to your users' browsers. At the time of writing, most browsers only fully support CookieStyle Netscape.

CookieTracking Directive

Description:	Enables tracking cookie
Syntax:	CookieTracking on|off
Default:	CookieTracking off
Context:	server config, virtual host, directory, .htaccess
Override:	FileInfo
Status:	Extension
Module:	mod_usertrack

When mod_usertrack is loaded, and CookieTracking on is set, Apache will send a user-tracking cookie for all new requests. This directive can be used to turn this behavior on or off on a per-server or per-directory basis. By default, enabling mod_usertrack will **not** activate cookies.

3.77 Apache Module mod_version

Description:	Version dependent configuration
Status:	Extension
Module Identifier:	version_module
Source File:	mod_version.c
Compatibility:	Available in version 2.0.56 and later

Summary

This module is designed for the use in test suites and large networks which have to deal with different httpd versions and different configurations. It provides a new container – <IfVersion>, which allows a flexible version checking including numeric comparisons and regular expressions.

Examples
```
<IfVersion 2.1.0>
    # current httpd version is exactly 2.1.0
</IfVersion>

<IfVersion >= 2.2>
    # use really new features :-)
</IfVersion>
```
See below for further possibilities.

Directives:

    <IfVersion>

IfVersion Directive

Description:	contains version dependent configuration
Syntax:	<IfVersion [[!]operator] version> ... </IfVersion>
Context:	server config, virtual host, directory, .htaccess
Override:	All
Status:	Extension
Module:	mod_version

The <IfVersion> section encloses configuration directives which are executed only if the httpd version matches the desired criteria. For normal (numeric) comparisons the *version* argument has the format *major*[.*minor*[.*patch*]], e.g. 2.1.0 or 2.2. *minor* and *patch* are optional. If these numbers are omitted, they are assumed to be zero. The following numerical *operators* are possible:

operator	description
= or ==	httpd version is equal
>	httpd version is greater than
>=	httpd version is greater or equal
<	httpd version is less than
<=	httpd version is less or equal

Example
```
<IfVersion >= 2.1>
    # this happens only in versions greater or
    # equal 2.1.0.
</IfVersion>
```

Besides the numerical comparison it is possible to match a regular expression against the httpd version. There are two ways to write it:

operator	description
= or ==	*version* has the form */regex/*
~	*version* has the form *regex*

Example
```
<IfVersion = /^2.1.[01234]$/>
    # e.g. workaround for buggy versions
</IfVersion>
```

In order to reverse the meaning, all operators can be preceded by an exclamation mark (!):

```
<IfVersion !~ ^2.1.[01234]$>
    # not for those versions
</IfVersion>
```

If the *operator* is omitted, it is assumed to be =.

3.78 Apache Module mod_vhost_alias

Description:	Provides for dynamically configured mass virtual hosting
Status:	Extension
Module Identifier:	vhost_alias_module
Source File:	mod_vhost_alias.c

Summary

This module creates dynamically configured virtual hosts, by allowing the IP address and/or the Host: header of the HTTP request to be used as part of the pathname to determine what files to serve. This allows for easy use of a huge number of virtual hosts with similar configurations.

> NOTE   If mod_alias or mod_userdir are used for translating URIs to filenames, they will override the directives of mod_vhost_alias described below. For example, the following configuration will map /cgi-bin/script.pl to /usr/local/apache2/cgi-bin/script.pl in all cases:
>
>   ScriptAlias /cgi-bin/ /usr/local/apache2/cgi-bin/
>   VirtualScriptAlias /never/found/%0/cgi-bin/

Directives:

    VirtualDocumentRoot
    VirtualDocumentRootIP
    VirtualScriptAlias
    VirtualScriptAliasIP

See also:

▷ UseCanonicalName (p. 134)

▷ Dynamically configured mass virtual hosting (p. 549)

3.78.1 Directory Name Interpolation

All the directives in this module interpolate a string into a pathname. The interpolated string (henceforth called the "name") may be either the server name (see the UseCanonicalName directive for details on how this is determined) or the IP address of the virtual host on the server in dotted-quad format. The interpolation is controlled by specifiers inspired by printf which have a number of formats:

%%	insert a %
%p	insert the port number of the virtual host
%N.M	insert (part of) the name

N and M are used to specify substrings of the name. N selects from the dot-separated components of the name, and M selects characters within whatever N has selected. M is optional and defaults to zero if it isn't present; the dot must be present if and only if M is present. The interpretation is as follows:

0	the whole name
1	the first part
2	the second part
-1	the last part
-2	the penultimate part
2+	the second and all subsequent parts
-2+	the penultimate and all preceding parts
1+ and -1+	the same as 0

If N or M is greater than the number of parts available a single underscore is interpolated.

3.78.2 Examples

For simple name-based virtual hosts you might use the following directives in your server configuration file:

```
UseCanonicalName Off
VirtualDocumentRoot /usr/local/apache/vhosts/%0
```

A request for http://www.example.com/directory/file.html will be satisfied by the file /usr/local/apache/vhosts/www.example.com/directory/file.html.

For a very large number of virtual hosts it is a good idea to arrange the files to reduce the size of the vhosts directory. To do this you might use the following in your configuration file:

```
UseCanonicalName Off
VirtualDocumentRoot
/usr/local/apache/vhosts/%3+/%2.1/%2.2/%2.3/%2
```

A request for http://www.domain.example.com/directory/file.html will be satisfied by the file /usr/local/apache/vhosts/example.com/d/o/m/domain/directory/file.html.

A more even spread of files can be achieved by hashing from the end of the name, for example:

```
VirtualDocumentRoot
/usr/local/apache/vhosts/%3+/%2.-1/%2.-2/%2.-3/%2
```

The example request would come from /usr/local/apache/vhosts/example.com/n/i/a/domain/directory/file.html.

Alternatively you might use:

```
VirtualDocumentRoot
/usr/local/apache/vhosts/%3+/%2.1/%2.2/%2.3/%2.4+
```

The example request would come from /usr/local/apache/vhosts/
example.com/d/o/m/ain/directory/file.html.

For IP-based virtual hosting you might use the following in your configuration
file:

```
UseCanonicalName DNS
VirtualDocumentRootIP /usr/local/apache/vhosts/%1/%2/%3/%4/docs
VirtualScriptAliasIP
/usr/local/apache/vhosts/%1/%2/%3/%4/cgi-bin
```

A request for http://www.domain.example.com/directory/file.html would
be satisfied by the file /usr/local/apache/vhosts/10/20/30/40/docs/
directory/file.html if the IP address of www.domain.example.com were
10.20.30.40.   A request for http://www.domain.example.com/cgi-bin/
script.pl would be satisfied by executing the program /usr/local/apache/
vhosts/10/20/30/40/cgi-bin/script.pl.

If you want to include the . character in a VirtualDocumentRoot directive, but
it clashes with a % directive, you can work around the problem in the following
way:

```
VirtualDocumentRoot /usr/local/apache/vhosts/%2.0.%3.0
```

A request for http://www.domain.example.com/directory/file.html will be
satisfied by the file /usr/local/apache/vhosts/domain.example/directory/
file.html.

The LogFormat directives %V and %A are useful in conjunction with this module.

VirtualDocumentRoot Directive

Description:	Dynamically configure the location of the document root for a given virtual host
Syntax:	VirtualDocumentRoot *interpolated-directory* |none
Default:	VirtualDocumentRoot none
Context:	server config, virtual host
Status:	Extension
Module:	mod_vhost_alias

The VirtualDocumentRoot directive allows you to determine where Apache will
find your documents based on the value of the server name. The result of
expanding *interpolated-directory* is used as the root of the document tree in
a similar manner to the DocumentRoot directive's argument. If *interpolated-directory* is none then VirtualDocumentRoot is turned off. This directive cannot
be used in the same context as VirtualDocumentRootIP.

VirtualDocumentRootIP Directive

Description:	Dynamically configure the location of the document root for a given virtual host
Syntax:	VirtualDocumentRootIP *interpolated-directory* |none
Default:	VirtualDocumentRootIP none
Context:	server config, virtual host
Status:	Extension
Module:	mod_vhost_alias

The VirtualDocumentRootIP directive is like the VirtualDocumentRoot directive, except that it uses the IP address of the server end of the connection for directory interpolation instead of the server name.

VirtualScriptAlias Directive

Description:	Dynamically configure the location of the CGI directory for a given virtual host
Syntax:	VirtualScriptAlias *interpolated-directory* |none
Default:	VirtualScriptAlias none
Context:	server config, virtual host
Status:	Extension
Module:	mod_vhost_alias

The VirtualScriptAlias directive allows you to determine where Apache will find CGI scripts in a similar manner to VirtualDocumentRoot does for other documents. It matches requests for URIs starting /cgi-bin/, much like ScriptAlias /cgi-bin/ would.

VirtualScriptAliasIP Directive

Description:	Dynamically configure the location of the cgi directory for a given virtual host
Syntax:	VirtualScriptAliasIP *interpolated-directory* |none
Default:	VirtualScriptAliasIP none
Context:	server config, virtual host
Status:	Extension
Module:	mod_vhost_alias

The VirtualScriptAliasIP directive is like the VirtualScriptAlias directive, except that it uses the IP address of the server end of the connection for directory interpolation instead of the server name.

3.79 Apache Module beos

Description:	This Multi-Processing Module is optimized for BeOS.
Status:	MPM
Module Identifier:	mpm_beos_module
Source File:	beos.c

Summary

This Multi-Processing Module (MPM) is the default for BeOS. It uses a single control process which creates threads to handle requests.

Directives:

CoreDumpDirectory (p. 517)   MinSpareThreads (p. 524)
Group (p. 519)   PidFile (p. 524)
Listen (p. 519)   ReceiveBufferSize (p. 525)
ListenBacklog (p. 521)   ScoreBoardFile (p. 525)
MaxClients (p. 522)   SendBufferSize (p. 526)
MaxMemFree (p. 522)   StartThreads (p. 527)
MaxRequestsPerThread   User (p. 529)
MaxSpareThreads (p. 523)

See also:

▷ Setting which addresses and ports Apache uses (p. 701)

MaxRequestsPerThread Directive

Description:	Limit on the number of requests that an individual thread will handle during its life
Syntax:	MaxRequestsPerThread *number*
Default:	MaxRequestsPerThread 0
Context:	server config
Status:	MPM
Module:	beos

The MaxRequestsPerThread directive sets the limit on the number of requests that an individual server thread will handle. After MaxRequestsPerThread requests, the thread will die. If MaxRequestsPerThread is 0, then the thread will never expire.

Setting MaxRequestsPerThread to a non-zero limit has two beneficial effects:

- it limits the amount of memory that a thread can consume by (accidental) memory leakage;
- by giving threads a finite lifetime, it helps reduce the number of threads when the server load reduces.

NOTE: *For KeepAlive requests, only the first request is counted towards this limit. In effect, it changes the behavior to limit the number of connections per thread.*

3.80 Apache Module mpm_common

Description:	A collection of directives that are implemented by more than one multi-processing module (MPM)
Status:	MPM

Directives:

AcceptMutex
ChrootDir
CoreDumpDirectory
EnableExceptionHook
GracefulShutdownTimeout
Group
Listen
ListenBackLog
LockFile
MaxClients
MaxMemFree
MaxRequestsPerChild
MaxSpareThreads

MinSpareThreads
PidFile
ReceiveBufferSize
ScoreBoardFile
SendBufferSize
ServerLimit
StartServers
StartThreads
ThreadLimit
ThreadStackSize
ThreadsPerChild
User

AcceptMutex Directive

Description:	Method that Apache uses to serialize multiple children accepting requests on network sockets
Syntax:	AcceptMutex Default|*method*
Default:	AcceptMutex Default
Context:	server config
Status:	MPM
Module:	prefork, worker

The AcceptMutex directive sets the method that Apache uses to serialize multiple children accepting requests on network sockets. Prior to Apache 2.0, the method was selectable only at compile time. The optimal method to use is highly architecture and platform dependent. For further details, see the performance tuning (p. 727) documentation.

If this directive is set to Default, then the compile-time selected default will be used. Other possible methods are listed below. Note that not all methods are available on all platforms. If a method is specified which is not available, a message will be written to the error log listing the available methods.

flock uses the flock(2) system call to lock the file defined by the LockFile directive.

fcntl uses the fcntl(2) system call to lock the file defined by the LockFile directive.

posixsem uses POSIX compatible semaphores to implement the mutex.

pthread uses POSIX mutexes as implemented by the POSIX Threads (PThreads) specification.

sysvsem uses SySV-style semaphores to implement the mutex.

If you want to find out the compile time chosen default for your system, you may set your LogLevel to debug. Then the default AcceptMutex will be written into the ErrorLog.

> WARNING *On most systems, when the pthread option is selected, if a child process terminates abnormally while holding the AcceptCntl mutex the server will stop responding to requests. When this occurs, the server will require a manual restart to recover.*
>
> *Solaris is a notable exception as it provides a mechanism, used by Apache, which usually allows the mutex to be recovered after a child process terminates abnormally while holding a mutex.*
>
> *If your system implements the pthread_mutexattr_setrobust_np() function, you may be able to use the pthread option safely.*

ChrootDir Directive

Description:	Directory for Apache to run chroot(8) after startup.
Syntax:	ChrootDir /path/to/directory
Default:	none
Context:	server config
Status:	MPM
Module:	event, prefork, worker
Compatibility:	Available in Apache 2.2.10 and later

This directive tells the server to *chroot(8)* to the specified directory after startup, but before accepting requests.

Note that running the server under chroot is not simple, and requires additional setup, particularly if you are running scripts such as CGI or PHP. Please make sure you are properly familiar with the operation of chroot before attempting to use this feature.

CoreDumpDirectory Directive

Description:	Directory where Apache attempts to switch before dumping core
Syntax:	CoreDumpDirectory directory
Default:	See usage for the default setting
Context:	server config
Status:	MPM
Module:	beos, mpm_winnt, prefork, worker

This controls the directory to which Apache attempts to switch before dumping core. The default is in the ServerRoot directory, however since this should not be writable by the user the server runs as, core dumps won't normally get written. If you want a core dump for debugging, you can use this directive to place it in a different location.

> CORE DUMPS ON LINUX *If Apache starts as root and switches to another user, the Linux kernel disables core dumps even if the directory is writable for the process. Apache (2.0.46 and later) reenables core dumps on Linux 2.4 and beyond, but only if you explicitly configure a* CoreDumpDirectory.

EnableExceptionHook Directive

Description:	Enables a hook that runs exception handlers after a crash
Syntax:	EnableExceptionHook On|Off
Default:	EnableExceptionHook Off
Context:	server config
Status:	MPM
Module:	prefork, worker
Compatibility:	Available in version 2.0.49 and later

For safety reasons this directive is only available if the server was configured with the --enable-exception-hook option. It enables a hook that allows external modules to plug in and do something after a child crashed.

There are already two modules, mod_whatkilledus and mod_backtrace that make use of this hook. Please have a look at Jeff Trawick's EnableExceptionHook site[64] for more information about these.

GracefulShutdownTimeout Directive

Description:	Specify a timeout after which a gracefully shutdown server will exit.
Syntax:	GracefulShutDownTimeout *seconds*
Default:	GracefulShutDownTimeout 0
Context:	server config
Status:	MPM
Module:	prefork, worker, event
Compatibility:	Available in version 2.2 and later

The GracefulShutdownTimeout specifies how many seconds after receiving a "graceful-stop" signal, a server should continue to run, handling the existing connections.

Setting this value to zero means that the server will wait indefinitely until all remaining requests have been fully served.

---

[64]http://www.apache.org/~trawick/exception_hook.html

Group Directive

Description:	Group under which the server will answer requests
Syntax:	Group *unix-group*
Default:	Group #-1
Context:	server config
Status:	MPM
Module:	beos, mpmt_os2, prefork, worker
Compatibility:	Only valid in global server config since Apache 2.0

The Group directive sets the group under which the server will answer requests. In order to use this directive, the server must be run initially as root. If you start the server as a non-root user, it will fail to change to the specified group, and will instead continue to run as the group of the original user. *Unix-group* is one of:

A group name Refers to the given group by name.

 # followed by a group number. Refers to a group by its number.

Example

Group www-group

It is recommended that you set up a new group specifically for running the server. Some admins use user nobody, but this is not always possible or desirable.

SECURITY *Don't set Group (or User) to root unless you know exactly what you are doing, and what the dangers are.*

Special note: Use of this directive in <VirtualHost> is no longer supported. To configure your server for suexec use SuexecUserGroup.

NOTE *Although the Group directive is present in the beos and mpmt_os2 MPMs, it is actually a no-op there and only exists for compatibility reasons.*

Listen Directive

Description:	IP addresses and ports that the server listens to
Syntax:	Listen [*IP-address*:]*portnumber* [*protocol*[a]]
Context:	server config
Status:	MPM
Module:	beos, mpm_netware, mpm_winnt, mpmt_os2, prefork, worker, event
Compatibility:	Required directive since Apache 2.0

---

[a]The *protocol* argument was added in 2.1.5

The Listen directive instructs Apache to listen to only specific IP addresses or ports; by default it responds to requests on all IP interfaces. Listen is now a required directive. If it is not in the config file, the server will fail to start. This is a change from previous versions of Apache.

The Listen directive tells the server to accept incoming requests on the specified port or address-and-port combination. If only a port number is specified, the server listens to the given port on all interfaces. If an IP address is given as well as a port, the server will listen on the given port and interface.

Multiple Listen directives may be used to specify a number of addresses and ports to listen to. The server will respond to requests from any of the listed addresses and ports.

For example, to make the server accept connections on both port 80 and port 8000, use:

```
Listen 80
Listen 8000
```

To make the server accept connections on two specified interfaces and port numbers, use

```
Listen 192.170.2.1:80
Listen 192.170.2.5:8000
```

IPv6 addresses must be surrounded in square brackets, as in the following example:

```
Listen [2001:db8::a00:20ff:fea7:ccea]:80
```

The optional *protocol* argument is not required for most configurations. If not specified, https is the default for port 443 and http the default for all other ports. The protocol is used to determine which module should handle a request, and to apply protocol specific optimizations with the AcceptFilter directive.

You only need to set the protocol if you are running on non-standard ports. For example, running an https site on port 8443:

```
Listen 192.170.2.1:8443 https
```

ERROR CONDITION *Multiple Listen directives for the same IP address and port will result in an Address already in use error message.*

See also:

▷ DNS Issues (p. 571)

▷ Setting which addresses and ports Apache uses (p. 701)

ListenBackLog Directive

Description:	Maximum length of the queue of pending connections
Syntax:	ListenBacklog *backlog*
Default:	ListenBacklog 511
Context:	server config
Status:	MPM
Module:	beos, mpm_netware, mpm_winnt, mpmt_os2, prefork, worker

The maximum length of the queue of pending connections. Generally no tuning is needed or desired, however on some systems it is desirable to increase this when under a TCP SYN flood attack. See the backlog parameter to the listen(2) system call.

This will often be limited to a smaller number by the operating system. This varies from OS to OS. Also note that many OSes do not use exactly what is specified as the backlog, but use a number based on (but normally larger than) what is set.

LockFile Directive

Description:	Location of the accept serialization lock file
Syntax:	LockFile *filename*
Default:	LockFile logs/accept.lock
Context:	server config
Status:	MPM
Module:	prefork, worker

The LockFile directive sets the path to the lockfile used when Apache is used with an AcceptMutex value of either fcntl or flock. This directive should normally be left at its default value. The main reason for changing it is if the logs directory is NFS mounted, since **the lockfile must be stored on a local disk**. The PID of the main server process is automatically appended to the filename.

SECURITY *It is best to avoid putting this file in a world writable directory such as /var/tmp because someone could create a denial of service attack and prevent the server from starting by creating a lockfile with the same name as the one the server will try to create.*

See also:

▷ AcceptMutex (p. 516)

MaxClients Directive

Description:	Maximum number of connections that will be processed simultaneously
Syntax:	MaxClients *number*
Default:	See usage for details
Context:	server config
Status:	MPM
Module:	beos, prefork, worker

The MaxClients directive sets the limit on the number of simultaneous requests that will be served. Any connection attempts over the MaxClients limit will normally be queued, up to a number based on the ListenBacklog directive. Once a child process is freed at the end of a different request, the connection will then be serviced.

For non-threaded servers (*i.e.*, prefork), MaxClients translates into the maximum number of child processes that will be launched to serve requests. The default value is 256; to increase it, you must also raise ServerLimit.

For threaded and hybrid servers (*e.g.* beos or worker) MaxClients restricts the total number of threads that will be available to serve clients. The default value for beos is 50. For hybrid MPMs the default value is 16 (ServerLimit) multiplied by the value of 25 (ThreadsPerChild). Therefore, to increase MaxClients to a value that requires more than 16 processes, you must also raise ServerLimit.

MaxMemFree Directive

Description:	Maximum amount of memory that the main allocator is allowed to hold without calling free()
Syntax:	MaxMemFree *KBytes*
Default:	MaxMemFree 0
Context:	server config
Status:	MPM
Module:	beos, mpm_netware, prefork, worker, mpm_winnt

The MaxMemFree directive sets the maximum number of free Kbytes that the main allocator is allowed to hold without calling free(). When not set, or when set to zero, the threshold will be set to unlimited.

MaxRequestsPerChild Directive

Description:	Limit on the number of requests that an individual child server will handle during its life
Syntax:	MaxRequestsPerChild *number*
Default:	MaxRequestsPerChild 10000
Context:	server config
Status:	MPM
Module:	mpm_netware, mpm_winnt, mpmt_os2, prefork, worker

The MaxRequestsPerChild directive sets the limit on the number of requests that an individual child server process will handle. After MaxRequestsPerChild requests, the child process will die. If MaxRequestsPerChild is 0, then the process will never expire.

DIFFERENT DEFAULT VALUES *The default value for mpm_netware and mpm_-winnt is 0.*

Setting MaxRequestsPerChild to a non-zero value limits the amount of memory that process can consume by (accidental) memory leakage.

NOTE *For KeepAlive requests, only the first request is counted towards this limit. In effect, it changes the behavior to limit the number of connections per child.*

MaxSpareThreads Directive

Description:	Maximum number of idle threads
Syntax:	MaxSpareThreads *number*
Default:	See usage for details
Context:	server config
Status:	MPM
Module:	beos, mpm_netware, mpmt_os2, worker

Maximum number of idle threads. Different MPMs deal with this directive differently.

For worker, the default is MaxSpareThreads 250. These MPMs deal with idle threads on a server-wide basis. If there are too many idle threads in the server then child processes are killed until the number of idle threads is less than this number.

For mpm_netware the default is MaxSpareThreads 100. Since this MPM runs a single-process, the spare thread count is also server-wide.

beos and mpmt_os2 work similar to mpm_netware. The default for beos is MaxSpareThreads 50. For mpmt_os2 the default value is 10.

RESTRICTIONS *The range of the MaxSpareThreads value is restricted. Apache will correct the given value automatically according to the following rules:*

- *mpm_netware wants the value to be greater than* MinSpareThreads.
- *For worker the value must be greater or equal than the sum of* MinSpareThreads *and* ThreadsPerChild.

See also:

▷ MinSpareThreads (p. 524)

▷ StartServers (p. 527)

MinSpareThreads Directive

Description:	Minimum number of idle threads available to handle request spikes
Syntax:	MinSpareThreads number
Default:	See usage for details
Context:	server config
Status:	MPM
Module:	beos, mpm_netware, mpmt_os2, worker

Minimum number of idle threads to handle request spikes. Different MPMs deal with this directive differently.

worker uses a default of MinSpareThreads 75 and deals with idle threads on a server-wide basis. If there aren't enough idle threads in the server then child processes are created until the number of idle threads is greater than number.

mpm_netware uses a default of MinSpareThreads 10 and, since it is a single-process MPM, tracks this on a server-wide bases.

beos and mpmt_os2 work similar to mpm_netware. The default for beos is MinSpareThreads 1. For mpmt_os2 the default value is 5.

See also:

▷ MaxSpareThreads (p. 523)

▷ StartServers (p. 527)

PidFile Directive

Description:	File where the server records the process ID of the daemon
Syntax:	PidFile filename
Default:	PidFile logs/httpd.pid
Context:	server config
Status:	MPM
Module:	beos, mpm_winnt, mpmt_os2, prefork, worker

The PidFile directive sets the file to which the server records the process id of the daemon. If the filename is not absolute then it is assumed to be relative to the ServerRoot.

Example
```
PidFile /var/run/apache.pid
```

It is often useful to be able to send the server a signal, so that it closes and then re-opens its ErrorLog and TransferLog, and re-reads its configuration files. This is done by sending a SIGHUP (kill -1) signal to the process id listed in the PidFile.

The PidFile is subject to the same warnings about log file placement and security (p. 677).

NOTE *As of Apache 2 it is recommended to use only the apachectl script for (re-)starting or stopping the server.*

ReceiveBufferSize Directive

Description:	TCP receive buffer size
Syntax:	ReceiveBufferSize *bytes*
Default:	ReceiveBufferSize 0
Context:	server config
Status:	MPM
Module:	beos, mpm_netware, mpm_winnt, mpmt_os2, prefork, worker

The server will set the TCP receive buffer size to the number of bytes specified.

If set to the value of 0, the server will use the OS default.

ScoreBoardFile Directive

Description:	Location of the file used to store coordination data for the child processes
Syntax:	ScoreBoardFile *file-path*
Default:	ScoreBoardFile logs/apache_status
Context:	server config
Status:	MPM
Module:	beos, mpm_winnt, prefork, worker

Apache uses a scoreboard to communicate between its parent and child processes. Some architectures require a file to facilitate this communication. If the file is left unspecified, Apache first attempts to create the scoreboard entirely in memory (using anonymous shared memory) and, failing that, will attempt to create the file on disk (using file-based shared memory). Specifying this directive causes Apache to always create the file on the disk.

Example
```
ScoreBoardFile /var/run/apache_status
```

File-based shared memory is useful for third-party applications that require direct access to the scoreboard.

If you use a ScoreBoardFile then you may see improved speed by placing it on a RAM disk. But be careful that you heed the same warnings about log file placement and security (p. 677).

See also:

▷ Stopping and Restarting Apache (p. 51)

SendBufferSize Directive

Description:	TCP buffer size
Syntax:	SendBufferSize *bytes*
Default:	SendBufferSize 0
Context:	server config
Status:	MPM
Module:	beos, mpm_netware, mpm_winnt, mpmt_os2, prefork, worker

The server will set the TCP send buffer size to the number of bytes specified. Very useful to increase past standard OS defaults on high speed high latency (*i.e.*, 100ms or so, such as transcontinental fast pipes).

If set to the value of 0, the server will use the OS default.

ServerLimit Directive

Description:	Upper limit on configurable number of processes
Syntax:	ServerLimit *number*
Default:	See usage for details
Context:	server config
Status:	MPM
Module:	prefork, worker

For the prefork MPM, this directive sets the maximum configured value for MaxClients for the lifetime of the Apache process. For the worker MPM, this directive in combination with ThreadLimit sets the maximum configured value for MaxClients for the lifetime of the Apache process. Any attempts to change this directive during a restart will be ignored, but MaxClients can be modified during a restart.

Special care must be taken when using this directive. If ServerLimit is set to a value much higher than necessary, extra, unused shared memory will be allocated. If both ServerLimit and MaxClients are set to values higher than the system can handle, Apache may not start or the system may become unstable.

With the prefork MPM, use this directive only if you need to set MaxClients higher than 256 (default). Do not set the value of this directive any higher than what you might want to set MaxClients to.

With worker use this directive only if your MaxClients and ThreadsPerChild settings require more than 16 server processes (default). Do not set the value of this directive any higher than the number of server processes required by what you may want for MaxClients and ThreadsPerChild.

NOTE *There is a hard limit of ServerLimit 20000 compiled into the server (for the prefork MPM 200000). This is intended to avoid nasty effects caused by typos.*

See also:

▷ Stopping and Restarting Apache (p. 51)

StartServers Directive

Description:	Number of child server processes created at startup
Syntax:	StartServers *number*
Default:	See usage for details
Context:	server config
Status:	MPM
Module:	mpmt_os2, prefork, worker

The StartServers directive sets the number of child server processes created on startup. As the number of processes is dynamically controlled depending on the load, there is usually little reason to adjust this parameter.

The default value differs from MPM to MPM. For worker the default is StartServers 3. For prefork defaults to 5 and for mpmt_os2 to 2.

StartThreads Directive

Description:	Number of threads created on startup
Syntax:	StartThreads *number*
Default:	See usage for details
Context:	server config
Status:	MPM
Module:	beos, mpm_netware

Number of threads created on startup. As the number of threads is dynamically controlled depending on the load, there is usually little reason to adjust this parameter.

For mpm_netware the default is StartThreads 50 and, since there is only a single process, this is the total number of threads created at startup to serve requests.

For beos the default is StartThreads 10. It also reflects the total number of threads created at startup to serve requests.

ThreadLimit Directive

Description:	Sets the upper limit on the configurable number of threads per child process
Syntax:	ThreadLimit *number*
Default:	See usage for details
Context:	server config
Status:	MPM
Module:	mpm_winnt, worker
Compatibility:	Available for mpm_winnt in Apache 2.0.41 and later

This directive sets the maximum configured value for ThreadsPerChild for the lifetime of the Apache process. Any attempts to change this directive during a restart will be ignored, but ThreadsPerChild can be modified during a restart up to the value of this directive.

Special care must be taken when using this directive. If ThreadLimit is set to a value much higher than ThreadsPerChild, extra unused shared memory will be allocated. If both ThreadLimit and ThreadsPerChild are set to values higher than the system can handle, Apache may not start or the system may become unstable. Do not set the value of this directive any higher than your greatest predicted setting of ThreadsPerChild for the current run of Apache.

The default value for ThreadLimit is 1920 when used with mpm_winnt and 64 when used with the others.

> NOTE   *There is a hard limit of ThreadLimit 20000 (or ThreadLimit 15000 with mpm_winnt) compiled into the server. This is intended to avoid nasty effects caused by typos.*

ThreadStackSize Directive

Description:	The size in bytes of the stack used by threads handling client connections
Syntax:	ThreadStackSize *size*
Default:	65536 on NetWare; varies on other operating systems
Context:	server config
Status:	MPM
Module:	mpm_netware, mpm_winnt, worker, event
Compatibility:	Available in Apache 2.1 and later

The ThreadStackSize directive sets the size of the stack (for autodata) of threads which handle client connections and call modules to help process those connections. In most cases the operating system default for stack size is reasonable, but there are some conditions where it may need to be adjusted:

- On platforms with a relatively small default thread stack size (e.g., HP-UX), Apache may crash when using some third-party modules which use a relatively large amount of autodata storage. Those same modules may have worked fine on other platforms where the default thread stack size is larger. This type of crash is resolved by setting `ThreadStackSize` to a value higher than the operating system default. This type of adjustment is necessary only if the provider of the third-party module specifies that it is required, or if diagnosis of an Apache crash indicates that the thread stack size was too small.

- On platforms where the default thread stack size is significantly larger than necessary for the web server configuration, a higher number of threads per child process will be achievable if `ThreadStackSize` is set to a value lower than the operating system default. This type of adjustment should only be made in a test environment which allows the full set of web server processing to be exercised, as there may be infrequent requests which require more stack to process. The minumum required stack size strongly depends on the modules used, but any change in the web server configuration can invalidate the current `ThreadStackSize` setting.

It is recommended to not reduce ThreadStackSize unless a high number of threads per child process is needed. On some platforms (including Linux), a setting of 128000 is already too low and causes crashes with some common modules.

ThreadsPerChild Directive

Description:	Number of threads created by each child process
Syntax:	`ThreadsPerChild number`
Default:	`See usage for details`
Context:	server config
Status:	MPM
Module:	`mpm_winnt, worker`

This directive sets the number of threads created by each child process. The child creates these threads at startup and never creates more. If using an MPM like mpm_winnt, where there is only one child process, this number should be high enough to handle the entire load of the server. If using an MPM like worker, where there are multiple child processes, the *total* number of threads should be high enough to handle the common load on the server.

The default value for ThreadsPerChild is 64 when used with mpm_winnt and 25 when used with the others.

User Directive

Description:	The userid under which the server will answer requests
Syntax:	`User unix-userid`
Default:	`User #-1`
Context:	server config
Status:	MPM
Module:	prefork, worker
Compatibility:	Only valid in global server config since Apache 2.0

The User directive sets the user ID as which the server will answer requests. In order to use this directive, the server must be run initially as root. If you start the server as a non-root user, it will fail to change to the lesser privileged user, and will instead continue to run as that original user. If you do start the server as root, then it is normal for the parent process to remain running as root. *Unix-userid* is one of:

A username Refers to the given user by name.

 # followed by a user number. Refers to a user by its number.

The user should have no privileges that result in it being able to access files that are not intended to be visible to the outside world, and similarly, the user should not be able to execute code that is not meant for HTTP requests. It is recommended that you set up a new user and group specifically for running the server. Some admins use user nobody, but this is not always desirable, since the nobody user can have other uses on the system.

> SECURITY *Don't set User (or Group) to root unless you know exactly what you are doing, and what the dangers are.*

Special note: Use of this directive in <VirtualHost> is no longer supported. To configure your server for suexec use SuexecUserGroup.

> NOTE *Although the User directive is present in the beos and mpmt_os2 MPMs, it is actually a no-op there and only exists for compatibility reasons.*

3.81 Apache Module event

Description:	An experimental variant of the standard worker MPM
Status:	MPM
Module Identifier:	mpm_event_module
Source File:	event.c

Summary

WARNING   *This MPM is experimental, so it may or may not work as expected.*

The event Multi-Processing Module (MPM) is designed to allow more requests to be served simultaneously by passing off some processing work to supporting threads, freeing up the main threads to work on new requests. It is based on the worker MPM, which implements a hybrid multi-process multi-threaded server. Run-time configuration directives are identical to those provided by worker.

To use the event MPM, add --with-mpm=event to the configure script's arguments when building the httpd.

Directives:

AcceptMutex (p. 516)
CoreDumpDirectory (p. 517)
EnableExceptionHook (p. 518)
Group (p. 519)
Listen (p. 519)
ListenBacklog (p. 521)
LockFile (p. 521)
MaxClients (p. 522)
MaxMemFree (p. 522)
MaxRequestsPerChild (p. 523)
MaxSpareThreads (p. 523)

MinSpareThreads (p. 524)
PidFile (p. 524)
ScoreBoardFile (p. 525)
SendBufferSize (p. 526)
ServerLimit (p. 526)
StartServers (p. 527)
ThreadLimit (p. 528)
ThreadStackSize (p. 528)
ThreadsPerChild (p. 529)
User (p. 529)

See also:

▷ The worker MPM (p. 537)

3.81.1 How it Works

This MPM tries to fix the 'keep alive problem' in HTTP. After a client completes the first request, the client can keep the connection open, and send further requests using the same socket. This can save signifigant overhead in creating TCP connections. However, Apache traditionally keeps an entire child process/thread waiting for data from the client, which brings its own disadvantages. To solve this problem, this MPM uses a dedicated thread to handle both the Listening sockets, and all sockets that are in a Keep Alive state.

The MPM assumes that the underlying apr_pollset implementation is reasonably threadsafe. This enables the MPM to avoid excessive high level locking, or having to wake up the listener thread in order to send it a keep-alive socket. This is currently only compatible with KQueue and EPoll.

3.81.2 Requirements

This MPM depends on APR's atomic compare-and-swap operations for thread synchronization. If you are compiling for an x86 target and you don't need to support 386s, or you are compiling for a SPARC and you don't need to run on pre-UltraSPARC chips, add --enable-nonportable-atomics=yes to the configure script's arguments. This will cause APR to implement atomic operations using efficient opcodes not available in older CPUs.

This MPM does not perform well on older platforms which lack good threading, but the requirement for EPoll or KQueue makes this moot.

- To use this MPM on FreeBSD, FreeBSD 5.3 or higher is recommended. However, it is possible to run this MPM on FreeBSD 5.2.1, if you use libkse (see man libmap.conf).

- For NetBSD, at least version 2.0 is recommended.

- For Linux, a 2.6 kernel is recommended. It is also necessary to ensure that your version of glibc has been compiled with support for EPoll.

3.82 Apache Module prefork

Description:	Implements a non-threaded, pre-forking web server
Status:	MPM
Module Identifier:	mpm_prefork_module
Source File:	prefork.c

Summary

This Multi-Processing Module (MPM) implements a non-threaded, pre-forking web server that handles requests in a manner similar to Apache 1.3. It is appropriate for sites that need to avoid threading for compatibility with non-thread-safe libraries. It is also the best MPM for isolating each request, so that a problem with a single request will not affect any other.

This MPM is very self-regulating, so it is rarely necessary to adjust its configuration directives. Most important is that MaxClients be big enough to handle as many simultaneous requests as you expect to receive, but small enough to assure that there is enough physical RAM for all processes.

Directives:

AcceptMutex (p. 516)   MaxSpareServers
CoreDumpDirectory (p. 517)   MinSpareServers
EnableExceptionHook (p. 518) PidFile (p. 524)
Group (p. 519)   ReceiveBufferSize (p. 525)
Listen (p. 519)   ScoreBoardFile (p. 525)
ListenBacklog (p. 521)   SendBufferSize (p. 526)
LockFile (p. 521)   ServerLimit (p. 526)
MaxClients (p. 522)   StartServers (p. 527)
MaxMemFree (p. 522)   User (p. 529)
MaxRequestsPerChild (p. 523)

See also:

▷ Setting which addresses and ports Apache uses (p. 701)

3.82.1 How it Works

A single control process is responsible for launching child processes which listen for connections and serve them when they arrive. Apache always tries to maintain several **spare** or idle server processes, which stand ready to serve incoming requests. In this way, clients do not need to wait for a new child processes to be forked before their requests can be served.

The StartServers, MinSpareServers, MaxSpareServers, and MaxClients regulate how the parent process creates children to serve requests. In general, Apache is very self-regulating, so most sites do not need to adjust these directives from their default values. Sites which need to serve more than 256 simultaneous requests may need to increase MaxClients, while sites with limited memory may need to decrease MaxClients to keep the server from thrashing (swapping memory to disk and back). More information about tuning process creation is provided in the performance hints (p. 727) documentation.

While the parent process is usually started as root under Unix in order to bind to port 80, the child processes are launched by Apache as a less-privileged user. The User and Group directives are used to set the privileges of the Apache child processes. The child processes must be able to read all the content that will be served, but should have as few privileges beyond that as possible.

MaxRequestsPerChild controls how frequently the server recycles processes by killing old ones and launching new ones.

MaxSpareServers Directive

Description:	Maximum number of idle child server processes
Syntax:	MaxSpareServers *number*
Default:	MaxSpareServers 10
Context:	server config
Status:	MPM
Module:	prefork

The MaxSpareServers directive sets the desired maximum number of *idle* child server processes. An idle process is one which is not handling a request. If there are more than MaxSpareServers idle, then the parent process will kill off the excess processes.

Tuning of this parameter should only be necessary on very busy sites. Setting this parameter to a large number is almost always a bad idea. If you are trying to set the value equal to or lower than MinSpareServers, Apache will automatically adjust it to MinSpareServers + 1.

See also:

▷ MinSpareServers (p. 534)

▷ StartServers (p. 527)

MinSpareServers Directive

Description:	Minimum number of idle child server processes
Syntax:	MinSpareServers *number*
Default:	MinSpareServers 5
Context:	server config
Status:	MPM
Module:	prefork

The MinSpareServers directive sets the desired minimum number of *idle* child server processes. An idle process is one which is not handling a request. If there are fewer than `MinSpareServers` idle, then the parent process creates new children at a maximum rate of 1 per second.

Tuning of this parameter should only be necessary on very busy sites. Setting this parameter to a large number is almost always a bad idea.

See also:

> ▷ MaxSpareServers (p. 534)
> ▷ StartServers (p. 527)

3.83 Apache Module mpm_winnt

Description:	This Multi-Processing Module is optimized for Windows NT.
Status:	MPM
Module Identifier:	mpm_winnt_module
Source File:	mpm_winnt.c

Summary

This Multi-Processing Module (MPM) is the default for the Windows NT operating systems. It uses a single control process which launches a single child process which in turn creates threads to handle requests

Directives:

CoreDumpDirectory (p. 517)   ScoreBoardFile (p. 525)
Listen (p. 519)   SendBufferSize (p. 526)
ListenBacklog (p. 521)   ThreadLimit (p. 528)
MaxMemFree (p. 522)   ThreadStackSize (p. 528)
MaxRequestsPerChild (p. 523)   ThreadsPerChild (p. 529)
PidFile (p. 524)   Win32DisableAcceptEx
ReceiveBufferSize (p. 525)

Win32DisableAcceptEx Directive

Description:	Use accept() rather than AcceptEx() to accept network connections
Syntax:	Win32DisableAcceptEx
Default:	AcceptEx() is enabled by default. Use this directive to disable use of AcceptEx()
Context:	server config
Status:	MPM
Module:	mpm_winnt
Compatibility:	Available in Version 2.0.49 and later

AcceptEx() is a Microsoft WinSock v2 API that provides some performance improvements over the use of the BSD style accept() API in certain circumstances. Some popular Windows products, typically virus scanning or virtual private network packages, have bugs that interfere with the proper operation of AcceptEx(). If you encounter an error condition like:

    [error] (730038)An operation was attempted on something that is
    not a socket.: winnt_accept: AcceptEx failed. Attempting to
    recover.

you should use this directive to disable the use of AcceptEx().

3.84 Apache Module worker

Description:	Multi-Processing Module implementing a hybrid multi-threaded multi-process web server
Status:	MPM
Module Identifier:	mpm_worker_module
Source File:	worker.c

Summary

This Multi-Processing Module (MPM) implements a hybrid multi-process multi-threaded server. By using threads to serve requests, it is able to serve a large number of requests with fewer system resources than a process-based server. However, it retains much of the stability of a process-based server by keeping multiple processes available, each with many threads.

The most important directives used to control this MPM are ThreadsPerChild, which controls the number of threads deployed by each child process and MaxClients, which controls the maximum total number of threads that may be launched.

Directives:

AcceptMutex (p. 516)	MinSpareThreads (p. 524)
CoreDumpDirectory (p. 517)	PidFile (p. 524)
EnableExceptionHook (p. 518)	ReceiveBufferSize (p. 525)
Group (p. 519)	ScoreBoardFile (p. 525)
Listen (p. 519)	SendBufferSize (p. 526)
ListenBacklog (p. 521)	ServerLimit (p. 526)
LockFile (p. 521)	StartServers (p. 527)
MaxClients (p. 522)	ThreadLimit (p. 528)
MaxMemFree (p. 522)	ThreadStackSize (p. 528)
MaxRequestsPerChild (p. 523)	ThreadsPerChild (p. 529)
MaxSpareThreads (p. 523)	User (p. 529)

See also:

▷ Setting which addresses and ports Apache uses (p. 701)

3.84.1 How it Works

A single control process (the parent) is responsible for launching child processes. Each child process creates a fixed number of server threads as specified in the ThreadsPerChild directive, as well as a listener thread which listens for connections and passes them to a server thread for processing when they arrive.

Apache always tries to maintain a pool of **spare** or idle server threads, which stand ready to serve incoming requests. In this way, clients do not need to wait for new threads or processes to be created before their requests can be served.

The number of processes that will initially launched is set by the StartServers directive. During operation, Apache assesses the total number of idle threads in all processes, and forks or kills processes to keep this number within the boundaries specified by MinSpareThreads and MaxSpareThreads. Since this process is very self-regulating, it is rarely necessary to modify these directives from their default values. The maximum number of clients that may be served simultaneously (i.e., the maximum total number of threads in all processes) is determined by the MaxClients directive. The maximum number of active child processes is determined by the MaxClients directive divided by the ThreadsPerChild directive.

Two directives set hard limits on the number of active child processes and the number of server threads in a child process, and can only be changed by fully stopping the server and then starting it again. ServerLimit is a hard limit on the number of active child processes, and must be greater than or equal to the MaxClients directive divided by the ThreadsPerChild directive. ThreadLimit is a hard limit of the number of server threads, and must be greater than or equal to the ThreadsPerChild directive. If non-default values are specified for these directives, they should appear before other worker directives.

In addition to the set of active child processes, there may be additional child processes which are terminating, but where at least one server thread is still handling an existing client connection. Up to MaxClients terminating processes may be present, though the actual number can be expected to be much smaller. This behavior can be avoided by disabling the termination of individual child processes, which is achieved using the following:

- set the value of MaxRequestsPerChild to zero
- set the value of MaxSpareThreads to the same value as MaxClients

A typical configuration of the process-thread controls in the worker MPM could look as follows:

```
ServerLimit 16
StartServers 2
MaxClients 150
MinSpareThreads 25
MaxSpareThreads 75
ThreadsPerChild 25
```

While the parent process is usually started as root under Unix in order to bind to port 80, the child processes and threads are launched by Apache as a less-privileged user. The User and Group directives are used to set the privileges of the Apache child processes. The child processes must be able to read all the content that will be served, but should have as few privileges beyond that as possible. In addition, unless suexec is used, these directives also set the privileges which will be inherited by CGI scripts.

MaxRequestsPerChild controls how frequently the server recycles processes by killing old ones and launching new ones.

4 Apache Virtual Host documentation

4.1 Apache Virtual Host documentation

The term Virtual Host refers to the practice of running more than one web site (such as www.company1.com and www.company2.com) on a single machine. Virtual hosts can be "IP-based (p. 547)", meaning that you have a different IP address for every web site, or "name-based (p. 543)", meaning that you have multiple names running on each IP address. The fact that they are running on the same physical server is not apparent to the end user.

Apache was one of the first servers to support IP-based virtual hosts right out of the box. Versions 1.1 and later of Apache support both IP-based and name-based virtual hosts (vhosts). The latter variant of virtual hosts is sometimes also called *host-based* or *non-IP virtual hosts*.

Below is a list of documentation pages which explain all details of virtual host support in Apache version 1.3 and later.

See also:

> ▷ mod_vhost_alias (p. 510)
> ▷ Name-based virtual hosts (p. 543)
> ▷ IP-based virtual hosts (p. 547)
> ▷ Virtual host examples (p. 555)
> ▷ File descriptor limits (p. 569)
> ▷ Mass virtual hosting (p. 549)
> ▷ Details of host matching (p. 563)

4.1.1 Virtual Host Support

- Name-based Virtual Hosts (p. 543) (More than one web site per IP address)
- IP-based Virtual Hosts (p. 547) (An IP address for each web site)
- Virtual Host examples for common setups (p. 555)
- File Descriptor Limits (p. 569) (or, *Too many log files*)
- Dynamically Configured Mass Virtual Hosting (p. 549)
- In-Depth Discussion of Virtual Host Matching (p. 563)

4.1.2 Configuration directives

- <VirtualHost>
- NameVirtualHost

- ServerName

- ServerAlias

- ServerPath

If you are trying to debug your virtual host configuration, you may find the Apache -S command line switch useful. That is, type the following command:

```
/usr/local/apache2/bin/httpd -S
```

This command will dump out a description of how Apache parsed the configuration file. Careful examination of the IP addresses and server names may help uncover configuration mistakes. (See the docs for the httpd program for other command line options.)

4.2 Name-based Virtual Host Support

This section describes when and how to use name-based virtual hosts.

See also:

- ▷ IP-based Virtual Host Support (p. 547)
- ▷ An In-Depth Discussion of Virtual Host Matching (p. 563)
- ▷ Dynamically configured mass virtual hosting (p. 549)
- ▷ Virtual Host examples for common setups (p. 555)
- ▷ ServerPath configuration example (p. 555)

4.2.1 Name-based vs. IP-based Virtual Hosts

IP-based virtual hosts use the IP address of the connection to determine the correct virtual host to serve. Therefore you need to have a separate IP address for each host. With name-based virtual hosting, the server relies on the client to report the hostname as part of the HTTP headers. Using this technique, many different hosts can share the same IP address.

Name-based virtual hosting is usually simpler, since you need only configure your DNS server to map each hostname to the correct IP address and then configure the Apache HTTP Server to recognize the different hostnames. Name-based virtual hosting also eases the demand for scarce IP addresses. Therefore you should use name-based virtual hosting unless there is a specific reason to choose IP-based virtual hosting. Some reasons why you might consider using IP-based virtual hosting:

- Some ancient clients are not compatible with name-based virtual hosting. For name-based virtual hosting to work, the client must send the HTTP Host header. This is required by HTTP/1.1, and is implemented by all modern HTTP/1.0 browsers as an extension. If you need to support obsolete clients and still use name-based virtual hosting, a possible technique is discussed at the end of this document.

- Name-based virtual hosting cannot be used with SSL secure servers because of the nature of the SSL protocol.

- Some operating systems and network equipment implement bandwidth management techniques that cannot differentiate between hosts unless they are on separate IP addresses.

4.2.2 Using Name-based Virtual Hosts

Related Modules	Related Directives
core	DocumentRoot
	NameVirtualHost
	ServerAlias
	ServerName
	ServerPath
	<VirtualHost>

To use name-based virtual hosting, you must designate the IP address (and possibly port) on the server that will be accepting requests for the hosts. This is configured using the NameVirtualHost directive. In the normal case where any and all IP addresses on the server should be used, you can use * as the argument to NameVirtualHost. If you're planning to use multiple ports (e.g. running SSL) you should add a Port to the argument, such as *:80. Note that mentioning an IP address in a NameVirtualHost directive does not automatically make the server listen to that IP address. See Setting which addresses and ports Apache uses (p. 701) for more details. In addition, any IP address specified here must be associated with a network interface on the server.

The next step is to create a <VirtualHost> block for each different host that you would like to serve. The argument to the <VirtualHost> directive must match a defined NameVirtualHost directive. (In this usual case, this will be "*:80"). Inside each <VirtualHost> block, you will need at minimum a ServerName directive to designate which host is served and a DocumentRoot directive to show where in the filesystem the content for that host lives.

> MAIN HOST GOES AWAY *If you are adding virtual hosts to an existing web server, you must also create a <VirtualHost> block for the existing host. The ServerName and DocumentRoot included in this virtual host should be the same as the global ServerName and DocumentRoot. List this virtual host first in the configuration file so that it will act as the default host.*

For example, suppose that you are serving the domain www.domain.tld and you wish to add the virtual host www.otherdomain.tld, which points at the same IP address. Then you simply add the following to httpd.conf:

```
NameVirtualHost *:80

<VirtualHost *:80>
    ServerName www.domain.tld
    ServerAlias domain.tld *.domain.tld
    DocumentRoot /www/domain
</VirtualHost>

<VirtualHost *:80>
    ServerName www.otherdomain.tld
```

```
    DocumentRoot /www/otherdomain
</VirtualHost>
```

You can alternatively specify an explicit IP address in place of the * in both the NameVirtualHost and <VirtualHost> directives. For example, you might want to do this in order to run some name-based virtual hosts on one IP address, and either IP-based, or another set of name-based virtual hosts on another address.

Many servers want to be accessible by more than one name. This is possible with the ServerAlias directive, placed inside the <VirtualHost> section. For example in the first <VirtualHost> block above, the ServerAlias directive indicates that the listed names are other names which people can use to see that same web site:

```
    ServerAlias domain.tld *.domain.tld
```

then requests for all hosts in the domain.tld domain will be served by the www.domain.tld virtual host. The wildcard characters * and ? can be used to match names. Of course, you can't just make up names and place them in ServerName or ServerAlias. You must first have your DNS server properly configured to map those names to an IP address associated with your server.

Finally, you can fine-tune the configuration of the virtual hosts by placing other directives inside the <VirtualHost> containers. Most directives can be placed in these containers and will then change the configuration only of the relevant virtual host. To find out if a particular directive is allowed, check the Context (p. 83) of the directive. Configuration directives set in the *main server context* (outside any <VirtualHost> container) will be used only if they are not overridden by the virtual host settings.

Now when a request arrives, the server will first check if it is using an IP address that matches the NameVirtualHost. If it is, then it will look at each <VirtualHost> section with a matching IP address and try to find one where the ServerName or ServerAlias matches the requested hostname. If it finds one, then it uses the configuration for that server. If no matching virtual host is found, then **the first listed virtual host** that matches the IP address will be used.

As a consequence, the first listed virtual host is the *default* virtual host. The DocumentRoot from the *main server* will **never** be used when an IP address matches the NameVirtualHost directive. If you would like to have a special configuration for requests that do not match any particular virtual host, simply put that configuration in a <VirtualHost> container and list it first in the configuration file.

4.2.3 Compatibility with Older Browsers

As mentioned earlier, there are some clients who do not send the required data for the name-based virtual hosts to work properly. These clients will always be sent the pages from the first virtual host listed for that IP address (the primary name-based virtual host).

HOW MUCH OLDER? *Please note that when we say older, we really do mean older. You are very unlikely to encounter one of these browsers in use today. All current versions of any browser send the Host header as required for name-based virtual hosts.*

There is a possible workaround with the ServerPath directive, albeit a slightly cumbersome one:

Example configuration:

```
NameVirtualHost 111.22.33.44

<VirtualHost 111.22.33.44>
    ServerName www.domain.tld
    ServerPath /domain
    DocumentRoot /web/domain
</VirtualHost>
```

What does this mean? It means that a request for any URI beginning with "/domain" will be served from the virtual host www.domain.tld. This means that the pages can be accessed as http://www.domain.tld/domain/ for all clients, although clients sending a Host: header can also access it as http://www.domain.tld/.

In order to make this work, put a link on your primary virtual host's page to http://www.domain.tld/domain/. Then, in the virtual host's pages, be sure to use either purely relative links (*e.g.*, "file.html" or "../icons/image.gif") or links containing the prefacing /domain/ (*e.g.*, "http://www.domain.tld/domain/misc/file.html" or "/domain/misc/file.html").

This requires a bit of discipline, but adherence to these guidelines will, for the most part, ensure that your pages will work with all browsers, new and old.

4.3 Apache IP-based Virtual Host Support

See also:

▷ Name-based Virtual Hosts Support (p. 543)

4.3.1 System requirements

As the term IP-based indicates, the server **must have a different IP address for each IP-based virtual host.** This can be achieved by the machine having several physical network connections, or by use of virtual interfaces which are supported by most modern operating systems (see system documentation for details, these are frequently called "IP aliases", and the "ifconfig" command is most commonly used to set them up).

4.3.2 How to set up Apache

There are two ways of configuring apache to support multiple hosts. Either by running a separate httpd daemon for each hostname, or by running a single daemon which supports all the virtual hosts.

Use multiple daemons when:

- There are security partitioning issues, such as company1 does not want anyone at company2 to be able to read their data except via the web. In this case you would need two daemons, each running with different User, Group, Listen, and ServerRoot settings.
- You can afford the memory and file descriptor requirements of listening to every IP alias on the machine. It's only possible to Listen to the "wildcard" address, or to specific addresses. So if you have a need to listen to a specific address for whatever reason, then you will need to listen to all specific addresses. (Although one httpd could listen to N-1 of the addresses, and another could listen to the remaining address.)

Use a single daemon when:

- Sharing of the httpd configuration between virtual hosts is acceptable.
- The machine services a large number of requests, and so the performance loss in running separate daemons may be significant.

4.3.3 Setting up multiple daemons

Create a separate httpd installation for each virtual host. For each installation, use the Listen directive in the configuration file to select which IP address (or virtual host) that daemon services. e.g.

```
Listen www.smallco.com:80
```

It is recommended that you use an IP address instead of a hostname (see DNS caveats (p. 571)).

4.3.4 Setting up a single daemon with virtual hosts

For this case, a single httpd will service requests for the main server and all the virtual hosts. The VirtualHost directive in the configuration file is used to set the values of ServerAdmin, ServerName, DocumentRoot, ErrorLog and TransferLog or CustomLog configuration directives to different values for each virtual host. e.g.

```
<VirtualHost www.smallco.com>
ServerAdmin webmaster@mail.smallco.com
DocumentRoot /groups/smallco/www
ServerName www.smallco.com
ErrorLog /groups/smallco/logs/error_log
TransferLog /groups/smallco/logs/access_log
</VirtualHost>

<VirtualHost www.baygroup.org>
ServerAdmin webmaster@mail.baygroup.org
DocumentRoot /groups/baygroup/www
ServerName www.baygroup.org
ErrorLog /groups/baygroup/logs/error_log
TransferLog /groups/baygroup/logs/access_log
</VirtualHost>
```

It is recommended that you use an IP address instead of a hostname (see DNS caveats (p. 571)).

Almost **any** configuration directive can be put in the VirtualHost directive, with the exception of directives that control process creation and a few other directives. To find out if a directive can be used in the VirtualHost directive, check the Context (p. 83) using the directive index (p. 805).

SuexecUserGroup may be used inside a VirtualHost directive if the suEXEC wrapper (p. 719) is used.

SECURITY: When specifying where to write log files, be aware of some security risks which are present if anyone other than the user that starts Apache has write access to the directory where they are written. See the security tips (p. 677) document for details.

4.4 Dynamically configured mass virtual hosting

This section describes how to efficiently serve an arbitrary number of virtual hosts with Apache.

4.4.1 Motivation

The techniques described here are of interest if your httpd.conf contains many <VirtualHost> sections that are substantially the same, for example:

```
NameVirtualHost 111.22.33.44
<VirtualHost 111.22.33.44>
    ServerName www.customer-1.com
    DocumentRoot /www/hosts/www.customer-1.com/docs
    ScriptAlias /cgi-bin/ /www/hosts/www.customer-1.com/cgi-bin
</VirtualHost>
<VirtualHost 111.22.33.44>
    ServerName www.customer-2.com
    DocumentRoot /www/hosts/www.customer-2.com/docs
    ScriptAlias /cgi-bin/ /www/hosts/www.customer-2.com/cgi-bin
</VirtualHost>
# blah blah blah
<VirtualHost 111.22.33.44>
    ServerName www.customer-N.com
    DocumentRoot /www/hosts/www.customer-N.com/docs
    ScriptAlias /cgi-bin/ /www/hosts/www.customer-N.com/cgi-bin
</VirtualHost>
```

The basic idea is to replace all of the static <VirtualHost> configuration with a mechanism that works it out dynamically. This has a number of advantages:

1. Your configuration file is smaller so Apache starts faster and uses less memory.

2. Adding virtual hosts is simply a matter of creating the appropriate directories in the filesystem and entries in the DNS - you don't need to reconfigure or restart Apache.

The main disadvantage is that you cannot have a different log file for each virtual host; however if you have very many virtual hosts then doing this is dubious anyway because it eats file descriptors. It is better to log to a pipe or a FIFO and arrange for the process at the other end to distribute the logs to the customers (it can also accumulate statistics, etc.).

4.4.2 Overview

A virtual host is defined by two pieces of information: its IP address, and the contents of the Host: header in the HTTP request. The dynamic mass virtual hosting technique is based on automatically inserting this information into the pathname of the file that is used to satisfy the request. This is done most easily using mod_vhost_alias, but if you are using a version of Apache up to 1.3.6 then you must use mod_rewrite. Both of these modules are disabled by default; you must enable one of them when configuring and building Apache if you want to use this technique.

A couple of things need to be 'faked' to make the dynamic virtual host look like a normal one. The most important is the server name which is used by Apache to generate self-referential URLs, etc. It is configured with the ServerName directive, and it is available to CGIs via the SERVER_NAME environment variable. The actual value used at run time is controlled by the UseCanonicalName setting. With UseCanonicalName Off the server name comes from the contents of the Host: header in the request. With UseCanonicalName DNS it comes from a reverse DNS lookup of the virtual host's IP address. The former setting is used for name-based dynamic virtual hosting, and the latter is used for IP-based hosting. If Apache cannot work out the server name because there is no Host: header or the DNS lookup fails then the value configured with ServerName is used instead.

The other thing to 'fake' is the document root (configured with DocumentRoot and available to CGIs via the DOCUMENT_ROOT environment variable). In a normal configuration this setting is used by the core module when mapping URIs to filenames, but when the server is configured to do dynamic virtual hosting that job is taken over by another module (either mod_vhost_alias or mod_rewrite) which has a different way of doing the mapping. Neither of these modules is responsible for setting the DOCUMENT_ROOT environment variable so if any CGIs or SSI documents make use of it they will get a misleading value.

4.4.3 Simple dynamic virtual hosts

This extract from httpd.conf implements the virtual host arrangement outlined in the Motivation section above, but in a generic fashion using mod_vhost_alias.

```
# get the server name from the Host:  header
UseCanonicalName Off

# this log format can be split per-virtual-host based on the
first field
LogFormat "%V %h %l %u %t \"%r\" %s %b" vcommon
CustomLog logs/access_log vcommon

# include the server name in the filenames used to satisfy
requests
VirtualDocumentRoot /www/hosts/%0/docs
VirtualScriptAlias /www/hosts/%0/cgi-bin
```

This configuration can be changed into an IP-based virtual hosting solution by just turning UseCanonicalName Off into UseCanonicalName DNS. The server name that is inserted into the filename is then derived from the IP address of the virtual host.

4.4.4 A virtually hosted homepages system

This is an adjustment of the above system tailored for an ISP's homepages
server. Using a slightly more complicated configuration we can select substrings of the server name to use in the filename so that e.g. the documents
for www.user.isp.com are found in /home/user/. It uses a single cgi-bin directory instead of one per virtual host.

```
# all the preliminary stuff is the same as above, then
# include part of the server name in the filenames
VirtualDocumentRoot /www/hosts/%2/docs
# single cgi-bin directory
ScriptAlias /cgi-bin/ /www/std-cgi/
```

There are examples of more complicated VirtualDocumentRoot settings in the
mod_vhost_alias documentation.

4.4.5 Using more than one virtual hosting system on the same server

With more complicated setups you can use Apache's normal <VirtualHost>
directives to control the scope of the various virtual hosting configurations. For
example, you could have one IP address for homepages customers and another
for commercial customers with the following setup. This can of course be combined with conventional <VirtualHost> configuration sections.

```
UseCanonicalName Off
LogFormat "%V %h %l %u %t \"%r\" %s %b" vcommon
<Directory /www/commercial>
    Options FollowSymLinks
    AllowOverride All
</Directory>
<Directory /www/homepages>
    Options FollowSymLinks
    AllowOverride None
</Directory>
<VirtualHost 111.22.33.44>
    ServerName www.commercial.isp.com
    CustomLog logs/access_log.commercial vcommon
    VirtualDocumentRoot /www/commercial/%0/docs
    VirtualScriptAlias /www/commercial/%0/cgi-bin
</VirtualHost>
<VirtualHost 111.22.33.45>
    ServerName www.homepages.isp.com
    CustomLog logs/access_log.homepages vcommon
    VirtualDocumentRoot /www/homepages/%0/docs
    ScriptAlias /cgi-bin/ /www/std-cgi/
```

```
</VirtualHost>
```

NOTE

If the first VirtualHost block does not include a ServerName direc-
tive, the reverse DNS of the relevant IP will be used instead. If this
is not the server name you wish to use, a bogus entry (ServerName
none.example.com) can be added to get around this behaviour.

4.4.6 More efficient IP-based virtual hosting

After the first example I noted that it is easy to turn it into an IP-based virtual
hosting setup. Unfortunately that configuration is not very efficient because it
requires a DNS lookup for every request. This can be avoided by laying out
the filesystem according to the IP addresses themselves rather than the corresponding names and changing the logging similarly. Apache will then usually
not need to work out the server name and so incur a DNS lookup.

```
# get the server name from the reverse DNS of the IP address
UseCanonicalName DNS

# include the IP address in the logs so they may be split
LogFormat "%A %h %l %u %t \"%r\" %s %b" vcommon
CustomLog logs/access_log vcommon

# include the IP address in the filenames
VirtualDocumentRootIP /www/hosts/%0/docs
VirtualScriptAliasIP /www/hosts/%0/cgi-bin
```

4.4.7 Simple dynamic virtual hosts using mod_rewrite

This extract from httpd.conf does the same thing as the first example. The
first half is very similar to the corresponding part above but with some changes
for backward compatibility and to make the mod_rewrite part work properly;
the second half configures mod_rewrite to do the actual work.

There are a couple of especially tricky bits: By default, mod_rewrite runs before
the other URI translation modules (mod_alias etc.) so if they are used then
mod_rewrite must be configured to accommodate them. Also, some magic must
be performed to do a per-dynamic-virtual-host equivalent of ScriptAlias.

```
# get the server name from the Host:  header
UseCanonicalName Off

# splittable logs
LogFormat "%{Host}i %h %l %u %t \"%r\" %s %b" vcommon
CustomLog logs/access_log vcommon

<Directory /www/hosts>
    # ExecCGI is needed here because we can't force
    # CGI execution in the way that ScriptAlias does
    Options FollowSymLinks ExecCGI
```

```
</Directory>
# now for the hard bit
RewriteEngine On
# a ServerName derived from a Host: header may be any case at
all
RewriteMap lowercase int:tolower
## deal with normal documents first:
# allow Alias /icons/ to work - repeat for other aliases
RewriteCond %{REQUEST_URI} !^/icons/
# allow CGIs to work
RewriteCond %{REQUEST_URI} !^/cgi-bin/
# do the magic
RewriteRule ^/(.*)$
/www/hosts/${lowercase:%{SERVER_NAME}}/docs/$1
## and now deal with CGIs - we have to force a MIME type
RewriteCond %{REQUEST_URI} ^/cgi-bin/
RewriteRule ^/(.*)$
/www/hosts/${lowercase:%{SERVER_NAME}}/cgi-bin/$1
[T=application/x-httpd-cgi]
# that's it!
```

4.4.8 A homepages system using mod_rewrite

This does the same thing as the second example.

```
RewriteEngine on
RewriteMap lowercase int:tolower
# allow CGIs to work
RewriteCond %{REQUEST_URI} !^/cgi-bin/
# check the hostname is right so that the RewriteRule works
RewriteCond ${lowercase:%{SERVER_NAME}} ^www\.[a-z-]+\.isp\.com$
# concatenate the virtual host name onto the start of the URI
# the [C] means do the next rewrite on the result of this one
RewriteRule ^(.+) ${lowercase:%{SERVER_NAME}}$1 [C]
# now create the real file name
RewriteRule ^www\.([a-z-]+)\.isp\.com/(.*) /home/$1/$2
# define the global CGI directory
ScriptAlias /cgi-bin/ /www/std-cgi/
```

4.4.9 Using a separate virtual host configuration file

This arrangement uses more advanced mod_rewrite features to get the translation from virtual host to document root from a separate configuration file. This provides more flexibility but requires more complicated configuration.

The vhost.map file contains something like this:

```
www.customer-1.com /www/customers/1
www.customer-2.com /www/customers/2
# ...
www.customer-N.com /www/customers/N
```

The http.conf contains this:

```
RewriteEngine on
RewriteMap lowercase int:tolower

# define the map file
RewriteMap vhost txt:/www/conf/vhost.map

# deal with aliases as above
RewriteCond %{REQUEST_URI} !^/icons/
RewriteCond %{REQUEST_URI} !^/cgi-bin/
RewriteCond ${lowercase:%{SERVER_NAME}} ^(.+)$
# this does the file-based remap
RewriteCond ${vhost:%1} ^(/.*)$
RewriteRule ^/(.*)$ %1/docs/$1

RewriteCond %{REQUEST_URI} ^/cgi-bin/
RewriteCond ${lowercase:%{SERVER_NAME}} ^(.+)$
RewriteCond ${vhost:%1} ^(/.*)$
RewriteRule ^/(.*)$ %1/cgi-bin/$1
```

4.5 VirtualHost Examples

This section attempts to answer the commonly-asked questions about setting up virtual hosts (p. 541). These scenarios are those involving multiple web sites running on a single server, via name-based (p. 543) or IP-based (p. 547) virtual hosts.

4.5.1 Running several name-based web sites on a single IP address.

Your server has a single IP address, and multiple aliases (CNAMES) point to this machine in DNS. You want to run a web server for www.example.com and www.example.org on this machine.

> NOTE *Creating virtual host configurations on your Apache server does not magically cause DNS entries to be created for those host names. You must have the names in DNS, resolving to your IP address, or nobody else will be able to see your web site. You can put entries in your hosts file for local testing, but that will work only from the machine with those hosts entries.*

Server configuration
```
# Ensure that Apache listens on port 80
Listen 80

# Listen for virtual host requests on all IP addresses
NameVirtualHost *:80

<VirtualHost *:80>
    DocumentRoot /www/example1
    ServerName www.example.com

    # Other directives here
</VirtualHost>

<VirtualHost *:80>
    DocumentRoot /www/example2
    ServerName www.example.org

    # Other directives here
</VirtualHost>
```

The asterisks match all addresses, so the main server serves no requests. Due to the fact that www.example.com is first in the configuration file, it has the highest priority and can be seen as the default or primary server. That means that if a request is received that does not match one of the specified ServerName directives, it will be served by this first VirtualHost.

> NOTE
>
> *You can, if you wish, replace * with the actual IP address of the system. In that case, the argument to VirtualHost must match the argument to NameVirtualHost:*
>
> *NameVirtualHost 172.20.30.40*

```
<VirtualHost 172.20.30.40>
# etc ...
```

*However, it is additionally useful to use * on systems where the IP address is not predictable - for example if you have a dynamic IP address with your ISP, and you are using some variety of dynamic DNS solution. Since * matches any IP address, this configuration would work without changes whenever your IP address changes.*

The above configuration is what you will want to use in almost all name-based virtual hosting situations. The only thing that this configuration will not work for, in fact, is when you are serving different content based on differing IP addresses or ports.

4.5.2 Name-based hosts on more than one IP address.

NOTE *Any of the techniques discussed here can be extended to any number of IP addresses.*

The server has two IP addresses. On one (172.20.30.40), we will serve the "main" server, server.domain.com and on the other (172.20.30.50), we will serve two or more virtual hosts.

Server configuration
```
Listen 80

# This is the "main" server running on 172.20.30.40
ServerName server.domain.com
DocumentRoot /www/mainserver

# This is the other address
NameVirtualHost 172.20.30.50

<VirtualHost 172.20.30.50>
    DocumentRoot /www/example1
    ServerName www.example.com

    # Other directives here ...
</VirtualHost>

<VirtualHost 172.20.30.50>
    DocumentRoot /www/example2
    ServerName www.example.org

    # Other directives here ...
</VirtualHost>
```

Any request to an address other than 172.20.30.50 will be served from the main server. A request to 172.20.30.50 with an unknown hostname, or no Host: header, will be served from www.example.com.

4.5.3 Serving the same content on different IP addresses (such as an internal and external address).

The server machine has two IP addresses (192.168.1.1 and 172.20.30.40). The machine is sitting between an internal (intranet) network and an external (internet) network. Outside of the network, the name server.example.com resolves to the external address (172.20.30.40), but inside the network, that same name resolves to the internal address (192.168.1.1).

The server can be made to respond to internal and external requests with the same content, with just one VirtualHost section.

Server configuration
```
NameVirtualHost 192.168.1.1
NameVirtualHost 172.20.30.40

<VirtualHost 192.168.1.1 172.20.30.40>
    DocumentRoot /www/server1
    ServerName server.example.com
    ServerAlias server
</VirtualHost>
```

Now requests from both networks will be served from the same VirtualHost.

NOTE: *On the internal network, one can just use the name* server *rather than the fully qualified host name* server.example.com.

Note also that, in the above example, you can replace the list of IP addresses with *, *which will cause the server to respond the same on all addresses.*

4.5.4 Running different sites on different ports.

You have multiple domains going to the same IP and also want to serve multiple ports. By defining the ports in the "NameVirtualHost" tag, you can allow this to work. If you try using <VirtualHost name:port> without the NameVirtualHost name:port or you try to use the Listen directive, your configuration will not work.

Server configuration
```
Listen 80
Listen 8080

NameVirtualHost 172.20.30.40:80
NameVirtualHost 172.20.30.40:8080

<VirtualHost 172.20.30.40:80>
    ServerName www.example.com
    DocumentRoot /www/domain-80
</VirtualHost>

<VirtualHost 172.20.30.40:8080>
    ServerName www.example.com
    DocumentRoot /www/domain-8080
```

```
</VirtualHost>

<VirtualHost 172.20.30.40:80>
    ServerName www.example.org
    DocumentRoot /www/otherdomain-80
</VirtualHost>

<VirtualHost 172.20.30.40:8080>
    ServerName www.example.org
    DocumentRoot /www/otherdomain-8080
</VirtualHost>
```

4.5.5 IP-based virtual hosting

The server has two IP addresses (172.20.30.40 and 172.20.30.50) which resolve to the names www.example.com and www.example.org respectively.

Server configuration
```
Listen 80

<VirtualHost 172.20.30.40>
    DocumentRoot /www/example1
    ServerName www.example.com
</VirtualHost>

<VirtualHost 172.20.30.50>
    DocumentRoot /www/example2
    ServerName www.example.org
</VirtualHost>
```

Requests for any address not specified in one of the <VirtualHost> directives (such as localhost, for example) will go to the main server, if there is one.

4.5.6 Mixed port-based and ip-based virtual hosts

The server machine has two IP addresses (172.20.30.40 and 172.20.30.50) which resolve to the names www.example.com and www.example.org respectively. In each case, we want to run hosts on ports 80 and 8080.

Server configuration
```
Listen 172.20.30.40:80
Listen 172.20.30.40:8080
Listen 172.20.30.50:80
Listen 172.20.30.50:8080

<VirtualHost 172.20.30.40:80>
    DocumentRoot /www/example1-80
    ServerName www.example.com
</VirtualHost>

<VirtualHost 172.20.30.40:8080>
    DocumentRoot /www/example1-8080
    ServerName www.example.com
```

```
</VirtualHost>
<VirtualHost 172.20.30.50:80>
    DocumentRoot /www/example2-80
    ServerName www.example.org
</VirtualHost>
<VirtualHost 172.20.30.50:8080>
    DocumentRoot /www/example2-8080
    ServerName www.example.org
</VirtualHost>
```

4.5.7 Mixed name-based and IP-based vhosts

On some of my addresses, I want to do name-based virtual hosts, and on others, IP-based hosts.

Server configuration

```
Listen 80

NameVirtualHost 172.20.30.40

<VirtualHost 172.20.30.40>
    DocumentRoot /www/example1
    ServerName www.example.com
</VirtualHost>

<VirtualHost 172.20.30.40>
    DocumentRoot /www/example2
    ServerName www.example.org
</VirtualHost>

<VirtualHost 172.20.30.40>
    DocumentRoot /www/example3
    ServerName www.example3.net
</VirtualHost>

# IP-based
<VirtualHost 172.20.30.50>
    DocumentRoot /www/example4
    ServerName www.example4.edu
</VirtualHost>

<VirtualHost 172.20.30.60>
    DocumentRoot /www/example5
    ServerName www.example5.gov
</VirtualHost>
```

4.5.8 Using `Virtual_host` and `mod_proxy` together

The following example allows a front-end machine to proxy a virtual host through to a server running on another machine. In the example, a virtual host of the same name is configured on a machine at 192.168.111.2. The

ProxyPreserveHost On directive is used so that the desired hostname is passed through, in case we are proxying multiple hostnames to a single machine.

```
<VirtualHost *:*>
ProxyPreserveHost On
ProxyPass / http://192.168.111.2/
ProxyPassReverse / http://192.168.111.2/
ServerName hostname.example.com
</VirtualHost>
```

4.5.9 Using _default_ vhosts

default vhosts for all ports

Catching *every* request to any unspecified IP address and port, *i.e.*, an address/port combination that is not used for any other virtual host.

```
Server configuration
<VirtualHost _default_:*>
    DocumentRoot /www/default
</VirtualHost>
```

Using such a default vhost with a wildcard port effectively prevents any request going to the main server.

A default vhost never serves a request that was sent to an address/port that is used for name-based vhosts. If the request contained an unknown or no Host: header it is always served from the primary name-based vhost (the vhost for that address/port appearing first in the configuration file).

You can use AliasMatch or RewriteRule to rewrite any request to a single information page (or script).

default vhosts for different ports

Same as setup 1, but the server listens on several ports and we want to use a second _default_ vhost for port 80.

```
Server configuration
<VirtualHost _default_:80>
    DocumentRoot /www/default80
    # ...
</VirtualHost>

<VirtualHost _default_:*>
    DocumentRoot /www/default
    # ...
</VirtualHost>
```

The default vhost for port 80 (which *must* appear before any default vhost with a wildcard port) catches all requests that were sent to an unspecified IP address. The main server is never used to serve a request.

default vhosts for one port

We want to have a default vhost for port 80, but no other default vhosts.

Server configuration
```
<VirtualHost _default_:80>
DocumentRoot /www/default
...
</VirtualHost>
```

A request to an unspecified address on port 80 is served from the default vhost. Any other request to an unspecified address and port is served from the main server.

4.5.10 Migrating a name-based vhost to an IP-based vhost

The name-based vhost with the hostname www.example.org (from our name-based example, setup 2) should get its own IP address. To avoid problems with name servers or proxies who cached the old IP address for the name-based vhost we want to provide both variants during a migration phase.

The solution is easy, because we can simply add the new IP address (172.20.30.50) to the VirtualHost directive.

Server configuration
```
Listen 80
ServerName www.example.com
DocumentRoot /www/example1

NameVirtualHost 172.20.30.40

<VirtualHost 172.20.30.40 172.20.30.50>
    DocumentRoot /www/example2
    ServerName www.example.org
    # ...
</VirtualHost>

<VirtualHost 172.20.30.40>
    DocumentRoot /www/example3
    ServerName www.example.net
    ServerAlias *.example.net
    # ...
</VirtualHost>
```

The vhost can now be accessed through the new address (as an IP-based vhost) and through the old address (as a name-based vhost).

4.5.11 Using the ServerPath directive

We have a server with two name-based vhosts. In order to match the correct virtual host a client must send the correct Host: header. Old HTTP/1.0 clients do not send such a header and Apache has no clue what vhost the client tried to reach (and serves the request from the primary vhost). To provide as much backward compatibility as possible we create a primary vhost which returns a single page containing links with an URL prefix to the name-based virtual hosts.

Server configuration

```
NameVirtualHost 172.20.30.40

<VirtualHost 172.20.30.40>
    # primary vhost
    DocumentRoot /www/subdomain
    RewriteEngine On
    RewriteRule ^/.* /www/subdomain/index.html
    # ...
</VirtualHost>

<VirtualHost 172.20.30.40>
DocumentRoot /www/subdomain/sub1
    ServerName www.sub1.domain.tld
    ServerPath /sub1/
    RewriteEngine On
    RewriteRule ^(/sub1/.*) /www/subdomain$1
    # ...
</VirtualHost>

<VirtualHost 172.20.30.40>
    DocumentRoot /www/subdomain/sub2
    ServerName www.sub2.domain.tld
    ServerPath /sub2/
    RewriteEngine On
    RewriteRule ^(/sub2/.*) /www/subdomain$1
    # ...
</VirtualHost>
```

Due to the ServerPath directive a request to the URL http://www.sub1.domain.tld/sub1/ is *always* served from the sub1-vhost. A request to the URL http://www.sub1.domain.tld/ is only served from the sub1-vhost if the client sent a correct Host: header. If no Host: header is sent the client gets the information page from the primary host.

Please note that there is one oddity: A request to http://www.sub2.domain.tld/sub1/ is also served from the sub1-vhost if the client sent no Host: header.

The RewriteRule directives are used to make sure that a client which sent a correct Host: header can use both URL variants, *i.e.*, with or without URL prefix.

4.6 An In-Depth Discussion of Virtual Host Matching

The virtual host code was completely rewritten in **Apache 1.3**. This section attempts to explain exactly what Apache does when deciding what virtual host to serve a hit from. With the help of the new NameVirtualHost directive virtual host configuration should be a lot easier and safer than with versions prior to 1.3.

If you just want to make it work without understanding how, here are some examples (p. 555).

4.6.1 Config File Parsing

There is a *main_server* which consists of all the definitions appearing outside of <VirtualHost> sections. There are virtual servers, called *vhosts*, which are defined by <VirtualHost> sections.

The directives ServerName and ServerPath can appear anywhere within the definition of a server. However, each appearance overrides the previous appearance (within that server).

The main_server has no default ServerPath, or ServerAlias. The default ServerName is deduced from the server's IP address.

Port numbers specified in the VirtualHost directive do not influence what port numbers Apache will listen on, they only discriminate between which VirtualHost will be selected to handle a request.

Each address appearing in the VirtualHost directive can have an optional port. If the port is unspecified it is treated as a wildcard port. The special port * indicates a wildcard that matches any port. Collectively the entire set of addresses (including multiple A record results from DNS lookups) are called the vhost's *address set*.

Unless a NameVirtualHost directive is used for the exact IP address and port pair in the VirtualHost directive, Apache selects the best match only on the basis of the IP address (or wildcard) and port number. If there are multiple identical best matches, the first VirtualHost appearing in the configuration file will be selected.

If you want Apache to *further* discriminate on the basis of the HTTP Host header supplied by the client, the NameVirtualHost directive *must* appear with the exact IP address (or wildcard) and port pair used in a correspnding set of VirtualHost directives.

The name-based virtual host selection occurs only after a single IP-based virtual host has been selected, and only considers the set of virtual hosts that carry an identical IP address and port pair.

Hostnames can be used in place of IP addresses in a virtual host definition, but it is resolved at startup and is not recommended.

Multiple `NameVirtualHost` directives can be used each with a set of `VirtualHost` directives but only one `NameVirtualHost` directive should be used for each specific IP:port pair.

The ordering of `NameVirtualHost` and `VirtualHost` directives is not important which makes the following two examples identical (only the order of the `VirtualHost` directives for *one* address set is important, see below):

```
NameVirtualHost 111.22.33.44        <VirtualHost 111.22.33.44>
<VirtualHost 111.22.33.44>          # server A
# server A                          </VirtualHost>
...                                 <VirtualHost 111.22.33.55>
</VirtualHost>                      # server C
<VirtualHost 111.22.33.44>          ...
# server B                          </VirtualHost>
...                                 <VirtualHost 111.22.33.44>
</VirtualHost>                      # server B
NameVirtualHost 111.22.33.55        ...
<VirtualHost 111.22.33.55>          </VirtualHost>
# server C                          <VirtualHost 111.22.33.55>
...                                 # server D
</VirtualHost>                      ...
<VirtualHost 111.22.33.55>          </VirtualHost>
# server D                          NameVirtualHost 111.22.33.44
...                                 NameVirtualHost 111.22.33.55
</VirtualHost>
```

(To aid the readability of your configuration you should prefer the left variant.)

During initialization a list for each IP address is generated and inserted into an hash table. If the IP address is used in a `NameVirtualHost` directive the list contains all name-based vhosts for the given IP address. If there are no vhosts defined for that address the `NameVirtualHost` directive is ignored and an error is logged. For an IP-based vhost the list in the hash table is empty.

Due to a fast hashing function the overhead of hashing an IP address during a request is minimal and almost not existent. Additionally the table is optimized for IP addresses which vary in the last octet.

For every vhost various default values are set. In particular:

1. If a vhost has no `ServerAdmin`, `Timeout`, `KeepAliveTimeout`, `KeepAlive`, `MaxKeepAliveRequests`, `ReceiveBufferSize`, or `SendBufferSize` directive then the respective value is inherited from the main_server. (That is, inherited from whatever the final setting of that value is in the main_server.)

2. The "lookup defaults" that define the default directory permissions for a vhost are merged with those of the main_server. This includes any per-directory configuration information for any module.

3. The per-server configs for each module from the main_server are merged into the vhost server.

Essentially, the main_server is treated as "defaults" or a "base" on which to build each vhost. But the positioning of these main_server definitions in the config file is largely irrelevant – the entire config of the main_server has been parsed when this final merging occurs. So even if a main_server definition appears after a vhost definition it might affect the vhost definition.

If the main_server has no ServerName at this point, then the hostname of the machine that httpd is running on is used instead. We will call the *main_server address set* those IP addresses returned by a DNS lookup on the ServerName of the main_server.

For any undefined ServerName fields, a name-based vhost defaults to the address given first in the VirtualHost statement defining the vhost.

Any vhost that includes the magic _default_ wildcard is given the same ServerName as the main_server.

4.6.2 Virtual Host Matching

The server determines which vhost to use for a request as follows:

Hash table lookup

When the connection is first made by a client, the IP address to which the client connected is looked up in the internal IP hash table.

If the lookup fails (the IP address wasn't found) the request is served from the _default_ vhost if there is such a vhost for the port to which the client sent the request. If there is no matching _default_ vhost the request is served from the main_server.

If the IP address is not found in the hash table then the match against the port number may also result in an entry corresponding to a NameVirtualHost *, which is subsequently handled like other name-based vhosts.

If the lookup succeeded (a corresponding list for the IP address was found) the next step is to decide if we have to deal with an IP-based or a name-base vhost.

IP-based vhost

If the entry we found has an empty name list then we have found an IP-based vhost, no further actions are performed and the request is served from that vhost.

Name-based vhost

If the entry corresponds to a name-based vhost the name list contains one or more vhost structures. This list contains the vhosts in the same order as the VirtualHost directives appear in the config file.

The first vhost on this list (the first vhost in the config file with the specified IP address) has the highest priority and catches any request to an unknown server name or a request without a Host: header field.

If the client provided a Host: header field the list is searched for a matching vhost and the first hit on a ServerName or ServerAlias is taken and the request is served from that vhost. A Host: header field can contain a port number, but Apache always matches against the real port to which the client sent the request.

If the client submitted a HTTP/1.0 request without Host: header field we don't know to what server the client tried to connect and any existing ServerPath is matched against the URI from the request. The first matching path on the list is used and the request is served from that vhost.

If no matching vhost could be found the request is served from the first vhost with a matching port number that is on the list for the IP to which the client connected (as already mentioned before).

Persistent connections

The IP lookup described above is only done *once* for a particular TCP/IP session while the name lookup is done on *every* request during a KeepAlive/persistent connection. In other words a client may request pages from different name-based vhosts during a single persistent connection.

Absolute URI

If the URI from the request is an absolute URI, and its hostname and port match the main server or one of the configured virtual hosts *and* match the address and port to which the client sent the request, then the scheme/hostname/port prefix is stripped off and the remaining relative URI is served by the corresponding main server or virtual host. If it does not match, then the URI remains untouched and the request is taken to be a proxy request.

Observations

- A name-based vhost can never interfere with an IP-base vhost and vice versa. An IP-based vhost can only be reached through an IP address of its own address set and never through any other address. The same applies to name-based vhosts; they can only be reached through an IP address of the corresponding address set which must be defined with a NameVirtualHost directive.

- ServerAlias and ServerPath checks are never performed for an IP-based vhost.

- The order of name-/IP-based, the _default_ vhost and the NameVirtualHost directive within the config file is not important. Only the ordering of name-based vhosts for a specific address set is significant. The one name-based vhosts that comes first in the configuration file has the highest priority for its corresponding address set.

- The Host: header field is never used during the matching process. Apache always uses the real port to which the client sent the request.

- If a ServerPath directive exists which is a prefix of another ServerPath directive that appears later in the configuration file, then the former will always be matched and the latter will never be matched. (That is assuming that no Host: header field was available to disambiguate the two.)

- If two IP-based vhosts have an address in common, the vhost appearing first in the config file is always matched. Such a thing might happen inadvertently. The server will give a warning in the error logfile when it detects this.

- A _default_ vhost catches a request only if there is no other vhost with a matching IP address *and* a matching port number for the request. The request is only caught if the port number to which the client sent the request matches the port number of your _default_ vhost which is your standard Listen by default. A wildcard port can be specified (*i.e.*, _default_:*) to catch requests to any available port. This also applies to NameVirtualHost * vhosts. Note that this is simply an extension of the "best match" principle, as a specific and exact match is favored over a wildcard.

- The main_server is only used to serve a request if the IP address and port number to which the client connected is unspecified and does not match any other vhost (including a _default_ vhost). In other words the main_server only catches a request for an unspecified address/port combination (unless there is a _default_ vhost which matches that port).

- A _default_ vhost or the main_server is *never* matched for a request with an unknown or missing Host: header field if the client connected to an address (and port) which is used for name-based vhosts, *e.g.*, in a NameVirtualHost directive.

- You should never specify DNS names in VirtualHost directives because it will force your server to rely on DNS to boot. Furthermore it poses a security threat if you do not control the DNS for all the domains listed. There's more information (p. 571) available on this and the next two topics.

- ServerName should always be set for each vhost. Otherwise A DNS lookup is required for each vhost.

4.6.3 Tips

In addition to the tips on the DNS Issues (p. 571) page, here are some further tips:

- Place all main_server definitions before any VirtualHost definitions. (This is to aid the readability of the configuration – the post-config merging process makes it non-obvious that definitions mixed in around virtual hosts might affect all virtual hosts.)

- Group corresponding `NameVirtualHost` and `VirtualHost` definitions in your configuration to ensure better readability.

- Avoid `ServerPaths` which are prefixes of other `ServerPaths`. If you cannot avoid this then you have to ensure that the longer (more specific) prefix vhost appears earlier in the configuration file than the shorter (less specific) prefix (*i.e.*, `"ServerPath /abc"` should appear after `"ServerPath /abc/def"`).

4.7 File Descriptor Limits

When using a large number of Virtual Hosts, Apache may run out of available file descriptors (sometimes called file handles) if each Virtual Host specifies different log files. The total number of file descriptors used by Apache is one for each distinct error log file, one for every other log file directive, plus 10-20 for internal use. Unix operating systems limit the number of file descriptors that may be used by a process; the limit is typically 64, and may usually be increased up to a large hard-limit.

Although Apache attempts to increase the limit as required, this may not work if:

1. Your system does not provide the setrlimit() system call.

2. The setrlimit(RLIMIT_NOFILE) call does not function on your system (such as Solaris 2.3)

3. The number of file descriptors required exceeds the hard limit.

4. Your system imposes other limits on file descriptors, such as a limit on stdio streams only using file descriptors below 256. (Solaris 2)

In the event of problems you can:

- Reduce the number of log files; don't specify log files in the <VirtualHost> sections, but only log to the main log files. (See Splitting up your log files, below, for more information on doing this.)

- If you system falls into 1 or 2 (above), then increase the file descriptor limit before starting Apache, using a script like

```
#!/bin/sh
ulimit -S -n 100
exec httpd
```

4.7.1 Splitting up your log files

If you want to log multiple virtual hosts to the same log file, you may want to split up the log files afterwards in order to run statistical analysis of the various virtual hosts. This can be accomplished in the following manner.

First, you will need to add the virtual host information to the log entries. This can be done using the LogFormat directive, and the %v variable. Add this to the beginning of your log format string:

```
LogFormat "%v %h %l %u %t \"%r\" %>s %b" vhost
CustomLog logs/multiple_vhost_log vhost
```

This will create a log file in the common log format, but with the canonical virtual host (whatever appears in the ServerName directive) prepended to each line. (See Custom Log Formats for more about customizing your log files.)

When you wish to split your log file into its component parts (one file per virtual host) you can use the program split-logfile (p. 48) to accomplish this. You'll find this program in the support directory of the Apache distribution.

Run this program with the command:

```
split-logfile < /logs/multiple_vhost_log
```

This program, when run with the name of your vhost log file, will generate one file for each virtual host that appears in your log file. Each file will be called hostname.log.

4.8 Issues Regarding DNS and Apache

This section could be summarized with the statement: don't configure Apache
in such a way that it relies on DNS resolution for parsing of the configuration
files. If Apache requires DNS resolution to parse the configuration files then
your server may be subject to reliability problems (i.e. it might not boot), or
denial and theft of service attacks (including users able to steal hits from other
users).

4.8.1 A Simple Example

```
<VirtualHost www.abc.dom>
ServerAdmin webgirl@abc.dom
DocumentRoot /www/abc
</VirtualHost>
```

In order for Apache to function properly, it absolutely needs to have two pieces
of information about each virtual host: the ServerName and at least one IP
address that the server will bind and respond to. The above example does
not include the IP address, so Apache must use DNS to find the address of
www.abc.dom. If for some reason DNS is not available at the time your server is
parsing its config file, then this virtual host **will not be configured**. It won't
be able to respond to any hits to this virtual host (prior to Apache version 1.2
the server would not even boot).

Suppose that www.abc.dom has address 192.0.2.1. Then consider this configuration snippet:

```
<VirtualHost 192.0.2.1>
ServerAdmin webgirl@abc.dom
DocumentRoot /www/abc
</VirtualHost>
```

This time Apache needs to use reverse DNS to find the ServerName for this virtualhost. If that reverse lookup fails then it will partially disable the virtualhost
(prior to Apache version 1.2 the server would not even boot). If the virtual host
is name-based then it will effectively be totally disabled, but if it is IP-based
then it will mostly work. However, if Apache should ever have to generate a full
URL for the server which includes the server name, then it will fail to generate
a valid URL.

Here is a snippet that avoids both of these problems:

```
<VirtualHost 192.0.2.1>
ServerName www.abc.dom
ServerAdmin webgirl@abc.dom
DocumentRoot /www/abc
</VirtualHost>
```

4.8.2 Denial of Service

There are (at least) two forms that denial of service can come in. If you are running a version of Apache prior to version 1.2 then your server will not even boot if one of the two DNS lookups mentioned above fails for any of your virtual hosts. In some cases this DNS lookup may not even be under your control; for example, if abc.dom is one of your customers and they control their own DNS, they can force your (pre-1.2) server to fail while booting simply by deleting the www.abc.dom record.

Another form is far more insidious. Consider this configuration snippet:

```
<VirtualHost www.abc.dom>
    ServerAdmin webgirl@abc.dom
    DocumentRoot /www/abc
</VirtualHost>

<VirtualHost www.def.dom>
    ServerAdmin webguy@def.dom
    DocumentRoot /www/def
</VirtualHost>
```

Suppose that you've assigned 192.0.2.1 to www.abc.dom and 192.0.2.2 to www.def.dom. Furthermore, suppose that def.dom has control of their own DNS. With this config you have put def.dom into a position where they can steal all traffic destined to abc.dom. To do so, all they have to do is set www.def.dom to 192.0.2.1. Since they control their own DNS you can't stop them from pointing the www.def.dom record wherever they wish.

Requests coming in to 192.0.2.1 (including all those where users typed in URLs of the form http://www.abc.dom/whatever) will all be served by the def.dom virtual host. To better understand why this happens requires a more in-depth discussion of how Apache matches up incoming requests with the virtual host that will serve it. A rough document describing this is available (p. 563).

4.8.3 The "main server" Address

The addition of name-based virtual host support (p. 543) in Apache 1.1 requires Apache to know the IP address(es) of the host that httpd is running on. To get this address it uses either the global ServerName (if present) or calls the C function gethostname (which should return the same as typing "hostname" at the command prompt). Then it performs a DNS lookup on this address. At present there is no way to avoid this lookup.

If you fear that this lookup might fail because your DNS server is down then you can insert the hostname in /etc/hosts (where you probably already have it so that the machine can boot properly). Then ensure that your machine is configured to use /etc/hosts in the event that DNS fails. Depending on what OS you are using this might be accomplished by editing /etc/resolv.conf, or maybe /etc/nsswitch.conf.

If your server doesn't have to perform DNS for any other reason then you might be able to get away with running Apache with the HOSTRESORDER environment variable set to "local". This all depends on what OS and resolver libraries you are using. It also affects CGIs unless you use mod_env to control the environment. It's best to consult the man pages or FAQs for your OS.

4.8.4 Tips to Avoid These Problems

- use IP addresses in VirtualHost
- use IP addresses in Listen
- ensure all virtual hosts have an explicit ServerName
- create a <VirtualHost _default_:*> server that has no pages to serve

4.8.5 Appendix: Future Directions

The situation regarding DNS is highly undesirable. For Apache 1.2 we've attempted to make the server at least continue booting in the event of failed DNS, but it might not be the best we can do. In any event, requiring the use of explicit IP addresses in configuration files is highly undesirable in today's Internet where renumbering is a necessity.

A possible work around to the theft of service attack described above would be to perform a reverse DNS lookup on the IP address returned by the forward lookup and compare the two names – in the event of a mismatch, the virtualhost would be disabled. This would require reverse DNS to be configured properly (which is something that most admins are familiar with because of the common use of "double-reverse" DNS lookups by FTP servers and TCP wrappers).

In any event, it doesn't seem possible to reliably boot a virtual-hosted web server when DNS has failed unless IP addresses are used. Partial solutions such as disabling portions of the configuration might be worse than not booting at all depending on what the webserver is supposed to accomplish.

As HTTP/1.1 is deployed and browsers and proxies start issuing the Host header it will become possible to avoid the use of IP-based virtual hosts entirely. In this case, a webserver has no requirement to do DNS lookups during configuration. But as of March 1997 these features have not been deployed widely enough to be put into use on critical webservers.

5 URL Rewriting Guide

5.1 Apache mod_rewrite

> "The great thing about mod_rewrite is it gives you all the configurability and flexibility of Sendmail. The downside to mod_rewrite is that it gives you all the configurability and flexibility of Sendmail."
>
> – Brian Behlendorf
> Apache Group

> "Despite the tons of examples and docs, mod_rewrite is voodoo. Damned cool voodoo, but still voodoo."
>
> – Brian Moore
> bem@news.cmc.net

Welcome to mod_rewrite, the Swiss Army Knife of URL manipulation!

This module uses a rule-based rewriting engine (based on a regular-expression parser) to rewrite requested URLs on the fly. It supports an unlimited number of rules and an unlimited number of attached rule conditions for each rule to provide a really flexible and powerful URL manipulation mechanism. The URL manipulations can depend on various tests, for instance server variables, environment variables, HTTP headers, time stamps and even external database lookups in various formats can be used to achieve granular URL matching.

This module operates on the full URLs (including the path-info part) both in per-server context (httpd.conf) and per-directory context (.htaccess files and <Directory> blocks) and can even generate query-string parts on result. The rewritten result can lead to internal sub-processing, external request redirection or even to an internal proxy throughput.

But all this functionality and flexibility has its drawback: complexity. So don't expect to understand this entire module in just one day.

See also:

- ▷ Mapping URLs to the Filesystem (p. 75)
- ▷ mod_rewrite wiki[1]
- ▷ Glossary (p. 795)

5.1.1 Documentation

- mod_rewrite reference documentation (p. 426)
- Introduction (p. 577)
- Flags (p. 582)

---

[1]http://wiki.apache.org/httpd/Rewrite

5.2 Apache mod_rewrite Introduction

This section supplements the mod_rewrite reference documentation (p. 426). It describes the basic concepts necessary for use of mod_rewrite. Other documents go into greater detail, but this doc should help the beginner get their feet wet.

See also:

▷ Module documentation (p. 426)

▷ Technical details (p. 588)

▷ Practical solutions to common problems (p. 591)

▷ Practical solutions to advanced problems (p. 599)

5.2.1 Introduction

The Apache module mod_rewrite is a very powerful and sophisticated module which provides a way to do URL manipulations. With it, you can do nearly all types of URL rewriting that you may need. It is, however, somewhat complex, and may be intimidating to the beginner. There is also a tendency to treat rewrite rules as magic incantation, using them without actually understanding what they do.

This section attempts to give sufficient background so that what follows is understood, rather than just copied blindly.

Remember that many common URL-manipulation tasks don't require the full power and complexity of mod_rewrite. For simple tasks, see mod_alias and the documentation on mapping URLs to the filesystem (p. 75).

Finally, before proceeding, be sure to configure the RewriteLog. Although this log file can give an overwhelming amount of information, it is indispensable in debugging problems with mod_rewrite configuration, since it will tell you exactly how each rule is processed.

5.2.2 Regular Expressions

mod_rewrite uses the Perl Compatible Regular Expression[2] vocabulary. In this section, we do not attempt to provide a detailed reference to regular expressions. For that, we recommend the PCRE man pages[3], the Perl regular expression man page[4], and Mastering Regular Expressions, by Jeffrey Friedl[5].

In this section, we attempt to provide enough of a regex vocabulary to get you started, without being overwhelming, in the hope that RewriteRules will be scientific formulae, rather than magical incantations.

---

[2]http://pcre.org/
[3]http://pcre.org/pcre.txt
[4]http://perldoc.perl.org/perlre.html
[5]http://www.oreilly.com/catalog/regex2/index.html

Regex vocabulary

The following are the minimal building blocks you will need, in order to write
regular expressions and RewriteRules. They certainly do not represent a complete regular expression vocabulary, but they are a good place to start, and
should help you read basic regular expressions, as well as write your own.

Character	Meaning	Example
.	Matches any single character	c.t will match cat, cot, cut, etc.
+	Repeats the previous match one or more times	a+ matches a, aa, aaa, etc
*	Repeats the previous match zero or more times.	a* matches all the same things a+ matches, but will also match an empty string.
?	Makes the match optional.	colou?r will match color and colour.
^	Called an anchor, matches the beginning of the string	^a matches a string that begins with a
$	The other anchor, this matches the end of the string.	a$ matches a string that ends with a.
( )	Groups several characters into a single unit, and captures a match for use in a backreference.	(ab)+ matches ababab - that is, the + applies to the group. For more on backreferences see below.
[ ]	A character class - matches one of the characters	c[uoa]t matches cut, cot or cat.
[^]	Negative character class - matches any character not specified	c[^/]t matches cat or c=t but not c/t

In mod_rewrite the ! character can be used before a regular expression to negate
it. This is, a string will be considered to have matched only if it does not match
the rest of the expression.

Regex Back-Reference Availability

One important thing here has to be remembered: Whenever you use parentheses
in *Pattern* or in one of the *CondPattern*, back-references are internally created
which can be used with the strings $N and %N (see below). These are available
for creating the strings *Substitution* and *TestString*. Figure 5.1 shows to which
locations the back-references are transferred for expansion.

5.2.3 RewriteRule basics

A RewriteRule consists of three arguments separated by spaces. The arguments
are

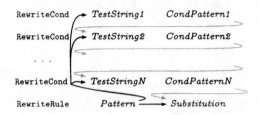

Figure 5.1: The back-reference flow through a rule.

1. *Pattern*: which incoming URLs should be affected by the rule;
2. *Substitution*: where should the matching requests be sent;
3. *[flags]*: options affecting the rewritten request.

The *Pattern* is always a regular expression matched against the URL-Path of the incoming request (the part after the hostname but before any question mark indicating the beginning of a query string).

The *Substitution* can itself be one of three things:

A full filesystem path to a resource

```
RewriteRule ^/games.* /usr/local/games/web
```

This maps a request to an arbitrary location on your filesystem, much like the `Alias` directive.

A web-path to a resource

```
RewriteRule ^/foo$ /bar
```

If `DocumentRoot` is set to `/usr/local/apache2/htdocs`, then this directive would map requests for `http://example.com/foo` to the path `/usr/local/apache2/htdocs/bar`.

An absolute URL

```
RewriteRule ^/product/view$
http://site2.example.com/seeproduct.html [R]
```

This tells the client to make a new request for the specified URL.

The *Substitution* can also contain *back-references* to parts of the incoming URL-path matched by the *Pattern*. Consider the following:

```
RewriteRule ^/product/(.*)/view$ /var/web/productdb/$1
```

The variable `$1` will be replaced with whatever text was matched by the expression inside the parenthesis in the *Pattern*. For example, a request for `http://example.com/product/r14df/view` will be mapped to the path `/var/web/productdb/r14df`.

If there is more than one expression in parenthesis, they are available in order
in the variables $1, $2, $3, and so on.

5.2.4 Rewrite Flags

The behavior of a RewriteRule can be modified by the application of one or
more flags to the end of the rule. For example, the matching behavior of a rule
can be made case-insensitive by the application of the [NC] flag:

```
RewriteRule ^puppy.html smalldog.html [NC]
```

For more details on the available flags, their meanings, and examples, see the
Rewrite Flags (p. 582) document.

5.2.5 Rewrite conditions

One or more RewriteCond directives can be used to restrict the types of requests
that will be subject to the following RewriteRule. The first argument is a
variable describing a characteristic of the request, the second argument is a
regular expression that must match the variable, and a third optional argument
is a list of flags that modify how the match is evaluated.

For example, to send all requests from a particular IP range to a different server,
you could use:

```
RewriteCond %{REMOTE_ADDR} ^10\.2\.
RewriteRule (.*) http://intranet.example.com$1
```

When more than one RewriteCond is specified, they must all match for the
RewriteRule to be applied. For example, to deny requests that contain the word
"hack" in their query string, except if they also contain a cookie containing the
word "go", you could use:

```
RewriteCond %{QUERY_STRING} hack
RewriteCond %{HTTP_COOKIE} !go
RewriteRule .* - [F]
```

Notice that the exclamation mark specifies a negative match, so the rule is only
applied if the cookie does not contain "go".

Matches in the regular expressions contained in the RewriteConds can be used
as part of the *Substitution* in the RewriteRule using the variables %1, %2, etc.
For example, this will direct the request to a different directory depending on
the hostname used to access the site:

```
RewriteCond %{HTTP_HOST} (.*)
RewriteRule ^/(.*) /sites/%1/$1
```

If the request was for http://example.com/foo/bar, then %1 would contain
example.com and $1 would contain foo/bar.

5.2.6 Rewrite maps

See `RewriteMap`.

5.2.7 .htaccess files

Rewriting is typically configured in the main server configuration setting (outside any `<Directory>` section) or inside `<VirtualHost>` containers. This is the easiest way to do rewriting and is recommended. It is possible, however, to do rewriting inside `<Directory>` sections or `.htaccess` files (p. 667) at the expense of some additional complexity. This technique is called per-directory rewrites.

The main difference with per-server rewrites is that the path prefix of the directory containing the `.htaccess` file is stripped before matching in the `RewriteRule`. In addition, the `RewriteBase` should be used to assure the request is properly mapped.

5.3 Apache mod_rewrite Flags

This section discusses the flags which are available to the RewriteRule directive, providing detailed explanations and examples. This is not necessarily a
comprehensive list of all flags available, so be sure to also consult the reference
documentation.

See also:

- ▷ Module documentation (p. 426)
- ▷ Technical details (p. 588)
- ▷ Rewrite Guide - useful examples (p. 591)
- ▷ Advanced Rewrite Guide - advanced useful examples (p. 599)

5.3.1 Introduction

RewriteRules can have their behavior modified by one or more flags. Flags
are included in square brackets at the end of the rule, and multiple flags are
separated by commas.

```
RewriteRule pattern target [Flag1,Flag2,Flag3]
```

The flags all have a short form, such as CO, as well as a longer form, such as
cookie. Some flags take one or more arguments. Flags are not case sensitive.

5.3.2 The flags

Each flag has a long and short form. While it is most common to use the short
form, it is recommended that you familiarize yourself with the long form, so
that you remember what each flag is supposed to do.

Presented here are each of the available flags, along with an example of how
you might use them.

C—chain

The [C] or [chain] flag indicates that the RewriteRule is chained to the next
rule. That is, if the rule matches, then it is processed as usual and control moves
on to the next rule. However, if it does not match, then the next rule, and any
other rules that are chained together, will be skipped.

CO—cookie

The [CO], or [cookie] flag, allows you to set a cookie when a particular
RewriteRule matches. The argument consists of three required fields and two
optional fields.

You must declare a name and value for the cookie to be set, and the domain
for which you wish the cookie to be valid. You may optionally set the lifetime
of the cookie, and the path for which it should be returned.

By default, the lifetime of the cookie is the current browser session.

By default, the path for which the cookie will be valid is "/" - that is, the entire website.

Several examples are offered here:

```
RewriteEngine On
RewriteRule ^/index.html - [CO=frontdoor:yes:.apache.org:1440:/]
```

This rule doesn't rewrite the request (the "-" rewrite target tells mod_rewrite to pass the request through unchanged) but sets a cookie called 'frontdoor' to a value of 'yes'. The cookie is valid for any host in the .apache.org domain. It will be set to expire in 1440 minutes (24 hours) and will be returned for all URIs.

E—env

With the [E], or [env] flag, you can set the value of an environment variable. Note that some environment variables may be set after the rule is run, thus unsetting what you have set. See the Environment Variables document (p. 705) for more details on how Environment variables work.

The following example sets an evironment variable called 'image' to a value of '1' if the requested URI is an image file. Then, that environment variable is used to exclude those requests from the access log.

```
RewriteRule \.(png|gif|jpg) - [E=image:1]
CustomLog logs/access_log combined env=!image
```

Note that this same effect can be obtained using SetEnvIf. This technique is offered as an example, not as a recommendation.

F—forbidden

Using the [F] flag causes Apache to return a 403 Forbidden status code to the client. While the same behavior can be accomplished using the Deny directive, this allows more flexibility in assigning a Forbidden status.

The following rule will forbid .exe files from being downloaded from your server.

```
RewriteRule \.exe - [F]
```

This example uses the "-" syntax for the rewrite target, which means that the requested URI is not modified. There's no reason to rewrite to another URI, if you're going to forbid the request.

G—gone

The [G] flag forces Apache to return a 410 Gone status with the response. This indicates that a resource used to be available, but is no longer available.

As with the [F] flag, you will typically use the "-" syntax for the rewrite target when using the [G] flag:

```
RewriteRule oldproduct - [G,NC]
```

H—handler

Forces the resulting request to be handled with the specified handler. For example, one might use this to force all files without a file extension to be parsed by the PHP handler:

```
RewriteRule !\.  - [H=application/x-httpd-php]
```

The regular expression above - !\. - will match any request that does not contain the literal . character.

L—last

The [L] flag causes mod_rewrite to stop processing the rule set. In most contexts, this means that if the rule matches, no further rules will be processed.

If you are using RewriteRule in either .htaccess files or in <Directory> sections, it is important to have some understanding of how the rules are processed. The simplified form of this is that once the rules have been processed, the rewritten request is handed back to the URL parsing engine to do what it may with it. It is possible that as the rewritten request is handled, the .htaccess file or <Directory> section may be encountered again, and thus the ruleset may be run again from the start. Most commonly this will happen if one of the rules causes a redirect - either internal or external - causing the request process to start over.

It is therefore important, if you are using RewriteRule directives in one of these context that you take explicit steps to avoid rules looping, and not count solely on the [L] flag to terminate execution of a series of rules, as shown below.

The example given here will rewrite any request to index.php, giving the original request as a query string argument to index.php, however, if the request is already for index.php, this rule will be skipped.

```
RewriteCond %{REQUEST_URI} !index\.php
RewriteRule ^(.*) index.php?req=$1 [L]
```

N—next

The [N] flag causes the ruleset to start over again from the top. Use with extreme caution, as it may result in loop.

The [Next] flag could be used, for example, if you wished to replace a certain string or letter repeatedly in a request. The example shown here will replace A with B everywhere in a request, and will continue doing so until there are no more As to be replaced.

```
RewriteRule (.*)A(.*) $1B$2 [N]
```

You can think of this as a while loop: While this pattern still matches, perform this substitution.

NC—nocase

Use of the [NC] flag causes the `RewriteRule` to be matched in a case-insensitive manner. That is, it doesn't care whether letters appear as upper-case or lower-case in the matched URI.

In the example below, any request for an image file will be proxied to your dedicated image server. The match is case-insensitive, so that `.jpg` and `.JPG` files are both acceptable, for example.

```
RewriteRule (.*\.(jpg|gif|png))$ http://images.example.com$1
[P,NC]
```

NE—noescape

By default, special characters, such as & and ?, for example, will be converted to their hexcode equivalent. Using the [NE] flag prevents that from happening.

```
RewriteRule ^/anchor/(.+) /bigpage.html#$1 [NE,R]
```

The above example will redirect `/anchor/xyz` to `/bigpage.html#xyz`. Omitting the [NE] will result in the # being converted to its hexcode equivalent, %23, which will then result in a 404 Not Found error condition.

NS—nosubreq

Use of the [NS] flag prevents the rule from being used on subrequests. For example, a page which is included using an SSI (Server Side Include) is a subrequest, and you may want to avoid rewrites happening on those subrequests.

Images, JavaScript files, or CSS files, loaded as part of an HTML page, are not subrequests - the browser requests them as separate HTTP requests.

P—proxy

Use of the [P] flag causes the request to be handled by mod_proxy, and handled via a proxy request. For example, if you wanted all image requests to be handled by a back-end image server, you might do something like the following:

```
RewriteRule (.*)\.(jpg|gif|png) http://images.example.com$1.$2
[P]
```

Use of the [P] flag implies [L] - that is, the request is immediately pushed through the proxy, and any following rules will not be considered.

PT—passthrough

The target (or substitution string) in a `RewriteRule` is assumed to be a file path, by default. The use of the [PT] flag causes it to be treated as a URI instead. That is to say, the use of the [PT] flag causes the result of the `RewriteRule` to be passed back through URL mapping, so that location-based mappings, such as `Alias`, for example, might have a chance to take effect.

If, for example, you have an `Alias` for `/icons`, and have a `RewriteRule` pointing there, you should use the [PT] flag to ensure that the `Alias` is evaluated.

```
Alias /icons /usr/local/apache/icons
RewriteRule /pics/(.+)\.jpg /icons/$1.gif [PT]
```

Omission of the [PT] flag in this case will cause the Alias to be ignored, resulting in a 'File not found' error being returned.

QSA—qsappend

When the replacement URI contains a query string, the default behavior of `RewriteRule` is to discard the existing query string, and replace it with the newly generated one. Using the [QSA] flag causes the query strings to be combined.

Consider the following rule:

```
RewriteRule /pages/(.+) /page.php?page=$1 [QSA]
```

With the [QSA] flag, a request for `/pages/123?one=two` will be mapped to `/page.php?page=123&one=two`. Without the [QSA] flag, that same request will be mapped to `/page.php?page=123` - that is, the existing query string will be discarded.

R—redirect

Use of the [R] flag causes a HTTP redirect to be issued to the browser. If a fully-qualified URL is specified (that is, including `http://servername/`) then a redirect will be issued to that location. Otherwise, the current servername will be used to generate the URL sent with the redirect.

A status code may be specified, in the range 300-399, with a 302 status code being used by default if none is specified.

You will almost always want to use [R] in conjunction with [L] (that is, use [R,L]) because on its own, the [R] flag prepends `http://thishost[:thisport]` to the URI, but then passes this on to the next rule in the ruleset, which can often result in 'Invalid URI in request' warnings.

S—skip

The [S] flag is used to skip rules that you don't want to run. This can be thought of as a goto statement in your rewrite ruleset. In the following example, we only want to run the `RewriteRule` if the requested URI doesn't correspond with an actual file.

```
# Is the request for a non-existent file?
RewriteCond %{REQUEST_FILENAME} !-f
RewriteCond %{REQUEST_FILENAME} !-d
# If so, skip these two RewriteRules
RewriteRule .? - [S=2]
RewriteRule (.*\.gif) images.php?$1
```

```
RewriteRule (.*\.html) docs.php?$1
```

This technique is useful because a `RewriteCond` only applies to the `RewriteRule` immediately following it. Thus, if you want to make a `RewriteCond` apply to several `RewriteRules`, one possible technique is to negate those conditions and use a [Skip] flag.

T—type

Sets the MIME type with which the resulting response will be sent. This has the same effect as the `AddType` directive.

For example, you might use the following technique to serve Perl source code as plain text, if requested in a particular way:

```
# Serve .pl files as plain text
RewriteRule \.pl$ - [T=text/plain]
```

Or, perhaps, if you have a camera that produces JPEG images without file extensions, you could force those images to be served with the correct MIME type by virtue of their file names:

```
# Files with 'IMG' in the name are jpg images.
RewriteRule IMG - [T=image/jpg]
```

Please note that this is a trivial example, and could be better done using `<FilesMatch>` instead. Always consider the alternate solutions to a problem before resorting to rewrite, which will invariably be a less efficient solution than the alternatives.

If used in per-directory context, use only - (dash) as the substitution *for the entire round of mod_rewrite processing*, otherwise the MIME-type set with this flag is lost due to an internal re-processing (including subsequent rounds of mod_rewrite processing). The L flag can be useful in this context to end the *current* round of mod_rewrite processing.

5.4 Apache mod_rewrite Technical Details

This section discusses some of the technical details of mod_rewrite and URL matching.

See also:

▷ Module documentation (p. 426)

▷ mod_rewrite introduction (p. 577)

▷ Rewrite Guide - useful examples (p. 591)

▷ Advanced Rewrite Guide - advanced useful examples (p. 599)

5.4.1 Internal Processing

The internal processing of this module is very complex but needs to be explained once even to the average user to avoid common mistakes and to let you exploit its full functionality.

5.4.2 API Phases

First you have to understand that when Apache processes a HTTP request it does this in phases. A hook for each of these phases is provided by the Apache API. mod_rewrite uses two of these hooks: the URL-to-filename translation hook which is used after the HTTP request has been read but before any authorization starts and the Fixup hook which is triggered after the authorization phases and after the per-directory config files (.htaccess) have been read, but before the content handler is activated.

So, after a request comes in and Apache has determined the corresponding server (or virtual server) the rewriting engine starts processing of all mod_-rewrite directives from the per-server configuration in the URL-to-filename phase. A few steps later when the final data directories are found, the per-directory configuration directives of mod_rewrite are triggered in the Fixup phase. In both situations mod_rewrite rewrites URLs either to new URLs or to filenames, although there is no obvious distinction between them. This is a usage of the API which was not intended to be this way when the API was designed, but as of Apache 1.x this is the only way mod_rewrite can operate. To make this point more clear remember the following two points:

1. Although mod_rewrite rewrites URLs to URLs, URLs to filenames and even filenames to filenames, the API currently provides only a URL-to-filename hook. In Apache 2.0 the two missing hooks will be added to make the processing more clear. But this point has no drawbacks for the user, it is just a fact which should be remembered: Apache does more in the URL-to-filename hook than the API intends for it.

2. Unbelievably mod_rewrite provides URL manipulations in per-directory context, i.e., within .htaccess files, although these are reached a very long time after the URLs have been translated to filenames. It has to be

this way because .htaccess files live in the filesystem, so processing has already reached this stage. In other words: According to the API phases at this time it is too late for any URL manipulations. To overcome this chicken and egg problem mod_rewrite uses a trick: When you manipulate a URL/filename in per-directory context mod_rewrite first rewrites the filename back to its corresponding URL (which is usually impossible, but see the RewriteBase directive below for the trick to achieve this) and then initiates a new internal sub-request with the new URL. This restarts processing of the API phases.

Again mod_rewrite tries hard to make this complicated step totally transparent to the user, but you should remember here: While URL manipulations in per-server context are really fast and efficient, per-directory rewrites are slow and inefficient due to this chicken and egg problem. But on the other hand this is the only way mod_rewrite can provide (locally restricted) URL manipulations to the average user.

Don't forget these two points!

5.4.3 Ruleset Processing

Now when mod_rewrite is triggered in these two API phases, it reads the configured rulesets from its configuration structure (which itself was either created on startup for per-server context or during the directory walk of the Apache kernel for per-directory context). Then the URL rewriting engine is started with the contained ruleset (one or more rules together with their conditions). The operation of the URL rewriting engine itself is exactly the same for both configuration contexts. Only the final result processing is different.

The order of rules in the ruleset is important because the rewriting engine processes them in a special (and not very obvious) order. The rule is this: The rewriting engine loops through the ruleset rule by rule (RewriteRule directives) and when a particular rule matches it optionally loops through existing corresponding conditions (RewriteCond directives). For historical reasons the conditions are given first, and so the control flow is a little bit long-winded. See Figure 5.2 for more details.

As you can see, first the URL is matched against the *Pattern* of each rule. When it fails mod_rewrite immediately stops processing this rule and continues with the next rule. If the *Pattern* matches, mod_rewrite looks for corresponding rule conditions. If none are present, it just substitutes the URL with a new value which is constructed from the string *Substitution* and goes on with its rule-looping. But if conditions exist, it starts an inner loop for processing them in the order in which they are listed. For conditions the logic is different: we don't match a pattern against the current URL. Instead we first create a string *TestString* by expanding variables, back-references, map lookups, *etc.* and then we try to match *CondPattern* against it. If the pattern doesn't match, the complete set of conditions and the corresponding rule fails. If the pattern matches, then the next condition is processed until no more conditions are

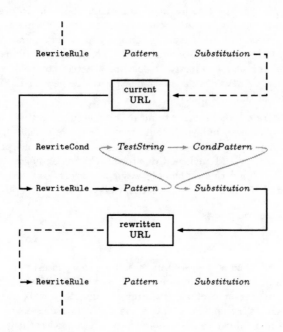

Figure 5.2: The control flow through the rewriting ruleset

available. If all conditions match, processing is continued with the substitution
of the URL with *Substitution*.

5.5 URL Rewriting Guide

This section supplements the mod_rewrite reference documentation (p. 426). It describes how one can use Apache's mod_rewrite to solve typical URL-based problems with which webmasters are commonly confronted. We give detailed descriptions on how to solve each problem by configuring URL rewriting rulesets.

> *ATTENTION: Depending on your server configuration it may be necessary to slightly change the examples for your situation, e.g. adding the [PT] flag when additionally using mod_alias and mod_userdir, etc. Or rewriting a ruleset to fit in .htaccess context instead of per-server context. Always try to understand what a particular ruleset really does before you use it. This avoids many problems.*

See also:

 ▷ Module documentation (p. 426)

 ▷ mod_rewrite introduction (p. 577)

 ▷ Advanced Rewrite Guide - advanced useful examples (p. 599)

 ▷ Technical details (p. 588)

5.5.1 Canonical URLs

Description: On some webservers there are more than one URL for a resource. Usually there are canonical URLs (which should be actually used and distributed) and those which are just shortcuts, internal ones, etc. Independent of which URL the user supplied with the request he should finally see the canonical one only.

Solution: We do an external HTTP redirect for all non-canonical URLs to fix them in the location view of the Browser and for all subsequent requests. In the example ruleset below we replace /~user by the canonical /u/user and fix a missing trailing slash for /u/user.

```
RewriteRule ^/~([^/]+)/?(.*)  /u/$1/$2  [R]
RewriteRule ^/u/([^/]+)$  /$1/$2/  [R]
```

5.5.2 Canonical Hostnames

Description: The goal of this rule is to force the use of a particular hostname, in preference to other hostnames which may be used to reach the same site. For example, if you wish to force the use of **www.example.com** instead of **example.com**, you might use a variant of the following recipe.

Solution: For sites running on a port other than 80:

```
RewriteCond %{HTTP_HOST}   !^www\.example\.com [NC]
RewriteCond %{HTTP_HOST}   !^$
RewriteCond %{SERVER_PORT} !^80$
RewriteRule ^/?(.*) http://www.example.com:
                            %{SERVER_PORT}/$1 [L,R,NE]
```

And for a site running on port 80

```
RewriteCond %{HTTP_HOST} !^www\.example\.com [NC]
RewriteCond %{HTTP_HOST} !^$
RewriteRule ^/?(.*) http://www.example.com/$1 [L,R,NE]
```

5.5.3 Moved DocumentRoot

Description: Usually the DocumentRoot of the webserver directly relates to
the URL "/". But often this data is not really of top-level priority. For
example, you may wish for visitors, on first entering a site, to go to a
particular subdirectory /about/. This may be accomplished using the
following ruleset:

Solution: We redirect the URL / to /about/:

```
RewriteEngine on
RewriteRule ^/$ /about/ [R]
```

Note that this can also be handled using the RedirectMatch directive:

```
RedirectMatch ^/$ http://example.com/e/www/
```

5.5.4 Trailing Slash Problem

Description: The vast majority of "trailing slash" problems can be dealt with
using the techniques discussed in the FAQ entry[6]. However, occasionally,
there is a need to use mod_rewrite to handle a case where a missing trailing
slash causes a URL to fail. This can happen, for example, after a series
of complex rewrite rules.

Solution: The solution to this subtle problem is to let the server add the trailing slash automatically. To do this correctly we have to use an external
redirect, so the browser correctly requests subsequent images etc. If we
only did a internal rewrite, this would only work for the directory page,
but would go wrong when any images are included into this page with
relative URLs, because the browser would request an in-lined object. For
instance, a request for image.gif in /~quux/foo/index.html would become /~quux/image.gif without the external redirect!

So, to do this trick we write:

```
RewriteEngine on
RewriteBase /~quux/
RewriteRule ^foo$ foo/ [R]
```

Alternately, you can put the following in a top-level .htaccess file in the
content directory. But note that this creates some processing overhead.

```
RewriteEngine on
RewriteBase /~quux/
RewriteCond %{REQUEST_FILENAME} -d
RewriteRule ^(.+[^/])$ $1/ [R]
```

---

[6]http://httpd.apache.org/docs/misc/FAQ-E.html#set-servername

5.5.5 Move Homedirs to Different Webserver

Description: Many webmasters have asked for a solution to the following situation: They wanted to redirect just all homedirs on a webserver to another webserver. They usually need such things when establishing a newer webserver which will replace the old one over time.

Solution: The solution is trivial with mod_rewrite. On the old webserver we just redirect all /~user/anypath URLs to http://newserver/~user/anypath.

```
RewriteEngine on
RewriteRule ^/~(.+) http://newserver/~$1 [R,L]
```

5.5.6 Search pages in more than one directory

Description: Sometimes it is necessary to let the webserver search for pages in more than one directory. Here MultiViews or other techniques cannot help.

Solution: We program a explicit ruleset which searches for the files in the directories.

```
RewriteEngine on

#   first try to find it in dir1/...
#   ...and if found stop and be happy:
RewriteCond /your/docroot/dir1/%{REQUEST_FILENAME} -f
RewriteRule ^(.+) /your/docroot/dir1/$1 [L]

#   second try to find it in dir2/...
#   ...and if found stop and be happy:
RewriteCond /your/docroot/dir2/%{REQUEST_FILENAME} -f
RewriteRule ^(.+) /your/docroot/dir2/$1 [L]

#   else go on for other Alias or ScriptAlias directives,
#   etc.
RewriteRule ^(.+) - [PT]
```

5.5.7 Set Environment Variables According To URL Parts

Description: Perhaps you want to keep status information between requests and use the URL to encode it. But you don't want to use a CGI wrapper for all pages just to strip out this information.

Solution: We use a rewrite rule to strip out the status information and remember it via an environment variable which can be later dereferenced from within XSSI or CGI. This way a URL /foo/S=java/bar/ gets translated to /foo/bar/ and the environment variable named STATUS is set to the value "java".

```
RewriteEngine on
RewriteRule ^(.*)/S=([^/]+)/(.*) $1/$3 [E=STATUS:$2]
```

5.5.8 Virtual User Hosts

Description: Assume that you want to provide www.username.host.domain.com for the homepage of username via just DNS A records to the same machine and without any virtualhosts on this machine.

Solution: For HTTP/1.0 requests there is no solution, but for HTTP/1.1 requests which contain a Host: HTTP header we can use the following ruleset to rewrite http://www.username.host.com/anypath internally to /home/username/anypath:

```
RewriteEngine on
RewriteCond %{HTTP_HOST} ^www\.[^.]+\.host\.com$
RewriteRule ^(.+) %{HTTP_HOST}$1 [C]
RewriteRule ^www\.([^.]+)\.host\.com(.*) /home/$1$2
```

5.5.9 Redirect Homedirs For Foreigners

Description: We want to redirect homedir URLs to another webserver www.somewhere.com when the requesting user does not stay in the local domain ourdomain.com. This is sometimes used in virtual host contexts.

Solution: Just a rewrite condition:

```
RewriteEngine on
RewriteCond %{REMOTE_HOST} !^.+\.ourdomain\.com$
RewriteRule ^(/~.+) http://www.somewhere.com/$1 [R,L]
```

5.5.10 Redirecting Anchors

Description: By default, redirecting to an HTML anchor doesn't work, because mod_rewrite escapes the # character, turning it into %23. This, in turn, breaks the redirection.

Solution: Use the [NE] flag on the RewriteRule. NE stands for No Escape.

5.5.11 Time-Dependent Rewriting

Description: When tricks like time-dependent content should happen a lot of webmasters still use CGI scripts which do for instance redirects to specialized pages. How can it be done via mod_rewrite?

Solution: There are a lot of variables named TIME_xxx for rewrite conditions. In conjunction with the special lexicographic comparison patterns <STRING, >STRING and =STRING we can do time-dependent redirects:

```
RewriteEngine on
RewriteCond %{TIME_HOUR}%{TIME_MIN} >0700
RewriteCond %{TIME_HOUR}%{TIME_MIN} <1900
```

```
RewriteRule ^foo\.html$ foo.day.html
RewriteRule ^foo\.html$ foo.night.html
```

This provides the content of `foo.day.html` under the URL `foo.html` from
07:00-19:00 and at the remaining time the contents of `foo.night.html`.
Just a nice feature for a homepage...

5.5.12 Backward Compatibility for YYYY to XXXX migration

Description: How can we make URLs backward compatible (still existing virtually) after migrating `document.YYYY` to `document.XXXX`, e.g. after translating a bunch of `.html` files to `.phtml`?

Solution: We just rewrite the name to its basename and test for existence of
the new extension. If it exists, we take that name, else we rewrite the
URL to its original state.

```
#   backward compatibility ruleset for
#   rewriting document.html to document.phtml
#   when and only when document.phtml exists
#   but no longer document.html
RewriteEngine on
RewriteBase /~quux/
#   parse out basename, but remember the fact
RewriteRule ^(.*)\.html$ $1 [C,E=WasHTML:yes]
#   rewrite to document.phtml if exists
RewriteCond %{REQUEST_FILENAME}.phtml -f
RewriteRule ^(.*)$ $1.phtml [S=1]
#   else reverse the previous basename cutout
RewriteCond %{ENV:WasHTML} ^yes$
RewriteRule ^(.*)$ $1.html
```

5.5.13 From Old to New (intern)

Description: Assume we have recently renamed the page `foo.html` to
`bar.html` and now want to provide the old URL for backward compatibility. Actually we want that users of the old URL even not recognize that
the pages was renamed.

Solution: We rewrite the old URL to the new one internally via the following
rule:

```
RewriteEngine on
RewriteBase /~quux/
RewriteRule ^foo\.html$ bar.html
```

5.5.14 From Old to New (extern)

Description: Assume again that we have recently renamed the page `foo.html`
to `bar.html` and now want to provide the old URL for backward compat-

ibility. But this time we want that the users of the old URL get hinted to the new one, i.e. their browser's Location field should change, too.

Solution: We force a HTTP redirect to the new URL which leads to a change of the browsers and thus the users view:

```
RewriteEngine on
RewriteBase /~quux/
RewriteRule ^foo\.html$ bar.html [R]
```

5.5.15 From Static to Dynamic

Description: How can we transform a static page foo.html into a dynamic variant foo.cgi in a seamless way, i.e. without notice by the browser/user.

Solution: We just rewrite the URL to the CGI-script and force the handler to be **cgi-script** so that it is executed as a CGI program. This way a request to /~quux/foo.html internally leads to the invocation of /~quux/foo.cgi.

```
RewriteEngine on
RewriteBase /~quux/
RewriteRule ^foo\.html$ foo.cgi [H=cgi-script]
```

5.5.16 Blocking of Robots

Description: How can we block a really annoying robot from retrieving pages of a specific webarea? A /robots.txt file containing entries of the "Robot Exclusion Protocol" is typically not enough to get rid of such a robot.

Solution: We use a ruleset which forbids the URLs of the webarea /~quux/foo/arc/ (perhaps a very deep directory indexed area where the robot traversal would create big server load). We have to make sure that we forbid access only to the particular robot, i.e. just forbidding the host where the robot runs is not enough. This would block users from this host, too. We accomplish this by also matching the User-Agent HTTP header information.

```
RewriteCond %{HTTP_USER_AGENT} ^NameOfBadRobot.*
RewriteCond %{REMOTE_ADDR}     ^123\.45\.67\.[8-9]$
RewriteRule ^/~quux/foo/arc/.+ - [F]
```

5.5.17 Blocked Inline-Images

Description: Assume we have under http://www.quux-corp.de/~quux/ some pages with inlined GIF graphics. These graphics are nice, so others directly incorporate them via hyperlinks to their pages. We don't like this practice because it adds useless traffic to our server.

Solution: While we cannot 100% protect the images from inclusion, we can at least restrict the cases where the browser sends a HTTP Referer header.

```
RewriteCond %{HTTP_REFERER} !^$
RewriteCond %{HTTP_REFERER}
```

```
                                   !^http://www.quux-corp.de/~quux/.*$ [NC]
        RewriteRule .*\.gif$ - [F]

        RewriteCond %{HTTP_REFERER} !^$
        RewriteCond %{HTTP_REFERER} !.*/foo-with-gif\.html$
        RewriteRule ^inlined-in-foo\.gif$ - [F]
```

5.5.18 Proxy Deny

Description: How can we forbid a certain host or even a user of a special host from using the Apache proxy?

Solution: We first have to make sure mod_rewrite is below(!) mod_proxy in the Configuration file when compiling the Apache webserver. This way it gets called *before* mod_proxy. Then we configure the following for a host-dependent deny...

```
        RewriteCond %{REMOTE_HOST} ^badhost\.mydomain\.com$
        RewriteRule !^http://[^/.]\.mydomain.com.* - [F]
```

...and this one for a user@host-dependent deny:

```
        RewriteCond %{REMOTE_IDENT}@%{REMOTE_HOST}
                                     ^badguy@badhost\.mydomain\.com$
        RewriteRule !^http://[^/.]\.mydomain.com.* - [F]
```

5.5.19 External Rewriting Engine

Description: A FAQ: How can we solve the FOO/BAR/QUUX/etc. problem? There seems no solution by the use of mod_rewrite...

Solution: Use an external RewriteMap, i.e. a program which acts like a RewriteMap. It is run once on startup of Apache receives the requested URLs on STDIN and has to put the resulting (usually rewritten) URL on STDOUT (same order!).

```
        RewriteEngine on
        RewriteMap quux-map prg:/path/to/map.quux.pl
        RewriteRule ^/~quux/(.*)$ /~quux/${quux-map:$1}

        #!/path/to/perl

        #   disable buffered I/O which would lead
        #   to deadloops for the Apache server
        $| = 1;

        #   read URLs one per line from stdin and
        #   generate substitution URL on stdout
        while (<>) {
            s|^foo/|bar/|;
            print $_;
        }
```

This is a demonstration-only example and just rewrites all URLs /~quux/foo/... to /~quux/bar/.... Actually you can program whatever you like. But notice that while such maps can be **used** also by an average user, only the system administrator can **define** it.

5.6 URL Rewriting Guide - Advanced topics

This section supplements the mod_rewrite reference documentation (p. 426). It describes how one can use Apache's mod_rewrite to solve typical URL-based problems with which webmasters are commonly confronted. We give detailed descriptions on how to solve each problem by configuring URL rewriting rulesets.

> *ATTENTION: Depending on your server configuration it may be necessary to adjust the examples for your situation, e.g., adding the [PT] flag if using mod_alias and mod_userdir, etc. Or rewriting a ruleset to work in .htaccess context instead of per-server context. Always try to understand what a particular ruleset really does before you use it; this avoids many problems.*

See also:

▷ Module documentation (p. 426)

▷ mod_rewrite introduction (p. 577)

▷ Rewrite Guide - useful examples (p. 591)

▷ Technical details (p. 588)

5.6.1 Web Cluster with Consistent URL Space

Description: We want to create a homogeneous and consistent URL layout across all WWW servers on an Intranet web cluster, i.e., all URLs (by definition server-local and thus server-dependent!) become server *independent*! What we want is to give the WWW namespace a single consistent layout: no URL should refer to any particular target server. The cluster itself should connect users automatically to a physical target host as needed, invisibly.

Solution: First, the knowledge of the target servers comes from (distributed) external maps which contain information on where our users, groups, and entities reside. They have the form:

```
user1   server_of_user1
user2   server_of_user2
  :        :
```

We put them into files map.xxx-to-host. Second we need to instruct all servers to redirect URLs of the forms:

```
/u/user/anypath
/g/group/anypath
/e/entity/anypath
```

to

```
http://physical-host/u/user/anypath
http://physical-host/g/group/anypath
http://physical-host/e/entity/anypath
```

when any URL path need not be valid on every server. The following
ruleset does this for us with the help of the map files (assuming that
server0 is a default server which will be used if a user has no entry in the
map):

```
RewriteEngine on

RewriteMap user-to-host txt:/path/to/map.user-to-host
RewriteMap group-to-host txt:/path/to/map.group-to-host
RewriteMap entity-to-host txt:/path/to/map.entity-to-host

RewriteRule ^/u/([^/]+)/?(.*)
               http://${user-to-host:$1|server0}/u/$1/$2
RewriteRule ^/g/([^/]+)/?(.*)
               http://${group-to-host:$1|server0}/g/$1/$2
RewriteRule ^/e/([^/]+)/?(.*)
               http://${entity-to-host:$1|server0}/e/$1/$2

RewriteRule ^/([uge])/([^/]+)/?$ /$1/$2/.www/
RewriteRule ^/([uge])/([^/]+)/([^.]+.+) /$1/$2/.www/$3\
```

5.6.2 Structured Homedirs

Description: Some sites with thousands of users use a structured homedir layout, *i.e.* each homedir is in a subdirectory which begins
(for instance) with the first character of the username. So,
/~foo/anypath is /home/f/foo/.www/anypath while /~bar/anypath is
/home/b/bar/.www/anypath.

Solution: We use the following ruleset to expand the tilde URLs into the above
layout.

```
RewriteEngine on
RewriteRule ^/~(([a-z])[a-z0-9]+)(.*) /home/$2/$1/.www$3
```

5.6.3 Filesystem Reorganization

Description: This really is a hardcore example: a killer application which
heavily uses per-directory RewriteRules to get a smooth look and feel
on the Web while its data structure is never touched or adjusted. Background: *net.sw* is my archive of freely available Unix software packages,
which I started to collect in 1992. It is both my hobby and job to do
this, because while I'm studying computer science I have also worked for
many years as a system and network administrator in my spare time. Every week I need some sort of software so I created a deep hierarchy of
directories where I stored the packages:

```
drwxrwxr-x   2 netsw   users    512 Aug  3 18:39 Audio/
drwxrwxr-x   2 netsw   users    512 Jul  9 14:37 Benchmark/
drwxrwxr-x  12 netsw   users    512 Jul  9 00:34 Crypto/
```

```
drwxrwxr-x   5 netsw   users    512 Jul  9 00:41 Database/
drwxrwxr-x   4 netsw   users    512 Jul 30 19:25 Dicts/
drwxrwxr-x  10 netsw   users    512 Jul  9 01:54 Graphic/
drwxrwxr-x   5 netsw   users    512 Jul  9 01:58 Hackers/
drwxrwxr-x   8 netsw   users    512 Jul  9 03:19 InfoSys/
drwxrwxr-x   3 netsw   users    512 Jul  9 03:21 Math/
drwxrwxr-x   3 netsw   users    512 Jul  9 03:24 Misc/
drwxrwxr-x   9 netsw   users    512 Aug  1 16:33 Network/
drwxrwxr-x   2 netsw   users    512 Jul  9 05:53 Office/
drwxrwxr-x   7 netsw   users    512 Jul  9 09:24 SoftEng/
drwxrwxr-x   7 netsw   users    512 Jul  9 12:17 System/
drwxrwxr-x  12 netsw   users    512 Aug  3 20:15 Typesetting/
drwxrwxr-x  10 netsw   users    512 Jul  9 14:08 X11/
```

In July 1996 I decided to make this archive public to the world via a nice
Web interface. "Nice" means that I wanted to offer an interface where
you can browse directly through the archive hierarchy. And "nice" means
that I didn't want to change anything inside this hierarchy - not even
by putting some CGI scripts at the top of it. Why? Because the above
structure should later be accessible via FTP as well, and I didn't want
any Web or CGI stuff mixed in there.

Solution: The solution has two parts: The first is a set of CGI scripts which
create all the pages at all directory levels on-the-fly. I put them under
/e/netsw/.www/ as follows:

```
-rw-r--r--   1 netsw   users   1318
                       Aug  1 18:10 .wwwacl
drwxr-xr-x  18 netsw   users    512
                       Aug  5 15:51 DATA/
-rw-rw-rw-   1 netsw   users 372982
                       Aug  5 16:35 LOGFILE
-rw-r--r--   1 netsw   users    659
                       Aug  4 09:27 TODO
-rw-r--r--   1 netsw   users   5697
                       Aug  1 18:01 netsw-about.html
-rwxr-xr-x   1 netsw   users    579
                       Aug  2 10:33 netsw-access.pl
-rwxr-xr-x   1 netsw   users   1532
                       Aug  1 17:35 netsw-changes.cgi
-rwxr-xr-x   1 netsw   users   2866
                       Aug  5 14:49 netsw-home.cgi
drwxr-xr-x   2 netsw   users    512
                       Jul  8 23:47 netsw-img/
-rwxr-xr-x   1 netsw   users  24050
                       Aug  5 15:49 netsw-lsdir.cgi
-rwxr-xr-x   1 netsw   users   1589
                       Aug  3 18:43 netsw-search.cgi
-rwxr-xr-x   1 netsw   users   1885
```

```
                              Aug  1 17:41 netsw-tree.cgi
      -rw-r--r--   1 netsw   users    234
                              Jul 30 16:35 netsw-unlimit.lst
```

The DATA/ subdirectory holds the above directory structure, *i.e.* the real
net.sw stuff, and gets automatically updated via rdist from time to time.
The second part of the problem remains: how to link these two structures
together into one smooth-looking URL tree? We want to hide the DATA/
directory from the user while running the appropriate CGI scripts for the
various URLs. Here is the solution: first I put the following into the per-
directory configuration file in the DocumentRoot of the server to rewrite
the public URL path /net.sw/ to the internal path /e/netsw:

```
RewriteRule ^net.sw$ net.sw/ [R]
RewriteRule ^net.sw/(.*)$ e/netsw/$1
```

The first rule is for requests which miss the trailing slash! The second rule
does the real thing. And then comes the killer configuration which stays
in the per-directory config file /e/netsw/.www/.wwwacl:

```
Options ExecCGI FollowSymLinks Includes MultiViews

RewriteEngine on

#  we are reached via /net.sw/ prefix
RewriteBase /net.sw/

#  first we rewrite the root dir to
#  the handling cgi script
RewriteRule ^$ netsw-home.cgi [L]
RewriteRule ^index\.html$ netsw-home.cgi [L]

#  strip out the subdirs when
#  the browser requests us from perdir pages
RewriteRule ^.+/(netsw-[^/]+/.+)$ $1 [L]

#  and now break the rewriting for local files
RewriteRule ^netsw-home\.cgi.* - [L]
RewriteRule ^netsw-changes\.cgi.* - [L]
RewriteRule ^netsw-search\.cgi.* - [L]
RewriteRule ^netsw-tree\.cgi$ - [L]
RewriteRule ^netsw-about\.html$ - [L]
RewriteRule ^netsw-img/.*$ - [L]

#  anything else is a subdir which gets handled
#  by another cgi script
RewriteRule !^netsw-lsdir\.cgi.* - [C]
RewriteRule (.*) netsw-lsdir.cgi/$1
```

Some hints for interpretation:

1. Notice the L (last) flag and no substitution field ('-') in the fourth part
2. Notice the ! (not) character and the C (chain) flag at the first rule in the last part
3. Notice the catch-all pattern in the last rule

5.6.4 Redirect Failing URLs to Another Web Server

Description: A typical FAQ about URL rewriting is how to redirect failing requests on webserver A to webserver B. Usually this is done via ErrorDocument CGI scripts in Perl, but there is also a mod_rewrite solution. But note that this performs more poorly than using an ErrorDocument CGI script!

Solution: The first solution has the best performance but less flexibility, and is less safe:

```
RewriteEngine on
RewriteCond /your/docroot/%{REQUEST_FILENAME} !-f
RewriteRule ^(.+) http://webserverB.dom/$1
```

The problem here is that this will only work for pages inside the DocumentRoot. While you can add more Conditions (for instance to also handle homedirs, etc.) there is a better variant:

```
RewriteEngine on
RewriteCond %{REQUEST_URI} !-U
RewriteRule ^(.+) http://webserverB.dom/$1
```

This uses the URL look-ahead feature of mod_rewrite. The result is that this will work for all types of URLs and is safe. But it does have a performance impact on the web server, because for every request there is one more internal subrequest. So, if your web server runs on a powerful CPU, use this one. If it is a slow machine, use the first approach or better an ErrorDocument CGI script.

5.6.5 Archive Access Multiplexer

Description: Do you know the great CPAN (Comprehensive Perl Archive Network) under http://www.perl.com/CPAN? CPAN automatically redirects browsers to one of many FTP servers around the world (generally one near the requesting client); each server carries a full CPAN mirror. This is effectively an FTP access multiplexing service. CPAN runs via CGI scripts, but how could a similar approach be implemented via mod_rewrite?

Solution: First we notice that as of version 3.0.0, mod_rewrite can also use the "ftp:" scheme on redirects. And second, the location approximation can be done by a RewriteMap over the top-level domain of the client. With a tricky chained ruleset we can use this top-level domain as a key to our multiplexing map.

```
RewriteEngine on
RewriteMap multiplex txt:/path/to/map.cxan
RewriteRule ^/CxAN/(.*) %{REMOTE_HOST}::$1 [C]
RewriteRule ^.+\.([a-zA-Z]+)::(.*)$
                    ${multiplex:$1|ftp.default.dom}$2   [R,L]

##
##  map.cxan -- Multiplexing Map for CxAN
##

de        ftp://ftp.cxan.de/CxAN/
uk        ftp://ftp.cxan.uk/CxAN/
com       ftp://ftp.cxan.com/CxAN/
 :
##EOF##
```

5.6.6 Browser Dependent Content

Description: At least for important top-level pages it is sometimes necessary
to provide the optimum of browser dependent content, i.e., one has to
provide one version for current browsers, a different version for the Lynx
and text-mode browsers, and another for other browsers.

Solution: We cannot use content negotiation because the browsers do not
provide their type in that form. Instead we have to act on the HTTP
header "User-Agent". The following config does the following: If the
HTTP header "User-Agent" begins with "Mozilla/3", the page foo.html
is rewritten to foo.NS.html and the rewriting stops. If the browser is
"Lynx" or "Mozilla" of version 1 or 2, the URL becomes foo.20.html.
All other browsers receive page foo.32.html. This is done with the following ruleset:

```
RewriteCond %{HTTP_USER_AGENT} ^Mozilla/3.*
RewriteRule ^foo\.html$ foo.NS.html [L]

RewriteCond %{HTTP_USER_AGENT} ^Lynx/.* [OR]
RewriteCond %{HTTP_USER_AGENT} ^Mozilla/[12].*
RewriteRule ^foo\.html$ foo.20.html [L]

RewriteRule ^foo\.html$ foo.32.html [L]
```

5.6.7 Dynamic Mirror

Description: Assume there are nice web pages on remote hosts we want to
bring into our namespace. For FTP servers we would use the mirror program which actually maintains an explicit up-to-date copy of the remote
data on the local machine. For a web server we could use the program
webcopy which runs via HTTP. But both techniques have a major drawback: The local copy is always only as up-to-date as the last time we ran

the program. It would be much better if the mirror was not a static one
we have to establish explicitly. Instead we want a dynamic mirror with
data which gets updated automatically as needed on the remote host(s).

Solution: To provide this feature we map the remote web page or even the
complete remote web area to our namespace by the use of the **Proxy
Throughput** feature (flag [P]):

```
RewriteEngine on
RewriteBase /~quux/
RewriteRule ^hotsheet/(.*)$
                    http://www.tstimpreso.com/hotsheet/$1   [P]

RewriteEngine on
RewriteBase /~quux/
RewriteRule ^usa-news\.html$
                    http://www.quux-corp.com/news/index.html   [P]
```

5.6.8 Reverse Dynamic Mirror

Description: ...

Solution:

```
RewriteEngine on
RewriteCond /mirror/of/remotesite/$1 -U
RewriteRule ^http://www\.remotesite\.com/(.*)$
                                /mirror/of/remotesite/$1
```

5.6.9 Retrieve Missing Data from Intranet

Description: This is a tricky way of virtually running a corporate (external) Internet web server (www.quux-corp.dom), while actually keeping and maintaining its data on an (internal) Intranet web server
(www2.quux-corp.dom) which is protected by a firewall. The trick is that
the external web server retrieves the requested data on-the-fly from the
internal one.

Solution: First, we must make sure that our firewall still protects the internal
web server and only the external web server is allowed to retrieve data
from it. On a packet-filtering firewall, for instance, we could configure a
firewall ruleset like the following:

```
ALLOW Host www.quux-corp.dom Port >1024
                        --> Host www2.quux-corp.dom Port 80
DENY  Host * Port *     --> Host www2.quux-corp.dom Port 80
```

Just adjust it to your actual configuration syntax. Now we can establish
the mod_rewrite rules which request the missing data in the background
through the proxy throughput feature:

```
RewriteRule ^/~([^/]+)/?(.*) /home/$1/.www/$2
RewriteCond %{REQUEST_FILENAME} !-f
```

```
RewriteCond %{REQUEST_FILENAME} !-d
RewriteRule ^/home/([^/]+)/.www/?(.*)
                    http://www2.quux-corp.dom/~$1/pub/$2 [P]
```

5.6.10 Load Balancing

Description: Suppose we want to load balance the traffic to www.example.com over www[0-5].example.com (a total of 6 servers). How can this be done?

Solution: There are many possible solutions for this problem. We will first discuss a common DNS-based method, and then one based on mod_rewrite:

1. **DNS Round-Robin**

   The simplest method for load-balancing is to use DNS round-robin. Here you just configure www[0-9].example.com as usual in your DNS with A (address) records, e.g.,

   ```
   www0   IN   A      1.2.3.1
   www1   IN   A      1.2.3.2
   www2   IN   A      1.2.3.3
   www3   IN   A      1.2.3.4
   www4   IN   A      1.2.3.5
   www5   IN   A      1.2.3.6
   ```

   Then you additionally add the following entries:

   ```
   www    IN   A      1.2.3.1
   www    IN   A      1.2.3.2
   www    IN   A      1.2.3.3
   www    IN   A      1.2.3.4
   www    IN   A      1.2.3.5
   ```

   Now when www.example.com gets resolved, BIND gives out www0-www5 - but in a permutated (rotated) order every time. This way the clients are spread over the various servers. But notice that this is not a perfect load balancing scheme, because DNS resolutions are cached by clients and other nameservers, so once a client has resolved www.example.com to a particular wwwN.example.com, all its subsequent requests will continue to go to the same IP (and thus a single server), rather than being distributed across the other available servers. But the overall result is okay because the requests are collectively spread over the various web servers.

2. **DNS Load-Balancing**

   A sophisticated DNS-based method for load-balancing is to use the program lbnamed which can be found at http://www.stanford.edu/~riepel/lbnamed/. It is a Perl 5 program which, in conjunction with auxilliary tools, provides real load-balancing via DNS.

3. **Proxy Throughput Round-Robin**

   In this variant we use mod_rewrite and its proxy throughput feature. First we dedicate www0.example.com to be actually www.example.com by using a single

```
www    IN  CNAME   www0.example.com.
```

entry in the DNS. Then we convert www0.example.com to a proxy-only server, i.e., we configure this machine so all arriving URLs are simply passed through its internal proxy to one of the 5 other servers (www1-www5). To accomplish this we first establish a ruleset which contacts a load balancing script lb.pl for all URLs.

```
RewriteEngine on
RewriteMap lb prg:/path/to/lb.pl
RewriteRule ^/(.+)$ ${lb:$1} [P,L]
```

Then we write lb.pl:

```
#!/path/to/perl
##
##  lb.pl -- load balancing script
##

$| = 1;

$name   = "www";       # the hostname base
$first  = 1;           # the first server (not 0 here,
                       #   because 0 is myself)
$last   = 5;           # the last server in the round-
                       #   robin
$domain = "foo.dom";   # the domainname

$cnt = 0;
while (<STDIN>) {
    $cnt = (($cnt+1) % ($last+1-$first));
    $server = sprintf("%s%d.%s",
                      $name, $cnt+$first, $domain);
    print "http://$server/$_";
}

##EOF##
```

A last notice: Why is this useful? Seems like www0.example.com still is overloaded? The answer is yes, it is overloaded, but with plain proxy throughput requests, only! All SSI, CGI, ePerl, etc. processing is handled done on the other machines. For a complicated site, this may work well. The biggest risk here is that www0 is now a single point of failure – if it crashes, the other servers are inaccessible.

4. **Dedicated Load Balancers**

There are more sophisticated solutions, as well. Cisco, F5, and several other companies sell hardware load balancers (typically used in pairs for redundancy), which offer sophisticated load balancing and auto-failover features. There are software packages which offer similar features on commodity hardware, as well. If you have enough

money or need, check these out. The lb-l mailing list[7] is a good
place to research.

5.6.11 New MIME-type, New Service

Description: On the net there are many nifty CGI programs. But their usage
is usually boring, so a lot of webmasters don't use them. Even Apache's
Action handler feature for MIME-types is only appropriate when the
CGI programs don't need special URLs (actually PATH_INFO and QUERY_-
STRINGS) as their input. First, let us configure a new file type with extension .scgi (for secure CGI) which will be processed by the popular
cgiwrap program. The problem here is that for instance if we use a Homogeneous URL Layout (see above) a file inside the user homedirs might
have a URL like /u/user/foo/bar.scgi, but cgiwrap needs URLs in the
form /~user/foo/bar.scgi/. The following rule solves the problem:

```
RewriteRule ^/[uge]/([^/]+)/\.www/(.+)\.scgi(.*) ...
... /internal/cgi/user/cgiwrap/~$1/$2.scgi$3
                        [NS,T=application/x-http-cgi]
```

Or assume we have some more nifty programs: wwwlog (which displays
the access.log for a URL subtree) and wwwidx (which runs Glimpse on
a URL subtree). We have to provide the URL area to these programs so
they know which area they are really working with. But usually this is
complicated, because they may still be requested by the alternate URL
form, i.e., typically we would run the swwidx program from within /u/
user/foo/ via hyperlink to

```
/internal/cgi/user/swwidx?i=/u/user/foo/
```

which is ugly, because we have to hard-code **both** the location of the
area **and** the location of the CGI inside the hyperlink. When we have to
reorganize, we spend a lot of time changing the various hyperlinks.

Solution: The solution here is to provide a special new URL format which
automatically leads to the proper CGI invocation. We configure the following:

```
RewriteRule ^/([uge])/([^/]+)(/?.*)/\*
                        /internal/cgi/user/wwwidx?i=/$1/$2$3/
RewriteRule ^/([uge])/([^/]+)(/?.*):log
                        /internal/cgi/user/wwwlog?f=/$1/$2$3
```

Now the hyperlink to search at /u/user/foo/ reads only

```
HREF="*"
```

which internally gets automatically transformed to

```
/internal/cgi/user/wwwidx?i=/u/user/foo/
```

The same approach leads to an invocation for the access log CGI program
when the hyperlink :log gets used.

---

[7]http://vegan.net/lb/

5.6.12 On-the-fly Content-Regeneration

Description: Here comes a really esoteric feature: Dynamically generated but statically served pages, i.e., pages should be delivered as pure static pages (read from the filesystem and just passed through), but they have to be generated dynamically by the web server if missing. This way you can have CGI-generated pages which are statically served unless an admin (or a cron job) removes the static contents. Then the contents gets refreshed.

Solution: This is done via the following ruleset:

```
RewriteCond %{REQUEST_FILENAME} !-s
RewriteRule ^page\.html$ page.cgi
                        [T=application/x-httpd-cgi,L]
```

Here a request for page.html leads to an internal run of a corresponding page.cgi if page.html is missing or has filesize null. The trick here is that page.cgi is a CGI script which (additionally to its STDOUT) writes its output to the file page.html. Once it has completed, the server sends out page.html. When the webmaster wants to force a refresh of the contents, he just removes page.html (typically from cron).

5.6.13 Document With Autorefresh

Description: Wouldn't it be nice, while creating a complex web page, if the web browser would automatically refresh the page every time we save a new version from within our editor? Impossible?

Solution: No! We just combine the MIME multipart feature, the web server NPH feature, and the URL manipulation power of mod_rewrite. First, we establish a new URL feature: Adding just :refresh to any URL causes the 'page' to be refreshed every time it is updated on the filesystem.

```
RewriteRule ^(/[uge]/[^/]+/?.*):refresh
                        /internal/cgi/apache/nph-refresh?f=$1
```

Now when we reference the URL

```
/u/foo/bar/page.html:refresh
```

this leads to the internal invocation of the URL

```
/internal/cgi/apache/nph-refresh?f=/u/foo/bar/page.html
```

The only missing part is the NPH-CGI script. Although one would usually say "left as an exercise to the reader" ;-) I will provide this, too.

```
#!/sw/bin/perl
##
##  nph-refresh -- NPH/CGI script for auto refreshing pages
##  Copyright (c) 1997 Ralf S. Engelschall, All Rights
##  Reserved.
##
$| = 1;
```

```perl
#    split the QUERY_STRING variable
@pairs = split(/&/, $ENV{'QUERY_STRING'});
foreach $pair (@pairs) {
    ($name, $value) = split(/=/, $pair);
    $name =~ tr/A-Z/a-z/;
    $name = 'QS_' . $name;
    $value =~
        s/%([a-fA-F0-9][a-fA-F0-9])/pack("C", hex($1))/eg;
    eval "\$$name = \"$value\"";
}
$QS_s = 1 if ($QS_s eq '');
$QS_n = 3600 if ($QS_n eq '');
if ($QS_f eq '') {
    print "HTTP/1.0 200 OK\n";
    print "Content-type: text/html\n\n";
    print "&lt;b&gt;ERROR&lt;/b&gt;: No file given\n";
    exit(0);
}
if (! -f $QS_f) {
    print "HTTP/1.0 200 OK\n";
    print "Content-type: text/html\n\n";
    print "&lt;b&gt;ERROR&lt;/b&gt;: File $QS_f not found\n";
    exit(0);
}

sub print_http_headers_multipart_begin {
    print "HTTP/1.0 200 OK\n";
    $bound = "ThisRandomString12345";
    print "Content-type:
            multipart/x-mixed-replace;boundary=$bound\n";
    &print_http_headers_multipart_next;
}

sub print_http_headers_multipart_next {
    print "\n--$bound\n";
}

sub print_http_headers_multipart_end {
    print "\n--$bound--\n";
}

sub displayhtml {
    local($buffer) = @_;
    $len = length($buffer);
    print "Content-type: text/html\n";
    print "Content-length: $len\n\n";
```

```perl
        print $buffer;
    }

sub readfile {
    local($file) = @_;
    local(*FP, $size, $buffer, $bytes);
    ($x, $x, $x, $x, $x, $x, $x, $size) = stat($file);
    $size = sprintf("%d", $size);
    open(FP, "&lt;$file");
    $bytes = sysread(FP, $buffer, $size);
    close(FP);
    return $buffer;
}


$buffer = &readfile($QS_f);
&print_http_headers_multipart_begin;
&displayhtml($buffer);

sub mystat {
    local($file) = $_[0];
    local($time);

    ($x, $x, $x, $x, $x, $x, $x, $x, $x, $mtime)
        = stat($file);
    return $mtime;
}


$mtimeL = &mystat($QS_f);
$mtime = $mtime;
for ($n = 0; $n &lt; $QS_n; $n++) {
    while (1) {
        $mtime = &mystat($QS_f);
        if ($mtime ne $mtimeL) {
            $mtimeL = $mtime;
            sleep(2);
            $buffer = &readfile($QS_f);
            &print_http_headers_multipart_next;
            &displayhtml($buffer);
            sleep(5);
            $mtimeL = &mystat($QS_f);
            last;
        }
        sleep($QS_s);
    }
}
```

```
&print_http_headers_multipart_end;

exit(0);

##EOF##
```

5.6.14 Mass Virtual Hosting

Description: The <VirtualHost> feature of Apache is nice and works great when you just have a few dozen virtual hosts. But when you are an ISP and have hundreds of virtual hosts, this feature is suboptimal.

Solution: To provide this feature we map the remote web page or even the complete remote web area to our namespace using the **Proxy Throughput** feature (flag [P]):

```
##
##   vhost.map
##
www.vhost1.dom:80    /path/to/docroot/vhost1
www.vhost2.dom:80    /path/to/docroot/vhost2
      :
www.vhostN.dom:80    /path/to/docroot/vhostN

##
##   httpd.conf
##
      :
#    use the canonical hostname on redirects, etc.
UseCanonicalName on

      :
#    add the virtual host in front of the CLF-format
CustomLog   /path/to/access_log
                          "%{VHOST}e %h %l %u %t \"%r\" %>s %b"
      :

#    enable the rewriting engine in the main server
RewriteEngine on

#    define two maps: one for fixing the URL and one which
#    defines the available virtual hosts with their
#    corresponding DocumentRoot.
RewriteMap lowercase int:tolower
RewriteMap vhost txt:/path/to/vhost.map

#    Now do the actual virtual host mapping
#    via a huge and complicated single rule:
#
```

```
#   1. make sure we don't map for common locations
RewriteCond %{REQUEST_URI} !^/commonurl1/.*
RewriteCond %{REQUEST_URI} !^/commonurl2/.*
    :
RewriteCond %{REQUEST_URI} !^/commonurlN/.*
#
#   2. make sure we have a Host header, because
#      currently our approach only supports
#      virtual hosting through this header
RewriteCond %{HTTP_HOST} !^$
#
#   3. lowercase the hostname
RewriteCond ${lowercase:%{HTTP_HOST}|NONE} ^(.+)$
#
#   4. lookup this hostname in vhost.map and
#      remember it only when it is a path
#      (and not "NONE" from above)
RewriteCond ${vhost:%1} ^(/.*)$
#
#   5. finally we can map the URL to its docroot location
#      and remember the virtual host for logging purposes
RewriteRule ^/(.*)$ %1/$1
                        [E=VHOST:${lowercase:%{HTTP_HOST}}]
    :
```

5.6.15 Host Deny

Description: How can we forbid a list of externally configured hosts from using our server?

Solution: For Apache >= 1.3b6:

```
RewriteEngine on
RewriteMap hosts-deny txt:/path/to/hosts.deny
RewriteCond ${hosts-deny:%{REMOTE_HOST}|NOT-FOUND}
                                        !=NOT-FOUND [OR]
RewriteCond ${hosts-deny:%{REMOTE_ADDR}|NOT-FOUND}
                                        !=NOT-FOUND
RewriteRule ^/.* - [F]
```

For Apache <= 1.3b6:

```
RewriteEngine on
RewriteMap hosts-deny txt:/path/to/hosts.deny
RewriteRule ^/(.*)$
                ${hosts-deny:%{REMOTE_HOST}|NOT-FOUND}/$1
RewriteRule !^NOT-FOUND/.* - [F]
RewriteRule ^NOT-FOUND/(.*)$
                ${hosts-deny:%{REMOTE_ADDR}|NOT-FOUND}/$1
RewriteRule !^NOT-FOUND/.* - [F]
```

```
RewriteRule ^NOT-FOUND/(.*)$ /$1

##
##  hosts.deny
##
##  ATTENTION! This is a map, not a list, even when
##            we treat it as such. mod_rewrite
##            parses it for key/value pairs, so at
##            least a dummy value "-" must be
##            present for each entry.
##

193.102.180.41  -
bsdti1.sdm.de   -
192.76.162.40   -
```

5.6.16 Proxy Deny

Description: How can we forbid a certain host or even a user of a special host from using the Apache proxy?

Solution: We first have to make sure mod_rewrite is below(!) mod_proxy in the Configuration file when compiling the Apache web server. This way it gets called *before* mod_proxy. Then we configure the following for a host-dependent deny...

```
RewriteCond %{REMOTE_HOST} ^badhost\.mydomain\.com$
RewriteRule !^http://[^/.]\.mydomain.com.* - [F]
```

...and this one for a user@host-dependent deny:

```
RewriteCond %{REMOTE_IDENT}@%{REMOTE_HOST}
                           ^badguy@badhost\.mydomain\.com$
RewriteRule !^http://[^/.]\.mydomain.com.* - [F]
```

5.6.17 Special Authentication Variant

Description: Sometimes very special authentication is needed, for instance authentication which checks for a set of explicitly configured users. Only these should receive access and without explicit prompting (which would occur when using Basic Auth via mod_auth_basic).

Solution: We use a list of rewrite conditions to exclude all except our friends:

```
RewriteCond %{REMOTE_IDENT}@%{REMOTE_HOST}
                           !^friend1@client1.quux-corp\.com$
RewriteCond %{REMOTE_IDENT}@%{REMOTE_HOST}
                           !^friend2@client2.quux-corp\.com$
RewriteCond %{REMOTE_IDENT}@%{REMOTE_HOST}
                           !^friend3@client3.quux-corp\.com$
RewriteRule ^/~quux/only-for-friends/ - [F]
```

5.6.18 Referer-based Deflector

Description: How can we program a flexible URL Deflector which acts on the
"Referer" HTTP header and can be configured with as many referring
pages as we like?

Solution: Use the following really tricky ruleset...

```
RewriteMap deflector txt:/path/to/deflector.map

RewriteCond %{HTTP_REFERER} !=""
RewriteCond ${deflector:%{HTTP_REFERER}} ^-$
RewriteRule ^.* %{HTTP_REFERER} [R,L]

RewriteCond %{HTTP_REFERER} !=""
RewriteCond ${deflector:%{HTTP_REFERER}|NOT-FOUND}
                                               !=NOT-FOUND
RewriteRule ^.* ${deflector:%{HTTP_REFERER}} [R,L]
```

... in conjunction with a corresponding rewrite map:

```
##
##  deflector.map
##

http://www.badguys.com/bad/index.html  -
http://www.badguys.com/bad/index2.html -
http://www.badguys.com/bad/index3.html http://somewhere.com/
```

This automatically redirects the request back to the referring page (when
"-" is used as the value in the map) or to a specific URL (when an URL
is specified in the map as the second argument).

5.7 SSL/TLS Strong Encryption: An Introduction

> "The nice thing about standards is that there are so many to
> choose from. And if you really don't like all the standards you just
> have to wait another year until the one arises you are looking for."
>
> – A. Tanenbaum, "Introduction to Computer Networks"

As an introduction this chapter is aimed at readers who are familiar with the
Web, HTTP, and Apache, but are not security experts. It is not intended to
be a definitive guide to the SSL protocol, nor does it discuss specific techniques
for managing certificates in an organization, or the important legal issues of
patents and import and export restrictions. Rather, it is intended to provide
a common background to mod_ssl users by pulling together various concepts,
definitions, and examples as a starting point for further exploration.

The presented content is mainly derived, with the author's permission, from the
article Introducing SSL and Certificates using SSLeay[8] by Frederick J. Hirsch[9],
of The Open Group Research Institute, which was published in Web Security:
A Matter of Trust[10], World Wide Web Journal, Volume 2, Issue 3, Summer
1997. Please send any positive feedback to Frederick Hirsch[11] (the original
article author) and all negative feedback to Ralf S. Engelschall[12] (the mod_ssl
author).

5.7.1 Cryptographic Techniques

Understanding SSL requires an understanding of cryptographic algorithms, message digest functions (aka. one-way or hash functions), and digital signatures.
These techniques are the subject of entire books (see for instance [AC96]) and
provide the basis for privacy, integrity, and authentication.

Cryptographic Algorithms

Suppose Alice wants to send a message to her bank to transfer some money.
Alice would like the message to be private, since it will include information
such as her account number and transfer amount. One solution is to use a
cryptographic algorithm, a technique that would transform her message into an
encrypted form, unreadable until it is decrypted. Once in this form, the message
can only be decrypted by using a secret key. Without the key the message
is useless: good cryptographic algorithms make it so difficult for intruders to
decode the original text that it isn't worth their effort.

There are two categories of cryptographic algorithms: conventional and public
key.

---

[8]http://home.comcast.net/~fjhirsch/Papers/wwwj/
[9]http://home.comcast.net/~fjhirsch/
[10]http://www.ora.com/catalog/wjsum97/
[11]mailto:hirsch@fjhirsch.com
[12]mailto:rse@engelschall.com

Conventional cryptography also known as symmetric cryptography, requires the sender and receiver to share a key: a secret piece of information that may be used to encrypt or decrypt a message. As long as this key is kept secret, nobody other than the sender or recipient can read the message. If Alice and the bank know a secret key, then they can send each other private messages. The task of sharing a key between sender and recipient before communicating, while also keeping it secret from others, can be problematic.

Public key cryptography also known as asymmetric cryptography, solves the key exchange problem by defining an algorithm which uses two keys, each of which may be used to encrypt a message. If one key is used to encrypt a message then the other must be used to decrypt it. This makes it possible to receive secure messages by simply publishing one key (the public key) and keeping the other secret (the private key).

Anyone can encrypt a message using the public key, but only the owner of the private key will be able to read it. In this way, Alice can send private messages to the owner of a key-pair (the bank), by encrypting them using their public key. Only the bank will be able to decrypt them.

Message Digests

Although Alice may encrypt her message to make it private, there is still a concern that someone might modify her original message or substitute it with a different one, in order to transfer the money to themselves, for instance. One way of guaranteeing the integrity of Alice's message is for her to create a concise summary of her message and send this to the bank as well. Upon receipt of the message, the bank creates its own summary and compares it with the one Alice sent. If the summaries are the same then the message has been received intact.

A summary such as this is called a **message digest**, *one-way function* or *hash function*. Message digests are used to create a short, fixed-length representation of a longer, variable-length message. Digest algorithms are designed to produce a unique digest for each message. Message digests are designed to make it impractically difficult to determine the message from the digest and (in theory) impossible to find two different messages which create the same digest – thus eliminating the possibility of substituting one message for another while maintaining the same digest.

Another challenge that Alice faces is finding a way to send the digest to the bank securely; if the digest is not sent securely, its integrity may be compromised and with it the possibility for the bank to determine the integrity of the original message. Only if the digest is sent securely can the integrity of the associated message be determined.

One way to send the digest securely is to include it in a digital signature.

Digital Signatures

When Alice sends a message to the bank, the bank needs to ensure that the message is really from her, so an intruder cannot request a transaction involving her account. A *digital signature*, created by Alice and included with the message, serves this purpose.

Digital signatures are created by encrypting a digest of the message and other information (such as a sequence number) with the sender's private key. Though anyone can *decrypt* the signature using the public key, only the sender knows the private key. This means that only the sender can have signed the message. Including the digest in the signature means the signature is only good for that message; it also ensures the integrity of the message since no one can change the digest and still sign it.

To guard against interception and reuse of the signature by an intruder at a later date, the signature contains a unique sequence number. This protects the bank from a fraudulent claim from Alice that she did not send the message – only she could have signed it (non-repudiation).

5.7.2 Certificates

Although Alice could have sent a private message to the bank, signed it and ensured the integrity of the message, she still needs to be sure that she is really communicating with the bank. This means that she needs to be sure that the public key she is using is part of the bank's key-pair, and not an intruder's. Similarly, the bank needs to verify that the message signature really was signed by the private key that belongs to Alice.

If each party has a certificate which validates the other's identity, confirms the public key and is signed by a trusted agency, then both can be assured that they are communicating with whom they think they are. Such a trusted agency is called a *Certificate Authority* and certificates are used for authentication.

Certificate Contents

A certificate associates a public key with the real identity of an individual, server, or other entity, known as the subject. As shown in Table 5.1, information about the subject includes identifying information (the distinguished name) and the public key. It also includes the identification and signature of the Certificate Authority that issued the certificate and the period of time during which the certificate is valid. It may have additional information (or extensions) as well as administrative information for the Certificate Authority's use, such as a serial number.

A distinguished name is used to provide an identity in a specific context – for instance, an individual might have a personal certificate as well as one for their identity as an employee. Distinguished names are defined by the X.509 standard [X509], which defines the fields, field names and abbreviations used to refer to the fields (see Table 5.2).

Table 5.1: Certificate Information

Subject	Distinguished Name, Public Key
Issuer	Distinguished Name, Signature
Period of Validity	Not Before Date, Not After Date
Administrative Information	Version, Serial Number
Extended Information	Basic Constraints, Netscape Flags, etc.

Table 5.2: Distinguished Name Information

DN Field	Abbrev.	Description	Example
Common Name	CN	Name being certified	CN=Joe Average
Organization or Company	O	Name is associated with this organization	O=Snake Oil, Ltd.
Organizational Unit	OU	Name is associated with this organization unit, such as a department	OU=Research Institute
City/Locality	L	Name is located in this City	L=Snake City
State/Province	ST	Name is located in this State/Province	ST=Desert
Country	C	Name is located in this Country (ISO code)	C=XZ

A Certificate Authority may define a policy specifying which distinguished field names are optional and which are required. It may also place requirements upon the field contents, as may users of certificates. For example, a browser can require that the Common Name for a certificate representing a server matches a wildcard pattern for the domain name of that server, such as *.snakeoil.com.

The binary format of a certificate is defined using the ASN.1 notation [X208] [PKCS]. This notation defines how to specify the contents and encoding rules define how this information is translated into binary form. The binary encoding of the certificate is defined using Distinguished Encoding Rules (DER), which are based on the more general Basic Encoding Rules (BER). For those transmissions which cannot handle binary, the binary form may be translated into an ASCII form by using Base64 encoding [MIME]. When placed between begin and end delimiter lines (as below), this encoded version is called a PEM ("Privacy Enhanced Mail") encoded certificate.

```
-----BEGIN CERTIFICATE-----
MIIC7jCCAlegAwIBAgIBATANBgkqhkiG9w0BAQQFADCBqTELMAkGA1UEBhMCWFkx
FTATBgNVBAgTDFNuYWtlIER1c2VydDETMBEGA1UEBxMKU25ha2UgVG93bjEXMBUG
A1UEChM0U25ha2UgT21sLCBMdGQxHjAcBgNVBAsTFUN1cnRpZm1jYXR1IEF1dGhv
cml0eTEVMBMGA1UEAxMMU25ha2UgT21sIENBMR4wHAYJKoZIhvcNAQkBFg9jYUBz
bmFrZW9pbC5kb20wHhcNOTgxMDIxMDg1ODM2WhcNOTkxMDIxMDg1ODM2WjCBpzEL
MAkGA1UEBhMCWFkxFTATBgNVBAgTDFNuYWtlIER1c2VydDETMBEGA1UEBxMKU25h
a2UgVG93bjEXMBUGA1UEChM0U25ha2UgT21sLCBMdGQxFzAVBgNVBAsTD1d1YnNl
cnZlciBUZWFtMRkwFwYDVQQDExB3d3cuc25ha2VvaWwuZG9tMR8wHQYJKoZIhvcN
AQkBFhB3d3dAc25ha2VvaWwuZG9tMIGfMA0GCSqGSIb3DQEBAQUAA4GNADCBiQKB
gQDH9Ge/s2zcH+da+rPTx/DPRp3xGjHZ4GG6pCmvADIEtBtKBFAcZ64n+Dy7Np8b
vKR+yy5DGQiijsH1D/j8H1GE+q4TZ80Fk7BNBFazHxFbYI40KMiCxdKzdif1yfaa
1WoANFlAzlSdbxeGVHoTOK+gT5w3UxwZKv2DLbCTzLZyPwIDAQABoyYwJDAPBgNV
HRMECDAGAQH/AgEAMBEGCWCGSAGG+EIBAQQEAwIAQDANBgkqhkiG9w0BAQQFAAOB
gQAZUIHAL4D09oE6Lv2k56Gp380BDuILvwLg1v1KL8mQR+KFjghCrtpqaztZqcDt
2q2QoyulCgSzHbEGmiOEsdkPfg6mpOpenssIFePYNI+/8u9HT4LuKMJX15hxBam7
dUHzICxBVC1lnHyYGjDuAMhe3961YAn8bC1d1/L4NMGBCQ==
-----END CERTIFICATE-----
```

Certificate Authorities

By verifying the information in a certificate request before granting the certificate, the Certificate Authority assures itself of the identity of the private key owner of a key-pair. For instance, if Alice requests a personal certificate, the Certificate Authority must first make sure that Alice really is the person the certificate request claims she is.

Certificate Chains

A Certificate Authority may also issue a certificate for another Certificate Authority. When examining a certificate, Alice may need to examine the certificate of the issuer, for each parent Certificate Authority, until reaching one which she has confidence in. She may decide to trust only certificates with a limited chain of issuers, to reduce her risk of a "bad" certificate in the chain.

Creating a Root-Level CA

As noted earlier, each certificate requires an issuer to assert the validity of the identity of the certificate subject, up to the top-level Certificate Authority (CA). This presents a problem: who can vouch for the certificate of the top-level authority, which has no issuer? In this unique case, the certificate is "self-signed", so the issuer of the certificate is the same as the subject. Browsers are preconfigured to trust well-known certificate authorities, but it is important to exercise extra care in trusting a self-signed certificate. The wide publication of a public key by the root authority reduces the risk in trusting this key – it would be obvious if someone else publicized a key claiming to be the authority.

A number of companies have established themselves as Certificate Authorities. These companies provide the following services:

- Verifying certificate requests
- Processing certificate requests
- Issuing and managing certificates

It is also possible to create your own Certificate Authority. Although risky in the Internet environment, it may be useful within an Intranet where the organization can easily verify the identities of individuals and servers.

Certificate Management

Establishing a Certificate Authority is a responsibility which requires a solid administrative, technical and management framework. Certificate Authorities not only issue certificates, they also manage them – that is, they determine for how long certificates remain valid, they renew them and keep lists of certificates that were issued in the past but are no longer valid (Certificate Revocation Lists, or CRLs).

For example, if Alice is entitled to a certificate as an employee of a company but has now left that company, her certificate may need to be revoked. Because certificates are only issued after the subject's identity has been verified and can then be passed around to all those with whom the subject may communicate, it is impossible to tell from the certificate alone that it has been revoked. Therefore when examining certificates for validity it is necessary to contact the issuing Certificate Authority to check CRLs – this is usually not an automated part of the process.

> NOTE *If you use a Certificate Authority that browsers are not configured to trust by default, it is necessary to load the Certificate Authority certificate into the browser, enabling the browser to validate server certificates signed by that Certificate Authority. Doing so may be dangerous, since once loaded, the browser will accept all certificates signed by that Certificate Authority.*

5.7.3 Secure Sockets Layer (SSL)

The Secure Sockets Layer protocol is a protocol layer which may be placed between a reliable connection-oriented network layer protocol (e.g. TCP/IP) and the application protocol layer (e.g. HTTP). SSL provides for secure communication between client and server by allowing mutual authentication, the use of digital signatures for integrity and encryption for privacy.

The protocol is designed to support a range of choices for specific algorithms used for cryptography, digests and signatures. This allows algorithm selection for specific servers to be made based on legal, export or other concerns and also enables the protocol to take advantage of new algorithms. Choices are negotiated between client and server when establishing a protocol session.

Table 5.3: Versions of the SSL protocol

Version	Source	Description	Browser Support
SSL v2.0	Vendor Standard (from Netscape Corp.) [SSL2]	First SSL protocol for which implementations exist	- NS Navigator 1.x/2.x - MS IE 3.x - Lynx/2.8+ OpenSSL
SSL v3.0	Expired Internet Draft (from Netscape Corp.) [SSL3]	Revisions to prevent specific security attacks, add non-RSA ciphers and support for certificate chains	- NS Navigator 2.x/3.x/4.x - MS IE 3.x/4.x - Lynx/2.8+ OpenSSL
TLS v1.0	Internet Standard (from IETF) [TLS1]	Revision of SSL 3.0 to update the MAC layer to HMAC, add block padding for block ciphers, message order standardization and more alert messages.	- Lynx/2.8+ OpenSSL

There are a number of versions of the SSL protocol, as shown in Table 5.3. As noted there, one of the benefits in SSL 3.0 is that it adds support of certificate chain loading. This feature allows a server to pass a server certificate along with issuer certificates to the browser. Chain loading also permits the browser to validate the server certificate, even if Certificate Authority certificates are not installed for the intermediate issuers, since they are included in the certificate chain. SSL 3.0 is the basis for the Transport Layer Security [TLS] protocol standard, currently in development by the Internet Engineering Task Force (IETF).

Establishing a Session

The SSL session is established by following a handshake sequence between client and server, as shown in Figure 5.3. This sequence may vary, depending on whether the server is configured to provide a server certificate or request a client certificate. Although cases exist where additional handshake steps are required for management of cipher information, this article summarizes one common scenario. See the SSL specification for the full range of possibilities.

NOTE *Once an SSL session has been established, it may be reused. This avoids the performance penalty of repeating the many steps needed to start a session. To do this, the server assigns each SSL session a unique session identifier which is cached in the server and which the client can use in future connections to reduce the handshake time (until the session identifer expires from the cache of the server).*

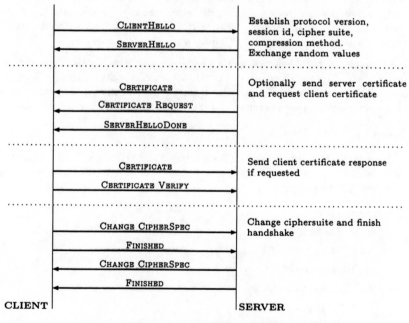

Figure 5.3: Simplified SSL Handshake Sequence

The elements of the handshake sequence, as used by the client and server, are listed below:

1. Negotiate the Cipher Suite to be used during data transfer

2. Establish and share a session key between client and server

3. Optionally authenticate the server to the client

4. Optionally authenticate the client to the server

The first step, Cipher Suite Negotiation, allows the client and server to choose a Cipher Suite supported by both of them. The SSL3.0 protocol specification defines 31 Cipher Suites. A Cipher Suite is defined by the following components:

- Key Exchange Method
- Cipher for Data Transfer
- Message Digest for creating the Message Authentication Code (MAC)

These three elements are described in the sections that follow.

Key Exchange Method

The key exchange method defines how the shared secret symmetric cryptography key used for application data transfer will be agreed upon by client and server. SSL 2.0 uses RSA key exchange only, while SSL 3.0 supports a choice of key exchange algorithms including RSA key exchange (when certificates are used), and Diffie-Hellman key exchange (for exchanging keys without certificates, or without prior communication between client and server).

One variable in the choice of key exchange methods is digital signatures – whether or not to use them, and if so, what kind of signatures to use. Signing with a private key provides protection against a man-in-the-middle-attack during the information exchange used to generating the shared key [AC96, p516].

Cipher for Data Transfer

SSL uses conventional symmetric cryptography, as described earlier, for encrypting messages in a session. There are nine choices of how to encrypt, including the option not to encrypt:

- No encryption
- Stream Ciphers
    - RC4 with 40-bit keys
    - RC4 with 128-bit keys
- CBC Block Ciphers
    - RC2 with 40 bit key
    - DES with 40 bit key
    - DES with 56 bit key
    - Triple-DES with 168 bit key
    - Idea (128 bit key)
    - Fortezza (96 bit key)

"CBC" refers to Cipher Block Chaining, which means that a portion of the previously encrypted cipher text is used in the encryption of the current block. "DES" refers to the Data Encryption Standard [AC96, ch12], which has a number of variants (including DES40 and 3DES_EDE). "Idea" is currently one of the best and cryptographically strongest algorithms available, and "RC2" is a proprietary algorithm from RSA DSI [AC96, ch13].

Digest Function

The choice of digest function determines how a digest is created from a record unit. SSL supports the following:

- No digest (Null choice)
- MD5, a 128-bit hash
- Secure Hash Algorithm (SHA-1), a 160-bit hash

The message digest is used to create a Message Authentication Code (MAC) which is encrypted with the message to verify integrity and to protect against replay attacks.

Handshake Sequence Protocol

The handshake sequence uses three protocols:

- The **SSL Handshake Protocol** for performing the client and server SSL session establishment.
- The **SSL Change Cipher Spec Protocol** for actually establishing agreement on the Cipher Suite for the session.
- The **SSL Alert Protocol** for conveying SSL error messages between client and server.

These protocols, as well as application protocol data, are encapsulated in the **SSL Record Protocol**, as shown in Figure 5.4. An encapsulated protocol is transferred as data by the lower layer protocol, which does not examine the data. The encapsulated protocol has no knowledge of the underlying protocol.

SSL Handshake Protocol	SSL Change Cipher Spec	SSL Alert Protocol	HTTP	Telnet	. . .
SSL Record Protocol					
TCP					
IP					

Figure 5.4: SSL Protocol Stack

The encapsulation of SSL control protocols by the record protocol means that if an active session is renegotiated the control protocols will be transmitted securely. If there was no previous session, the Null cipher suite is used, which means there will be no encryption and messages will have no integrity digests, until the session has been established.

Data Transfer

The SSL Record Protocol, shown in Figure 5.4, is used to transfer application and SSL Control data between the client and server, where necessary fragmenting this data into smaller units, or combining multiple higher level protocol data messages into single units. It may compress, attach digest signatures, and encrypt these units before transmitting them using the underlying reliable transport protocol (Note: currently, no major SSL implementations include support for compression).

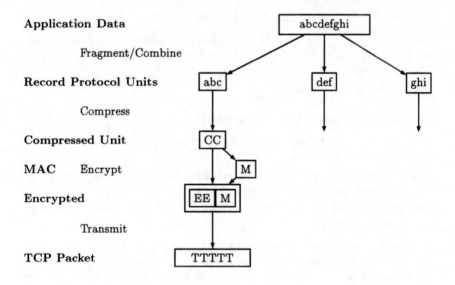

Figure 5.5: SSL Record Protocol

Securing HTTP Communication

One common use of SSL is to secure Web HTTP communication between a browser and a webserver. This does not preclude the use of non-secured HTTP - the secure version (called HTTPS) is the same as plain HTTP over SSL, but uses the URL scheme https rather than http, and a different server port (by default, port 443). This functionality is a large part of what mod_ssl provides for the Apache webserver.

5.7.4 References

[AC96] Bruce Schneier, Applied Cryptography, 2nd Edition, Wiley, 1996. See http://www.counterpane.com/ for various other materials by Bruce Schneier.

[X208] ITU-T Recommendation X.208, Specification of Abstract Syntax Notation One (ASN.1), 1988. See for instance http://www.itu.int/ rec/recommendation.asp?type=items&lang=e&parent=T-REC-X.208-198811-I.

[X509] ITU-T Recommendation X.509, The Directory - Authentication Framework. See for instance http://www.itu.int/rec/ recommendation.asp?type=folders&lang=e&parent=T-REC-X.509.

[PKCS] Public Key Cryptography Standards (PKCS), RSA Laboratories Technical Notes, See http://www.rsasecurity.com/rsalabs/pkcs/.

[MIME] N. Freed, N. Borenstein, Multipurpose Internet Mail Extensions (MIME) Part One: Format of Internet Message Bodies, RFC2045. See for instance http://ietf.org/rfc/rfc2045.txt.

[SSL2] Kipp E.B. Hickman, The SSL Protocol, 1995. See http://www.netscape.com/eng/security/SSL_2.html.

[SSL3] Alan O. Freier, Philip Karlton, Paul C. Kocher, The SSL Protocol Version 3.0, 1996. See http://www.netscape.com/eng/ssl3/draft302.txt.

[TLS1] Tim Dierks, Christopher Allen, The TLS Protocol Version 1.0, 1999. See http://ietf.org/rfc/rfc2246.txt.

6 Authentication, Authorization and Access Control

Authentication is any process by which you verify that someone is who they claim they are. Authorization is any process by which someone is allowed to be where they want to go, or to have information that they want to have.

6.1 Related Modules and Directives

There are three types of modules involved in the authentication and authorization process. You will usually need to choose at least one module from each group.

- Authentication type (see the AuthType directive)
    - mod_auth_basic
    - mod_auth_digest
- Authentication provider
    - mod_authn_alias
    - mod_authn_anon
    - mod_authn_dbd
    - mod_authn_dbm
    - mod_authn_default
    - mod_authn_file
    - mod_authnz_ldap
- Authorization (see the Require directive)
    - mod_authnz_ldap
    - mod_authz_dbm
    - mod_authz_default
    - mod_authz_groupfile
    - mod_authz_owner
    - mod_authz_user

The module mod_authnz_ldap is both an authentication and authorization provider. The module mod_authn_alias is not an authentication provider in itself, but allows other authentication providers to be configured in a flexible manner.

The module mod_authz_host provides authorization and access control based on hostname, IP address or characteristics of the request, but is not part of the authentication provider system.

You probably also want to take a look at the Access Control (p. 635) howto, which discusses the various ways to control access to your server.

6.2 Introduction

If you have information on your web site that is sensitive or intended for only a small group of people, the techniques in this article will help you make sure that the people that see those pages are the people that you wanted to see them.

This article covers the "standard" way of protecting parts of your web site that most of you are going to use.

NOTE: *If your data really needs to be secure, consider using mod_ssl in addition to any authentication.*

6.3 The Prerequisites

The directives discussed in this article will need to go either in your main server configuration file (typically in a <Directory> section), or in per-directory configuration files (.htaccess files).

If you plan to use .htaccess files, you will need to have a server configuration that permits putting authentication directives in these files. This is done with the AllowOverride directive, which specifies which directives, if any, may be put in per-directory configuration files.

Since we're talking here about authentication, you will need an AllowOverride directive like the following:

```
AllowOverride AuthConfig
```

Or, if you are just going to put the directives directly in your main server configuration file, you will of course need to have write permission to that file.

And you'll need to know a little bit about the directory structure of your server, in order to know where some files are kept. This should not be terribly difficult, and I'll try to make this clear when we come to that point.

6.4 Getting it working

Here's the basics of password protecting a directory on your server.

First, you need to create a password file. Exactly how you do this will vary depending on what authentication provider you have chosen. More on that later. To start with, we'll use a text password file.

This file should be placed somewhere not accessible from the web. This is so that folks cannot download the password file. For example, if your documents are served out of /usr/local/apache/htdocs you might want to put the password file(s) in /usr/local/apache/passwd.

To create the file, use the htpasswd utility that came with Apache. This will be located in the bin directory of wherever you installed Apache. If you have installed Apache from a third-party package, it may be in your execution path.

To create the file, type:

```
htpasswd -c /usr/local/apache/passwd/passwords rbowen
```

htpasswd will ask you for the password, and then ask you to type it again to confirm it:

```
# htpasswd -c /usr/local/apache/passwd/passwords rbowen
New password: mypassword
Re-type new password: mypassword
Adding password for user rbowen
```

If htpasswd is not in your path, of course you'll have to type the full path to the file to get it to run. With a default installation, it's located at /usr/local/ apache2/bin/htpasswd

Next, you'll need to configure the server to request a password and tell the server which users are allowed access. You can do this either by editing the httpd.conf file or using an .htaccess file. For example, if you wish to protect the directory /usr/local/apache/htdocs/secret, you can use the following directives, either placed in the file /usr/local/apache/htdocs/secret/.htaccess, or placed in httpd.conf inside a <Directory /usr/local/apache/apache/htdocs/secret> section.

```
AuthType Basic
AuthName "Restricted Files"
# (Following line optional)
AuthBasicProvider file
AuthUserFile /usr/local/apache/passwd/passwords
Require user rbowen
```

Let's examine each of those directives individually. The AuthType directive selects that method that is used to authenticate the user. The most common method is Basic, and this is the method implemented by mod_auth_basic. It is important to be aware, however, that Basic authentication sends the password from the client to the server unencrypted. This method should therefore not be used for highly sensitive data, unless accompanied by mod_ssl. Apache supports one other authentication method: AuthType Digest. This method is implemented by mod_auth_digest and is much more secure. Most recent browsers support Digest authentication.

The AuthName directive sets the **Realm** to be used in the authentication. The realm serves two major functions. First, the client often presents this information to the user as part of the password dialog box. Second, it is used by the client to determine what password to send for a given authenticated area.

So, for example, once a client has authenticated in the "Restricted Files" area, it will automatically retry the same password for any area on the same server that is marked with the "Restricted Files" Realm. Therefore, you can prevent a user from being prompted more than once for a password by letting multiple restricted areas share the same realm. Of course, for security reasons, the client will always need to ask again for the password whenever the hostname of the server changes.

The `AuthBasicProvider` is, in this case, optional, since `file` is the default value for this directive. You'll need to use this directive if you are choosing a different source for authentication, such as mod_authn_dbm or mod_authn_dbd.

The `AuthUserFile` directive sets the path to the password file that we just created with `htpasswd`. If you have a large number of users, it can be quite slow to search through a plain text file to authenticate the user on each request. Apache also has the ability to store user information in fast database files. The mod_authn_dbm module provides the `AuthDBMUserFile` directive. These files can be created and manipulated with the dbmmanage program. Many other types of authentication options are available from third party modules in the Apache Modules Database[1].

Finally, the `Require` directive provides the authorization part of the process by setting the user that is allowed to access this region of the server. In the next section, we discuss various ways to use the `Require` directive.

6.5 Letting more than one person in

The directives above only let one person (specifically someone with a username of rbowen) into the directory. In most cases, you'll want to let more than one person in. This is where the `AuthGroupFile` comes in.

If you want to let more than one person in, you'll need to create a group file that associates group names with a list of users in that group. The format of this file is pretty simple, and you can create it with your favorite editor. The contents of the file will look like this:

```
GroupName:   rbowen dpitts sungo rshersey
```

That's just a list of the members of the group in a long line separated by spaces.

To add a user to your already existing password file, type:

```
htpasswd /usr/local/apache/passwd/passwords dpitts
```

You'll get the same response as before, but it will be appended to the existing file, rather than creating a new file. (It's the -c that makes it create a new password file).

Now, you need to modify your `.htaccess` file to look like the following:

```
AuthType Basic
AuthName "By Invitation Only"
# Optional line:
AuthBasicProvider file
AuthUserFile /usr/local/apache/passwd/passwords
AuthGroupFile /usr/local/apache/passwd/groups
Require group GroupName
```

---

[1]http://modules.apache.org/

Now, anyone that is listed in the group GroupName, and has an entry in the password file, will be let in, if they type the correct password.

There's another way to let multiple users in that is less specific. Rather than creating a group file, you can just use the following directive:

```
Require valid-user
```

Using that rather than the Require user rbowen line will allow anyone in that is listed in the password file, and who correctly enters their password. You can even emulate the group behavior here, by just keeping a separate password file for each group. The advantage of this approach is that Apache only has to check one file, rather than two. The disadvantage is that you have to maintain a bunch of password files, and remember to reference the right one in the AuthUserFile directive.

6.6 Possible problems

Because of the way that Basic authentication is specified, your username and password must be verified every time you request a document from the server. This is even if you're reloading the same page, and for every image on the page (if they come from a protected directory). As you can imagine, this slows things down a little. The amount that it slows things down is proportional to the size of the password file, because it has to open up that file, and go down the list of users until it gets to your name. And it has to do this every time a page is loaded.

A consequence of this is that there's a practical limit to how many users you can put in one password file. This limit will vary depending on the performance of your particular server machine, but you can expect to see slowdowns once you get above a few hundred entries, and may wish to consider a different authentication method at that time.

6.7 Alternate password storage

Because storing passwords in plain text files has the above problems, you may wish to store your passwords somewhere else, such as in a database.

mod_authn_dbm and mod_authn_dbd are two modules which make this possible. Rather than selecting AuthBasicProvider file, instead you can choose dbm or dbd as your storage format.

To select a DBD file rather than a text file, for example:

```
<Directory /www/docs/private>
AuthName "Private"
AuthType Basic
AuthBasicProvider dbm
AuthDBMUserFile /www/passwords/passwd.dbm
Require valid-user
</Directory>
```

Other options are available. Consult the mod_authn_dbm documentation for more details.

6.8 More information

You should also read the documentation for mod_auth_basic and mod_authz_-host which contain some more information about how this all works. mod_-authn_alias can also help in simplifying certain authentication configurations.

The various ciphers supported by Apache for authentication data are explained in Password Encryptions (p. 771).

And you may want to look at the Access Control (p. 635) howto, which discusses a number of related topics.

7 Access Control

Access control refers to any means of controlling access to any resource. This is separate from authentication and authorization (p. 629).

7.1 Related Modules and Directives

Access control can be done by several different modules. The most important of these is mod_authz_host. Other modules discussed in this section include mod_setenvif and mod_rewrite.

7.2 Access control by host

If you wish to restrict access to portions of your site based on the host address of your visitors, this is most easily done using mod_authz_host.

The Allow and Deny directives let you allow and deny access based on the host name, or host address, of the machine requesting a document. The Order directive goes hand-in-hand with these two, and tells Apache in which order to apply the filters.

The usage of these directives is:

```
Allow from address
```

where *address* is an IP address (or a partial IP address) or a fully qualified domain name (or a partial domain name); you may provide multiple addresses or domain names, if desired.

For example, if you have someone spamming your message board, and you want to keep them out, you could do the following:

```
Deny from 10.252.46.165
```

Visitors coming from that address will not be able to see the content covered by this directive. If, instead, you have a machine name, rather than an IP address, you can use that.

```
Deny from host.example.com
```

And, if you'd like to block access from an entire domain, you can specify just part of an address or domain name:

```
Deny from 192.168.205
Deny from phishers.example.com moreidiots.example
Deny from ke
```

Using Order will let you be sure that you are actually restricting things to the group that you want to let in, by combining a Deny and an Allow directive:

```
Order deny,allow
Deny from all
```

Allow from *dev.example.com*

Listing just the Allow directive would not do what you want, because it will let
folks from that host in, in addition to letting everyone in. What you want is to
let *only* those folks in.

7.3 Access control by environment variable

mod_authz_host, in conjunction with mod_setenvif, can be used to restrict access to your website based on the value of arbitrary environment variables. This
is done with the Allow from env= and Deny from env= syntax.

```
SetEnvIf User-Agent BadBot GoAway=1
Order allow,deny
Allow from all
Deny from env=GoAway
```

> WARNING: *Access control by User-Agent is an unreliable technique, since
> the User-Agent header can be set to anything at all, at the whim of the
> end user.*

In the above example, the environment variable GoAway is set to 1 if the
User-Agent matches the string BadBot. Then we deny access for any request
when this variable is set. This blocks that particular user agent from the site.

An environment variable test can be negated using the =! syntax:

```
Allow from env=!GoAway
```

7.4 Access control with mod_rewrite

The [F] RewriteRule flag causes a 403 Forbidden response to be sent. Using
this, you can deny access to a resource based on arbitrary criteria.

For example, if you wish to block access to a resource between 8pm and 6am,
you can do this using mod_rewrite.

```
RewriteEngine On
RewriteCond %{TIME_HOUR} >20 [OR]
RewriteCond %{TIME_HOUR} <07
RewriteRule ^/fridge - [F]
```

This will return a 403 Forbidden response for any request after 8pm or before
7am. This technique can be used for any criteria that you wish to check. You can
also redirect, or otherwise rewrite these requests, if that approach is preferred.

7.5 More information

You should also read the documentation for mod_auth_basic and mod_authz_-
host which contain some more information about how this all works. mod_-
authn_alias can also help in simplifying certain authentication configurations.

See the Authentication and Authorization (p. 629) howto.

8 Caching Guide

This section supplements the mod_cache, mod_disk_cache, mod_mem_cache, mod_-file_cache and htcacheclean (p. 33) reference documentation. It describes how to use Apache's caching features to accelerate web and proxy serving, while avoiding common problems and misconfigurations.

8.1 Introduction

As of Apache HTTP server version 2.2 mod_cache and mod_file_cache are no longer marked experimental and are considered suitable for production use. These caching architectures provide a powerful means to accelerate HTTP handling, both as an origin webserver and as a proxy.

mod_cache and its provider modules mod_mem_cache and mod_disk_cache provide intelligent, HTTP-aware caching. The content itself is stored in the cache, and mod_cache aims to honour all of the various HTTP headers and options that control the cachability of content. It can handle both local and proxied content. mod_cache is aimed at both simple and complex caching configurations, where you are dealing with proxied content, dynamic local content or have a need to speed up access to local files which change with time.

mod_file_cache on the other hand presents a more basic, but sometimes useful, form of caching. Rather than maintain the complexity of actively ensuring the cachability of URLs, mod_file_cache offers file-handle and memory-mapping tricks to keep a cache of files as they were when Apache was last started. As such, mod_file_cache is aimed at improving the access time to local static files which do not change very often.

As mod_file_cache presents a relatively simple caching implementation, apart from the specific sections on CacheFile and MMapFile, the explanations in this guide cover the mod_cache caching architecture.

To get the most from this section, you should be familiar with the basics of HTTP, and have read the Users' Guides to Mapping URLs to the Filesystem (p. 75) and Content negotiation (p. 687).

8.2 Caching Overview

Related Modules	Related Directives
mod_cache	CacheEnable
mod_mem_cache	CacheDisable
mod_disk_cache	CacheFile
mod_file_cache	MMapFile
	UseCanonicalName
	CacheNegotiatedDocs

There are two main stages in mod_cache that can occur in the lifetime of a request. First, mod_cache is a URL mapping module, which means that if a URL has been cached, and the cached version of that URL has not expired, the request will be served directly by mod_cache.

This means that any other stages that might ordinarily happen in the process of serving a request – for example being handled by mod_proxy, or mod_rewrite – won't happen. But then this is the point of caching content in the first place.

If the URL is not found within the cache, mod_cache will add a filter (p. 715) to the request handling. After Apache has located the content by the usual means, the filter will be run as the content is served. If the content is determined to be cacheable, the content will be saved to the cache for future serving.

If the URL is found within the cache, but also found to have expired, the filter is added anyway, but mod_cache will create a conditional request to the backend, to determine if the cached version is still current. If the cached version is still current, its meta-information will be updated and the request will be served from the cache. If the cached version is no longer current, the cached version will be deleted and the filter will save the updated content to the cache as it is served.

8.2.1 Improving Cache Hits

When caching locally generated content, ensuring that UseCanonicalName is set to On can dramatically improve the ratio of cache hits. This is because the hostname of the virtual-host serving the content forms a part of the cache key. With the setting set to On virtual-hosts with multiple server names or aliases will not produce differently cached entities, and instead content will be cached as per the canonical hostname.

Because caching is performed within the URL to filename translation phase, cached documents will only be served in response to URL requests. Ordinarily this is of little consequence, but there is one circumstance in which it matters: If you are using Server Side Includes (p. 659);

```
<!-- The following include can be cached -->
<!--#include virtual="/footer.html" -->

<!-- The following include can not be cached -->
<!--#include file="/path/to/footer.html" -->
```

If you are using Server Side Includes, and want the benefit of speedy serves from the cache, you should use virtual include types.

8.2.2 Expiry Periods

The default expiry period for cached entities is one hour, however this can be easily over-ridden by using the CacheDefaultExpire directive. This default is only used when the original source of the content does not specify an expire time or time of last modification.

If a response does not include an Expires header but does include a
Last-Modified header, mod_cache can infer an expiry period based on the use
of the CacheLastModifiedFactor directive.

For local content, mod_expires may be used to fine-tune the expiry period.

The maximum expiry period may also be controlled by using the
CacheMaxExpire.

8.2.3 A Brief Guide to Conditional Requests

When content expires from the cache and is re-requested from the backend or
content provider, rather than pass on the original request, Apache will use a
conditional request instead.

HTTP offers a number of headers which allow a client, or cache to discern
between different versions of the same content. For example if a resource was
served with an "Etag:" header, it is possible to make a conditional request with
an "If-None-Match:" header. If a resource was served with a "Last-Modified:"
header it is possible to make a conditional request with an "If-Modified-Since:"
header, and so on.

When such a conditional request is made, the response differs depending on
whether the content matches the conditions. If a request is made with an "If-
Modified-Since:" header, and the content has not been modified since the time
indicated in the request then a terse "304 Not Modified" response is issued.

If the content has changed, then it is served as if the request were not conditional
to begin with.

The benefits of conditional requests in relation to caching are twofold. Firstly,
when making such a request to the backend, if the content from the backend
matches the content in the store, this can be determined easily and without the
overhead of transferring the entire resource.

Secondly, conditional requests are usually less strenuous on the backend. For
static files, typically all that is involved is a call to stat() or similar system
call, to see if the file has changed in size or modification time. As such, even if
Apache is caching local content, even expired content may still be served faster
from the cache if it has not changed. As long as reading from the cache store
is faster than reading from the backend (e.g. an in-memory cache compared to
reading from disk).

8.2.4 What Can be Cached?

As mentioned already, the two styles of caching in Apache work differently,
mod_file_cache caching maintains file contents as they were when Apache was
started. When a request is made for a file that is cached by this module, it is
intercepted and the cached file is served.

mod_cache caching on the other hand is more complex. When serving a request, if it has not been cached previously, the caching module will determine if the content is cacheable. The conditions for determining cachability of a response are;

1. Caching must be enabled for this URL. See the CacheEnable and CacheDisable directives.

2. The response must have a HTTP status code of 200, 203, 300, 301 or 410.

3. The request must be a HTTP GET request.

4. If the request contains an "Authorization:" header, the response will not be cached.

5. If the response contains an "Authorization:" header, it must also contain an "s-maxage", "must-revalidate" or "public" option in the "Cache-Control:" header.

6. If the URL included a query string (e.g. from an HTML form GET method) it will not be cached unless the response specifies an explicit expiration by including an "Expires:" header or the max-age or s-maxage directive of the "Cache-Control:" header, as per RFC2616 sections 13.9 and 13.2.1.

7. If the response has a status of 200 (OK), the response must also include at least one of the "Etag", "Last-Modified" or the "Expires" headers, or the max-age or s-maxage directive of the "Cache-Control:" header, unless the CacheIgnoreNoLastMod directive has been used to require otherwise.

8. If the response includes the "private" option in a "Cache-Control:" header, it will not be stored unless the CacheStorePrivate has been used to require otherwise.

9. Likewise, if the response includes the "no-store" option in a "Cache-Control:" header, it will not be stored unless the CacheStoreNoStore has been used.

10. A response will not be stored if it includes a "Vary:" header containing the match-all "*".

8.2.5 What Should Not be Cached?

In short, any content which is highly time-sensitive, or which varies depending on the particulars of the request that are not covered by HTTP negotiation, should not be cached.

If you have dynamic content which changes depending on the IP address of the requester, or changes every 5 minutes, it should almost certainly not be cached.

If on the other hand, the content served differs depending on the values of various HTTP headers, it might be possible to cache it intelligently through the use of a "Vary" header.

8.2.6 Variable/Negotiated Content

If a response with a "Vary" header is received by mod_cache when requesting content by the backend it will attempt to handle it intelligently. If possible, mod_cache will detect the headers attributed in the "Vary" response in future requests and serve the correct cached response.

If for example, a response is received with a vary header such as;

    Vary: negotiate,accept-language,accept-charset

mod_cache will only serve the cached content to requesters with accept-language and accept-charset headers matching those of the original request.

8.3 Security Considerations

8.3.1 Authorization and Access Control

Using mod_cache is very much like having a built in reverse-proxy. Requests will be served by the caching module unless it determines that the backend should be queried. When caching local resources, this drastically changes the security model of Apache.

As traversing a filesystem hierarchy to examine potential .htaccess files would be a very expensive operation, partially defeating the point of caching (to speed up requests), mod_cache makes no decision about whether a cached entity is authorised for serving. In other words; if mod_cache has cached some content, it will be served from the cache as long as that content has not expired.

If, for example, your configuration permits access to a resource by IP address you should ensure that this content is not cached. You can do this by using the CacheDisable directive, or mod_expires. Left unchecked, mod_cache - very much like a reverse proxy - would cache the content when served and then serve it to any client, on any IP address.

8.3.2 Local exploits

As requests to end-users can be served from the cache, the cache itself can become a target for those wishing to deface or interfere with content. It is important to bear in mind that the cache must at all times be writable by the user which Apache is running as. This is in stark contrast to the usually recommended situation of maintaining all content unwritable by the Apache user.

If the Apache user is compromised, for example through a flaw in a CGI process, it is possible that the cache may be targeted. When using mod_disk_cache, it is relatively easy to insert or modify a cached entity.

This presents a somewhat elevated risk in comparison to the other types of attack it is possible to make as the Apache user. If you are using mod_disk_-cache you should bear this in mind - ensure you upgrade Apache when security upgrades are announced and run CGI processes as a non-Apache user using suEXEC (p. 719) if possible.

8.3.3 Cache Poisoning

When running Apache as a caching proxy server, there is also the potential for so-called cache poisoning. Cache Poisoning is a broad term for attacks in which an attacker causes the proxy server to retrieve incorrect (and usually undesirable) content from the backend.

For example if the DNS servers used by your system running Apache are vulnerable to DNS cache poisoning, an attacker may be able to control where Apache connects to when requesting content from the origin server. Another example is so-called HTTP request-smuggling attacks.

This section is not the correct place for an in-depth discussion of HTTP request smuggling (instead, try your favourite search engine) however it is important to be aware that it is possible to make a series of requests, and to exploit a vulnerability on an origin webserver such that the attacker can entirely control the content retrieved by the proxy.

8.4 File-Handle Caching

Related Modules	Related Directives
mod_file_cache	CacheFile
mod_mem_cache	CacheEnable
	CacheDisable

The act of opening a file can itself be a source of delay, particularly on network filesystems. By maintaining a cache of open file descriptors for commonly served files, Apache can avoid this delay. Currently Apache provides two different implementations of File-Handle Caching.

8.4.1 CacheFile

The most basic form of caching present in Apache is the file-handle caching provided by mod_file_cache. Rather than caching file-contents, this cache maintains a table of open file descriptors. Files to be cached in this manner are specified in the configuration file using the CacheFile directive.

The CacheFile directive instructs Apache to open the file when Apache is started and to re-use this file-handle for all subsequent access to this file.

```
CacheFile /usr/local/apache2/htdocs/index.html
```

If you intend to cache a large number of files in this manner, you must ensure that your operating system's limit for the number of open files is set appropriately.

Although using CacheFile does not cause the file-contents to be cached per-se, it does mean that if the file changes while Apache is running these changes will not be picked up. The file will be consistently served as it was when Apache was started.

If the file is removed while Apache is running, Apache will continue to maintain an open file descriptor and serve the file as it was when Apache was started. This usually also means that although the file will have been deleted, and not show up on the filesystem, extra free space will not be recovered until Apache is stopped and the file descriptor closed.

8.4.2 CacheEnable fd

mod_mem_cache also provides its own file-handle caching scheme, which can be enabled via the CacheEnable directive.

```
CacheEnable fd /
```

As with all of mod_cache this type of file-handle caching is intelligent, and handles will not be maintained beyond the expiry time of the cached content.

8.5 In-Memory Caching

Related Modules	Related Directives
mod_mem_cache	CacheEnable
mod_file_cache	CacheDisable
	MMapFile

Serving directly from system memory is universally the fastest method of serving content. Reading files from a disk controller or, even worse, from a remote network is orders of magnitude slower. Disk controllers usually involve physical processes, and network access is limited by your available bandwidth. Memory access on the other hand can take mere nano-seconds.

System memory isn't cheap though, byte for byte it's by far the most expensive type of storage and it's important to ensure that it is used efficiently. By caching files in memory you decrease the amount of memory available on the system. As we'll see, in the case of operating system caching, this is not so much of an issue, but when using Apache's own in-memory caching it is important to make sure that you do not allocate too much memory to a cache. Otherwise the system will be forced to swap out memory, which will likely degrade performance.

8.5.1 Operating System Caching

Almost all modern operating systems cache file-data in memory managed directly by the kernel. This is a powerful feature, and for the most part operating systems get it right. For example, on Linux, let's look at the difference in the time it takes to read a file for the first time and the second time;

```
colm@coroebus:~$ time cat testfile > /dev/null
```

```
real      0m0.065s
user      0m0.000s
sys       0m0.001s
colm@coroebus:~$ time cat testfile > /dev/null
real      0m0.003s
user      0m0.003s
sys       0m0.000s
```

Even for this small file, there is a huge difference in the amount of time it takes to read the file. This is because the kernel has cached the file contents in memory.

By ensuring there is "spare" memory on your system, you can ensure that more and more file-contents will be stored in this cache. This can be a very efficient means of in-memory caching, and involves no extra configuration of Apache at all.

Additionally, because the operating system knows when files are deleted or modified, it can automatically remove file contents from the cache when neccessary. This is a big advantage over Apache's in-memory caching which has no way of knowing when a file has changed.

Despite the performance and advantages of automatic operating system caching there are some circumstances in which in-memory caching may be better performed by Apache.

Firstly, an operating system can only cache files it knows about. If you are running Apache as a proxy server, the files you are caching are not locally stored but remotely served. If you still want the unbeatable speed of in-memory caching, Apache's own memory caching is needed.

8.5.2 MMapFile Caching

mod_file_cache provides the MMapFile directive, which allows you to have Apache map a static file's contents into memory at start time (using the mmap system call). Apache will use the in-memory contents for all subsequent accesses to this file.

```
MMapFile /usr/local/apache2/htdocs/index.html
```

As with the CacheFile directive, any changes in these files will not be picked up by Apache after it has started.

The MMapFile directive does not keep track of how much memory it allocates, so you must ensure not to over-use the directive. Each Apache child process will replicate this memory, so it is critically important to ensure that the files mapped are not so large as to cause the system to swap memory.

8.5.3 mod_mem_cache Caching

mod_mem_cache provides a HTTP-aware intelligent in-memory cache. It also uses heap memory directly, which means that even if *MMap* is not supported on your system, mod_mem_cache may still be able to perform caching.

Caching of this type is enabled via;

```
# Enable memory caching
CacheEnable mem /

# Limit the size of the cache to 1 Megabyte
MCacheSize 1024
```

8.6 Disk-based Caching

Related Modules	Related Directives
mod_disk_cache	CacheEnable
	CacheDisable

mod_disk_cache provides a disk-based caching mechanism for mod_cache. As with mod_mem_cache this cache is intelligent and content will be served from the cache only as long as it is considered valid.

Typically the module will be configured as so;

```
CacheRoot      /var/cache/apache/
CacheEnable disk /
CacheDirLevels 2
CacheDirLength 1
```

Importantly, as the cached files are locally stored, operating system in-memory caching will typically be applied to their access also. So although the files are stored on disk, if they are frequently accessed it is likely the operating system will ensure that they are actually served from memory.

8.6.1 Understanding the Cache-Store

To store items in the cache, mod_disk_cache creates a 22 character hash of the URL being requested. This hash incorporates the hostname, protocol, port, path and any CGI arguments to the URL, to ensure that multiple URLs do not collide.

Each character may be any one of 64-different characters, which mean that overall there are 64^22 possible hashes. For example, a URL might be hashed to xyTGxSMO2b68mBCykqkp1w. This hash is used as a prefix for the naming of the files specific to that URL within the cache, however first it is split up into directories as per the CacheDirLevels and CacheDirLength directives.

CacheDirLevels specifies how many levels of subdirectory there should be, and

CacheDirLength specifies how many characters should be in each directory. With the example settings given above, the hash would be turned into a filename prefix as /var/cache/apache/x/y/TGxSMO2b68mBCykqkp1w.

The overall aim of this technique is to reduce the number of subdirectories or files that may be in a particular directory, as most file-systems slow down as this number increases. With setting of "1" for CacheDirLength there can at most be 64 subdirectories at any particular level. With a setting of 2 there can be 64 * 64 subdirectories, and so on. Unless you have a good reason not to, using a setting of "1" for CacheDirLength is recommended.

Setting CacheDirLevels depends on how many files you anticipate to store in the cache. With the setting of "2" used in the above example, a grand total of 4096 subdirectories can ultimately be created. With 1 million files cached, this works out at roughly 245 cached URLs per directory.

Each URL uses at least two files in the cache-store. Typically there is a ".header" file, which includes meta-information about the URL, such as when it is due to expire and a ".data" file which is a verbatim copy of the content to be served.

In the case of a content negotiated via the "Vary" header, a ".vary" directory will be created for the URL in question. This directory will have multiple ".data" files corresponding to the differently negotiated content.

8.6.2 Maintaining the Disk Cache

Although mod_disk_cache will remove cached content as it is expired, it does not maintain any information on the total size of the cache or how little free space may be left.

Instead, provided with Apache is the htcacheclean (p. 33) tool which, as the name suggests, allows you to clean the cache periodically. Determining how frequently to run htcacheclean (p. 33) and what target size to use for the cache is somewhat complex and trial and error may be needed to select optimal values.

htcacheclean (p. 33) has two modes of operation. It can be run as persistent daemon, or periodically from cron. htcacheclean (p. 33) can take up to an hour or more to process very large (tens of gigabytes) caches and if you are running it from cron it is recommended that you determine how long a typical run takes, to avoid running more than one instance at a time.

Because mod_disk_cache does not itself pay attention to how much space is used you should ensure that htcacheclean (p. 33) is configured to leave enough "grow room" following a clean.

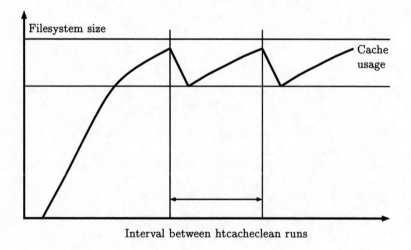

Figure 8.1: Typical cache growth / clean sequence.

9 Apache Tutorial: Dynamic Content with CGI

9.1 Introduction

Related Modules	Related Directives
mod_alias	AddHandler
mod_cgi	Options
	ScriptAlias

The CGI (Common Gateway Interface) defines a way for a web server to interact with external content-generating programs, which are often referred to as CGI programs or CGI scripts. It is the simplest, and most common, way to put dynamic content on your web site. This section will be an introduction to setting up CGI on your Apache web server, and getting started writing CGI programs.

9.2 Configuring Apache to permit CGI

In order to get your CGI programs to work properly, you'll need to have Apache configured to permit CGI execution. There are several ways to do this.

9.2.1 ScriptAlias

The ScriptAlias

directive tells Apache that a particular directory is set aside for CGI programs. Apache will assume that every file in this directory is a CGI program, and will attempt to execute it, when that particular resource is requested by a client.

The ScriptAlias directive looks like:

```
ScriptAlias /cgi-bin/ /usr/local/apache2/cgi-bin/
```

The example shown is from your default httpd.conf configuration file, if you installed Apache in the default location. The ScriptAlias directive is much like the Alias directive, which defines a URL prefix that is to mapped to a particular directory. Alias and ScriptAlias are usually used for directories that are outside of the DocumentRoot directory. The difference between Alias and ScriptAlias is that ScriptAlias has the added meaning that everything under that URL prefix will be considered a CGI program. So, the example above tells Apache that any request for a resource beginning with /cgi-bin/ should be served from the directory /usr/local/apache2/cgi-bin/, and should be treated as a CGI program.

For example, if the URL http://www.example.com/cgi-bin/test.pl is requested, Apache will attempt to execute the file /usr/local/apache2/cgi-bin/ test.pl and return the output. Of course, the file will have to exist, and be executable, and return output in a particular way, or Apache will return an error message.

9.2.2 CGI outside of ScriptAlias directories

CGI programs are often restricted to ScriptAlias'ed directories for security reasons. In this way, administrators can tightly control who is allowed to use CGI programs. However, if the proper security precautions are taken, there is no reason why CGI programs cannot be run from arbitrary directories. For example, you may wish to let users have web content in their home directories with the UserDir directive. If they want to have their own CGI programs, but don't have access to the main cgi-bin directory, they will need to be able to run CGI programs elsewhere.

There are two steps to allowing CGI execution in an arbitrary directory. First, the cgi-script handler must be activated using the AddHandler or SetHandler directive. Second, ExecCGI must be specified in the Options directive.

9.2.3 Explicitly using Options to permit CGI execution

You could explicitly use the Options directive, inside your main server configuration file, to specify that CGI execution was permitted in a particular directory:

```
<Directory /usr/local/apache2/htdocs/somedir>
    Options +ExecCGI
</Directory>
```

The above directive tells Apache to permit the execution of CGI files. You will also need to tell the server what files are CGI files. The following AddHandler directive tells the server to treat all files with the cgi or pl extension as CGI programs:

```
AddHandler cgi-script .cgi .pl
```

9.2.4 .htaccess files

The .htaccess tutorial (p. 667) shows how to activate CGI programs if you do not have access to httpd.conf.

9.2.5 User Directories

To allow CGI program execution for any file ending in .cgi in users' directories, you can use the following configuration.

```
<Directory /home/*/public_html>
    Options +ExecCGI
    AddHandler cgi-script .cgi
</Directory>
```

If you wish designate a cgi-bin subdirectory of a user's directory where everything will be treated as a CGI program, you can use the following.

```
<Directory /home/*/public_html/cgi-bin>
```

```
    Options ExecCGI
    SetHandler cgi-script
</Directory>
```

9.3 Writing a CGI program

There are two main differences between "regular" programming, and CGI programming.

First, all output from your CGI program must be preceded by a MIME-type header. This is HTTP header that tells the client what sort of content it is receiving. Most of the time, this will look like:

```
Content-type:  text/html
```

Secondly, your output needs to be in HTML, or some other format that a browser will be able to display. Most of the time, this will be HTML, but occasionally you might write a CGI program that outputs a gif image, or other non-HTML content.

Apart from those two things, writing a CGI program will look a lot like any other program that you might write.

9.3.1 Your first CGI program

The following is an example CGI program that prints one line to your browser. Type in the following, save it to a file called first.pl, and put it in your cgi-bin directory.

```
#!/usr/bin/perl
print "Content-type:  text/html\n\n";
print "Hello, World.";
```

Even if you are not familiar with Perl, you should be able to see what is happening here. The first line tells Apache (or whatever shell you happen to be running under) that this program can be executed by feeding the file to the interpreter found at the location /usr/bin/perl. The second line prints the content-type declaration we talked about, followed by two carriage-return newline pairs. This puts a blank line after the header, to indicate the end of the HTTP headers, and the beginning of the body. The third line prints the string "Hello, World.". And that's the end of it.

If you open your favorite browser and tell it to get the address

```
http://www.example.com/cgi-bin/first.pl
```

or wherever you put your file, you will see the one line Hello, World. appear in your browser window. It's not very exciting, but once you get that working, you'll have a good chance of getting just about anything working.

9.4 But it's still not working!

There are four basic things that you may see in your browser when you try to access your CGI program from the web:

The output of your CGI program Great! That means everything worked fine. If the output is correct, but the browser is not processing it correctly, make sure you have the correct Content-Type set in your CGI program.

The source code of your CGI program or a "POST Method Not Allowed" message
> That means that you have not properly configured Apache to process your CGI program. Reread the section on configuring Apache and try to find what you missed.

A message starting with "Forbidden" That means that there is a permissions problem. Check the Apache error log and the section below on file permissions.

A message saying "Internal Server Error" If you check the Apache error log, you will probably find that it says "Premature end of script headers", possibly along with an error message generated by your CGI program. In this case, you will want to check each of the below sections to see what might be preventing your CGI program from emitting the proper HTTP headers.

9.4.1 File permissions

Remember that the server does not run as you. That is, when the server starts up, it is running with the permissions of an unprivileged user - usually nobody, or www - and so it will need extra permissions to execute files that are owned by you. Usually, the way to give a file sufficient permissions to be executed by nobody is to give everyone execute permission on the file:

```
chmod a+x first.pl
```

Also, if your program reads from, or writes to, any other files, those files will need to have the correct permissions to permit this.

9.4.2 Path information and environment

When you run a program from your command line, you have certain information that is passed to the shell without you thinking about it. For example, you have a PATH, which tells the shell where it can look for files that you reference.

When a program runs through the web server as a CGI program, it may not have the same PATH. Any programs that you invoke in your CGI program (like sendmail, for example) will need to be specified by a full path, so that the shell can find them when it attempts to execute your CGI program.

A common manifestation of this is the path to the script interpreter (often perl) indicated in the first line of your CGI program, which will look something like:

```
#!/usr/bin/perl
```

Make sure that this is in fact the path to the interpreter.

In addition, if your CGI program depends on other environment variables, you will need to assure that those variables are passed by Apache.

9.4.3 Program errors

Most of the time when a CGI program fails, it's because of a problem with the program itself. This is particularly true once you get the hang of this CGI stuff, and no longer make the above two mistakes. The first thing to do is to make sure that your program runs from the command line before testing it via the web server. For example, try:

```
cd /usr/local/apache2/cgi-bin
./first.pl
```

(Do not call the perl interpreter. The shell and Apache should find the interpreter using the path information on the first line of the script.)

The first thing you see written by your program should be a set of HTTP headers, including the Content-Type, followed by a blank line. If you see anything else, Apache will return the Premature end of script headers error if you try to run it through the server. See Writing a CGI program above for more details.

9.4.4 Error logs

The error logs are your friend. Anything that goes wrong generates message in the error log. You should always look there first. If the place where you are hosting your web site does not permit you access to the error log, you should probably host your site somewhere else. Learn to read the error logs, and you'll find that almost all of your problems are quickly identified, and quickly solved.

9.4.5 Suexec

The suexec (p. 719) support program allows CGI programs to be run under different user permissions, depending on which virtual host or user home directory they are located in. Suexec has very strict permission checking, and any failure in that checking will result in your CGI programs failing with Premature end of script headers.

To check if you are using suexec, run apachectl -V and check for the location of SUEXEC_BIN. If Apache finds an suexec binary there on startup, suexec will be activated.

Unless you fully understand suexec, you should not be using it. To disable suexec, simply remove (or rename) the suexec binary pointed to by SUEXEC_BIN and then restart the server. If, after reading about suexec (p. 719), you still wish to use it, then run suexec -V to find the location of the suexec log file, and use that log file to find what policy you are violating.

9.5 What's going on behind the scenes?

As you become more advanced in CGI programming, it will become useful to understand more about what's happening behind the scenes. Specifically, how the browser and server communicate with one another. Because although it's all very well to write a program that prints "Hello, World.", it's not particularly useful.

9.5.1 Environment variables

Environment variables are values that float around you as you use your computer. They are useful things like your path (where the computer searches for the actual file implementing a command when you type it), your username, your terminal type, and so on. For a full list of your normal, every day environment variables, type env at a command prompt.

During the CGI transaction, the server and the browser also set environment variables, so that they can communicate with one another. These are things like the browser type (Firefox, IE, Lynx), the server type (Apache, IIS, WebSite), the name of the CGI program that is being run, and so on.

These variables are available to the CGI programmer, and are half of the story of the client-server communication. The complete list of required variables is at http://hoohoo.ncsa.uiuc.edu/cgi/env.html.

This simple Perl CGI program will display all of the environment variables that are being passed around. Two similar programs are included in the cgi-bin directory of the Apache distribution. Note that some variables are required, while others are optional, so you may see some variables listed that were not in the official list. In addition, Apache provides many different ways for you to add your own environment variables (p. 705) to the basic ones provided by default.

```perl
#!/usr/bin/perl
print "Content-type:  text/html\n\n";
foreach $key (keys %ENV) {
    print "$key --> $ENV{$key}<br>";
}
```

9.5.2 STDIN and STDOUT

Other communication between the server and the client happens over standard input (STDIN) and standard output (STDOUT). In normal everyday context, STDIN means the keyboard, or a file that a program is given to act on, and STDOUT usually means the console or screen.

When you POST a web form to a CGI program, the data in that form is bundled up into a special format and gets delivered to your CGI program over STDIN.

The program then can process that data as though it was coming in from the keyboard, or from a file

The "special format" is very simple. A field name and its value are joined together with an equals (=) sign, and pairs of values are joined together with an ampersand (&). Inconvenient characters like spaces, ampersands, and equals signs, are converted into their hex equivalent so that they don't gum up the works. The whole data string might look something like:

```
name=Rich%20Bowen&city=Lexington&sidekick=Squirrel%20Monkey
```

You'll sometimes also see this type of string appended to a URL. When that is done, the server puts that string into the environment variable called QUERY_-STRING. That's called a GET request. Your HTML form specifies whether a GET or a POST is used to deliver the data, by setting the METHOD attribute in the FORM tag.

Your program is then responsible for splitting that string up into useful information. Fortunately, there are libraries and modules available to help you process this data, as well as handle other of the aspects of your CGI program.

9.6 CGI modules/libraries

When you write CGI programs, you should consider using a code library, or module, to do most of the grunt work for you. This leads to fewer errors, and faster development.

If you're writing CGI programs in Perl, modules are available on CPAN[1]. The most popular module for this purpose is CGI.pm. You might also consider CGI::Lite, which implements a minimal set of functionality, which is all you need in most programs.

If you're writing CGI programs in C, there are a variety of options. One of these is the CGIC library, from http://www.boutell.com/cgic/.

9.7 For more information

There are a large number of CGI resources on the web. You can discuss CGI problems with other users on the Usenet group comp.infosystems.www.authoring.cgi[2]. And the -servers mailing list from the HTML Writers Guild is a great source of answers to your questions. You can find out more at http://www.hwg.org/lists/hwg-servers/.

And, of course, you should probably read the CGI specification, which has all the details on the operation of CGI programs. You can find the original version at the NCSA[3] and there is an updated draft at the Common Gateway Interface RFC project[4].

---

[1] http://www.cpan.org/
[2] news:comp.infosystems.www.authoring.cgi
[3] http://hoohoo.ncsa.uiuc.edu/cgi/interface.html
[4] http://www.w3.org/CGI/

When you post a question about a CGI problem that you're having, whether
to a mailing list, or to a newsgroup, make sure you provide enough information
about what happened, what you expected to happen, and how what actually
happened was different, what server you're running, what language your CGI
program was in, and, if possible, the offending code. This will make finding
your problem much simpler.

Note that questions about CGI problems should **never** be posted to the Apache
bug database unless you are sure you have found a problem in the Apache source
code.

10 Apache Tutorial: Introduction to Server Side Includes

Server-side includes provide a means to add dynamic content to existing HTML documents.

10.1 Introduction

Related Modules	Related Directives
mod_include	Options
mod_cgi	XBitHack
mod_expires	AddType
	SetOutputFilter
	BrowserMatchNoCase

This article deals with Server Side Includes, usually called simply SSI. In this article, I'll talk about configuring your server to permit SSI, and introduce some basic SSI techniques for adding dynamic content to your existing HTML pages.

In the latter part of the article, we'll talk about some of the somewhat more advanced things that can be done with SSI, such as conditional statements in your SSI directives.

10.2 What are SSI?

SSI (Server Side Includes) are directives that are placed in HTML pages, and evaluated on the server while the pages are being served. They let you add dynamically generated content to an existing HTML page, without having to serve the entire page via a CGI program, or other dynamic technology.

The decision of when to use SSI, and when to have your page entirely generated by some program, is usually a matter of how much of the page is static, and how much needs to be recalculated every time the page is served. SSI is a great way to add small pieces of information, such as the current time. But if the majority of your page is being generated at the time that it is served, you need to look for some other solution.

10.3 Configuring your server to permit SSI

To permit SSI on your server, you must have the following directive either in your httpd.conf file, or in a .htaccess file:

    Options +Includes

This tells Apache that you want to permit files to be parsed for SSI directives. Note that most configurations contain multiple Options directives that can override each other. You will probably need to apply the Options to the specific directory where you want SSI enabled in order to assure that it gets evaluated last.

Not just any file is parsed for SSI directives. You have to tell Apache which files should be parsed. There are two ways to do this. You can tell Apache to parse any file with a particular file extension, such as .shtml, with the following directives:

```
AddType text/html .shtml
AddOutputFilter INCLUDES .shtml
```

One disadvantage to this approach is that if you wanted to add SSI directives to an existing page, you would have to change the name of that page, and all links to that page, in order to give it a .shtml extension, so that those directives would be executed.

The other method is to use the XBitHack directive:

```
XBitHack on
```

XBitHack tells Apache to parse files for SSI directives if they have the execute bit set. So, to add SSI directives to an existing page, rather than having to change the file name, you would just need to make the file executable using chmod.

```
chmod +x pagename.html
```

A brief comment about what not to do. You'll occasionally see people recommending that you just tell Apache to parse all .html files for SSI, so that you don't have to mess with .shtml file names. These folks have perhaps not heard about XBitHack. The thing to keep in mind is that, by doing this, you're requiring that Apache read through every single file that it sends out to clients, even if they don't contain any SSI directives. This can slow things down quite a bit, and is not a good idea.

Of course, on Windows, there is no such thing as an execute bit to set, so that limits your options a little.

In its default configuration, Apache does not send the last modified date or content length HTTP headers on SSI pages, because these values are difficult to calculate for dynamic content. This can prevent your document from being cached, and result in slower perceived client performance. There are two ways to solve this:

1. Use the XBitHack Full configuration. This tells Apache to determine the last modified date by looking only at the date of the originally requested file, ignoring the modification date of any included files.

2. Use the directives provided by mod_expires to set an explicit expiration time on your files, thereby letting browsers and proxies know that it is acceptable to cache them.

10.4 Basic SSI directives

SSI directives have the following syntax:

```
<!--#element attribute=value attribute=value ...  -->
```

It is formatted like an HTML comment, so if you don't have SSI correctly enabled, the browser will ignore it, but it will still be visible in the HTML source. If you have SSI correctly configured, the directive will be replaced with its results.

The element can be one of a number of things, and we'll talk some more about most of these in the next installment of this series. For now, here are some examples of what you can do with SSI

10.4.1 Today's date

```
<!--#echo var="DATE_LOCAL" -->
```

The echo element just spits out the value of a variable. There are a number of standard variables, which include the whole set of environment variables that are available to CGI programs. Also, you can define your own variables with the set element.

If you don't like the format in which the date gets printed, you can use the config element, with a timefmt attribute, to modify that formatting.

```
<!--#config timefmt="%A %B %d, %Y" -->
Today is <!--#echo var="DATE_LOCAL" -->
```

10.4.2 Modification date of the file

```
This document last modified <!--#flastmod file="index.html" -->
```

This element is also subject to timefmt format configurations.

10.4.3 Including the results of a CGI program

This is one of the more common uses of SSI - to output the results of a CGI program, such as everybody's favorite, a "hit counter."

```
<!--#include virtual="/cgi-bin/counter.pl" -->
```

10.5 Additional examples

Following are some specific examples of things you can do in your HTML documents with SSI.

10.5.1 When was this section modified?

Earlier, we mentioned that you could use SSI to inform the user when the document was most recently modified. However, the actual method for doing that was left somewhat in question. The following code, placed in your HTML document, will put such a time stamp on your page. Of course, you will have to have SSI correctly enabled, as discussed above.

```
<!--#config timefmt="%A %B %d, %Y" -->
This file last modified <!--#flastmod file="ssi.shtml" -->
```

Of course, you will need to replace the ssi.shtml with the actual name of the file that you're referring to. This can be inconvenient if you're just looking for a generic piece of code that you can paste into any file, so you probably want to use the LAST_MODIFIED variable instead:

```
<!--#config timefmt="%D" -->
This file last modified <!--#echo var="LAST_MODIFIED" -->
```

For more details on the timefmt format, go to your favorite search site and look for strftime. The syntax is the same.

10.5.2 Including a standard footer

If you are managing any site that is more than a few pages, you may find that making changes to all those pages can be a real pain, particularly if you are trying to maintain some kind of standard look across all those pages.

Using an include file for a header and/or a footer can reduce the burden of these updates. You just have to make one footer file, and then include it into each page with the include SSI command. The include element can determine what file to include with either the file attribute, or the virtual attribute. The file attribute is a file path, *relative to the current directory*. That means that it cannot be an absolute file path (starting with /), nor can it contain ../ as part of that path. The virtual attribute is probably more useful, and should specify a URL relative to the document being served. It can start with a /, but must be on the same server as the file being served.

```
<!--#include virtual="/footer.html" -->
```

I'll frequently combine the last two things, putting a LAST_MODIFIED directive inside a footer file to be included. SSI directives can be contained in the included file, and includes can be nested - that is, the included file can include another file, and so on.

10.6 What else can I config?

In addition to being able to config the time format, you can also config two other things.

Usually, when something goes wrong with your SSI directive, you get the message

```
[an error occurred while processing this directive]
```

If you want to change that message to something else, you can do so with the errmsg attribute to the config element:

```
<!--#config errmsg="[It appears that you don't know how to use
SSI]" -->
```

Hopefully, end users will never see this message, because you will have resolved all the problems with your SSI directives before your site goes live. (Right?)

And you can config the format in which file sizes are returned with the sizefmt attribute. You can specify bytes for a full count in bytes, or abbrev for an abbreviated number in Kb or Mb, as appropriate.

10.7 Executing commands

You can actually have SSI execute a command using the shell (/bin/sh, to be precise - or the DOS shell, if you're on Win32). The following, for example, will give you a directory listing.

```
<pre>
<!--#exec cmd="ls" -->
</pre>
```

or, on Windows

```
<pre>
<!--#exec cmd="dir" -->
</pre>
```

You might notice some strange formatting with this directive on Windows, because the output from dir contains the string "<dir>" in it, which confuses browsers.

Note that this feature is exceedingly dangerous, as it will execute whatever code happens to be embedded in the exec tag. If you have any situation where users can edit content on your web pages, such as with a "guestbook", for example, make sure that you have this feature disabled. You can allow SSI, but not the exec feature, with the IncludesNOEXEC argument to the Options directive.

10.8 Advanced SSI techniques

In addition to spitting out content, Apache SSI gives you the option of setting variables, and using those variables in comparisons and conditionals.

10.8.1 Caveat

Most of the features discussed in this article are only available to you if you are running Apache 1.2 or later. Of course, if you are not running Apache 1.2 or later, you need to upgrade immediately, if not sooner. Go on. Do it now. We'll wait.

10.8.2 Setting variables

Using the set directive, you can set variables for later use. We'll need this later in the discussion, so we'll talk about it here. The syntax of this is as follows:

```
<!--#set var="name" value="Rich" -->
```

In addition to merely setting values literally like that, you can use any other variable, including environment variables (p. 705) or the variables discussed above (like LAST_MODIFIED, for example) to give values to your variables. You will specify that something is a variable, rather than a literal string, by using the dollar sign ($) before the name of the variable.

```
<!--#set var="modified" value="$LAST_MODIFIED" -->
```

To put a literal dollar sign into the value of your variable, you need to escape the dollar sign with a backslash.

```
<!--#set var="cost" value="\$100" -->
```

Finally, if you want to put a variable in the midst of a longer string, and there's a chance that the name of the variable will run up against some other characters, and thus be confused with those characters, you can place the name of the variable in braces, to remove this confusion. (It's hard to come up with a really good example of this, but hopefully you'll get the point.)

```
<!--#set var="date" value="${DATE_LOCAL}_${DATE_GMT}" -->
```

10.8.3 Conditional expressions

Now that we have variables, and are able to set and compare their values, we can use them to express conditionals. This lets SSI be a tiny programming language of sorts. mod_include provides an if, elif, else, endif structure for building conditional statements. This allows you to effectively generate multiple logical pages out of one actual page.

The structure of this conditional construct is:

```
<!--#if expr="test_condition" -->
<!--#elif expr="test_condition" -->
<!--#else -->
<!--#endif -->
```

A *test_condition* can be any sort of logical comparison - either comparing values to one another, or testing the "truth" of a particular value. (A given string is true if it is nonempty.) For a full list of the comparison operators available to you, see the mod_include documentation. Here are some examples of how one might use this construct.

In your configuration file, you could put the following line:

```
BrowserMatchNoCase macintosh Mac
BrowserMatchNoCase MSIE InternetExplorer
```

This will set environment variables "Mac" and "InternetExplorer" to true, if the client is running Internet Explorer on a Macintosh.

Then, in your SSI-enabled document, you might do the following:

```
<!--#if expr="${Mac} && ${InternetExplorer}" -->
Apologetic text goes here
<!--#else -->
Cool JavaScript code goes here
<!--#endif -->
```

Not that I have anything against IE on Macs - I just struggled for a few hours last week trying to get some JavaScript working on IE on a Mac, when it was working everywhere else. The above was the interim workaround.

Any other variable (either ones that you define, or normal environment variables) can be used in conditional statements. With Apache's ability to set environment variables with the SetEnvIf directives, and other related directives, this functionality can let you do some pretty involved dynamic stuff without ever resorting to CGI.

10.9 Conclusion

SSI is certainly not a replacement for CGI, or other technologies used for generating dynamic web pages. But it is a great way to add small amounts of dynamic content to pages, without doing a lot of extra work.

11 Apache Tutorial: .htaccess files

.htaccess files provide a way to make configuration changes on a per-directory basis.

11.1 .htaccess files

Related Modules	Related Directives
core	AccessFileName
mod_authn_file	AllowOverride
mod_authz_groupfile	Options
mod_cgi	AddHandler
mod_include	SetHandler
mod_mime	AuthType
	AuthName
	AuthUserFile
	AuthGroupFile
	Require

11.2 What they are/How to use them

.htaccess files (or "distributed configuration files") provide a way to make configuration changes on a per-directory basis. A file, containing one or more configuration directives, is placed in a particular document directory, and the directives apply to that directory, and all subdirectories thereof.

> NOTE: *If you want to call your .htaccess file something else, you can change the name of the file using the AccessFileName directive. For example, if you would rather call the file .config then you can put the following in your server configuration file:*
>
> *AccessFileName .config*

In general, .htaccess files use the same syntax as the main configuration files (p. 54). What you can put in these files is determined by the AllowOverride directive. This directive specifies, in categories, what directives will be honored if they are found in a .htaccess file. If a directive is permitted in a .htaccess file, the documentation for that directive will contain an Override section, specifying what value must be in AllowOverride in order for that directive to be permitted.

For example, if you look at the documentation for the AddDefaultCharset directive, you will find that it is permitted in .htaccess files. (See the Context line in the directive summary.) The Override (p. 83) line reads FileInfo. Thus, you must have at least AllowOverride FileInfo in order for this directive to be honored in .htaccess files.

Example:

Context:	(p. 83)	server config, virtual host, directory, .htaccess
Override:	(p. 83)	FileInfo

If you are unsure whether a particular directive is permitted in a .htaccess file, look at the documentation for that directive, and check the Context line for ".htaccess".

11.3 When (not) to use .htaccess files

In general, you should never use .htaccess files unless you don't have access to the main server configuration file. There is, for example, a prevailing misconception that user authentication should always be done in .htaccess files. This is simply not the case. You can put user authentication configurations in the main server configuration, and this is, in fact, the preferred way to do things.

.htaccess files should be used in a case where the content providers need to make configuration changes to the server on a per-directory basis, but do not have root access on the server system. In the event that the server administrator is not willing to make frequent configuration changes, it might be desirable to permit individual users to make these changes in .htaccess files for themselves. This is particularly true, for example, in cases where ISPs are hosting multiple user sites on a single machine, and want their users to be able to alter their configuration.

However, in general, use of .htaccess files should be avoided when possible. Any configuration that you would consider putting in a .htaccess file, can just as effectively be made in a <Directory> section in your main server configuration file.

There are two main reasons to avoid the use of .htaccess files.

The first of these is performance. When AllowOverride is set to allow the use of .htaccess files, Apache will look in every directory for .htaccess files. Thus, permitting .htaccess files causes a performance hit, whether or not you actually even use them! Also, the .htaccess file is loaded every time a document is requested.

Further note that Apache must look for .htaccess files in all higher-level directories, in order to have a full complement of directives that it must apply. (See section on how directives are applied.) Thus, if a file is requested out of a directory /www/htdocs/example, Apache must look for the following files:

```
/.htaccess
/www/.htaccess
/www/htdocs/.htaccess
/www/htdocs/example/.htaccess
```

And so, for each file access out of that directory, there are 4 additional filesystem accesses, even if none of those files are present. (Note that this would only be the case if .htaccess files were enabled for /, which is not usually the case.)

The second consideration is one of security. You are permitting users to modify server configuration, which may result in changes over which you have no control. Carefully consider whether you want to give your users this privilege. Note also that giving users less privileges than they need will lead to additional technical support requests. Make sure you clearly tell your users what level of privileges you have given them. Specifying exactly what you have set AllowOverride to, and pointing them to the relevant documentation, will save yourself a lot of confusion later.

Note that it is completely equivalent to put a .htaccess file in a directory /www/htdocs/example containing a directive, and to put that same directive in a Directory section <Directory /www/htdocs/example> in your main server configuration:

.htaccess file in /www/htdocs/example:

Contents of .htaccess file in /www/htdocs/example
```
AddType text/example .exm
```

Section from your httpd.conf file
```
<Directory /www/htdocs/example>
    AddType text/example .exm
</Directory>
```

However, putting this configuration in your server configuration file will result in less of a performance hit, as the configuration is loaded once when Apache starts, rather than every time a file is requested.

The use of .htaccess files can be disabled completely by setting the AllowOverride directive to none:

```
AllowOverride None
```

11.4 How directives are applied

The configuration directives found in a .htaccess file are applied to the directory in which the .htaccess file is found, and to all subdirectories thereof. However, it is important to also remember that there may have been .htaccess files in directories higher up. Directives are applied in the order that they are found. Therefore, a .htaccess file in a particular directory may override directives found in .htaccess files found higher up in the directory tree. And those, in turn, may have overridden directives found yet higher up, or in the main server configuration file itself.

Example:

In the directory /www/htdocs/example1 we have a .htaccess file containing the following:

```
Options +ExecCGI
```

(Note: you must have "AllowOverride Options" in effect to permit the use of the "Options" directive in .htaccess files.)

In the directory /www/htdocs/example1/example2 we have a .htaccess file containing:

```
Options Includes
```

Because of this second .htaccess file, in the directory /www/htdocs/example1/ example2, CGI execution is not permitted, as only Options Includes is in effect, which completely overrides any earlier setting that may have been in place.

11.4.1 Merging of .htaccess with the main configuration files

As discussed in the documentation on Configuration Sections (p. 57), .htaccess files can override the <Directory> sections for the corresponding directory, but will be overriden by other types of configuration sections from the main configuration files. This fact can be used to enforce certain configurations, even in the presence of a liberal AllowOverride setting. For example, to prevent script execution while allowing anything else to be set in .htaccess you can use:

```
<Directory />
    Allowoverride All
</Directory>

<Location />
    Options +IncludesNoExec -ExecCGI
</Location>
```

11.5 Authentication example

If you jumped directly to this part of the document to find out how to do authentication, it is important to note one thing. There is a common misconception that you are required to use .htaccess files in order to implement password authentication. This is not the case. Putting authentication directives in a <Directory> section, in your main server configuration file, is the preferred way to implement this, and .htaccess files should be used only if you don't have access to the main server configuration file. See above for a discussion of when you should and should not use .htaccess files.

Having said that, if you still think you need to use a .htaccess file, you may find that a configuration such as what follows may work for you.

.htaccess file contents:

```
AuthType Basic
AuthName "Password Required"
AuthUserFile /www/passwords/password.file
AuthGroupFile /www/passwords/group.file
```

```
Require Group admins
```

Note that `AllowOverride AuthConfig` must be in effect for these directives to have any effect.

Please see the authentication tutorial (p. 629) for a more complete discussion of authentication and authorization.

11.6 Server Side Includes example

Another common use of `.htaccess` files is to enable Server Side Includes for a particular directory. This may be done with the following configuration directives, placed in a `.htaccess` file in the desired directory:

```
Options +Includes
AddType text/html shtml
AddHandler server-parsed shtml
```

Note that `AllowOverride Options` and `AllowOverride FileInfo` must both be in effect for these directives to have any effect.

Please see the SSI tutorial (p. 659) for a more complete discussion of server-side includes.

11.7 CGI example

Finally, you may wish to use a `.htaccess` file to permit the execution of CGI programs in a particular directory. This may be implemented with the following configuration:

```
Options +ExecCGI
AddHandler cgi-script cgi pl
```

Alternately, if you wish to have all files in the given directory be considered to be CGI programs, this may be done with the following configuration:

```
Options +ExecCGI
SetHandler cgi-script
```

Note that `AllowOverride Options` and `AllowOverride FileInfo` must both be in effect for these directives to have any effect.

Please see the CGI tutorial (p. 651) for a more complete discussion of CGI programming and configuration.

11.8 Troubleshooting

When you put configuration directives in a `.htaccess` file, and you don't get the desired effect, there are a number of things that may be going wrong.

Most commonly, the problem is that `AllowOverride` is not set such that your configuration directives are being honored. Make sure that you don't have a `AllowOverride None` in effect for the file scope in question. A good test for this is to put garbage in your .htaccess file and reload. If a server error is not generated, then you almost certainly have AllowOverride None in effect.

If, on the other hand, you are getting server errors when trying to access documents, check your Apache error log. It will likely tell you that the directive used in your .htaccess file is not permitted. Alternately, it may tell you that you had a syntax error, which you will then need to fix.

12 Per-user web directories

On systems with multiple users, each user can be permitted to have a web site in their home directory using the UserDir directive. Visitors to a URL http://example.com/~username/ will get content out of the home directory of the user "username", out of the subdirectory specified by the UserDir directive.

See also:

▷ Mapping URLs to the Filesystem (p. 75)

12.1 Per-user web directories

Related Modules	Related Directives
mod_userdir	UserDir
	DirectoryMatch
	AllowOverride

12.2 Setting the file path with UserDir

The UserDir directive specifies a directory out of which per-user content is loaded. This directive may take several different forms.

If a path is given which does not start with a leading slash, it is assumed to be a directory path relative to the home directory of the specified user. Given this configuration:

    UserDir public_html

the URL http://example.com/~rbowen/file.html will be translated to the file path /home/rbowen/public_html/file.html

If a path is given starting with a slash, a directory path will be constructed using that path, plus the username specified. Given this configuration:

    UserDir /var/html

the URL http://example.com/~rbowen/file.html will be translated to the file path /var/html/rbowen/file.html

If a path is provided which contains an asterisk (*), a path is used in which the asterisk is replaced with the username. Given this configuration:

    UserDir /var/www/*/docs

the URL http://example.com/~rbowen/file.html will be translated to the file path /var/www/rbowen/docs/file.html

Multiple directories or directory paths can also be set.

```
UserDir public_html /var/html
```

For the URL http://example.com/~rbowen/file.html, Apache will search for ~rbowen. If it isn't found, Apache will search for rbowen in /var/html. If found, the above URL will then be translated to the file path /var/html/rbowen/file.html

12.3 Redirecting to external URLs

The UserDir directive can be used to redirect user directory requests to external URLs.

```
UserDir http://example.org/users/*/
```

The above example will redirect a request for http://example.com/~bob/abc.html to http://example.org/users/bob/abc.html.

12.4 Restricting what users are permitted to use this feature

Using the syntax shown in the UserDir documentation, you can restrict what users are permitted to use this functionality:

```
UserDir disabled root jro fish
```

The configuration above will enable the feature for all users except for those listed in the disabled statement. You can, likewise, disable the feature for all but a few users by using a configuration like the following:

```
UserDir disabled
UserDir enabled rbowen krietz
```

See UserDir documentation for additional examples.

12.5 Enabling a cgi directory for each user

In order to give each user their own cgi-bin directory, you can use a <Directory> directive to make a particular subdirectory of a user's home directory cgi-enabled.

```
<Directory /home/*/public_html/cgi-bin/>
Options ExecCGI
SetHandler cgi-script
</Directory>
```

Then, presuming that UserDir is set to public_html, a cgi program example.cgi could be loaded from that directory as:

```
http://example.com/~rbowen/cgi-bin/example.cgi
```

12.6 Allowing users to alter configuration

If you want to allows users to modify the server configuration in their web space, they will need to use .htaccess files to make these changed. Ensure that you

have set `AllowOverride` to a value sufficient for the directives that you want
to permit the users to modify. See the .htaccess tutorial (p. 667) for additional
details on how this works.

13 Security Tips

Some hints and tips on security issues in setting up a web server. Some of the suggestions will be general, others specific to Apache.

13.1 Keep up to Date

The Apache HTTP Server has a good record for security and a developer community highly concerned about security issues. But it is inevitable that some problems – small or large – will be discovered in software after it is released. For this reason, it is crucial to keep aware of updates to the software. If you have obtained your version of the HTTP Server directly from Apache, we highly recommend you subscribe to the Apache HTTP Server Announcements List[1] where you can keep informed of new releases and security updates. Similar services are available from most third-party distributors of Apache software.

Of course, most times that a web server is compromised, it is not because of problems in the HTTP Server code. Rather, it comes from problems in add-on code, CGI scripts, or the underlying Operating System. You must therefore stay aware of problems and updates with all the software on your system.

13.2 Permissions on ServerRoot Directories

In typical operation, Apache is started by the root user, and it switches to the user defined by the User directive to serve hits. As is the case with any command that root executes, you must take care that it is protected from modification by non-root users. Not only must the files themselves be writeable only by root, but so must the directories, and parents of all directories. For example, if you choose to place ServerRoot in /usr/local/apache then it is suggested that you create that directory as root, with commands like these:

```
mkdir /usr/local/apache
cd /usr/local/apache
mkdir bin conf logs
chown 0 .  bin conf logs
chgrp 0 .  bin conf logs
chmod 755 .  bin conf logs
```

It is assumed that /, /usr, and /usr/local are only modifiable by root. When you install the httpd executable, you should ensure that it is similarly protected:

```
cp httpd /usr/local/apache/bin
chown 0 /usr/local/apache/bin/httpd
chgrp 0 /usr/local/apache/bin/httpd
chmod 511 /usr/local/apache/bin/httpd
```

---

[1] http://httpd.apache.org/lists.html#http-announce

You can create an htdocs subdirectory which is modifiable by other users – since root never executes any files out of there, and shouldn't be creating files in there.

If you allow non-root users to modify any files that root either executes or writes on then you open your system to root compromises. For example, someone could replace the httpd binary so that the next time you start it, it will execute some arbitrary code. If the logs directory is writeable (by a non-root user), someone could replace a log file with a symlink to some other system file, and then root might overwrite that file with arbitrary data. If the log files themselves are writeable (by a non-root user), then someone may be able to overwrite the log itself with bogus data.

13.3 Server Side Includes

Server Side Includes (SSI) present a server administrator with several potential security risks.

The first risk is the increased load on the server. All SSI-enabled files have to be parsed by Apache, whether or not there are any SSI directives included within the files. While this load increase is minor, in a shared server environment it can become significant.

SSI files also pose the same risks that are associated with CGI scripts in general. Using the exec cmd element, SSI-enabled files can execute any CGI script or program under the permissions of the user and group Apache runs as, as configured in httpd.conf.

There are ways to enhance the security of SSI files while still taking advantage of the benefits they provide.

To isolate the damage a wayward SSI file can cause, a server administrator can enable suexec (p. 719) as described in the CGI in General section.

Enabling SSI for files with .html or .htm extensions can be dangerous. This is especially true in a shared, or high traffic, server environment. SSI-enabled files should have a separate extension, such as the conventional .shtml. This helps keep server load at a minimum and allows for easier management of risk.

Another solution is to disable the ability to run scripts and programs from SSI pages. To do this replace Includes with IncludesNOEXEC in the Options directive. Note that users may still use <--#include virtual="..." --> to execute CGI scripts if these scripts are in directories designated by a ScriptAlias directive.

13.4 CGI in General

First of all, you always have to remember that you must trust the writers of the CGI scripts/programs or your ability to spot potential security holes in CGI, whether they were deliberate or accidental. CGI scripts can run essentially arbitrary commands on your system with the permissions of the web server user and can therefore be extremely dangerous if they are not carefully checked.

All the CGI scripts will run as the same user, so they have potential to conflict (accidentally or deliberately) with other scripts e.g. User A hates User B, so he writes a script to trash User B's CGI database. One program which can be used to allow scripts to run as different users is suEXEC (p. 719) which is included with Apache as of 1.2 and is called from special hooks in the Apache server code. Another popular way of doing this is with CGIWrap[2].

13.5 Non Script Aliased CGI

Allowing users to execute CGI scripts in any directory should only be considered if:

- You trust your users not to write scripts which will deliberately or accidentally expose your system to an attack.
- You consider security at your site to be so feeble in other areas, as to make one more potential hole irrelevant.
- You have no users, and nobody ever visits your server.

13.6 Script Aliased CGI

Limiting CGI to special directories gives the admin control over what goes into those directories. This is inevitably more secure than non script aliased CGI, but only if users with write access to the directories are trusted or the admin is willing to test each new CGI script/program for potential security holes.

Most sites choose this option over the non script aliased CGI approach.

13.7 Other sources of dynamic content

Embedded scripting options which run as part of the server itself, such as mod_-php, mod_perl, mod_tcl, and mod_python, run under the identity of the server itself (see the User directive), and therefore scripts executed by these engines potentially can access anything the server user can. Some scripting engines may provide restrictions, but it is better to be safe and assume not.

13.8 Protecting System Settings

To run a really tight ship, you'll want to stop users from setting up .htaccess files which can override security features you've configured. Here's one way to do it.

In the server configuration file, put

```
<Directory />
AllowOverride None
</Directory>
```

---

[2]http://cgiwrap.sourceforge.net/

This prevents the use of .htaccess files in all directories apart from those specifically enabled.

13.9 Protect Server Files by Default

One aspect of Apache which is occasionally misunderstood is the feature of default access. That is, unless you take steps to change it, if the server can find its way to a file through normal URL mapping rules, it can serve it to clients.

For instance, consider the following example:

```
# cd /; ln -s / public_html
Accessing http://localhost/~root/
```

This would allow clients to walk through the entire filesystem. To work around this, add the following block to your server's configuration:

```
<Directory />
Order Deny,Allow
Deny from all
</Directory>
```

This will forbid default access to filesystem locations. Add appropriate Directory blocks to allow access only in those areas you wish. For example,

```
<Directory /usr/users/*/public_html>
Order Deny,Allow
Allow from all
</Directory>
<Directory /usr/local/httpd>
Order Deny,Allow
Allow from all
</Directory>
```

Pay particular attention to the interactions of Location and Directory directives; for instance, even if <Directory /> denies access, a <Location /> directive might overturn it.

Also be wary of playing games with the UserDir directive; setting it to something like ./ would have the same effect, for root, as the first example above. If you are using Apache 1.3 or above, we strongly recommend that you include the following line in your server configuration files:

```
UserDir disabled root
```

13.10 Watching Your Logs

To keep up-to-date with what is actually going on against your server you have to check the Log Files (p. 66). Even though the log files only reports what has already happened, they will give you some understanding of what attacks is thrown against the server and allow you to check if the necessary level of security is present.

A couple of examples:

```
grep -c "/jsp/source.jsp?/jsp/ /jsp/source.jsp??" access_log
grep "client denied" error_log | tail -n 10
```

The first example will list the number of attacks trying to exploit the Apache Tomcat Source.JSP Malformed Request Information Disclosure Vulnerability[3], the second example will list the ten last denied clients, for example:

```
[Thu Jul 11 17:18:39 2002] [error] [client foo.example.com]
client denied by server configuration:
/usr/local/apache/htdocs/.htpasswd
```

As you can see, the log files only report what already has happened, so if the client had been able to access the .htpasswd file you would have seen something similar to:

```
foo.example.com - - [12/Jul/2002:01:59:13 +0200] "GET /.htpasswd
HTTP/1.1"
```

in your Access Log (p. 66). This means you probably commented out the following in your server configuration file:

```
<Files ~ "^\.ht">
Order allow,deny
Deny from all
</Files>
```

---

[3]http://online.securityfocus.com/bid/4876/info/

14 Dynamic Shared Object (DSO) Support

The Apache HTTP Server is a modular program where the administrator can choose the functionality to include in the server by selecting a set of modules. The modules can be statically compiled into the httpd binary when the server is built. Alternatively, modules can be compiled as Dynamic Shared Objects (DSOs) that exist separately from the main httpd binary file. DSO modules may be compiled at the time the server is built, or they may be compiled and added at a later time using the Apache Extension Tool (apxs).

This section describes how to use DSO modules as well as the theory behind their use.

14.1 Implementation

Related Modules	Related Directives
mod_so	LoadModule

The DSO support for loading individual Apache modules is based on a module named mod_so which must be statically compiled into the Apache core. It is the only module besides core which cannot be put into a DSO itself. Practically all other distributed Apache modules can then be placed into a DSO by individually enabling the DSO build for them via configure's --enable-*module*=shared option as discussed in the install documentation (p. 775). After a module is compiled into a DSO named mod_foo.so you can use mod_so's LoadModule command in your httpd.conf file to load this module at server startup or restart.

To simplify this creation of DSO files for Apache modules (especially for third-party modules) a new support program named apxs (**APache eXtenSion**) is available. It can be used to build DSO based modules *outside of* the Apache source tree. The idea is simple: When installing Apache the configure's make install procedure installs the Apache C header files and puts the platform-dependent compiler and linker flags for building DSO files into the apxs program. This way the user can use apxs to compile his Apache module sources without the Apache distribution source tree and without having to fiddle with the platform-dependent compiler and linker flags for DSO support.

14.2 Usage Summary

To give you an overview of the DSO features of Apache 2.x, here is a short and concise summary:

1. Build and install a *distributed* Apache module, say mod_foo.c, into its own DSO mod_foo.so:

   ```
   $ ./configure --prefix=/path/to/install --enable-foo=shared
   $ make install
   ```

2. Build and install a *third-party* Apache module, say mod_foo.c, into its
   own DSO mod_foo.so:

```
$ ./configure
--add-module=module_type:/path/to/3rdparty/mod_foo.c \
    --enable-foo=shared
$ make install
```

3. Configure Apache for *later installation* of shared modules:

```
$ ./configure --enable-so
$ make install
```

4. Build and install a *third-party* Apache module, say mod_foo.c, into its
   own DSO mod_foo.so *outside of* the Apache source tree using apxs:

```
$ cd /path/to/3rdparty
$ apxs -c mod_foo.c
$ apxs -i -a -n foo mod_foo.la
```

In all cases, once the shared module is compiled, you must use a LoadModule
directive in httpd.conf to tell Apache to activate the module.

14.3 Background

On modern Unix derivatives there exists a nifty mechanism usually called dynamic linking/loading of *Dynamic Shared Objects* (DSO) which provides a way
to build a piece of program code in a special format for loading it at run-time
into the address space of an executable program.

This loading can usually be done in two ways: Automatically by a system
program called ld.so when an executable program is started or manually from
within the executing program via a programmatic system interface to the Unix
loader through the system calls dlopen()/dlsym().

In the first way the DSO's are usually called *shared libraries* or *DSO libraries*
and named libfoo.so or libfoo.so.1.2. They reside in a system directory
(usually /usr/lib) and the link to the executable program is established at
build-time by specifying -lfoo to the linker command. This hard-codes library
references into the executable program file so that at start-time the Unix loader
is able to locate libfoo.so in /usr/lib, in paths hard-coded via linker-options
like -R or in paths configured via the environment variable LD_LIBRARY_PATH.
It then resolves any (yet unresolved) symbols in the executable program which
are available in the DSO.

Symbols in the executable program are usually not referenced by the DSO
(because it's a reusable library of general code) and hence no further resolving
has to be done. The executable program has no need to do anything on its own
to use the symbols from the DSO because the complete resolving is done by the
Unix loader. (In fact, the code to invoke ld.so is part of the run-time startup
code which is linked into every executable program which has been bound non-
static). The advantage of dynamic loading of common library code is obvious:

the library code needs to be stored only once, in a system library like libc.so, saving disk space for every program.

In the second way the DSO's are usually called *shared objects* or *DSO files* and can be named with an arbitrary extension (although the canonical name is foo.so). These files usually stay inside a program-specific directory and there is no automatically established link to the executable program where they are used. Instead the executable program manually loads the DSO at run-time into its address space via dlopen(). At this time no resolving of symbols from the DSO for the executable program is done. But instead the Unix loader automatically resolves any (yet unresolved) symbols in the DSO from the set of symbols exported by the executable program and its already loaded DSO libraries (especially all symbols from the ubiquitous libc.so). This way the DSO gets knowledge of the executable program's symbol set as if it had been statically linked with it in the first place.

Finally, to take advantage of the DSO's API the executable program has to resolve particular symbols from the DSO via dlsym() for later use inside dispatch tables *etc.* In other words: The executable program has to manually resolve every symbol it needs to be able to use it. The advantage of such a mechanism is that optional program parts need not be loaded (and thus do not spend memory) until they are needed by the program in question. When required, these program parts can be loaded dynamically to extend the base program's functionality.

Although this DSO mechanism sounds straightforward there is at least one difficult step here: The resolving of symbols from the executable program for the DSO when using a DSO to extend a program (the second way). Why? Because "reverse resolving" DSO symbols from the executable program's symbol set is against the library design (where the library has no knowledge about the programs it is used by) and is neither available under all platforms nor standardized. In practice the executable program's global symbols are often not re-exported and thus not available for use in a DSO. Finding a way to force the linker to export all global symbols is the main problem one has to solve when using DSO for extending a program at run-time.

The shared library approach is the typical one, because it is what the DSO mechanism was designed for, hence it is used for nearly all types of libraries the operating system provides. On the other hand using shared objects for extending a program is not used by a lot of programs.

14.4 Advantages and Disadvantages

The above DSO based features have the following advantages:

- The server package is more flexible at run-time because the actual server process can be assembled at run-time via LoadModule httpd.conf configuration commands instead of configure options at build-time. For instance this way one is able to run different server instances (standard &

SSL version, minimalistic & powered up version [mod_perl, PHP3], *etc.*) with only one Apache installation.

- The server package can be easily extended with third-party modules even after installation. This is at least a great benefit for vendor package maintainers who can create a Apache core package and additional packages containing extensions like PHP3, mod_perl, mod_fastcgi, *etc.*

- Easier Apache module prototyping because with the DSO/apxs pair you can both work outside the Apache source tree and only need an apxs -i command followed by an apachectl restart to bring a new version of your currently developed module into the running Apache server.

DSO has the following disadvantages:

- The DSO mechanism cannot be used on every platform because not all operating systems support dynamic loading of code into the address space of a program.

- The server is approximately 20% slower at startup time because of the symbol resolving overhead the Unix loader now has to do.

- The server is approximately 5% slower at execution time under some platforms because position independent code (PIC) sometimes needs complicated assembler tricks for relative addressing which are not necessarily as fast as absolute addressing.

- Because DSO modules cannot be linked against other DSO-based libraries (ld -lfoo) on all platforms (for instance a.out-based platforms usually don't provide this functionality while ELF-based platforms do) you cannot use the DSO mechanism for all types of modules. Or in other words, modules compiled as DSO files are restricted to only use symbols from the Apache core, from the C library (libc) and all other dynamic or static libraries used by the Apache core, or from static library archives (libfoo.a) containing position independent code. The only chances to use other code is to either make sure the Apache core itself already contains a reference to it or loading the code yourself via dlopen().

15 Content Negotiation

Apache supports content negotiation as described in the HTTP/1.1 specification. It can choose the best representation of a resource based on the browser-supplied preferences for media type, languages, character set and encoding. It also implements a couple of features to give more intelligent handling of requests from browsers that send incomplete negotiation information.

Content negotiation is provided by the mod_negotiation module, which is compiled in by default.

15.1 About Content Negotiation

A resource may be available in several different representations. For example, it might be available in different languages or different media types, or a combination. One way of selecting the most appropriate choice is to give the user an index page, and let them select. However it is often possible for the server to choose automatically. This works because browsers can send, as part of each request, information about what representations they prefer. For example, a browser could indicate that it would like to see information in French, if possible, else English will do. Browsers indicate their preferences by headers in the request. To request only French representations, the browser would send

```
Accept-Language:  fr
```

Note that this preference will only be applied when there is a choice of representations and they vary by language.

As an example of a more complex request, this browser has been configured to accept French and English, but prefer French, and to accept various media types, preferring HTML over plain text or other text types, and preferring GIF or JPEG over other media types, but also allowing any other media type as a last resort:

```
Accept-Language:  fr; q=1.0, en; q=0.5
Accept:  text/html; q=1.0, text/*; q=0.8, image/gif; q=0.6,
image/jpeg; q=0.6, image/*; q=0.5, */*; q=0.1
```

Apache supports 'server driven' content negotiation, as defined in the HTTP/1.1 specification. It fully supports the Accept, Accept-Language, Accept-Charset andAccept-Encoding request headers. Apache also supports 'transparent' content negotiation, which is an experimental negotiation protocol defined in RFC 2295 and RFC 2296. It does not offer support for 'feature negotiation' as defined in these RFCs.

A **resource** is a conceptual entity identified by a URI (RFC 2396). An HTTP server like Apache provides access to **representations** of the resource(s) within its namespace, with each representation in the form of a sequence of bytes with a defined media type, character set, encoding, etc. Each resource may be associated with zero, one, or more than one representation at any given time. If multiple representations are available, the resource is referred to as **negotiable** and each of its representations is termed a **variant**. The ways in which the variants for a negotiable resource vary are called the **dimensions** of negotiation.

15.2 Negotiation in Apache

In order to negotiate a resource, the server needs to be given information about each of the variants. This is done in one of two ways:

- Using a type map (*i.e.*, a *.var file) which names the files containing the variants explicitly, or

- Using a 'MultiViews' search, where the server does an implicit filename pattern match and chooses from among the results.

15.2.1 Using a type-map file

A type map is a document which is associated with the handler named type-map (or, for backwards-compatibility with older Apache configurations, the MIME-type application/x-type-map). Note that to use this feature, you must have a handler set in the configuration that defines a file suffix as type-map; this is best done with

```
AddHandler type-map .var
```

in the server configuration file.

Type map files should have the same name as the resource which they are describing, and have an entry for each available variant; these entries consist of contiguous HTTP-format header lines. Entries for different variants are separated by blank lines. Blank lines are illegal within an entry. It is conventional to begin a map file with an entry for the combined entity as a whole (although this is not required, and if present will be ignored). An example map file is shown below. This file would be named foo.var, as it describes a resource named foo.

```
URI: foo

URI: foo.en.html
Content-type:  text/html
Content-language:  en

URI: foo.fr.de.html
Content-type:  text/html;charset=iso-8859-2
Content-language:  fr, de
```

Note also that a typemap file will take precedence over the filename's extension, even when Multiviews is on. If the variants have different source qualities, that may be indicated by the "qs" parameter to the media type, as in this picture (available as JPEG, GIF, or ASCII-art):

```
URI: foo
```

```
URI: foo.jpeg
Content-type:   image/jpeg; qs=0.8
URI: foo.gif
Content-type:   image/gif; qs=0.5
URI: foo.txt
Content-type:   text/plain; qs=0.01
```

qs values can vary in the range 0.000 to 1.000. Note that any variant with a qs value of 0.000 will never be chosen. Variants with no 'qs' parameter value are given a qs factor of 1.0. The qs parameter indicates the relative 'quality' of this variant compared to the other available variants, independent of the client's capabilities. For example, a JPEG file is usually of higher source quality than an ASCII file if it is attempting to represent a photograph. However, if the resource being represented is an original ASCII art, then an ASCII representation would have a higher source quality than a JPEG representation. A qs value is therefore specific to a given variant depending on the nature of the resource it represents.

The full list of headers recognized is available in the mod_negotiation typemap (p. 367) documentation.

15.2.2 Multiviews

MultiViews is a per-directory option, meaning it can be set with an Options directive within a <Directory>, <Location> or <Files> section in httpd.conf, or (if AllowOverride is properly set) in .htaccess files. Note that Options All does not set MultiViews; you have to ask for it by name.

The effect of MultiViews is as follows: if the server receives a request for /some/dir/foo, if /some/dir has MultiViews enabled, and /some/dir/foo does *not* exist, then the server reads the directory looking for files named foo.*, and effectively fakes up a type map which names all those files, assigning them the same media types and content-encodings it would have if the client had asked for one of them by name. It then chooses the best match to the client's requirements.

MultiViews may also apply to searches for the file named by the DirectoryIndex directive, if the server is trying to index a directory. If the configuration files specify

```
DirectoryIndex index
```

then the server will arbitrate between index.html and index.html3 if both are present. If neither are present, and index.cgi is there, the server will run it.

If one of the files found when reading the directory does not have an extension recognized by mod_mime to designate its Charset, Content-Type, Language, or Encoding, then the result depends on the setting of the MultiViewsMatch directive. This directive determines whether handlers, filters, and other extension types can participate in MultiViews negotiation.

15.3 The Negotiation Methods

After Apache has obtained a list of the variants for a given resource, either from a type-map file or from the filenames in the directory, it invokes one of two methods to decide on the 'best' variant to return, if any. It is not necessary to know any of the details of how negotiation actually takes place in order to use Apache's content negotiation features. However the rest of this section explains the methods used for those interested.

There are two negotiation methods:

1. **Server driven negotiation with the Apache algorithm** is used in the normal case. The Apache algorithm is explained in more detail below. When this algorithm is used, Apache can sometimes 'fiddle' the quality factor of a particular dimension to achieve a better result. The ways Apache can fiddle quality factors is explained in more detail below.

2. **Transparent content negotiation** is used when the browser specifically requests this through the mechanism defined in RFC 2295. This negotiation method gives the browser full control over deciding on the 'best' variant, the result is therefore dependent on the specific algorithms used by the browser. As part of the transparent negotiation process, the browser can ask Apache to run the 'remote variant selection algorithm' defined in RFC 2296.

15.3.1 Dimensions of Negotiation

Dimension	Notes
Media Type	Browser indicates preferences with the `Accept` header field. Each item can have an associated quality factor. Variant description can also have a quality factor (the `"qs"` parameter).
Language	Browser indicates preferences with the `Accept-Language` header field. Each item can have a quality factor. Variants can be associated with none, one or more than one language.
Encoding	Browser indicates preference with the `Accept-Encoding` header field. Each item can have a quality factor.
Charset	Browser indicates preference with the `Accept-Charset` header field. Each item can have a quality factor. Variants can indicate a charset as a parameter of the media type.

15.3.2 Apache Negotiation Algorithm

Apache can use the following algorithm to select the 'best' variant (if any) to return to the browser. This algorithm is not further configurable. It operates as follows:

1. First, for each dimension of the negotiation, check the appropriate *Accept** header field and assign a quality to each variant. If the *Accept** header

for any dimension implies that this variant is not acceptable, eliminate it. If no variants remain, go to step 4.

2. Select the 'best' variant by a process of elimination. Each of the following tests is applied in order. Any variants not selected at each test are eliminated. After each test, if only one variant remains, select it as the best match and proceed to step 3. If more than one variant remains, move on to the next test.

   a) Multiply the quality factor from the Accept header with the quality-of-source factor for this variants media type, and select the variants with the highest value.

   b) Select the variants with the highest language quality factor.

   c) Select the variants with the best language match, using either the order of languages in the Accept-Language header (if present), or else the order of languages in the LanguagePriority directive (if present).

   d) Select the variants with the highest 'level' media parameter (used to give the version of text/html media types).

   e) Select variants with the best charset media parameters, as given on the Accept-Charset header line. Charset ISO-8859-1 is acceptable unless explicitly excluded. Variants with a text/* media type but not explicitly associated with a particular charset are assumed to be in ISO-8859-1.

   f) Select those variants which have associated charset media parameters that are *not* ISO-8859-1. If there are no such variants, select all variants instead.

   g) Select the variants with the best encoding. If there are variants with an encoding that is acceptable to the user-agent, select only these variants. Otherwise if there is a mix of encoded and non-encoded variants, select only the unencoded variants. If either all variants are encoded or all variants are not encoded, select all variants.

   h) Select the variants with the smallest content length.

   i) Select the first variant of those remaining. This will be either the first listed in the type-map file, or when variants are read from the directory, the one whose file name comes first when sorted using ASCII code order.

3. The algorithm has now selected one 'best' variant, so return it as the response. The HTTP response header Vary is set to indicate the dimensions of negotiation (browsers and caches can use this information when caching the resource). End.

4. To get here means no variant was selected (because none are acceptable to the browser). Return a 406 status (meaning "No acceptable representation") with a response body consisting of an HTML document listing the available variants. Also set the HTTP Vary header to indicate the dimensions of variance.

15.4 Fiddling with Quality Values

Apache sometimes changes the quality values from what would be expected by
a strict interpretation of the Apache negotiation algorithm above. This is to
get a better result from the algorithm for browsers which do not send full or
accurate information. Some of the most popular browsers send `Accept` header
information which would otherwise result in the selection of the wrong variant
in many cases. If a browser sends full and correct information these fiddles will
not be applied.

15.4.1 Media Types and Wildcards

The `Accept:` request header indicates preferences for media types. It can also
include 'wildcard' media types, such as "image/*" or "*/*" where the * matches
any string. So a request including:

```
Accept:  image/*, */*
```

would indicate that any type starting "image/" is acceptable, as is any other
type. Some browsers routinely send wildcards in addition to explicit types they
can handle. For example:

```
Accept:  text/html, text/plain, image/gif, image/jpeg, */*
```

The intention of this is to indicate that the explicitly listed types are preferred,
but if a different representation is available, that is ok too. Using explicit quality
values, what the browser really wants is something like:

```
Accept:  text/html, text/plain, image/gif, image/jpeg, */*;
q=0.01
```

The explicit types have no quality factor, so they default to a preference of 1.0
(the highest). The wildcard */* is given a low preference of 0.01, so other types
will only be returned if no variant matches an explicitly listed type.

If the `Accept:` header contains *no* q factors at all, Apache sets the q value of
"*/*", if present, to 0.01 to emulate the desired behavior. It also sets the q
value of wildcards of the format "type/*" to 0.02 (so these are preferred over
matches against "*/*". If any media type on the `Accept:` header contains a
q factor, these special values are *not* applied, so requests from browsers which
send the explicit information to start with work as expected.

15.4.2 Language Negotiation Exceptions

New in Apache 2.0, some exceptions have been added to the negotiation algorithm to allow graceful fallback when language negotiation fails to find a match.

When a client requests a page on your server, but the server cannot find a
single page that matches the `Accept-language` sent by the browser, the server
will return either a "No Acceptable Variant" or "Multiple Choices" response to
the client. To avoid these error messages, it is possible to configure Apache to
ignore the `Accept-language` in these cases and provide a document that does

not explicitly match the client's request. The `ForceLanguagePriority` directive can be used to override one or both of these error messages and substitute the servers judgement in the form of the `LanguagePriority` directive.

The server will also attempt to match language-subsets when no other match can be found. For example, if a client requests documents with the language en-GB for British English, the server is not normally allowed by the HTTP/1.1 standard to match that against a document that is marked as simply en. (Note that it is almost surely a configuration error to include en-GB and not en in the `Accept-Language` header, since it is very unlikely that a reader understands British English, but doesn't understand English in general. Unfortunately, many current clients have default configurations that resemble this.) However, if no other language match is possible and the server is about to return a "No Acceptable Variants" error or fallback to the `LanguagePriority`, the server will ignore the subset specification and match en-GB against en documents. Implicitly, Apache will add the parent language to the client's acceptable language list with a very low quality value. But note that if the client requests "en-GB; q=0.9, fr; q=0.8", and the server has documents designated "en" and "fr", then the "fr" document will be returned. This is necessary to maintain compliance with the HTTP/1.1 specification and to work effectively with properly configured clients.

In order to support advanced techniques (such as cookies or special URL-paths) to determine the user's preferred language, since Apache 2.0.47 mod_-negotiation recognizes the environment variable (p. 705) prefer-language. If it exists and contains an appropriate language tag, mod_negotiation will try to select a matching variant. If there's no such variant, the normal negotiation process applies.

Example
```
SetEnvIf Cookie "language=(.+)" prefer-language=$1
Header append Vary cookie
```

15.5 Extensions to Transparent Content Negotiation

Apache extends the transparent content negotiation protocol (RFC 2295) as follows. A new {encoding ..} element is used in variant lists to label variants which are available with a specific content-encoding only. The implementation of the RVSA/1.0 algorithm (RFC 2296) is extended to recognize encoded variants in the list, and to use them as candidate variants whenever their encodings are acceptable according to the `Accept-Encoding` request header. The RVSA/1.0 implementation does not round computed quality factors to 5 decimal places before choosing the best variant.

15.6 Note on hyperlinks and naming conventions

If you are using language negotiation you can choose between different naming conventions, because files can have more than one extension, and the order of the extensions is normally irrelevant (see the mod_mime (p. 348) documentation for details).

A typical file has a MIME-type extension (*e.g.*, html), maybe an encoding extension (*e.g.*, gz), and of course a language extension (*e.g.*, en) when we have different language variants of this file.

Examples:

- foo.en.html
- foo.html.en
- foo.en.html.gz

Here are some more examples of filenames together with valid and invalid hyperlinks:

Filename	Valid hyperlink	Invalid hyperlink
foo.html.en	foo	-
	foo.html	
foo.en.html	foo	foo.html
foo.html.en.gz	foo	foo.gz
	foo.html	foo.html.gz
foo.en.html.gz	foo	foo.html
		foo.html.gz
		foo.gz
foo.gz.html.en	foo	foo.html
	foo.gz	
	foo.gz.html	
foo.html.gz.en	foo	foo.gz
	foo.html	
	foo.html.gz	

Looking at the table above, you will notice that it is always possible to use the name without any extensions in a hyperlink (*e.g.*, foo). The advantage is that you can hide the actual type of a document and can change it later, *e.g.*, from html to shtml or cgi without changing any hyperlink references.

If you want to continue to use a MIME-type in your hyperlinks (*e.g.* foo.html) the language extension (including an encoding extension if there is one) must be on the right hand side of the MIME-type extension (*e.g.*, foo.html.en).

15.7 Note on Caching

When a cache stores a representation, it associates it with the request URL. The next time that URL is requested, the cache can use the stored representation. But, if the resource is negotiable at the server, this might result in only the first requested variant being cached and subsequent cache hits might return the wrong response. To prevent this, Apache normally marks all responses that are returned after content negotiation as non-cacheable by HTTP/1.0 clients.

Apache also supports the HTTP/1.1 protocol features to allow caching of negotiated responses.

For requests which come from a HTTP/1.0 compliant client (either a browser or a cache), the directive `CacheNegotiatedDocs` can be used to allow caching of responses which were subject to negotiation. This directive can be given in the server config or virtual host, and takes no arguments. It has no effect on requests from HTTP/1.1 clients.

For HTTP/1.1 clients, Apache sends a `Vary` HTTP response header to indicate the negotiation dimensions for the response. Caches can use this information to determine whether a subsequent request can be served from the local copy. To encourage a cache to use the local copy regardless of the negotiation dimensions, set the `force-no-vary` environment variable (p. 705).

16 Custom Error Responses

Additional functionality allows webmasters to configure the response of Apache to some error or problem.

Customizable responses can be defined to be activated in the event of a server detected error or problem.

If a script crashes and produces a "500 Server Error" response, then this response can be replaced with either some friendlier text or by a redirection to another URL (local or external).

16.1 Behavior

16.1.1 Old Behavior

NCSA httpd 1.3 would return some boring old error/problem message which would often be meaningless to the user, and would provide no means of logging the symptoms which caused it.

16.1.2 New Behavior

The server can be asked to:

1. Display some other text, instead of the NCSA hard coded messages, or
2. redirect to a local URL, or
3. redirect to an external URL.

Redirecting to another URL can be useful, but only if some information can be passed which can then be used to explain and/or log the error/problem more clearly.

To achieve this, Apache will define new CGI-like environment variables:

```
REDIRECT_HTTP_ACCEPT=*/*, image/gif, image/x-xbitmap, image/jpeg
REDIRECT_HTTP_USER_AGENT=Mozilla/1.1b2 (X11; I; HP-UX A.09.05
9000/712)
REDIRECT_PATH=.:/bin:/usr/local/bin:/etc
REDIRECT_QUERY_STRING=
REDIRECT_REMOTE_ADDR=121.345.78.123
REDIRECT_REMOTE_HOST=ooh.ahhh.com
REDIRECT_SERVER_NAME=crash.bang.edu
REDIRECT_SERVER_PORT=80
REDIRECT_SERVER_SOFTWARE=Apache/0.8.15
REDIRECT_URL=/cgi-bin/buggy.pl
```

Note the REDIRECT_ prefix.

At least REDIRECT_URL and REDIRECT_QUERY_STRING will be passed to the new URL (assuming it's a cgi-script or a cgi-include). The other variables will exist only if they existed prior to the error/problem. **None** of these will be set if your ErrorDocument is an *external* redirect (anything starting with a scheme name like http:, even if it refers to the same host as the server).

16.2 Configuration

Use of ErrorDocument is enabled for .htaccess files when the AllowOverride is set accordingly.

Here are some examples...

```
ErrorDocument 500 /cgi-bin/crash-recover
ErrorDocument 500 "Sorry, our script crashed.  Oh dear"
ErrorDocument 500 http://xxx/
ErrorDocument 404 /Lame_excuses/not_found.html
ErrorDocument 401 /Subscription/how_to_subscribe.html
```

The syntax is,

```
ErrorDocument <3-digit-code> <action>
```

where the action can be,

1. Text to be displayed. Wrap the text with quotes (").

2. An external URL to redirect to.

3. A local URL to redirect to.

16.3 Custom Error Responses and Redirects

Apache's behavior to redirected URLs has been modified so that additional environment variables are available to a script/server-include.

16.3.1 Old behavior

Standard CGI vars were made available to a script which has been redirected to. No indication of where the redirection came from was provided.

16.3.2 New behavior

A new batch of environment variables will be initialized for use by a script which has been redirected to. Each new variable will have the prefix REDIRECT_. REDIRECT_ environment variables are created from the CGI environment variables which existed prior to the redirect, they are renamed with a REDIRECT_ prefix, *i.e.*, HTTP_USER_AGENT becomes REDIRECT_HTTP_USER_AGENT. In addition to these new variables, Apache will define REDIRECT_URL and REDIRECT_STATUS to help the script trace its origin. Both the original URL and the URL being redirected to can be logged in the access log.

If the ErrorDocument specifies a local redirect to a CGI script, the script should include a "Status:" header field in its output in order to ensure the propagation all the way back to the client of the error condition that caused it to be invoked. For instance, a Perl ErrorDocument script might include the following:

```
...
print "Content-type:  text/html\n";
printf "Status:  %s Condition Intercepted\n",
$ENV{"REDIRECT_STATUS"};
...
```

If the script is dedicated to handling a particular error condition, such as 404 Not Found, it can use the specific code and error text instead.

Note that the script *must* emit an appropriate Status: header (such as 302 Found), if the response contains a Location: header (in order to issue a client side redirect). Otherwise the Location: header may have no effect.

17 Binding

Configuring Apache to listen on specific addresses and ports.

See also:

> ▷ Virtual Hosts (p. 541)
>
> ▷ DNS Issues (p. 571)

17.1 Overview

Related Modules	Related Directives
core	<VirtualHost>
mpm_common	Listen

When Apache starts, it binds to some port and address on the local machine and waits for incoming requests. By default, it listens to all addresses on the machine. However, it may need to be told to listen on specific ports, or only on selected addresses, or a combination of both. This is often combined with the Virtual Host feature, which determines how Apache responds to different IP addresses, hostnames and ports.

The Listen directive tells the server to accept incoming requests only on the specified ports or address-and-port combinations. If only a port number is specified in the Listen directive, the server listens to the given port on all interfaces. If an IP address is given as well as a port, the server will listen on the given port and interface. Multiple Listen directives may be used to specify a number of addresses and ports to listen on. The server will respond to requests from any of the listed addresses and ports.

For example, to make the server accept connections on both port 80 and port 8000, on all interfaces, use:

```
Listen 80
Listen 8000
```

To make the server accept connections on port 80 for one interface, and port 8000 on another, use

```
Listen 192.0.2.1:80
Listen 192.0.2.5:8000
```

IPv6 addresses must be enclosed in square brackets, as in the following example:

```
Listen [2001:db8::a00:20ff:fea7:ccea]:80
```

17.2 Special IPv6 Considerations

A growing number of platforms implement IPv6, and APR supports IPv6 on most of these platforms, allowing Apache to allocate IPv6 sockets, and to handle requests sent over IPv6.

One complicating factor for Apache administrators is whether or not an IPv6 socket can handle both IPv4 connections and IPv6 connections. Handling IPv4 connections with an IPv6 socket uses IPv4-mapped IPv6 addresses, which are allowed by default on most platforms, but are disallowed by default on FreeBSD, NetBSD, and OpenBSD, in order to match the system-wide policy on those platforms. On systems where it is disallowed by default, a special `configure` parameter can change this behavior for Apache.

On the other hand, on some platforms, such as Linux and Tru64, the **only** way to handle both IPv6 and IPv4 is to use mapped addresses. If you want Apache to handle IPv4 and IPv6 connections with a minimum of sockets, which requires using IPv4-mapped IPv6 addresses, specify the `--enable-v4-mapped` `configure` option.

`--enable-v4-mapped` is the default on all platforms except FreeBSD, NetBSD, and OpenBSD, so this is probably how your Apache was built.

If you want Apache to handle IPv4 connections only, regardless of what your platform and APR will support, specify an IPv4 address on all `Listen` directives, as in the following examples:

```
Listen 0.0.0.0:80
Listen 192.0.2.1:80
```

If your platform supports it and you want Apache to handle IPv4 and IPv6 connections on separate sockets (i.e., to disable IPv4-mapped addresses), specify the `--disable-v4-mapped` `configure` option. `--disable-v4-mapped` is the default on FreeBSD, NetBSD, and OpenBSD.

17.3 How This Works With Virtual Hosts

The `Listen` directive does not implement Virtual Hosts - it only tells the main server what addresses and ports to listen on. If no `<VirtualHost>` directives are used, the server will behave in the same way for all accepted requests. However, `<VirtualHost>` can be used to specify a different behavior for one or more of the addresses or ports. To implement a VirtualHost, the server must first be told to listen to the address and port to be used. Then a `<VirtualHost>` section should be created for the specified address and port to set the behavior of this virtual host. Note that if the `<VirtualHost>` is set for an address and port that the server is not listening to, it cannot be accessed.

18 Multi-Processing Modules (MPMs)

This section describes what a Multi-Processing Module is and how they are used by the Apache HTTP Server.

18.1 Introduction

The Apache HTTP Server is designed to be a powerful and flexible web server that can work on a very wide variety of platforms in a range of different environments. Different platforms and different environments often require different features, or may have different ways of implementing the same feature most efficiently. Apache has always accommodated a wide variety of environments through its modular design. This design allows the webmaster to choose which features will be included in the server by selecting which modules to load either at compile-time or at run-time.

Apache 2.0 extends this modular design to the most basic functions of a web server. The server ships with a selection of Multi-Processing Modules (MPMs) which are responsible for binding to network ports on the machine, accepting requests, and dispatching children to handle the requests.

Extending the modular design to this level of the server allows two important benefits:

- Apache can more cleanly and efficiently support a wide variety of operating systems. In particular, the Windows version of Apache is now much more efficient, since mpm_winnt can use native networking features in place of the POSIX layer used in Apache 1.3. This benefit also extends to other operating systems that implement specialized MPMs.

- The server can be better customized for the needs of the particular site. For example, sites that need a great deal of scalability can choose to use a threaded MPM like worker or event, while sites requiring stability or compatibility with older software can use a prefork.

At the user level, MPMs appear much like other Apache modules. The main difference is that one and only one MPM must be loaded into the server at any time. The list of available MPMs appears on the module index page (p. 801).

18.2 Choosing an MPM

MPMs must be chosen during configuration, and compiled into the server. Compilers are capable of optimizing a lot of functions if threads are used, but only if they know that threads are being used.

To actually choose the desired MPM, use the argument --with-mpm=*NAME* with the configure script. *NAME* is the name of the desired MPM.

Once the server has been compiled, it is possible to determine which MPM was chosen by using ./httpd -l. This command will list every module that is compiled into the server, including the MPM.

18.3 MPM Defaults

The following table lists the default MPMs for various operating systems. This will be the MPM selected if you do not make another choice at compile-time.

BeOS	beos
Netware	mpm_netware
OS/2	mpmt_os2
Unix	prefork
Windows	mpm_winnt

19 Environment Variables in Apache

The Apache HTTP Server provides a mechanism for storing information in named variables that are called *environment variables*. This information can be used to control various operations such as logging or access control. The variables are also used as a mechanism to communicate with external programs such as CGI scripts. This section discusses different ways to manipulate and use these variables.

Although these variables are referred to as *environment variables*, they are not the same as the environment variables controlled by the underlying operating system. Instead, these variables are stored and manipulated in an internal Apache structure. They only become actual operating system environment variables when they are provided to CGI scripts and Server Side Include scripts. If you wish to manipulate the operating system environment under which the server itself runs, you must use the standard environment manipulation mechanisms provided by your operating system shell.

19.1 Setting Environment Variables

Related Modules	Related Directives
mod_env	BrowserMatch
mod_rewrite	BrowserMatchNoCase
mod_setenvif	PassEnv
mod_unique_id	RewriteRule
	SetEnv
	SetEnvIf
	SetEnvIfNoCase
	UnsetEnv

19.1.1 Basic Environment Manipulation

The most basic way to set an environment variable in Apache is using the unconditional SetEnv directive. Variables may also be passed from the environment of the shell which started the server using the PassEnv directive.

19.1.2 Conditional Per-Request Settings

For additional flexibility, the directives provided by mod_setenvif allow environment variables to be set on a per-request basis, conditional on characteristics of particular requests. For example, a variable could be set only when a specific browser (User-Agent) is making a request, or only when a specific Referer [sic] header is found. Even more flexibility is available through the mod_rewrite's RewriteRule which uses the [E=...] option to set environment variables.

19.1.3 Unique Identifiers

Finally, mod_unique_id sets the environment variable UNIQUE_ID for each request to a value which is guaranteed to be unique across "all" requests under very specific conditions.

19.1.4 Standard CGI Variables

In addition to all environment variables set within the Apache configuration and passed from the shell, CGI scripts and SSI pages are provided with a set of environment variables containing meta-information about the request as required by the CGI specification[1].

19.1.5 Some Caveats

- It is not possible to override or change the standard CGI variables using the environment manipulation directives.

- When suexec is used to launch CGI scripts, the environment will be cleaned down to a set of *safe* variables before CGI scripts are launched. The list of *safe* variables is defined at compile-time in suexec.c.

- For portability reasons, the names of environment variables may contain only letters, numbers, and the underscore character. In addition, the first character may not be a number. Characters which do not match this restriction will be replaced by an underscore when passed to CGI scripts and SSI pages.

- The SetEnv directive runs late during request processing meaning that directives such as SetEnvIf and RewriteCond will not see the variables set with it.

19.2 Using Environment Variables

Related Modules	Related Directives
mod_authz_host	Allow
mod_cgi	CustomLog
mod_ext_filter	Deny
mod_headers	ExtFilterDefine
mod_include	Header
mod_log_config	LogFormat
mod_rewrite	RewriteCond
	RewriteRule

19.2.1 CGI Scripts

One of the primary uses of environment variables is to communicate information to CGI scripts. As discussed above, the environment passed to CGI scripts in-

---

[1]http://www.w3.org/CGI/

cludes standard meta-information about the request in addition to any variables set within the Apache configuration. For more details, see the CGI tutorial (p. 651).

19.2.2 SSI Pages

Server-parsed (SSI) documents processed by mod_include's INCLUDES filter can print environment variables using the echo element, and can use environment variables in flow control elements to makes parts of a page conditional on characteristics of a request. Apache also provides SSI pages with the standard CGI environment variables as discussed above. For more details, see the SSI tutorial (p. 659).

19.2.3 Access Control

Access to the server can be controlled based on the value of environment variables using the allow from env= and deny from env= directives. In combination with SetEnvIf, this allows for flexible control of access to the server based on characteristics of the client. For example, you can use these directives to deny access to a particular browser (User-Agent).

19.2.4 Conditional Logging

Environment variables can be logged in the access log using the LogFormat option %e. In addition, the decision on whether or not to log requests can be made based on the status of environment variables using the conditional form of the CustomLog directive. In combination with SetEnvIf this allows for flexible control of which requests are logged. For example, you can choose not to log requests for filenames ending in gif, or you can choose to only log requests from clients which are outside your subnet.

19.2.5 Conditional Response Headers

The Header directive can use the presence or absence of an environment variable to determine whether or not a certain HTTP header will be placed in the response to the client. This allows, for example, a certain response header to be sent only if a corresponding header is received in the request from the client.

19.2.6 External Filter Activation

External filters configured by mod_ext_filter using the ExtFilterDefine directive can by activated conditional on an environment variable using the disableenv= and enableenv= options.

19.2.7 URL Rewriting

The %{ENV:*variable*} form of *TestString* in the RewriteCond allows mod_-rewrite's rewrite engine to make decisions conditional on environment variables. Note that the variables accessible in mod_rewrite without the ENV: prefix are not actually environment variables. Rather, they are variables special to mod_rewrite which cannot be accessed from other modules.

19.3 Special Purpose Environment Variables

Interoperability problems have led to the introduction of mechanisms to modify the way Apache behaves when talking to particular clients. To make these mechanisms as flexible as possible, they are invoked by defining environment variables, typically with BrowserMatch, though SetEnv and PassEnv could also be used, for example.

19.3.1 downgrade-1.0

This forces the request to be treated as a HTTP/1.0 request even if it was in a later dialect.

19.3.2 force-gzip

If you have the DEFLATE filter activated, this environment variable will ignore the accept-encoding setting of your browser and will send compressed output unconditionally.

19.3.3 force-no-vary

This causes any Vary fields to be removed from the response header before it is sent back to the client. Some clients don't interpret this field correctly; setting this variable can work around this problem. Setting this variable also implies **force-response-1.0**.

19.3.4 force-response-1.0

This forces an HTTP/1.0 response to clients making an HTTP/1.0 request. It was originally implemented as a result of a problem with AOL's proxies. Some HTTP/1.0 clients may not behave correctly when given an HTTP/1.1 response, and this can be used to interoperate with them.

19.3.5 gzip-only-text/html

When set to a value of "1", this variable disables the DEFLATE output filter provided by mod_deflate for content-types other than text/html. If you'd rather use statically compressed files, mod_negotiation evaluates the variable as well (not only for gzip, but for all encodings that differ from "identity").

19.3.6 no-gzip

When set, the DEFLATE filter of mod_deflate will be turned off and mod_-negotiation will refuse to deliver encoded resources.

19.3.7 no-cache

Available in versions 2.2.12 and later

When set, mod_cache will not save an otherwise cacheable response. This environment variable does not influence whether a response already in the cache will be served for the current request.

19.3.8 nokeepalive

This disables KeepAlive when set.

19.3.9 prefer-language

This influences mod_negotiation's behaviour. If it contains a language tag (such as en, ja or x-klingon), mod_negotiation tries to deliver a variant with that language. If there's no such variant, the normal negotiation (p. 687) process applies.

19.3.10 redirect-carefully

This forces the server to be more careful when sending a redirect to the client. This is typically used when a client has a known problem handling redirects. This was originally implemented as a result of a problem with Microsoft's Web-Folders software which has a problem handling redirects on directory resources via DAV methods.

19.3.11 suppress-error-charset

Available in versions after 2.0.54

When Apache issues a redirect in response to a client request, the response includes some actual text to be displayed in case the client can't (or doesn't) automatically follow the redirection. Apache ordinarily labels this text according to the character set which it uses, which is ISO-8859-1.

However, if the redirection is to a page that uses a different character set, some broken browser versions will try to use the character set from the redirection text rather than the actual page. This can result in Greek, for instance, being incorrectly rendered.

Setting this environment variable causes Apache to omit the character set for the redirection text, and these broken browsers will then correctly use that of the destination page.

SECURITY NOTE

Sending error pages without a specified character set may allow a cross-site-scripting attack for existing browsers (MSIE) which do not follow the HTTP/1.1 specification and attempt to "guess" the character set from the content. Such browsers can be easily fooled into using the UTF-7 character set, and UTF-7 content from input data (such as the request-URI) will not be escaped by the usual escaping mechanisms designed to prevent cross-site-scripting attacks.

19.3.12 force-proxy-request-1.0, proxy-nokeepalive, proxy-sendchunked, proxy-sendcl, proxy-chain-auth, proxy-interim-response, proxy-initial-not-pooled

These directives alter the protocol behavior of mod_proxy. See the mod_proxy and mod_proxy_http documentation for more details.

19.4 Examples

19.4.1 Changing protocol behavior with misbehaving clients

Earlier versions recommended that the following lines be included in httpd.conf to deal with known client problems. Since the affected clients are no longer seen in the wild, this configuration is likely no-longer necessary.

```
#
# The following directives modify normal HTTP response
# behavior. The first directive disables keepalive for
# Netscape 2.x and browsers that spoof it. There are
# known problems with these browser implementations.
# The second directive is for Microsoft Internet
# Explorer 4.0b2 which has a broken HTTP/1.1
# implementation and does not properly support
# keepalive when it is used on 301 or 302 (redirect)
# responses.
#
BrowserMatch "Mozilla/2" nokeepalive
BrowserMatch "MSIE 4\.0b2;" nokeepalive
              downgrade-1.0 force-response-1.0


#
# The following directive disables HTTP/1.1 responses
# to browsers which are in violation of the HTTP/1.0
# spec by not being able to grok a basic 1.1 response.
#
BrowserMatch "RealPlayer 4\.0" force-response-1.0
BrowserMatch "Java/1\.0" force-response-1.0
BrowserMatch "JDK/1\.0" force-response-1.0
```

19.4.2 Do not log requests for images in the access log

This example keeps requests for images from appearing in the access log. It can be easily modified to prevent logging of particular directories, or to prevent logging of requests coming from particular hosts.

```
SetEnvIf Request_URI \.gif image-request
```

```
SetEnvIf Request_URI \.jpg image-request
SetEnvIf Request_URI \.png image-request
CustomLog logs/access_log common env=!image-request
```

19.4.3 Prevent "Image Theft"

This example shows how to keep people not on your server from using images on your server as inline-images on their pages. This is not a recommended configuration, but it can work in limited circumstances. We assume that all your images are in a directory called /web/images.

```
SetEnvIf Referer "^http://www\.example\.com/" local_referal #
Allow browsers that do not send Referer info SetEnvIf Referer
"^$" local_referal <Directory /web/images>
    Order Deny,Allow
    Deny from all
    Allow from env=local_referal
</Directory>
```

For more information about this technique, see the "Keeping Your Images from Adorning Other Sites[2]" tutorial on ServerWatch.

---

[2]http://www.serverwatch.com/tutorials/article.php/1132731

20 Apache's Handler Use

This section describes the use of Apache's Handlers.

20.1 What is a Handler

Related Modules	Related Directives
mod_actions	Action
mod_asis	AddHandler
mod_cgi	RemoveHandler
mod_imagemap	SetHandler
mod_info	
mod_mime	
mod_negotiation	
mod_status	

A "handler" is an internal Apache representation of the action to be performed when a file is called. Generally, files have implicit handlers, based on the file type. Normally, all files are simply served by the server, but certain file types are "handled" separately.

Handlers may also be configured explicitly, based on either filename extensions or on location, without relation to file type. This is advantageous both because it is a more elegant solution, and because it also allows for both a type and a handler to be associated with a file. (See also Files with Multiple Extensions (p. 348).)

Handlers can either be built into the server or included in a module, or they can be added with the Action directive. The built-in handlers in the standard distribution are as follows:

- **default-handler**: Send the file using the default_handler(), which is the handler used by default to handle static content. (core)
- **send-as-is**: Send file with HTTP headers as is. (mod_asis)
- **cgi-script**: Treat the file as a CGI script. (mod_cgi)
- **imap-file**: Parse as an imagemap rule file. (mod_imagemap)
- **server-info**: Get the server's configuration information. (mod_info)
- **server-status**: Get the server's status report. (mod_status)
- **type-map**: Parse as a type map file for content negotiation. (mod_-negotiation)

20.2 Examples

20.2.1 Modifying static content using a CGI script

The following directives will cause requests for files with the html extension to trigger the launch of the footer.pl CGI script.

```
Action add-footer /cgi-bin/footer.pl
AddHandler add-footer .html
```

Then the CGI script is responsible for sending the originally requested document (pointed to by the PATH_TRANSLATED environment variable) and making whatever modifications or additions are desired.

20.2.2 Files with HTTP headers

The following directives will enable the send-as-is handler, which is used for files which contain their own HTTP headers. All files in the /web/htdocs/ asis/ directory will be processed by the send-as-is handler, regardless of their filename extensions.

```
<Directory /web/htdocs/asis>
SetHandler send-as-is
</Directory>
```

20.3 Programmer's Note

In order to implement the handler features, an addition has been made to the Apache API[1] that you may wish to make use of. Specifically, a new record has been added to the request_rec structure:

```
char *handler
```

If you wish to have your module engage a handler, you need only to set r->handler to the name of the handler at any time prior to the invoke_handler stage of the request. Handlers are implemented as they were before, albeit using the handler name instead of a content type. While it is not necessary, the naming convention for handlers is to use a dash-separated word, with no slashes, so as to not invade the media type name-space.

---

[1]http://httpd.apache.org/docs/2.2/developer/API.html

21 Filters

This section describes the use of filters in Apache.

21.1 Filtering in Apache 2

Related Modules	Related Directives
mod_filter	FilterChain
mod_deflate	FilterDeclare
mod_ext_filter	FilterProtocol
mod_include	FilterProvider
mod_charset_lite	AddInputFilter
	AddOutputFilter
	RemoveInputFilter
	RemoveOutputFilter
	ExtFilterDefine
	ExtFilterOptions
	SetInputFilter
	SetOutputFilter

The Filter Chain is available in Apache 2.0 and higher, and enables applications to process incoming and outgoing data in a highly flexible and configurable manner, regardless of where the data comes from. We can pre-process incoming data, and post-process outgoing data, at will. This is basically independent of the traditional request processing phases.

Some examples of filtering in the standard Apache distribution are:

- mod_include, implements server-side includes.
- mod_ssl, implements SSL encryption (https).
- mod_deflate, implements compression/decompression on the fly.
- mod_charset_lite, transcodes between different character sets.
- mod_ext_filter, runs an external program as a filter.

Apache also uses a number of filters internally to perform functions like chunking and byte-range handling.

A wider range of applications are implemented by third-party filter modules available from modules.apache.org[1] and elsewhere. A few of these are:

- HTML and XML processing and rewriting
- XSLT transforms and XIncludes
- XML Namespace support

---

[1]http://modules.apache.org/

Request Processing in Apache

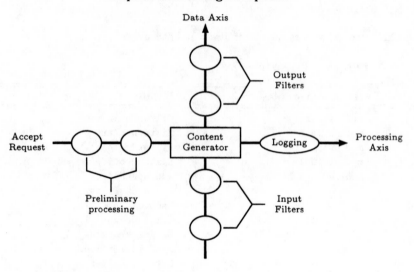

- File Upload handling and decoding of HTML Forms
- Image processing
- Protection of vulnerable applications such as PHP scripts
- Text search-and-replace editing

21.2 Smart Filtering

mod_filter, included in Apache 2.1 and later, enables the filter chain to be configured dynamically at run time. So for example you can set up a proxy to rewrite HTML with an HTML filter and JPEG images with a completely separate filter, despite the proxy having no prior information about what the origin server will send. This works by using a filter harness, that dispatches to different providers according to the actual contents at runtime. Any filter may be either inserted directly in the chain and run unconditionally, or used as a provider and inserted dynamically. For example,

- an HTML processing filter will only run if the content is text/html or application/xhtml+xml
- A compression filter will only run if the input is a compressible type and not already compressed
- A charset conversion filter will be inserted if a text document is not already in the desired charset

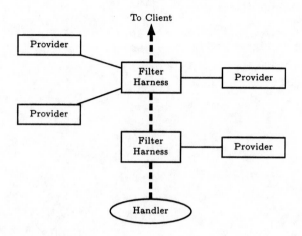

21.3 Using Filters

There are two ways to use filtering: Simple and Dynamic. In general, you should use one or the other; mixing them can have unexpected consequences (although simple Input filtering can be mixed freely with either simple or dynamic Output filtering).

The Simple Way is the only way to configure input filters, and is sufficient for output filters where you need a static filter chain. Relevant directives are `SetInputFilter`, `SetOutputFilter`, `AddInputFilter`, `AddOutputFilter`, `RemoveInputFilter`, and `RemoveOutputFilter`.

The Dynamic Way enables both static and flexible, dynamic configuration of output filters, as discussed in the mod_filter page. Relevant directives are `FilterChain`, `FilterDeclare`, and `FilterProvider`.

One further directive `AddOutputFilterByType` is still supported, but may be problematic and is now deprecated. Use dynamic configuration instead.

22 suEXEC Support

The **suEXEC** feature provides Apache users the ability to run **CGI** and **SSI** programs under user IDs different from the user ID of the calling web server. Normally, when a CGI or SSI program executes, it runs as the same user who is running the web server.

Used properly, this feature can reduce considerably the security risks involved with allowing users to develop and run private CGI or SSI programs. However, if suEXEC is improperly configured, it can cause any number of problems and possibly create new holes in your computer's security. If you aren't familiar with managing *setuid root* programs and the security issues they present, we highly recommend that you not consider using suEXEC.

22.1 Before we begin

Before jumping head-first into this section, you should be aware of the assumptions made on the part of the Apache Group and this section.

First, it is assumed that you are using a UNIX derivative operating system that is capable of **setuid** and **setgid** operations. All command examples are given in this regard. Other platforms, if they are capable of supporting suEXEC, may differ in their configuration.

Second, it is assumed you are familiar with some basic concepts of your computer's security and its administration. This involves an understanding of **setuid/setgid** operations and the various effects they may have on your system and its level of security.

Third, it is assumed that you are using an **unmodified** version of suEXEC code. All code for suEXEC has been carefully scrutinized and tested by the developers as well as numerous beta testers. Every precaution has been taken to ensure a simple yet solidly safe base of code. Altering this code can cause unexpected problems and new security risks. It is **highly** recommended you not alter the suEXEC code unless you are well versed in the particulars of security programming and are willing to share your work with the Apache Group for consideration.

Fourth, and last, it has been the decision of the Apache Group to **NOT** make suEXEC part of the default installation of Apache. To this end, suEXEC configuration requires of the administrator careful attention to details. After due consideration has been given to the various settings for suEXEC, the administrator may install suEXEC through normal installation methods. The values for these settings need to be carefully determined and specified by the administrator to properly maintain system security during the use of suEXEC functionality. It is through this detailed process that the Apache Group hopes to limit suEXEC installation only to those who are careful and determined enough to use it.

Still with us? Yes? Good. Let's move on!

22.2 suEXEC Security Model

Before we begin configuring and installing suEXEC, we will first discuss the security model you are about to implement. By doing so, you may better understand what exactly is going on inside suEXEC and what precautions are taken to ensure your system's security.

suEXEC is based on a setuid "wrapper" program that is called by the main Apache web server. This wrapper is called when an HTTP request is made for a CGI or SSI program that the administrator has designated to run as a userid other than that of the main server. When such a request is made, Apache provides the suEXEC wrapper with the program's name and the user and group IDs under which the program is to execute.

The wrapper then employs the following process to determine success or failure – if any one of these conditions fail, the program logs the failure and exits with an error, otherwise it will continue:

1. **Is the user executing this wrapper a valid user of this system?**

   This is to ensure that the user executing the wrapper is truly a user of the system.

2. **Was the wrapper called with the proper number of arguments?**

   The wrapper will only execute if it is given the proper number of arguments. The proper argument format is known to the Apache web server. If the wrapper is not receiving the proper number of arguments, it is either being hacked, or there is something wrong with the suEXEC portion of your Apache binary.

3. **Is this valid user allowed to run the wrapper?**

   Is this user the user allowed to run this wrapper? Only one user (the Apache user) is allowed to execute this program.

4. **Does the target CGI or SSI program have an unsafe hierarchical reference?**

   Does the target CGI or SSI program's path contain a leading '/' or have a '..' backreference? These are not allowed; the target CGI/SSI program must reside within suEXEC's document root (see --with-suexec-docroot=*DIR* below).

5. **Is the target user name valid?**

   Does the target user exist?

6. **Is the target group name valid?**

   Does the target group exist?

7. **Is the target user *NOT* superuser?**

   Presently, suEXEC does not allow *root* to execute CGI/SSI programs.

8. **Is the target userid *ABOVE* the minimum ID number?**

   The minimum user ID number is specified during configuration. This allows you to set the lowest possible userid that will be allowed to execute CGI/SSI programs. This is useful to block out "system" accounts.

9. **Is the target group *NOT* the superuser group?**

   Presently, suEXEC does not allow the *root* group to execute CGI/SSI programs.

10. **Is the target groupid *ABOVE* the minimum ID number?**

    The minimum group ID number is specified during configuration. This allows you to set the lowest possible groupid that will be allowed to execute CGI/SSI programs. This is useful to block out "system" groups.

11. **Can the wrapper successfully become the target user and group?**

    Here is where the program becomes the target user and group via setuid and setgid calls. The group access list is also initialized with all of the groups of which the user is a member.

12. **Can we change directory to the one in which the target CGI/SSI program resides?**

    If it doesn't exist, it can't very well contain files. If we can't change directory to it, it might aswell not exist.

13. **Is the directory within the Apache webspace?**

    If the request is for a regular portion of the server, is the requested directory within suEXEC's document root? If the request is for a UserDir, is the requested directory within the directory configured as suEXEC's userdir (see suEXEC's configuration options)?

14. **Is the directory *NOT* writable by anyone else?**

    We don't want to open up the directory to others; only the owner user may be able to alter this directories contents.

15. **Does the target CGI/SSI program exist?**

    If it doesn't exists, it can't very well be executed.

16. **Is the target CGI/SSI program *NOT* writable by anyone else?**

    We don't want to give anyone other than the owner the ability to change the CGI/SSI program.

17. **Is the target CGI/SSI program *NOT* setuid or setgid?**

    We do not want to execute programs that will then change our UID/GID again.

18. **Is the target user/group the same as the program's user/group?**

    Is the user the owner of the file?

19. **Can we successfully clean the process environment to ensure safe operations?**

suEXEC cleans the process' environment by establishing a safe execution PATH (defined during configuration), as well as only passing through those variables whose names are listed in the safe environment list (also created during configuration).

20. **Can we successfully become the target CGI/SSI program and execute?**

Here is where suEXEC ends and the target CGI/SSI program begins.

This is the standard operation of the suEXEC wrapper's security model. It is somewhat stringent and can impose new limitations and guidelines for CGI/SSI design, but it was developed carefully step-by-step with security in mind.

For more information as to how this security model can limit your possibilities in regards to server configuration, as well as what security risks can be avoided with a proper suEXEC setup, see the "Beware the Jabberwock" section of this section.

22.3 Configuring & Installing suEXEC

Here's where we begin the fun.

suEXEC configuration options

--enable-suexec This option enables the suEXEC feature which is never installed or activated by default. At least one --with-suexec-xxxxx option has to be provided together with the --enable-suexec option to let APACI accept your request for using the suEXEC feature.

--with-suexec-bin=*PATH* The path to the suexec binary must be hard-coded in the server for security reasons. Use this option to override the default path. *e.g.* --with-suexec-bin=/usr/sbin/suexec

--with-suexec-caller=*UID* The username (p. 516) under which Apache normally runs. This is the only user allowed to execute this program.

--with-suexec-userdir=*DIR* Define to be the subdirectory under users' home directories where suEXEC access should be allowed. All executables under this directory will be executable by suEXEC as the user so they should be "safe" programs. If you are using a "simple" UserDir directive (ie. one without a "*" in it) this should be set to the same value. suEXEC will not work properly in cases where the UserDir directive points to a location that is not the same as the user's home directory as referenced in the passwd file. Default value is "public_html".
If you have virtual hosts with a different UserDir for each, you will need to define them to all reside in one parent directory; then name that parent directory here. **If this is not defined properly, "~userdir" cgi requests will not work!**

--with-suexec-docroot=*DIR* Define as the DocumentRoot set for Apache. This will be the only hierarchy (aside from UserDirs) that can be used for suEXEC behavior. The default directory is the --datadir value with the suffix "/htdocs", *e.g.* if you configure with "--datadir=/home/apache" the directory "/home/apache/htdocs" is used as document root for the suEXEC wrapper.

--with-suexec-uidmin=*UID* Define this as the lowest UID allowed to be a target user for suEXEC. For most systems, 500 or 100 is common. Default value is 100.

--with-suexec-gidmin=*GID* Define this as the lowest GID allowed to be a target group for suEXEC. For most systems, 100 is common and therefore used as default value.

--with-suexec-logfile=*FILE* This defines the filename to which all suEXEC transactions and errors are logged (useful for auditing and debugging purposes). By default the logfile is named "suexec_log" and located in your standard logfile directory (--logfiledir).

--with-suexec-safepath=*PATH* Define a safe PATH environment to pass to CGI executables. Default value is "/usr/local/bin:/usr/bin:/bin".

22.3.1 Compiling and installing the suEXEC wrapper

If you have enabled the suEXEC feature with the --enable-suexec option the suexec binary (together with Apache itself) is automatically built if you execute the make command.

After all components have been built you can execute the command make install to install them. The binary image suexec is installed in the directory defined by the --sbindir option. The default location is "/usr/local/apache2/bin/suexec".

Please note that you need *root privileges* for the installation step. In order for the wrapper to set the user ID, it must be installed as owner *root* and must have the setuserid execution bit set for file modes.

22.3.2 Setting paranoid permissions

Although the suEXEC wrapper will check to ensure that its caller is the correct user as specified with the --with-suexec-caller configure option, there is always the possibility that a system or library call suEXEC uses before this check may be exploitable on your system. To counter this, and because it is best-practise in general, you should use filesystem permissions to ensure that only the group Apache runs as may execute suEXEC.

If for example, your web server is configured to run as:

```
User www
Group webgroup
```

and suexec is installed at "/usr/local/apache2/bin/suexec", you should run:

```
chgrp webgroup /usr/local/apache2/bin/suexec
chmod 4750 /usr/local/apache2/bin/suexec
```

This will ensure that only the group Apache runs as can even execute the suEXEC wrapper.

22.4 Enabling & Disabling suEXEC

Upon startup of Apache, it looks for the file suexec in the directory defined by the --sbindir option (default is "/usr/local/apache/sbin/suexec"). If Apache finds a properly configured suEXEC wrapper, it will print the following message to the error log:

```
[notice] suEXEC mechanism enabled (wrapper:  /path/to/suexec)
```

If you don't see this message at server startup, the server is most likely not finding the wrapper program where it expects it, or the executable is not installed *setuid root*.

If you want to enable the suEXEC mechanism for the first time and an Apache server is already running you must kill and restart Apache. Restarting it with a simple HUP or USR1 signal will not be enough.

If you want to disable suEXEC you should kill and restart Apache after you have removed the suexec file.

22.5 Using suEXEC

Requests for CGI programs will call the suEXEC wrapper only if they are for a virtual host containing a SuexecUserGroup directive or if they are processed by mod_userdir.

Virtual Hosts:
One way to use the suEXEC wrapper is through the SuexecUserGroup directive in VirtualHost definitions. By setting this directive to values different from the main server user ID, all requests for CGI resources will be executed as the *User* and *Group* defined for that <VirtualHost>. If this directive is not specified for a <VirtualHost> then the main server userid is assumed.

User directories:
Requests that are processed by mod_userdir will call the suEXEC wrapper to execute CGI programs under the userid of the requested user directory. The only requirement needed for this feature to work is for CGI execution to be enabled for the user and that the script must meet the scrutiny of the security checks above. See also the --with-suexec-userdir compile time option.

22.6 Debugging suEXEC

The suEXEC wrapper will write log information to the file defined with the --with-suexec-logfile option as indicated above. If you feel you have configured and installed the wrapper properly, have a look at this log and the error_log for the server to see where you may have gone astray.

22.7 Beware the Jabberwock: Warnings & Examples

There are a few points of interest regarding the wrapper that can cause limitations on server setup. Please review these before submitting any "bugs" regarding suEXEC.

- **suEXEC Points Of Interest**
- Hierarchy limitations

  For security and efficiency reasons, all suEXEC requests must remain within either a top-level document root for virtual host requests, or one top-level personal document root for userdir requests. For example, if you have four VirtualHosts configured, you would need to structure all of your VHosts' document roots off of one main Apache document hierarchy to take advantage of suEXEC for VirtualHosts. (Example forthcoming.)

- suEXEC's PATH environment variable

  This can be a dangerous thing to change. Make certain every path you include in this define is a **trusted** directory. You don't want to open people up to having someone from across the world running a trojan horse on them.

- Altering the suEXEC code

  Again, this can cause **Big Trouble** if you try this without knowing what you are doing. Stay away from it if at all possible.

23 Apache Performance Tuning

Apache 2.x is a general-purpose webserver, designed to provide a balance of flexibility, portability, and performance. Although it has not been designed specifically to set benchmark records, Apache 2.x is capable of high performance in many real-world situations.

Compared to Apache 1.3, release 2.x contains many additional optimizations to increase throughput and scalability. Most of these improvements are enabled by default. However, there are compile-time and run-time configuration choices that can significantly affect performance. This section describes the options that a server administrator can configure to tune the performance of an Apache 2.x installation. Some of these configuration options enable the httpd to better take advantage of the capabilities of the hardware and OS, while others allow the administrator to trade functionality for speed.

23.1 Hardware and Operating System Issues

The single biggest hardware issue affecting webserver performance is RAM. A webserver should never ever have to swap, as swapping increases the latency of each request beyond a point that users consider "fast enough". This causes users to hit stop and reload, further increasing the load. You can, and should, control the MaxClients setting so that your server does not spawn so many children it starts swapping. This procedure for doing this is simple: determine the size of your average Apache process, by looking at your process list via a tool such as top, and divide this into your total available memory, leaving some room for other processes.

Beyond that the rest is mundane: get a fast enough CPU, a fast enough network card, and fast enough disks, where "fast enough" is something that needs to be determined by experimentation.

Operating system choice is largely a matter of local concerns. But some guidelines that have proven generally useful are:

- Run the latest stable release and patchlevel of the operating system that you choose. Many OS suppliers have introduced significant performance improvements to their TCP stacks and thread libraries in recent years.

- If your OS supports a sendfile(2) system call, make sure you install the release and/or patches needed to enable it. (With Linux, for example, this means using Linux 2.4 or later. For early releases of Solaris 8, you may need to apply a patch.) On systems where it is available, sendfile enables Apache 2 to deliver static content faster and with lower CPU utilization.

23.2 Run-Time Configuration Issues

Related Modules	Related Directives
mod_dir	AllowOverride
mpm_common	DirectoryIndex
mod_status	HostnameLookups
	EnableMMAP
	EnableSendfile
	KeepAliveTimeout
	MaxSpareServers
	MinSpareServers
	Options
	StartServers

23.2.1 HostnameLookups and other DNS considerations

Prior to Apache 1.3, HostnameLookups defaulted to On. This adds latency to every request because it requires a DNS lookup to complete before the request is finished. In Apache 1.3 this setting defaults to Off. If you need to have addresses in your log files resolved to hostnames, use the logresolve program that comes with Apache, or one of the numerous log reporting packages which are available.

It is recommended that you do this sort of postprocessing of your log files on some machine other than the production web server machine, in order that this activity not adversely affect server performance.

If you use any Allow from domain or Deny from domain directives (i.e., using a hostname, or a domain name, rather than an IP address) then you will pay for two DNS lookups (a reverse, followed by a forward lookup to make sure that the reverse is not being spoofed). For best performance, therefore, use IP addresses, rather than names, when using these directives, if possible.

Note that it's possible to scope the directives, such as within a <Location /server-status> section. In this case the DNS lookups are only performed on requests matching the criteria. Here's an example which disables lookups except for .html and .cgi files:

```
HostnameLookups off
<Files ~ "\.(html|cgi)$">
    HostnameLookups on
</Files>
```

But even still, if you just need DNS names in some CGIs you could consider doing the gethostbyname call in the specific CGIs that need it.

23.2.2 FollowSymLinks and SymLinksIfOwnerMatch

Wherever in your URL-space you do not have an Options FollowSymLinks, or you do have an Options SymLinksIfOwnerMatch Apache will have to issue extra system calls to check up on symlinks. One extra call per filename component. For example, if you had:

```
DocumentRoot /www/htdocs
<Directory />
    Options SymLinksIfOwnerMatch
</Directory>
```

and a request is made for the URI /index.html. Then Apache will perform lstat(2) on /www, /www/htdocs, and /www/htdocs/index.html. The results of these lstats are never cached, so they will occur on every single request. If you really desire the symlinks security checking you can do something like this:

```
DocumentRoot /www/htdocs
<Directory />
    Options FollowSymLinks
</Directory>

<Directory /www/htdocs>
    Options -FollowSymLinks +SymLinksIfOwnerMatch
</Directory>
```

This at least avoids the extra checks for the DocumentRoot path. Note that you'll need to add similar sections if you have any Alias or RewriteRule paths outside of your document root. For highest performance, and no symlink protection, set FollowSymLinks everywhere, and never set SymLinksIfOwnerMatch.

23.2.3 AllowOverride

Wherever in your URL-space you allow overrides (typically .htaccess files) Apache will attempt to open .htaccess for each filename component. For example,

```
DocumentRoot /www/htdocs
<Directory />
    AllowOverride all
</Directory>
```

and a request is made for the URI /index.html. Then Apache will attempt to open /.htaccess, /www/.htaccess, and /www/htdocs/.htaccess. The solutions are similar to the previous case of Options FollowSymLinks. For highest performance use AllowOverride None everywhere in your filesystem.

23.2.4 Negotiation

If at all possible, avoid content-negotiation if you're really interested in every last ounce of performance. In practice the benefits of negotiation outweigh the performance penalties. There's one case where you can speed up the server. Instead of using a wildcard such as:

```
DirectoryIndex index
```

Use a complete list of options:

```
DirectoryIndex index.cgi index.pl index.shtml index.html
```

where you list the most common choice first.

Also note that explicitly creating a type-map file provides better performance than using MultiViews, as the necessary information can be determined by reading this single file, rather than having to scan the directory for files.

If your site needs content negotiation consider using type-map files, rather than the Options MultiViews directive to accomplish the negotiation. See the Content Negotiation (p. 687) documentation for a full discussion of the methods of negotiation, and instructions for creating type-map files.

23.2.5 Memory-mapping

In situations where Apache 2.x needs to look at the contents of a file being delivered–for example, when doing server-side-include processing–it normally memory-maps the file if the OS supports some form of mmap(2).

On some platforms, this memory-mapping improves performance. However, there are cases where memory-mapping can hurt the performance or even the stability of the httpd:

- On some operating systems, mmap does not scale as well as read(2) when the number of CPUs increases. On multiprocessor Solaris servers, for example, Apache 2.x sometimes delivers server-parsed files faster when mmap is disabled.

- If you memory-map a file located on an NFS-mounted filesystem and a process on another NFS client machine deletes or truncates the file, your process may get a bus error the next time it tries to access the mapped file content.

For installations where either of these factors applies, you should use EnableMMAP off to disable the memory-mapping of delivered files. (Note: This directive can be overridden on a per-directory basis.)

23.2.6 Sendfile

In situations where Apache 2.x can ignore the contents of the file to be delivered – for example, when serving static file content – it normally uses the kernel sendfile support the file if the OS supports the sendfile(2) operation.

On most platforms, using sendfile improves performance by eliminating separate read and send mechanics. However, there are cases where using sendfile can harm the stability of the httpd:

- Some platforms may have broken sendfile support that the build system did not detect, especially if the binaries were built on another box and moved to such a machine with broken sendfile support.

- With an NFS-mounted files, the kernel may be unable to reliably serve the network file through its own cache.

For installations where either of these factors applies, you should use EnableSendfile off to disable sendfile delivery of file contents. (Note: This directive can be overridden on a per-directory basis.)

23.2.7 Process Creation

Prior to Apache 1.3 the MinSpareServers, MaxSpareServers, and StartServers settings all had drastic effects on benchmark results. In particular, Apache required a "ramp-up" period in order to reach a number of children sufficient to serve the load being applied. After the initial spawning of StartServers children, only one child per second would be created to satisfy the MinSpareServers setting. So a server being accessed by 100 simultaneous clients, using the default StartServers of 5 would take on the order 95 seconds to spawn enough children to handle the load. This works fine in practice on real-life servers, because they aren't restarted frequently. But does really poorly on benchmarks which might only run for ten minutes.

The one-per-second rule was implemented in an effort to avoid swamping the machine with the startup of new children. If the machine is busy spawning children it can't service requests. But it has such a drastic effect on the perceived performance of Apache that it had to be replaced. As of Apache 1.3, the code will relax the one-per-second rule. It will spawn one, wait a second, then spawn two, wait a second, then spawn four, and it will continue exponentially until it is spawning 32 children per second. It will stop whenever it satisfies the MinSpareServers setting.

This appears to be responsive enough that it's almost unnecessary to twiddle the MinSpareServers, MaxSpareServers and StartServers knobs. When more than 4 children are spawned per second, a message will be emitted to the ErrorLog. If you see a lot of these errors then consider tuning these settings. Use the mod_status output as a guide.

Related to process creation is process death induced by the MaxRequestsPerChild setting. By default this is 0, which means that there is no limit to the number of requests handled per child. If your config-uration currently has this set to some very low number, such as 30, you may want to bump this up significantly. If you are running SunOS or an old version of Solaris, limit this to 10000 or so because of memory leaks.

When keep-alives are in use, children will be kept busy doing nothing waiting for more requests on the already open connection. The default KeepAliveTimeout of 5 seconds attempts to minimize this effect. The tradeoff here is between network bandwidth and server resources. In no event should you raise this above about 60 seconds, as most of the benefits are lost[1].

23.3 Compile-Time Configuration Issues

23.3.1 Choosing an MPM

Apache 2.x supports pluggable concurrency models, called Multi-Processing Modules (p. 703) (MPMs). When building Apache, you must choose an MPM to use. There are platform-specific MPMs for some platforms: beos, mpm_-netware, mpmt_os2, and mpm_winnt. For general Unix-type systems, there are several MPMs from which to choose. The choice of MPM can affect the speed and scalability of the httpd:

- The worker MPM uses multiple child processes with many threads each. Each thread handles one connection at a time. Worker generally is a good choice for high-traffic servers because it has a smaller memory footprint than the prefork MPM.

- The prefork MPM uses multiple child processes with one thread each. Each process handles one connection at a time. On many systems, prefork is comparable in speed to worker, but it uses more memory. Prefork's threadless design has advantages over worker in some situations: it can be used with non-thread-safe third-party modules, and it is easier to debug on platforms with poor thread debugging support.

For more information on these and other MPMs, please see the MPM documentation (p. 703).

23.3.2 Modules

Since memory usage is such an important consideration in performance, you should attempt to eliminate modules that you are not actually using. If you have built the modules as DSOs (p. 683), eliminating modules is a simple matter of commenting out the associated LoadModule directive for that module. This allows you to experiment with removing modules, and seeing if your site still functions in their absense.

If, on the other hand, you have modules statically linked into your Apache binary, you will need to recompile Apache in order to remove unwanted modules.

An associated question that arises here is, of course, what modules you need, and which ones you don't. The answer here will, of course, vary from one web site to another. However, the *minimal* list of modules which you can get by with tends to include mod_mime, mod_dir, and mod_log_config. mod_log_config is, of course, optional, as you can run a web site without log files. This is, however, not recommended.

---

[1]http://www.hpl.hp.com/techreports/Compaq-DEC/WRL-95-4.html

23.3.3 Atomic Operations

Some modules, such as mod_cache and recent development builds of the worker MPM, use APR's atomic API. This API provides atomic operations that can be used for lightweight thread synchronization.

By default, APR implements these operations using the most efficient mechanism available on each target OS/CPU platform. Many modern CPUs, for example, have an instruction that does an atomic compare-and-swap (CAS) operation in hardware. On some platforms, however, APR defaults to a slower, mutex-based implementation of the atomic API in order to ensure compatibility with older CPU models that lack such instructions. If you are building Apache for one of these platforms, and you plan to run only on newer CPUs, you can select a faster atomic implementation at build time by configuring Apache with the --enable-nonportable-atomics option:

```
./buildconf
./configure --with-mpm=worker --enable-nonportable-atomics=yes
```

The --enable-nonportable-atomics option is relevant for the following platforms:

- Solaris on SPARC
  By default, APR uses mutex-based atomics on Solaris/SPARC. If you configure with --enable-nonportable-atomics, however, APR generates code that uses a SPARC v8plus opcode for fast hardware compare-and-swap. If you configure Apache with this option, the atomic operations will be more efficient (allowing for lower CPU utilization and higher concurrency), but the resulting executable will run only on UltraSPARC chips.

- Linux on x86
  By default, APR uses mutex-based atomics on Linux. If you configure with --enable-nonportable-atomics, however, APR generates code that uses a 486 opcode for fast hardware compare-and-swap. This will result in more efficient atomic operations, but the resulting executable will run only on 486 and later chips (and not on 386).

23.3.4 mod_status and ExtendedStatus On

If you include mod_status and you also set ExtendedStatus On when building and running Apache, then on every request Apache will perform two calls to gettimeofday(2) (or times(2) depending on your operating system), and (pre-1.3) several extra calls to time(2). This is all done so that the status report contains timing indications. For highest performance, set ExtendedStatus off (which is the default).

23.3.5 accept Serialization - multiple sockets

WARNING: *This section has not been fully updated to take into account changes made in the 2.x version of the Apache HTTP Server. Some of the information may still be relevant, but please use it with care.*

This discusses a shortcoming in the Unix socket API. Suppose your web server uses multiple Listen statements to listen on either multiple ports or multiple addresses. In order to test each socket to see if a connection is ready Apache uses select(2). select(2) indicates that a socket has *zero* or *at least one* connection waiting on it. Apache's model includes multiple children, and all the idle ones test for new connections at the same time. A naive implementation looks something like this (these examples do not match the code, they're contrived for pedagogical purposes):

```
for (;;) {
    for (;;) {
        fd_set accept_fds;
        FD_ZERO (&accept_fds);
        for (i = first_socket; i <= last_socket; ++i) {
            FD_SET (i, &accept_fds);
        }
        rc = select (last_socket+1, &accept_fds, NULL, NULL,
        NULL);
        if (rc < 1) continue;
        new_connection = -1;
        for (i = first_socket; i <= last_socket; ++i) {
            if (FD_ISSET (i, &accept_fds)) {
                new_connection = accept (i, NULL, NULL);
                if (new_connection != -1) break;
            }
        }
        if (new_connection != -1) break;
    }
    process the new_connection;
}
```

But this naive implementation has a serious starvation problem. Recall that multiple children execute this loop at the same time, and so multiple children will block at select when they are in between requests. All those blocked children will awaken and return from select when a single request appears on any socket (the number of children which awaken varies depending on the operating system and timing issues). They will all then fall down into the loop and try to accept the connection. But only one will succeed (assuming there's still only one connection ready), the rest will be *blocked* in accept. This effectively locks those children into serving requests from that one socket and no other sockets, and they'll be stuck there until enough new requests appear on that socket to wake them all up. This starvation problem was first documented in PR#467[2]. There are at least two solutions.

One solution is to make the sockets non-blocking. In this case the accept won't block the children, and they will be allowed to continue immediately. But

---

[2]http://bugs.apache.org/index/full/467

this wastes CPU time. Suppose you have ten idle children in select, and one connection arrives. Then nine of those children will wake up, try to accept the connection, fail, and loop back into select, accomplishing nothing. Meanwhile none of those children are servicing requests that occurred on other sockets until they get back up to the select again. Overall this solution does not seem very fruitful unless you have as many idle CPUs (in a multiprocessor box) as you have idle children, not a very likely situation.

Another solution, the one used by Apache, is to serialize entry into the inner loop. The loop looks like this (differences highlighted):

```
for (;;) {
    accept_mutex_on ();
    for (;;) {
        fd_set accept_fds;
        FD_ZERO (&accept_fds);
        for (i = first_socket; i <= last_socket; ++i) {
            FD_SET (i, &accept_fds);
        }
        rc = select (last_socket+1, &accept_fds, NULL, NULL,
        NULL);
        if (rc < 1) continue;
        new_connection = -1;
        for (i = first_socket; i <= last_socket; ++i) {
            if (FD_ISSET (i, &accept_fds)) {
                new_connection = accept (i, NULL, NULL);
                if (new_connection != -1) break;
            }
        }
        if (new_connection != -1) break;
    }
    accept_mutex_off ();
    process the new_connection;
}
```

The functions accept_mutex_on and accept_mutex_off implement a mutual exclusion semaphore. Only one child can have the mutex at any time. There are several choices for implementing these mutexes. The choice is defined in src/conf.h (pre-1.3) or src/include/ap_config.h (1.3 or later). Some architectures do not have any locking choice made, on these architectures it is unsafe to use multiple Listen directives.

The directive AcceptMutex can be used to change the selected mutex implementation at run-time.

AcceptMutex flock This method uses the flock(2) system call to lock a lock file (located by the LockFile directive).

AcceptMutex fcntl This method uses the fcntl(2) system call to lock a lock file (located by the LockFile directive).

AcceptMutex sysvsem (1.3 or later) This method uses SysV-style semaphores
to implement the mutex. Unfortunately SysV-style semaphores have some
bad side-effects. One is that it's possible Apache will die without cleaning
up the semaphore (see the ipcs(8) man page). The other is that the
semaphore API allows for a denial of service attack by any CGIs running under the same uid as the webserver (*i.e.*, all CGIs, unless you use
something like suexec or cgiwrapper). For these reasons this method is
not used on any architecture except IRIX (where the previous two are
prohibitively expensive on most IRIX boxes).

AcceptMutex pthread (1.3 or later) This method uses POSIX mutexes and
should work on any architecture implementing the full POSIX threads
specification, however appears to only work on Solaris (2.5 or later), and
even then only in certain configurations. If you experiment with this you
should watch out for your server hanging and not responding. Static
content only servers may work just fine.

AcceptMutex posixsem (2.0 or later) This method uses POSIX semaphores.
The semaphore ownership is not recovered if a thread in the process hold-
ing the mutex segfaults, resulting in a hang of the web server.

If your system has another method of serialization which isn't in the above list
then it may be worthwhile adding code for it to APR.

Another solution that has been considered but never implemented is to partially
serialize the loop – that is, let in a certain number of processes. This would
only be of interest on multiprocessor boxes where it's possible multiple children
could run simultaneously, and the serialization actually doesn't take advantage
of the full bandwidth. This is a possible area of future investigation, but priority
remains low because highly parallel web servers are not the norm.

Ideally you should run servers without multiple Listen statements if you want
the highest performance. But read on.

23.3.6 accept Serialization - single socket

The above is fine and dandy for multiple socket servers, but what about single
socket servers? In theory they shouldn't experience any of these same problems
because all children can just block in accept(2) until a connection arrives,
and no starvation results. In practice this hides almost the same "spinning"
behaviour discussed above in the non-blocking solution. The way that most
TCP stacks are implemented, the kernel actually wakes up all processes blocked
in accept when a single connection arrives. One of those processes gets the
connection and returns to user-space, the rest spin in the kernel and go back
to sleep when they discover there's no connection for them. This spinning is
hidden from the user-land code, but it's there nonetheless. This can result in
the same load-spiking wasteful behaviour that a non-blocking solution to the
multiple sockets case can.

For this reason we have found that many architectures behave more "nicely" if we serialize even the single socket case. So this is actually the default in almost all cases. Crude experiments under Linux (2.0.30 on a dual Pentium pro 166 w/128Mb RAM) have shown that the serialization of the single socket case causes less than a 3% decrease in requests per second over unserialized single-socket. But unserialized single-socket showed an extra 100ms latency on each request. This latency is probably a wash on long haul lines, and only an issue on LANs. If you want to override the single socket serialization you can define SINGLE_LISTEN_UNSERIALIZED_ACCEPT and then single-socket servers will not serialize at all.

23.3.7 Lingering Close

As discussed in draft-ietf-http-connection-00.txt[3] section 8, in order for an HTTP server to **reliably** implement the protocol it needs to shutdown each direction of the communication independently (recall that a TCP connection is bi-directional, each half is independent of the other). This fact is often overlooked by other servers, but is correctly implemented in Apache as of 1.2.

When this feature was added to Apache it caused a flurry of problems on various versions of Unix because of a shortsightedness. The TCP specification does not state that the FIN_WAIT_2 state has a timeout, but it doesn't prohibit it. On systems without the timeout, Apache 1.2 induces many sockets stuck forever in the FIN_WAIT_2 state. In many cases this can be avoided by simply upgrading to the latest TCP/IP patches supplied by the vendor. In cases where the vendor has never released patches (*i.e.*, SunOS4 – although folks with a source license can patch it themselves) we have decided to disable this feature.

There are two ways of accomplishing this. One is the socket option SO_LINGER. But as fate would have it, this has never been implemented properly in most TCP/IP stacks. Even on those stacks with a proper implementation (*i.e.*, Linux 2.0.31) this method proves to be more expensive (cputime) than the next solution.

For the most part, Apache implements this in a function called lingering_close (in http_main.c). The function looks roughly like this:

```
void lingering_close (int s)
{
    char junk_buffer[2048];
    /* shutdown the sending side */
    shutdown (s, 1);
    signal (SIGALRM, lingering_death);
    alarm (30);
    for (;;) {
        select (s for reading, 2 second timeout);
        if (error) break;
```

---

[3]http://www.ics.uci.edu/pub/ietf/http/draft-ietf-http-connection-00.txt

```
        if (s is ready for reading) {
            if (read (s, junk_buffer, sizeof (junk_buffer)) <=
            0) {
                break;
            }
            /* just toss away whatever is here */
        }
    }
    close (s);
}
```

This naturally adds some expense at the end of a connection, but it is required for a reliable implementation. As HTTP/1.1 becomes more prevalent, and all connections are persistent, this expense will be amortized over more requests. If you want to play with fire and disable this feature you can define NO_LINGCLOSE, but this is not recommended at all. In particular, as HTTP/1.1 pipelined persistent connections come into use lingering_close is an absolute necessity (and pipelined connections are faster[4], so you want to support them).

23.3.8 Scoreboard File

Apache's parent and children communicate with each other through something called the scoreboard. Ideally this should be implemented in shared memory. For those operating systems that we either have access to, or have been given detailed ports for, it typically is implemented using shared memory. The rest default to using an on-disk file. The on-disk file is not only slow, but it is unreliable (and less featured). Peruse the src/main/conf.h file for your architecture and look for either USE_MMAP_SCOREBOARD or USE_SHMGET_SCOREBOARD. Defining one of those two (as well as their companions HAVE_MMAP and HAVE_-SHMGET respectively) enables the supplied shared memory code. If your system has another type of shared memory, edit the file src/main/http_main.c and add the hooks necessary to use it in Apache. (Send us back a patch too please.)

> *Historical note: The Linux port of Apache didn't start to use shared memory until version 1.2 of Apache. This oversight resulted in really poor and unreliable behaviour of earlier versions of Apache on Linux.*

23.3.9 DYNAMIC_MODULE_LIMIT

If you have no intention of using dynamically loaded modules (you probably don't if you're reading this and tuning your server for every last ounce of performance) then you should add -DDYNAMIC_MODULE_LIMIT=0 when building your server. This will save RAM that's allocated only for supporting dynamically loaded modules.

---

[4]http://www.w3.org/Protocols/HTTP/Performance/Pipeline.html

23.4 Appendix: Detailed Analysis of a Trace

Here is a system call trace of Apache 2.0.38 with the worker MPM on Solaris 8. This trace was collected using:

```
truss -l -p httpd_child_pid.
```

The -l option tells truss to log the ID of the LWP (lightweight process–Solaris's form of kernel-level thread) that invokes each system call.

Other systems may have different system call tracing utilities such as strace, ktrace, or par. They all produce similar output.

In this trace, a client has requested a 10KB static file from the httpd. Traces of non-static requests or requests with content negotiation look wildly different (and quite ugly in some cases).

```
/67:    accept(3, 0x00200BEC, 0x00200C0C, 1) (sleeping...)
/67:    accept(3, 0x00200BEC, 0x00200C0C, 1) = 9
```

In this trace, the listener thread is running within LWP #67.

Note the lack of accept(2) serialization. On this particular platform, the worker MPM uses an unserialized accept by default unless it is listening on multiple ports.

```
/65:    lwp_park(0x00000000, 0) = 0
/67:    lwp_unpark(65, 1) = 0
```

Upon accepting the connection, the listener thread wakes up a worker thread to do the request processing. In this trace, the worker thread that handles the request is mapped to LWP #65.

```
/65:    getsockname(9, 0x00200BA4, 0x00200BC4, 1) = 0
```

In order to implement virtual hosts, Apache needs to know the local socket address used to accept the connection. It is possible to eliminate this call in many situations (such as when there are no virtual hosts, or when Listen directives are used which do not have wildcard addresses). But no effort has yet been made to do these optimizations.

```
/65:    brk(0x002170E8) = 0
/65:    brk(0x002190E8) = 0
```

The brk(2) calls allocate memory from the heap. It is rare to see these in a system call trace, because the httpd uses custom memory allocators (apr_pool and apr_bucket_alloc) for most request processing. In this trace, the httpd has just been started, so it must call malloc(3) to get the blocks of raw memory with which to create the custom memory allocators.

```
/65:    fcntl(9, F_GETFL, 0x00000000) = 2
/65:    fstat64(9, 0xFAF7B818) = 0
/65:    getsockopt(9, 65535, 8192, 0xFAF7B918,
                0xFAF7B910, 2190656) = 0
```

```
/65:    fstat64(9, 0xFAF7B818) = 0
/65:    getsockopt(9, 65535, 8192, 0xFAF7B918,
                 0xFAF7B914, 2190656) = 0
/65:    setsockopt(9, 65535, 8192, 0xFAF7B918,
                 4, 2190656) = 0
/65:    fcntl(9, F_SETFL, 0x00000082) = 0
```

Next, the worker thread puts the connection to the client (file descriptor 9) in non-blocking mode. The setsockopt(2) and getsockopt(2) calls are a side-effect of how Solaris's libc handles fcntl(2) on sockets.

```
/65:    read(9, " G E T   / 1 0 k . h t m".., 8000) = 97
```

The worker thread reads the request from the client.

```
/65:    stat("/var/httpd/apache/httpd-8999/htdocs/10k.html",
             0xFAF7B978) = 0
/65:    open("/var/httpd/apache/httpd-8999/htdocs/10k.html",
             O_RDONLY) = 10
```

This httpd has been configured with Options FollowSymLinks and AllowOverride None. Thus it doesn't need to lstat(2) each directory in the path leading up to the requested file, nor check for .htaccess files. It simply calls stat(2) to verify that the file: 1) exists, and 2) is a regular file, not a directory.

```
/65:    sendfilev(0, 9, 0x00200F90, 2, 0xFAF7B53C) = 10269
```

In this example, the httpd is able to send the HTTP response header and the requested file with a single sendfilev(2) system call. Sendfile semantics vary among operating systems. On some other systems, it is necessary to do a write(2) or writev(2) call to send the headers before calling sendfile(2).

```
/65:    write(4, " 1 2 7 . 0 . 0 . 1   -  ".., 78) = 78
```

This write(2) call records the request in the access log. Note that one thing missing from this trace is a time(2) call. Unlike Apache 1.3, Apache 2.x uses gettimeofday(3) to look up the time. On some operating systems, like Linux or Solaris, gettimeofday has an optimized implementation that doesn't require as much overhead as a typical system call.

```
/65:    shutdown(9, 1, 1) = 0
/65:    poll(0xFAF7B980, 1, 2000) = 1
/65:    read(9, 0xFAF7BC20, 512) = 0
/65:    close(9) = 0
```

The worker thread does a lingering close of the connection.

```
/65:    close(10) = 0
/65:    lwp_park(0x00000000, 0) (sleeping...)
```

Finally the worker thread closes the file that it has just delivered and blocks until the listener assigns it another connection.

```
/67:    accept(3, 0x001FEB74, 0x001FEB94, 1) (sleeping...)
```

Meanwhile, the listener thread is able to accept another connection as soon as it has dispatched this connection to a worker thread (subject to some flow-control logic in the worker MPM that throttles the listener if all the available workers are busy). Though it isn't apparent from this trace, the next accept(2) can (and usually does, under high load conditions) occur in parallel with the worker thread's handling of the just-accepted connection.

24 Frequently Asked Questions

This section is not a traditional FAQ, but rather a quick guide showing you what to do when you run into problems with the Apache HTTP Server.

A more traditional but quite outdated document is the Apache 1.3 FAQ[1].

24.1 "Why can't I ...? Why won't ... work?" What to do in case of problems

If you are having trouble with your Apache server software, you should take the following steps:

Check the ErrorLog! Apache tries to be helpful when it encounters a problem. In many cases, it will provide some details by writing one or more messages to the server error log. Sometimes this is enough for you to diagnose and fix the problem yourself (such as file permissions or the like). The default location of the error log is /usr/local/apache2/logs/error_log, but see the ErrorLog directive in your config files for the location on your server.

If you end up in any of the support forums this is quite likely to be the first place they will ask you retrieve information from. Please ensure you know where to find your errorlog. If you are unsure, the wiki page here[2] can give you some ideas where to look.

Consult the wiki The Apache HTTP Server Wiki[3] contains guides to solving many common problems.

Check the Apache bug database Most problems that get reported to The Apache Group are recorded in the bug database[4]. **Do not** submit a new bug report until you have checked existing reports (open *and* closed) and asked about your problem in a user-support forum (see below). If you find that your issue has already been reported, please *don't* add a "me, too" report.

Ask in a user support forum Apache has an active community of users who are willing to share their knowledge. Participating in this community is usually the best and fastest way to get answers to your questions and problems.

Users mailing list[5]

#httpd on Freenode IRC[6] is also available for user support issues.

---

[1] http://httpd.apache.org/docs/misc/FAQ.html
[2] http://wiki.apache.org/httpd/DistrosDefaultLayout
[3] http://wiki.apache.org/httpd/
[4] http://httpd.apache.org/bug_report.html
[5] http://httpd.apache.org/userslist.html
[6] http://freenode.net

Please use the bug database for bugs! If you've gone through those steps above that are appropriate and have obtained no relief, then please *do* let the httpd developers know about the problem by logging a bug report[7].

If your problem involves the server crashing and generating a core dump, please include a backtrace[8] (if possible).

24.2 Whom do I contact for support?

With millions of users and fewer than sixty volunteer developers, we cannot provide personal support for Apache. For free support, we suggest participating in a user forum (see above).

Professional, commercial support for Apache is available from a number of companies.

---

[7]http://httpd.apache.org/bug_report.html
[8]http://httpd.apache.org/dev/debugging.html

25 Using Apache HTTP Server on Microsoft Windows

This section explains how to install, configure and run Apache 2.2 under Microsoft Windows. If you have questions after reviewing the documentation (and any event and error logs), you should consult the peer-supported users' mailing list[1].

This section assumes that you are installing a binary distribution of Apache. If you want to compile Apache yourself (possibly to help with development or tracking down bugs), see Compiling Apache for Microsoft Windows (p. 755).

25.1 Operating System Requirements

The primary Windows platform for running Apache 2.2 is Windows 2000 or later. The binary installer only works with the x86 family of processors, such as Intel and AMD processors. Always obtain and install the current service pack to avoid operating system bugs.

> Running Apache on Windows 9x is ignored by the developers, and is strongly discouraged. On Windows NT 4.0, installing Service Pack 6 is required. Apache HTTP Server versions later than 2.2 will not run on any operating system earlier than Windows 2000.

25.2 Downloading Apache for Windows

Information on the latest versions of Apache can be found on the web site of the Apache web server at http://httpd.apache.org/download.cgi. There you will find the current release, as well as more recent alpha or beta test versions, and a list of HTTP and FTP mirrors from which you can download the Apache web server. Please use a mirror near to you for a fast and reliable download.

For Windows installations you should download the version of Apache for Windows with the .msi extension. This is a single Microsoft Installer file, which contains a ready-to-run build of Apache. There is a separate .zip file, which contains only the source code, see the summary above.

25.3 Installing Apache for Windows

You need Microsoft Installer 2.0 or above for the installation to work. For Windows NT 4.0 and 2000 refer to Microsoft's article KB 292539[2]. Windows XP and later do not require this update. The Windows 98/ME installer engine appears to no longer be available from Microsoft, and these instructions no longer detail such prerequisites.

Note that you cannot install two versions of Apache 2.2 on the same computer with the binary installer. You can, however, install a version of the 1.3 series

---

[1]http://httpd.apache.org/userslist.html
[2]http://support.microsoft.com/kb/292539/

and a version of the 2.2 series on the same computer without problems. If you need to have two different 2.2 versions on the same computer, you have to compile and install Apache from the source (p. 755).

Run the Apache .msi file you downloaded above. The installation will ask you for these things:

1. **Network Domain.** Enter the DNS domain in which your server is or will be registered in. For example, if your server's full DNS name is server.mydomain.net, you would type mydomain.net here.

2. **Server Name.** Your server's full DNS name. From the example above, you would type server.mydomain.net here.

3. **Administrator's Email Address.** Enter the server administrator's or webmaster's email address here. This address will be displayed along with error messages to the client by default.

4. **For whom to install Apache.** Select for All Users, on Port 80, as a Service - Recommended if you'd like your new Apache to listen at port 80 for incoming traffic. It will run as a service (that is, Apache will run even if no one is logged in on the server at the moment) Select only for the Current User, on Port 8080, when started Manually if you'd like to install Apache for your personal experimenting or if you already have another WWW server running on port 80.

5. **The installation type.** Select Typical for everything except the source code and libraries for module development. With Custom you can specify what to install. A full install will require about 13 megabytes of free disk space. This does *not* include the size of your web site(s).

6. **Where to install.** The default path is C:\Program Files\Apache Software Foundation under which a directory called Apache2.2 will be created by default.

During the installation, Apache will configure the files in the conf subdirectory to reflect the chosen installation directory. However, if any of the configuration files in this directory already exist, they will not be overwritten. Instead, the new copy of the corresponding file will be left with the extension .default. So, for example, if conf\httpd.conf already exists, it will be renamed as conf\httpd.conf.default. After the installation you should manually check to see what new settings are in the .default file, and if necessary, update your existing configuration file.

Also, if you already have a file called htdocs\index.html, it will not be overwritten (and no index.html.default will be installed either). This means it should be safe to install Apache over an existing installation, although you would have to stop the existing running server before doing the installation, and then start the new one after the installation is finished.

After installing Apache, you must edit the configuration files in the conf subdirectory as required. These files will be configured during the installation so that Apache is ready to be run from the directory it was installed into, with the documents server from the subdirectory htdocs. There are lots of other options which you should set before you really start using Apache. However, to get started quickly, the files should work as installed.

25.4 Customizing Apache for Windows

Apache is configured by the files in the conf subdirectory. These are the same files used to configure the Unix version, but there are a few different directives for Apache on Windows. See the directive index (p. 805) for all the available directives.

The main differences in Apache for Windows are:

- Because Apache for Windows is multithreaded, it does not use a separate process for each request, as Apache can on Unix. Instead there are usually only two Apache processes running: a parent process, and a child which handles the requests. Within the child process each request is handled by a separate thread.

  The process management directives are also different:

  MaxRequestsPerChild: Like the Unix directive, this controls how many requests (actually, connections) which a single child process will serve before exiting. However, unlike on Unix, a replacement process is not instantly available. Use the default MaxRequestsPerChild 0, unless instructed to change the behavior to overcome a memory leak in third party modules or in-process applications.

  Warning: The server configuration file is reread when a new child process is started. If you have modified httpd.conf, *the new child may not start or you may receive unexpected results.*

  ThreadsPerChild: This directive is new. It tells the server how many threads it should use. This is the maximum number of connections the server can handle at once, so be sure to set this number high enough for your site if you get a lot of hits. The recommended default is ThreadsPerChild 150, but this must be adjusted to reflect the greatest anticipated number of simultaneous connections to accept.

- The directives that accept filenames as arguments must use Windows file-names instead of Unix ones. However, because Apache may interpret backslashes as an "escape character" sequence, you should consistently use forward slashes in path names, not backslashes. Drive letters can be used; if omitted, the drive of the SystemRoot directive (or -d command line option) becomes the default.

- While filenames are generally case-insensitive on Windows, URLs are still treated internally as case-sensitive before they are mapped to the filesystem. For example, the <Location>, Alias, and ProxyPass directives all use case-sensitive arguments. For this reason, it is particularly important to use the <Directory> directive when attempting to limit access to content in the filesystem, since this directive applies to any content in a directory, regardless of how it is accessed. If you wish to assure that only lowercase is used in URLs, you can use something like:

```
RewriteEngine On
RewriteMap lowercase int:tolower
RewriteCond %{REQUEST_URI} [A-Z]
RewriteRule (.*) ${lowercase:$1} [R,L]
```

- When running, Apache needs write access only to the logs directory and any configured cache directory tree. Due to the issue of case insensitive and short 8.3 format names, Apache must validate all path names given. This means that each directory which Apache evaluates, from the drive root up to the directory leaf, must have read, list and traverse directory permissions. If Apache2.2 is installed at C:\Program Files, then the root directory, Program Files and Apache2.2 must all be visible to Apache.

- Apache for Windows contains the ability to load modules at runtime, without recompiling the server. If Apache is compiled normally, it will install a number of optional modules in the \Apache2.2\modules directory. To activate these or other modules, the new LoadModule directive must be used. For example, to activate the status module, use the following (in addition to the status-activating directives in access.conf):

```
LoadModule status_module modules/mod_status.so
```

Information on creating loadable modules (p. 453) is also available.

- Apache can also load ISAPI (Internet Server Application Programming Interface) extensions such as those used by Microsoft IIS and other Windows servers. More information is available (p. 318). Note that Apache **cannot** load ISAPI Filters, and ISAPI Handlers with some Microsoft feature extensions will not work.

- When running CGI scripts, the method Apache uses to find the interpreter for the script is configurable using the ScriptInterpreterSource directive.

- Since it is often difficult to manage files with names like .htaccess in Windows, you may find it useful to change the name of this per-directory configuration file using the AccessFilename directive.

- Any errors during Apache startup are logged into the Windows event log when running on Windows NT. This mechanism acts as a backup for those situations where Apache is not yet prepared to use the error.log file. You can review the Windows Applicat Event Log by using the Event Viewer, e.g. Start - Settings - Control Panel - Administrative Tools - Event Viewer.

25.5 Running Apache as a Service

You can install Apache as a service automatically during the installation. If you chose to install for all users, the installation will create an Apache service for you. If you specify to install for yourself only, you can manually register Apache as a service after the installation. You have to be a member of the Administrators group for the service installation to succeed.

Apache comes with a utility called the Apache Service Monitor. With it you can see and manage the state of all installed Apache services on any machine on your network. To be able to manage an Apache service with the monitor, you have to first install the service (either automatically via the installation or manually).

You can install Apache as a Windows NT service as follows from the command prompt at the Apache bin subdirectory:

```
httpd.exe -k install
```

If you need to specify the name of the service you want to install, use the following command. You have to do this if you have several different service installations of Apache on your computer.

```
httpd.exe -k install -n "MyServiceName"
```

If you need to have specifically named configuration files for different services, you must use this:

```
httpd.exe -k install -n "MyServiceName" -f "c:\files\my.conf"
```

If you use the first command without any special parameters except -k install, the service will be called Apache2.2 and the configuration will be assumed to be conf\httpd.conf.

Removing an Apache service is easy. Just use:

```
httpd.exe -k uninstall
```

The specific Apache service to be uninstalled can be specified by using:

```
httpd.exe -k uninstall -n "MyServiceName"
```

Normal starting, restarting and shutting down of an Apache service is usually done via the Apache Service Monitor, by using commands like NET START Apache2.2 and NET STOP Apache2.2 or via normal Windows service management. Before starting Apache as a service by any means, you should test the service's configuration file by using:

```
httpd.exe -n "MyServiceName" -t
```

You can control an Apache service by its command line switches, too. To start an installed Apache service you'll use this:

```
httpd.exe -k start
```

To stop an Apache service via the command line switches, use this:

    httpd.exe -k stop

or

    httpd.exe -k shutdown

You can also restart a running service and force it to reread its configuration file by using:

    httpd.exe -k restart

By default, all Apache services are registered to run as the system user (the LocalSystem account). The LocalSystem account has no privileges to your network via any Windows-secured mechanism, including the file system, named pipes, DCOM, or secure RPC. It has, however, wide privileges locally.

> *Never grant any network privileges to the* LocalSystem *account! If you need Apache to be able to access network resources, create a separate account for Apache as noted below.*

It is recommended that users create a separate account for running Apache service(s). If you have to access network resources via Apache, this is required.

1. Create a normal domain user account, and be sure to memorize its password.

2. Grant the newly-created user a privilege of Log on as a service and Act as part of the operating system. On Windows NT 4.0 these privileges are granted via User Manager for Domains, but on Windows 2000 and XP you probably want to use Group Policy for propagating these settings. You can also manually set these via the Local Security Policy MMC snap-in.

3. Confirm that the created account is a member of the Users group.

4. Grant the account read and execute (RX) rights to all document and script folders (htdocs and cgi-bin for example).

5. Grant the account change (RWXD) rights to the Apache logs directory.

6. Grant the account read and execute (RX) rights to the httpd.exe binary executable.

> *It is usually a good practice to grant the user the Apache service runs as read and execute (RX) access to the whole Apache2.2 directory, except the* logs *subdirectory, where the user has to have at least change (RWXD) rights.*

If you allow the account to log in as a user and as a service, then you can log on with that account and test that the account has the privileges to execute the scripts, read the web pages, and that you can start Apache in a console window. If this works, and you have followed the steps above, Apache should execute as a service with no problems.

> *Error code 2186 is a good indication that you need to review the "Log On As" configuration for the service, since Apache cannot access a required network resource. Also, pay close attention to the privileges of the user Apache is configured to run as.*

When starting Apache as a service you may encounter an error message from the Windows Service Control Manager. For example, if you try to start Apache by using the Services applet in the Windows Control Panel, you may get the following message:

```
Could not start the Apache2.2 service on \\COMPUTER
Error 1067; The process terminated unexpectedly.
```

You will get this generic error if there is any problem with starting the Apache service. In order to see what is really causing the problem you should follow the instructions for Running Apache for Windows from the Command Prompt.

If you are having problems with the service, it is suggested you follow the instructions below to try starting httpd.exe from a console window, and work out the errors before struggling to start it as a service again.

25.6 Running Apache as a Console Application

Running Apache as a service is usually the recommended way to use it, but it is sometimes easier to work from the command line (on Windows 9x running Apache from the command line is the recommended way due to the lack of reliable service support.)

To run Apache from the command line as a console application, use the following command:

```
httpd.exe
```

Apache will execute, and will remain running until it is stopped by pressing Control-C.

You can also run Apache via the shortcut Start Apache in Console placed to Start Menu --> Programs --> Apache HTTP Server 2.2.xx --> Control Apache Server during the installation. This will open a console window and start Apache inside it. If you don't have Apache installed as a service, the window will remain visible until you stop Apache by pressing Control-C in the console window where Apache is running in. The server will exit in a few seconds. However, if you do have Apache installed as a service, the shortcut starts the service. If the Apache service is running already, the shortcut doesn't do anything.

You can tell a running Apache to stop by opening another console window and entering:

```
httpd.exe -k shutdown
```

This should be preferred over pressing Control-C because this lets Apache end any current operations and clean up gracefully.

You can also tell Apache to restart. This forces it to reread the configuration file. Any operations in progress are allowed to complete without interruption. To restart Apache, either press Control-Break in the console window you used for starting Apache, or enter

```
httpd.exe -k restart
```

in any other console window.

> *Note for people familiar with the Unix version of Apache: these com-
> mands provide a Windows equivalent to* `kill -TERM pid` *and* `kill`
> `-USR1 pid`. *The command line option used, -k, was chosen as a re-
> minder of the* `kill` *command used on Unix.*

If the Apache console window closes immediately or unexpectedly after startup, open the Command Prompt from the Start Menu -> Programs. Change to the folder to which you installed Apache, type the command `httpd.exe`, and read the error message. Then change to the logs folder, and review the `error.log` file for configuration mistakes. If you accepted the defaults when you installed Apache, the commands would be:

```
c:
cd "\Program Files\Apache Software Foundation\Apache2.2\bin"
httpd.exe
```

Then wait for Apache to stop, or press Control-C. Then enter the following:

```
cd ..\logs
more < error.log
```

When working with Apache it is important to know how it will find the con-figuration file. You can specify a configuration file on the command line in two ways:

- `-f` specifies an absolute or relative path to a particular configuration file:

  ```
  httpd.exe -f "c:\my server files\anotherconfig.conf"
  ```

  or

  ```
  httpd.exe -f files\anotherconfig.conf
  ```

- `-n` specifies the installed Apache service whose configuration file is to be used:

  ```
  httpd.exe -n "MyServiceName"
  ```

In both of these cases, the proper `ServerRoot` should be set in the configuration file.

If you don't specify a configuration file with `-f` or `-n`, Apache will use the file name compiled into the server, such as `conf\httpd.conf`. This built-in path is relative to the installation directory. You can verify the compiled file name

from a value labelled as SERVER_CONFIG_FILE when invoking Apache with the
-V switch, like this:

    httpd.exe -V

Apache will then try to determine its ServerRoot by trying the following, in
this order:

1. A ServerRoot directive via the -C command line switch.
2. The -d switch on the command line.
3. Current working directory.
4. A registry entry which was created if you did a binary installation.
5. The server root compiled into the server. This is /apache by default,
   you can verify it by using httpd.exe -V and looking for a value labelled
   as HTTPD_ROOT.

During the installation, a version-specific registry key is created in the Windows
registry. The location of this key depends on the type of the installation. If
you chose to install Apache for all users, the key is located under the HKEY_-
LOCAL_MACHINE hive, like this (the version numbers will of course vary between
different versions of Apache:

    HKEY_LOCAL_MACHINE\SOFTWARE\Apache Software
    Foundation\Apache\2.2.2

Correspondingly, if you chose to install Apache for the current user only, the
key is located under the HKEY_CURRENT_USER hive, the contents of which are
dependent of the user currently logged on:

    HKEY_CURRENT_USER\SOFTWARE\Apache Software
    Foundation\Apache\2.2.2

This key is compiled into the server and can enable you to test new versions
without affecting the current version. Of course, you must take care not to
install the new version in the same directory as another version.

If you did not do a binary install, Apache will in some scenarios complain about
the missing registry key. This warning can be ignored if the server was otherwise
able to find its configuration file.

The value of this key is the ServerRoot directory which contains the conf
subdirectory. When Apache starts it reads the httpd.conf file from that directory. If this file contains a ServerRoot directive which contains a different
directory from the one obtained from the registry key above, Apache will forget
the registry key and use the directory from the configuration file. If you copy
the Apache directory or configuration files to a new location it is vital that
you update the ServerRoot directive in the httpd.conf file to reflect the new
location.

25.7 Testing the Installation

After starting Apache (either in a console window or as a service) it will be listening on port 80 (unless you changed the Listen directive in the configuration files or installed Apache only for the current user). To connect to the server and access the default page, launch a browser and enter this URL:

    http://localhost/

Apache should respond with a welcome page and you should see "It Works!". If nothing happens or you get an error, look in the error.log file in the logs subdirectory. If your host is not connected to the net, or if you have serious problems with your DNS (Domain Name Service) configuration, you may have to use this URL:

    http://127.0.0.1/

If you happen to be running Apache on an alternate port, you need to explicitly put that in the URL:

    http://127.0.0.1:8080/

Once your basic installation is working, you should configure it properly by editing the files in the conf subdirectory. Again, if you change the configuration of the Windows NT service for Apache, first attempt to start it from the command line to make sure that the service starts with no errors.

Because Apache **cannot** share the same port with another TCP/IP application, you may need to stop, uninstall or reconfigure certain other services before running Apache. These conflicting services include other WWW servers, some firewall implementations, and even some client applications (such as Skype) which will use port 80 to attempt to bypass firewall issues.

26 Compiling Apache for Microsoft Windows

There are many important points before you begin compiling Apache. See Using
Apache with Microsoft Windows (p. 745) before you begin.

26.1 Requirements

Compiling Apache requires the following environment to be properly installed:

- Disk Space

  Make sure you have at least 200 MB of free disk space available. After installation Apache requires approximately 80 MB of disk space, plus
  space for log and cache files, which can grow rapidly. The actual disk
  space requirements will vary considerably based on your chosen configuration and any third-party modules or libraries, especially when OpenSSL
  is also built. Because many files are text and very easily compressed,
  NTFS filesystem compression cuts these requirements in half.

- Appropriate Patches

  The httpd binary is built with the help of several patches to third party
  packages, which ensure the released code is buildable and debuggable.
  These patches are available and distributed from http://www.apache.org/
  dist/httpd/binaries/win32/patches_applied/ and are recommended to be
  applied to obtain identical results as the "official" ASF distributed binaries.

- Microsoft Visual C++ 6.0 (Visual Studio 97) or later.

  Apache can be built using the command line tools, or from within the
  Visual Studio IDE Workbench. The command line build requires the
  environment to reflect the PATH, INCLUDE, LIB and other variables that
  can be configured with the vcvars32.bat script.

  *You may want the Visual Studio Processor Pack for your older
  version of Visual Studio, or a full (not Express) version of newer
  Visual Studio editions, for the ml.exe assembler. This will allow
  you to build OpenSSL, if desired, using the more efficient assembly
  code implementation.*

  *Only the Microsoft compiler tool chain is actively supported by the
  active httpd contributors. Although the project regularly accepts
  patches to ensure MinGW and other alternative builds work and
  improve upon them, they are not actively maintained and are often
  broken in the course of normal development.*

- Updated Microsoft Windows Platform SDK, February 2003 or later.

  An appropriate Windows Platform SDK is included by default in the full
  (not express/lite) versions of Visual C++ 7.1 (Visual Studio 2002) and

later, these users can ignore these steps unless explicitly choosing a newer or different version of the Platform SDK.

To use Visual C++ 6.0 or 7.0 (Studio 2000 .NET), the Platform SDK environment must be prepared using the `setenv.bat` script (installed by the Platform SDK) before starting the command line build or launching the msdev/devenv GUI environment. Installing the Platform SDK for Visual Studio Express versions (2003 and later) should adjust the default environment appropriately.

```
"c:\Program Files\Microsoft Visual
Studio\VC98\Bin\VCVARS32"
"c:\Program Files\Platform SDK\setenv.bat"
```

- Perl and awk

  Several steps recommended here require a perl interpreter during the build preparation process, but it is otherwise not required.

  To install Apache within the build system, several files are modified using the `awk.exe` utility. awk was chosen since it is a very small download (compared with Perl or WSH/VB) and accomplishes the task of modifying configuration files upon installation. Brian Kernighan's http://www.cs.princeton.edu/~bwk/btl.mirror/ site has a compiled native Win32 binary, http://www.cs.princeton.edu/~bwk/btl.mirror/awk95.exe which you must save with the name `awk.exe` (rather than `awk95.exe`).

  > If `awk.exe` is not found, Makefile.win's install target will not perform substitutions in the installed .conf files. You must manually modify the installed .conf files to allow the server to start. Search and replace all "@token@" tags as appropriate.

  > The Visual Studio IDE will only find `awk.exe` from the PATH, or executable path specified in the menu option Tools -> Options -> (Projects ->) Directories. Ensure awk.exe is in your system path.

  > Also note that if you are using Cygwin tools (http://www.cygwin.com/) the awk utility is named `gawk.exe` and that the file `awk.exe` is really a symlink to the `gawk.exe` file. The Windows command shell does not recognize symlinks, and because of this building InstallBin will fail. A workaround is to delete `awk.exe` from the cygwin installation and copy `gawk.exe` to `awk.exe`. Also note the cygwin/mingw ports of gawk 3.0.x were buggy, please upgrade to 3.1.x before attempting to use any gawk port.

- [Optional] zlib library (for mod_deflate)

  Zlib must be installed into a `srclib` subdirectory named `zlib`. This must be built in-place. Zlib can be obtained from http://www.zlib.net/ – the mod_deflate is confirmed to work correctly with version 1.2.3.

```
nmake -f win32\Makefile.msc
nmake -f win32\Makefile.msc test
```

- [Optional] OpenSSL libraries (for mod_ssl and ab.exe with ssl support)

    The OpenSSL library is cryptographic software. The country in which you currently reside may have restrictions on the import, possession, use, and/or re-export to another country, of encryption software. BEFORE using any encryption software, please check your country's laws, regulations and policies concerning the import, possession, or use, and re-export of encryption software, to see if this is permitted. See http://www.wassenaar.org/ for more information.

    Configuring and building OpenSSL requires perl to be installed.

    OpenSSL must be installed into a srclib subdirectory named openssl, obtained from http://www.openssl.org/source/, in order to compile mod_ssl or the abs.exe project, which is ab.c with SSL support enabled. To prepare OpenSSL to be linked to Apache mod_ssl or abs.exe, and disable patent encumbered features in OpenSSL, you might use the following build commands:

    ```
    perl Configure no-rc5 no-idea enable-mdc2 enable-zlib
    VC-WIN32 -Ipath/to/srclib/zlib -Lpath/to/srclib/zlib
    ms\do_masm.bat
    nmake -f ms\ntdll.mak
    ```

    It is not advisable to use zlib-dynamic, as that transfers the cost of deflating SSL streams to the first request which must load the zlib dll. Note the suggested patch enables the -L flag to work with windows builds, corrects the name of zdll.lib and ensures .pdb files are generated for troubleshooting. If the assembler is not installed, you would add no-asm above and use ms\do_ms.bat instead of the ms\do_masm.bat script.

- [Optional] Database libraries (for mod_dbd and mod_authn_dbm)

    The apr-util library exposes DBM (keyed database) and DBD (query oriented database) client functionality to the httpd server and its modules, such as authentication and authorization. The SDBM DBM and ODBC DBD providers are compiled unconditionally.

    The DBD support includes the Oracle instantclient package, MySQL, PostgreSQL and sqlite. To build these all, for example, set up the LIB to include the library path, INCLUDE to include the headers path, and PATH to include the DLL bin path of all four SDK's, and set the DBD_LIST environment variable to inform the build which client driver SDKs are installed correctly, e.g.;

    ```
    set DBD_LIST=sqlite3 pgsql oracle mysql
    ```

    Similarly, the dbm support can be extended with DBM_LIST to build a Berkeley DB provider (db) and/or gdbm provider, by similarly configuring LIB, INCLUDE and PATH first to ensure the client library libs and headers are available.

```
set DBM_LIST=db gdbm
```

Depending on the choice of database distributions, it may be nec-essary to change the actual link target name (e.g. gdbm.lib vs. libgdb.lib) that are listed in the corresponding .dsp/.mak files within the directories srclib\apr-util\dbd or ... \dbm.

See the README-win32.txt file for more hints on obtaining the various database driver SDKs.

26.2 Command-Line Build

Makefile.win is the top level Apache makefile. To compile Apache on Windows, simply use one of the following commands to build the release or debug flavor:

```
nmake /f Makefile.win _apacher

nmake /f Makefile.win _apached
```

Either command will compile Apache. The latter will disable optimization of the resulting files, making it easier to single step the code to find bugs and track down problems.

You can add your apr-util DBD and DBM provider choices with the additional make (environment) variables DBD_LIST and DBM_LIST, see the comments about [Optional] Database libraries, above. Review the initial comments in Makefile.win for additional options that can be provided when invoking the build.

26.3 Developer Studio Workspace IDE Build

Apache can also be compiled using VC++'s Visual Studio development environment. To simplify this process, a Visual Studio workspace, Apache.dsw, is provided. This workspace exposes the entire list of working .dsp projects that are required for the complete Apache binary release. It includes dependencies between the projects to assure that they are built in the appropriate order.

Open the Apache.dsw workspace, and select InstallBin (Release or Debug build, as desired) as the Active Project. InstallBin causes all related project to be built, and then invokes Makefile.win to move the compiled executables and dlls. You may personalize the INSTDIR= choice by changing InstallBin's Settings, General tab, Build command line entry. INSTDIR defaults to the /Apache2 directory. If you only want a test compile (without installing) you may build the BuildBin project instead.

The .dsp project files are distributed in Visual Studio 6.0 (98) format. Visual C++ 5.0 (97) will recognize them. Visual Studio 2002 (.NET) and later users must convert Apache.dsw plus the .dsp files into an Apache.sln plus .msproj files. Be sure you reconvert the .msproj file again if its source .dsp file changes! This is really trivial, just open Apache.dsw in the VC++ 7.0 IDE once again and reconvert.

There is a flaw in the .vcproj conversion of .dsp files. devenv.exe will mis-parse the /D flag for RC flags containing long quoted /D'efines which contain spaces. The command:

```
perl srclib\apr\build\cvtdsp.pl -2005
```

will convert the /D flags for RC flags to use an alternate, parseable syntax; unfortunately this syntax isn't supported by Visual Studio 97 or its exported .mak files. These /D flags are used to pass the long description of the mod_apachemodule.so files to the shared .rc resource version-identifier build.

Visual Studio 2002 (.NET) and later users should also use the Build menu, Configuration Manager dialog to uncheck both the Debug and Release Solution modules abs, mod_deflate and mod_ssl components, as well as every component starting with apr_db*. These modules are built by invoking nmake, or the IDE directly with the BinBuild target, which builds those modules conditionally if the srclib directories openssl and/or zlib exist, and based on the setting of DBD_LIST and DBM_LIST environment variables.

26.4 Exporting command-line .mak files

Exported .mak files pose a greater hassle, but they are required for Visual C++ 5.0 users to build mod_ssl, abs (ab with SSL support) and/or mod_deflate. The .mak files also support a broader range of C++ tool chain distributions, such as Visual Studio Express.

You must first build all projects in order to create all dynamic auto-generated targets, so that dependencies can be parsed correctly. Build the entire project from within the Visual Studio 6.0 (98) IDE, using the BuildAll target, then use the Project Menu Export for all makefiles (checking on "with dependencies".) Run the following command to correct absolute paths into relative paths so they will build anywhere:

```
perl srclib\apr\build\fixwin32mak.pl
```

You must type this command from the *top level* directory of the httpd source tree. Every .mak and .dep project file within the current directory and below will be corrected, and the timestamps adjusted to reflect the .dsp.

Always review the generated .mak and .dep files for Platform SDK or other local, machine specific file paths. The DevStudio\Common\MSDev98\bin\ (VC6) directory contains a sysincl.dat file, which lists all exceptions. Update this file (including both forward and backslashed paths, such as both sys/time.h and sys\time.h) to ignore such newer dependencies. Including local-install paths in a distributed .mak file will cause the build to fail completely.

If you contribute back a patch that revises project files, we must commit project files in Visual Studio 6.0 format. Changes should be simple, with minimal compilation and linkage flags that can be recognized by all Visual Studio environments.

26.5 Installation

Once Apache has been compiled, it needs to be installed in its server root directory. The default is the \Apache2 directory, of the same drive.

To build and install all the files into the desired folder *dir* automatically, use one of the following nmake commands:

```
nmake /f Makefile.win installr INSTDIR=dir
nmake /f Makefile.win installd INSTDIR=dir
```

The *dir* argument to INSTDIR provides the installation directory; it can be omitted if Apache is to be installed into \Apache22 (of the current drive).

26.6 Warning about building Apache from the development tree

Note only the .dsp files are maintained between release builds. The .mak files are NOT regenerated, due to the tremendous waste of reviewer's time. Therefore, you cannot rely on the NMAKE commands above to build revised .dsp project files unless you then export all .mak files yourself from the project. This is unnecessary if you build from within the Microsoft Developer Studio environment.

27 The Apache EBCDIC Port

Warning: This section has not been updated to take into account changes made in the 2.0 version of the Apache HTTP Server. Some of the information may still be relevant, but please use it with care.

27.1 Overview of the Apache EBCDIC Port

Version 1.3 of the Apache HTTP Server is the first version which includes a port to a (non-ASCII) mainframe machine which uses the EBCDIC character set as its native codeset.

(It is the SIEMENS family of mainframes running the BS2000/OSD operating system[1]. This mainframe OS nowadays features a SVR4-derived POSIX subsystem).

The port was started initially to

- prove the feasibility of porting the Apache HTTP server[2] to this platform
- find a "worthy and capable" successor for the venerable CERN-3.0[3] daemon (which was ported a couple of years ago), and to
- prove that Apache's preforking process model can on this platform easily outperform the accept-fork-serve model used by CERN by a factor of 5 or more.

This section serves as a rationale to describe some of the design decisions of the port to this machine.

27.2 Design Goals

One objective of the EBCDIC port was to maintain enough backwards compatibility with the (EBCDIC) CERN server to make the transition to the new server attractive and easy. This required the addition of a configurable method to define whether a HTML document was stored in ASCII (the only format accepted by the old server) or in EBCDIC (the native document format in the POSIX subsystem, and therefore the only realistic format in which the other POSIX tools like grep or sed could operate on the documents). The current solution to this is a "pseudo-MIME-format" which is intercepted and interpreted by the Apache server (see below). Future versions might solve the problem by defining an "ebcdic-handler" for all documents which must be converted.

---

[1]http://www.siemens.de/servers/bs2osd/osdbc_us.htm
[2]http://httpd.apache.org/
[3]http://www.w3.org/Daemon/

27.3 Technical Solution

Since all Apache input and output is based upon the BUFF data type and its methods, the easiest solution was to add the conversion to the BUFF handling routines. The conversion must be settable at any time, so a BUFF flag was added which defines whether a BUFF object has currently enabled conversion or not. This flag is modified at several points in the HTTP protocol:

- **set** before a request is received (because the request and the request header lines are always in ASCII format)
- **set/unset** when the request body is received - depending on the content type of the request body (because the request body may contain ASCII text or a binary file)
- **set** before a reply header is sent (because the response header lines are always in ASCII format)
- **set/unset** when the response body is sent - depending on the content type of the response body (because the response body may contain text or a binary file)

27.4 Porting Notes

1. The relevant changes in the source are #ifdef'ed into two categories:

   #ifdef CHARSET_EBCDIC Code which is needed for any EBCDIC based machine. This includes character translations, differences in contiguity of the two character sets, flags which indicate which part of the HTTP protocol has to be converted and which part doesn't *etc.*

   #ifdef _OSD_POSIX Code which is needed for the SIEMENS BS2000/OSD mainframe platform only. This deals with include file differences and socket implementation topics which are only required on the BS2000/OSD platform.

2. The possibility to translate between ASCII and EBCDIC at the socket level (on BS2000 POSIX, there is a socket option which supports this) was intentionally *not* chosen, because the byte stream at the HTTP protocol level consists of a mixture of protocol related strings and non-protocol related raw file data. HTTP protocol strings are always encoded in ASCII (the GET request, any Header: lines, the chunking information *etc.*) whereas the file transfer parts (*i.e.*, GIF images, CGI output *etc.*) should usually be just "passed through" by the server. This separation between "protocol string" and "raw data" is reflected in the server code by functions like bgets() or rvputs() for strings, and functions like bwrite() for binary data. A global translation of everything would therefore be inadequate.

   (In the case of text files of course, provisions must be made so that EBCDIC documents are always served in ASCII)

3. This port therefore features a built-in protocol level conversion for the server-internal strings (which the compiler translated to EBCDIC strings) and thus for all server-generated documents. The hard coded ASCII escapes \012 and \015 which are ubiquitous in the server code are an exception: they are already the binary encoding of the ASCII \n and \r and must not be converted to ASCII a second time. This exception is only relevant for server-generated strings; and *external* EBCDIC documents are not expected to contain ASCII newline characters.

4. By examining the call hierarchy for the BUFF management routines, I added an "EBCDIC/ASCII conversion layer" which would be crossed on every puts/write/get/gets, and a conversion flag which allowed enabling/disabling the conversions on-the-fly. Usually, a document crosses this layer twice from its origin source (a file or CGI output) to its destination (the requesting client): file -> Apache, and Apache -> client.

   The server can now read the header lines of a CGI-script output in EBCDIC format, and then find out that the remainder of the script's output is in ASCII (like in the case of the output of a WWW Counter program: the document body contains a GIF image). All header processing is done in the native EBCDIC format; the server then determines, based on the type of document being served, whether the document body (except for the chunking information, of course) is in ASCII already or must be converted from EBCDIC.

5. For Text documents (MIME types text/plain, text/html *etc.*), an implicit translation to ASCII can be used, or (if the users prefer to store some documents in raw ASCII form for faster serving, or because the files reside on a NFS-mounted directory tree) can be served without conversion.

   Example:

   to serve files with the suffix .ahtml as a raw ASCII text/html document without implicit conversion (and suffix .ascii as ASCII text/plain), use the directives:

   ```
   AddType text/x-ascii-html .ahtml
   AddType text/x-ascii-plain .ascii
   ```

   Similarly, any text/foo MIME type can be served as "raw ASCII" by configuring a MIME type "text/x-ascii-foo" for it using AddType.

6. Non-text documents are always served "binary" without conversion. This seems to be the most sensible choice for, *e.g.*, GIF/ZIP/AU file types. This of course requires the user to copy them to the mainframe host using the "rcp -b" binary switch.

7. Server parsed files are always assumed to be in native (*i.e.*, EBCDIC) format as used on the machine, and are converted after processing.

8. For CGI output, the CGI script determines whether a conversion is needed or not: by setting the appropriate Content-Type, text files can be converted, or GIF output can be passed through unmodified. An example for the latter case is the wwwcount program which we ported as well.

27.5 Document Storage Notes

27.5.1 Binary Files

All files with a Content-Type: which does not start with text/ are regarded as *binary files* by the server and are not subject to any conversion. Examples for binary files are GIF images, gzip-compressed files and the like.

When exchanging binary files between the mainframe host and a Unix machine or Windows PC, be sure to use the ftp "binary" (TYPE I) command, or use the rcp -b command from the mainframe host (the -b switch is not supported in unix rcp's).

27.5.2 Text Documents

The default assumption of the server is that Text Files (*i.e.*, all files whose Content-Type: starts with text/) are stored in the native character set of the host, EBCDIC.

27.5.3 Server Side Included Documents

SSI documents must currently be stored in EBCDIC only. No provision is made to convert it from ASCII before processing.

27.6 Apache Modules' Status

Module	Status	Notes
core	+	
mod_access	+	
mod_actions	+	
mod_alias	+	
mod_asis	+	
mod_auth	+	
mod_auth_anon	+	
mod_auth_dbm	?	with own libdb.a
mod_autoindex	+	
mod_cern_meta	?	
mod_cgi	+	
mod_digest	+	
mod_dir	+	
mod_so	−	no shared libs
mod_env	+	
mod_example	−	(test bed only)
mod_expires	+	
mod_headers	+	
mod_imagemap	+	
mod_include	+	
mod_info	+	
mod_log_agent	+	

```
mod_log_config      +
mod_log_referer     +
mod_mime            +
mod_mime_magic      ?       not ported yet
mod_negotiation     +
mod_proxy           +
mod_rewrite         +       untested
mod_setenvif        +
mod_speling         +
mod_status          +
mod_unique_id       +
mod_userdir         +
mod_usertrack       ?       untested
```

27.7 Third Party Modules' Status

Module	Status	Notes
mod_jserv[4]	–	JAVA still being ported.
mod_php3[5]	+	mod_php3 runs fine, with LDAP and GD and FreeType libraries.
mod_put[6]	?	untested
mod_session	–	untested

---

[4]http://java.apache.org/
[5]http://www.php.net/
[6]http://hpwww.ec-lyon.fr/~vincent/apache/mod_put.html

28 Relevant Standards

This section documents all the relevant standards that the Apache HTTP Server follows, along with brief descriptions.

In addition to the information listed below, the following resources should be consulted:

- http://purl.org/NET/http-errata[1] - HTTP/1.1 Specification Errata
- http://www.rfc-editor.org/errata.html[2] - RFC Errata
- http://ftp.ics.uci.edu/pub/ietf/http/#RFC[3] - A pre-compiled list of HTTP related RFCs

NOTICE *This section is not yet complete.*

28.1 HTTP Recommendations

Regardless of what modules are compiled and used, Apache as a basic web server complies with the following IETF recommendations:

RFC 1945[4] (Informational) The Hypertext Transfer Protocol (HTTP) is an application-level protocol with the lightness and speed necessary for distributed, collaborative, hypermedia information systems. This documents HTTP/1.0.

RFC 2616[5] (Standards Track) The Hypertext Transfer Protocol (HTTP) is an application-level protocol for distributed, collaborative, hypermedia information systems. This documents HTTP/1.1.

RFC 2396[6] (Standards Track) A Uniform Resource Identifier (URI) is a compact string of characters for identifying an abstract or physical resource.

28.2 HTML Recommendations

Regarding the Hypertext Markup Language, Apache complies with the following IETF and W3C recommendations:

RFC 2854[7] (Informational) This document summarizes the history of HTML development, and defines the "text/html" MIME type by pointing to the relevant W3C recommendations.

---

[1] http://purl.org/NET/http-errata
[2] http://www.rfc-editor.org/errata.html
[3] http://ftp.ics.uci.edu/pub/ietf/http/#RFC
[4] http://www.rfc-editor.org/rfc/rfc1945.txt
[5] http://www.rfc-editor.org/rfc/rfc2616.txt
[6] http://www.rfc-editor.org/rfc/rfc2396.txt
[7] http://www.rfc-editor.org/rfc/rfc2854.txt

HTML 4.01 Specification[8] **(Errata**[9]**)** This specification defines the HyperText Markup Language (HTML), the publishing language of the World Wide Web. This specification defines HTML 4.01, which is a subversion of HTML 4.

HTML 3.2 Reference Specification[10] The HyperText Markup Language (HTML) is a simple markup language used to create hypertext documents that are portable from one platform to another. HTML documents are SGML documents.

XHTML 1.1 - Module-based XHTML[11] **(Errata**[12]**)** This Recommendation defines a new XHTML document type that is based upon the module framework and modules defined in Modularization of XHTML.

XHTML 1.0 The Extensible HyperText Markup Language (Second Edition)[13] **(Errata**[14]**)**
This specification defines the Second Edition of XHTML 1.0, a reformulation of HTML 4 as an XML 1.0 application, and three DTDs corresponding to the ones defined by HTML 4.

28.3 Authentication

Concerning the different methods of authentication, Apache follows the following IETF recommendations:

RFC 2617[15] **(Draft standard)** "HTTP/1.0", includes the specification for a Basic Access Authentication scheme.

28.4 Language/Country Codes

The following links document ISO and other language and country code information:

ISO 639-2[16] ISO 639 provides two sets of language codes, one as a two-letter code set (639-1) and another as a three-letter code set (this part of ISO 639) for the representation of names of languages.

ISO 3166-1[17] These pages document the country names (official short names in English) in alphabetical order as given in ISO 3166-1 and the corresponding ISO 3166-1-alpha-2 code elements.

BCP 47[18] **(Best Current Practice), RFC 3066**[19] This document describes a language tag for use in cases where it is desired to indicate the

---

[8]http://www.w3.org/TR/html401
[9]http://www.w3.org/MarkUp/html4-updates/errata
[10]http://www.w3.org/TR/REC-html32
[11]http://www.w3.org/TR/xhtml11/
[12]http://www.w3.org/2001/04/REC-xhtml-modularization-20010410-errata
[13]http://www.w3.org/TR/xhtml1
[14]http://www.w3.org/2002/08/REC-xhtml1-20020801-errata
[15]http://www.rfc-editor.org/rfc/rfc2617.txt
[16]http://www.loc.gov/standards/iso639-2/
[17]http://www.iso.ch/iso/en/prods-services/iso3166ma/02iso-3166-code-lists/index.html

language used in an information object, how to register values for use in this language tag, and a construct for matching such language tags.

RFC 3282[20] **(Standards Track)** This document defines a "Content-language:" header, for use in cases where one desires to indicate the language of something that has RFC 822-like headers, like MIME body parts or Web documents, and an "Accept-Language:" header for use in cases where one wishes to indicate one's preferences with regard to language.

---

[18]http://www.rfc-editor.org/rfc/bcp/bcp47.txt
[19]http://www.rfc-editor.org/rfc/rfc3066.txt
[20]http://www.rfc-editor.org/rfc/rfc3282.txt

29 Password Formats

Notes about the password encryption formats generated and understood by Apache.

29.1 Basic Authentication

There are four formats that Apache recognizes for basic-authentication passwords. Note that not all formats work on every platform:

PLAIN TEXT (i.e. *unencrypted*) Windows, BEOS, & Netware only.

CRYPT Unix only. Uses the traditional Unix crypt(3) function with a randomly-generated 32-bit salt (only 12 bits used) and the first 8 characters of the password.

SHA1 "{SHA}" + Base64-encoded SHA-1 digest of the password.

MD5 "$apr1$" + the result of an Apache-specific algorithm using an iterated (1,000 times) MD5 digest of various combinations of a random 32-bit salt and the password. See the APR source file apr_md5.c[1] for the details of the algorithm.

29.1.1 Generating values with htpasswd

MD5
```
$ htpasswd -nbm myName myPassword
myName:$apr1$r31.....$HqJZimcKQFAMYayBlzkrA/
```

SHA1
```
$ htpasswd -nbs myName myPassword
myName:{SHA}VBPuJHI7uixaa6LQGWx4s+5GKNE=
```

CRYPT
```
$ htpasswd -nbd myName myPassword
myName:rqXexS6ZhobKA
```

29.1.2 Generating CRYPT and MD5 values with the OpenSSL command-line program

OpenSSL knows the Apache-specific MD5 algorithm.

MD5
```
$ openssl passwd -apr1 myPassword
$apr1$qHDFfhPC$nITSVHgYbDAK1YOacGRnYO
```

CRYPT
```
openssl passwd -crypt myPassword
qQ5vTYO3c8dsU
```

---

[1]http://svn.apache.org/viewvc/apr/apr-util/branches/1.3.x/crypto/apr_md5.c?view=co

29.1.3 Validating CRYPT or MD5 passwords with the OpenSSL command line program

The salt for a CRYPT password is the first two characters (converted to a binary value). To validate myPassword against rqXexS6ZhobKA

CRYPT
```
$ openssl passwd -crypt -salt rq myPassword
Warning:  truncating password to 8 characters
rqXexS6ZhobKA
```

Note that using myPasswo instead of myPassword will produce the same result because only the first 8 characters of CRYPT passwords are considered.

The salt for an MD5 password is between $apr1$ and the following $ (as a Base64-encoded binary value - max 8 chars). To validate myPassword against $apr1$r31.....$HqJZimcKQFAMYayBlzkrA/

MD5
```
$ openssl passwd -apr1 -salt r31.....  myPassword
$apr1$r31.....$HqJZimcKQFAMYayBlzkrA/
```

29.1.4 Database password fields for mod_dbd

The SHA1 variant is probably the most useful format for DBD authentication. Since the SHA1 and Base64 functions are commonly available, other software can populate a database with encrypted passwords that are usable by Apache basic authentication.

To create Apache SHA1-variant basic-authentication passwords in various languages:

PHP
```
'{SHA}' .  base64_encode(sha1($password, TRUE))
```

Java
```
"{SHA}" + new sun.misc.BASE64Encoder().encode(
java.security.MessageDigest.getInstance("SHA1").digest(
password.getBytes()))
```

ColdFusion
```
"{SHA}" & ToBase64(BinaryDecode(Hash(password, "SHA1"), "Hex"))
```

Ruby
```
require 'digest/sha1'
require 'base64'
'{SHA}' + Base64.encode64(Digest::SHA1.digest(password))
```

C or C++
```
Use the APR function:  apr_sha1_base64
```

PostgreSQL (with the contrib/pgcrypto functions installed)
```
'{SHA}'||encode(digest(password,'sha1'),'base64')
```

29.2 Digest Authentication

Apache recognizes one format for digest-authentication passwords - the MD5
hash of the string user:realm:password as a 32-character string of hexadecimal
digits. realm is the Authorization Realm argument to the AuthName directive
in httpd.conf.

29.2.1 Database password fields for mod_dbd

Since the MD5 function is commonly available, other software can populate a
database with encrypted passwords that are usable by Apache digest authentication.

To create Apache digest-authentication passwords in various languages:

PHP
```
md5($user . ':' . $realm . ':' .$password)
```

Java
```
byte b[] =
java.security.MessageDigest.getInstance("MD5").digest( (user +
":" + realm + ":" + password ).getBytes());
java.math.BigInteger bi = new java.math.BigInteger(1, b);
String s = bi.toString(16);
while (s.length() < 32)
    s = "0" + s;
// String s is the encrypted password
```

ColdFusion
```
LCase(Hash( (user & ":" & realm & ":" & password) , "MD5"))
```

Ruby
```
require 'digest/md5'
Digest::MD5.hexdigest(user + ':' + realm + ':' + password)
```

PostgreSQL (with the contrib/pgcrypto functions installed)
```
encode(digest( user || ':' || realm || ':' || password ,
'md5'), 'hex')
```

30 Release Notes

30.1 Compiling and Installing

This section covers compilation and installation of the Apache HTTP Server on Unix and Unix-like systems only. For compiling and installation on Windows, see Using Apache HTTPd with Microsoft Windows (p. 745). For other platforms, see the platform (p. 745) documentation.

Apache HTTPd uses libtool and autoconf to create a build environment that looks like many other Open Source projects.

If you are upgrading from one minor version to the next (for example, 2.2.50 to 2.2.51), please skip down to the upgrading section.

See also:

▷ Configure the source tree (p. 18)

▷ Starting the Apache HTTP Server (p. 49)

▷ Stopping and Restarting (p. 51)

30.1.1 Overview for the impatient

Download	`$ lynx http://httpd.apache.org/download.cgi`
Extract	`$ gzip -d httpd-NN.tar.gz`
	`$ tar xvf httpd-NN.tar`
	`$ cd httpd-NN`
Configure	`$ ./configure --prefix=PREFIX`
Compile	`$ make`
Install	`$ make install`
Customize	`$ vi PREFIX/conf/httpd.conf`
Test	`$ PREFIX/bin/apachectl -k start`

NN must be replaced with the current version number, and *PREFIX* must be replaced with the filesystem path under which the server should be installed. If *PREFIX* is not specified, it defaults to /usr/local/apache2.

Each section of the compilation and installation process is described in more detail below, beginning with the requirements for compiling and installing Apache HTTP Server.

30.1.2 Requirements

The following requirements exist for building Apache HTTPd:

Disk Space Make sure you have at least 50 MB of temporary free disk space available. After installation Apache occupies approximately 10 MB of disk space. The actual disk space requirements will vary considerably based on your chosen configuration options and any third-party modules.

ANSI-C Compiler and Build System Make sure you have an ANSI-C compiler installed. The GNU C compiler (GCC)[1] from the Free Software Foundation (FSF)[2] is recommended. If you don't have GCC then at least make sure your vendor's compiler is ANSI compliant. In addition, your PATH must contain basic build tools such as make.

Accurate time keeping Elements of the HTTP protocol are expressed as the time of day. So, it's time to investigate setting some time synchronization facility on your system. Usually the ntpdate or xntpd programs are used for this purpose which are based on the Network Time Protocol (NTP). See the NTP homepage[3] for more details about NTP software and public time servers.

Perl 5[4] [OPTIONAL] For some of the support scripts like apxs or dbmmanage (which are written in Perl) the Perl 5 interpreter is required (versions 5.003 or newer are sufficient). If you have multiple Perl interpreters (for example, a systemwide install of Perl 4, and your own install of Perl 5), you are advised to use the --with-perl option (see below) to make sure the correct one is used by configure. If no Perl 5 interpreter is found by the configure script, you will not be able to use the affected support scripts. Of course, you will still be able to build and use Apache HTTPd.

apr/apr-util >= 1.2[5] apr and apr-util are bundled with the Apache HTTPd source releases, and will be used without any problems in almost all circumstances. However, if apr or apr-util, versions 1.0 or 1.1, are installed on your system, you must either upgrade your apr/apr-util installations to 1.2, force the use of the bundled libraries or have httpd use separate builds. To use the bundled apr/apr-util sources specify the --with-included-apr option to configure:

> NOTE *The –with-included-apr option was added in version 2.2.3*

```
# Force the use of the bundled apr/apr-util
./configure --with-included-apr
```

To build Apache HTTPd against a manually installed apr/apr-util:

```
# Build and install apr 1.2
cd srclib/apr
./configure --prefix=/usr/local/apr-httpd/
make
make install
# Build and install apr-util 1.2
cd ../apr-util
```

---

[1]http://www.gnu.org/software/gcc/gcc.html
[2]http://www.gnu.org/
[3]http://www.ntp.org
[4]http://www.perl.org/

```
./configure --prefix=/usr/local/apr-util-httpd/
--with-apr=/usr/local/apr-httpd/
make
make install
```

```
# Configure httpd
cd ../../
./configure --with-apr=/usr/local/apr-httpd/
--with-apr-util=/usr/local/apr-util-httpd/
```

30.1.3 Download

The Apache HTTP Server can be downloaded from the Apache HTTP Server download site[6], which lists several mirrors. Most users of Apache HTTPd on unix-like systems will be better off downloading and compiling a source version. The build process (described below) is easy, and it allows you to customize your server to suit your needs. In addition, binary releases are often not up to date with the latest source releases. If you do download a binary, follow the instructions in the INSTALL.bindist file inside the distribution.

After downloading, it is important to verify that you have a complete and unmodified version of the Apache HTTP Server. This can be accomplished by testing the downloaded tarball against the PGP signature. Details on how to do this are available on the download page[7] and an extended example is available describing the use of PGP[8].

30.1.4 Extract

Extracting the source from the Apache HTTPd tarball is a simple matter of uncompressing, and then untarring:

```
$ gzip -d httpd-NN.tar.gz
$ tar xvf httpd-NN.tar
```

This will create a new directory under the current directory containing the source code for the distribution. You should cd into that directory before proceeding with compiling the server.

30.1.5 Configuring the source tree

The next step is to configure the Apache HTTPd source tree for your particular platform and personal requirements. This is done using the script configure included in the root directory of the distribution. (Developers downloading an unreleased version of the Apache HTTPd source tree will need to have autoconf and libtool installed and will need to run buildconf before proceeding with the next steps. This is not necessary for official releases.)

---

[5] http://apr.apache.org
[6] http://httpd.apache.org/download.cgi
[7] http://httpd.apache.org/download.cgi#verify
[8] http://httpd.apache.org/dev/verification.html

To configure the source tree using all the default options, simply type ./
configure. To change the default options, configure accepts a variety of variables and command line options.

The most important option is the location --prefix where the Apache HTTP
Server is to be installed later, because Apache HTTPd has to be configured for
this location to work correctly. More fine-tuned control of the location of files
is possible with additional configure options (p. 18).

Also at this point, you can specify which features (p. 18) you want included
in Apache HTTPd by enabling and disabling modules (p. 801). The Apache
HTTP Server comes with a Base (p. 81) set of modules included by default.
Other modules are enabled using the --enable-*module* option, where *module*
is the name of the module with the mod_ string removed and with any underscore
converted to a dash. You can also choose to compile modules as shared objects
(DSOs) (p. 683) – which can be loaded or unloaded at runtime – by using
the option --enable-*module*=shared. Similarly, you can disable Base modules
with the --disable-*module* option. Be careful when using these options, since
configure cannot warn you if the module you specify does not exist; it will
simply ignore the option.

In addition, it is sometimes necessary to provide the configure script with
extra information about the location of your compiler, libraries, or header files.
This is done by passing either environment variables or command line options
to configure. For more information, see the configure manual page.

For a short impression of what possibilities you have, here is a typical example
which compiles Apache for the installation tree /sw/pkg/apache with a particular compiler and flags plus the two additional modules mod_rewrite and
mod_speling for later loading through the DSO mechanism:

```
$ CC="pgcc" CFLAGS="-02" \
./configure --prefix=/sw/pkg/apache \
--enable-rewrite=shared \
--enable-speling=shared
```

When configure is run it will take several minutes to test for the availability of
features on your system and build Makefiles which will later be used to compile
the server.

Details on all the different configure options are available on the configure
manual page.

30.1.6 Build

Now you can build the various parts which form the Apache HTTPd package
by simply running the command:

```
$ make
```

Please be patient here, since a base configuration takes several minutes to compile and the time will vary widely depending on your hardware and the number of modules that you have enabled.

30.1.7 Install

Now it's time to install the package under the configured installation *PREFIX* (see `--prefix` option above) by running:

```
$ make install
```

If you are upgrading, the installation will not overwrite your configuration files or documents.

30.1.8 Customize

Next, you can customize your Apache HTTP Server by editing the configuration files (p. 54) under *PREFIX*/conf/.

```
$ vi PREFIX/conf/httpd.conf
```

Have a look at the Apache HTTP Server manual under docs/manual/ or consult http://httpd.apache.org/docs/2.2/ for the most recent version of this manual and a complete reference of available configuration directives (p. 805).

30.1.9 Test

Now you can start (p. 49) your Apache HTTP Server by immediately running:

```
$ PREFIX/bin/apachectl -k start
```

and then you should be able to request your first document via URL http://localhost/. The web page you see is located under the `DocumentRoot`, which will usually be *PREFIX*/htdocs/. Then stop (p. 51) the server again by running:

```
$ PREFIX/bin/apachectl -k stop
```

30.1.10 Upgrading

The first step in upgrading is to read the release announcement and the file `CHANGES` in the source distribution to find any changes that may affect your site. When changing between major releases (for example, from 1.3 to 2.0 or from 2.0 to 2.2), there will likely be major differences in the compile-time and run-time configuration that will require manual adjustments. All modules will also need to be upgraded to accomodate changes in the module API.

Upgrading from one minor version to the next (for example, from 2.2.55 to 2.2.57) is easier. The `make install` process will not overwrite any of your existing documents, log files, or configuration files. In addition, the developers make every effort to avoid incompatible changes in the `configure` options, run-time configuration, or the module API between minor versions. In most cases you should be able to use an identical `configure` command line, an identical configuration file, and all of your modules should continue to work.

To upgrade across minor versions, start by finding the file `config.nice` in the build directory of your installed server or at the root of the source tree for your old install. This will contain the exact `configure` command line that you used to configure the source tree. Then to upgrade from one version to the next, you need only copy the `config.nice` file to the source tree of the new version, edit it to make any desired changes, and then run:

```
$ ./config.nice
$ make
$ make install
$ PREFIX/bin/apachectl -k graceful-stop
$ PREFIX/bin/apachectl -k start
```

You should always test any new version in your environment before putting it into production. For example, you can install and run the new version along side the old one by using a different --prefix and a different port (by adjusting the Listen directive) to test for any incompatibilities before doing the final upgrade.

30.2 Upgrading to 2.2 from 2.0

In order to assist folks upgrading, we maintain a document describing information critical to existing Apache users. These are intended to be brief notes, and you should be able to find more information in either the New Features (p. 783) document, or in the src/CHANGES file.

This section describes only the changes from 2.0 to 2.2. If you are upgrading from version 1.3, you should also consult the 1.3 to 2.0 upgrading document.[9]

See also:

▷ Overview of new features in Apache 2.2 (p. 783)

30.2.1 Compile-Time Configuration Changes

The compilation process is very similar to the one used in version 2.0. Your old configure command line (as found in build/config.nice in the installed server directory) can be used in some cases. The most significant change required will be to account for changes in module names, in particular for the authentication and authorization modules. Some details of changes:

- mod_imap has been renamed to mod_imagemap
- mod_auth has been split up into mod_auth_basic, mod_authn_file, mod_authz_user, and mod_authz_groupfile
- mod_access has been renamed to mod_authz_host
- mod_auth_ldap has been renamed to mod_authnz_ldap
- Upgraded to require the APR 1.0 API.
- Updated bundled PCRE version to 5.0

30.2.2 Run-Time Configuration Changes

Your existing version 2.0 config files and startup scripts can usually be used unchanged in version 2.2. Some small adjustments may be necessary for particular configurations as discussed below. In addition, if you dynamically load the standard modules using the LoadModule directive, then you will need to account for the module name changes mentioned above.

If you choose to use the new default configuration file for version 2.2, you will find that it has been greatly simplified by removing all but the most essential configuration settings. A set of example configuration settings for more advanced features is present in the conf/extra/ directory of the installed server. Default configuration files are installed in the conf/original directory.

Some runtime configuration changes that you may notice:

- The apachectl option startssl is no longer available. To enable SSL support, you should edit httpd.conf to include the relevant

---

[9]http://httpd.apache.org/docs/2.0/upgrading.html

mod_ssl directives and then use `apachectl start` to start the server. An example configuration to activate mod_ssl has been included in `conf/extra/httpd-ssl.conf`.

- The default setting of `UseCanonicalName` is now `Off`. If you did not have this directive in your config file, you can add `UseCanonicalName On` to retain the old behavior.

- The module `mod_userdir` will no longer act on requests unless a `UserDir` directive specifying a directory name is present in the config file. To restore the old default behavior, place the directive `UserDir public_html` in your config file.

- The directive `AuthDigestFile` from `mod_auth_digest` has been merged with `AuthUserFile` and is now part of `mod_authn_file`.

30.2.3 Misc Changes

- The module `mod_cache`, which was experimental in Apache 2.0, is now a standard module.

- The module `mod_disk_cache`, which was experimental in Apache 2.0, is now a standard module.

- The module `mod_mem_cache`, which was experimental in Apache 2.0, is now a standard module.

- The module `mod_charset_lite`, which was experimental in Apache 2.0, is now a standard module.

- The module `mod_dumpio`, which was experimental in Apache 2.0, is now a standard module.

30.2.4 Third Party Modules

Many third-party modules designed for version 2.0 will work unchanged with the Apache HTTP Server version 2.2. But all modules must be recompiled before being loaded.

30.3 Overview of new features in Apache 2.2

This section describes some of the major changes between the 2.0 and 2.2 versions of the Apache HTTP Server. For new features since version 1.3, see the 2.0 new features (p. 787) document.

30.3.1 Core Enhancements

Authn/Authz The bundled authentication and authorization modules have been refactored. The new mod_authn_alias module can greatly simplify certain authentication configurations. See module name changes, and the developer changes for more information about how these changes affects users and module writers.

Caching mod_cache, mod_disk_cache, and mod_mem_cache have undergone a lot of changes, and are now considered production-quality. htcacheclean has been introduced to clean up mod_disk_cache setups.

Configuration The default configuration layout has been simplified and modularised. Configuration snippets which can be used to enable commonly-used features are now bundled with Apache, and can be easily added to the main server config.

Graceful stop The prefork, worker and event MPMs now allow httpd to be shutdown gracefully via the graceful-stop (p. 51) signal. The GracefulShutdownTimeout directive has been added to specify an optional timeout, after which httpd will terminate regardless of the status of any requests being served.

Proxying The new mod_proxy_balancer module provides load balancing services for mod_proxy. The new mod_proxy_ajp module adds support for the Apache JServ Protocol version 1.3 used by Apache Tomcat[10].

Regular Expression Library Updated Version 5.0 of the Perl Compatible Regular Expression Library[11] (PCRE) is now included. httpd can be configured to use a system installation of PCRE by passing the --with-pcre flag to configure.

Smart Filtering mod_filter introduces dynamic configuration to the output filter chain. It enables filters to be conditionally inserted, based on any Request or Response header or environment variable, and dispenses with the more problematic dependencies and ordering problems in the 2.0 architecture.

Large File Support httpd is now built with support for files larger than 2GB on modern 32-bit Unix systems. Support for handling >2GB request bodies has also been added.

Event MPM The event MPM uses a separate thread to handle Keep Alive requests and accepting connections. Keep Alive requests have traditionally

---

[10]http://jakarta.apache.org/tomcat/
[11]http://www.pcre.org/

required httpd to dedicate a worker to handle it. This dedicated worker could not be used again until the Keep Alive timeout was reached.

SQL Database Support mod_dbd, together with the apr_dbd framework, brings direct SQL support to modules that need it. Supports connection pooling in threaded MPMs.

30.3.2 Module Enhancements

Authn/Authz Modules in the aaa directory have been renamed and offer better support for digest authentication. For example, mod_auth is now split into mod_auth_basic and mod_authn_file; mod_auth_dbm is now called mod_authn_dbm; mod_access has been renamed mod_authz_host. There is also a new mod_authn_alias module for simplifying certain authentication configurations.

mod_authnz_ldap This module is a port of the 2.0 mod_auth_ldap module to the 2.2 Authn/Authz framework. New features include using LDAP attribute values and complicated search filters in the Require directive.

mod_authz_owner A new module that authorizes access to files based on the owner of the file on the file system

mod_version A new module that allows configuration blocks to be enabled based on the version number of the running server.

mod_info Added a new ?config argument which will show the configuration directives as parsed by Apache, including their file name and line number. The module also shows the order of all request hooks and additional build information, similar to httpd -V.

mod_ssl Added a support for RFC 2817[12], which allows connections to upgrade from clear text to TLS encryption.

mod_imagemap mod_imap has been renamed to mod_imagemap to avoid user confusion.

30.3.3 Program Enhancements

httpd A new command line option -M has been added that lists all modules that are loaded based on the current configuration. Unlike the -l option, this list includes DSOs loaded via mod_so.

httxt2dbm A new program used to generate dbm files from text input, for use in RewriteMap with the dbm map type.

30.3.4 Module Developer Changes

APR 1.0 API Apache 2.2 uses the APR 1.0 API. All deprecated functions and symbols have been removed from APR and APR-Util. For details, see the APR Website[13].

---

[12]http://www.ietf.org/rfc/rfc2817.txt
[13]http://apr.apache.org/

Authn/Authz The bundled authentication and authorization modules have been renamed along the following lines:

- mod_auth_* -> Modules that implement an HTTP authentication mechanism
- mod_authn_* -> Modules that provide a backend authentication provider
- mod_authz_* -> Modules that implement authorization (or access)
- mod_authnz_* -> Module that implements both authentication & authorization

There is a new authentication backend provider scheme which greatly eases the construction of new authentication backends.

Connection Error Logging A new function, ap_log_cerror has been added to log errors that occur with the client's connection. When logged, the message includes the client IP address.

Test Configuration Hook Added A new hook, test_config has been added to aid modules that want to execute special code only when the user passes -t to httpd.

Set Threaded MPM's Stacksize A new directive, ThreadStackSize has been added to set the stack size on all threaded MPMs. This is required for some third-party modules on platforms with small default thread stack size.

Protocol handling for output filters In the past, every filter has been responsible for ensuring that it generates the correct response headers where it affects them. Filters can now delegate common protocol management to mod_filter, using the ap_register_output_filter_protocol or ap_filter_protocol calls.

Monitor hook added Monitor hook enables modules to run regular/scheduled jobs in the parent (root) process.

Regular expression API changes The pcreposix.h header is no longer available; it is replaced by the new ap_regex.h header. The POSIX.2 regex.h implementation exposed by the old header is now available under the ap_ namespace from ap_regex.h. Calls to regcomp, regexec and so on can be replaced by calls to ap_regcomp, ap_regexec.

DBD Framework (SQL Database API) With Apache 1.x and 2.0, modules requiring an SQL backend had to take responsibility for managing it themselves. Apart from reinventing the wheel, this can be very inefficient, for example when several modules each maintain their own connections.

Apache 2.1 and later provides the ap_dbd API for managing database connections (including optimised strategies for threaded and unthreaded MPMs), while APR 1.2 and later provides the apr_dbd API for interacting with the database.

New modules SHOULD now use these APIs for all SQL database operations. Existing applications SHOULD be upgraded to use it where
feasible, either transparently or as a recommended option to their users.

30.4 Overview of new features in Apache 2.0

This section describes some of the major changes between the 1.3 and 2.0 versions of the Apache HTTP Server.

See also:

 ▷ Upgrading to 2.0 from 1.3 (p. 781)

30.4.1 Core Enhancements

Unix Threading On Unix systems with POSIX threads support, Apache can now run in a hybrid multiprocess, multithreaded mode. This improves scalability for many, but not all configurations.

New Build System The build system has been rewritten from scratch to be based on autoconf and libtool. This makes Apache's configuration system more similar to that of other packages.

Multiprotocol Support Apache now has some of the infrastructure in place to support serving multiple protocols. mod_echo has been written as an example.

Better support for non-Unix platforms Apache 2.0 is faster and more stable on non-Unix platforms such as BeOS, OS/2, and Windows. With the introduction of platform-specific multi-processing modules (p. 703) (MPMs) and the Apache Portable Runtime (APR), these platforms are now implemented in their native API, avoiding the often buggy and poorly performing POSIX-emulation layers.

New Apache API The API for modules has changed significantly for 2.0. Many of the module-ordering/-priority problems from 1.3 should be gone. 2.0 does much of this automatically, and module ordering is now done per-hook to allow more flexibility. Also, new calls have been added that provide additional module capabilities without patching the core Apache server.

IPv6 Support On systems where IPv6 is supported by the underlying Apache Portable Runtime library, Apache gets IPv6 listening sockets by default. Additionally, the Listen, NameVirtualHost, and VirtualHost directives support IPv6 numeric address strings (e.g., "Listen [2001:db8::1]:8080").

Filtering Apache modules may now be written as filters which act on the stream of content as it is delivered to or from the server. This allows, for example, the output of CGI scripts to be parsed for Server Side Include directives using the INCLUDES filter in mod_include. The module mod_ext_filter allows external programs to act as filters in much the same way that CGI programs can act as handlers.

Multilanguage Error Responses Error response messages to the browser are now provided in several languages, using SSI documents. They may be customized by the administrator to achieve a consistent look and feel.

Simplified configuration Many confusing directives have been simplified. The often confusing Port and BindAddress directives are gone; only the Listen directive is used for IP address binding; the ServerName directive specifies the server name and port number only for redirection and vhost recognition.

Native Windows NT Unicode Support Apache 2.0 on Windows NT now uses utf-8 for all filename encodings. These directly translate to the underlying Unicode file system, providing multilanguage support for all Windows NT-based installations, including Windows 2000 and Windows XP. *This support does not extend to Windows 95, 98 or ME, which continue to use the machine's local codepage for filesystem access.*

Regular Expression Library Updated Apache 2.0 includes the Perl Compatible Regular Expression Library[14] (PCRE). All regular expression evaluation now uses the more powerful Perl 5 syntax.

30.4.2 Module Enhancements

mod_ssl New module in Apache 2.0. This module is an interface to the SSL/TLS encryption protocols provided by OpenSSL.

mod_dav New module in Apache 2.0. This module implements the HTTP Distributed Authoring and Versioning (DAV) specification for posting and maintaining web content.

mod_deflate New module in Apache 2.0. This module allows supporting browsers to request that content be compressed before delivery, saving network bandwidth.

mod_auth_ldap New module in Apache 2.0.41. This module allows an LDAP database to be used to store credentials for HTTP Basic Authentication. A companion module, mod_ldap provides connection pooling and results caching.

mod_auth_digest Includes additional support for session caching across processes using shared memory.

mod_charset_lite New module in Apache 2.0. This experimental module allows for character set translation or recoding.

mod_file_cache New module in Apache 2.0. This module includes the functionality of mod_mmap_static in Apache 1.3, plus adds further caching abilities.

mod_headers This module is much more flexible in Apache 2.0. It can now modify request headers used by mod_proxy, and it can conditionally set response headers.

mod_proxy The proxy module has been completely rewritten to take advantage of the new filter infrastructure and to implement a more reliable,

---

[14]http://www.pcre.org/

HTTP/1.1 compliant proxy. In addition, new <Proxy> configuration sections provide more readable (and internally faster) control of proxied sites; overloaded <Directory "proxy:..."> configuration are not supported. The module is now divided into specific protocol support modules including proxy_connect, proxy_ftp and proxy_http.

mod_negotiation A new ForceLanguagePriority directive can be used to assure that the client receives a single document in all cases, rather than NOT ACCEPTABLE or MULTIPLE CHOICES responses. In addition, the negotiation and MultiViews algorithms have been cleaned up to provide more consistent results and a new form of type map that can include document content is provided.

mod_autoindex Autoindex'ed directory listings can now be configured to use HTML tables for cleaner formatting, and allow finer-grained control of sorting, including version-sorting, and wildcard filtering of the directory listing.

mod_include New directives allow the default start and end tags for SSI elements to be changed and allow for error and time format configuration to take place in the main configuration file rather than in the SSI document. Results from regular expression parsing and grouping (now based on Perl's regular expression syntax) can be retrieved using mod_include's variables $0 .. $9.

mod_auth_dbm Now supports multiple types of DBM-like databases using the AuthDBMType directive.

30.5 The Apache License, Version 2.0

Apache License
Version 2.0, January 2004
http://www.apache.org/licenses/

TERMS AND CONDITIONS FOR USE, REPRODUCTION, AND DISTRI-
BUTION

1. **Definitions**

    "License" shall mean the terms and conditions for use, reproduction, and
    distribution as defined by Sections 1 through 9 of this section.

    "Licensor" shall mean the copyright owner or entity authorized by the
    copyright owner that is granting the License.

    "Legal Entity" shall mean the union of the acting entity and all other
    entities that control, are controlled by, or are under common control with
    that entity. For the purposes of this definition, "control" means (i) the
    power, direct or indirect, to cause the direction or management of such
    entity, whether by contract or otherwise, or (ii) ownership of fifty percent
    (50%) or more of the outstanding shares, or (iii) beneficial ownership of
    such entity.

    "You" (or "Your") shall mean an individual or Legal Entity exercising
    permissions granted by this License.

    "Source" form shall mean the preferred form for making modifications,
    including but not limited to software source code, documentation source,
    and configuration files.

    "Object" form shall mean any form resulting from mechanical transforma-
    tion or translation of a Source form, including but not limited to compiled
    object code, generated documentation, and conversions to other media
    types.

    "Work" shall mean the work of authorship, whether in Source or Object
    form, made available under the License, as indicated by a copyright notice
    that is included in or attached to the work (an example is provided in the
    Appendix below).

    "Derivative Works" shall mean any work, whether in Source or Object
    form, that is based on (or derived from) the Work and for which the
    editorial revisions, annotations, elaborations, or other modifications rep-
    resent, as a whole, an original work of authorship. For the purposes of this
    License, Derivative Works shall not include works that remain separable
    from, or merely link (or bind by name) to the interfaces of, the Work and
    Derivative Works thereof.

    "Contribution" shall mean any work of authorship, including the original
    version of the Work and any modifications or additions to that Work or

Derivative Works thereof, that is intentionally submitted to Licensor for inclusion in the Work by the copyright owner or by an individual or Legal Entity authorized to submit on behalf of the copyright owner. For the purposes of this definition, "submitted" means any form of electronic, verbal, or written communication sent to the Licensor or its representatives, including but not limited to communication on electronic mailing lists, source code control systems, and issue tracking systems that are managed by, or on behalf of, the Licensor for the purpose of discussing and improving the Work, but excluding communication that is conspicuously marked or otherwise designated in writing by the copyright owner as "Not a Contribution."

"Contributor" shall mean Licensor and any individual or Legal Entity on behalf of whom a Contribution has been received by Licensor and subsequently incorporated within the Work.

2. **Grant of Copyright License.** Subject to the terms and conditions of this License, each Contributor hereby grants to You a perpetual, worldwide, non-exclusive, no-charge, royalty-free, irrevocable copyright license to reproduce, prepare Derivative Works of, publicly display, publicly perform, sublicense, and distribute the Work and such Derivative Works in Source or Object form.

3. **Grant of Patent License.** Subject to the terms and conditions of this License, each Contributor hereby grants to You a perpetual, worldwide, non-exclusive, no-charge, royalty-free, irrevocable (except as stated in this section) patent license to make, have made, use, offer to sell, sell, import, and otherwise transfer the Work, where such license applies only to those patent claims licensable by such Contributor that are necessarily infringed by their Contribution(s) alone or by combination of their Contribution(s) with the Work to which such Contribution(s) was submitted. If You institute patent litigation against any entity (including a cross-claim or counterclaim in a lawsuit) alleging that the Work or a Contribution incorporated within the Work constitutes direct or contributory patent infringement, then any patent licenses granted to You under this License for that Work shall terminate as of the date such litigation is filed.

4. **Redistribution.** You may reproduce and distribute copies of the Work or Derivative Works thereof in any medium, with or without modifications, and in Source or Object form, provided that You meet the following conditions:

   a) You must give any other recipients of the Work or Derivative Works a copy of this License; and

   b) You must cause any modified files to carry prominent notices stating that You changed the files; and

   c) You must retain, in the Source form of any Derivative Works that You distribute, all copyright, patent, trademark, and attribution notices from the Source form of the Work, excluding those notices that do not pertain to any part of the Derivative Works; and

d) If the Work includes a "NOTICE" text file as part of its distribution, then any Derivative Works that You distribute must include a readable copy of the attribution notices contained within such NOTICE file, excluding those notices that do not pertain to any part of the Derivative Works, in at least one of the following places: within a NOTICE text file distributed as part of the Derivative Works; within the Source form or documentation, if provided along with the Derivative Works; or, within a display generated by the Derivative Works, if and wherever such third-party notices normally appear. The contents of the NOTICE file are for informational purposes only and do not modify the License. You may add Your own attribution notices within Derivative Works that You distribute, alongside or as an addendum to the NOTICE text from the Work, provided that such additional attribution notices cannot be construed as modifying the License.

You may add Your own copyright statement to Your modifications and may provide additional or different license terms and conditions for use, reproduction, or distribution of Your modifications, or for any such Derivative Works as a whole, provided Your use, reproduction, and distribution of the Work otherwise complies with the conditions stated in this License.

5. **Submission of Contributions.** Unless You explicitly state otherwise, any Contribution intentionally submitted for inclusion in the Work by You to the Licensor shall be under the terms and conditions of this License, without any additional terms or conditions. Notwithstanding the above, nothing herein shall supersede or modify the terms of any separate license agreement you may have executed with Licensor regarding such Contributions.

6. **Trademarks.** This License does not grant permission to use the trade names, trademarks, service marks, or product names of the Licensor, except as required for reasonable and customary use in describing the origin of the Work and reproducing the content of the NOTICE file.

7. **Disclaimer of Warranty.** Unless required by applicable law or agreed to in writing, Licensor provides the Work (and each Contributor provides its Contributions) on an "AS IS" BASIS, WITHOUT WARRANTIES OR CONDITIONS OF ANY KIND, either express or implied, including, without limitation, any warranties or conditions of TITLE, NON-INFRINGEMENT, MERCHANTABILITY, or FITNESS FOR A PARTICULAR PURPOSE. You are solely responsible for determining the appropriateness of using or redistributing the Work and assume any risks associated with Your exercise of permissions under this License.

8. **Limitation of Liability.** In no event and under no legal theory, whether in tort (including negligence), contract, or otherwise, unless required by applicable law (such as deliberate and grossly negligent acts) or agreed to in writing, shall any Contributor be liable to You for damages, including any direct, indirect, special, incidental, or consequential damages of any

character arising as a result of this License or out of the use or inability to use the Work (including but not limited to damages for loss of goodwill, work stoppage, computer failure or malfunction, or any and all other commercial damages or losses), even if such Contributor has been advised of the possibility of such damages.

9. **Accepting Warranty or Additional Liability.** While redistributing the Work or Derivative Works thereof, You may choose to offer, and charge a fee for, acceptance of support, warranty, indemnity, or other liability obligations and/or rights consistent with this License. However, in accepting such obligations, You may act only on Your own behalf and on Your sole responsibility, not on behalf of any other Contributor, and only if You agree to indemnify, defend, and hold each Contributor harmless for any liability incurred by, or claims asserted against, such Contributor by reason of your accepting any such warranty or additional liability.

END OF TERMS AND CONDITIONS

APPENDIX: How to apply the Apache License to your work.

To apply the Apache License to your work, attach the following boilerplate notice, with the fields enclosed by brackets "[]" replaced with your own identifying information. (Don't include the brackets!) The text should be enclosed in the appropriate comment syntax for the file format. We also recommend that a file or class name and description of purpose be included on the same "printed page" as the copyright notice for easier identification within third-party archives.

```
Copyright [yyyy] [name of copyright owner]

Licensed under the Apache License, Version 2.0 (the "License");
you may not use this file except in compliance with the License.
You may obtain a copy of the License at

    http://www.apache.org/licenses/LICENSE-2.0

Unless required by applicable law or agreed to in writing,
software distributed under the License is distributed on an "AS
IS" BASIS, WITHOUT WARRANTIES OR CONDITIONS OF ANY KIND, either
express or implied. See the License for the specific language
governing permissions and limitations under the License.
```

30.6 NOTICE

The NOTICE file from the Apache distribution is reproduced here:

Apache HTTP Server
Copyright 2009 The Apache Software Foundation.

This product includes software developed at The Apache Software Foundation (`http://www.apache.org/`).

Portions of this software were developed at the National Center for Supercomputing Applications (NCSA) at the University of Illinois at Urbana-Champaign.

This software contains code derived from the RSA Data Security Inc. MD5 Message-Digest Algorithm, including various modifications by Spyglass Inc., Carnegie Mellon University, and Bell Communications Research, Inc (Bellcore).

31 Glossary and Index

31.1 Glossary

This glossary defines some of the common terminology related to Apache in particular, and web serving in general. More information on each concept is provided in the links.

31.1.1 Definitions

Access Control The restriction of access to network realms. In an Apache context usually the restriction of access to certain *URLs*.
See: Authentication, Authorization, and Access Control (p. 629)

Algorithm An unambiguous formula or set of rules for solving a problem in a finite number of steps. Algorithms for encryption are usually called **Ciphers**.

APache eXtension Tool (apxs) A perl script that aids in compiling module sources into Dynamic Shared Objects (DSOs) and helps install them in the Apache Web server.
See: Manual Page: apxs

Apache Portable Runtime (APR) A set of libraries providing many of the basic interfaces between the server and the operating system. APR is developed parallel to the Apache HTTP Server as an independent project.
See: Apache Portable Runtime Project[1]

Authentication The positive identification of a network entity such as a server, a client, or a user.
See: Authentication, Authorization, and Access Control (p. 629)

Certificate A data record used for authenticating network entities such as a server or a client. A certificate contains X.509 information pieces about its owner (called the subject) and the signing Certification Authority (called the issuer), plus the owner's public key and the signature made by the CA. Network entities verify these signatures using CA certificates.
See: SSL/TLS Encryption (p. 616)

Certificate Signing Request (CSR) An unsigned certificate for submission to a Certification Authority, which signs it with the Private Key of their CA *Certificate*. Once the CSR is signed, it becomes a real certificate.
See: SSL/TLS Encryption (p. 616)

Certification Authority (CA) A trusted third party whose purpose is to sign certificates for network entities it has authenticated using secure means. Other network entities can check the signature to verify that a CA has authenticated the bearer of a certificate.
See: SSL/TLS Encryption (p. 616)

---

[1] http://apr.apache.org/

Cipher An algorithm or system for data encryption. Examples are DES, IDEA, RC4, etc.
See: SSL/TLS Encryption (p. 616)

Ciphertext The result after Plaintext is passed through a Cipher.
See: SSL/TLS Encryption (p. 616)

Common Gateway Interface (CGI) A standard definition for an interface between a web server and an external program that allows the external program to service requests. The interface was originally defined by NCSA[2] but there is also an RFC project[3].
See: Dynamic Content with CGI (p. 651)

Configuration Directive See: Directive

Configuration File A text file containing Directives that control the configuration of Apache.
See: Configuration Files (p. 54)

CONNECT An HTTP method for proxying raw data channels over HTTP. It can be used to encapsulate other protocols, such as the SSL protocol.

Context An area in the configuration files where certain types of directives are allowed.
See: Terms Used to Describe Apache Directives (p. 83)

Digital Signature An encrypted text block that validates a certificate or other file. A Certification Authority creates a signature by generating a hash of the *Public Key* embedded in a *Certificate*, then encrypting the hash with its own *Private Key*. Only the CA's public key can decrypt the signature, verifying that the CA has authenticated the network entity that owns the *Certificate*.
See: SSL/TLS Encryption (p. 616)

Directive A configuration command that controls one or more aspects of Apache's behavior. Directives are placed in the Configuration File
See: Directive Index (p. 805)

Dynamic Shared Object (DSO) Modules compiled separately from the Apache httpd binary that can be loaded on-demand.
See: Dynamic Shared Object Support (p. 683)

Environment Variable (env-variable) Named variables managed by the operating system shell and used to store information and communicate between programs. Apache also contains internal variables that are referred to as environment variables, but are stored in internal Apache structures, rather than in the shell environment.
See: Environment Variables in Apache (p. 705)

Export-Crippled Diminished in cryptographic strength (and security) in order to comply with the United States' Export Administration Regulations

---

[2]http://hoohoo.ncsa.uiuc.edu/cgi/overview.html
[3]http://www.w3.org/CGI/

(EAR). Export-crippled cryptographic software is limited to a small key size, resulting in *Ciphertext* which usually can be decrypted by brute force.
See: SSL/TLS Encryption (p. 616)

Filter A process that is applied to data that is sent or received by the server. Input filters process data sent by the client to the server, while output filters process documents on the server before they are sent to the client. For example, the INCLUDES output filter processes documents for Server Side Includes.
See: Filters (p. 715)

Fully-Qualified Domain-Name (FQDN) The unique name of a network entity, consisting of a hostname and a domain name that can resolve to an IP address. For example, www is a hostname, example.com is a domain name, and www.example.com is a fully-qualified domain name.

Handler An internal Apache representation of the action to be performed when a file is called. Generally, files have implicit handlers, based on the file type. Normally, all files are simply served by the server, but certain file types are "handled" separately. For example, the cgi-script handler designates files to be processed as CGIs.
See: Apache's Handler Use (p. 713)

Hash A mathematical one-way, irreversible algorithm generating a string with fixed-length from another string of any length. Different input strings will usually produce different hashes (depending on the hash function).

Header The part of the HTTP request and response that is sent before the actual content, and that contains meta-information describing the content.

.htaccess A configuration file that is placed inside the web tree and applies configuration directives to the directory where it is placed and all sub-directories. Despite its name, this file can hold almost any type of directive, not just access-control directives.
See: Configuration Files (p. 54)

httpd.conf The main Apache configuration file. The default location is /usr/local/apache2/conf/httpd.conf, but it may be moved using run-time or compile-time configuration.
See: Configuration Files (p. 54)

HyperText Transfer Protocol (HTTP) The standard transmission protocol used on the World Wide Web. Apache implements version 1.1 of the protocol, referred to as HTTP/1.1 and defined by RFC 2616[4].

HTTPS The HyperText Transfer Protocol (Secure), the standard encrypted communication mechanism on the World Wide Web. This is actually just HTTP over SSL.
See: SSL/TLS Encryption (p. 616)

---

[4]http://ietf.org/rfc/rfc2616.txt

Method In the context of HTTP, an action to perform on a resource, specified on the request line by the client. Some of the methods available in HTTP are GET, POST, and PUT.

Message Digest A hash of a message, which can be used to verify that the contents of the message have not been altered in transit.
See: SSL/TLS Encryption (p. 616)

MIME-type A way to describe the kind of document being transmitted. Its name comes from that fact that its format is borrowed from the Multipurpose Internet Mail Extensions. It consists of a major type and a minor type, separated by a slash. Some examples are text/html, image/gif, and application/octet-stream. In HTTP, the MIME-type is transmitted in the Content-Type header.
See: mod_mime (p. 348)

Module An independent part of a program. Much of Apache's functionality is contained in modules that you can choose to include or exclude. Modules that are compiled into the Apache httpd binary are called **static modules**, while modules that are stored separately and can be optionally loaded at run-time are called **dynamic modules** or DSOs. Modules that are included by default are called **base modules**. Many modules are available for Apache that are not distributed as part of the Apache HTTP Server tarball. These are referred to as **third-party modules**.
See: Module Index (p. 801)

Module Magic Number (MMN) Module Magic Number is a constant defined in the Apache source code that is associated with binary compatibility of modules. It is changed when internal Apache structures, function calls and other significant parts of API change in such a way that binary compatibility cannot be guaranteed any more. On MMN change, all third party modules have to be at least recompiled, sometimes even slightly changed in order to work with the new version of Apache.

OpenSSL The Open Source toolkit for SSL/TLS
See http://www.openssl.org/#

Pass Phrase The word or phrase that protects private key files. It prevents unauthorized users from encrypting them. Usually it's just the secret encryption/decryption key used for Ciphers.
See: SSL/TLS Encryption (p. 616)

Plaintext The unencrypted text.

Private Key The secret key in a Public Key Cryptography system, used to decrypt incoming messages and sign outgoing ones.
See: SSL/TLS Encryption (p. 616)

Proxy An intermediate server that sits between the client and the *origin server*. It accepts requests from clients, transmits those requests on to the origin server, and then returns the response from the origin server to the client. If several clients request the same content, the proxy can deliver that

content from its cache, rather than requesting it from the origin server each time, thereby reducing response time.
See: mod_proxy (p. 374)

Public Key The publicly available key in a Public Key Cryptography system, used to encrypt messages bound for its owner and to decrypt signatures made by its owner.
See: SSL/TLS Encryption (p. 616)

Public Key Cryptography The study and application of asymmetric encryption systems, which use one key for encryption and another for decryption. A corresponding pair of such keys constitutes a key pair. Also called Asymmetric Cryptography.
See: SSL/TLS Encryption (p. 616)

Regular Expression (Regex) A way of describing a pattern in text - for example, "all the words that begin with the letter A" or "every 10-digit phone number" or even "Every sentence with two commas in it, and no capital letter Q". Regular expressions are useful in Apache because they let you apply certain attributes against collections of files or resources in very flexible ways - for example, all .gif and .jpg files under any "images" directory could be written as "/images/.*(jpg|gif)$". Apache uses Perl Compatible Regular Expressions provided by the PCRE[5] library. You can find more documentation about PCRE's regular expression syntax at that site, or at Wikipedia[6].

Reverse Proxy A proxy server that appears to the client as if it is an *origin server*. This is useful to hide the real origin server from the client for security reasons, or to load balance.

Secure Sockets Layer (SSL) A protocol created by Netscape Communications Corporation for general communication authentication and encryption over TCP/IP networks. The most popular usage is *HTTPS*, i.e. the HyperText Transfer Protocol (HTTP) over SSL.
See: SSL/TLS Encryption (p. 616)

Server Name Indication (SNI) An SSL function that allows passing the desired server hostname in the initial SSL handshake message, so that the web server can select the correct virtual host configuration to use in processing the SSL handshake. It was added to SSL starting with the TLS extensions, RFC 3546.
See: the SSL FAQ (p. 616) and RFC 3546[7]

Server Side Includes (SSI) A technique for embedding processing directives inside HTML files.
See: Introduction to Server Side Includes (p. 659)

Session The context information of a communication in general.

---

[5] http://www.pcre.org/
[6] http://en.wikipedia.org/wiki/PCRE
[7] http://www.ietf.org/rfc/rfc3546.txt

SSLeay The original SSL/TLS implementation library developed by Eric A. Young

Symmetric Cryptography The study and application of *Ciphers* that use a single secret key for both encryption and decryption operations.
See: SSL/TLS Encryption (p. 616)

Tarball A package of files gathered together using the tar utility. Apache distributions are stored in compressed tar archives or using pkzip.

Transport Layer Security (TLS) The successor protocol to SSL, created by the Internet Engineering Task Force (IETF) for general communication authentication and encryption over TCP/IP networks. TLS version 1 is nearly identical with SSL version 3.
See: SSL/TLS Encryption (p. 616)

Uniform Resource Locator (URL) The name/address of a resource on the Internet. This is the common informal term for what is formally called a Uniform Resource Identifier. URLs are usually made up of a scheme, like http or https, a hostname, and a path. A URL for this page might be http://httpd.apache.org/docs/2.2/glossary.html.

Uniform Resource Identifier (URI) A compact string of characters for identifying an abstract or physical resource. It is formally defined by RFC 2396[8]. URIs used on the world-wide web are commonly referred to as URLs.

Virtual Hosting Serving multiple websites using a single instance of Apache. *IP virtual hosting* differentiates between websites based on their IP address, while *name-based virtual hosting* uses only the name of the host and can therefore host many sites on the same IP address.
See: Apache Virtual Host documentation (p. 541)

X.509 An authentication certificate scheme recommended by the International Telecommunication Union (ITU-T) which is used for SSL/TLS authentication.
See: SSL/TLS Encryption (p. 616)

---

[8]http://www.ietf.org/rfc/rfc2396.txt

31.2 Module Index

Below is a list of all of the modules that come as part of the Apache distribution. See also the complete alphabetical list of all Apache directives (p. 805).

See also:

▷ Multi-Processing Modules (MPMs) (p. 703)

▷ Directive Quick Reference (p. 805)

Core Features and Multi-Processing Modules

core (p. 87) Core Apache HTTP Server features that are always available

mpm_common (p. 516) A collection of directives that are implemented by more than one multi-processing module (MPM)

beos (p. 514) This Multi-Processing Module is optimized for BeOS.

event (p. 531) An experimental variant of the standard worker MPM

mpm_netware Multi-Processing Module implementing an exclusively threaded web server optimized for Novell NetWare

mpmt_os2 Hybrid multi-process, multi-threaded MPM for OS/2

prefork (p. 533) Implements a non-threaded, pre-forking web server

mpm_winnt (p. 536) This Multi-Processing Module is optimized for Windows NT.

worker (p. 537) Multi-Processing Module implementing a hybrid multi-threaded multi-process web server

Other Modules

mod_actions (p. 138) This module provides for executing CGI scripts based on media type or request method.

mod_alias (p. 141) Provides for mapping different parts of the host filesystem in the document tree and for URL redirection

mod_asis (p. 148) Sends files that contain their own HTTP headers

mod_authnz_ldap (p. 172) Allows an LDAP directory to be used to store the database for HTTP Basic authentication.

mod_authn_alias (p. 158) Provides the ability to create extended authentication providers based on actual providers

mod_authn_anon (p. 160) Allows "anonymous" user access to authenticated areas

mod_authn_dbd (p. 164) User authentication using an SQL database

mod_authn_dbm (p. 167) User authentication using DBM files

mod_authn_default (p. 169) Authentication fallback module

mod_authn_file (p. 170) User authentication using text files

mod_authz_dbm (p. 187) Group authorization using DBM files

mod_authz_default (p. 190) Authorization fallback module

mod_authz_groupfile (p. 191) Group authorization using plaintext files

mod_authz_host (p. 193) Group authorizations based on host (name or IP address)

mod_authz_owner (p. 198) Authorization based on file ownership

mod_authz_user (p. 201) User Authorization

mod_auth_basic (p. 150) Basic authentication

mod_auth_digest (p. 152) User authentication using MD5 Digest Authentication.

mod_autoindex (p. 202) Generates directory indexes, automatically, similar to the Unix ls command or the Win32 dir shell command

mod_cache (p. 215) Content cache keyed to URIs.

mod_cern_meta (p. 227) CERN httpd metafile semantics

mod_cgi (p. 229) Execution of CGI scripts

mod_cgid (p. 233) Execution of CGI scripts using an external CGI daemon

mod_charset_lite (p. 235) Specify character set translation or recoding

mod_dav (p. 238) Distributed Authoring and Versioning (WebDAV[9]) functionality

mod_dav_fs (p. 242) filesystem provider for mod_dav

mod_dav_lock (p. 243) generic locking module for mod_dav

mod_dbd (p. 245) Manages SQL database connections

mod_deflate (p. 251) Compress content before it is delivered to the client

mod_dir (p. 257) Provides for "trailing slash" redirects and serving directory index files

mod_disk_cache (p. 260) Content cache storage manager keyed to URIs

mod_dumpio (p. 263) Dumps all I/O to error log as desired.

mod_echo (p. 265) A simple echo server to illustrate protocol modules

mod_env (p. 266) Modifies the environment which is passed to CGI scripts and SSI pages

mod_example (p. 268) Illustrates the Apache module API

mod_expires (p. 270) Generation of Expires and Cache-Control HTTP headers according to user-specified criteria

mod_ext_filter (p. 274) Pass the response body through an external program before delivery to the client

---

[9]http://www.webdav.org/

mod_so (p. 453) Loading of executable code and modules into the server at start-up or restart time

mod_speling (p. 456) Attempts to correct mistaken URLs that users might have entered by ignoring capitalization and by allowing up to one misspelling

mod_ssl (p. 458) Strong cryptography using the Secure Sockets Layer (SSL) and Transport Layer Security (TLS) protocols

mod_status (p. 492) Provides information on server activity and performance

mod_substitute (p. 495) Perform search and replace operations on response bodies

mod_suexec (p. 497) Allows CGI scripts to run as a specified user and Group

mod_unique_id (p. 498) Provides an environment variable with a unique identifier for each request

mod_userdir (p. 501) User-specific directories

mod_usertrack (p. 504) *Clickstream* logging of user activity on a site

mod_version (p. 508) Version dependent configuration

mod_vhost_alias (p. 510) Provides for dynamically configured mass virtual hosting

31.3 Directive Quick Reference

The directive quick reference shows the usage, default, status, and context of each Apache configuration directive. For more information about each of these, see the Directive Dictionary (p. 83).

The first line of each entry gives the directive name and usage. The default value of the directive is shown in the right hand column, if a default exists. If the default is too large to display, the first characters will be followed by "+".

The contexts where the directive is allowed, and the status of the directive, are shown in square brackets using the following abbreviations:

s	server config	C	Core
v	virtual host	M	MPM
d	directory	B	Base
h	.htaccess	E	Extension
		X	Experimental

`AcceptFilter` *protocol accept_filter*   [s,C]
Configures optimizations for a Protocol's Listener Sockets. (p. 88)

`AcceptMutex Default|`*method*   Default [s,M]
Method that Apache uses to serialize multiple children accepting requests on network sockets. (p. 516)

`AcceptPathInfo On|Off|Default`   Default [svdh,C]
Resources accept trailing pathname information. (p. 89)

`AccessFileName` *filename* `[`*filename*`]` ...   .htaccess [sv,C]
Name of the distributed configuration file. (p. 90)

`Action` *action-type cgi-script* `[virtual]`   [svdh,B]
Activates a CGI script for a particular handler or content-type. (p. 138)

`AddAlt` *string file* `[`*file*`]` ...   [svdh,B]
Alternate text to display for a file, instead of an icon selected by filename. (p. 204)

`AddAltByEncoding` *string MIME-encoding* `[`*MIME-encoding*`]` ...   [svdh,B]
Alternate text to display for a file instead of an icon selected by MIME-encoding. (p. 205)

`AddAltByType` *string MIME-type* `[`*MIME-type*`]` ...   [svdh,B]
Alternate text to display for a file, instead of an icon selected by MIME content-type. (p. 205)

`AddCharset` *charset extension* `[`*extension*`]` ...   [svdh,B]
Maps the given filename extensions to the specified content charset. (p. 351)

`AddDefaultCharset On|Off|`*charset*   Off [svdh,C]
Default charset parameter to be added when a response content-type is text/plain or text/html. (p. 90)

`AddDescription` *string file* `[`*file*`]` ...   [svdh,B]
Description to display for a file. (p. 205)

`AddEncoding` *MIME-enc extension* `[`*extension*`]` ...   [svdh,B]
Maps the given filename extensions to the specified encoding type. (p. 352)

AddHandler *handler-name extension* [*extension*] ...   [svdh,B]
    Maps the filename extensions to the specified handler. (p. 353)

AddIcon *icon name* [*name*] ...   [svdh,B]
    Icon to display for a file selected by name. (p. 206)

AddIconByEncoding *icon MIME-encoding* [*MIME-encoding*] ...   [svdh,B]
    Icon to display next to files selected by MIME content-encoding. (p. 207)

AddIconByType *icon MIME-type* [*MIME-type*] ...   [svdh,B]
    Icon to display next to files selected by MIME content-type. (p. 207)

AddInputFilter *filter* [;*filter*...] *extension* [*extension*] ...   [svdh,B]
    Maps filename extensions to the filters that will process client requests. (p. 353)

AddLanguage *MIME-lang extension* [*extension*] ...   [svdh,B]
    Maps the given filename extension to the specified content language. (p. 354)

AddModuleInfo *module-name string*   [sv,E]
    Adds additional information to the module information displayed by the server-
    info handler. (p. 317)

AddOutputFilter *filter* [;*filter*...] *extension* [*extension*] ...   [svdh,B]
    Maps filename extensions to the filters that will process responses from the
    server. (p. 355)

AddOutputFilterByType *filter* [;*filter*...] *MIME-type* [*MIME-type*]
    ...   [svdh,C]
    Assigns an output filter to a particular MIME-type. (p. 91)

AddType *MIME-type extension* [*extension*] ...   [svdh,B]
    Maps the given filename extensions onto the specified content type. (p. 355)

Alias *URL-path file-path|directory-path*   [sv,B]
    Maps URLs to filesystem locations. (p. 142)

AliasMatch *regex file-path|directory-path*   [sv,B]
    Maps URLs to filesystem locations using regular expressions. (p. 143)

Allow from all|*host*|env=[!]*env-variable* [*host*|env=[!]*env-variable*]
    ...   [dh,B]
    Controls which hosts can access an area of the server. (p. 193)

AllowCONNECT *port* [*port*] ...   443 563   [sv,E]
    Ports that are allowed to CONNECT through the proxy. (p. 380)

AllowEncodedSlashes On|Off   Off   [sv,C]
    Determines whether encoded path separators in URLs are allowed to be passed
    through. (p. 92)

AllowOverride All|None|*directive-type* [*directive-type*] ...   All   [d,C]
    Types of directives that are allowed in .htaccess files. (p. 93)

Anonymous *user* [*user*] ...   [dh,E]
    Specifies userIDs that are allowed access without password verification. (p. 161)

Anonymous_LogEmail On|Off   On   [dh,E]
    Sets whether the password entered will be logged in the error log. (p. 162)

Anonymous_MustGiveEmail On|Off   On   [dh,E]
    Specifies whether blank passwords are allowed. (p. 162)

`Anonymous_NoUserID On|Off`   Off [dh,E]
    Sets whether the userID field may be empty. (p. 162)

`Anonymous_VerifyEmail On|Off`   Off [dh,E]
    Sets whether to check the password field for a correctly formatted email address.
    (p. 163)

`AuthBasicAuthoritative On|Off`   On [dh,B]
    Sets whether authorization and authentication are passed to lower level modules.
    (p. 150)

`AuthBasicProvider provider-name [provider-name] ...`   file [dh,B]
    Sets the authentication provider(s) for this location. (p. 151)

`AuthDBDUserPWQuery query`   [d,E]
    SQL query to look up a password for a user. (p. 165)

`AuthDBDUserRealmQuery query`   [d,E]
    SQL query to look up a password hash for a user and realm. . (p. 166)

`AuthDBMGroupFile file-path`   [dh,E]
    Sets the name of the database file containing the list of user groups for autho-
    rization. (p. 187)

`AuthDBMType default|SDBM|GDBM|NDBM|DB`   default [dh,E]
    Sets the type of database file that is used to store passwords. (p. 167)

`AuthDBMUserFile file-path`   [dh,E]
    Sets the name of a database file containing the list of users and passwords for
    authentication. (p. 168)

`AuthDefaultAuthoritative On|Off`   On [dh,B]
    Sets whether authentication is passed to lower level modules. (p. 169)

`AuthDigestAlgorithm MD5|MD5-sess`   MD5 [dh,E]
    Selects the algorithm used to calculate the challenge and response hashes in
    digest authentication. (p. 154)

`AuthDigestDomain URI [URI] ...`   [dh,E]
    URIs that are in the same protection space for digest authentication. (p. 154)

`AuthDigestNcCheck On|Off`   Off [s,E]
    Enables or disables checking of the nonce-count sent by the server. (p. 155)

`AuthDigestNonceFormat format`   [dh,E]
    Determines how the nonce is generated. (p. 155)

`AuthDigestNonceLifetime seconds`   300 [dh,E]
    How long the server nonce is valid. (p. 155)

`AuthDigestProvider provider-name [provider-name] ...`   file [dh,E]
    Sets the authentication provider(s) for this location. (p. 155)

`AuthDigestQop none|auth|auth-int [auth|auth-int]`   auth [dh,E]
    Determines the quality-of-protection to use in digest authentication. (p. 156)

`AuthDigestShmemSize size`   1000 [s,E]
    The amount of shared memory to allocate for keeping track of clients. (p. 156)

`AuthGroupFile file-path`   [dh,B]
    Sets the name of a text file containing the list of user groups for authorization.
    (p. 191)

AuthLDAPBindAuthoritative*off*/*on*   on [dh,E]
> Determines if other authentication providers are used when a user can be mapped
> to a DN but the server cannot successfully bind with the user's credentials..
> (p. 180)

AuthLDAPBindDN *distinguished-name*   [dh,E]
> Optional DN to use in binding to the LDAP server. (p. 181)

AuthLDAPBindPassword *password*   [dh,E]
> Password used in conjuction with the bind DN. (p. 181)

AuthLDAPCharsetConfig *file-path*   [s,E]
> Language to charset conversion configuration file. (p. 181)

AuthLDAPCompareDNOnServer on|off   on [dh,E]
> Use the LDAP server to compare the DNs. (p. 182)

AuthLDAPDereferenceAliases never|searching|finding|always   Always [dh,E]
> When will the module de-reference aliases. (p. 182)

AuthLDAPGroupAttribute *attribute*   member uniquemember + [dh,E]
> LDAP attributes used to check for group membership. (p. 182)

AuthLDAPGroupAttributeIsDN on|off   on [dh,E]
> Use the DN of the client username when checking for group membership. (p. 183)

AuthLDAPRemoteUserAttribute uid   [dh,E]
> Use the value of the attribute returned during the user query to set the RE-
> MOTE_USER environment variable. (p. 183)

AuthLDAPRemoteUserIsDN on|off   off [dh,E]
> Use the DN of the client username to set the REMOTE_USER environment
> variable. (p. 184)

AuthLDAPUrl *url [NONE|SSL|TLS|STARTTLS]*   [dh,E]
> URL specifying the LDAP search parameters. (p. 184)

AuthName *auth-domain*   [dh,C]
> Authorization realm for use in HTTP authentication. (p. 94)

AuthType Basic|Digest   [dh,C]
> Type of user authentication. (p. 95)

AuthUserFile *file-path*   [dh,B]
> Sets the name of a text file containing the list of users and passwords for au-
> thentication. (p. 170)

<AuthnProviderAlias *baseProvider Alias*> ...   </AuthnProviderAlias>   [s,E]
> Enclose a group of directives that represent an extension of a base authentication
> provider and referenced by the specified alias. (p. 159)

AuthzDBMAuthoritative On|Off   On [dh,E]
> Sets whether authorization will be passed on to lower level modules. (p. 188)

AuthzDBMType default|SDBM|GDBM|NDBM|DB   default [dh,E]
> Sets the type of database file that is used to store list of user groups. (p. 189)

AuthzDefaultAuthoritative On|Off   On [dh,B]
> Sets whether authorization is passed to lower level modules. (p. 190)

AuthzGroupFileAuthoritative On|Off   On [dh,B]
> Sets whether authorization will be passed on to lower level modules. (p. 192)

AuthzLDAPAuthoritative on|off   on [dh,E]
Prevent other authentication modules from authenticating the user if this one fails. (p. 186)

AuthzOwnerAuthoritative On|Off   On [dh,E]
Sets whether authorization will be passed on to lower level modules. (p. 200)

AuthzUserAuthoritative On|Off   On [dh,B]
Sets whether authorization will be passed on to lower level modules. (p. 201)

BalancerMember [balancerurl] url [key=value [key=value ...]]   [d,E]
Add a member to a load balancing group. (p. 380)

BrowserMatch regex [!]env-variable[=value] [[!]env-variable[=value]]
  ...   [svdh,B]
Sets environment variables conditional on HTTP User-Agent . (p. 449)

BrowserMatchNoCase regex [!]env-variable[=value] [[!]env-variable[=value]]
  ...   [svdh,B]
Sets environment variables conditional on User-Agent without respect to case. (p. 450)

BufferedLogs On|Off   Off [s,B]
Buffer log entries in memory before writing to disk. (p. 337)

CGIMapExtension cgi-path .extension   [dh,C]
Technique for locating the interpreter for CGI scripts. (p. 95)

CacheDefaultExpire seconds   3600 (one hour) [sv,E]
The default duration to cache a document when no expiry date is specified.. (p. 218)

CacheDirLength length   2 [sv,E]
The number of characters in subdirectory names. (p. 260)

CacheDirLevels levels   3 [sv,E]
The number of levels of subdirectories in the cache.. (p. 261)

CacheDisable url-string   [sv,E]
Disable caching of specified URLs. (p. 218)

CacheEnable cache_type url-string   [sv,E]
Enable caching of specified URLs using a specified storage manager. (p. 219)

CacheFile file-path [file-path] ...   [s,X]
Cache a list of file handles at startup time. (p. 280)

CacheIgnoreCacheControl On|Off   Off [sv,E]
Ignore request to not serve cached content to client. (p. 220)

CacheIgnoreHeaders header-string [header-string] ...   None [sv,E]
Do not store the given HTTP header(s) in the cache. . (p. 220)

CacheIgnoreNoLastMod On|Off   Off [sv,E]
Ignore the fact that a response has no Last Modified header.. (p. 221)

CacheIgnoreQueryString On|Off   Off [sv,E]
Ignore query string when caching. (p. 222)

CacheIgnoreURLSessionIdentifiers identifier [identifier] ...   None [sv,E]
Ignore defined session identifiers encoded in the URL when caching . (p. 222)

CacheLastModifiedFactor *float*   0.1 [sv,E]
    The factor used to compute an expiry date based on the LastModified date..
    (p. 223)

CacheLock *on/off*   off [sv,E]
    Enable the thundering herd lock.. (p. 223)

CacheLockMaxAge *integer*   5 [sv,E]
    Set the maximum possible age of a cache lock.. (p. 224)

CacheLockPath *directory*   /tmp/mod_cache-lock + [sv,E]
    Set the lock path directory.. (p. 224)

CacheMaxExpire *seconds*   86400 (one day) [sv,E]
    The maximum time in seconds to cache a document. (p. 224)

CacheMaxFileSize *bytes*   1000000 [sv,E]
    The maximum size (in bytes) of a document to be placed in the cache. (p. 261)

CacheMinFileSize *bytes*   1 [sv,E]
    The minimum size (in bytes) of a document to be placed in the cache. (p. 261)

CacheNegotiatedDocs On|Off   Off [sv,B]
    Allows content-negotiated documents to be cached by proxy servers. (p. 369)

CacheRoot *directory*   [sv,E]
    The directory root under which cache files are stored. (p. 262)

CacheStoreNoStore On|Off   Off [sv,E]
    Attempt to cache requests or responses that have been marked as no-store..
    (p. 225)

CacheStorePrivate On|Off   Off [sv,E]
    Attempt to cache responses that the server has marked as private. (p. 225)

CharsetDefault *charset*   [svdh,E]
    Charset to translate into. (p. 236)

CharsetOptions *option* [*option*] ...   DebugLevel=0 NoImpl + [svdh,E]
    Configures charset translation behavior. (p. 236)

CharsetSourceEnc *charset*   [svdh,E]
    Source charset of files. (p. 237)

CheckCaseOnly on|off   Off [svdh,E]
    Limits the action of the speling module to case corrections. (p. 456)

CheckSpelling on|off   Off [svdh,E]
    Enables the spelling module. (p. 457)

ChrootDir */path/to/directory*   [s,M]
    Directory for Apache to run chroot(8) after startup.. (p. 517)

ContentDigest On|Off   Off [svdh,C]
    Enables the generation of Content-MD5 HTTP Response headers. (p. 95)

CookieDomain *domain*   [svdh,E]
    The domain to which the tracking cookie applies. (p. 505)

CookieExpires *expiry-period*   [svdh,E]
    Expiry time for the tracking cookie. (p. 506)

CookieLog *filename*   [sv,B]
    Sets filename for the logging of cookies. (p. 338)

CookieName *token*   Apache [svdh,E]
    Name of the tracking cookie. (p. 506)

CookieStyle *Netscape/Cookie/Cookie2/RFC2109/RFC2965*   Netscape [svdh,E]
    Format of the cookie header field. (p. 506)

CookieTracking on|off   off [svdh,E]
    Enables tracking cookie. (p. 507)

CoreDumpDirectory *directory*   [s,M]
    Directory where Apache attempts to switch before dumping core. (p. 517)

CustomLog *file|pipe format|nickname* [env=[!]*environment-variable*]   [sv,B]
    Sets filename and format of log file. (p. 338)

DBDExptime *time-in-seconds*   300 [sv,E]
    Keepalive time for idle connections. (p. 248)

DBDKeep *number*   2 [sv,E]
    Maximum sustained number of connections. (p. 248)

DBDMax *number*   10 [sv,E]
    Maximum number of connections. (p. 248)

DBDMin *number*   1 [sv,E]
    Minimum number of connections. (p. 248)

DBDParams *param1=value1*[,*param2=value2*]   [sv,E]
    Parameters for database connection. (p. 249)

DBDPersist On|Off   [sv,E]
    Whether to use persistent connections. (p. 249)

DBDPrepareSQL *"SQL statement" label*   [sv,E]
    Define an SQL prepared statement. (p. 250)

DBDriver *name*   [sv,E]
    Specify an SQL driver. (p. 250)

Dav On|Off|*provider-name*   Off [d,E]
    Enable WebDAV HTTP methods. (p. 240)

DavDepthInfinity on|off   off [svd,E]
    Allow PROPFIND, Depth: Infinity requests. (p. 241)

DavGenericLockDB *file-path*   [svd,E]
    Location of the DAV lock database. (p. 243)

DavLockDB *file-path*   [sv,E]
    Location of the DAV lock database. (p. 242)

DavMinTimeout *seconds*   0 [svd,E]
    Minimum amount of time the server holds a lock on a DAV resource. (p. 241)

DefaultIcon *url-path*   [svdh,B]
    Icon to display for files when no specific icon is configured. (p. 207)

DefaultLanguage *MIME-lang*   [svdh,B]
    Sets all files in the given scope to the specified language. (p. 356)

DefaultType *MIME-type/none*   text/plain [svdh,C]
    MIME content-type that will be sent if the server cannot determine a type in
    any other way. (p. 96)

DeflateBufferSize *value*   8096 [sv,E]
    Fragment size to be compressed at one time by zlib. (p. 254)

DeflateCompressionLevel *value*   [sv,E]
    How much compression do we apply to the output. (p. 254)

DeflateFilterNote [*type*] *notename*   [sv,E]
    Places the compression ratio in a note for logging. (p. 254)

DeflateMemLevel *value*   9 [sv,E]
    How much memory should be used by zlib for compression. (p. 255)

DeflateWindowSize *value*   15 [sv,E]
    Zlib compression window size. (p. 255)

Deny from all|*host*|env=[!]*env-variable* [*host*|env=[!]*env-variable*]
    ...   [dh,B]
    Controls which hosts are denied access to the server. (p. 195)

<Directory *directory-path*> ... </Directory>   [sv,C]
    Enclose a group of directives that apply only to the named file-system directory
    and sub-directories. (p. 97)

DirectoryIndex *local-url* [*local-url*] ...   index.html [svdh,B]
    List of resources to look for when the client requests a directory. (p. 257)

<DirectoryMatch *regex*> ... </DirectoryMatch>   [sv,C]
    Enclose directives that apply to file-system directories matching a regular ex-
    pression and their subdirectories. (p. 98)

DirectorySlash On|Off   On [svdh,B]
    Toggle trailing slash redirects on or off. (p. 258)

DocumentRoot *directory-path*   /usr/local/apache/h + [sv,C]
    Directory that forms the main document tree visible from the web. (p. 99)

DumpIOInput On|Off   Off [s,E]
    Dump all input data to the error log. (p. 263)

DumpIOLogLevel *level*   debug [s,E]
    Controls the logging level of the DumpIO output. (p. 264)

DumpIOOutput On|Off   Off [s,E]
    Dump all output data to the error log. (p. 264)

EnableExceptionHook On|Off   Off [s,M]
    Enables a hook that runs exception handlers after a crash. (p. 518)

EnableMMAP On|Off   On [svdh,C]
    Use memory-mapping to read files during delivery. (p. 99)

EnableSendfile On|Off   On [svdh,C]
    Use the kernel sendfile support to deliver files to the client. (p. 100)

ErrorDocument *error-code* *document*   [svdh,C]
    What the server will return to the client in case of an error. (p. 101)

ErrorLog *file-path*|syslog[:*facility*]   logs/error_log (Uni + [sv,C]
    Location where the server will log errors. (p. 103)

Example [svdh,X]
    Demonstration directive to illustrate the Apache module API. (p. 269)

ExpiresActive On|Off [svdh,E]
    Enables generation of Expires headers. (p. 271)

ExpiresByType *MIME-type* <*code*>*seconds* [svdh,E]
    Value of the Expires header configured by MIME type. (p. 272)

ExpiresDefault <*code*>*seconds* [svdh,E]
    Default algorithm for calculating expiration time. (p. 273)

ExtFilterDefine *filtername parameters* [s,E]
    Define an external filter. (p. 276)

ExtFilterOptions *option* [*option*] ...   DebugLevel=0 NoLogS + [d,E]
    Configure mod_ext_filter options. (p. 278)

ExtendedStatus On|Off Off [s,B]
    Keep track of extended status information for each request. (p. 493)

FallbackResource *local-url* [svdh,B]
    Define a default URL for requests that don't map to a file. (p. 259)

FileETag *component* ...   INode MTime Size [svdh,C]
    File attributes used to create the ETag HTTP response header for static files.
    (p. 104)

<Files *filename*> ... </Files> [svdh,C]
    Contains directives that apply to matched filenames. (p. 105)

<FilesMatch *regex*> ... </FilesMatch> [svdh,C]
    Contains directives that apply to regular-expression matched filenames. (p. 105)

FilterChain [+=-@!]*filter-name* ... [svdh,B]
    Configure the filter chain. (p. 286)

FilterDeclare *filter-name [type]* [svdh,B]
    Declare a smart filter. (p. 286)

FilterProtocol *filter-name* [*provider-name*] *proto-flags* [svdh,B]
    Deal with correct HTTP protocol handling. (p. 287)

FilterProvider *filter-name provider-name* [req|resp|env]=*dispatch*
        match [svdh,B]
    Register a content filter. (p. 287)

FilterTrace *filter-name level* [svd,B]
    Get debug/diagnostic information from mod_filter. (p. 288)

ForceLanguagePriority None|Prefer|Fallback [Prefer|Fallback] Prefer [svdh,B]
    Action to take if a single acceptable document is not found. (p. 369)

ForceType *MIME-type*|None [dh,C]
    Forces all matching files to be served with the specified MIME content-type.
    (p. 106)

ForensicLog *filename*|*pipe* [sv,E]
    Sets filename of the forensic log. (p. 342)

GracefulShutDownTimeout *seconds* [s,M]
    Specify a timeout after which a gracefully shutdown server will exit.. (p. 518)

IndexHeadInsert *"markup ..."*   [svdh,B]
    Inserts text in the HEAD section of an index page.. (p. 209)

IndexIgnore *file* [*file*] ...   [svdh,B]
    Adds to the list of files to hide when listing a directory. (p. 209)

IndexOptions [+|-]*option* [[+|-]*option*] ...   [svdh,B]
    Various configuration settings for directory indexing. (p. 209)

IndexOrderDefault Ascending|Descending Name|Date|Size|Description
        Ascending Name [svdh,B]
    Sets the default ordering of the directory index. (p. 213)

IndexStyleSheet *url-path*   [svdh,B]
    Adds a CSS stylesheet to the directory index. (p. 214)

KeepAlive On|Off   On [sv,C]
    Enables HTTP persistent connections. (p. 110)

KeepAliveTimeout *seconds*   5 [sv,C]
    Amount of time the server will wait for subsequent requests on a persistent connection. (p. 110)

LDAPCacheEntries *number*   1024 [s,E]
    Maximum number of entries in the primary LDAP cache. (p. 329)

LDAPCacheTTL *seconds*   600 [s,E]
    Time that cached items remain valid. (p. 329)

LDAPConnectionTimeout *seconds*   [s,E]
    Specifies the socket connection timeout in seconds. (p. 329)

LDAPOpCacheEntries *number*   1024 [s,E]
    Number of entries used to cache LDAP compare operations. (p. 330)

LDAPOpCacheTTL *seconds*   600 [s,E]
    Time that entries in the operation cache remain valid. (p. 330)

LDAPSharedCacheFile *directory-path/filename*   [s,E]
    Sets the shared memory cache file. (p. 330)

LDAPSharedCacheSize *bytes*   500000 [s,E]
    Size in bytes of the shared-memory cache. (p. 330)

LDAPTrustedClientCert *type directory-path/filename/nickname*
        [*password*]   [svdh,E]
    Sets the file containing or nickname referring to a per connection client certificate. Not all LDAP toolkits support per connection client certificates.. (p. 331)

LDAPTrustedGlobalCert *type directory-path/filename* [*password*]   [s,E]
    Sets the file or database containing global trusted Certificate Authority or global client certificates. (p. 331)

LDAPTrustedMode *type*   [sv,E]
    Specifies the SSL/TLS mode to be used when connecting to an LDAP server.. (p. 332)

LDAPVerifyServerCert On|Off   On [s,E]
    Force server certificate verification. (p. 332)

LanguagePriority *MIME-lang* [*MIME-lang*] ...   [svdh,B]
    The precedence of language variants for cases where the client does not express
    a preference. (p. 370)

<Limit *method* [*method*] ... > ... </Limit>   [svdh,C]
    Restrict enclosed access controls to only certain HTTP methods. (p. 111)

<LimitExcept *method* [*method*] ... > ... </LimitExcept>   [svdh,C]
    Restrict access controls to all HTTP methods except the named ones. (p. 112)

LimitInternalRecursion *number* [*number*]   10 [sv,C]
    Determine maximum number of internal redirects and nested subrequests.
    (p. 112)

LimitRequestBody *bytes*   0 [svdh,C]
    Restricts the total size of the HTTP request body sent from the client. (p. 113)

LimitRequestFieldSize *bytes*   8190 [s,C]
    Limits the size of the HTTP request header allowed from the client. (p. 113)

LimitRequestFields *number*   100 [s,C]
    Limits the number of HTTP request header fields that will be accepted from
    the client. (p. 114)

LimitRequestLine *bytes*   8190 [s,C]
    Limit the size of the HTTP request line that will be accepted from the client.
    (p. 115)

LimitXMLRequestBody *bytes*   1000000 [svdh,C]
    Limits the size of an XML-based request body. (p. 115)

Listen [*IP-address*:]*portnumber* [*protocol*]   [s,M]
    IP addresses and ports that the server listens to. (p. 519)

ListenBacklog *backlog*   [s,M]
    Maximum length of the queue of pending connections. (p. 521)

LoadFile *filename* [*filename*] ...   [s,E]
    Link in the named object file or library. (p. 454)

LoadModule *module* *filename*   [s,E]
    Links in the object file or library, and adds to the list of active modules. (p. 455)

<Location *URL-path*|*URL*> ... </Location>   [sv,C]
    Applies the enclosed directives only to matching URLs. (p. 116)

<LocationMatch *regex*> ... </LocationMatch>   [sv,C]
    Applies the enclosed directives only to regular-expression matching URLs.
    (p. 117)

LockFile *filename*   logs/accept.lock [s,M]
    Location of the accept serialization lock file. (p. 521)

LogFormat *format*|*nickname* [*nickname*]   "%h %l %u %t \"%r\" + [sv,B]
    Describes a format for use in a log file. (p. 339)

LogLevel *level*   warn [sv,C]
    Controls the verbosity of the ErrorLog. (p. 118)

MCacheMaxObjectCount *value*   1009 [s,E]
    The maximum number of objects allowed to be placed in the cache. (p. 345)

`MCacheMaxObjectSize` *bytes*   10000 [s,E]
    The maximum size (in bytes) of a document allowed in the cache. (p. 345)

`MCacheMaxStreamingBuffer` *size_in_bytes*   the smaller of 1000 + [s,E]
    Maximum amount of a streamed response to buffer in memory before declaring
    the response uncacheable. (p. 345)

`MCacheMinObjectSize` *bytes*   1 [s,E]
    The minimum size (in bytes) of a document to be allowed in the cache. (p. 346)

`MCacheRemovalAlgorithm LRU|GDSF`   GDSF [s,E]
    The algorithm used to select documents for removal from the cache. (p. 346)

`MCacheSize` *KBytes*   100 [s,E]
    The maximum amount of memory used by the cache in KBytes. (p. 347)

`MMapFile` *file-path* [*file-path*] ...   [s,X]
    Map a list of files into memory at startup time. (p. 281)

`MaxClients` *number*   [s,M]
    Maximum number of connections that will be processed simultaneously. (p. 522)

`MaxKeepAliveRequests` *number*   100 [sv,C]
    Number of requests allowed on a persistent connection. (p. 119)

`MaxMemFree` *KBytes*   0 [s,M]
    Maximum amount of memory that the main allocator is allowed to hold without
    calling free(). (p. 522)

`MaxRequestsPerChild` *number*   10000 [s,M]
    Limit on the number of requests that an individual child server will handle
    during its life. (p. 523)

`MaxRequestsPerThread` *number*   0 [s,M]
    Limit on the number of requests that an individual thread will handle during
    its life. (p. 514)

`MaxSpareServers` *number*   10 [s,M]
    Maximum number of idle child server processes. (p. 534)

`MaxSpareThreads` *number*   [s,M]
    Maximum number of idle threads. (p. 523)

`MetaDir` *directory*   .web [svdh,E]
    Name of the directory to find CERN-style meta information files. (p. 227)

`MetaFiles on|off`   off [svdh,E]
    Activates CERN meta-file processing. (p. 228)

`MetaSuffix` *suffix*   .meta [svdh,E]
    File name suffix for the file containing CERN-style meta information. (p. 228)

`MimeMagicFile` *file-path*   [sv,E]
    Enable MIME-type determination based on file contents using the specified
    magic file. (p. 366)

`MinSpareServers` *number*   5 [s,M]
    Minimum number of idle child server processes. (p. 534)

`MinSpareThreads` *number*   [s,M]
    Minimum number of idle threads available to handle request spikes. (p. 524)

ModMimeUsePathInfo On|Off   Off [d,B]
    Tells mod_mime to treat path_info components as part of the filename. (p. 357)

MultiviewsMatch Any|NegotiatedOnly|Filters|Handlers
        [Handlers|Filters]   NegotiatedOnly [svdh,B]
    The types of files that will be included when searching for a matching file with
    MultiViews. (p. 357)

NWSSLTrustedCerts filename [filename] ...   [s,B]
    List of additional client certificates. (p. 372)

NWSSLUpgradeable [IP-address:]portnumber   [s,B]
    Allows a connection to be upgraded to an SSL connection upon request. (p. 372)

NameVirtualHost addr[:port]   [s,C]
    Designates an IP address for name-virtual hosting. (p. 119)

NoProxy host [host] ...   [sv,E]
    Hosts, domains, or networks that will be connected to directly. (p. 380)

Options [+|-]option [[+|-]option] ...   All [svdh,C]
    Configures what features are available in a particular directory. (p. 120)

Order ordering   Deny,Allow [dh,B]
    Controls the default access state and the order in which Allow and Deny are
    evaluated.. (p. 195)

PassEnv env-variable [env-variable] ...   [svdh,B]
    Passes environment variables from the shell. (p. 266)

PidFile filename   logs/httpd.pid [s,M]
    File where the server records the process ID of the daemon. (p. 524)

ProtocolEcho On|Off   Off [sv,X]
    Turn the echo server on or off. (p. 265)

<Proxy wildcard-url> ...</Proxy>   [sv,E]
    Container for directives applied to proxied resources. (p. 382)

ProxyBadHeader IsError|Ignore|StartBody   IsError [sv,E]
    Determines how to handle bad header lines in a response. (p. 383)

ProxyBlock *|word|host|domain [word|host|domain] ...   [sv,E]
    Words, hosts, or domains that are banned from being proxied. (p. 383)

ProxyDomain Domain   [sv,E]
    Default domain name for proxied requests. (p. 384)

ProxyErrorOverride On|Off   Off [sv,E]
    Override error pages for proxied content. (p. 384)

ProxyFtpDirCharset character set   ISO-8859-1 [svd,E]
    Define the character set for proxied FTP listings. (p. 384)

ProxyIOBufferSize bytes   8192 [sv,E]
    Determine size of internal data throughput buffer. (p. 385)

<ProxyMatch regex> ...</ProxyMatch>   [sv,E]
    Container for directives applied to regular-expression-matched proxied resources.
    (p. 385)

ProxyMaxForwards number   -1 [sv,E]
    Maximum number of proxies that a request can be forwarded through. (p. 385)

ProxyPass [path] !|url [key=value key=value ...]]   [nocanon]
    [interpolate]   [svd,E]
    Maps remote servers into the local server URL-space. (p. 386)

ProxyPassInterpolateEnv On|Off   Off [svd,E]
    Enable Environment Variable interpolation in Reverse Proxy configurations.
    (p. 391)

ProxyPassMatch [regex] !|url [key=value [key=value ...]]   [svd,E]
    Maps remote servers into the local server URL-space using regular expressions.
    (p. 392)

ProxyPassReverse [path] url [interpolate]   [svd,E]
    Adjusts the URL in HTTP response headers sent from a reverse proxied server.
    (p. 393)

ProxyPassReverseCookieDomain internal-domain public-domain
    [interpolate]   [svd,E]
    Adjusts the Domain string in Set-Cookie headers from a reverse-proxied server.
    (p. 394)

ProxyPassReverseCookiePath internal-path public-path [interpolate] [svd,E]
    Adjusts the Path string in Set-Cookie headers from a reverse- proxied server.
    (p. 394)

ProxyPreserveHost On|Off   Off [sv,E]
    Use incoming Host HTTP request header for proxy request. (p. 394)

ProxyReceiveBufferSize bytes   0 [sv,E]
    Network buffer size for proxied HTTP and FTP connections. (p. 395)

ProxyRemote match remote-server   [sv,E]
    Remote proxy used to handle certain requests. (p. 395)

ProxyRemoteMatch regex remote-server   [sv,E]
    Remote proxy used to handle requests matched by regular expressions. (p. 396)

ProxyRequests On|Off   Off [sv,E]
    Enables forward (standard) proxy requests. (p. 396)

ProxySCGIInternalRedirect On|Off   On [svd,E]
    Enable or disable internal redirect responses from the backend. (p. 422)

ProxySCGISendfile On|Off|Headername   Off [svd,E]
    Enable evaluation of X-Sendfile pseudo response header. (p. 422)

ProxySet url key=value [key=value ...]   [d,E]
    Set various Proxy balancer or member parameters. (p. 396)

ProxyStatus Off|On|Full   Off [sv,E]
    Show Proxy LoadBalancer status in mod_status. (p. 397)

ProxyTimeout seconds   [sv,E]
    Network timeout for proxied requests. (p. 397)

ProxyVia On|Off|Full|Block   Off [sv,E]
    Information provided in the Via HTTP response header for proxied requests.
    (p. 398)

RLimitCPU seconds|max [seconds|max]   [svdh,C]
    Limits the CPU consumption of processes launched by Apache children. (p. 122)

RLimitMEM *bytes*|max [*bytes*|max]   [svdh,C]
    Limits the memory consumption of processes launched by Apache children.
    (p. 122)

RLimitNPROC *number*|max [*number*|max]   [svdh,C]
    Limits the number of processes that can be launched by processes launched by
    Apache children. (p. 123)

ReadmeName *filename*   [svdh,B]
    Name of the file that will be inserted at the end of the index listing. (p. 214)

ReceiveBufferSize *bytes*   0 [s,M]
    TCP receive buffer size. (p. 525)

Redirect [*status*] *URL-path URL*   [svdh,B]
    Sends an external redirect asking the client to fetch a different URL. (p. 144)

RedirectMatch [*status*] *regex URL*   [svdh,B]
    Sends an external redirect based on a regular expression match of the current
    URL. (p. 145)

RedirectPermanent *URL-path URL*   [svdh,B]
    Sends an external permanent redirect asking the client to fetch a different URL.
    (p. 145)

RedirectTemp *URL-path URL*   [svdh,B]
    Sends an external temporary redirect asking the client to fetch a different URL.
    (p. 146)

RemoveCharset *extension* [*extension*] ...   [vdh,B]
    Removes any character set associations for a set of file extensions. (p. 358)

RemoveEncoding *extension* [*extension*] ...   [vdh,B]
    Removes any content encoding associations for a set of file extensions. (p. 359)

RemoveHandler *extension* [*extension*] ...   [vdh,B]
    Removes any handler associations for a set of file extensions. (p. 359)

RemoveInputFilter *extension* [*extension*] ...   [vdh,B]
    Removes any input filter associations for a set of file extensions. (p. 360)

RemoveLanguage *extension* [*extension*] ...   [vdh,B]
    Removes any language associations for a set of file extensions. (p. 360)

RemoveOutputFilter *extension* [*extension*] ...   [vdh,B]
    Removes any output filter associations for a set of file extensions. (p. 361)

RemoveType *extension* [*extension*] ...   [vdh,B]
    Removes any content type associations for a set of file extensions. (p. 361)

RequestHeader set|append|merge|add|unset|edit *header* [*value*] [*replacement*]
        [early|env=[!]*variable*]   [svdh,E]
    Configure HTTP request headers. (p. 293)

RequestReadTimeout [header=*timeout*[[-*maxtimeout*],MinRate=*rate*]
        [body=*timeout*[[-*maxtimeout*],MinRate=*rate*]   [sv,X]
    Set timeout values for receiving request headers and body from client. . (p. 424)

Require *entity-name* [*entity-name*] ...   [dh,C]
    Selects which authenticated users can access a resource. (p. 124)

RewriteBase *URL-path*   [dh,E]
    Sets the base URL for per-directory rewrites. (p. 427)

RewriteCond *TestString CondPattern*   [svdh,E]
    Defines a condition under which rewriting will take place . (p. 429)

RewriteEngine on|off   off [svdh,E]
    Enables or disables runtime rewriting engine. (p. 434)

RewriteLock *file-path*   [s,E]
    Sets the name of the lock file used for RewriteMap synchronization. (p. 435)

RewriteLog *file-path*   [sv,E]
    Sets the name of the file used for logging rewrite engine processing. (p. 435)

RewriteLogLevel *Level*   0 [sv,E]
    Sets the verbosity of the log file used by the rewrite engine. (p. 436)

RewriteMap *MapName MapType:MapSource*   [sv,E]
    Defines a mapping function for key-lookup. (p. 436)

RewriteOptions *Options*   [svdh,E]
    Sets some special options for the rewrite engine. (p. 439)

RewriteRule *Pattern Substitution [flags]*   [svdh,E]
    Defines rules for the rewriting engine. (p. 440)

SSIETag on|off   off [dh,B]
    Controls whether ETags are generated by the server.. (p. 310)

SSIEnableAccess on|off   off [dh,B]
    Enable the -A flag during conditional flow control processing.. (p. 311)

SSIEndTag *tag*   "->" [sv,B]
    String that ends an include element. (p. 311)

SSIErrorMsg *message*   "[an error occurred + [svdh,B]
    Error message displayed when there is an SSI error. (p. 312)

SSILastModified on|off   off [dh,B]
    Controls whether Last-Modified headers are generated by the server.. (p. 312)

SSIStartTag *tag*   "<!-#" [sv,B]
    String that starts an include element. (p. 313)

SSITimeFormat *formatstring*   "%A, %d-%b-%Y %H:%M + [svdh,B]
    Configures the format in which date strings are displayed. (p. 313)

SSIUndefinedEcho *string*   "(none)" [svdh,B]
    String displayed when an unset variable is echoed. (p. 314)

SSLCACertificateFile *file-path*   [sv,E]
    File of concatenated PEM-encoded CA Certificates for Client Auth. (p. 461)

SSLCACertificatePath *directory-path*   [sv,E]
    Directory of PEM-encoded CA Certificates for Client Auth. (p. 461)

SSLCADNRequestFile *file-path*   [sv,E]
    File of concatenated PEM-encoded CA Certificates for defining acceptable CA
    names. (p. 461)

SSLCADNRequestPath *directory-path*   [sv,E]
    Directory of PEM-encoded CA Certificates for defining acceptable CA names.
    (p. 462)

SSLCARevocationFile *file-path*   [sv,E]
  File of concatenated PEM-encoded CA CRLs for Client Auth. (p. 463)

SSLCARevocationPath *directory-path*   [sv,E]
  Directory of PEM-encoded CA CRLs for Client Auth. (p. 463)

SSLCertificateChainFile *file-path*   [sv,E]
  File of PEM-encoded Server CA Certificates. (p. 463)

SSLCertificateFile *file-path*   [sv,E]
  Server PEM-encoded X.509 Certificate file. (p. 464)

SSLCertificateKeyFile *file-path*   [sv,E]
  Server PEM-encoded Private Key file. (p. 464)

SSLCipherSuite *cipher-spec*   ALL:!ADH:RC4+RSA:+H + [svdh,E]
  Cipher Suite available for negotiation in SSL handshake. (p. 465)

SSLCryptoDevice *engine*   builtin [s,E]
  Enable use of a cryptographic hardware accelerator. (p. 467)

SSLEngine on|off|optional   off [sv,E]
  SSL Engine Operation Switch. (p. 469)

SSLFIPS on|off   off [s,E]
  SSL FIPS mode Switch. (p. 469)

SSLHonorCipherOrder *flag*   [sv,E]
  Option to prefer the server's cipher preference order. (p. 470)

SSLInsecureRenegotiation *flag*   off [sv,E]
  Option to enable support for insecure renegotiation. (p. 470)

SSLMutex *type*   none [s,E]
  Semaphore for internal mutual exclusion of operations. (p. 471)

SSLOptions [+|-]*option* ...   [svdh,E]
  Configure various SSL engine run-time options. (p. 472)

SSLPassPhraseDialog *type*   builtin [s,E]
  Type of pass phrase dialog for encrypted private keys. (p. 474)

SSLProtocol [+|-]*protocol* ...   all [sv,E]
  Configure usable SSL protocol flavors. (p. 475)

SSLProxyCACertificateFile *file-path*   [sv,E]
  File of concatenated PEM-encoded CA Certificates for Remote Server Auth.
  (p. 476)

SSLProxyCACertificatePath *directory-path*   [sv,E]
  Directory of PEM-encoded CA Certificates for Remote Server Auth. (p. 476)

SSLProxyCARevocationFile *file-path*   [sv,E]
  File of concatenated PEM-encoded CA CRLs for Remote Server Auth. (p. 477)

SSLProxyCARevocationPath *directory-path*   [sv,E]
  Directory of PEM-encoded CA CRLs for Remote Server Auth. (p. 477)

SSLProxyCheckPeerCN on|off   off [sv,E]
  Whether to check the remote server certificates CN field . (p. 478)

SSLProxyCheckPeerExpire on|off   off [sv,E]
  Whether to check if remote server certificate is expired . (p. 478)

SSLProxyCipherSuite *cipher-spec*   ALL:!ADH:RC4+RSA:+H + [svdh,E]
    Cipher Suite available for negotiation in SSL proxy handshake. (p. 478)

SSLProxyEngine on|off   off [sv,E]
    SSL Proxy Engine Operation Switch. (p. 479)

SSLProxyMachineCertificateFile *filename*   [s,E]
    File of concatenated PEM-encoded client certificates and keys to be used by the
    proxy. (p. 479)

SSLProxyMachineCertificatePath *directory*   [s,E]
    Directory of PEM-encoded client certificates and keys to be used by the proxy.
    (p. 480)

SSLProxyProtocol [+|-]*protocol* ...   all [sv,E]
    Configure usable SSL protocol flavors for proxy usage. (p. 480)

SSLProxyVerify *level*   none [svdh,E]
    Type of remote server Certificate verification. (p. 480)

SSLProxyVerifyDepth *number*   1 [svdh,E]
    Maximum depth of CA Certificates in Remote Server Certificate verification.
    (p. 481)

SSLRandomSeed *context source [bytes]*   [s,E]
    Pseudo Random Number Generator (PRNG) seeding source. (p. 482)

SSLRenegBufferSize *bytes*   131072 [dh,E]
    Set the size for the SSL renegotiation buffer. (p. 484)

SSLRequire *expression*   [dh,E]
    Allow access only when an arbitrarily complex boolean expression is true.
    (p. 484)

SSLRequireSSL   [dh,E]
    Deny access when SSL is not used for the HTTP request. (p. 486)

SSLSessionCache *type*   none [s,E]
    Type of the global/inter-process SSL Session Cache. (p. 488)

SSLSessionCacheTimeout *seconds*   300 [sv,E]
    Number of seconds before an SSL session expires in the Session Cache. (p. 489)

SSLStrictSNIVHostCheck on|off   off [sv,E]
    Whether to allow non SNI clients to access a name based virtual host. . (p. 489)

SSLUserName *varname*   [sdh,E]
    Variable name to determine user name. (p. 490)

SSLVerifyClient *level*   none [svdh,E]
    Type of Client Certificate verification. (p. 490)

SSLVerifyDepth *number*   1 [svdh,E]
    Maximum depth of CA Certificates in Client Certificate verification. (p. 491)

Satisfy Any|All   All [dh,C]
    Interaction between host-level access control and user authentication. (p. 125)

ScoreBoardFile *file-path*   logs/apache_status [s,M]
    Location of the file used to store coordination data for the child processes.
    (p. 525)

Script *method* *cgi-script*   [svd,B]
    Activates a CGI script for a particular request method.. (p. 139)

ScriptAlias *URL-path* *file-path|directory-path*   [sv,B]
    Maps a URL to a filesystem location and designates the target as a CGI script.
    (p. 146)

ScriptAliasMatch *regex* *file-path|directory-path*   [sv,B]
    Maps a URL to a filesystem location using a regular expression and designates
    the target as a CGI script. (p. 147)

ScriptInterpreterSource Registry|Registry-Strict|Script   Script [svdh,C]
    Technique for locating the interpreter for CGI scripts. (p. 126)

ScriptLog *file-path*   [sv,B]
    Location of the CGI script error logfile. (p. 231)

ScriptLogBuffer *bytes*   1024 [sv,B]
    Maximum amount of PUT or POST requests that will be recorded in the
    scriptlog. (p. 231)

ScriptLogLength *bytes*   10385760 [sv,B]
    Size limit of the CGI script logfile. (p. 232)

ScriptSock *file-path*   logs/cgisock [s,B]
    The filename prefix of the socket to use for communication with the CGI daemon.
    (p. 233)

SecureListen *[IP-address:]portnumber* *Certificate-Name* [MUTUAL]   [s,B]
    Enables SSL encryption for the specified port. (p. 373)

SeeRequestTail On|Off   Off [s,B]
    Determine if mod_status displays the first 63 characters of a request or the last
    63, assuming the request itself is greater than 63 chars.. (p. 493)

SendBufferSize *bytes*   0 [s,M]
    TCP buffer size. (p. 526)

ServerAdmin *email-address|URL*   [sv,C]
    Email address that the server includes in error messages sent to the client.
    (p. 127)

ServerAlias *hostname* *[hostname]* ...   [v,C]
    Alternate names for a host used when matching requests to name-virtual hosts.
    (p. 127)

ServerLimit *number*   [s,M]
    Upper limit on configurable number of processes. (p. 526)

ServerName *[scheme://]fully-qualified-domain-name[:port]*   [sv,C]
    Hostname and port that the server uses to identify itself. (p. 128)

ServerPath *URL-path*   [v,C]
    Legacy URL pathname for a name-based virtual host that is accessed by an
    incompatible browser. (p. 129)

ServerRoot *directory-path*   /usr/local/apache [s,C]
    Base directory for the server installation. (p. 129)

ServerSignature On|Off|EMail   Off [svdh,C]
    Configures the footer on server-generated documents. (p. 130)

ServerTokens Major|Minor|Min[imal]|Prod[uctOnly]|OS|Full   Full [s,C]
    Configures the Server HTTP response header. (p. 130)

SetEnv *env-variable value*   [svdh,B]
    Sets environment variables. (p. 266)

SetEnvIf *attribute regex [!]env-variable*[=*value*] [[[!]*env-variable*[=*value*]]
    ...   [svdh,B]
    Sets environment variables based on attributes of the request . (p. 450)

SetEnvIfNoCase *attribute regex [!]env-variable*[=*value*]
    [[!]*env-variable*[=*value*]] ...   [svdh,B]
    Sets environment variables based on attributes of the request without respect
    to case. (p. 452)

SetHandler *handler-name*|None   [svdh,C]
    Forces all matching files to be processed by a handler. (p. 131)

SetInputFilter *filter*[;*filter*...]   [svdh,C]
    Sets the filters that will process client requests and POST input. (p. 132)

SetOutputFilter *filter*[;*filter*...]   [svdh,C]
    Sets the filters that will process responses from the server. (p. 132)

StartServers *number*   [s,M]
    Number of child server processes created at startup. (p. 527)

StartThreads *number*   [s,M]
    Number of threads created on startup. (p. 527)

Substitute *s/pattern/substitution/[infq]*   [dh,E]
    Pattern to filter the response content. (p. 495)

SuexecUserGroup *User Group*   [sv,E]
    User and group for CGI programs to run as. (p. 497)

ThreadLimit *number*   [s,M]
    Sets the upper limit on the configurable number of threads per child process.
    (p. 528)

ThreadStackSize *size*   [s,M]
    The size in bytes of the stack used by threads handling client connections.
    (p. 528)

ThreadsPerChild *number*   [s,M]
    Number of threads created by each child process. (p. 529)

TimeOut *seconds*   300 [sv,C]
    Amount of time the server will wait for certain events before failing a request.
    (p. 133)

TraceEnable *[on|off|extended]*   on [s,C]
    Determines the behaviour on TRACE requests. (p. 133)

TransferLog *file|pipe*   [sv,B]
    Specify location of a log file. (p. 340)

TypesConfig *file-path*   conf/mime.types [s,B]
    The location of the mime.types file. (p. 362)

UnsetEnv *env-variable* [*env-variable*] ...   [svdh,B]
    Removes variables from the environment. (p. 267)

UseCanonicalName On|Off|DNS   Off [svd,C]
    Configures how the server determines its own name and port. (p. 134)

UseCanonicalPhysicalPort On|Off   Off [svd,C]
    Configures how the server determines its own name and port. (p. 135)

User *unix-userid*   #-1 [s,M]
    The userid under which the server will answer requests. (p. 529)

UserDir *directory-filename* [*directory-filename*] ...   [sv,B]
    Location of the user-specific directories. (p. 501)

VirtualDocumentRoot *interpolated-directory*|none   none [sv,E]
    Dynamically configure the location of the document root for a given virtual
    host. (p. 512)

VirtualDocumentRootIP *interpolated-directory*|none   none [sv,E]
    Dynamically configure the location of the document root for a given virtual
    host. (p. 513)

<VirtualHost *addr*[:*port*] [*addr*[:*port*]] ...> ... </VirtualHost>   [s,C]
    Contains directives that apply only to a specific hostname or IP address. (p. 135)

VirtualScriptAlias *interpolated-directory*|none   none [sv,E]
    Dynamically configure the location of the CGI directory for a given virtual host.
    (p. 513)

VirtualScriptAliasIP *interpolated-directory*|none   none [sv,E]
    Dynamically configure the location of the cgi directory for a given virtual host.
    (p. 513)

Win32DisableAcceptEx   [s,M]
    Use accept() rather than AcceptEx() to accept network connections. (p. 536)

XBitHack on|off|full   off [svdh,B]
    Parse SSI directives in files with the execute bit set. (p. 314)

Other books from the publisher

Network Theory publishes books about free software under free documentation licenses. Our current catalogue includes the following titles:

- **The Perl Language Reference Manual** Larry Wall et al. (ISBN 978-1-906966-02-7) $39.95 (£29.95)

  This manual is a printed edition of the official Perl reference documentation from the Perl 5.12.1 distribution. It describes the syntax of Perl and its built-in datatypes, operators, functions, variables, regular expressions and diagnostic messages. For each copy of this manual sold, $1 is donated to The Perl Foundation.

- **PostgreSQL Reference Manual: Volumes 1A, 1B, 2, 3** (ISBN 978-1-906966-04-1) $19.95 (£14.95), (ISBN 978-1-906966-05-8) $19.95 (£14.95), (ISBN 978-1-906966-06-5) $19.95 (£14.95), (ISBN 978-1-906966-07-2) $14.95 (£9.95)

  These manuals document the SQL language and commands of PostgreSQL 9.0, its client and server programming interfaces, and the configuration and maintenance of PostgreSQL servers. For each copy of these manuals sold, $1 is donated to the PostgreSQL project.

- **The Org Mode 7 Reference Manual** Carsten Dominik (ISBN: 978-1-906966-08-9) $14.95 (£9.95)

  This manual is a printed edition of the official Org reference documentation from the Org 7.3 distribution. Org mode is a powerful system for organizing projects, tasks and notes in the Emacs editor. For each copy of this manual sold, $1 is donated to the Org Project.

- **The XML 1.0 Standard (5th Edition)** W3C XML Working Group (ISBN 0954612094) $12.95 (£8.95)

  This manual is a printed edition of the Extensible Markup Language (XML) 1.0 standard from the World Wide Web Consortium. It also includes the Namespaces in XML 1.0 specification (Third Edition) and XML Information Set (Second Edition).

- **XML Path Language (XPath) 2.0 Standard** W3C XML Query and XSL Working Groups (ISBN 978-1-906966-01-0) $12.95 (£8.95)

  This manual is a printed edition of the XPath 2.0 standard from the World Wide Web Consortium.

- **GNU Bash Reference Manual** by Chet Ramey and Brian Fox (ISBN 0-9541617-7-7) $29.95 (£19.95)

  This manual is the definitive reference for GNU Bash, the standard GNU command-line interpreter. GNU Bash is a complete implementation of the POSIX.2 Bourne shell specification, with additional features from the

C-shell and Korn shell. For each copy of this manual sold, $1 is donated to the Free Software Foundation.

- **An Introduction to Python** by Guido van Rossum and Fred L. Drake, Jr. (ISBN 0-9541617-6-9) $19.95 (£12.95)

  This tutorial provides an introduction to Python, an easy to learn object oriented programming language. For each copy of this manual sold, $1 is donated to the Python Software Foundation.

- **Python Language Reference Manual** by Guido van Rossum and Fred L. Drake, Jr. (ISBN 0-9541617-8-5) $19.95 (£12.95)

  This manual is the official reference for the Python language itself. It describes the syntax of Python and its built-in datatypes in depth, This manual is suitable for readers who need to be familiar with the details and rules of the Python language and its object system. For each copy of this manual sold, $1 is donated to the Python Software Foundation.

- **An Introduction to GCC** by Brian J. Gough, foreword by Richard M. Stallman. (ISBN 0-9541617-9-3) $19.95 (£12.95)

  This manual provides a tutorial introduction to the GNU C and C++ compilers, gcc and g++. Many books teach the C and C++ languages, but this book explains how to use the compiler itself. Based on years of observation of questions posted on mailing lists, it guides the reader straight to the important options of GCC.

- **Valgrind 3.3** by J. Seward, N. Nethercote, J. Weidendorfer et al. (ISBN 0-9546120-5-1) $19.95 (£12.95)

  This manual describes how to use Valgrind, an award-winning suite of tools for debugging and profiling GNU/Linux programs. Valgrind detects memory and threading bugs automatically, avoiding hours of frustrating bug-hunting and making programs more stable. For each copy of this manual sold, $1 is donated to the Valgrind developers.

- **Comparing and Merging Files with GNU diff and patch** by David MacKenzie, Paul Eggert, and Richard Stallman (ISBN 0-9541617-5-0) $19.95 (£12.95)

  This manual describes how to compare and merge files using GNU diff and patch. It includes an extensive tutorial that guides the reader through all the options of the diff and patch commands. For each copy of this manual sold, $1 is donated to the Free Software Foundation.

- **Version Management with CVS** by Per Cederqvist et al. (ISBN 0-9541617-1-8) $29.95 (£19.95)

  This manual describes how to use CVS, the concurrent versioning system—one of the most widely-used source-code management systems available today. The manual provides tutorial examples for new users of CVS, as well as the definitive reference documentation for every CVS command and configuration option.

- **An Introduction to R** by W.N. Venables, D.M. Smith and the R Development Core Team (ISBN 0-9541617-4-2) $19.95 (£12.95)

This tutorial manual provides a comprehensive introduction to GNU R, a free software package for statistical computing and graphics.

- **GNU Scientific Library Reference Manual—Third Edition** by M. Galassi, et al (ISBN 0-9546120-7-8) $39.95 (£24.95)

This reference manual is the definitive guide to the GNU Scientific Library (GSL), a numerical library for C and C++ programmers. The manual documents over 1,000 mathematical routines needed for solving problems in science and engineering. All the money raised from the sale of this book supports the development of the GNU Scientific Library.

- **GNU Octave Manual Version 3** by John W. Eaton et al. (ISBN 0-9546120-6-X) $39.95 (£24.95)

This manual is the definitive guide to GNU Octave, an interactive environment for numerical computation with matrices and vectors. This edition covers version 3 of GNU Octave. For each copy sold $1 is donated to the GNU Octave Development Fund.

All titles are available for order from bookstores worldwide. Sales of the manuals fund the development of more free software and documentation.

For details, visit the website http://www.network-theory.co.uk/. For questions or comments, please contact sales@network-theory.co.uk.

Index

Page numbers in **bold** are definitions, others are general references.

Please note that page numbers given here may point to the start of the section containing the reference, rather than the exact location of the reference itself (this is due to limitations in the original document format).

10/14 ⑥ 6/14

CPSIA information can be obtained at www.ICGtesting.com
Printed in the USA
LVOW051312290413

331370LV00003B/323/P

Yearbook of Intensive Care and Emergency Medicine 2005

Edited by J.-L. Vincent